Lecture Notes in Computer Science 15806

The series Lecture Notes in Computer Science (LNCS), including its subseries Lecture Notes in Artificial Intelligence (LNAI) and Lecture Notes in Bioinformatics (LNBI), has established itself as a medium for the publication of new developments in computer science and information technology research, teaching, and education.

LNCS enjoys close cooperation with the computer science R & D community, the series counts many renowned academics among its volume editors and paper authors, and collaborates with prestigious societies. Its mission is to serve this international community by providing an invaluable service, mainly focused on the publication of conference and workshop proceedings and postproceedings. LNCS commenced publication in 1973.

Brian K. Smith · Marcela Borge
Editors

Learning and Collaboration Technologies

12th International Conference, LCT 2025
Held as Part of the 27th HCI International Conference, HCII 2025
Gothenburg, Sweden, June 22–27, 2025
Proceedings, Part I

Springer

Editors
Brian K. Smith
Boston College
Chestnut Hill, MA, USA

Marcela Borge
The Pennsylvania State University
University Park, PA, USA

ISSN 0302-9743 ISSN 1611-3349 (electronic)
Lecture Notes in Computer Science
ISBN 978-3-031-93563-3 ISBN 978-3-031-93564-0 (eBook)
https://doi.org/10.1007/978-3-031-93564-0

This Springer imprint is published by the registered company Springer Nature Switzerland AG
The registered company address is: Gewerbestrasse 11, 6330 Cham, Switzerland

Foreword

The HCI International (HCII) conference was founded in 1984 by Gavriel Salvendy (Purdue University, USA, Tsinghua University, P.R. China, and University of Central Florida, USA) and the first event of the series, "1st USA-Japan Conference on Human-Computer Interaction", was held in Honolulu, Hawaii, USA, 18–20 August. Since then, HCI International is held jointly with several Thematic Areas and Affiliated Conferences, with each one under the auspices of a distinguished international Program Board and under one management and one registration. Twenty-seven HCI International Conferences have been organized so far (every two years until 2013, and annually thereafter).

Last year, we celebrated 40 years since the establishment of the HCII conference, which has been a hub for presenting groundbreaking research and novel ideas and collaboration for people from all over the world. Over the years, this conference has served as a platform for scholars, researchers, industry experts, and students to exchange ideas, connect, and address challenges in the ever-evolving HCI field. The conference has evolved itself, adapting to new technologies and emerging trends, while staying committed to its core mission of advancing knowledge and driving change.

The 27th International Conference on Human-Computer Interaction, HCI International 2025 (HCII 2025), was held as an 'on-site' conference at the Gothia Towers Hotel and Swedish Exhibition & Congress Centre, in Gothenburg, Sweden, on June 22–27, 2025, with the additional option for 'on-line' participation. It incorporated the 21 thematic areas and affiliated conferences listed below.

A total of 7972 individuals from academia, research institutes, industry, and government agencies from 92 countries submitted contributions. 1430 papers and 355 posters (as short research papers) are included in the volumes of the proceedings published just before the start of the conference, and which are listed below. The contributions thoroughly cover the entire field of human-computer interaction, highlight the evolving role of computers in diverse contexts, and demonstrate how HCI research is shaping and improving user experiences across a wide range of domains, influencing technological progress and its effective integration into various sectors.

The HCII conference also offers the option of presenting 'Late Breaking Work', both for papers and posters, with the corresponding proceedings volumes published after the conference. Full papers are included in the 'HCII 2025 - Late Breaking Papers' volumes of the proceedings published in the Springer LNCS series, while 'Poster Extended Abstracts' are included as short research papers in the 'HCII 2025 - Late Breaking Posters' volumes published in the Springer CCIS series.

I would like to thank the Program Board Chairs and the members of the Program Boards of all thematic areas and affiliated conferences for their contribution towards the high scientific quality and overall success of the HCI International 2025 conference. Their manifold support including paper reviews (via a single-blind review process, with a minimum of two reviews per submission), session organization, and their willingness to act as goodwill ambassadors for the conference is most highly appreciated.

This conference would not have been possible without the continuous and unwavering support and advice of Gavriel Salvendy, founder, General Chair Emeritus, and Scientific Advisor. For his outstanding efforts, I would like to express my sincere appreciation to Abbas Moallem, Communications Chair and Editor of HCI International News.

June 2025 Constantine Stephanidis

HCI International 2025 Thematic Areas and Affiliated Conferences

- HCI: Human-Computer Interaction Thematic Area
- HIMI: Human Interface and the Management of Information Thematic Area
- EPCE: 22nd International Conference on Engineering Psychology and Cognitive Ergonomics
- AC: 19th International Conference on Augmented Cognition
- UAHCI: 19th International Conference on Universal Access in Human-Computer Interaction
- CCD: 17th International Conference on Cross-Cultural Design
- SCSM: 17th International Conference on Social Computing and Social Media
- VAMR: 17th International Conference on Virtual, Augmented and Mixed Reality
- DHM: 16th International Conference on Digital Human Modeling and Applications in Health, Safety, Ergonomics and Risk Management
- DUXU: 14th International Conference on Design, User Experience, and Usability
- C&C: 13th International Conference on Culture and Computing
- DAPI: 13th International Conference on Distributed, Ambient and Pervasive Interactions
- HCIBGO: 12th International Conference on HCI in Business, Government and Organizations
- LCT: 12th International Conference on Learning and Collaboration Technologies
- ITAP: 11th International Conference on Human Aspects of IT for the Aged Population
- AIS: 7th International Conference on Adaptive Instructional Systems
- HCI-CPT: 7th International Conference on HCI for Cybersecurity, Privacy and Trust
- HCI-Games: 7th International Conference on HCI in Games
- MobiTAS: 7th International Conference on HCI in Mobility, Transport and Automotive Systems
- AI-HCI: 6th International Conference on Artificial Intelligence in HCI
- MOBILE: 6th International Conference on Human-Centered Design, Operation and Evaluation of Mobile Communications

List of Conference Proceedings Volumes Appearing Before the Conference

1. LNCS 15766, Human-Computer Interaction - Part I, edited by Masaaki Kurosu and Ayako Hashizume
2. LNCS 15767, Human-Computer Interaction - Part II, edited by Masaaki Kurosu and Ayako Hashizume
3. LNCS 15768, Human-Computer Interaction - Part III, edited by Masaaki Kurosu and Ayako Hashizume
4. LNCS 15769, Human-Computer Interaction - Part IV, edited by Masaaki Kurosu and Ayako Hashizume
5. LNCS 15770, Human-Computer Interaction - Part V, edited by Masaaki Kurosu and Ayako Hashizume
6. LNCS 15771, Human-Computer Interaction - Part VI, edited by Masaaki Kurosu and Ayako Hashizume
7. LNCS 15772, Human-Computer Interaction - Part VII, edited by Masaaki Kurosu and Ayako Hashizume
8. LNCS 15773, Human Interface and the Management of Information: Part I, edited by Hirohiko Mori and Yumi Asahi
9. LNCS 15774, Human Interface and the Management of Information: Part II, edited by Hirohiko Mori and Yumi Asahi
10. LNCS 15775, Human Interface and the Management of Information: Part III, edited by Hirohiko Mori and Yumi Asahi
11. LNAI 15776, Engineering Psychology and Cognitive Ergonomics: Part I, edited by Don Harris and Wen-Chin Li
12. LNAI 15777, Engineering Psychology and Cognitive Ergonomics: Part II, edited by Don Harris and Wen-Chin Li
13. LNAI 15778, Augmented Cognition: Part I, edited by Dylan D. Schmorrow and Cali M. Fidopiastis
14. LNAI 15779, Augmented Cognition: Part II, edited by Dylan D. Schmorrow and Cali M. Fidopiastis
15. LNCS 15780, Universal Access in Human-Computer Interaction: Part I, edited by Margherita Antona and Constantine Stephanidis
16. LNCS 15781, Universal Access in Human-Computer Interaction: Part II, edited by Margherita Antona and Constantine Stephanidis
17. LNCS 15782, Cross-Cultural Design: Part I, edited by Pei-Luen Patrick Rau
18. LNCS 15783, Cross-Cultural Design: Part II, edited by Pei-Luen Patrick Rau
19. LNCS 15784, Cross-Cultural Design: Part III, edited by Pei-Luen Patrick Rau
20. LNCS 15785, Cross-Cultural Design: Part IV, edited by Pei-Luen Patrick Rau

21. LNCS 15786, Social Computing and Social Media: Part I, edited by Adela Coman and Simona Vasilache
22. LNCS 15787, Social Computing and Social Media: Part II, edited by Adela Coman and Simona Vasilache
23. LNCS 15788, Virtual, Augmented and Mixed Reality: Part I, edited by Jessie Y. C. Chen and Gino Fragomeni
24. LNCS 15789, Virtual, Augmented and Mixed Reality: Part II, edited by Jessie Y. C. Chen and Gino Fragomeni
25. LNCS 15790, Virtual, Augmented and Mixed Reality: Part III, edited by Jessie Y. C. Chen and Gino Fragomeni
26. LNCS 15791, Digital Human Modeling and Applications in Health, Safety, Ergonomics and Risk Management: Part I, edited by Vincent G. Duffy
27. LNCS 15792, Digital Human Modeling and Applications in Health, Safety, Ergonomics and Risk Management: Part II, edited by Vincent G. Duffy
28. LNCS 15793, Digital Human Modeling and Applications in Health, Safety, Ergonomics and Risk Management: Part III, edited by Vincent G. Duffy
29. LNCS 15794, Design, User Experience, and Usability: Part I, edited by Martin Schrepp
30. LNCS 15795, Design, User Experience, and Usability: Part II, edited by Martin Schrepp
31. LNCS 15796, Design, User Experience, and Usability: Part III, edited by Martin Schrepp
32. LNCS 15797, Design, User Experience, and Usability: Part IV, edited by Martin Schrepp
33. LNCS 15798, Design, User Experience, and Usability: Part V, edited by Martin Schrepp
34. LNCS 15799, Design, User Experience, and Usability: Part VI, edited by Martin Schrepp
35. LNCS 15800, Culture and Computing: Part I, edited by Matthias Rauterberg
36. LNCS 15801, Culture and Computing: Part II, edited by Matthias Rauterberg
37. LNCS 15802, Distributed, Ambient and Pervasive Interactions: Part I, edited by Norbert A. Streitz and Shin'ichi Konomi
38. LNCS 15803, Distributed, Ambient and Pervasive Interactions: Part II, edited by Norbert A. Streitz and Shin'ichi Konomi
39. LNCS 15804, HCI in Business, Government and Organizations: Part I, edited by Fiona Fui-Hoon Nah and Keng Leng Siau
40. LNCS 15805, HCI in Business, Government and Organizations: Part II, edited by Fiona Fui-Hoon Nah and Keng Leng Siau
41. LNCS 15806, Learning and Collaboration Technologies: Part I, edited by Brian K. Smith and Marcela Borge
42. LNCS 15807, Learning and Collaboration Technologies: Part II, edited by Brian K. Smith and Marcela Borge
43. LNCS 15808, Learning and Collaboration Technologies: Part III, edited by Brian K. Smith and Marcela Borge

44. LNCS 15809, Human Aspects of IT for the Aged Population: Part I, edited by Qin Gao and Jia Zhou
45. LNCS 15810, Human Aspects of IT for the Aged Population: Part II, edited by Qin Gao and Jia Zhou
46. LNCS 15811, Human Aspects of IT for the Aged Population: Part III, edited by Qin Gao and Jia Zhou
47. LNCS 15812, Adaptive Instructional System: Part I, edited by Robert A. Sottilare and Jessica Schwarz
48. LNCS 15813, Adaptive Instructional System: Part II, edited by Robert A. Sottilare and Jessica Schwarz
49. LNCS 15814, HCI for Cybersecurity, Privacy and Trust: Part I, edited by Abbas Moallem
50. LNCS 15815, HCI for Cybersecurity, Privacy and Trust: Part II, edited by Abbas Moallem
51. LNCS 15816, HCI in Games, edited by Xiaowen Fang
52. LNCS 15817, HCI in Mobility, Transport and Automotive Systems: Part I, edited by Heidi Krömker
53. LNCS 15818, HCI in Mobility, Transport and Automotive Systems: Part II, edited by Heidi Krömker
54. LNAI 15819, Artificial Intelligence in HCI: Part I, edited by Helmut Degen and Stavroula Ntoa
55. LNAI 15820, Artificial Intelligence in HCI: Part II, edited by Helmut Degen and Stavroula Ntoa
56. LNAI 15821, Artificial Intelligence in HCI: Part III, edited by Helmut Degen and Stavroula Ntoa
57. LNAI 15822, Artificial Intelligence in HCI: Part IV, edited by Helmut Degen and Stavroula Ntoa
58. LNCS 15823, Human-Centered Design, Operation and Evaluation of Mobile Communications: Part I, edited by June Wei and George Margetis
59. LNCS 15824, Human-Centered Design, Operation and Evaluation of Mobile Communications: Part II, edited by June Wei and George Margetis
60. CCIS 2522, HCI International 2025 Posters - Part I, edited by Constantine Stephanidis, Margherita Antona, Stavroula Ntoa and Gavriel Salvendy
61. CCIS 2523, HCI International 2025 Posters - Part II, edited by Constantine Stephanidis, Margherita Antona, Stavroula Ntoa and Gavriel Salvendy
62. CCIS 2524, HCI International 2025 Posters - Part III, edited by Constantine Stephanidis, Margherita Antona, Stavroula Ntoa and Gavriel Salvendy
63. CCIS 2525, HCI International 2025 Posters - Part IV, edited by Constantine Stephanidis, Margherita Antona, Stavroula Ntoa and Gavriel Salvendy
64. CCIS 2526, HCI International 2025 Posters - Part V, edited by Constantine Stephanidis, Margherita Antona, Stavroula Ntoa and Gavriel Salvendy
65. CCIS 2527, HCI International 2025 Posters - Part VI, edited by Constantine Stephanidis, Margherita Antona, Stavroula Ntoa and Gavriel Salvendy

66. CCIS 2528, HCI International 2025 Posters - Part VII, edited by Constantine Stephanidis, Margherita Antona, Stavroula Ntoa and Gavriel Salvendy
67. CCIS 2529, HCI International 2025 Posters - Part VIII, edited by Constantine Stephanidis, Margherita Antona, Stavroula Ntoa and Gavriel Salvendy

https://2025.hci.international/proceedings

Preface

In today's knowledge society, learning and collaboration are fundamental and interrelated aspects of knowledge acquisition and creation. Learning technology is the broad range of communication, information, and related technologies that can support learning, teaching, and assessment, often collaboratively. Collaboration technology, on the other hand, is targeted to support individuals working in teams towards a common goal, which may be educational. Collaboration technologies may support communication, the management of activities, and/or problem-solving processes. In this context, interactive technologies affect and improve the existing educational system and become a transformative force that can generate radically new ways of knowing, learning, and collaborating.

The 12th International Conference on Learning and Collaboration Technologies (LCT 2025), affiliated with HCI International 2025, addressed the theoretical foundations, design and implementation, and effectiveness and impact issues related to interactive technologies for learning and collaboration. Papers focused on design methodologies, tools, theoretical models, learning design or learning experience (LX) design, and technology adoption and use in formal, non-formal, and informal educational contexts.

K-20 (kindergarten to higher education) classrooms and lifelong learning contexts are increasingly adopting learning and collaboration technologies. Technology can support expansive forms of collaboration, deepen empathy, coordinate complex interactions among people, materials, and purposes, and develop skill sets that are essential across twenty-first-century workspaces. The general themes of the LCT conference aim to address challenges in designing better learning and collaboration with technology, supporting learners to develop relevant approaches and skills, and assessing or evaluating gains and outcomes. To this end, topics such as extended reality (XR) learning, embodied and immersive learning, mobile learning and ubiquitous technologies, serious games and gamification, and virtual teachers, among others, are explored in the LCT conference proceedings. Learning experience design and user experience design continue to pose challenges in the realm of learning environments and collaboration technology. LCT seeks to foster continuous dialogue while synthesizing current knowledge.

Three volumes of the HCII 2025 proceedings are dedicated to this year's edition of the LCT 2025 conference.

- Learning and Collaboration Technologies - Part I: Designing Learning Experiences; Technological Innovation in Education
- Learning and Collaboration Technologies - Part II: From Human Teachers to AI Educators; Intelligent Learning Environments
- Learning and Collaboration Technologies - Part III: Serious Games and Gamification; Immersive Learning; Understanding Learning Experiences

These volumes' papers were accepted for publication after a minimum of two single-blind reviews from the members of the LCT Program Board or, in some cases, from members of the Program Boards of other affiliated conferences. We would like to thank them all for their invaluable contributions, support, and efforts.

June 2025

Brian K. Smith
Marcela Borge

12th International Conference on Learning and Collaboration Technologies (LCT 2025)

The full list with the Program Board Chairs and the members of the Program Boards of all thematic areas and affiliated conferences of HCII 2025 is available online at:

http://www.hci.international/board-members-2025.php

HCI International 2026 Conference

The 28th International Conference on Human-Computer Interaction, HCI International 2026, will be held jointly with the affiliated conferences at the Montréal Convention Centre (Palais des congrès de Montréal), in Montreal, Canada, 26–31 July 2026. It will cover a broad spectrum of themes related to Human-Computer Interaction, including theoretical issues, methods, tools, processes, and case studies in HCI design, as well as novel interaction techniques, interfaces, and applications. The proceedings will be published by Springer (part of Springer Nature) in a multi-volume set. More information will become available on the conference website: https://2026.hci.international/.

General Chair
Prof. Constantine Stephanidis
University of Crete and ICS-FORTH
Heraklion, Crete, Greece
Email: general_chair@2026.hci.international

https://2026.hci.international/

Contents – Part I

Technological Innovation in Education

Contents – Part II

Contents – Part III

Immersive Learning

Understanding Learning Experiences

Designing Learning Experiences

Effects of an AI-Guided Musical Blocks System on Children's Learning Engagement and Emotions

Chia-Hui Feng[1,2](✉), Hao-Chiang Koong Lin[1], Chu-Yu Christine Cheng[2], Jing-Lin Huang[3], and Yu-Xin Zhou[2]

[1] Department of Information and Learning Technology, National University of Tainan, No. 33, Sec. 2, Shulin St., West Central District, Tainan, Taiwan R.O.C.
wanda@stust.edu.tw
[2] Department of Creative Product Design, Southern Taiwan University of Science and Technology, No. 1, Nan-Tai St., Yongkang District, Tainan, Taiwan R.O.C.
[3] Hillsborough High-School, 466 Raider Blvd, Hillsborough, NJ 08844, USA

Abstract. This study presents the development of an innovative music learning system that integrates artificial intelligence-based image recognition technology, employing interactive musical storybooks and intelligent musical blocks as core pedagogical tools to establish a novel digital learning paradigm for musical literacy. Using a quasi-experimental design, 27 participants aged 7–12 years were randomly assigned to experimental and control groups. The system integrates Robflow's image recognition technology with the YOLOv11 deep learning model, achieving 99.5% mean precision in musical note recognition tasks. Analysis using the Achievement Emotions Questionnaire (AEQ) revealed that the experimental group exhibited significantly higher positive emotions (enjoyment, hope, and pride) while demonstrating notable reductions in negative emotions (boredom, shame, and hopelessness). From a human-computer interaction perspective, the system employs CNC precision machining and epoxy resin filling techniques to develop transparent musical blocks that blend aesthetics with functionality. The research validates the feasibility and effectiveness of AI-assisted music education in fostering musical literacy, providing new directions for future digital interactive learning development.

Keywords: Musical Literacy · Image Recognition · AIGC · Digital Learning

1 Introduction

In the context of the rapid advancement of digital technologies, innovative models and teaching strategies for music education have become an important topic of educational research. Modern children, as digital natives [1–3], are immersed in the digital environment from birth. They prefer digital interactions and are more adept at receiving and processing information through visualization, demonstrating learning characteristics and cognitive patterns that significantly differ from previous generations. This shift in digital literacy requires a reevaluation in digital music education, specifically in cultivating musical literacy of children.

B. K. Smith and M. Borge (Eds.): HCII 2025, LNCS 15806, pp. 3–16, 2025.
https://doi.org/10.1007/978-3-031-93564-0_1

Traditional musical education faces multiple challenges. Teachers focus on delivering curriculum context, while the students passively absorb and process the context, such as music theories or playing techniques, making it difficult for them to grasp the essence of piano playing [4]. This model neglects the learning interests and creative development of children. Teaching methods lack interactivity and engagement, leading to low motivation for learning. Moreover, abstract music theory creates significant cognitive barriers for children. According to McPherson, cultivating music talent requires an early start and an enriched environment that provides diverse training [5], allowing the students to develop comprehensively in performance, creativity, and listening.

The integration of digital learning into children's music education significantly enhances the development of students′ music literacy, fosters self-esteem, and promotes cognitive development [6]. By strengthening both musical and emotional cognition, digital learning increases students′ interest and aesthetic appreciation. Moreover, multisensory stimulation supports the holistic development of cognitive functions [5, 7]. Systematic training can cultivate musical abilities in students, rather than relying solely on innate talent. When children engage with educational material that integrates visual, auditory, and interactive elements, notable improvements are observed in cognitive functions such as working memory, problem-solving skills, and emotional regulation [8].

A multimodal learning pattern can effectively activate neural connections across different regions in the brain, promoting a balanced development of multiple intelligences. Specifically, in the field of music education, Li demonstrated that incorporating deep learning technology for instrument recognition significantly enhanced children′s engagement and motivation in piano education [4]. Students prefer game-based teaching, which enhances the effectiveness of their piano learning outcomes while improving their music-reading and sight-singing abilities. The integration of digital learning not only enriches the ways of present learning materials but also builds an integral foundation for constructing a comprehensive cognitive development framework. By incorporating educational technology into this innovative teaching model, this approach opens a new direction for traditional music education development and offers a fresh perspective for advancing STEAM education.

This study aims at exploring the impact of combining artificial intelligence (AI) image recognition technology with an interactive musical note blocks learning system on children's development of music literacy. The primary objective is to develop an interactive music block learning system that integrates AI image recognition technology, providing intuitive and gamified learning. In addition, this study assesses the impact of interactive music block learning system on children's learning emotions and learning outcomes.

2 Literature Review

2.1 Digital Music Learning

The application of multimedia in music education has demonstrated significant educational benefits over the years. Multimedia tools not only enhance cognitive development in preschool children but also effectively increase their learning engagement. A comparative study between mobile applications and the Montessori method revealed that mobile games effectively support kindergarten children's ear training, sound discrimination, and musical composition skills [9]. Research has demonstrated that multimedia teaching significantly enhances both autonomous and non-autonomous attention in children′s music courses, with this deep engagement playing a crucial role in cognitive development [10].

In terms of cognitive skills, empirical research demonstrates that integrating multimedia into music education effectively improves memory, language, and mathematical abilities, thereby promoting overall learning performance [11]. Studies have documented that children participating in digital music activities demonstrate excellence in problem-solving abilities and emotional regulation [12]. Furthermore, investigations into piano education have revealed that the application of multimedia technology can deepen children's musical appreciation abilities and creative skills [13]. Recent research has shown that digital music teaching tools, incorporating artificial intelligence and multimedia resources, significantly improved students' rhythm sense by 30% and creativity by 25% compared to traditional methods, enhancing innovative thinking [14]. Advanced studies utilizing deep learning algorithms have successfully integrated traditional music culture with modern vocal education, strengthening students' vocal skills and artistic literacy to achieve higher learning objectives [15].

2.2 Convolutional Neural Networks

Convolutional Neural Networks (CNN) [16–18] serves as the core technological framework for note recognition. CNN, through its unique multi-layer feature extraction capability, can effectively process the visual features of musical symbols. In the note recognition task, the input staff image goes through multiple layers of convolutional operations, allowing the system to automatically learn and extract key features of the notes, such as the circular structure of a whole note, and the head and stem features of a quarter note. These features are processed through pooling layers for dimensionality reduction. Max pooling retains the most significant note features, while average pooling considers the overall distribution of features. This effectively reduces computational complexity and helps prevent overfitting. After multiple convolution and pooling operations, the feature map is transformed into a one-dimensional vector through the flattened layer, and ultimately, classification is performed in the fully connected layer, as shown in Fig. 1.

2.3 Roboflow

Roboflow plays a pivotal role in the development and application of AI-enhanced systems, particularly in the domains of robotics, computer vision, and image processing [19–22]. In the field of traffic monitoring, Roboflow has processed 5,000 license plate

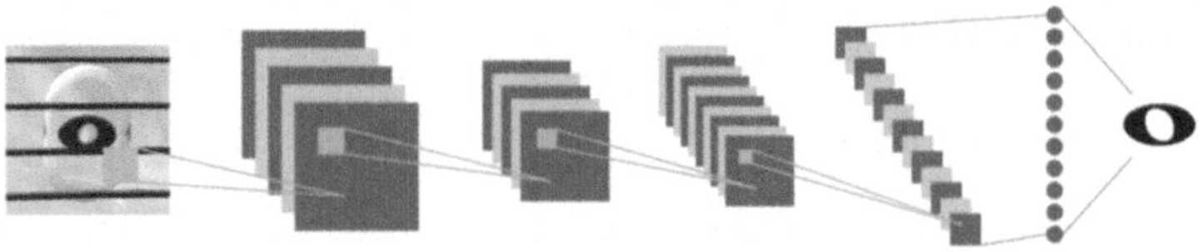

Fig. 1. Musical Note Recognition Using Convolutional Neural Networks.

images, generating 10,000 high-quality bounding box annotations and integrating interpretable data [23]. For facility monitoring, its dataset demonstrates significant advantages in railway crossing object detection, especially in data augmentation and spatial geometry computation [24]. Roboflow's comprehensive functionalities including image annotation, data augmentation, dataset management, and format conversion establish a robust data processing foundation for training and evaluating machine learning models. In this study, Roboflow is primarily utilized for image processing and music note annotation, handling image datasets, labeling musical notes, enhancing data, and assisting in the training and deployment of deep learning models. Specifically, it facilitates the annotation of whole notes, half notes, and quarter notes based on their distinctive features. Using a deep learning-based approach to musical note recognition, a dataset comprising tens of thousands of annotated musical notes was trained and validated, achieving a mean average precision (mAP) of 99.5% in note recognition.

2.4 Yolo

YOLO (You Only Look Once) is an object detection model specifically designed for real-time target detection, providing both classification and bounding box localization for each detected object. By integrating object detection and classification, YOLO achieves remarkable processing speed, making it particularly well-suited for real-time applications. The YOLO architecture has been extensively adopted in diverse domains, including object detection, scene understanding, and medical image analysis. In this study, we integrate the YOLO model with CNN, wherein YOLO partitions images into grids, with each grid cell responsible for detecting objects within its designated region. This framework ensures an optimal balance between accuracy and computational efficiency while enhancing feature extraction capabilities. The CNN component serves as the foundational layer for image feature extraction and classification.

According to Du the YOLO architecture has surpassed the computational speed limitations inherent in conventional CNN-based approaches while maintaining a balance between processing speed and accuracy [25]. Its rapid feature extraction capability is particularly crucial for applications requiring real-time computation and processing, such as real-time surveillance and edge computing [26–29]. In our implementation, YOLO processes the dynamic arrangement of musical blocks in real time, demonstrating robust recognition performance. However, classification challenges may arise under suboptimal lighting conditions or when blocks overlap on the musical staff. To mitigate these limitations, the model incorporates advanced mechanisms for handling inter-block occlusions and variations in ambient lighting conditions, thereby reducing recognition errors. Furthermore, the model's pre-training strategy incorporates environmental lighting considerations tailored to specific educational settings, ensuring effective real-time feedback and interactive learning capabilities in musical block applications.

2.5 Design and Fabrication of Recognizable Musical Note Blocks

To ensure precise image recognition, the transparent musical note blocks are fabricated using high-precision Computer Numerical Control (CNC) machining technology, as shown in Fig. 2. The acrylic material undergoes meticulous processing with specialized alloy milling cutters, where CNC machining enables the precise cutting of both the outer structural frame and the internal musical note patterns. During the machining process, an advanced liquid spray cooling system is employed to effectively prevent material deformation, thereby ensuring high dimensional accuracy and manufacturing precision. Furthermore, a black epoxy resin filling technique is applied, utilizing a thermosetting material synthesized through the chemical reaction of two liquid polymers. The molecular characteristics of epoxy resin facilitate stable interfacial bonding with the acrylic material, significantly enhancing the structural integrity of the transparent musical note blocks. This integration not only reinforces the mechanical stability of the blocks but also improves the accuracy of image recognition, optimizing their performance in vision-based applications.

Fig. 2. Interactive Music Building Blocks.

2.6 AIGC-Based Interactive Storybooks

The integration of AI into the design process enhances the early stages of conceptualization through representation creation, empathy triggers, and engagement mechanisms, facilitating cognitive activities based on knowledge-driven and decompose-and-integrate approaches [30]. Artificial Intelligence-Generated Content (AIGC) is increasingly incorporated into educational environments, supporting the co-creation of instructional materials and driving the digital transformation of education. In programming education, the integration of AIGC into higher-level abstract learning has been shown to significantly improve learning outcomes and computational thinking skills by enhancing interactivity and authenticity [30, 31].

Furthermore, AIGC technology enables the generation of personalized and dynamic educational content, enhancing both learning comprehension and efficiency. As shown in Fig. 3, this study employs AIGC in the context of musical education through interactive storytelling, providing a gamified learning experience. Ultimately, AIGC facilitates the development of higher-order cognitive skills, transforms educational assessment methodologies, and reshapes teaching and learning processes [32].

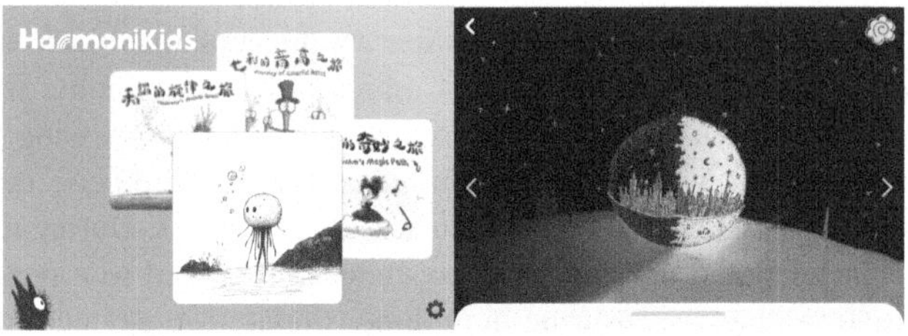

Fig. 3. Presents AIGC-based interactive storybooks designed to enhance musical education.

3 Methodology

An innovative music learning system was developed to integrate artificial intelligence-based image recognition technology. The system architecture encompasses two primary components: interactive musical storybooks and intelligent musical blocks, implementing gamification strategies to facilitate children's comprehension of foundational musical concepts. The learning progression is systematically designed and empirically structured to advance incrementally, beginning with fundamental note recognition before progressing through rhythm mastery to melodic composition.

3.1 Research Participants and Experimental Design

The research employed a pre-test/post-test control group design involving 27 participants aged 7–12 years, who were randomly assigned using a stratified sampling method to either the control group (n = 13) using traditional musical dot boards or the experimental group (n = 14) using intelligent musical blocks. To assess learners' emotional responses during fundamental music learning, the Achievement Emotions Questionnaire (AEQ) was administered, comprising 30 items measuring eight distinct emotions: Enjoyment, Hope, Pride, Anger, Anxiety, Boredom, Shame, and Hopelessness. Prior to the instructional intervention, both groups completed a 15-min pre-test to measure learning effectiveness and emotional states using the AEQ. The control group engaged with conventional musical dot boards, while the experimental group utilized intelligent musical blocks integrated with storybooks, creating a distinct multisensory learning experience. Following the 40-min learning sessions, both groups completed post-tests evaluating learning outcomes and emotional responses through the AEQ, as shown in Fig. 4.

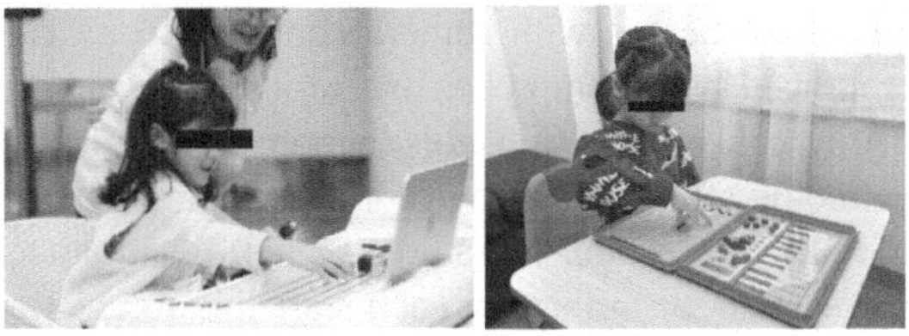

Fig. 4. Participants engaged in learning using musical instructional materials.

3.2 System Development Process

The development process focused on creating a proprietary musical note positioning and pitch recognition technology. The core system employs the Roboflow platform for musical note feature annotation, enabling precise identification of various musical note types, including whole notes, half notes, and quarter notes through AI model training, as shown in Fig. 5.

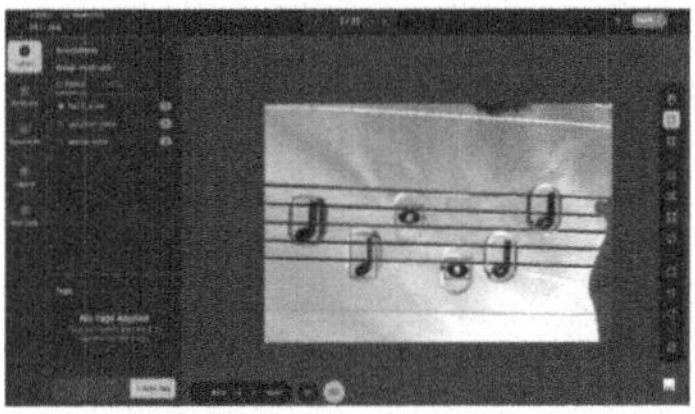

Fig. 5. Musical note annotation on Roboflow with bounding box data.

The system architecture integrates the efficient object detection capabilities of the YOLOv11 deep learning model with OpenCV, an open-source computer vision and machine learning library. This integration maintains an optimal balance between processing speed and accuracy in extracting musical notes from camera-detected note blocks positioned on the staff lines. The image preprocessing phase, recognized as a critical component affecting the performance of all system modules, significantly influences overall system efficiency [33]. The system operation workflow is depicted, as shown in Fig. 6.

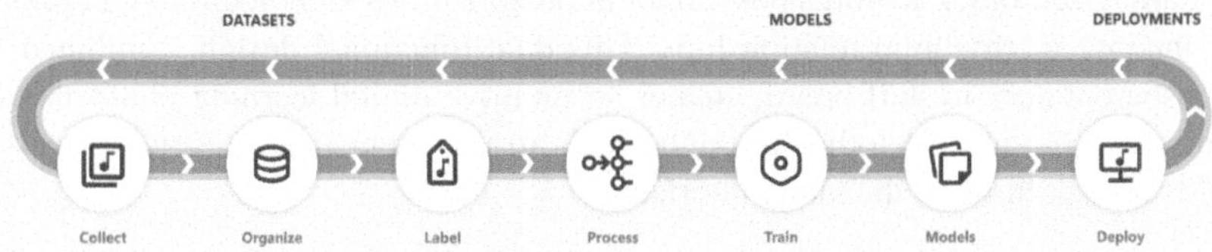

Fig. 6. Machine learning process for musical blocks.

System implementation begins with camera capture of musical note block positions on the staff, followed by a comprehensive series of image preprocessing steps. These steps include grayscale binarization, noise suppression, and the implementation of Hough transform technology for detecting and correcting staff line tilt angles. The black-and-white binarization process establishes a precise staff positioning system, assigning location markers and sequence numbers to each staff line to create a definitive correspondence between note positions and actual pitch values. To maintain system accuracy across diverse environmental conditions, significant emphasis was placed on addressing interference factors such as varying lighting conditions, perspective distortions, and environmental noise. The system culminates in a JavaScript-integrated frontend interface, delivering a responsive and interactive music learning platform.

3.3 Hardware and Software Integration

The development of an innovative music learning system integrates AI recognition technology through meticulously engineered hardware components, as shown in Fig. 7. The core system incorporates an AI recognition camera positioned beneath a transparent acrylic staff board, enabling stable detection of pitch and beat patterns from below. The system processes these visual inputs of musical notes and generates corresponding melodies through the tablet interface.

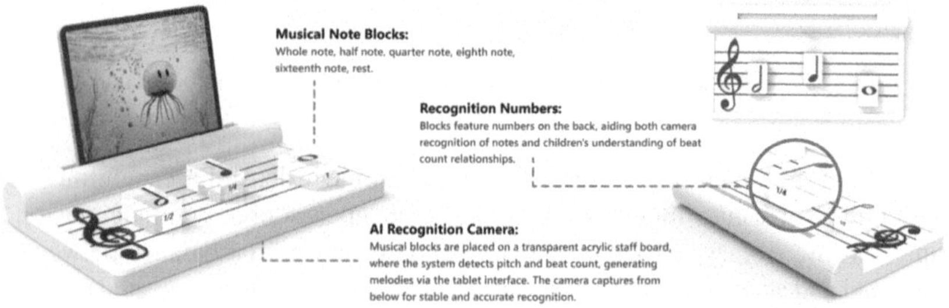

Fig. 7. Conceptual Hardware Design of the Musical Block Recognition System.

The musical note block system encompasses various note values, including whole notes, half notes, quarter notes, and rests, which can be positioned on the transparent staff board. Each block features beat count indicators on its side, facilitating children′s understanding of rhythmic relationships. This dual-functional design, combined with the transparent acrylic staff board, creates an intuitive digital learning platform where students can compose melodies through block arrangement while receiving real-time digital feedback through the tablet interface.

4 Results

4.1 Deep Learning Model Training and Evaluation for Musical Note Blocks

The Roboflow deep learning methodology was implemented for training the musical note recognition dataset, which comprised 15,644 images at 640 × 640 pixel resolution, featuring annotations for whole notes, half notes, and quarter notes. The system enhanced musical note data processing capabilities through image annotation and data augmentation techniques. The training process was conducted in two phases: initially focusing on single musical note blocks positioned at various pitches, followed by training with three or more note blocks placed on the staff under diverse background conditions.

Model performance was evaluated through metrics during the Roboflow training process, with results indicating favorable convergence trends across all loss functions. Specifically, the box loss decreased from an initial value of 1.2 to 0.4, classification loss reduced from 3.0 to 0.3, and distribution focal loss declined from 1.4 to 0.8. The validation loss curves maintained high consistency with the training set, demonstrating effective prevention of overfitting.

Regarding evaluation metrics, the model exhibited exceptional performance: precision and recall rates rapidly approached 1.0, while mean Average Precision (mAP) showed outstanding results across various IoU thresholds. The mAP50 achieved optimal performance, with the more stringent mAP50–95 consistently maintaining values above 99.5%. As shown in Fig. 8, these comprehensive results indicate that the model achieved excellent convergence and superior recognition capabilities across both training and validation datasets.

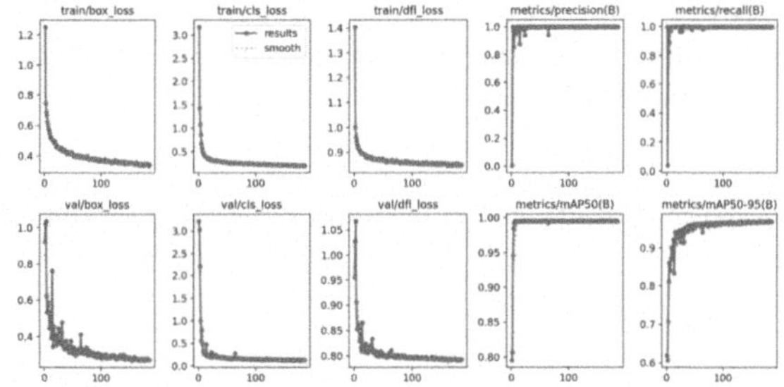

Fig. 8. Training and Validation Metrics for Musical Note Recognition Using Roboflow.

4.2 AEQ Learning Emotion Scale Statistical Analysis

This study investigated the emotional effects of an intelligent musical block with storybooks versus compared to traditional dot boards on children's comprehension of musical rhythm, notation, and melody. Using a quasi-experimental design, 27 child participants were randomly assigned to either an experimental group or a control group. Data analysis was conducted using SPSS 27, employing analysis of covariance (ANCOVA), independent samples t-tests, and regression analysis to test the research hypotheses.

ANCOVA was conducted to examine differences in learning emotions between the experimental group (N = 14) and control group (N = 13). The post-test scores served as the dependent variable (Y), with pre-test scores as the covariate (X), and different group students as independent samples. The homogeneity of regression slopes was confirmed $p > .05$, validating the fundamental assumption for ANCOVA, as shown Table 1. This result supported accepting the null hypothesis, demonstrating homogeneous regression coefficients between groups and confirming the appropriateness of proceeding with the covariance analysis.

Table 1. Intra-group Regression Analysis of AEQ Learning Emotions.

Source of variation	*SS*	*df*	*MS*	*F*	*p*
Group	.013	1	.013	.767	.390
Pre-test score	1.640	1	1.64	95.732	.001
Group * Pre-test score	.001	1	.001	.049	.826
Error (between groups)	.394	23	.017		

ANCOVA was conducted to compare post-learning emotional responses between the experimental group (N = 14) and control group (N = 13). After adjusting for the covariate, the mean scores on the AEQ were 2.958 ($SD = .4099$) for the experimental group and 2.883 ($SD = .2511$) for the control group. After controlling for the effect of pre-test scores (covariate) on post-test scores (dependent variable), analysis revealed a significant difference between groups ($F = 27.188$, $p < .001$), with a large effect size ($\eta 2 = .531$), as shown Table 2. These results indicate that different learning approaches significantly influenced the AEQ scores.

Table 2. Analysis of Covariance Results for Post-test AEQ Learning Emotions.

Group	*SS*	*df*	*MS*	*F*	*p*	$\eta 2$
EG	.447	1	.447	22.188	.001	.531
CG	.395	24	.016			

Experimental group, EG (N = 14); control group, CG (N = 13).

4.3 Analysis of Children's Emotional Responses

Comparative analysis of children's learning emotions examined an experimental group (N = 14) using the interactive musical block system and a control group (N = 13) using traditional musical dot boards, evaluating eight emotional dimensions through the AEQ. Independent samples t-test results revealed significantly higher positive emotions in the experimental group, with Enjoyment (t = −0.052, p = .001), Hope (t = −5403, p =

.001), and Pride (t = −7827, p = .001) all showing significant differences (p < .05), as shown in Table 3. These results indicate substantial enhancement in children's learning enjoyment and self-confidence through the interactive musical block system.

Furthermore, the experimental group demonstrated significantly lower negative emotions compared to the control group, particularly in Hopelessness (t = 4.219, p = .001), Shame (t = 2.962, p = .007), Boredom (t = 2.361, p = .026), and Anger (t = 1.966, p = .006). The substantial reduction in Hopelessness (EG: M = 1.8571 vs. CG: M = 2.7115) is especially noteworthy, suggesting that the system effectively mitigates feelings of despair in the learning process. Only Anxiety (t = 1.415, p = 1.61) showed no significant difference between groups.

The experimental group showed markedly higher scores in positive emotions (Enjoyment: M = 4.1429 vs. 2.8846; Hope: M = 3.8335 vs. 2.7946; Pride: M = 3.6785 vs. 2.3653) while maintaining lower scores in negative emotions. Overall, these results strongly support the effectiveness of the interactive musical block system in enhancing elementary school students' learning emotions and motivation, demonstrating superior capability in fostering positive emotional engagement compared to traditional learning methods.

Table 3. AEQ Learning Emotion scale – *t* test analysis results.

Emotion	Group	*M*	*SD*	*t*	*df*	*p*
Enjoyment	CG	2.8846	.64239	6.052	25	.001*
	EG	4.1429	.40089			
Hope	CG	2.7946	.47209	5.403	25	.001*
	EG	3.8335	.52689			
Pride	CG	2.3653	.49598	7.827	25	.001*
	EG	3.6785	.35933			
Anger	CG	2.8846	.40331	1.966	25	.006
	EG	2.3928	.81284			
Anxiety	CG	3.3140	.54451	1.415	25	1.61
	EG	3.0059	.58381			
Boredom	CG	3.1025	.60494	2.361	25	.026
	EG	2.5000	.71167			
Shame	CG	3.0064	.51311	2.962	25	.007
	EG	2.2499	.77622			
Hopelessness	CG	2.7115	.50874	4.219	25	.001*
	EG	1.8571	.54344			

* $p < 0.05$. Experimental group, EG ($N = 14$); control group, CG ($N = 13$).

5 Conclusions

The development of an innovative music learning system integrates AI image recognition technology, utilizing interactive musical storybooks and intelligent musical blocks as core pedagogical tools to establish a novel paradigm in music education. The findings indicate significant improvements in children′s music learning experiences and educational outcomes. Analysis using the AEQ revealed that the experimental group exhibited significantly higher levels of positive emotions (enjoyment, hope, and pride) while demonstrating notable reductions in negative emotions (boredom, shame, and helplessness), validating the system′s effectiveness in fostering emotional engagement and learning motivation [34, 35].

From the perspective of learning emotions, this study provides empirical evidence for the effectiveness of enhancing children′s emotional engagement in music education. Quantitative results reveal a significant increase in positive emotions and a notable decrease in negative emotions, underscoring the positive impact of technology-assisted teaching tools on the learning experience. Nonetheless, the limited sample size in this study necessitates an increase in the number of participants for broader applicability. Given the growing emphasis on social-emotional learning in contemporary educational research, these findings hold particular importance [36].

Secondly, from a human-computer interaction perspective, this study represents a breakthrough in applying deep learning technology to digital music education tools. The integration of Roboflow′s image recognition technology enables real-time recognition and interaction with musical blocks, creating a more intuitive and engaging learning experience. Furthermore, the teaching aid design incorporates CNC precision machining and epoxy resin filling techniques to develop transparent musical blocks that blend aesthetics with functionality. These blocks, when placed on the staff, enhance image recognition accuracy and address challenges associated with top-down camera recognition, offering new directions for the development of teaching aids in music education.

Several limitations were identified, including constraints in human resources, time, and financial factors. The research sample was restricted to elementary school students within a specific age range, and variables such as participants' gender, learning backgrounds, and developmental environments could not be fully accounted for. Consequently, the findings may not be entirely generalizable to other educational contexts.

Acknowledgments. This research work was funded by the National Science and Technology Council, Taiwan, under the Undergraduate Student Research Program, with grant number NSTC 113–2813-C-218–003-H.

References

1. Akçayır, M., Dündar, H., Akçayır, G.: What makes you a digital native? is it enough to be born after 1980? Comput. Hum. Behav. **60**, 435–440 (2016)
2. Vodanovich, S., Sundaram, D., Myers, M.: Research commentary digital natives and ubiquitous information systems. Inf. Syst. Res. **21**, 711–723 (2010)

3. Prensky, M.H.: Sapiens digital: from digital immigrants and digital natives to digital wisdom. Innovate: J. online Edu. **5**(3) (2009)
4. Li, H.: Piano education of children using musical instrument recognition and deep learning technologies under the educational psychology. Front. Psychol. **12** (2021)
5. McPherson, G.E.: Giftedness and talent in music. J. Aesthetic Educ. **31**(4), 65–77 (1997)
6. He, Y.: Practical teaching of college music courses based on vocal rhythmic pedagogy. Appl. Math. Nonlinear Sci. **9** (2024)
7. Woody, R.H.: Musicians' use of harmonic cognitive strategies when playing by ear. Psychol. Music **48**(5), 674–692 (2020)
8. Yafie, E., et al.: Supporting cognitive development through multimedia learning and scientific approach: an experimental study in preschool. Univ. J. Educ. Res. **8**(11), 113–123 (2020)
9. Paule-Ruiz, M., et al.: Music learning in preschool with mobile devices. Behav. Inf. Technol. **36**(1), 95–111 (2017)
10. Dotsenko, S., Zhang, Y.: Multimedia technologies in music education of preschool children. New Collegium (2023)
11. Turyamureeba, S.: Integrating music education into the curriculum for cognitive development. J. Res. Educ. **4**, 50–54 (2024)
12. Shore, R.A.: Music and cognitive development: from notes to neural networks. NHSA DIALOG **13**(1), 53–65 (2010)
13. Liu, J.: An automatic classification method for multiple music genres by integrating emotions and intelligent algorithms. Appl. Artif. Intell. **37**(1), 2211458 (2023)
14. Shi, S.: Research on the innovation path of music education in higher vocational colleges and universities in the context of the new era. Appl. Math. Nonlinear Sci. **9** (2024)
15. Zhang, N.: Informatization integration strategy of modern vocal music teaching and traditional music culture in colleges and universities in the era of artificial intelligence. Appl. Math. Nonlinear Sci. **9** (2023)
16. LeCun, Y., Bengio, Y., Hinton, G.: Deep learning. Nature **521**(7553), 436–444 (2015)
17. O′Shea, K.: An introduction to convolutional neural networks. arXiv preprint arXiv:1511.08458 (2015)
18. Li, Z., et al.: A survey of convolutional neural networks: analysis, applications, and prospects. IEEE Trans. Neural Netw. Learn. Syst. **33**(12), 6999–7019 (2021)
19. Baldovino, R.G., et al.: A visual aid system using image processing and deep learning with audio haptic feedback for the blind and visually-impaired. Procedia Comput. Sci. **246**, 2974–2983 (2024)
20. Halder, S., et al.: AI-based seagrass morphology measurement. J. Environ. Manage. **369**, 122246 (2024)
21. Kumar, M., et al.: YOLOv5x-based brain tumor detection for healthcare applications. Procedia Comput. Sci. **233**, 950–959 (2024)
22. Soni, V., et al.: Introducing AOD 4: a dataset for air borne object detection. Data Brief **56**, 110801 (2024)
23. Agarwal, V., Bansal, G.: Automatic number plate detection and recognition using YOLO world. Comput. Electr. Eng. **120**, 109646 (2024)
24. Amin, A.L., Chimba, D., Hasan, K.: Integrating AI and edge computing for advanced safety at railroad grade crossings. J. Rail Transport Planning Manag. **33**, 100501 (2025)
25. Du, J.: Understanding of object detection based on CNN family and YOLO. In: Journal of Physics: Conference Series. IOP Publishing (2018)
26. Bahhar, C., et al.: Wildfire and smoke detection using staged YOLO model and ensemble CNN. Electronics (2023)
27. El-Bana, S., Al-Kabbany, A., Sharkas, M.: A multi-task pipeline with specialized streams for classification and segmentation of infection manifestations in COVID-19 scans. PeerJ Comput. Sci. **6**, e303 (2020)

28. Li, M., et al.: Agricultural greenhouses detection in high-resolution satellite images based on convolutional neural networks: comparison of faster R-CNN, YOLO v3 and SSD. Sensors **20** (2020)
29. Liu, Y., et al.: Attention to task-aligned object detection for end–edge–cloud video surveillance. IEEE Internet Things J. **11**, 13781–13792 (2024)
30. Liao, J., Hansen, P., Chai, C.: A framework of artificial intelligence augmented design support. Hum. Comput. Interact. **35**(5–6), 511–544 (2020)
31. Shanshan, S., Sen, G.: Empowering learners with AI-generated content for programming learning and computational thinking: the lens of extended effective use theory. J. Comput. Assist. Learn. **40**(4), 1941–1958 (2024)
32. Li, J., et al.: What does artificial intelligence generated content bring to teaching and learning? a literature review on AIGC in education. In: 2024 International Symposium on Educational Technology. IEEE (2024)
33. Choi, A.E., et al.: SKIMusic: a mobile sheet music player. in DLSU research congress (2017)
34. Koong Lin, H.C., et al.: Application of WSQ (watch-summary-question) flipped teaching in affective conversational robots: impacts on learning emotion, self-directed learning, and learning effectiveness of senior high school students. Int. J. Hum. Comput. Interact. 1–18 (2024)
35. Plass, J.L., Homer, B.D., Kinzer, C.K.: Foundations of game-based learning. Educ. Psychol. **50**(4), 258–283 (2015)
36. Wu, T.T., et al.: Leveraging computer vision for adaptive learning in STEM education: Effect of engagement and self-efficacy. Int. J. Educ. Technol. High. Educ. **20**(1), 53 (2023)

Enhancing Engineering Education Through User-Centred Design Integration

Lilit Hakobyan(✉) and Abinaya Sowriraghavan

Aston University, Birmingham B4 7ET, UK
{hakobyl2,a.sowriraghavan}@aston.ac.uk

Abstract. As engineering education evolves to meet the demands of rapidly advancing technology, there is an increasing need for professionals who can design intuitive, user-centred applications. This paper explores the integration of User-Centred Design (UCD) principles within a Human-Computer Interaction (HCI) module taught at both undergraduate (UG) and postgraduate (PG) levels. Employing a structured four-phase framework that integrates theoretical instruction, practical application, peer collaboration, and reflective practice, the research assesses student performance over three academic years to examine how embedding UCD principles enhances student learning and problem-solving abilities, promoting empathetic thinking within design. Findings indicate significant improvements in design-related assessments, particularly among undergraduates, highlighting the value of hands-on application. Challenges persist in areas such as Knowledge Elicitation (KE) and Usability Evaluation (UE), where undergraduates struggle with analytical reasoning and research methodologies, while postgraduates demonstrate stronger competencies. The study contributes to engineering education by advocating for a balanced curriculum that integrates UCD principles, ensuring future engineers develop both technical expertise and a user-centred mindset essential for designing effective, user-focused systems.

Keywords: User-centred Design · Engineering education · Research-based learning

1 Introduction

Modern engineering disciplines increasingly require professionals who can design intuitive, user-centred systems that align with user needs and expectations. While technical proficiency remains a core aspect of engineering education, traditional curricula often overlook the importance of user-centred approaches to design [34]. This results in a gap between the technical skills acquired by graduates and their ability to engage with real-world user needs. Consequently, engineering professionals may find themselves limited in their effectiveness in workplace environments that prioritise user satisfaction and human factors [16]. The interdisciplinary nature of HCI, however, presents a valuable opportunity

B. K. Smith and M. Borge (Eds.): HCII 2025, LNCS 15806, pp. 17–36, 2025.
https://doi.org/10.1007/978-3-031-93564-0_2

to bridge this gap, as it combines technical knowledge with a strong emphasis on understanding user needs and behaviours. Core HCI principles (e.g., user research,usability evaluation) inherently align with UCD, which encourages students to think critically from a user's perspective and develop problem-solving skills that extend beyond technical implementation [13]. By engaging with UCD methodologies, students not only enhance their ability to create more intuitive and accessible systems but also cultivate a more empathetic approach to engineering challenges [33]. This integration of UCD into engineering curricula can equip future professionals with the essential skills to design systems that not only meet technical requirements but also prioritise user experience. By embedding these principles into their education, graduates are better prepared to meet industry demands, where UCD is increasingly recognised as a key factor in successful product and system development. This approach aligns with a broader shift towards student-centred learning, where hands-on, iterative processes mirror real-world problem-solving methods [25]. By actively applying theoretical knowledge in practical contexts, students gain deeper insights, fostering critical thinking and reflective learning—skills that extend beyond traditional teaching models and into professional practice.

This paper explores the integration of UCD principles into a HCI module delivered at both the second-year UG and PG taught levels. The aim is to evaluate how embedding UCD practices within an engineering curriculum enhances student engagement and their ability to tackle complex, real-world problems. By incorporating UCD methodologies early in students' academic journeys, this study offers insights from an instructor's perspective on how such an approach deepens students' understanding of course content and its practical applications. The HCI modules in question are structured around three core UCD processes: knowledge elicitation (KE), user interface (UI) design, and usability evaluation (UE). Students are assessed on their ability to apply these principles to real-world challenges, with the curriculum designed to introduce each process sequentially. This gradual progression allows students to develop their skills in empathy-driven design while reinforcing their theoretical understanding through practical application. The scaffolding of these concepts aligns with best practices in flipped classroom pedagogy [23], where students engage in independent pre-class study before applying their learning in collaborative, problem-based activities.

The integration of UCD into the HCI module at both levels has yielded positive outcomes, particularly in enhancing student engagement and fostering a stronger connection between technical design and user needs. It is important to note that while the findings are not exhaustive and reflect a range of experiences shared by instructors, they provide valuable contributions to the ongoing discussion on the effective integration of the UCD framework into educational practices. The following sections will further explore the impact of this integration through an analysis of student performance trends, challenges encountered when applying UCD principles, and opportunities for future research to refine pedagogical strategies and enhance student learning outcomes.

2 Literature Review

In higher education, the way students learn has changed significantly over the years: the traditional lecture-based model, once the dominant mode of instruction, has increasingly been complemented by more interactive, learner-driven pedagogies [1]. This transition is driven by the recognition that learning is most effective when students engage in active construction of knowledge rather than passive receipt of information, which is where pedagogical approaches like research-based learning can be advantageous. Similarly, Flipped Classroom Model [20] is a pedagogical approach that reverses traditional teaching methods by delivering instructional content outside of the classroom, often through video lectures, while in-class time is devoted to engaging in active learning activities. While improvements seen in flipped classrooms may be attributed to the introduction of active learning strategies rather than the flipped format itself, the effectiveness of this approach can be hindered by challenges such as students not reviewing materials before the session, limiting their ability to fully engage in classroom activities [20].

HCI education has adapted to this shift, incorporating methods that promote student engagement and collaboration [19]. The interdisciplinary nature of HCI allows students to develop a range of skills, with a particular focus on empathetic, user-centered design [10,33]. Through the application of core principles such as understanding user needs, HCI courses foster critical thinking and problem-solving abilities, with an emphasis on the user perspective [22]. When it comes to teaching HCI, various pedagogical approaches have emerged, such as the "prototype walkthrough" method, where students engage with the design process in studio settings and receive iterative feedback from peers and instructors [18]. This approach was found to encourage active participation in the design cycle, helping students develop both technical and interpersonal skills. A similar studio-based approach focused on KE, prototype implementation, and UE as core elements of UCD (which mirrors the structure of the HCI modules in this study) [24]. Another approach involved students identifying urban problems, designing a system to address them, and presenting the design to a panel of judges [29]. This hands-on methodology integrates problem identification, design, and evaluation, closing the loop between user needs and design outcomes. Research suggests that aligning this approach with international standards for software engineering education allows students to gain a deeper understanding of theoretical concepts by working on real projects [35]. This, in turn, fosters collaboration, creativity, and critical thinking as they work in teams to tackle complex problems, simulating the challenges they will face in the professional world.

At the heart of these approaches is UCD, which has evolved into a central tenet of HCI education [7]. The integration of UCD within higher education curricula is particularly important, as it prepares students to solve real-world problems through a user-first lens. It is often suggested that engineering curricula should strike a balance between technical subjects and practical design skills [14], as the demand for designers skilled in UCD principles has increased, particularly in software engineering and technology [15]. These skills, however, are often challenging for engineering students, who are typically more accustomed to scientific and computational thinking [2,11]. The integration of UCD into engineering education has been successfully demonstrated in some cases, where project-based learning, involving the application of UCD principles, was found to significantly enhance students' understanding of both HCI and UCD [26].

While pedagogical methods for teaching UCD can vary, they often include hands-on, practical experiences that engage students directly with users, providing invaluable learning opportunities. Active learning, an educational strategy that incorporates techniques such as teamwork, problem-based learning, discussions, and peer-learning, has been found to improve critical thinking and problem-solving abilities among CS undergraduates [27]. Multiple studies have positively reviewed the application of active learning in education and reported benefits such as improved self-efficacy [31], higher grades [30] and increased retention in their programs [6]. The combination of flipped classroom with active learning promotes learner participation, as structured in-class activities can root the materials learned independently [12,37].

As new technologies continue to evolve, however, teaching UCD within this context presents challenges related to balancing innovation with ethical considerations, especially when involving human subjects. Further, within the context of UCD, empathetic thinking emerges as a key skill for developers and designers, enabling them to understand and address user needs in a way that goes beyond simply ensuring user satisfaction. One effective method for promoting empathetic thinking is the incorporation of Design Thinking (DT) principles, which prioritise empathy as a central component [10,28]. DT is an interactive, user-centred approach that is both structured and flexible, often referred to in the literature as innovative, creative, or intuitive thinking [9]. This approach has been applied across multiple domains, including engineering, education, technology, and healthcare, addressing a wide range of problem areas [32]. Another key aspect of DT is its inherently collaborative nature, which fosters inclusivity and encourages interdisciplinary teams to unite diverse skills and perspectives [21]. The application of DT in nursing education, for example, was shown to not only help students develop empathy and teamwork skills but also enhance their ability to tackle complex real-world challenges [4], while reinforcing the critical role of empathy in healthcare education [17]. Similarly, the application of DT in early childhood education has been shown to foster creativity and cognitive flexibility, further demonstrating the versatility of this approach across various educational contexts [36].

It is evident from the discussion that incorporating active learning into Engineering education, specifically within HCI courses, presents an opportunity to extend these benefits into a technical, design-focused field. Within HCI, engaging students in UCD has the potential to enable them to directly apply theoretical concepts to practical, real-world problems. This approach has the potential to not only help students build core skills but also encourage reflective thinking and problem-solving abilities. Below, we outline how such a model has been effectively incorporated within the proposed HCI UG and PG modules.

3 Module Design and Structure

The HCI modules introduces active learning through the practical application of UCD principles. Students engage in activities that mirror the stages of and design typical in real-world HCI projects, integrating both theoretical knowledge and hands-on practice in the user interface (UI) design process. This structure fosters essential problem-solving skills, focusing on knowledge elicitation, UI design, and usability evaluation—core components of HCI. Figure 1 provides a visual summary of the key activities and associated methods for each phase: KE, User-Centred UI Design, and UE. This overview highlights the skills and approaches students adopt as they progress through each phase of the module. By guiding students through these structured UCD processes, the module encourages critical and empathetic thinking about user needs, preparing them for future roles in both academic and professional settings that demand proficiency in research and problem-solving.

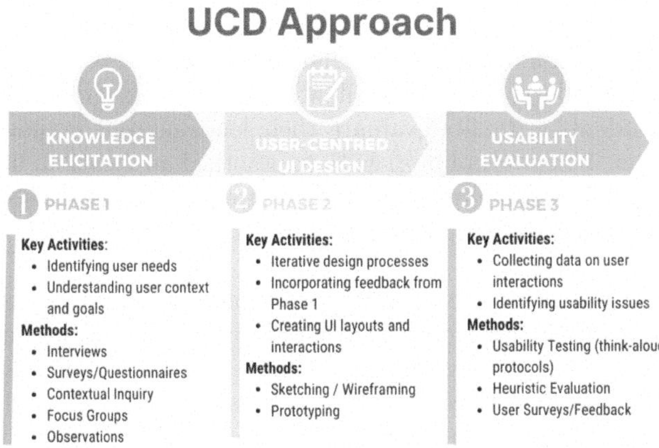

Fig. 1. Key activities and methods associated with the three core phases of the HCI module: KE, Design, and UE.

Through participation in UCD activities, students are expected to achieve key learning outcomes aligned with developing essential HCI competencies:

- Mastery of KE techniques that allow students to gather and interpret user requirements effectively in the context of UI design.
- Ability to adopt and apply UCD methods that consider end-user needs, fostering an empathetic approach to design.

- Proficiency in evaluating and analysing UI designs with a specific focus on usability, informed by a foundational understanding of HCI principles.
- Development of transferable skills in reflective practice, teamwork, and self-directed learning, promoting critical and empathetic perspectives essential for ongoing professional growth.

The module adopts a flipped classroom approach, integrating theoretical and practical components within a flexible learning cycle. To maximise the value of in-class time, students are first provided with video recordings of essential lecture content covering the foundational theories and principles students are expected to grasp. During the practical sessions, students apply the knowledge gained from these video lectures to work through real-world problems, focusing on tasks that require them to prepare for fieldwork activities outside of the classroom. These activities are structured around key phases of HCI design processes - beginning with knowledge elicitation, followed by UI design, and concluding with usability evaluation. In each phase, students are encouraged to integrate their theoretical understanding with practical application, reinforcing both skill sets.

Between sessions, students have allocated time to engage in practical activities such as data collection and user studies according to their plans developed during class. This is an important phase, as it forms the basis of their fieldwork and contributes directly to the assessment components. Once the fieldwork is completed, students return to class sessions where they analyse results, reflect on their research and findings, discuss challenges encountered, and refine their approaches. These reflective sessions allow peer feedback and instructor guidance, helping students critically evaluate their learning and prepare for subsequent assessments. This cycle of preparation, practical application, fieldwork and reflection not only supports students' immediate learning, but also helps them build essential research and problem-solving skills that are critical in professional HCI practice.

The module assessments are organised into cohesive activities, each designed to advance students' engagement with a primary learning outcome, aligning with the stages of UCD to develop analytical, empathetic and reflective skills essential for HCI practice. It consists of interrelated group tasks that create a cohesive portfolio of work, simulating the iterative nature of research-based HCI projects. Each assessment builds upon the previous one, with formative feedback provided at each stage, guiding students through the continuous refinement of their designs. Each year, students work on projects that vary in theme, ranging from topics such as healthy eating and sustainability in shopping, to others that resonate with current trends and student interests.

- KE: Students collaborate to conduct user research by selecting and applying relevant KE techniques. They reflect on their methodological choices and analyse findings, enhancing their analytical thinking and team communication skills.
- User-Centred UI Design: Using insights from the KE phase, students, as a team, engage in user-centred design, refining UI elements to address real-world

requirements. This phase promotes empathetic thinking, practical application of design methods, and team reflection through presentations that justify design choices.

- UE: Students devise and execute a usability evaluation plan for their UI prototypes, collecting and analysing usability data to refine their designs further. This component encourages reflective thinking and familiarity with research-driven evaluation processes. This assessment component is completed as a team task in the undergraduate cohort, but individually in the postgraduate cohort, reflecting slight differences in learning outcomes.

4 Data Analysis and Results

For this study, data was gathered from end-of-term evaluation questionnaires for the UG HCI module over the past three academic years (2021-2022, 2022-2023, and 2023-2024) to examine student satisfaction and experience. Open-ended responses within the questionnaire provided qualitative insights into student experiences and perceptions of teaching approaches. Due to the very low response rate for the PG cohort evaluation questionnaire, with only one or two responses received, it was not included in the qualitative analysis. In addition to the questionnaires, module reports for both modules were analysed to assess student performance across different assessment components.

Ethical approval for this study was obtained from the relevant Research Ethics Committee, ensuring compliance with institutional guidelines for data protection and participant confidentiality. No identifiable information was included in the questionnaire feedback to protect individuals' confidentiality. The goal of this study is not to focus on individual students' engagement or participation levels; as such, all data extracted is anonymised and is not linked to specific individuals.

The quantitative data were analysed using inferential and descriptive statistical techniques. For student satisfaction, trends in module evaluation scores were examined across the three academic years. For student performance, descriptive statistics were applied to assess pass rates, mean marks, and the distribution of scores across different assessment components for both modules. Table 1 presents the number of registered UG students alongside the mid-module response rate. While we acknowledge that only a small proportion of students completed the end-of-term module evaluation questionnaire, these responses provide valuable insights as discussed below.

Table 2 details students' Likert scale ratings on key aspects of the module. Academic support received consistently high ratings across all years, suggesting sustained satisfaction with available resources and guidance. Interestingly, self-reported engagement remained stable, with only minor fluctuations across years, indicating a continued connection to the module content. There was a gradual decrease in satisfaction with the "mode of delivery" across the three years, which likely reflects changing circumstances in teaching arrangements post-COVID-19.

Table 1. Student registrations and responses to the mid-module questionnaire across three academic years.

Academic Year	No of students registered	No of responses received
2021–2022	199	20
2022–2023	225	27
2023–2024	263	32

During the initial 2021–22 cohort, when fully online learning was more familiar, students may have found it easier to engage remotely with both lectures and collaborative work. As in-person teaching reintroduced a blended format in later years, it appears that some students faced new challenges adapting to the mix of asynchronous and face-to-face elements.

Table 2. Student responses to selected module evaluation questions for the HCI module across three academic years.

Question	2021–2022	2022–2023	2023–2024
The mode of delivery works well	4.5 out of 5	4.1 out of 5	3.7 out of 5
I have received sufficient academic support	4.4 out of 5	4.5 out of 5	4.3 out of 5
I have engaged well with this module	4.2 out of 5	4.3 out of 5	4.2 out of 5

Despite these fluctuations in delivery mode preference, student satisfaction with academic support remained robust, with consistently high scores over 4.0 each year. This suggests that reliable tutor support has been essential in sustaining student engagement. Together, these insights highlight both the potential for online flexibility and the importance of structured support in the blended learning model. Although we do not claim that these results are wholly representative, the scores seem to reflect significant elements of students' learning experiences, as observed from our perspective. The feedback collected here complements our direct observations allowing us to understand better the impact of the module's design and delivery on student satisfaction and perceived support.

As shown in Fig. 2a, the undergraduate module has experienced a steady increase in student numbers over the past three academic years (199 in 2021, 225 in 2022, and 263 in 2023). Pass rates and mean marks have remained relatively stable, with a notable dip in 2022 (87.11% pass rate, mean mark of 53.67) before recovering in 2023 (93.77% pass rate, mean mark of 55.98). While the module structure remained unchanged, the observed dip may align with broader shifts in student engagement and expectations, as reflected in the gradual decline in satisfaction with the mode of delivery over the same period (see Table 2).

In contrast, Fig. 2b shows greater variability in the postgraduate module's performance. Student numbers have fluctuated (28 in 2021, 34 in 2022, 26 in

2023), with pass rates ranging from 61.76% in 2022 to 100% in 2023, and mean marks rising from 46.54 in 2022 to 64.23 in 2023. These inconsistencies can likely be attributed to the nature of the MSc Computer Science programme, a conversion course where many students enter with little to no prior computing background. Given the intensive one-year structure, students may have varying levels of preparedness for HCI and UCD, contributing to the observed performance differences.

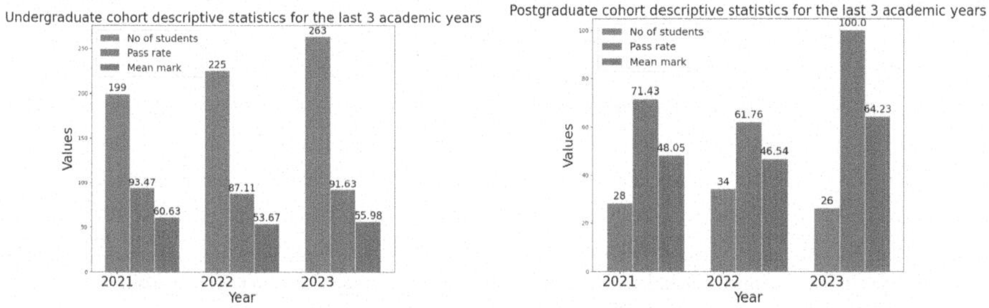

(a) Undergraduate cohort performance (b) Postgraduate cohort performance

Fig. 2. Undergraduate and postgraduate cohort performance (2021–2023), showing student numbers, pass rates, and mean marks across three academic years.

Table 3. Comparative performance of UG and PG students across Knowledge Elicitation, Design, and Usability Evaluation assessments, by academic year.

Cohort	Comparison	2021/22 (%)	2022/23 (%)	2023/24 (%)
UG	(KE > Design)	18.59	23.11	16.35
	(Design > UE)	61.31	69.33	89.35
	(Design > KE)	79.40	60.00	79.85
	(UE > KE)	45.23	40.00	47.91
	(UE > Design)	34.17	19.56	7.22
	(KE > UE)	45.23	47.56	47.53
PG	(KE > Design)	0.00	5.88	53.85
	(Design > UE)	78.57	76.47	65.38
	(Design > KE)	75.00	82.35	46.15
	(UE > KE)	21.43	35.29	46.15
	(UE > Design)	0.00	8.82	30.77
	(KE > UE)	57.14	50.00	50.00

To explore how student performance varied across the three assessment components over time and between cohorts, student performance data were analysed.

This analysis aimed to provide insights into how students engage with assessments that differ in cognitive demands and to highlight any significant differences in performance between the UG and PG groups, as shown in Table 3.

The design assessment consistently demonstrated higher performance across both cohorts. In 2021/22, 61.31% of UG students performed better in this assessment compared to the UE, increasing to 89.35% in 2023/24. In contrast, PG students showed a slight decline from 78.57% to 65.38% over the same period. This trend can likely be attributed to the highly practical and creative nature of the design assessment. The iterative and hands-on nature of design tasks allows students to directly apply theoretical knowledge to the activity, often leading to higher engagement and a more tangible sense of accomplishment.

In contrast, performance in both KE and UE assessments was more variable and generally lagged behind that of the design assessment. For KE, the proportion of undergraduate students who performed better in this assessment than in the design task fluctuated over the three years, showing no consistent upward or downward trend. The PG cohort outperformed the undergraduates in KE, with 53.85% of PG students performing better in this assessment than in the design task in 2023/24, compared to just 16.35% of UG students, which clearly shows a positive sign in the first step towards understanding users and their requirements. The stronger performance of PG students in KE can likely be attributed to their more advanced academic experience. As they are typically expected to engage more deeply with theoretical concepts, including research methods and data analysis, they may be better equipped for tasks requiring critical thinking, analysis, and synthesis of data. In contrast, the lower UG performance in KE may reflect their earlier stage in developing these skills, as well as the challenge of transitioning from creative, practical tasks (e.g., programming) to more theoretical, research-based work. Interestingly, however, no PG students performed better in KE than in the design task in 2021/22. Across the three years, the proportion of students who performed better in the UE assessment compared to KE or the design task fluctuated, with a notable decline in those outperforming the design task in UE by 2023/24. Performance relative to KE showed a slight increase in the final year (47.91%).

For the PG cohort, the percentage of students who performed better in UE compared to KE increased steadily from 21.43% in 2021/22 to 46.15% in 2023/24, which shows that students value and empathise with users and close-the-loop from knowledge elicitation to evaluation. A similar trend was observed when comparing UE and design performance: while no PG students performed better in UE than in the design task in 2021/22, this increased to 30.77% in 2023/24.

Overall, both cohorts appear to face greater difficulties engaging in evaluation activities, which is evident from their analysis, compared to design or KE tasks. The UE assessment typically requires students to apply analytical thinking to identify strengths and weaknesses in their prototype designs, demanding both evaluative and critical skills. This process is often more challenging as it involves critiquing and assessing their own work, a cognitively complex task compared to engaging in design activities, something that ought to be considered for future pedagogical improvements within curricula.

The decline in UE performance may also stem from other factors, such as structural and scheduling aspects of the module. Since UE is the final assessment component, fewer support sessions are available, and students are expected to complete much of the work independently outside of tutorial sessions. This lack of structured guidance may make it more challenging for students to develop the necessary evaluative skills, particularly if they have had limited prior experience with critical analysis and self-assessment.

4.1 Qualitative Results: A Thematic Analysis

The qualitative data were analysed using thematic analysis [3] to identify key themes reflecting undergraduate students' experiences and perceptions of the module. The process began with familiarisation, where feedback was reviewed multiple times to identify recurring patterns. Responses were then systematically coded, capturing insights related to module design, collaboration, and the practical application of UCD principles. Ultimately, four key themes were identified: (1) Module Design and Structure, (2) Application of UCD Principles, (3) Collaborative and Structured Learning Environment, and (4) Positive Learning Experience. Figure 3 presents the resulting codes and their alignment with the four identified themes, offering a visual summary of the thematic structure.

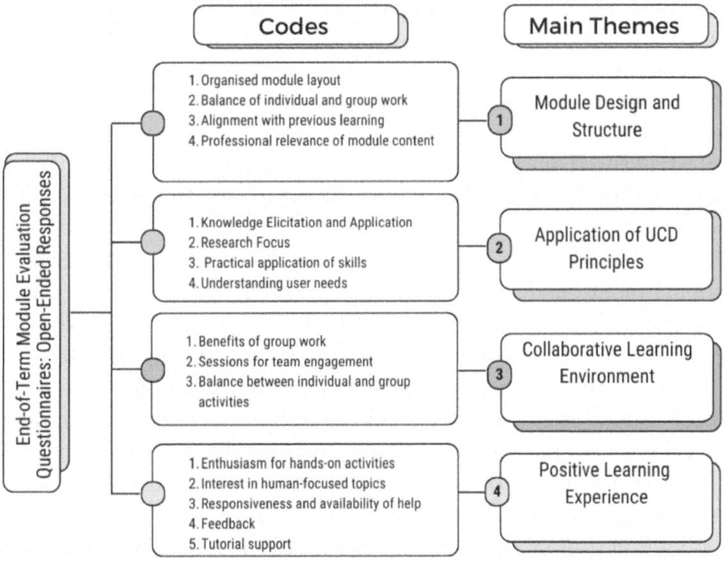

Fig. 3. Thematic analysis of qualitative responses from end-of-term module evaluations, highlighting key themes and codes.

It is important to note, that a subset of miscellaneous comments around scheduling difficulties, or personal availability conflicts was excluded from the analysis to ensure that the thematic analysis remained focused on constructive insights related to the module's core design, structure, and pedagogical impact. These comments reflected either logistical challenges or personal circumstances rather than patterns directly linked to the module's learning objectives and student engagement with content. For instance, several comments referred to scheduling difficulties, issues with group dynamics, or personal availability conflicts. While these reflections are important, these were not substantive enough to inform the broader analysis which focused on pedagogical and experiential aspects of the module. Instead, they highlighted situational issues outside the intended learning activities and outcomes. These outlier comments are nonetheless noted for potential future consideration, especially where structural adjustments may enhance students' overall experience.

Each of the themes below highlights distinct aspects of the module that contributed to student engagement, from the design and practical application of UCD principles to the collaborative nature of the learning environment. The emergent themes are explored in more detail below, drawing on student feedback to demonstrate how different elements of the module influenced student learning and engagement.

(1) *Module Design and Structure*
This theme captures students' appreciation for the clarity, structure, and organisation of the module, as well as the relevance of the content to their professional aspirations. One of the most frequently mentioned codes was the "structured and organised module layout", with students expressing satisfaction with how the course content was presented. Many students felt that the clear organisation helped them understand the flow of the module and the expectations associated with each task. As exemplified by the following quote "everything has been really well structured and clear, and the tasks are reasonable", the module's design succeeded in fostering clarity and providing students with a strong sense of direction.

Another key aspect was the alignment of the module with prior learning. Many students mentioned that the module's content was presented in a way that built upon knowledge gained in earlier modules. This sense of continuity helped students understand the relevance of the current module and its integration with previous modules, thereby enhancing their learning experience.

The "professional relevance of module content" was another prominent point of feedback. Students appreciated the real-world application of the module's content, which they felt would be valuable in their future careers. The structure of the course content, including real-world tasks and opportunities to engage in problem-solving activities, helped students connect academic theory with practice. The combination of different delivery methods allowed for both independent learning and hands-on application as exemplified by the following quote: "The use of asynchronous lectures and in-person tutorial sessions are well balanced".

Overall, students' feedback on the module design and structure suggests that the course is effectively structured to facilitate learning. The clarity of course objectives and the professional relevance of the content all contributed to a positive learning environment. The design of the module, with its well-considered combination of synchronous and asynchronous activities, provides a clear framework for students to engage with the material and apply their learning in a practical, collaborative manner. This structured approach, supported by timely feedback and guidance, appears to have helped students navigate the complexities of the module and develop their knowledge and skills in a systematic, effective way.

(2) ***Application of UCD Principles***

This theme focuses on the students' engagement with the UCD principles integrated into the module. Central to this theme is the students' recognition of the real-world applicability of UCD processes, such as knowledge elicitation, feedback gathering, and understanding user requirements. Many students expressed that learning and applying these principles not only broadened their understanding of the design process but also helped them develop a more holistic approach to problem-solving: one that incorporates user perspectives alongside technical considerations. As one student suggested, "I like the element of gathering our research," reinforcing the value placed on UCD's real-world application.

One common thread in their responses is the recognition that the focus on user needs, rather than merely technical specifications, sets the module apart from others. For example, students highlighted the value of gathering user research and learning methods for designing systems that genuinely meet users' needs. As one student noted, "I enjoy the practical work as I think it gives insight into software building [...] and makes you think in a larger scope, particularly about what the users require."

The emphasis on knowledge elicitation, particularly gathering and analysing user feedback, was noted as an important learning experience. Students appreciated the opportunity to conduct research and understand the importance of aligning design decisions with actual user needs. The practical application of these skills was seen as beneficial for future careers, as students felt better equipped to approach design challenges from a user-focused standpoint. As one student suggested, "I like the element of gathering our research," reinforcing the value placed on UCD's real-world application.

Overall, this theme demonstrates how the application of UCD principles enhances students' ability to approach design challenges from a practical, user-centred perspective, which is perceived as vital for both academic growth and professional readiness.

(3) ***Collaborative Learning Environment***

The collaborative learning environment established within the module emerged as a key element in shaping students' experiences, particularly in fostering effective teamwork and engagement. Feedback from students indicates that the balance between individual tasks and group activities is a key element of the module's design, promoting effective teamwork and active engagement.

Feedback from students highlighted the importance of group work, both in terms of balancing the workload and enhancing collaborative skills. Many students appreciated the opportunity to work closely with peers, recognising the value of shared problem-solving and collective learning. The positive student feedback regarding the collaborative nature of the module indicates that the integration of group tasks with individual responsibilities struck an effective balance, contributing to a productive learning experience as one student noted, "The group work is something I enjoy as it spreads the workload you have to do [...]" highlighting the practical benefits of working together while reducing individual pressure.

The inclusion of in-person group sessions played a significant role in keeping teams engaged and ensuring that group members remained active participants throughout the module. As one student noted, "On-campus lessons ensure that most of the team members are engaging, which is essential for a team project." This insight reflects the value of having dedicated time for students to collaborate face-to-face, fostering active communication and providing opportunities for direct feedback from the teaching staff.

Similarly, students appreciated the proactive approach to managing group dynamics, especially in terms of addressing "disengaged" or "unproductive" team members. The structured environment helped ensure that all team members were contributing, with some students noting that their groups had strategies to address instances of unequal participation. By fostering an environment where students can work together, reflect on their progress, and receive immediate support, the module successfully cultivates a collaborative learning space that enhances both individual and collective achievement.

(3) *Positive Learning Experience*

The final theme highlights students' appreciation for the supportive and engaging learning experience offered by the module, particularly through hands-on activities, accessible teaching staff, and consistent feedback. Many students expressed enjoyment and motivation to engage with the module's "human-focused" topics, noting how these resonated with their interests and professional aspirations. The practical tutorials, led by "enthusiastic lecturers", emerged as a central feature in creating a positive learning experience.

The detailed feedback and tutorial support provided by teaching staff played an important role in enhancing students' experiences. Comments highlighted the value of receiving thorough, timely feedback that helped students better understand concepts and improve their work iteratively. For many, the responsiveness of the teaching staff during tutorials added an extra layer of encouragement, reinforcing a supportive environment conducive to active, engaged learning.

While several elements within this theme, such as detailed feedback, tutorial support, and group work, may also align with previous themes (e.g., Collaborative Learning Environment), they are discussed here due to the consistently positive sentiments students associated with these aspects. This categorisation emphasises students' holistic appreciation for the module's structure, support systems, and active learning opportunities as factors that enhanced their engagement and satisfaction.

5 Discussion and Reflections

The integration of UCD principles into the HCI modules highlighted several patterns in student engagement and achievement. The structured four-phase framework (Fig. 4) provides a scaffolded learning experience that integrates UCD principles and research-driven learning to enhance student engagement. By delineating activities into distinct "before-class," "during-class," and "after-class" stages based on the framework outlined in a study on the flipped classroom model's impact on student achievement [5], the module ensures that students gradually build their knowledge and skills in a structured and iterative manner. The thematic analysis of student feedback and performance trends across different assessments underscores both the strengths of this approach and areas for potential refinement.

The module's design begins with the **(1) Preparation Phase** (Before-Class), where students engage with pre-recorded lectures, directed readings, and independent learning activities. This phase is instrumental in introducing theoretical concepts and grounding students in foundational knowledge before engaging in interactive class discussions. The effectiveness of this phase is reflected in the positive student feedback on academic support, as structured materials provide students with the flexibility to learn at their own pace. It was, however, observed that during initial weeks, students showed some hesitancy in committing to this pre-class work. It often took a few sessions for them to recognise the importance of completing these activities as foundational preparation for in-class discussions and planning exercises. As students adapted, engagement with pre-recorded materials increased, encouraging them to arrive prepared, which positively impacted their collaborative work. This is in line with findings in flipped classroom pedagogy, where students initially underestimate the significance of self-study until they experience the in-class demands [23]. It is important to note that students who struggled with KE tasks may have benefited from additional scaffolding during this stage, particularly undergraduates who had less prior experience with research methodologies.

The second phase, the **(2) Exploration Phase** (During-Class), represents the in-class component of the flipped model. During this stage, students put their theoretical learning gained from the previous stage into practice through hands-on activities such as group work, planning exercises, and exploratory tasks that support their fieldwork preparation. The success of this approach is evident in the strong student engagement and higher performance in design-related assessments. The iterative process enabled students to develop a deeper understanding of UCD principles, highlighting the effectiveness of interactive classroom sessions in bridging theory and practice. The variability in student satisfaction with the mode of delivery, however, suggests that further refinements could be made to balance in-person and asynchronous elements, particularly

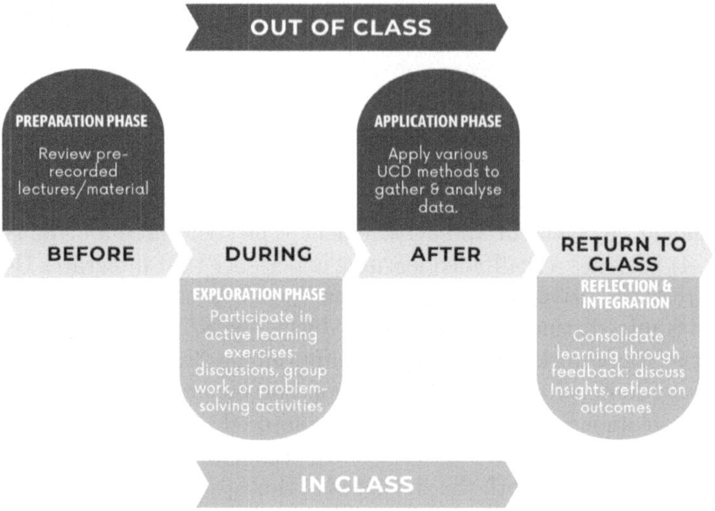

Fig. 4. A four-step blended learning framework for the HCI module

for students who may require additional guidance. Facilitating group work in this way also introduced further challenges related to student participation and group dynamics, as some students initially struggled with the active and collaborative demands of the session. The module staff placed particular emphasis on supporting teams where engagement was observed to be inconsistent. By closely monitoring group dynamics, staff were able to identify instances where certain students were less involved in collaborative tasks. To address this, module staff facilitated discussions with all groups, encouraging students to articulate their decision-making processes and to reflect on their individual contributions. These interactions aimed to prompt each team member to participate fully in activities, fostering a more accountable and cohesive team environment. Through guided questioning students were encouraged to engage critically with the tasks at hand, enhancing group cohesion and ensuring a collaborative approach to learning. By mid-module, students appeared more comfortable and effective in their group work, applying theoretical concepts more critically and engaging in class activities more meaningfully.

Following this is the **(3) Application Phase** (After-Class), an out-of-class stage where students apply UCD methodologies in real-world contexts. During this phase, students conduct data collection based on the plans developed in class, using methods such as interviews, surveys, and observational techniques to gather insights relevant to their design goals. This phase highlighted a key challenge: some students initially struggled with the autonomy required to carry out these UCD activities (including UE) effectively. This phase was important for students to bridge theoretical understanding with real-world application, often involving iterative planning, data collection, and data analysis. For many students, this hands-on application of learning helped them develop both independence and self-efficacy. In line with Kolb's Experiential Learning Theory [8], the fieldwork gave students a concrete experience to reflect upon, strengthening their learning cycle. Nevertheless, the observed decline in performance in UE assessment, particularly among undergraduates, suggests that students may require additional structured guidance during this phase.

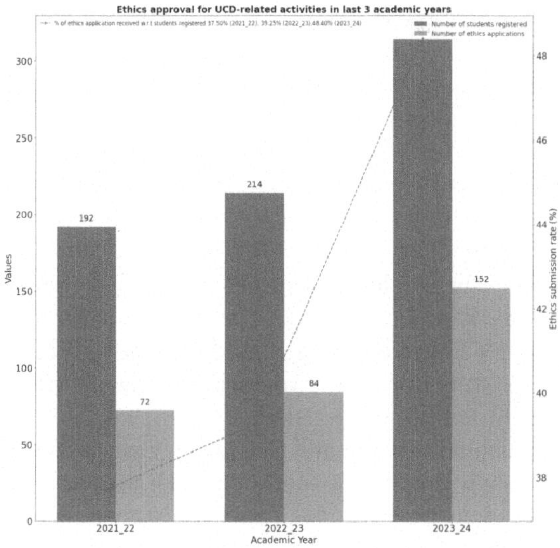

Fig. 5. Ethics Submission Overview: Student Numbers and Submission Rates for Final-Year UG

While the structured learning approach in the HCI module supports the development of research skills and critical engagement with UCD methodologies, it remains challenging to assess its long-term impact beyond the module itself. One potential indicator of its influence can be observed in the increasing proportion of final-year students applying for ethical approval for their final-year projects (see Fig. 5). Over the past three years, the percentage of final-year students submitting ethics applications has steadily increased, from 38% in 2021/22 to 48% in 2023/24. This suggests that students may be developing a greater awareness of ethical considerations when conducting research or designing user-facing systems. Although this trend cannot be directly attributed to the HCI module, it aligns with the module's emphasis on knowledge elicitation, usability evaluation, and iterative design—components that encourage students to critically reflect on ethical implications in research and system development. Further investigation would be required to establish a more direct causal link, but this trend highlights the potential for structured HCI learning to foster a more empathetic and ethically aware student cohort.

6 Conclusions

The findings of this study offer valuable insights into the design and delivery of HCI curricula, particularly in the integration of UCD principles within UG and PG education. The structured four-phase framework has proven effective in guiding students through an iterative learning process, fostering engagement through hands-on application, reflection, and feedback. Notably, the upward trend in UG performance on the design assessment highlights the benefits of practical, creative tasks in reinforcing design principles and enhancing both student motivation and learning outcomes.

Despite these positive outcomes, challenges remain particularly in KE and UE assessments. UG students, in particular, may require additional support in research methodologies and data analysis techniques to develop the higher-order thinking skills necessary for engaging with UCD activities. Similarly, a stronger emphasis on usability testing could benefit both UG and PG cohorts, ensuring a more comprehensive understanding of evaluation methods. Refinements to the after-class and reflection phases of the module, such as integrating more structured formative feedback and clearer guidance for self-directed assessments, could further enhance students' ability to critically engage with research findings and translate them into informed decisions.

Future research should investigate the underlying causes of observed performance trends through qualitative methods, such as interviews or surveys, to better understand student perceptions of each assessment type. Studying empathetic thinking skills over a longer period of time by comparing performance and application across other taught subjects, by involving students as key stakeholders in observing their sentiments towards a design-centric curriculum could shed light on scope for pedagogy-based improvements. This would help determine whether differences in engagement and outcomes stem from prior experience, perceived difficulty, or personal learning preferences. Overall, the structured approach not only provides a clear learning framework but also supports students in bridging the gap between theory and practice. While the findings are limited by the small cohort size and reliance on instructor reflections, they offer preliminary insights into the benefits and challenges of this pedagogical approach. The next phase of research will seek to expand the evidence base by incorporating direct student perspectives, contributing to the ongoing refinement of HCI education and informing future curriculum development.

Disclosure of Interests. The authors have no competing interests to declare that are relevant to the content of this article.

References

1. Ang, K.C., Afzal, F., Crawford, L.H.: Transitioning from passive to active learning: preparing future project leaders. Project Leadership Soc. **2**, 100016 (2021)
2. Beneroso, D., Robinson, J.: Online project-based learning in engineering design: supporting the acquisition of design skills. Educ. Chem. Eng. **38**, 38–47 (2022)

3. Braun, V., Clarke, V.: Using thematic analysis in psychology. Qual. Res. Psychol. **3**(2), 77–101 (2006)
4. Bravo, K.: Design thinking in nursing education and health sciences education. Nurs. Educ. Perspect. **44**(3), 164–168 (2023)
5. Cabı, E.: The impact of the flipped classroom model on students' academic achievement. Int. Rev. Res. Open Distributed Learn. **19**(3) (2018)
6. Calvin, J.J., et al.: Research group-led undergraduate research program: analyzing and improving a versatile springboard for first-year undergraduates. J. Chem. Educ. **99**(2), 799–809 (2021)
7. Cho, Y., Park, H.J., Lim, H.: Research in user-centered design 2009 to 2018: a systematic keyword network analysis. In: HCI International 2020-Posters: 22nd International Conference, HCII 2020, Copenhagen, Denmark, July 19–24, 2020, Proceedings, Part I 22, pp. 11–18. Springer (2020)
8. Da, K.: Experiential learning. Experience as the Source of Learning and Development **41** (1984)
9. Dahiya, A., Kujur, A., Kumar, J.: A neurophysiological investigation of design thinking process in human-computer interaction design. In: Proceedings of the 14th International Conference on Interfaces and Human Computer Interaction 2020 and 13th International Conference on Game and Entertainment Technologies 2020 (2020)
10. Dias, I., Costa, E., Mealha, Ó.: Involving older adults in the design process: a human-centric design thinking approach. IxD&A **54**, 85–110 (2022)
11. Dym, C.L., Agogino, A.M., Eris, O., Frey, D.D., Leifer, L.J.: Engineering design thinking, teaching, and learning. J. Eng. Educ. **94**(1), 103–120 (2005)
12. Entezari, M., Javdan, M.: Active learning and flipped classroom, hand in hand approach to improve students learning in human anatomy and physiology. Int. J. High. Educ. **5**(4), 222–231 (2016)
13. Faiola, A., Davis, S.B., Edwards, R.L.: Extending knowledge domains for new media education: integrating interaction design theory and methods. New Media Soc. **12**(5), 691–709 (2010)
14. Fernando, A.R., Ghazali, N.E., Al Haddad, S.A.H., Mohd-Yusof, K.: Work in progress: Framework for developing design-centric engineering curricula. In: 2022 IEEE World Engineering Education Conference (EDUNINE), pp. 1–4. IEEE (2022)
15. Gondomar, R., Mor, E.: From ucd to hcd and beyond. conciliating the human aims between philosophy and design education. In: International Conference on Human-Computer Interaction, pp. 108–122. Springer (2020)
16. Hasanain, B.: The role of ergonomic and human factors in sustainable manufacturing: a review. Machines **12**(3), 159 (2024)
17. Hawkins, J., Baaki, J., Tremblay, B., Hawkins, R.J.: Impact of a design thinking educational activity on graduate students' knowledge, confidence, and perceived benefits. Nurse Educator, pp. 10–1097 (2024)
18. Hundhausen, C.D., Fairbrother, D., Petre, M.: An empirical study of the "prototype walkthrough" a studio-based activity for hci education. ACM Trans. Comput.-Hum. Interact. (TOCHI) **19**(4), 1–36 (2012)
19. Iantorno, M., Pandeliev, V.: Teaching software to diverse ux design cohorts: from flipped classrooms to computer-based scaffolding. In: Proceedings of the 6th Annual Symposium on HCI Education, pp. 1–11 (2024)
20. Jensen, J.L., Kummer, T.A., Godoy, P.D.d.M.: Improvements from a flipped classroom may simply be the fruits of active learning. CBE—Life Sci. Educ. **14**(1), ar5 (2015)

21. Jiang, H., Yen, C.C.: Design thinking in conceptual design processes: a comparison between industrial and engineering design students. Advances in Industrial Design Engineering, p. 29 (2013)
22. Martinelli, S.R., Zaina, L.A.: Learning hci from a virtual flipped classroom: improving the students' experience in times of covid-19. In: Proceedings of the xx Brazilian Symposium on Human Factors in Computing Systems, pp. 1–11 (2021)
23. O'Flaherty, J., Phillips, C.: The use of flipped classrooms in higher education: a scoping review. Internet High. Educ. **25**, 85–95 (2015)
24. Reimer, Y.J., Douglas, S.A.: Teaching hci design with the studio approach. Comput. Sci. Educ. **13**(3), 191–205 (2003)
25. Salto, L.M., Riggs, M.L., Delgado De Leon, D., Casiano, C.A., De Leon, M.: underrepresented minority high school and college students report stem-pipeline sustaining gains after participating in the loma linda university summer health disparities research program. PloS one **9**(9), e108497 (2014)
26. Santana-Mancilla, P.C., Rodriguez-Ortiz, M.A., Garcia-Ruiz, M.A., Gaytan-Lugo, L.S., Fajardo-Flores, S.B., Contreras-Castillo, J.: Teaching hci skills in higher education through game design: a study of students' perceptions. In: Informatics, vol. 6, p. 22. MDPI (2019)
27. Santoso, H.B., Sari, E.: Transforming undergraduate hci course in indonesia: a preliminary study. In: Proceedings of the Asia Pacific HCI and UX Design Symposium, pp. 55–59 (2015)
28. She, J., Belanger, E., Bartels, C., Reeling, H.: Improve syntax correctness and breadth of design space exploration in functional analysis. J. Mech. Des. **144**(11), 111402 (2022)
29. Solano, A.: Teaching experience of the human-computer interaction course at the universidad autónoma de occidente of colombia. In: Proceedings of the XVIII International Conference on Human Computer Interaction, pp. 1–2 (2017)
30. Sternquist, B., Huddleston, P., Fairhurst, A.: Framing the undergraduate research experience: discovery involvement in retailing undergraduate education. J. Mark. Educ. **40**(1), 76–84 (2018)
31. Stump, G.S., Husman, J., Corby, M.: Engineering students' intelligence beliefs and learning. J. Eng. Educ. **103**(3), 369–387 (2014)
32. Vesudevan, M., Rozee, I., Shamsuddin, W., Wei, L.C.: Impacts of design thinking course for undergraduate students in a private higher education institution. Sciences **3**(13), 39–45 (2020)
33. Wallisch, A., Briede-Westermeyer, J.C., Luzardo-Briceno, M.: Fostering user-empathy skills of engineering students by collaborative teaching. Int. J. Eng. Educ. **37**(1), 223–243 (2021)
34. Woodill, S., Akiyama, Y.: Integrating user-centred design approaches for a course design framework for interdisciplinary studies in teaching and learning. J. Teach. Learn. **14**(1), 93–107 (2020)
35. Xu, H., Wu, Z., Lin, T., Tang, N., Chen, Y.: Research on teaching model of project-driven hci course. In: International Conference on Education, Management and Computing Technology (ICEMCT-16), pp. 909–914. Atlantis Press (2016)
36. Yalçın, V.: Design thinking model in early childhood education. Int. J. Psychol. Educ. Stud. **9**(1), 196–210 (2022)
37. Zappe, S., Leicht, R., Messner, J., Litzinger, T., Lee, H.W.: "flipping" the classroom to explore active learning in a large undergraduate course. In: 2009 Annual Conference & Exposition, pp. 14–1385 (2009)

Co-designing User Experience of Moodle Workspaces in Higher Education - Process and Principles

Laura Havinen[1(✉)], Juho-Pekka Mäkipää[1], and Rebekah Rousi[1,2]

[1] University of Vaasa, Wolffintie 32, 65200 Vaasa, Finland
{laura.havinen,juho-pekka.makipaa,rebekah.rousi}@uwasa.fi
[2] University of Jyväskylä, PO Box 35, 40014 Jyväskylä, Finland

Abstract. Studies have shown that user experience (UX) in course learning platforms impacts learning. UX not only stems from user interface design, but the design of instructional information within the workspace. This study examines the teacher-led design elements that students experience to improve the UX of Moodle workspaces. During the study, students were asked to re-design their course workspace for better UX. The study was implemented in two UX courses in 2021 (N = 35) and 2024 (N = 31). Through co-design workshops, students identified problematic object-level UX issues in the workspaces. We conducted a content analysis on student reports to identify themes describing the issues. From these themes, we derived design principles to improve UX in the Moodle workspace. The results indicate connections between practical improvements and the intended UX in the context of course workspaces. In addition, the study demonstrates how co-design can be used to improve the UX of a course workspace.

Keywords: User Experience · Co-Design · Learning Platforms · Course Workspaces

1 Introduction

As e-learning and blended learning becomes more popular, the value of user experience (UX) within online learning platforms rises to play an important role in the learning experience. Learning platforms in higher education (HE) that feature effective design and interaction promote learning engagement [1, 2]. Poorly designed workspaces that incite negative UX may lead to low rates of use, failures to understand or accept tasks, interrupt learning performance, and may even lead to course dropouts [1, 3]. In contrast, positive UX in workspaces can help students achieve learning goals [4], and lead to significantly improved learning performance [5]. Teachers, however, have limited skills in designing course workspaces in learning platforms. This particularly holds from the perspective of designing for positive UX [6]. Involving students in the workspace design process has proven valuable in the context of instructional design [7]. This paper explores the results of co-designing with students in improving the UX of a course workspace in Moodle.

B. K. Smith and M. Borge (Eds.): HCII 2025, LNCS 15806, pp. 37–56, 2025.
https://doi.org/10.1007/978-3-031-93564-0_3

Moodle is one of the most popular open-source learning platforms in HE and it has millions of users globally [8]. Like any other product, it should not be seen as simply functional, delivering usability, but should tap into the psychological and social dimensions of users enabling a deeper connection between users, systems, and what the systems represent [9]. In learning platforms other critical factors than simply effectiveness is at play, such as engagement in learning method, selection of appropriate and effective pedagogical methods, and accounting for diverse learning styles (see e.g., [10, 11]). Moodle is a platform that serves as a base for teachers and educational designers to be able to design contents, learning processes and learning progress. This is enabled through careful consideration of information chunking and sequences, hierarchies and order of logic, meaningful tasks and exercises, and effective evaluation methods [12]. Thus, teachers and educational designers enact a level of Moodle UX design that directly impacts the reception, interaction, and learning of required contents.

In the present paper we investigate the teacher and educational designer level of design in Moodle workspaces. The aim of the study was to examine what teacher-led design elements students experience to contribute to better UX in course workspaces. The intention was to give the students the floor as learning and instructional design experts, as well as co-designers of the workspace in question, and for future workspaces on future courses to come. A co-design method was implemented in which students as end-users were asked to re-design the workspace. The re-design task supported mutual learning between students and teachers and empowered them to be involved in influencing students' own learning's future. This was achieved through their participation in designing the pedagogical level of digital learning technology [13].

The current paper outlines a study that engaged students in co-design of the Moodle workspace for their own course. It begins with a brief review of related literature focusing on pedagogical and UX design on e-learning platforms as well as UX attributes. The method section describes the procedure, recruitment, and approach of the study, while the results outline the main findings of the students' object-level design suggestions for the Moodle workspace. In the discussion, we ponder the findings and what they mean in the context of an evolving digital world. For example, in the near future Moodle will most likely have an 'artificial intelligence (AI) design' component that can aid educators and educational designers in effectively designing workspaces. Yet, to arrive at this stage, detailed knowledge of how students perceive, engage with, and re-design the course workspace level of the platform is critical.

2 Learning Platforms and Related Literature

A learning platform is a computer mediated environment that facilitates collaboration via discussions, content sharing, documentation, tracking, evaluation, automation, reporting and these days more [14]. Understandings and applications of learning platforms have fast moved from ideas of virtual traditional classrooms with one standardized format to potentially highly personalized spaces that, with the help of AI and learning analytics, can tailor content and delivery on an individual level [15]. Since the introduction of learning platforms during the late-1990s, educational professionals and researchers have engendered to decipher how the domains of education and information technology can effectively be combined to achieve the best possible learning outcomes [16]. Particularly in the fields of educational science and educational technology, frameworks, guidelines, heuristics, and other measures for critical success factors have been developed [10, 16, 17].

From the perspective of the design of e-learning technology, scholars such as Nokelainen [18] and Pham, Singh and Jahnke [19] have developed and built on the concept of pedagogical usability. In his earlier efforts to establish usability criteria that accounted for the learning aspects of educational technology design, Nokelainen outlined that pedagogical usability needs to support: learner control; learner activity; cooperative or collaborative learning; goal orientation; applicability (suitability for support and applied learning); added value; motivation; advancing previous knowledge; flexibility; and feedback. Conversely, the Technology Pedagogical Content Knowledge framework (TPACK) by Koehler and associates [20] focuses on the design of content in e-learning technology. Where Nokelainen's pedagogical usability can be as an extension of traditional technical usability observations, TPACK accounts for the information or content level of the design. It outlines the relationship between the content, the teacher or educational designer, and the students within the context of the technology. Kenttälä, Kankaanranta and Rousi [10] took this further to emphasize the importance of the interplay between UX and learning. Their framework, LETUS – Learning experience technology usability – sought to combine previous usability and technology design insights with an understanding that experience is everything when designing content and technology for learning purposes. LETUS incorporates scholarship in UX to draw the connections between the instrumental, the experiential [21], as well as the hedonic and their role to promote learning with educational technology.

One area of research that requires more attention is the role of students and their expert insight in the design of learning platforms and course workspaces. Regarding Moodle, Moyo [11] studied Moodle from the student perspective in relation to their perceptions of authenticity. Authenticity is a contested concept, as it is value-laden regarding power and authority, hierarchies and rankings, in terms of what is deemed as *authentic* or genuine [22]. This particularly holds in the AI-driven digital era where phenomena such as AI-generated cultural products are becoming commonplace. Yet, Moyo [11] argued that authenticity is a crucial quality in terms of establishing integrity within the learner, technology, and pedagogical delivery relationship. The COVID-19 pandemic also spurred an increase in student-centered studies of learning platforms and other aspects of remote learning UX. Arima and associates [23] studied activities in which students were asked to re-design the face-to-face course workspace in Moodle. Another study by Sheridan and Gigliotti [24] explored re-design of workspaces to optimize learning engagement for all students. They cite that participation in design not only increases the likelihood of improving design for all but instills a sense of ownership that serves to boost motivation to use and to learn. These factors are important to consider when approaching UX in the context of learning technology.

2.1 Previous Studies on UX Attributes

Hassenzahl [9] defined the key elements of design products (c.f. Moodle) as that of on content, presentational style, functionality, and interactional style which conveys a product's characteristics. While time and UX research have moved on, we want to reflect on these elements to provide grounding for how the Moodle workspace and its additional educational design layer can and should be understood. Thus, the characteristics of UX design are marked by pragmatic qualities (useful or practical), hedonic qualities (not directly functional, more aesthetic, semantic and motivational), and attractiveness (and the combination of these) [9, 25, 26]. In this study, we approach UX by applying the six UX attributes identified by Schrepp [26]: attractiveness, perspicuity, efficiency, dependability, stimulation, and novelty. Attractiveness is not only contested but complex in aesthetic and psychological scholarship (see [27, 28]). It however can be described as pertaining to appeal, pleasantness, enjoyment, and a psychological 'pull' that incites sentiments and motivation towards innovativeness and creativity [29–32]. Also, back in the 1990s, Tractinsky [33] emphasized that aesthetics and attractiveness have a significant impact on ease-of-use, through influencing choices and encouraging engagement. This has been furthered by numerous studies over the years that show how beautiful things evoke positivity and motivate users [34] while additionally inducing a sense of perceived usability and trust [3, 35, 36]. Studies [e.g., 37, 38] also show, that more visually complex web pages lead to more negative first impressions than medium or low complexity web pages.

Perspicuity has been defined as ease-of-use and comprehensibility. Clear contents can be understood quickly when they are beautiful and rationally organized [39–41], and culturally appropriate for users [42]. Efficiency is often equated with speed, i.e., how quickly a user can perform the desired task [43, 44]. Efficiency also refers to whether the task is possible to perform simply and easily [45]. In evaluating the effectiveness, attention is often paid towards whether the investigated platform offers shortcuts, whether it processes information quickly [46] or whether the most important information is presented first [45]. Dependability refers to the reliability, predictability, logic and correspondence with expectations of the design in question [29]. Functionality is also an important factor in dependability, that connects with user expectations and how the system design supports the user in achieving use goals. Thus, in visual design, it is critical that the function and behavior of the system corresponds with how the user understands the visual information, and thus user interface [47].

Stimulation is one of the hedonistic features of the UX that is highly relevant to learning. The characteristics of stimulation include excitement, curiosity, interest, motivation, creativity, and innovation. Additionally, randomness adds to the factor of surprise for the user, as it creates new starting points and directs the flow state towards further exploration [48, 49]. Furthermore, stimulation affects an individual's personal development, the accumulation of skills and the growth of knowledge [50]. However, stimulation loses its intensity over time [51, 52]. Thus, novelty and the introduction of new elements as time progresses, help sustain the user's (student's) attention. The novelty attribute is converted into whether the product is innovative and creative, and how it gets the user's attention [53]. In relation to products considered essential, the significance of novelty diminishes due to their mandatory use [54].

2.2 Participatory and Co-design for the UX of Learning Platforms

In UX scholarship, participatory design and co-design have been discussed as a family of methods that seek to involve stakeholders in the design process, and as co-designers [55]. Considering the e-learning context, these stakeholders include students, administrators, educational designers and teachers [56]. This strain of methodology is particularly valuable from cognitive-affective and social perspectives as it affords designers insight into both the pragmatic attributes of the design spaces, as well as the hedonic, semantic, and experiential dimensions. Designers are thus afforded details concerning the conditions and contexts in which courses are held, and learning occurs. Similarly to ethnography, co-design allows practitioners to more closely align with the multi-dimensional circumstances users (students and learners) face when potentially encountering the design. By encouraging stakeholders to participate in design processes, designers – and in this case, teachers and educational designers who formulate the information content and instructional level of the Moodle workspace – have ample opportunity to design for more effective and enrichening user and learning experiences [57].

Through engaging students in the design and re-design of workspaces, students become involved in learning from a different, instructional perspective, in a deeper and more meaningful way. This is not a simple question of improving UX to ease human-learning technology interaction. Rather, the platform contents are embedded with the mental structuration of students, while at the same time, through the design-lead sense-making processes of organizing the contents, students cognitively structure (understand) and process the content for themselves. There is also an instilled ownership, conveyed through identity – as designers – within the course and its goals [11]. In other words, co-design and various forms of participatory design encourage engagement, identification, and learning [55, 58].

3 Methodology

The study involved two groups of university students enrolled in a master's-level stand-alone UX course (5 ECTS) at the University of Vaasa, Finland during the years 2021 and 2024. The course was taught by two teachers (author 1 and 2 of this paper). In these courses students were assigned to evaluate the UX of the course's Moodle workspace. Upon the evaluation results, in small groups, students were instructed to formulate suggestions for improvements. The improvement suggestions collected during both 2021 (Study 1 – January–March 2021) and 2024 (Study 2 – January–March 2024) serve as data for the current paper. We analyzed the project work reports delivered by students via qualitative content analysis. Focus was placed on identifying what students find problematic and how they would improve the Moodle workspace for better UX. In the next sub-sections, we elaborate on how we recruited participants, the procedure, data collection, and steps taken within the qualitative content analysis.

3.1 Participants

For Study 1, we recruited 35 master level university students, of which 29 responded to a questionnaire about their demographics. Out of these participants, 18 (62%) were female and 11 (37%) were male. The age range of respondents was 21 to 42 years, with an average age of 27 years. For Study 2, we recruited 31 master level university students of which 25 responded to a questionnaire about their demographics. Out of these participants, 15 (60%) were female and 10 (40%) were male. The age range of the respondents was 20–53 years, and the average age was 30 years. Participants of both studies contributed to the research voluntarily. From a research ethics perspective, the students were asked individually for permission to use their coursework generated data in this research. The authors stressed that the decision not to participate had no influence on the students' grades. All students enrolled in these courses agreed to participate.

3.2 Procedure

We established groups of three to four students that each were assigned to address one UX attribute as a UX goal (see [46]). For Study 1 there were 11 groups and in Study 2 there were eight groups. The UX attributes were adapted from Schrepp et al. [26] and are listed as: attractiveness, perspicuity, efficiency, dependability, stimulation, and novelty. The application of the study was the Moodle workspace of the course they were enrolled in, excluding the content of the appendices (e.g., PDF files such as lecture slides). The workspace was designed by one of the teachers on the course. As the course in question was the same in both studies, the workspace was mostly similar. The differences were that the workspace was improved for Study 2 based on the suggestions made in Study 1, and the Moodle platform was updated to another version between the studies, which led to changes in some of the features of the workspace and platform overall.

The course workspace during Study 1 had the following structure of six subpages:

- Home page, which included basic information about the course.
- Lectures page, which included lecture slides and recordings.
- Workshops page, which included materials related to information seeking workshop and co-design workshops.
- Seminars page, which included content related to the project work presentations.
- Project work page, which included materials related to the project work.
- Literature and related materials page, that had references to additional reading.

The course workspace in Study 2 had a similar structure, but the contents of the workshops page and seminars page were merged into the project work page. In addition, one page was added to include readings from a mandatory previous course.

During the project work, the groups conducted a literature review to discover existing knowledge of UX principles and attributes in the context of learning platforms. Following this, each group prepared, planned, and facilitated one co-design workshop. The workshop participants were other students participating in the course, instilling multi-perspective learning experience in terms of co-design UX methods and processes. Lastly, groups presented their findings via a written report. Next, the workshops in both studies are described in more detail.

Study 1. In Study 1, students held 11 workshops in total. In both studies, the students could choose whether to have the workshops onsite or online. In Study 1, all workshops were held online, which was influenced by the outbreak of COVID-19 in 2020. During the co-design workshops, the groups were tasked with finding answers to questions about the users and their aims, as well as to the use context and key functionalities. In addition, they were asked to find out how the participants currently perceived the UX attribute and how perceiving the UX attribute could be improved.

The groups, the UX attributes they addressed, and the techniques they used in the workshops in Study 1 are presented in Table 1.

Table 1. Groups and the techniques used in the co-design workshops in Study 1.

Group ID	Group size	UX attribute	Techniques	Workshop participants
G1	3	Attractiveness	Personas, interview, sketching	2
G2	3	Attractiveness	Interview, task analysis, personas, experience map	2
G3	3	Perspicuity	Semi-structured interview, personas, user story	3
G4	3	Perspicuity	Heuristics [59] used for evaluation	4
G5	4	Efficiency	Personas, journey map, sketching	3
G6	3	Efficiency	Task analysis, interview	3
G7	3	Dependability	Semi-structured interview, experience map, personas	1
G8	3	Dependability	Personas, empathy map	3
G9	3	Stimulation	Personas, interview, empathy map	3
G10	4	Stimulation	Personas, AttrakDiff questionnaire, interview, discussion	4
G11	3	Novelty	Interview, discussion, sketching	3
Total	**N = 35**			**N = 31**

Study 2. In Study 2, students held eight workshops in total. One workshop was held at the campus, while other workshops were held online. The groups conducted co-design sessions aiming to find the answers to the same questions as in Study 1. The groups, the UX attributes they addressed, and the techniques they used in the workshops in Study 2 are presented in Table 2.

As a difference from Study 1, no groups in Study 2 focused on stimulation and novelty.

Table 2. Groups and the techniques used in the co-design workshops in Study 2.

Group ID	Group size	UX attribute	Techniques	Workshop participants
G12	3	Attractiveness	Word cloud, focus group interview, visual card sorting, survey	4
G13	4	Attractiveness	Sentence completion, self-expression template	4
G14	4	Perspicuity	Survey, sentence completion, group interview	5
G15	4	Perspicuity	Focus group interview, sentence completion, self-expression template	4
G16	4	Efficiency	Sentence completion, usability testing with thinking aloud	4
G17	3	Efficiency	Sentence completion, self-expression template	3
G18	5	Dependability	Pre-survey, UEQ, co-creation	3
G19	4	Dependability	Personas, sentence completion, self-expression template	4
Total	**N = 31**			**N = 31**

3.3 Data Collection and Data Analysis

The data collected from Studies 1 and 2 consisted of 19 project work reports. The data included on average 22 pages per report, with a total of 435 pages. The documents consisted of theoretical background, description of the methods of the studies, and results section including notes from the workshops and sketches of the workspace illustrating the findings.

After anonymizing the reports, we analyzed them via qualitative content analysis [60]. We coded the reports by asking the following three questions:

1. What is the problem the students have identified in the course workspace?
2. Why is it important to make improvements to solve this problem? What are the negative or positive consequences related to the problem?
3. How do students suggest that the identified problem should be solved?

The content analysis was started by two of the authors individually going through the research data and marking initial findings. Only those problems were included in the analysis that were related to the course workspace and notions related to other parts of the learning platform, e.g., platform home page, were excluded. Also, only those improvement suggestions were included in the analysis which could be implemented with the functionalities that were found in the current installation and did not require altering the design of Moodle learning platform. For example, suggestions such as creating a mobile application to improve efficiency (G6) were excluded. As the focus of the study was on the design of the workspace, comments that solely focused on altering the documents shared through the workspace were excluded. Then we cross-referenced, discussed, and categorized our findings. After combining and comparing the findings, the content analysis resulted in 12 themes. These themes were then divided into four groups by utilizing Hassenzahl´s [9] product features (content, presentational style, functionality, interaction style) to pinpoint which feature they were most related to.

4 Results

The resulting themes, the product features the themes are related to, and the UX attributes the themes were reported to influence are illustrated in Table 3.

Table 3. Themes, their related product features, and the affected UX attributes (abbreviations in the table: attractiveness (A); perspicuity (P); efficiency (E); dependability (D); stimulation (S); and novelty (N)).

Feature	Theme	(A)	(P)	(E)	(D)	(S)	(N)
Content	Information structure	x	x	x	x	x	x
	Content relevancy	x		x	x	x	x
	Text	x	x	x	x	x	x
	Information completeness		x		x	x	x
Presentational style	Visuals	x	x	x	x	x	x
	Fonts	x	x		x		
	Colors	x			x		
	Organizational consistency	x	x	x	x		
Functionality	Course navigation	x	x	x	x	x	
	Study progress		x	x	x	x	x
	Community		x			x	
Interaction style	Internal consistency	x	x	x	x	x	

Next, each theme is described alongside examples from the object-level findings. The sub-sections follow the order of the above-mentioned product features, which emphasize the relevant aspects of the workspace, and the issues connected to these aspects.

4.1 Content

Most of the students' findings were related to the workspace content. The four themes that focus on how the content affects UX are information structure, content relevancy, text, and information completeness, with information structure attracting the highest number of notions. In both Studies 1 and 2 students stressed that the most important information, such as deadlines and instructions for main assignments, should be presented first (G1, G3, G6, G10, G15, G16, G17). Students highlighted that the clarity of the home page caters to both first-time users and returning users. On the first visit, the home page offers an overall picture of the course (G15) and later supports the effective use of the workspace (G17). Information relevant to all students should be more visible, whereas information relevant to only some should be under subsections (G17). It was also seen as critical that important information was not scattered around the workspace (G4, G14). Rather, this information should be collected and accessible in one place. Additionally, students felt that similar or related content should be placed together in a common section (G17, G19). Students gave suggestions on how to structure the pages to utilize horizontal (G1, G5) and vertical space (G1, G6, G11) more effectively. For example, vertical space could be separated with visual lines (G1) to assist in finding information. Using two column horizontal layouts would minimize unnecessary empty space (G1) and improve novelty through innovation (G11).

Related to content relevancy, the main pain points related to irrelevant information, irrelevant placing of information, and irrelevant ways to express information. Unused modules and unnecessary information should be removed which would add white space that supports attractiveness (G13). Also, students indicated that certain information on the home page should be moved to another place as it was not experienced as important enough to be featured there (G1, G6, G9, G10). Lastly, related to content relevancy, students valued the most effective ways to express information. For example, using PDF files was not seen as necessary if the file content could be expressed directly on the page (G7). As another example, students pointed out that long lists of information (e.g., links) indicate laboriousness and make the user refuse the content (G3, G11). Rather, that kind of content should be compiled and presented on a subpage or in a specific folder (G1, G9, G11).

Related to text, students expressed the consistency and quality of text to affect UX. Titles and materials should be named descriptively, improving dependability (G18) and efficiency (G17). The title of the material should indicate its type (e.g., lecture) (G17). In both Studies 1 and 2 students stressed that to support findability the date that the material was related to should be indicated (G2, G3, G4, G6, G6, G10, G17). Short descriptions should be provided at the beginning of a new page and in relation to materials, such as links (G1, G2, G3, G6, G10, G11). Providing content without description was seen as unattractive and oppressive (G3, G11), whereas descriptions were seen to support efficiency (G1, G3, G6). Using English concepts in a course that did not utilize English as the main language was experienced as disturbing. Central concepts should preferably be provided in the language used on the course (G4, G5) and foreign loan words should be described (G4). Spelling mistakes were felt to indicate the unreliability of the workspace or that it was made in haste (G1) which had a negative effect on attractiveness.

Information completeness referred to instances where the workspace did not feel ready-made. Understandably workspaces have some content that will be updated during the course, but students indicated that when it felt that the teachers just had not had time to update the workspace it had a negative effect on the UX in terms of dependability

(G8). Also, un-ready content such as broken links did not support effective use (G14). But on the other hand, students experienced placeholders indicating that updates were coming as stimulating (G10) and supporting the sense of novelty (G11).

4.2 Presentational Style

In relation to the workspace's presentational style, four themes can be depicted as relating to the UX of the course workspace. These are visuals, fonts, colors, and organizational consistency. Regarding visuals, students discussed the use of images from many different viewpoints. Firstly, they reported that the use of videos and images can make the workspace more attractive (G1, G13), as they can awaken interest and increase aesthetic pleasantness (G11), but the images should be of high quality and relevant. For example, in a UX course, an image of two people was felt to indicate interaction (G18) and thus relevant for the course. Students preferred images of people (G18), as images of objects were identified as distant (G12). Using free stock images was experienced as not supporting credibility (G7), and AI generated images were experienced as giving an unauthentic feel (G18). Recommendations supported the use of 'real' or original images – i.e., photographs and drawings. Images of course teachers were positively experienced, as the images supported recognizing who the teacher responsible for the course is (G17). Utilizing images should not be done at the expense of slowing Moodle down, as that would affect efficiency negatively (G17).

Students also experienced fonts as holding significance for the UX. Students pinpointed that the fonts should be legible (G18), and a large font size was mentioned as something that would help to distinguish important information faster (G2, G4, G13). Inconsistent use of fonts was experienced to lead to distrust and unattractiveness, in addition to evoking feelings that the workspace was generated in haste (G1).

Colors were mainly mentioned in Study 2, but in both studies students pinpointed how the colors affect especially the attractiveness (G1, G12). The use of colors was also experienced as supporting the informing of students (G13) and in eliciting trust (G18). Simple and light colors were experienced as boring (G12). The main color of the workspace was yellow in both studies. This was experienced as a preferred choice both in general (G12), and as it was the same as the organizational color. This made the workspace feel familiar and dependable (G18, G12).

The last theme was organizational consistency, which appeared in Study 2 and pertained to the color-related findings mentioned above. Yet, beyond color, students pointed out that there was no uniform layout of workspaces designed by different teachers. This always required learning a new structure and logic when students entered a new workspace. Students wished for a unified structure for each workspace, as familiarity was experienced to support effective use (G14, G16). Also, uniform layout of structure, information and images was experienced to enhance attractiveness (G13).

4.3 Functionality

Three themes are related to the functionality of the workspace. These three themes are course navigation, study progress, and community. The course navigation was experienced as a central functionality. In the workspace of Study 1, the course navigation was statically located in the upper right corner of the workspace, which was reported as difficult to use (G1, G3, G5, G6, G10). Students found it inefficient and frustrating as it forced them to scroll up on the page when wanting to navigate to another page. In the workspace of Study 2, the course navigation was a collapsible menu (i.e., course index) on the left side of the screen that automatically generated items based on the materials teachers included in their workspace. This led to the course navigation becoming information-dense and unorganized. Students identified that teachers should consider this and aim for a smaller number of items to be included in the course navigation. Teachers should also focus on clearly naming the items they know will be included in the course navigation (G19). This would make it easier to find the information needed (G15).

Within the theme of study progress, students hoped for more possibilities to follow course advancement and returned assignments. As ways to implement this, students mentioned the visual progress bar (G14, G16, G19), course calendar (G9, G11, G16), and checkboxes to mark sections done (G14). Being able to monitor study progress would improve perspicuity (G14) and support effective course completion (G16).

Lastly, in Study 1 students pinpointed that the course workspace had no functionalities that would support communication within the class (G10), or with the teachers (G4). The fact that community was not emphasized in the workspace was felt to be discouraging (G10). A discussion forum was suggested as a solution, which was also later implemented in the workspace. Notions related to the theme of community did not appear in Study 2. This most likely relates to the fact that improvement was made in this respect, so the problem was solved by the time Study 2 was undertaken.

4.4 Interaction Style

The last feature, interaction style, was least represented in the students' findings. The basic interaction style in Moodle's user interface design is a dimension in which teachers have no impact. In relation to interaction style, internal consistency was raised as a key theme. Internal consistency was apparent in both Study 1 and Study 2. In this theme, students reported issues where the workspace functions worked differently than they expected or differently than in other parts of the system. For example, a picture of a video that seemed to be embedded was experienced as misleading (G1). As another example, in both studies, students mentioned that here was inconsistency on how links opened (G4, G6, G10, G15, G19) – whether in the same window, in a new tab, or in a new window. This was experienced as frustrating (G10, G19). In Study 2, the students criticized the unstandardized way that links were indicated within a text (G15, G19). The link text was dark blue in color which did not have enough contrast to be distinguishable from the main black text. Although teachers cannot change the way the platform indicates links, students suggested a workaround where teachers could reference the links in the text (G15).

5 Discussion

As a result of this study, 12 themes depicting the object-level UX issues were created and divided into four groups presenting product features. Next, we will elaborate the findings related to each product feature (content, presentational style, functionality, and interaction style) and illustrate them in the form of 12 design principles to support the practical applicability of the results. These design principles are formed based on the student-reported conclusions from student-led co-design workshops. Features especially related to the content and presentational style of the workspace were seen as possessing the greatest potential to improve the UX.

Regarding content, the findings can be illustrated with the following four design principles:

1. Organize content based on importance and relevance, and group similar content in one place.
2. Select the most appropriate way to present information and remove unnecessary content.
3. Use descriptive titles and precise language.
4. Avoid providing incomplete information.

The main findings related to content focused on aspects associated with the information structure. The importance of logical order, consistency and grouping of contents were emphasized. Especially the easy findability of the most important issues was seen as crucial, and arising in improvement suggestions related to each of the six UX attributes. This was also well in line with content relevance, which included suggestions aiming to avoid the presentation of irrelevant information or irrelevant ways to distribute the information. Providing clear indicators, such as descriptions and dates, were seen to improve, among other things, findability. Lastly, the feeling of incompleteness of the workspace should be avoided. Instead, the updates should be implemented to stimulate and support a sense of novelty while reinforcing the impression that the course is up-to-date and relevant with continuous developments in the field. From a UX perspective, novelty additionally serves to insight curiosity, motivating engagement and fueling the will to learn more – both about the design, but in this case, about the course and its contents [37, 38]. Thus, the impression of the course and its flow should be communicating a sense that the phenomena presented do not exist in a stationary state, rather, they are dynamic and evolving. This alludes to the idea that through curiosity in the course, students may be a part of the future directions of the taught phenomena. As for product design aesthetics, it is important to emphasize that completeness does not equal novelty, rather, it refers to the impression of a package that has been carefully designed with the user (students) and functional objectives (learning) in mind. This alludes to an understanding that the package as a whole is within grasp in the workspace [61, 62]. So, while the content and progress of the knowledge shared and fostered within the course should maintain a sense of incompleteness, the aesthetics of the workspace should bear an aura of 'progre8ssive completeness'. That is, the student should feel the safety of being held competently in the teacher's and Moodle's hands while preparing for impact after the course is completed.

When it came to presentation style, the power of using the right type of visuals, fonts, colors, as well as following institutional consistency, was depicted to lead to improved UX, as is illustrated with the following design principles:

5. Use relevant visuals.
6. Use legible fonts and maintain font consistency.
7. how colors affect attractiveness.
8. Follow and support organizational consistency.

Although images and videos were seen to improve workspace attractiveness, selecting unsuitable images might lead to depressing UX attributes such as dependability. The selection of font type and size had significance for efficient use, and the consistent use of fonts supported attractiveness and trust. The possibilities of utilizing colors were not merely related to improving attractiveness and efficiency, but color was also seen to communicate dependability when the organizational colors were utilized. Following organizational consistency in the workspace structure, colors, and visuals was seen to improve attractiveness and efficiency. This additionally entails systematic operationalization of the familiar, rendering prototypicality [63, 64] as critical at some level.

The findings related to functionalities and interaction style highlight the importance of the functions and the ways to interact with them for the experienced UX. The findings can be described with the following design principles:

9. Limit the number of items in course navigation.
10. Offer ways to follow course progress.
11. Offer ways to interact.

As central functions in a course workspace, the students identified the tools related to course navigation and monitoring study progress. The course navigation was mentioned in relation to problems and solutions of the information structure, and the expressed notions are intertwined. For example, the course navigation was mentioned when considering information architecture, and in relation to the items aimed at improving efficient use. It was noticed that the course navigation also enhances the clarity of the workspace content. The ability to monitor study progress was linked to efficiency and perspicuity. An interesting finding was the importance of the community for the students. Students felt not being able to interact within the course to suppress stimulation. In other words, students are stimulated via social interaction within learning processes. This finding corresponds with results from other studies that indicate how virtual environments should be designed to enhance social interaction between learners to enable deep and meaningful learning (see e.g., [65]).

Related to the interaction style, the key finding can be illustrated with the following design principle:

12. Follow internal consistency.

Violations to consistency depressed several of the UX attributes, especially perspicuity. This connects with the dimension of pedagogical usability as described by Nokelainen [18], in that the design of the technology and its interaction styles should support seamless engagement with learning materials and processes (see also [10] and [20]).

Internal consistency promotes efficient learning of interaction, which enables learners to focus on the learning design itself rather than on how to operate the workspace.

As a research contribution, this study indicates how co-design can be used to improve the UX of a course workspace, while engaging students in deeper and more meaningful learning. The co-design workshops functioned well in extracting improvement ideas for the course workspace, learning about UX design, and instilling greater involvement in the subject matter of the course. Through re-designing the workspace students actively operationalized theories and principles that were embedded within the course content and learning objectives. Students understood their engagement in the course work by improving their current and future workspaces, rendering it a meaningful task. This strongly resonates with Moyo [11] and others (i.e., [67, 68]).

This study also contributes to research on the UX of course workspaces by indicating possible connections between practical improvements and intended UX. It draws attention to levels of design that are added onto the basic core of interactional products. These are user-designed and implemented levels that also require attention – both at the instructional design level as well as user interface and information architecture levels. The reason being is that, in reality, teachers and educational designers do not have ample amounts of time to invest in careful consideration for the layout and progress of course contents. Studies such as the present one are instrumental in further development of products (learning platforms) from the perspectives of current technological developments, i.e., generative AI. Generative AI, for instance, has the potential to aid teachers and educational designers in producing, arranging, and suggesting effective workspace designs, in which all the teachers would need to do is feed the material required in the course. Prompts may include learning objectives and certain priorities, then the generative AI can produce alternative packages. Thus, this study offers several practical implications for teachers and instructional designers, learning platform designers, and future directions in AI on how to improve the UX of course workspaces.

This study has several limitations. The reported effect of the object-level improvements on UX was done based on the students' reports. The participants represent a homogenous group in terms of nationality and culture. We understand that the findings (e.g., related to colors, images, and information presentation) could and most likely would vary depending on the cultural context. The number of students working with different attributes was not even, as the theme of novelty was only chosen by one group, and stimulation was chosen by two groups, whereas the other attributes were chosen respectively by a total of four groups. Moreover, further analysis from the combined learning experience and UX perspectives, i.e., operationalizing models such as LETUS [10] - to ascertain the balance and presence of essential pedagogical design features and how these influence the learning process and experience in its entirety would be fruitful. In addition, this study was conducted in a specific context: a HE level UX course that utilized a Moodle workspace. The generalizability of the results regarding courses held in other subjects or utilizing other types of digital learning environments should be further studied. On the other hand, one feature that improves the reliability of the results is the fact that the data was gathered in two timepoints with the years difference and within two different versions of learning platforms.

In this study, we were open to discovering the role of UX attributes overall in the context of learning in a Moodle workspace. The UX attributes are intertwined as can be seen from the results. This corresponds with earlier research results on pedagogical usability and learning experience in digital technology design (see [10, 18]). As highlighted before, the main goal of the course workspace is to support learning, and thus this research could be continued by looking more deeply into the connection between UX and learning. Moreover, future research should emphasize the role of generative AI in assisting teachers and educational designers in course workspace design. This could also be done by examining the ways in which students could co-design with AI.

6 Conclusion

In this paper, we presented the results of co-designing the UX of a course workspace in Moodle with students. The results are illustrated with 12 design principles describing the possibilities for teacher-led improvements of UX. The findings emphasize the importance of logical order of contents, with a focus on using the most appropriate way to present relevant information. In addition, the workspace should avoid a feeling of incompleteness. Effective use of visuals, fonts, and colors, along with institutional consistency, was found to improve UX. Central functions identified included tools related to course navigation and monitoring study progress. Social interaction within the course was highlighted as crucial for stimulation and meaningful learning. Internal consistency in interaction styles was important for supporting seamless engagement with learning materials. The results of this study offer several practical implications for teachers, instructional designers, and learning platform designers. Also, this study demonstrates how co-design can be effectively used to improve the UX of a course workspace.

Acknowledgments. The authors would like to acknowledge the Research Council of Finland for funding the "Emotional experience of ethics and privacy in everyday pervasive systems (BUGGED)" project (decision number 348391) and the "Multifaceted ripple effects and limitations of human-AI interplay at work, business and society (SYNTHETICA)" project (358714).

Disclosure of Interests. The authors have no competing interests to declare that are relevant to the content of this article.

References

1. Majors, J., Bengs, A., Granlund, S., Ylitalo, A., Byholm, M.: Moodle moods? a user experience study of a small private online course for higher teacher education. In: Proceedings of the 22nd International Academic Mindtrek Conference, pp. 228–235. ACM, Tampere Finland (2018). https://doi.org/10.1145/3275116.3275146
2. Maslov, I., Nikou, S., Hansen, P.: Exploring user experience of learning management system. Int. J. Inf. Learn. Technol. **38**, 344–363 (2021)
3. Norman, D.: Emotion & design: attractive things work better. Interactions **9**, 36–42 (2002). https://doi.org/10.1145/543434.543435

4. Demir, F., Bruce-Kotey, C., Alenezi, F.: User experience matters: does one size fit all? evaluation of learning management systems. Technol. Knowl. Learn. (2021). https://doi.org/10.1007/s10758-021-09518-1
5. de Kock, E., van Biljon, J., Botha, A.: User experience of academic staff in the use of a learning management system tool. In: Proceedings of the Annual Conference of the South African Institute of Computer Scientists and Information Technologists on SAICSIT '16, pp. 1–10. ACM Press, Johannesburg, South Africa (2016). https://doi.org/10.1145/2987491.2987514
6. Walker, S., Prytherch, D., Turner, J.: The pivotal role of staff user experiences in Moodle and the potential impact on student learning. In: 2013 Second International Conference on E-Learning and E-Technologies in Education (ICEEE), pp. 192–197. IEEE (2013)
7. Könings, K.D., Seidel, T., van Merriënboer, J.J.: Participatory design of learning environments: integrating perspectives of students, teachers, and designers. Instr. Sci. **42**, 1–9 (2014). https://doi.org/10.1007/s11251-013-9305-2
8. Hasan, L.: Usability problems on desktop and mobile interfaces of the moodle learning management system (LMS). In: Proceedings of the 2018 International Conference on E-Business and Applications, pp. 69–73. ACM, New York, NY, USA (2018). https://doi.org/10.1145/3194188.3194192
9. Hassenzahl, M.: the thing and i: understanding the relationship between user and product. In: Blythe, M.A., Overbeeke, K., Monk, A.F., and Wright, P.C. (eds.) Funology, pp. 31–42. Springer Netherlands, Dordrecht (2003). https://doi.org/10.1007/1-4020-2967-5_4
10. Kenttälä, V., Rousi, R., Kankaanranta, M.: Towards the learning experience technology usability framework. In: Handbook of Research on Instructional Systems and Educational Technology, pp. 128–140. IGI global (2017). https://doi.org/10.4018/978-1-5225-2399-4.ch012
11. Moyo, N.E.: Students' perceptions of the authenticity of e-learning design within Moodle at Lupane State University, Matebeleland North, Zimbabwe. PhD Thesis, University of Johannesburg (2023)
12. Gobet, F., et al.: Chunking mechanisms in human learning. Trends Cogn. Sci. **5**, 236–243 (2001). https://doi.org/10.1016/S1364-6613(00)01662-4
13. Bødker, S., Dindler, C., Iversen, O.S., Smith, R.C.: Participatory design. Springer International Publishing, San Rafael, California (2021)
14. Ellis, R.K.: Field guide to learning management. ASTD Learn. Circ. **11**(1), (2009)
15. Tapalova, O., Zhiyenbayeva, N.: Artificial intelligence in education: AIEd for personalised learning pathways. Electron. J. E-Learn. **20**, 639–653 (2022). https://doi.org/10.34190/ejel.20.5.2597
16. Gunasekaran, A., McNeil, R.D., Shaul, D.: E-learning: research and applications. Ind. Commer. Train. **34**, 44–53 (2002). https://doi.org/10.1108/00197850210417528
17. Kurhila, J., Miettinen, M., Nokelainen, P., Tirri, H.: The role of the learning platform in student-centred e-learning. In: IEEE International Conference on Advanced Learning Technologies, 2004. Proceedings, pp. 540–544. IEEE (2004). https://doi.org/10.1109/ICALT.2004.1357473
18. Nokelainen, P.: An empirical assessment of pedagogical usability criteria for digital learning material with elementary school students. J. Educ. Technol. Soc. **9**, 178–197 (2006)
19. Pham, M., Singh, K., Jahnke, I.: Socio-technical-pedagogical usability of online courses for older adult learners. Interact. Learn. Environ. **31**, 2855–2871 (2023). https://doi.org/10.1080/10494820.2021.1912784
20. Koehler, M.J., Mishra, P., Kereluik, K., Shin, T.S., Graham, C.R.: The technological pedagogical content knowledge framework. In: Spector, J.M., Merrill, M.D., Elen, J., and Bishop, M.J. (eds.) Handbook of Research on Educational Communications and Technology, pp. 101–111. Springer New York, New York, NY (2014). https://doi.org/10.1007/978-1-4614-3185-5_9

21. Hassenzahl, M., Tractinsky, N.: User experience a research agenda. Behav. Inf. Technol. **25**, 91–97 (2006). https://doi.org/10.1080/01449290500330331
22. Handler, R.: Authenticity. Anthropol. Today **2**(1), 2–4 (1986)
23. Arima, S., Yasui, M., Okawa, K.: Re-design classroom into MOOC-like content with remote face-to-face sessions during the COVID-19 pandemic: a case study in graduate school. In: Proceedings of the Eighth ACM Conference on Learning @ Scale, pp. 299–302. ACM, Virtual Event Germany (2021). https://doi.org/10.1145/3430895.3460163
24. Sheridan, L., Gigliotti, A.: Designing online teaching curriculum to optimise learning for all students in higher education. Curric. J. **34**, 651–673 (2023). https://doi.org/10.1002/curj.208
25. Hassenzahl, M.: The effect of perceived hedonic quality on product appealingness. Int. J. Hum. Comput. Interact. **13**, 481–499 (2001). https://doi.org/10.1207/S15327590IJHC1304_07
26. Schrepp, M., Held, T., Laugwitz, B.: The influence of hedonic quality on the attractiveness of user interfaces of business management software. Interact. Comput. **18**, 1055–1069 (2006). https://doi.org/10.1016/j.intcom.2006.01.002
27. Rousi, R.: From cute to content: user experience from a cognitive semiotic perspective. PhD Thesis, University of Jyväskylä (2013)
28. Rousi, R., Silvennoinen, J.: Simplicity and the art of something more: a cognitive-semiotic approach to simplicity and complexity in human-technology interaction and design experience. Hum. Technol. **14** (2018). https://doi.org/10.17011/ht/urn.201805242752
29. Hinderks, A., Schrepp, M., Domínguez Mayo, F.J., Escalona, M.J., Thomaschewski, J.: Developing a UX KPI based on the user experience questionnaire. Comput. Stand. Interfaces **65**, 38–44 (2019). https://doi.org/10.1016/j.csi.2019.01.007
30. Laugwitz, B., Held, T., Schrepp, M.: Construction and evaluation of a user experience questionnaire. In: Holzinger, A. (ed.) HCI and Usability for Education and Work, pp. 63–76. Springer, Berlin, Heidelberg (2008). https://doi.org/10.1007/978-3-540-89350-9_6
31. Rauschenberger, M., Schrepp, M., Perez-Cota, M., Olschner, S., Thomaschewski, J.: Efficient measurement of the user experience of interactive products. how to use the user experience questionnaire (UEQ). example: spanish language version. Int. J. Interact. Multimed. Artif. Intell. **2**, 39–45 (2013). https://doi.org/10.9781/ijimai.2013.215
32. Schrepp, M.: User experience questionnaire handbook (2015). https://doi.org/10.13140/RG.2.1.2815.0245
33. Tractinsky, N.: Aesthetics and apparent usability: empirically assessing cultural and methodological issues. In: Proceedings of the ACM SIGCHI Conference on Human factors in computing systems, pp. 115–122. ACM, New York, NY, USA (1997). https://doi.org/10.1145/258549.258626
34. Jiang, Z., Wang, W., Tan, B.C.Y., Yu, J.: The determinants and impacts of aesthetics in users' first interaction with websites. J. Manag. Inf. Syst. **33**, 229–259 (2016). https://doi.org/10.1080/07421222.2016.1172443
35. Miniukovich, A., Figl, K.: The effect of prototypicality on webpage aesthetics, usability, and trustworthiness. Int. J. Hum. Comput. Stud. **179**, 103103 (2023)
36. Tractinsky, N., Katz, A.S., Ikar, D.: What is beautiful is usable. Interact. Comput. **13**, 127–145 (2000). https://doi.org/10.1016/S0953-5438(00)00031-X
37. Tuch, A.N., Presslaber, E.E., Stöcklin, M., Opwis, K., Bargas-Avila, J.A.: The role of visual complexity and prototypicality regarding first impression of websites: Working towards understanding aesthetic judgments. Int. J. Hum. Comput. Stud. **70**, 794–811 (2012). https://doi.org/10.1016/j.ijhcs.2012.06.003
38. Yablonski, J.: Laws of UX: Using Psychology to Design Better Products and Services. Inc, O'Reilly Media (2024)
39. Al-Hunaiyyan, A., Alhajri, R., Alghannam, B., Al-Shaher, A.: Student information system: investigating user experience (UX). Int. J. Adv. Comput. Sci. Appl. **12**, (2021). https://doi.org/10.14569/IJACSA.2021.0120210

40. Schrepp, M., Otten, R., Blum, K., Thomaschewski, J.: What causes the dependency between perceived aesthetics and perceived usability? Int. J. Interact. Multimed. Artif. Intell. **6**, 78 (2021). https://doi.org/10.9781/ijimai.2020.12.005
41. Sterz, S., Baum, K., Lauber-Rönsberg, A., Hermanns, H.: Towards perspicuity requirements. In: 2021 IEEE 29th International Requirements Engineering Conference Workshops (REW), pp. 159–163 (2021). https://doi.org/10.1109/REW53955.2021.00029
42. Reinecke, K., Bernstein, A.: Improving performance, perceived usability, and aesthetics with culturally adaptive user interfaces. ACM Trans. Comput. Hum. Interact. **18**(8), 1–8:29 (2011). https://doi.org/10.1145/1970378.1970382
43. Fatima, A., Luca, C., Wilson, G.: User experience and efficiency for semantic search engine. In: 2014 International Conference on Optimization of Electrical and Electronic Equipment (OPTIM), pp. 924–929 (2014). https://doi.org/10.1109/OPTIM.2014.6851023
44. Nielsen, J.: Enhancing the explanatory power of usability heuristics. In: Proceedings of the SIGCHI Conference on Human Factors in Computing Systems Celebrating Interdependence CHI '94, pp. 152–158. ACM Press, Boston, Massachusetts, United States (1994). https://doi.org/10.1145/191666.191729
45. Marques, L., et al.: Understanding UX better: a new technique to go beyond emotion assessment. Sensors. **21**, 7183 (2021). https://doi.org/10.3390/s21217183
46. Varsaluoma, J.: Approaches to improve user experience in product development: UX goals, long-term evaluations and usage data logging. PhD Thesis, Tampere University of Technology (2018)
47. Ricciardi, S., et al.: Dependability issues in visual–haptic interfaces. J. Vis. Lang. Comput. **21**, 33–40 (2010). https://doi.org/10.1016/j.jvlc.2009.07.001
48. Hassenzahl, M.: User experience (UX): towards an experiential perspective on product quality. In: Proceedings of the 20th International Conference of the Association Francophone d'Interaction Homme-Machine on IHM '08. p. 11. ACM Press, Metz, France (2008). https://doi.org/10.1145/1512714.1512717
49. Hassenzahl, M., Platz, A., Burmester, M., Lehner, K.: Hedonic and ergonomic quality aspects determine a software's appeal. In: Proceedings of the SIGCHI conference on Human Factors in Computing Systems, pp. 201–208. ACM, New York, NY, USA (2000). https://doi.org/10.1145/332040.332432
50. Väätäjä, H., Koponen, T., Roto, V.: Developing practical tools for user experience evaluation: a case from mobile news journalism. VTT Symp. **258**, 240–247 (2009)
51. Kujala, S., Roto, V., Väänänen-Vainio-Mattila, K., Karapanos, E., Sinnelä, A.: UX Curve: a method for evaluating long-term user experience. Interact. Comput. **23**, 473–483 (2011). https://doi.org/10.1016/j.intcom.2011.06.005
52. von Wilamowitz-Moellendorff, M., Hassenzahl, M., Platz, A.: Dynamics of user experience: how the perceived quality of mobile phones changes over time. In: User experience-towards a unified view, Workshop at the 4th Nordic conference on human-computer interaction, pp. 74–78 (2006)
53. Schrepp, M., Hinderks, A., Thomaschewski, J.: Construction of a benchmark for the user experience questionnaire (UEQ). Int. J. Interact. Multimed. Artif. Intell. **4**, 40–44 (2017). https://doi.org/10.9781/ijimai.2017.445
54. Prakoso, B.S., Subriadi, A.P.: User experience on e-government online services: a case study on the SIMPATIKA service application at the ministry of religious affairs of Indonesia. J. Inf. Technol. Comput. Sci. **3**, 67–76 (2018). https://doi.org/10.25126/jitecs.20183152
55. Bødker, S., Dindler, C., Iversen, O.S., Smith, R.C.: What can we learn from the history of participatory design? In: Participatory Design, pp. 15–29. Springer International Publishing, Cham (2022). https://doi.org/10.1007/978-3-031-02235-7_3
56. Tuhkala, A.: A systematic literature review of participatory design studies involving teachers. Eur. J. Educ. **56**, 641–659 (2021). https://doi.org/10.1111/ejed.12471

57. Rajanen, D., Tornberg, A., Rajanen, M.: Heuristics for course workspace design and evaluation. In: 34th British HCI Conference, pp. 60–75 (2021). https://doi.org/10.14236/ewic/HCI2021.5
58. Smith, P.: Engaging online students through peer-comparison progress dashboards. J. Appl. Res. High. Educ. **12**, 38–56 (2019). https://doi.org/10.1108/JARHE-11-2018-0249
59. Reeves, T.C., et al.: Usability and instructional design heuristics for e-learning evaluation. association for the advancement of computing in education (AACE), pp. 1615–1621 (2002)
60. Krippendorff, K.: Content analysis. Int. Encycl. Commun. **1**, 403–407 (1989)
61. Patrick, V.M.: Everyday consumer aesthetics. Curr. Opin. Psychol. **10**, 60–64 (2016). https://doi.org/10.1016/j.copsyc.2015.12.007
62. Sevilla, J., Kahn, B.E.: The completeness heuristic: product shape completeness influences size perceptions, preference, and consumption. J. Mark. Res. **51**, 57–68 (2014). https://doi.org/10.1509/jmr.12.0153
63. Coope, M., Huisman, G., Hekkert, P.: Haptic aesthetics in product design: designing headphones that feel beautiful. In: De Sainz Molestina, D., Galluzzo, L., Rizzo, F., and Spallazzo, D. (eds.), IASDR 2023: Life-Changing Design, pp. 9–13. Milan, Italy (2023). https://doi.org/10.21606/iasdr.2023.303
64. Hekkert, P., Thurgood, C., Whitfield, T.A.: The mere exposure effect for consumer products as a consequence of existing familiarity and controlled exposure. Acta Psychol. **144**, 411–417 (2013). https://doi.org/10.1016/j.actpsy.2013.07.015
65. Mystakidis, S., Berki, E., Valtanen, J.-P.: Deep and meaningful e-learning with social virtual reality environments in higher education: a systematic literature review. Appl. Sci. **11**, 2412 (2021). https://doi.org/10.3390/app11052412
66. Demırbas, D., Ogut, S.T.: Re-designing the design brief as a digital learning tool with participatory design approach. Turk. Online J. Distance Educ. **21**, 83–100 (2020). https://doi.org/10.17718/tojde.690356
67. Dindler, C., Smith, R., Iversen, O.S.: Computational empowerment: participatory design in education. CoDesign **16**, 66–80 (2020). https://doi.org/10.1080/15710882.2020.1722173

International Telecommunication Project as a Basis for Formation of Interactive Learning Proto-Ecosystem

Marina S. Kogan[1(✉)], Inga S. Lutskaya[2], Nina V. Popova[1], Anna V. Gavrilova[1], Galina V. Tretyakova[3], Syed Raihan-Ul-Islam[4], Ehatasham Ul Hoque Eiten[4], and Wang Lin[5]

[1] Peter the Great St Petersburg Polytechnic University, 29 Polytechnicheskaya Str, 195251 St. Petersburg, Russia
kogan_ms@spbstu.ru
[2] Higher School of Economics, HSE University, 123 Griboyedova Canal Emb, 190068 St Petersburg, Russia
[3] Financial University Under the Government of the Russian Federation, 49/2 Leningradsky Prospekt, Moscow 125167, Russia
[4] Daffodil International University, Daffodil Smart City, Birulia, Savar, Dhaka 1216, Bangladesh
[5] Tangshan Oriental Education Corporation, Jiqingli, Daqing Road, Development Zone, Tangshan 063000, Hebei, China

Abstract. Telecommunication projects are widely used by the English teachers across the world. This type of activity engages students to use their linguistic skills as well as negotiation skills whenever necessary. Competent allocation of the responsibilities within the student groups makes the discussion more effective and useful for each participant. A telecommunication project might also have a goal to create a new intellectual product. In this case the students enhance their linguistic skills while working on other issues. A telecommunication project is a complex system made of many components including technology, people and content. Whenever any component is changed it impacts the whole system. This study shows that a telecommunication project conducted outside of the main curriculum can be considered as a learning ecosystem prototype, which brings many benefits to its participants including enhanced intercultural communicative competence, negotiation skills, awareness and curiosity about other cultures and better understanding of one's own culture.

Keywords: Telecollaboration · Intercultural Learning · Learning Ecosystem · Interactive Learning Proto-Ecosystem

1 Introduction

Information and Communication Technologies (ICTs) have changed educational landscape ever since they emerged and gained popularity [1]. Modern students are used to work in a multitasking environment: they have to maintain a particular public image

B. K. Smith and M. Borge (Eds.): HCII 2025, LNCS 15806, pp. 57–70, 2025.
https://doi.org/10.1007/978-3-031-93564-0_4

in numerous social media; they have to submit papers online and in time via online studying platforms; they have to speak on camera and use microphone via group conferences etc. Learning process nowadays is not restricted to any formal context [2] and students are free to study from a more comfortable environment. Using ICTs can also give many benefits for intercultural communicative competence: it can involve students, who are geographically located far from the class, in the same project and create a new intellectual product [3].

For many years teachers have been using telecollaboration to communicate with geographically distant partner students to provide an opportunity for authentic communication, meaningful collaboration and first-hand experience of working and learning with partners from other cultural backgrounds [4]. Some authors from our team also had such experience in the past [5, 6]. Online exchange projects of this kind can develop learners' independent work, linguistic accuracy, intercultural awareness, international communication competence [7] and technical literacy. Telecollaboration has gone far beyond individual classroom initiatives and now plays a big role for internationalization, intercultural development and virtual mobility in universities across the world.

Educators from different countries have been using online intercultural exchange for several decades by now. Different types of online exchange activities were developing in isolation from one another, which led to numerous names they have today, such as *telecollaboration, virtual exchange, internet-mediated intercultural foreign language education, globally networked learning environments, e-tandem, teletandem* [8]. The difference between the names means that the educators set various goals for an intercultural telecollaboration and have different approach towards their realization. But there are similar characteristics for all these projects, such as: they are internet-based, include more than one group of students, united by the same culture or/and country, they are conducted within an institution and aimed at developing linguistic skills and international communicative competence [9]. All these features are interconnected and create a kind of system.

This form of online learning involves learners from different classes to take part in a collaboration and interact with the learners from geographically remote places. It happens using technology and under the guidance of teachers and/or trained facilitators [10, p. 291]. International telecollaboration means that intercultural dialogue is at the center of learning. It is interaction and collaboration that create understanding and give new knowledge. Intercultural model of telecollaboration involves international partnership into the project. It also emphasizes the developing cultural awareness and other aspects of intercultural communicative competence, in addition to linguistic competence [10, p. 294]. That is why one of the main activities of a telecommunication project is a collaborative research project comparing both cultures. Such telecollaboration can be comprehensively integrated into the students' study programs and play an important role in the future career of the graduates. But at the same time there are many advantages of a telecommunication project, which is an out-of-class activity.

It is obvious from the above description that an intercultural telecollaboration consists of several components such as: groups of learners, partners from other cultures and/or countries, educational program, educators, facilitators, technology etc. Groups of learners can vary and engage more people interested in intercultural exchanges. Sometimes mutual work can lead to further academic results such as a publication, or to an intercultural friendship expressed, for example, in lasting pen pal correspondence/e-mail exchange. Thus, we can say that a telecommunication project can be considered as an interactive learning proto-ecosystem, consisting of multiple stakeholders aiming at human-centered learning [11]. To conduct an intercultural telecollaboration concentrating on a single stakeholder is not enough. An intercultural telecommunication is a far more complex system than a language tandem, which involves two learners from different cultures exchanging their opinions in a foreign language.

The stakeholders, who communicate via telecollaboration, might come from different backgrounds (industries, professions, cultures etc.) [12], but they are united by the same goal. Whenever a change happens inside this ecosystem, all of its components are impacted one way or another. Usually a learning ecosystem consists of two groups of components: biotic or social or simply – people, and abiotic ones [13]. Biotic group includes students, teachers, invited guests, facilitators etc. Abiotic group includes technology, contents of the project, tools etc. [2, 11].

International telecollaboration can help to solve the most difficult task in a foreign language learning – creating the environment which requires using the foreign language naturally to reach the goal [14, 15]. All participants become involved in the same learning ecosystem where they have to use their cultural knowledge as well as technological and communicative skills.

Our case study was conducted by two hosting universities: Peter the Great Polytechnic University (Saint Petersburg, Russia) and Daffodil International University (Dhaka, Bangladesh). Polytechnic University is one of the oldest state universities, which offers 138 majors for bachelor students; it has a developed network of international partners across the world. English as a foreign language is taught to all bachelor students of the university. Daffodil International University (DIU) is one of the top universities in Bangladesh, recognized in many national and international rankings. Currently, DIU has over 22,000 students across 6 different faculties and 30 departments, including around 200 international students from various countries. The university has established collaborations with over 620 universities worldwide and is a member of leading international organizations. The university constantly engages its students in different exchange programs, international internships, research collaborations, short-term training programs, virtual mobility, etc. Both universities encourage the students to raise their cultural curiosity and organize special laboratories for learning English. The telecommunication project organized by these two universities was an out-of-class activity aimed at enhancing the students' English skills and intercultural communication skills.

2 Research Questions

This research was aimed at resolving the following questions:

- Can an intercultural telecollaboration project form a learning proto-ecosystem as the environment for its realization?
- Can an international telecollaboration project contribute to reducing disparity between "small" and "big" cultures in terms of students' genuine interest in them?
- What is students' motivation to participate in this kind of out-of-class activity?

3 Telecommunication Project as an Interactive Learning Proto-Ecosystem

3.1 Pedagogical Goals and Means for Their Implementation

Modern ICTs allow communication with native speakers of any language, which helps to overcome artificiality in foreign language learning when it is being learned in a non-native language environment. International telecollaboration projects can make independent student work more efficient and intensive.

The learning process becomes more efficient when it is directed by a problem to be solved. While the students look for a solution they not only think, they also look for information, analyze and generalize. Group work also can stimulate students' ability to research, discuss and create. When they create new ideas, they rely on their previous experience and knowledge. Telecommunication is a supervised activity, so the students have to consider the interests of the whole group, be more attentive to their groupmates and respect their point of view – all these components form a team. In case of an international telecollaboration the team work runs entirely (or almost entirely) in a foreign language without any artificiality. A lot of skills which are hard to train in the classroom settings (polite interrupting, compensatory techniques, ways of clarifying /negotiating meaning, expressing different degrees of agreement/disagreement, etc., to name just a few) are acquired and developed in the course of such projects.

The participants concentrate their attention on solving the problem rather than on their language, which means they are more attentive to the contents of their learning. They enhance their soft skills: they learn how to deliver their ideas in a short and convincing form; they listen to their team members; they actively participate in the discussion and learn how to interrupt it according to the rules; they make their point of view argumentative; they are able to find consensus and state the mutual decision. The students become more active in an inter-cultural dialogue and they are eager to take initiative.

An online exchange project between the students from different countries reinforces the ability of the students to use a foreign language in everyday life: they enrich their practical English not only with new grammar and new vocabulary, but also with specific cultural information. In general, their range of vision expands. Active independent work and participation in the discussion makes them use their creativity and show their talents, which is more difficult to do during ordinary classes.

Participation in an intercultural telecommunication project can give the results that are useful outside of the project itself. The participants become more motivated to develop their language skills: they practice listening, speaking, reading, the art of monologue, using the dictionary; they find the ways of integrating their knowledge of other cultures into real life. In other words, they become a part of the cultural dialogue. Besides that, the students advance their technical skills. Their work within the project creates in them the need to speak a foreign language.

Among the main goals set before this project we can mention the following:

- To give the students a unique experience of an intercultural communication and representing their own culture in a foreign language [16];
- To strengthen their sense of cultural and ethnical identity [17];

- To make the students more respectful towards other opinions and cultures [20, p.41];
- To make the students more curious and broaden their range of vision [7];
- To advance the students' ability to set educational goals and find means to achieve them;
- To teach the students how to work with information and foreign colleagues within a project;
- To make the students understand how their foreign peers live, work and study;
- To make the students see how English is used in other countries. [18]

We tried to reach most of the goals by selecting motivated students from the two universities who had to create a new intellectual product using digital tools and their prior knowledge and experience.

3.2 Technological Component

Participating students were supposed to work synchronously during mutual meetings and then independently within their small groups to prepare their final product. To make their work more convenient, we selected the following online instruments:

Zoom. The meetings were conducted on Zoom Platform for several reasons: it has a clear interface; it allows teachers to divide the participants into breakout rooms for private discussion; it allows up to 100 people to join the meeting without registration. Zoom was a very convenient tool not only for the common discussion but also for displaying the final presentations and sharing videos about the Bangladeshi and Russian cultures. To entertain the participants there was also a customized countdown designed by technical support team from Bangladesh.

Overall, there were three synchronous online meetings in Zoom: one meeting in a week. The meetings were not recorded. Zoom was also used for two preliminary meetings of the organizers.

WhatsApp. Group discussion was conducted via the messenger WhatsApp. Here, the students and organizers mostly communicated to fix meeting dates and share relevant information among themselves. There was one group chat that included all participants of the project and later each group launched their own separate group chats for further discussion of the final product. These group chats were not supervised by the teachers. From the very beginning it was decided that the students from different countries would be divided into three random inter-cultural groups, which made them speak English only.

Google Docs. Each group of students had their own Google Doc file where they typed down their ideas and later – chose the final topic for their presentations. These files were accessible for the teachers and the students could see the teachers' comments there whenever it was applicable. The second synchronous meeting was concentrated on generating ideas in the Google Docs file so that the supervisors had a chance to follow the way the students developed their ideas.

PowerPoint. The students were given the task to present their final intellectual product in any possible format: a leaflet, a presentation, a banner etc. All three groups chose to use PowerPoint for their presentations because PowerPoint is easy to use, it can include text along with suitable visuals and the students had experience in preparing presentations using this software.

4 Procedure

4.1 Content

The students were given the main topic for the whole project: Bangladesh and Russia towards better education. The students were asked to think on how students from both countries can unite to improve their intercultural communicative competence and their English. Prior to the group discussion they were tasked to present themselves and describe themselves as 'typical' representatives of their culture. Many students used popular stereotypes as a basis for their self-introduction. For example, it is usually said that Russians never smile and one student said that she rarely smiles 'as a typical Russian'.

Then the students were divided into three groups and were given the task: in the next three weeks they were supposed to prepare a presentation showing how Bangladesh and Russia might help each other to learn better considering the strongest points of both countries. The first meeting lasted for about an hour.

The second meeting also lasted for approximately an hour and was conducted almost entirely in Zoom breakout rooms: the groups were supposed to continue developing their ideas and they were asked to elaborate on them by answering particular questions in the Google Docs file. They typed down both countries' strongest and weakest points, then chose the most interesting of them. Then they also thought on mutual interests of both countries and how these interests can be used for the students' interaction.

On the third meeting the students presented their final product in a digital form. Approximately 30 min were dedicated to presenting the suggestions by the groups. The first group suggested that further telecollaboration projects could be dedicated to narrow science specialties such as Nuclear Power, Textile Engineering, Pharmaceuticals, and Genetic Engineering, which would help to create new hopes for the engineering industry. The second group talked about making larger groups for science projects and research in the fields, which they prefer: this might lead to new creative ideas and more comprehensive cultural exchange. The third group stated that it would be wonderful to create a guidebook covering such topics as traditional food, tourist attractions, cultural heritage, etc. of both countries, and the guidebook could also be given to those students who are going to take part in such telecollaboration projects in the future. The preliminary scenario of the third synchronous meeting is presented in Table 1.

4.2 Data Collection

Data came from two main sources: the researchers' observations of Zoom meetings and the questionnaire completed by the participants after the project was over. The questionnaire was made up in electronic format using Google Forms. It consisted of 9 closed multiple-choice questions with a single possible answer and 2 open-ended questions. By conducting this survey, we wanted to understand if the participation in

Table 1. The preliminary scenario of the third synchronous meeting.

Russia-Bangladesh Virtual Exchange Project-2021			
Seq	Segment	Responsible Person	Duration
1	Host Introduction	Inga Lutskaya, Coordinator of the Program	2 min
2	Background Briefing • How we started? • Russia Day 2020 video	Mr. Syed Raihan-Ul-Islam, Sr. Assistant Director, International Affairs, DIU	5 min
3	Previous 3 sessions' activity summary	Dr. Ehatasham Ul Hoque Eiten, Lecturer, Dept. of English, DIU & Coordinator of the Program	3 min
4	Presentation rules briefing and calling groups	Inga Lutskaya, Coordinator of the Program	3 min
5	Presentations	• Group 1 • Group 2 • Group 3	30 min
6	Review on presentations	• Nina V. Popova, Professor, Graduate School of Applied Linguistics, Interpreting & Translation, SPbPU • Dr. Liza Sharmin, Head, Dept. of English, DIU	10 min
7	Experience Sharing by participants	• Russia (NAME) • Bangladesh (NAME)	10 min
8	Congratulatory Speech	Mr. Dobrokhotov Maxim Director of the Russian Center for Science and Culture, Dhaka	10 min
9	Group Photo	Mr. Syed Raihan-Ul-Islam, Sr. Assistant Director, International Affairs, DIU	2 min
10	Discussing future of the project & closing remark	Inga Lutskaya, Coordinator of the Program	5 min
Sign Out			

the project met the students' initial expectations; if the project helped the students to improve any of their skills; if the students reached any unexpected results.

The questionnaire was anonymous, but the respondents were asked to identify their country of origin. Out of 12 participating students 10 filled out the questionnaire: 4 students from Russia and 6 students from Bangladesh.

4.3 Selection of Participants

Students. Students are the main asset of the whole project. This project was not anticipated to be a part of the students' curriculum. That is why the students should have been ready to dedicate their free time to online synchronous meetings as well as time to independent group work in group chats. The biggest challenge was to attract students for this activity as we couldn't promise them good marks in any of their subjects. Possible participants were offered inter-cultural interaction, interesting tasks to solve, prospects for their future publication and certificates of participation.

It was not hard to engage the students from Bangladesh: they were well-informed about Russia, which is an active party of different bilateral projects since Bangladesh became an independent state in 1971, and had interest in communicating with Russian students. Bangladeshi students were selected through random sampling. First, there was a call for participation in the project. Interested students applied and after a primary screening based on their availability and communication skills (the medium of communication between Russian and Bangladeshi students was English), the participants of the project were selected. The students participated in the project voluntarily and with consent. No under-aged (below 18) students took part in the project. The selection process was strictly monitored to avoid any gender, religious, regional, or cultural bias.

At the same time Russian students did not know much about Bangladesh and didn't have that much interest in learning about it: by the time the project was about to start, in the Russian-language media field there was the only single video about Bangladesh, and this video did not show the country's merits, including, for example, information about the rich country's natural features such as the longest sea beach in the world, or the state's outstanding people such as the Nobel peace prize laureate Muhammad Yunus[1] (current Chief Advisor of the Interim Government of Bangladesh), or about the beautiful national language, which was the reason to launch the International Mother Language day. Potential participants were searched for in student social media groups and social clubs with the help of volunteered colleagues who advertised the project during their English classes. Finding interested students gave the organizers some headache resulting in postponing the project for two months, which actually was launched on March, 21 and lasted for three weeks.

Eventually, 12 motivated students were found for the project: 6 students from each country, who formed three mixed groups with four participants in each: two Bangladeshi and two Russian students. The students had different majors in their universities: they were students of science, law, international relations, linguistics, and engineering. They also were of different years of study: from the second to the fourth year of Bachelor degree. But all of them met the main requirement: they learned English as a foreign language and they were able to communicate in English.

Teachers. First of all, the teachers contacted online and agreed on the project implementation. They designed the project framework, decided what online instruments should be

[1] Muhammad Yunus and Grameen Bank were awarded the Nobel Peace Prize for 2006 for their work to "create economic and social development from below". Grameen Bank′s objective since its establishment in 1983 has been to grant poor people small loans on easy terms – so-called micro-credit – and Yunus was the bank′s founder. His Nobel Lecture is available here: https://www.nobelprize.org/prizes/peace/2006/yunus/lecture/.

used and when, then discussed the main topic for the project and prepared schedules for each synchronous meeting. After that, separately, the teachers went on to find interested students at their universities. Totally, two meetings between teachers were held at the preliminary stage of the project.

During the meetings one of the teachers supported them technologically, another teacher presented the tasks and all of them supervised the communication inside and outside the breakout rooms.

Specially Invited Guests. The first two Zoom-meetings were closed events and no guests were invited. The third meeting was opened for all the interested. That is why the press-release for the third meeting was published on the official web-sites of the hosting universities. Around 20 students, who didn't get the chance to become the participants, visited the last meeting, critically observed it and afterwards shared their feedback with the facilitators.

The third meeting was also attended by specially invited professors from the hosting universities, who shared their feedback and gave valuable insight for future work.

Readers. When the project was over, two students took the initiative to prepare an article for a daily newspaper 'The Bangladesh Today' thus familiarizing its readers with the project results.

All together they formed an interactive learning proto-ecosystem schematically shown in Fig. 1.

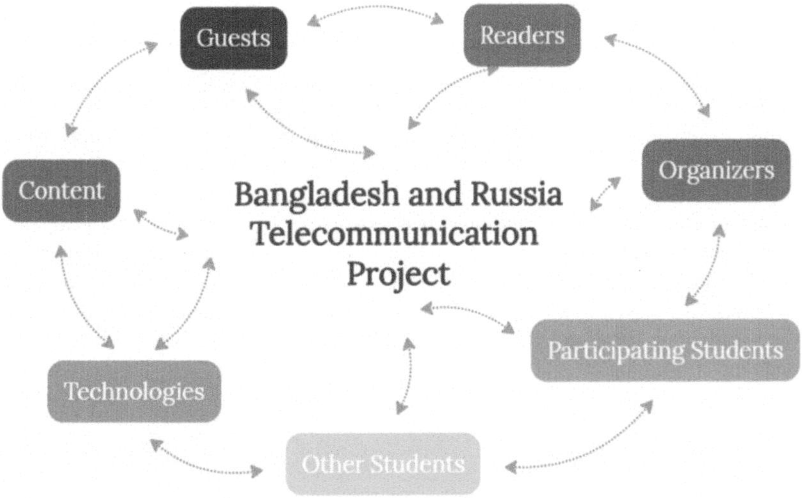

Fig. 1. Learning proto-ecosystem created during the telecommunication project between Bangladeshi and Russian students.

5 Results and Discussion

5.1 Observation of the Meetings

During the meetings there were several unplanned issues that might be anticipated in future presented in Table 2.

Table 2. Main issues faced by the organizers during the synchronous meetings.

No	Issue	How it was solved	How it can be anticipated
1	"Silent" participants. We were slightly surprised to encounter a sort of extreme manifestation of unwillingness to speak in our project. Two students in one of the groups turned off their cameras and microphones as soon as they were invited to their breakout room during the second meeting	We had to talk to those students personally and explain to them the importance of the person's 'presence' for this work	We assume that in future this kind of talk should be done in advance equipping students with the techniques preventing communication breaks and allowing students to choose roles according to their temper in order to make everyone speak As English teachers we have first-hand knowledge of "silent students' problem", and try different approaches to make them speak, e.g. in online comics-based English course [19]
2	Technical issues. Unfortunately, when the students worked independently their communication was sometimes interrupted by poor connection or other technical issues, which made their work more complicated and time-consuming	During our meetings there was a person in charge of technical issues and he did his best to resolve the issue as quickly as possible	It is necessary to be technically equipped and to have a plan "B" in case technical issues arise at one or both sides. Ideally during synchronous meetings there should be a person solely responsible for technical well-being

5.2 Questionnaire Analysis

Based on the questionnaire we can assert that this telecollaboration project made a positive impact on its participants. During the synchronous meeting some students mentioned that they were a part of this type of activity for the first time in their life and they didn't expect it would become that useful. Some students did not finish their interaction with the completion of the project: they continued friendly communication afterwards.

Their English became more flexible, on the one hand, but, on the other hand, the language was the main obstacle for several students. The English used in Bangladesh, as well as the English taught in Russia have their specifics impacted by the local culture. It is applied not only to the pronunciation but also to the vocabulary and word-formation. Understanding English of their international peers was one of the challenges for almost all students during the sessions. We think that the students didn't have enough time to get used to the language of their foreign colleagues, which affected their time-management.

Being nervous also affected overall performance: more time was spent for adjusting to each other; during the first session some participants turned off their cameras and microphones not to participate in the discussion.

Among the features that attracted the students to this activity were: interest in another culture, a chance to practice their English, the opportunity to make international friends, prospect of a new publication and, last but not least, memorable certificates signed by the officials from two hosting universities.

5.3 Discussion

The students from both countries were learning English as a foreign language. But as they came from two entirely different cultures, they saw the learning process from different angles. Different views on mutual work, sharing responsibilities and the value of the final presentation made them apply more effort and be more diplomatic. Interestingly, the participating students were attracted to the project mainly due to their cultural interest, which means they did have interest in digital diplomacy, negotiations and tolerance – the topics becoming increasingly popular worldwide nowadays [20, p. 42; 21].

The results of the project implementation outlined that intercultural telecollaboration, as it was put by the students, improved their international communicative competence. It made them more responsible for the cumulative work of their group and for their personal working area: they took initiative to perform particular tasks within the group and kept on to this initiative. It also enhanced their negotiation skills and made them more prone to start communication in a foreign language. The participants also became more curious about other cultures: several students mentioned that they were surprised they didn't know much about Bangladesh and that they learned more about it during the project. Russian students also said that it was hard for them to understand English of their Bangladeshi peers but it was interesting to overcome this language barrier. They also understood how important cultural diversity is and started to value it more.

The study indicated its effectiveness in promoting cross-cultural understanding and collaboration. The usage of services such as WhatsApp and Zoom provided smooth communication, group coordination, and cultural exchange presentations, allowing participants to highlight the rich traditions of both Bangladesh and Russia. A fair and inclusive selection method based on English communication abilities and availability guaranteed diversity avoiding bias. According to the students' self-estimation and the teachers' observation, students improved such important skills as efficient communication, collaboration, and presentation. Certificates issued by both universities recognized the efforts of the participants and facilitators, lending credibility to their participation. The project received considerable coverage in social networks and even in Bangladeshi national newspapers such as *The Bangladesh Today*[2], where participants discussed their enriching experiences and the initiative′s originality. Voluntary participation and assent reinforced ethical standards, making the initiative an excellent model for future collaborations.

The project had immediate accomplishments: the participating students prepared short presentations for the English class and shared their experiences with their groupmates, which was followed by Q&A session. One of the organizers used the data collected during the project for preparing and successful defense of her Master thesis[3]. Beyond these results we can assume that the project lays the groundwork for mid and long-term effects, such as inspiring similar cross-cultural initiatives, strengthening international relationships, and encouraging students to participate in global teamwork and cultural exchange.

After the completion of the project, students and facilitators were awarded with certificates signed by the authorities of both universities. The post-release of the conducted telecommunication was also published on the official web-sites of both hosting universities and attracted more attention from the interested teachers and students.

6 Conclusions and Further Work

The results of the research showed that telecollaboration might be a powerful tool in enhancing students' soft skills. It would be useful to move this activity into the class and see how the forming interactive learning proto-ecosystem helps make such telecollaboration projects more sustainable. We believe that such exchange projects can promote innovative thinking and broaden students' minds.

An intercultural telecollaboration project definitely forms an interactive learning system prototype: it has different components depending on each other and which produce specific results working as a whole. This ecosystem makes the students use the target language without asking to do so resulting in intercultural communicative competence enhancement.

Moreover, during the study we saw how the students' interest grew towards the culture that was unknown for them. Now the participants know some interesting facts about the other participating country and that country is a bit closer to them.

We hope that in future these students will be more motivated to participate in this kind of activity and they might develop even more remarkable ideas during their work.

At the same time to make the work more efficient we have to think about several issues. First of all, the benefits for the students should be more transparent. The content of an online cultural exchange should be interesting and engaging enough for the students to become involved in the discussion for the sake of the discussion itself.

The second issue is that such projects require more thorough preparation including:

[2] The Bangladesh Today is a daily newspaper in Bangladesh published in English. The circulation of the newspaper is over 25000. Online version is available via the link: https://thebangladeshtoday.com/.

[3] The details of the graduate qualification work titled "Actualization of polylogue of cultures in foreign language teaching in higher educational establishments in the form of telecommunication project" are available via the link: https://elib.spbstu.ru/dl/3/2022/vr/vr22-118.pdf/en/info.

- preliminary introduction of the culture and history of the partner's country to potential participants;
- familiarization of the participants with specific accent and other peculiarities of the specific English language variety of the other party involved;
- an elaborated but flexible scenario having room for ad hoc adjustments of the whole project;
- description of the participant roles for stimulating active intra group discussion.

The organizers should also remember how important technology is for a telecommunication project.

To sum up, it should be pointed out that the interactive learning proto-ecosystem created during this telecollaboration project had a positive impact on both the students and the teachers. The teachers enhanced their abilities to manage unforeseen situations, overcome unexpected difficulties, make quick decisions and find alternative solutions. The students enhanced their language skills, enriched their awareness about their own and the partners' culture, and boosted their intercultural communicative competence.

Disclosure of Interests. The authors have no competing interests to declare that are relevant to the content of this article.

References

1. Fonseca, D., Conde, M.Á., García-Peñalvo, F.J.: Improving the information society skills: is knowledge accessible for all? Univers. Access Inf. Soc. **17**, 229–245 (2018). https://doi.org/10.1007/s10209-017-0548-6
2. Jeladze, E., Pata, K., Sunney Quaicoe, J.: Factors determining digital learning ecosystem smartness in schools. Interact. Des. Archit. J. **35**, 32–55 (2017). https://doi.org/10.55612/s-5002-035-002
3. O′Dowd, R., Dooly Owenby, M.: Intercultural communicative competence through telecollaboration and VE. In: J. Jackson (ed.) The Routledge handbook of language and intercultural communication. 2nd edn, pp. 361–375 (2020) https://doi.org/10.4324/9781003036210
4. O'Dowd, R., Lewis, T.: Online intercultural exchange: policy, pedagogy, practice. Routledge, New York (2016)
5. Kogan M., Popova N., Shestakov K., Harrison L.: Out-of-class online language learning partnership between Russian and American students: Analysis of tandem project results. In: Stephanidis C. (ed.) HCI International 2015 Posters' Extended Abstracts. HCI 2015. Communications in Computer and Information Science, vol. 529. pp. 271–276. Springer, Cham. (2015). https://doi.org/10.1007/978-3-319-21383-5_46
6. Popova, N.V., Tretyakova, G.V.: Telekommunikacionnyj proekt kak realizacija poliloga kul'tur v obuchenii ino-strannomu jazyku v vuze [Telecommunication project as realization of polylogue of cultures during foreign language classes at University]. Inostrannye jazyki v shkole [Foreign Lang. Schools]. **2**, 29–38 (2017). [in Russian]
7. Marull, C., Kumar, S.: Authentic language learning through telecollaboration in online courses. TechTrends **64**, 628–635 (2020). https://doi.org/10.1007/s11528-020-00488-2
8. O'Dowd, R.: From telecollaboration to virtual exchange: state-of-the-art and the role of UNICollaboration in moving forward. J. Virtual Exch. **1**, 1–23 (2018) https://doi.org/10.14705/rpnet.2018.jve.1

9. Godwin-Jones, R.: Telecollaboration as an approach to developing intercultural communication competence. Lang. Learn. Technol. **23**(3), 8–28 (2019) http://hdl.han-dle.net/10125/44691
10. O'Dowd, R.: Emerging trends and new directions in telecollaborative learning. CALICO J. **33**(3), 291–310 (2016) https://www.jstor.org/stable/90014362
11. Chigbu, B.I., Ngwevu, V., Jojo, A.: The effectiveness of innovative pedagogy in the industry 4.0: educational ecosystem perspective. Soc. Sci. Humanit. Open. **7**(1), 100419 (2023) https://doi.org/10.1016/j.ssaho.2023.100419
12. de Souza Rodrigues, M.A., Chimenti, P., Nogueira, A.R.R.: An exploration of eLearning adoption in the educational ecosystem. Educ. Inf. Technol. **26**, 585–615 (2021). https://doi.org/10.1007/s10639-020-10276-3
13. Nguyen, L.T., Tuamsuk, K.: Digital learning ecosystem at educational institutions: a content analysis of scholarly discourse. Cogent Educ. **9**(1) (2022) https://doi.org/10.1080/2331186X.2022.2111033
14. Polat, E.S.: Metod proektov na urokah inostrannogo jazyka [project method at foreign language classes]. Inostrannye jazyki v shkole [Foreign Lang. Schools], **2000**(4), 3–10 (2000) [in Russian]
15. Polat, E.S.: The project method. In A.A. Miroljubov (ed.) Foreign Language Pedagogy: Teaching: Traditions and Modern Approaches, pp. 254–264.Titul, Obninsk (2010) [in Russian]
16. Alonso-Belmonte, I., Vinagre, M.: Interculturality and identity in computer-mediated communication: findings from L2 teaching contexts. Comput. Assist. Lang. Learn. **30**(5), 343–350 (2017). https://doi.org/10.1080/09588221.2017.1321329
17. Kern, R.: Perspectives on technology in learning and teaching languages. TESOL Q. **40**(1), 183–210 (2006). https://doi.org/10.2307/40264516
18. Golubeva, L.M.: Mezhdunarodnyye telekommunikatsyonnyye proyekty. [international telecommunication projects]. In: Ilina, N.F. (ed.) Regional Innovative Platforms as a Resource for Regional Education Development, pp. 64–68. KK IPK, Krasnoyarsk (2018) [in Russian]
19. Kogan, M.S., Gavrilova, A.V., Anosova, N.E., Petrikova, E.D.: Comics-based online course as a learning resource for encouraging students' speaking activity through intensive independent learning. In: Zaphiris, P., et al. (eds.) HCI International 2023 Late Breaking Papers. HCII 2023. LNCS, vol. 14060. pp. 139–153. Springer, Cham (2023) https://doi.org/10.1007/978-3-031-48060-7_11
20. Helm, F.: A dialogic model for telecollaboration. Bellaterra J. Teach. Learn. Lang. Lit. **6**(2), 28–48 (2013). https://doi.org/10.5565/rev/jtl3.522
21. Aranha, S., Rampazzo, L.: Towards a working definition of negotiation in telecollaboration: analysis of teletandem oral sessions. Colomb. Appl. Linguist. J. **24**(2), 234–245 (2022) https://doi.org/10.14483/22487085/17191

The AI Workbench - An Interactive No-Code Tool for Fostering AI Literacy

Jessica Laufer(✉) and Jasminko Novak

University of Applied Sciences Stralsund, 18437 Stralsund, Germany
jessica.laufer@hochschule-stralsund.de

Abstract. This paper describes the design and a preliminary evaluation of the AI Workbench, an interactive tool for fostering AI literacy for secondary school students by enabling them to prototype user-facing AI applications without programming. It is based on a competence model for AI literacy that combines technical exploration and ethical reflection, in order to support a critical understanding while also encouraging responsible engagement with AI systems. The workbench focuses on building simple image recognition applications, but goes beyond related tools by providing customizable multimedia outputs and a dual view interface allowing students to explore the perspectives of both developers and end-users. In this way, it highlights the problem of the opacity of AI and its real-world implications, encouraging students to critically examine issues such as transparency, fairness, and ethical considerations. The results of a preliminary evaluation in two workshops with 57 secondary school students provided positive indications of the effectiveness of the tool to support experiential learning about AI. Participants reported a better understanding of both AI mechanics and basic ethical issues, as well as high user satisfaction. Further development will include scenario-based simulations, such as autonomous driving test environments, to better contextualize technical and ethical decisions.

Keywords: AI Literacy · AI Education · No-Code AI Prototyping · Experiential Learning

1 Introduction

Artificial intelligence (AI) is an essential component of digital ecosystems with which adolescents interact on a daily basis. Platforms such as Instagram and TikTok use AI algorithms to select personalized content, and frequently operate as opaque "black-box" systems. Users are often unaware of how these systems operate, resulting in limited comprehension and engagement with AI [1,2]. This divergence emphasizes the essential need to cultivate AI literacy as a capacity that empowers people to critically analyze, interact with and understand AI technology and its societal implications [2,3].

B. K. Smith and M. Borge (Eds.): HCII 2025, LNCS 15806, pp. 71–88, 2025.
https://doi.org/10.1007/978-3-031-93564-0_5

AI literacy is thus emerging as a crucial set of skills for competently and safely navigating a world increasingly permeated by AI. It includes understanding fundamental AI principles, recognizing ethical implications, and evaluating the limitations and biases inherent in AI systems. Educational initiatives, such as AI4K12 [10], aim to address this by making AI concepts accessible to K-12 students, fostering informed and responsible digital citizenship [3]. Experiential learning principles can provide a robust framework to foster this understanding through hands-on reflective activities that bridge the gap between abstract theory and practical application, as they have proven in other domains [4]. These principles have proven effective in various domains, such as healthcare simulations, engineering projects, and teacher education, demonstrating their broad applicability across disciplines [4].

Research highlights the need for learning approaches that go beyond technical proficiency, incorporating critical reflection on AI's ethical and societal implications [2,3]. While many existing educational tools introduce students to core machine learning concepts, they often prioritize usability and accessibility over deeper engagement with transparency, bias, and fairness in AI systems [1,8]. At the same time, the experiential learning approach has shown in different domains how it can help with learning to understand complex issues in real-world contexts, typically combining theoretical concepts and practice in directly experienceable situations.

This paper outlines the conceptual design, implementation, and evaluation of the AI Workbench, discussing its potential to support experiential learning and foster critical thinking in AI education. In the next section, we first briefly review related work, focusing on existing tools and their shortcomings for reaching this goal. We then present the design of the AI workbench and what kind of basic competences for AI literacy it aims to support. Finally, we discuss the main insights and results from a preliminary evaluation in two workshops with school students.

2 Related Work

The increasing integration of AI into everyday life has led to a growing emphasis on AI literacy in education. This section will discuss AI education tools and gaps in the approaches.

2.1 Existing ML-Tools for AI Education

Existing educational tools such as Google's Teachable Machine (GTM) [5] and Machine Learning for Kids (ML4Kids) [6] have played an important role in introducing AI concepts to school students. These tools simplify complex AI processes and provide a simple visual user interface to make them accessible to students without requiring advanced coding skills [3,7]. Both tools focus on enabling users to train basic AI models for image recognition through highly visual, interactive interfaces. This accessibility has made them popular resources for teaching fundamental principles of machine learning (ML) [2].

A key advantage of these tools is their ability to facilitate hands-on, interactive learning. GTM, for instance, allows students to train classification models quickly by supplying labeled training examples, demonstrating the basics of supervised learning in an intuitive way [8]. The immediate feedback provided by these tools in model testing helps learners understand how training data influences AI model performance. This enables them to experiment with different datasets, adjust labels, and observe real-time changes in classification results, reinforcing the basic principles of machine learning through trial and error [1]. ML4Kids extends this interactive approach by integrating AI with block-based coding platforms like Scratch, allowing students to create AI-driven applications [3,7]. This feature enables learners to combine machine learning with programming logic, fostering computational thinking and problem-solving skills. Beyond basic training and classification, some tools also allow for some level of customization and real-world applications beyond image recognition. GTM supports various input types such as images, audio, and pose estimation, broadening the scope of AI experimentation beyond standard text or image classification [8]. This flexibility enables students to explore different AI applications, from speech recognition to gesture-based interactions, aligning with real-world AI use cases [1]. ML4Kids further supports project-based learning by enabling students to integrate AI models into real-world applications. Through guided activities, students can train models using their own datasets and apply them to interactive projects, reinforcing the importance of data quality and ethical considerations in AI development [2].

Overall, such tools demonstrate that AI education can be both accessible and engaging through visual and interactive learning approaches. They introduce fundamental machine learning concepts while fostering creativity, experimentation, and computational thinking. Research highlights these aspects as essential components of effective AI education [7].

2.2 Gaps in Current Approaches

While existing AI education tools offer interactive experiences, they primarily focus on technical implementation, often neglecting ethical considerations and experiential learning in user-facing AI applications. Key aspects such as the influence of the composition of training data on system outcomes, bias, and fairness are insufficiently addressed. The importance of guiding students to critically engage with these issues to foster a more comprehensive understanding of AI's societal implications has been highlighted in the literature [8]. Similarly, AI transparency remains a challenge, as many tools do not sufficiently address the complexities of AI decision-making, making it difficult for students to grasp the opaque nature of AI models and the challenges users face in interpreting AI outputs [1]. Furthermore, the role of human developers in shaping AI behavior, such as defining system outputs and their presentation to users, has received limited attention in interactive ML tools for AI education. This limits the possibilities to address the awareness of AI's broader societal impact, including fairness, accountability, and user trust [2].

Although existing tools incorporate interactive elements, they often lack the structured reflection necessary for experiential learning, which is essential for critically assessing AI development decisions. Google's Teachable Machine (GTM), for example, enables users to create classification models without prior ML experience but has limitations in fostering deep understanding. It offers some customization of model parameters but does not explicitly address ethical considerations such as bias, fairness, and transparency [8]. In particular, GTM focuses primarily on training and testing of AI models [5], offering little exposure to post-training considerations such as model evaluation, deployment, and presentation of results to end-users. Without this perspective, students may struggle to understand how design choices, such as data selection and output representation, affect user trust and AI system transparency.

To bridge these gaps, AI education tools should go beyond training and testing as well as provide structured opportunities for reflection and ethical discussion. This requires tools that incorporate experiential learning principles, allowing students to engage with AI both as developers and end-users, fostering deeper critical reflection on AI's ethical dimensions and real-world applications.

3 Design of the AI Workbench

The AI Workbench has been developed to address the described gaps by providing a hands-on, interactive, no-code platform that allows secondary school students to engage with AI development through experiential learning. Its design aims to support students in actively constructing knowledge by experimenting with building simple user-facing AI applications, reflecting on their design choices, and analyzing the impact of their decisions. Grounded in a well-defined AI literacy model [9], the Workbench enables students to explore AI from both developer and user perspectives through a dual-view approach. It introduces customizable outputs, allowing students to reflect on the consequences of AI design decisions and the ethical responsibilities developers bear in shaping AI systems. This section outlines the design of the AI Workbench, its alignment with AI literacy competences, and the structured methodology adopted to integrate hands-on and experiential learning activities effectively.

3.1 Tool Design and Features

The AI Workbench is designed as an accessible, structured environment that allows students to engage with AI concepts in a hands-on manner. It follows a guided approach, ensuring that learners can systematically progress through the development of an AI model while gaining an understanding of key machine learning principles. The tool is built around two primary perspectives: the *developer view* and the *end-user view*, allowing students to engage with AI models

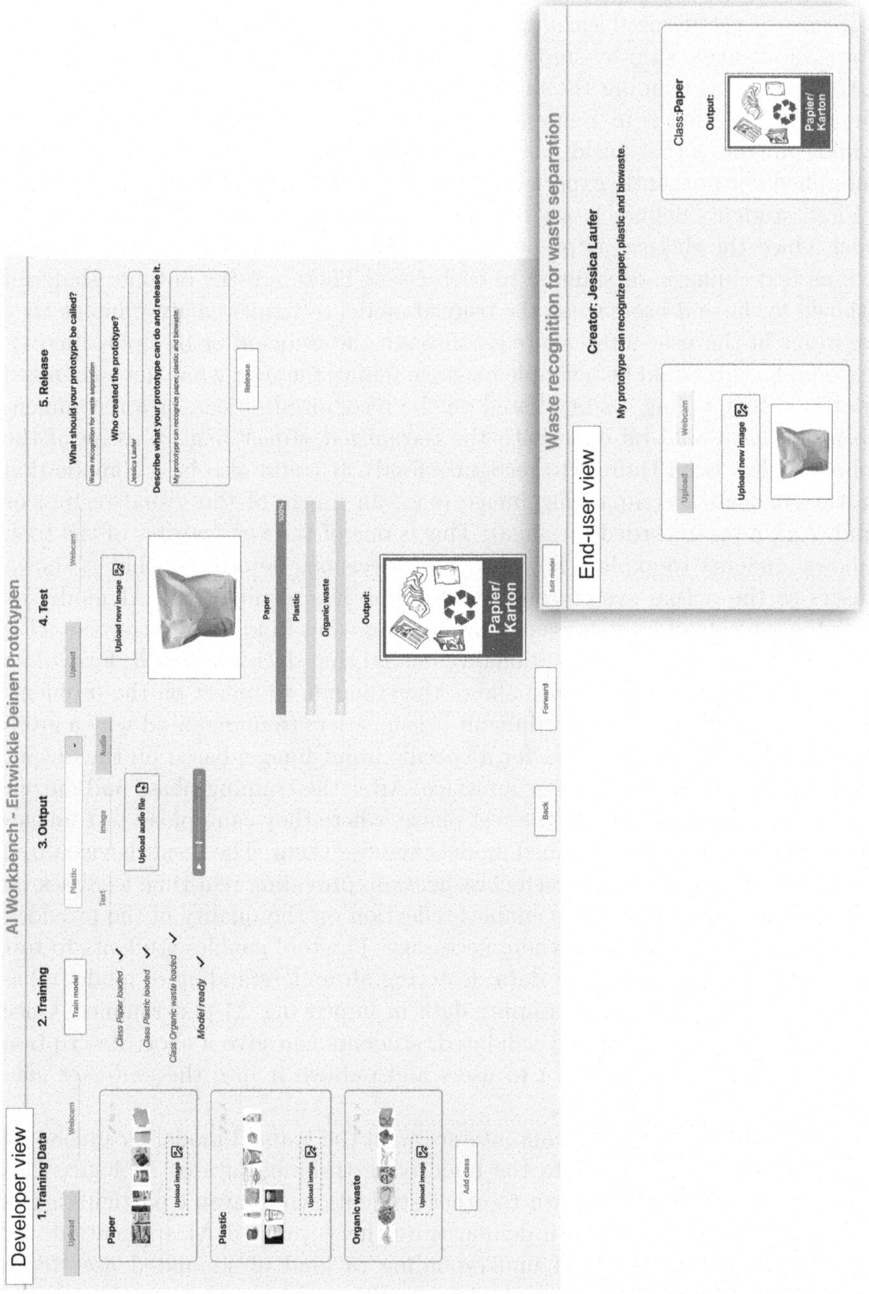

Fig. 1. The AI Workbench: Developer view (left) and end-user view (right)

both as system designers and as end-users interacting with a simple AI application based on the developed AI model.

To ensure a structured learning experience, the interface of the AI Workbench follows an intuitive step-by-step workflow in the *developer view* (Fig. 1): selecting training data, training the model, defining outputs, testing the model, and ultimately deploying it in a simple user interface for end-users. This structured workflow mirrors a real-world AI development process. It provides students with a simplified yet authentic experience of model creation, evaluation, and use.

First, students define classes by name, upload training data, and train their model. Once the dataset is prepared, they assign specific multimedia outputs (such as text, images, or sounds) to each class. These are the outputs that will be shown to the end-users when the trained model recognizes a given image they have input in the user interface (e.g., through the webcam or by uploading it). For example, this could be a simple message telling the user what the recognized object is, a text telling a story based on the recognized object, or a recommendation of what could be done with the recognized object (e.g., a recipe if the application has been trained to recognize food). It could also be a combination of a text and an accompanying image (e.g., an image of the visual recipe) or sound (e.g., a pre-recorded message). This is one of the key features of the tool. It allows students to explore how developer decisions determine what is shown to users as the actual system output based on the result of the AI model. It highlights the role of human agency in deciding what kind of behavior the AI is supposed to mimic and the intentionality behind that decision and the form of its presentation. Importantly, it also allows the students to reflect on the problems of in-transparency: how easy or difficult it is for users to understand why a given output has been shown to them for a specific input image, based on the output they are provided in the end-user interface. After the training phase and output definition, students proceed to the test phase, where they can upload test images and observe how well their trained model classifies them. The result is visualized through confidence scores for each classification, providing real-time feedback on model performance. This stage enables reflection on the quality of the provided training data and refinement where necessary. The tool enables students to test their models with independent data, fostering an understanding of model reliability and the role of diverse training data in improving AI performance. Once the model has been tested and validated, students can give a short description of their AI system to be shown to users and publish it into the *end-user view* (Fig. 1).

In the *end-user view*, students interact with the trained model by uploading images without direct access to the underlying training data or AI logic. This end-user view can also be shown to other students who haven't participated in building a given model to both demonstrate the developed AI application and to explore their reactions and understanding (a kind of simulated user test). This transition to the user view highlights the problems associated with the black-box nature of AI and the challenges users face in interpreting AI-based system outputs. This allows the students to directly experience and reflect on the transparency problems of AI applications. By integrating these elements, the workbench not only supports technical learning but can also be used to facilitate discussions on the ethical implications of AI, including bias, fairness, and transparency.

3.2 Alignment with A Competence Model for AI Literacy

The AI Workbench is specifically designed to align with main AI literacy competences by offering a guided yet flexible environment for hands-on exploration. Existing frameworks for AI literacy highlight key competences such as understanding main AI mechanisms, assessing system limitations, and reflecting on ethical and societal implications [2,3]. Such frameworks provide a theoretical foundation for educational tools that aim to help learners develop practical AI knowledge. Experiential learning can play a crucial role in this process by fostering active experimentation and reflective observation, thereby transforming abstract concepts into tangible experiences [4].

The described design of the AI Workbench follows a specific AI literacy competence model proposed by Gnoth et al. [9] This competence model provides a structured framework to support students in acquiring basic competences for a better understanding of AI systems in everyday life. Table 1 outlines the key competences covered by this competence model.

The AI Workbench closely aligns with this competence model by addressing the eight defined competences directly or indirectly. It also goes beyond that by addressing a further refined and detailed version of this competence model developed in the iKIDO project [11]. For the purposes of this paper, in the following, we will focus only on the basic competence model presented in Table 1.

The AI Workbench briefly introduces students to a basic understanding of the main principle of the underlying nature of AI (*Competence 1*): by allowing them to engage with model training and testing, students can observe that AI essentially learns from example data. While this provides a concrete hands-on experience with an example class of ML models (image recognition), it does not address the broader theoretical foundations of AI. For *Competence 2*, the AI Workbench effectively guides students with its structured user interface in the *developer view* through the key components of an AI system-training data input, model learning, and output generation and testing. Students label datasets, train models, and evaluate outputs with test data, gaining practical insights into how AI systems learn from data. While the tool does not explore the internal mechanisms of AI algorithms in depth, it provides an accessible framework for understanding the relationship between input data, model learning, and model predictions (or, in this case, classifications).

Through training and testing their models, students observe how AI generalizes from existing data to classify new inputs, which partly addresses *Competence 3*. At a basic level, this helps school students understand that AI systems recognize patterns in training data and apply learned knowledge to new instances of such data. For *Competence 4*, the AI Workbench emphasizes the importance of training data composition and quantity in determining model accuracy. Students

Table 1. Competence model for basic AI Literacy proposed in [9]

What do we mean by AI?	
1	Artificial Intelligence, commonly abbreviated AI, is a specific type of algorithm that is applied in technological systems, which are referred to as AI systems.
2	AI systems consist of three components following a logical order:
	1. Input → training data
	2. Processing of input → learning algorithm
	3. Output → prediction based on test data
How does an AI system learn?	
3	[a] An AI system learns by recognizing patterns in its training data. [b] The significant advantage of an AI system is that it learns from historic data and applies the generated knowledge to new problems within the same domain.
4	Since training data is vital for the learning process of an AI system, both its [a] composition and [b] quantity determine the accuracy of the outcomes.
5	Since an AI system has no understanding of a given subject, it relies on human knowledge to define the meaning of training data (e.g., labelling that data).
6	The learning algorithm in an AI system is sensitive to minor variations in input: small changes in the training data can lead to significant changes in the output.
What should one be aware of when interacting with an AI system?	
7	An AI system cannot transfer its knowledge to other areas, making it a highly specialized system.
8	AI systems can exhibit a lack of transparency. This occurs because [a] AI algorithms are often hidden in many applications without explicitly informing users, leading to potentially unrecognized influences on their perceptions, and [b] even if users are made aware of the use of AI, they still face significant difficulties in understanding the system's inner workings due to the opacity and complexity of AI "decision-making" processes, including hidden properties of AI.

engage in selecting, labeling, and structuring datasets, witnessing firsthand how data quality impacts prediction reliability. The ability to refine training data and reassess model performance makes this competence a central focus of the tool. The necessity of human knowledge in AI training, as outlined in *Competence 5*, is reinforced by requiring students to manually label their datasets. This process illustrates that AI systems do not inherently understand content but rely entirely on human-provided annotations. While the tool demonstrates this principle practically, it does not explicitly guide students through deeper discussions on annotation biases or knowledge representation. However, it can be used to stimulate such discussions, facilitated by a teacher or workshop facilitator. *Competence 6* is addressed by allowing students to explore how small variations in training data influence AI outcomes. Through iterative testing, students can see that minor changes in image selection or labeling can significantly impact classification results. While statistical measures of sensitivity and specificity are not directly introduced, the hands-on experimentation supports the development of an intuitive understanding of the dependency between input data and model performance.

Competence 7 is addressed indirectly as students experience firsthand that AI models are highly specialized and can only classify images that align by type with their training data. By testing their models with new or slightly different images, students can observe the limitations in model performance and in its capability to generalize beyond its training set. For *Competence 8*, the AI Workbench emphasizes the challenges of AI in-transparency through the dual-view interface. When switching from the developer to the end-user perspective, students recognize how an AI system functions as a "black box," where users must rely on the provided description without access to the internal decision-making process. This hands-on experience highlights both the hidden nature of AI algorithms in real-world applications and the challenges users face in understanding AI-generated outputs. It also underscores the importance of the decisions in the development process regarding how AI outputs should be presented to end-users (e.g., what accompanying information or explanations are provided). The structured experimentation with different training data and model outputs further encourages students to reflect on the role of transparency in AI systems and the ethical implications of opaque decision-making processes.

In conclusion, engaging with AI through interactive tasks allows students to experience key competences firsthand, but it is also through guided discussions that these experiences are examined. By reflecting on challenges such as the limitations of AI specialization or the opacity of AI decision-making and their possible impact on end-users, students can develop a better understanding of the societal and ethical dimensions of AI. These discussions provide an opportunity to connect individual observations to broader AI literacy concepts, fostering critical thinking and awareness. Ultimately, the combination of active experimentation and structured reflection supports students in learning not only how AI systems function but also in gaining the ability to assess their implications in real-world contexts.

3.3 Technical Implementation of the AI Workbench

The AI Workbench is developed as a web-based application. It is built using modern web technologies to ensure accessibility, responsiveness, and ease of use, enabling students to engage with AI concepts interactively. The front end is implemented in JavaScript and HTML with the use of Preact [12], a lightweight alternative to React, optimized for performance and scalability. Preact is a fast JavaScript library that provides the same modern component-based architecture as React but with a significantly smaller footprint, making it well-suited for web applications that prioritize performance and scalability [12]. For ML model training and testing, the workbench utilizes TensorFlow.js [13], allowing students to train and test models directly in the browser without requiring additional installations. The underlying AI model is based on MobileNet [14], a pre-trained convolutional neural network (CNN) architecture designed for efficient image classification tasks. Using transfer learning, students provide training data through image uploads, which are then processed and fed into the model to generate predictions. This approach enables real-time feedback on model performance, supporting an interactive learning experience.

4 Preliminary Evaluation

To assess the effectiveness of the AI Workbench, a preliminary evaluation was conducted in two workshops. The goal was to examine how well the tool supports students in understanding key AI concepts, including model training, ethical considerations, and the dual perspective of developers and end-users. Additionally, the evaluation aimed to determine whether the AI Workbench could effectively be used to convey these concepts within different time constraints.

4.1 Methodology

Two different evaluation formats were used for this purpose: evaluation of standalone use of the workbench and evaluation of its use embedded into a broader workshop context. The standalone session was designed as a short workshop (1h), allowing students to explore the AI Workbench in a compact timeframe with minimal theoretical input and with voluntary participation. This format served to test whether the tool could facilitate meaningful learning experiences even with limited instructional time.

The session embedded into a broader context was conducted as part of a structured 2-day workshop performed as part of obligatory school project days, providing students with a more comprehensive, guided learning experience. This format allowed participants to build a deeper understanding of AI concepts by going through multiple pre-structured challenges (i.e., tasks) before using the AI workbench in an AI development challenge. There, the participants freely used the AI workbench to develop a prototype of an AI application idea of their choice. By conducting the evaluation across both workshop formats, the evaluation aimed to gain insights into the adaptability and effectiveness of the AI Workbench in different educational settings, considering both structured learning environments and self-motivated exploration.

User feedback for the evaluation of the AI Workbench was collected with Likert-scale questionnaires and group discussions in both the embedded and standalone session. Thereby, in the standalone workshop, the questions focused specifically on the tool's usability and educational impact (e.g., "The AI Workbench helped me understand how AI models learn from training data"). In the embedded session, collected feedback addressed the entire workshop but included specific questions about the developer challenge, where the AI workbench was used. However, the embedded session served as an initial test of the AI Workbench to validate the concept, with feedback primarily gathered through discussions. Guided by prompts from the moderator, group discussions explored the differences between developer and end-user perspectives, the importance of training data, and the ethical "power" of developers in shaping AI outputs. These qualitative insights underscored key learning outcomes.

4.2 Embedded Session

The embedded session was performed as a dedicated 2h session with the AI Workbench within a two-day workshop designed to provide students with a comprehensive understanding of AI systems for image recognition and generation. The entire workshop took place as part of school project days, and participation was obligatory for all students from the participating school class. 27 participants with a nearly balanced gender distribution attended the workshop. All of the students were in the eighth school year and around 14 years old.

Session Design. Following a hands-on experiential learning approach, workshop participants actively engaged with AI technologies, allowing them to explore their fundamental mechanisms and limitations. The workshop featured a series of challenges that introduced AI applications in everyday life, guided students in understanding the training process, selecting appropriate training data, assessing model reliability, and experimenting with advanced concepts such as deepfakes and image generation.

Building on extensive foundational input, at the end of the first day of the workshop, students participated in the *Developer Challenge* lasting two hours. In this challenge, they followed a structured workflow depicted in Fig. 2. They worked in teams and first brainstormed an idea for an AI application based on image recognition, addressing a societal issue. They defined the problem the application would aim to solve, considered the target users that the application should support, and decided what exactly the AI model should do (e.g., recognizing faces, identifying objects). They then applied the knowledge acquired in the previous guided part of the workshop (ca. 2h) to develop a prototype of this idea using the AI workbench. They collected their own training data, trained a specialized image recognition model for their application scenario, tested its performance with appropriate test data, and refined the training data and the model if necessary. They also defined the multimedia system outputs to be shown to end-users in the user view for each of the image classes for which the model was trained. The prototypes were then exchanged between the teams, with each team testing the prototypes of one or more other teams as end-users, unfamiliar with the training data or the model design. This phase emphasized the challenges of interpreting specialized AI systems and the ethical implications of developer decisions, such as intentionally misleading outputs.

The described hands-on experience provided students with a structured and creative environment to translate theoretical concepts into practical AI solutions.

The session concluded with group presentations of the developed AI application prototypes, followed by a plenary discussion where students critically reflected on their key insights and ethical considerations.

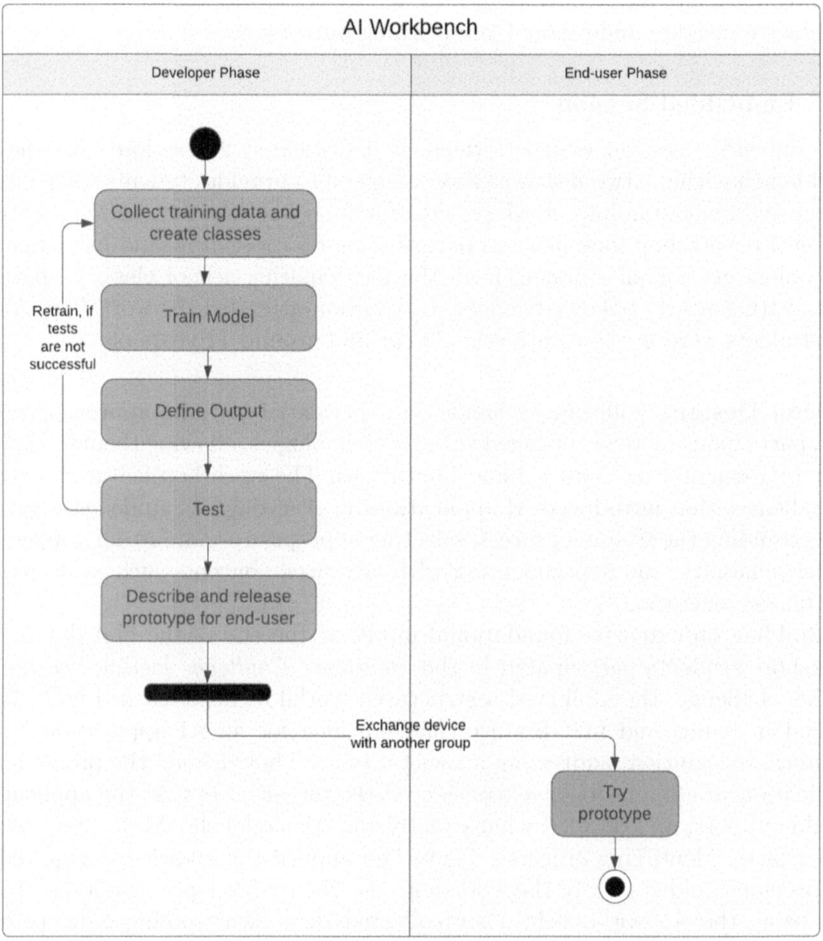

Fig. 2. Visualization of the AI Workbench workflow in the AI Developer Challenge sessions

Results. For this session, 14 out of 27 students provided feedback after the workshop through a questionnaire assessing the entire workshop, and all 27 students attended the group discussion, touching also specifically upon the session with the AI Workbench. The overall workshop feedback highlighted an improvement in their understanding of AI transparency issues, surpassing outcomes from prior workshops that had utilized Google's Teachable Machine (GTM). Many students demonstrated an awareness of AI as a "black box" system, recognizing the challenges associated with interpreting and understanding AI decision-making.

The questionnaire contained no specific questions about the tools used in the workshop in order to avoid overloading the school students with too many questions after a long day, following the teacher's concerns pointing to this as a critical issue. The embedded session was thus evaluated only qualitatively based on the insights from the group discussions.

Observations from the group discussions indicated that students recognized that the quality, diversity, and quantity of training data played a crucial role in determining the performance and reliability of AI models. Many participants observed that minor variations in the dataset significantly affected classification results, reinforcing the necessity of carefully choosing training inputs. Another recurring theme was the understanding of AI as a "black box" system. Students testing the prototypes of other teams found it challenging to determine the purpose and decision-making processes of an AI model based only on the given descriptions of the application provided by the developing teams. This highlighted the opacity of AI systems. The end-user view of the AI Workbench played a crucial role in illustrating these challenges, allowing students to experience firsthand the gap between AI developers and users.

A final common theme was the influence of developers on AI behavior. Students engaged in discussions about how AI developers have significant control over how models behave and how users interact with them. Many participants acknowledged the potential for unintentional bias in AI outputs and reflected on the ethical responsibilities associated with AI system design. These discussions underscored the importance of transparency and accountability in AI development.

4.3 Standalone Session

Due to the short duration of the standalone session (1h), only a brief theoretical introduction has been provided at the beginning before transitioning directly into hands-on work with the AI Workbench, also framed as an AI Developer Challenge. This short format was intentionally designed to evaluate whether the tool could effectively convey key AI concepts within a restricted time frame. This session was conducted as part of an event to familiarize school students with technical topics. The participation was voluntary, and a total of 30 students aged between 13 and 15, with a nearly equal gender distribution, attended the session.

Session Design. The session began with a brief introduction to fundamental AI principles, including image recognition, the basics of training and testing AI models, and the importance of diverse and well-structured training data. However, rather than delving deeply into theoretical aspects, the focus was on quickly equipping students with just enough context to begin practical experimentation.

The session then followed the same structured workflow described above in the embedded session and depicted in Fig. 2.

A key element of this session was the dual-view experience, which allowed students to engage with AI both as developers and as end-users. This structure encouraged them to reflect on AI as a "black box" system, emphasizing how design choices, such as training data selection and output configuration, influence user interactions and system reliability.

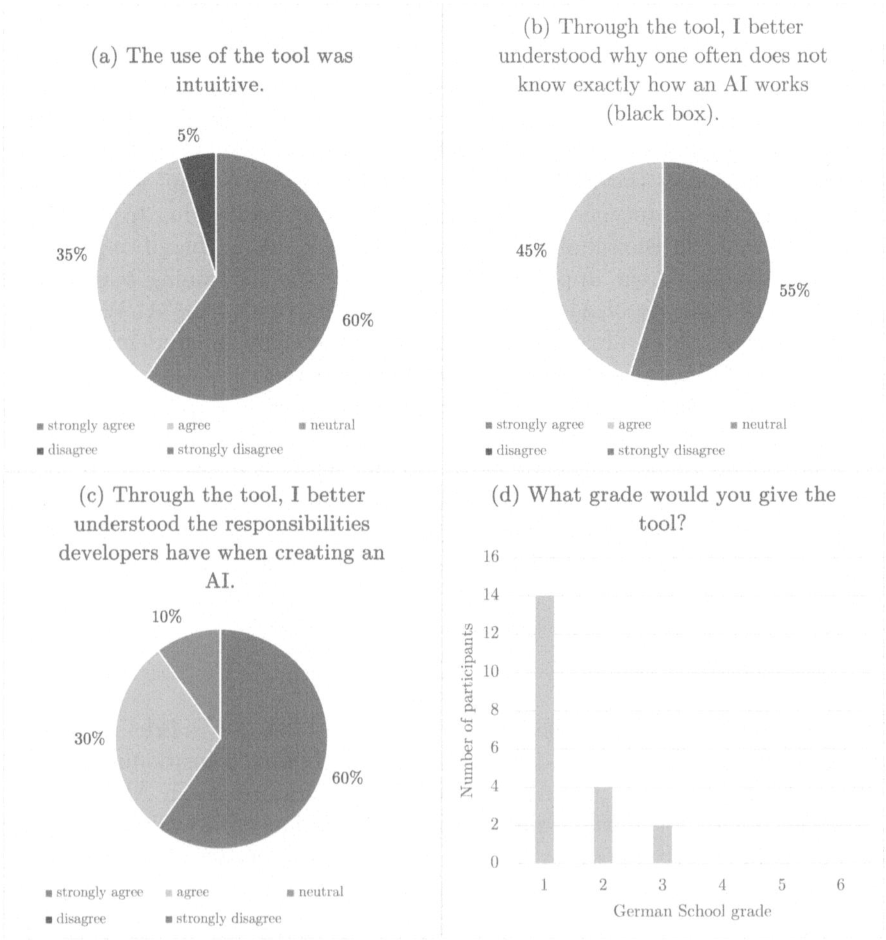

Fig. 3. User Feedback on the AI Workbench

Results. In this session, a high level of student engagement and satisfaction, as reflected in the questionnaire responses, could be observed despite the limited time frame. 20 out of 30 participants provided feedback. 95% of the respondents agreed or strongly agreed that the tool was intuitive to use. Similarly, all respondents either agreed or strongly agreed that their understanding of AI as a "black box" system had improved. Furthermore, 85% of the respondents agreed that they had gained a greater awareness of the developer's influence on AI behavior, particularly in terms of selecting training data and defining system outputs. The overall satisfaction with the tool was reflected in an average rating of 1.4 on the German school grading scale (range between "1 = very good" and "6 = deficient"), where 1.0 signifies the highest level of approval. The results are visualized in Fig. 3. Other evaluation results indicate that participants responded positively to various aspects of the AI Workbench, including its clarity, ease of use, and navigation (See Fig. 4). Most students strongly agreed that the tool effectively supported independent learning and provided a clear understanding of the AI model development process. While a small proportion of students expressed neutral or disagreeing opinions, the overall feedback suggests that the structured, hands-on approach successfully fosters AI literacy, with minor areas for potential refinement in instructional support (See Fig. 5).

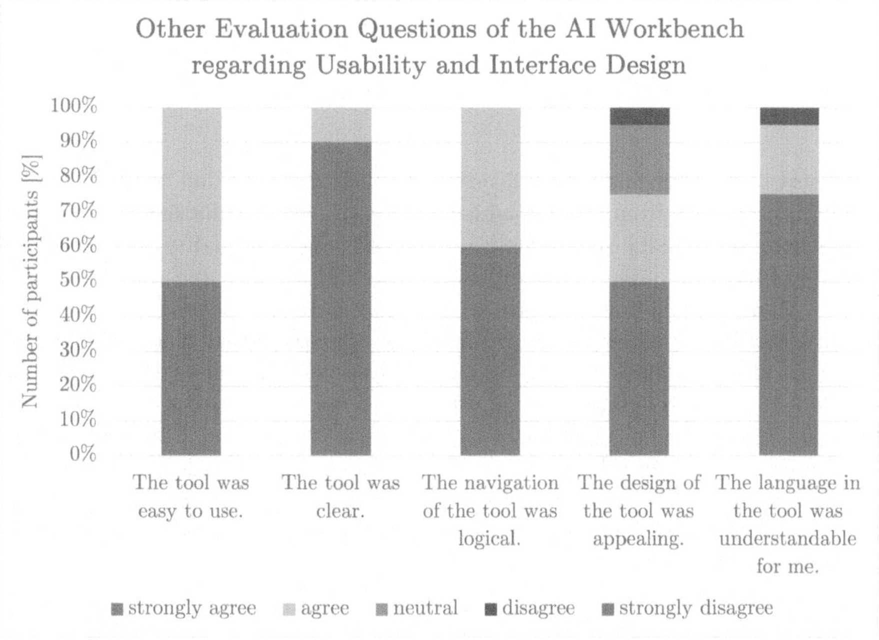

Fig. 4. Other User Feedback on the AI Workbench's Design and Usability

These results suggest that the structured design of the AI Workbench and of this session allowed students to quickly build and test AI models while developing a foundational understanding of AI principles.

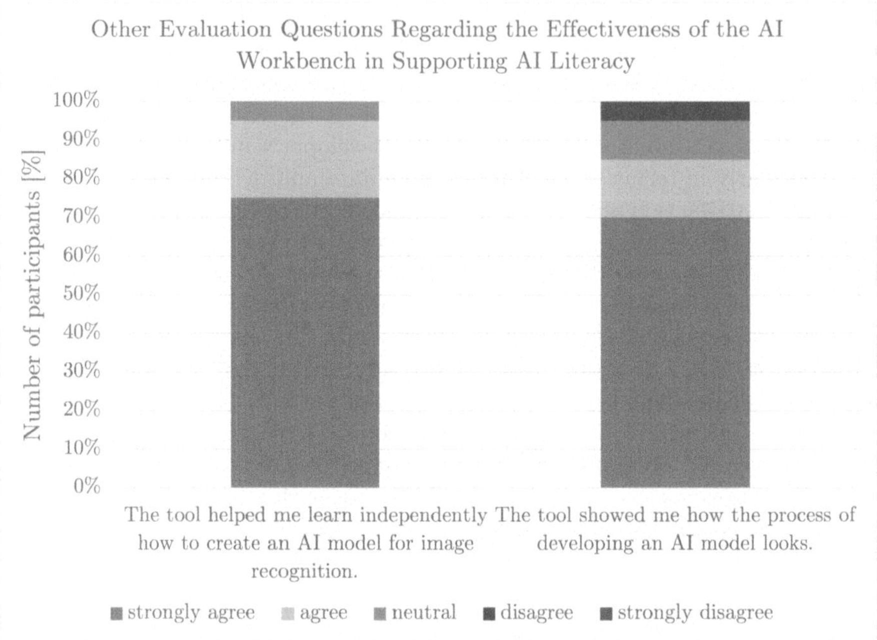

Fig. 5. Other User Feedback on the AI Workbench's supporting AI Literacy

Observations from the group discussion, which was attended by all 30 participants, mirror those from the embedded session. In spite of the shorter duration, in this session students also quickly recognized that the quality, diversity, and quantity of training data greatly influenced the performance and reliability of AI models. Many participants also observed that already small changes in the training dataset affected classification results. The opacity of the "black box" nature of AI was also addressed in the discussion. The descriptions of the prototypes provided by the development teams were found not sufficient for understanding the actual operation and purpose of the underlying AI model. This confirms the importance of providing the end-user view in the AI Workbench for experiencing the gap between AI developers and users. A final common theme was the discussion about how AI developers have significant control over how models behave and how users interact with them.

5 Conclusions

In this paper, we have presented the design and a preliminary (formative) evaluation of the AI Workbench, an interactive tool supporting the development of AI literacy for secondary school students, enabling them to build simple AI applications without programming. The structured approach of the AI Workbench supports the development of both technical proficiency and ethical awareness.

By integrating hands-on experimentation with ethical reflection, the tool bridges the gap between theoretical knowledge and practical application, allowing students to critically engage with issues such as transparency, fairness, and the societal impact of AI.

Although the preliminary evaluation was limited in scope and was performed in an exploratory manner, the obtained results already indicate that the design of the AI Workbench is well-suited to support the development of basic AI competences through experiential learning. The observed student engagement in the workshop sessions, the feedback from the questionnaire, and qualitative observations from group discussions indicate that the tool design effectively addresses key gaps in existing related tools for AI education. Students gained practical insights into AI mechanics, the role of the training data and its influence on the reliability of AI models, the impact of design decisions in AI development, and related ethical considerations. In particular, the dual-view interface played an important role, allowing the students to experience firsthand the gap between the perspective of the developers of AI systems and the end-users, fostering critical thinking and the awareness of the problems of intransparency and opacity in the design of AI applications.

While the current version of the AI Workbench has already effectively enabled school students to explore foundational AI concepts, further developments are planned to enhance its functionality and broaden its educational impact. To this end, we are working on including a scenario-based simulation module that will allow students to test their AI prototypes in a simulated autonomous driving test environment, allowing them to deepen their understanding of AI development and ethical issues in a real-world scenario. This will be accompanied by gamification elements, introducing interactive, game-like challenges to further stimulate engagement and reinforce learning outcomes. We also plan to extend the options for defining system outputs with the possibility of attaching URLs to be called for each recognized class. This allows extending system behavior with dynamic, real-time responses such as displaying search results for an identified image, calling up a predefined scripts, or even connecting to an LLM. Through these enhancements, the AI Workbench aims to further its goals of fostering critical thinking, ethical awareness, and practical skills in AI literacy, ensuring it remains a comprehensive and adaptable tool for AI education.

While the workbench has proven effective for supporting AI literacy education, there are limitations to consider. The tool has currently only been tested in small groups and in an exploratory manner. Further studies are needed to more systematically assess the impact on students' understanding and application of AI literacy competences.

Acknowledgement. The AI Workbench was developed as part of the iKIDO project at the Institute of Applied Computer Science of the University of Applied Science Stralsund, funded by the German Federal Ministry for Family, Senior Citizens, Women and Youth.

References

1. Van Brummelen, J., Heng, T., Tabunshchyk, V.: Teaching Tech to Talk: K-12 conversational artificial intelligence literacy curriculum and development tools. Proc. AAAI Conf. Artif. Intell. 35(17), pp. 15655-15663. (2021) arXiv2009.05653
2. Long, D., Magerko, B.: What is AI literacy? competencies and design considerations. In: Proc. 2020 CHI Conf. Hum. Factors Comput. Syst. ACM, Honolulu HI USA, pp 1–16. (2020). https://doi.org/10.1145/3313831.3376727
3. Touretzky D, Gardner-McCune C, Martin F, Seehorn D.: Envisioning AI for K-12: what should every child know about AI? Proc AAAI Conf Artif Intell. 33(01), pp. 9795– 9799 (2019). https://doi.org/10.1609/aaai.v33i01.33019795
4. Kolb, D.A.: Experiential learning: experience as the source of learning and development, 2nd edn. Pearson Education Inc., Upper Saddle River (2015)
5. Google Teachable Machine. https://teachablemachine.withgoogle.com. Accessed 28 Jan 2025
6. Machine Learning 4 Kids. https://machinelearningforkids.co.uk/?lang=en. Accessed 28 Jan 2025
7. Gresse Von Wangenheim, C., Hauck, J.C.R., Pacheco, F.S., Bertonceli Bueno, M.F.: Visual tools for teaching machine learning in K-12: a ten-year systematic mapping. Educ. Inf. Technol. **26**(5), 5733–5778. (2021). https://doi.org/10.1007/s10639-021-10570-8
8. Williams, R., Ali, S., Devasia, N., et al.: AI+ethics curricula for middle school youth: lessons learned from three project-based curricula. Int. J. Artif. Intell. Educ. **33**, 325–383 (2013). https://doi.org/10.1007/s40593-022-00298-y
9. Gnoth, S., Novak, J.: Supporting AI Literacy Through Experiential Learning: An Exploratory Study. HCII, Gothenburg (2025)
10. Artificial Intelligence (AI) for K-12 initiative (AI4K12). https://ai4k12.org. Accessed 28 Jan 2025
11. iKIDO project website. https://ikido.info. Accessed 28 Jan 2025
12. Preact. https://preactjs.com. Accessed 29 Jan 2025
13. Tensorflow JS. https://www.tensorflow.org/js. Accessed 29 Jan 2025
14. mobileNet_v3. https://www.kaggle.com/models/google/mobilenet-v3. Accessed 29 Jan 2025

Role-Playing as an Embodied Cognition Strategy to Enhance Learning Outcomes in the Empathize and Define Stages of Design Thinking Within Project-Based Design Courses

Yuhan Luo[1](✉), Pengxiang Jia[2], Bingjian Liu[1], Nai Yeen Gavin Lai[1], Guang Li[1], and Wai Siong Chai[1]

[1] University of Nottingham Ningbo China, 199 Taikang East Road, Ningbo 315100, China
{yuhan.luo,bingjian.liu,gavin.lai,guang.li,wai-siong.chai}@nottingham.edu.cn

[2] Zhejiang Wanli University, 8 Qianhu Road, Ningbo 315100, China

Abstract. In design education, project-based learning and design thinking emphasize the development of higher-order cognitive skills, including critical thinking and problem-solving. However, students often rely on intuitive, fast thinking (System 1), leading to premature solutions during the empathize and define stages. Dual Process Theory suggests that design thinking requires slower, reflective thinking (System 2) for effective problem analysis. Role-playing, as an embodied learning strategy, provides an opportunity to bridge the gap between these two types of thinking by engaging students physically and emotionally. However, its impact on learning outcomes during these stages remains unclear. This study explored how role-playing with varying embodiment levels influenced comprehension, retention, and transferability in the empathize and define stages of design thinking. Ninety undergraduate design students were randomly assigned to three groups: high-embodiment, low-embodiment, and control. The high-embodiment group engaged in sensorimotor role-playing, while the low-embodiment group focused on verbal interactions, and the control group followed a lecture-based approach. The study included pre-tests, post-tests, and delayed tests to assess outcomes. Results showed that role-playing, particularly high-embodiment, significantly improved comprehension, retention, and the ability to transfer knowledge to new contexts. These findings suggest that embodied learning strategies, especially high-embodiment role-playing, enhance cognitive engagement and support deeper reflective thinking in design education.

Keywords: Embodied Learning · Design Thinking · Role Playing

1 Introduction

The rise of Industry 4.0 is reshaping design education through emerging technologies including artificial intelligence (AI), the Internet of Things (IoT), big data, and smart manufacturing. Designers in the future must acquire interdisciplinary expertise

B. K. Smith and M. Borge (Eds.): HCII 2025, LNCS 15806, pp. 89–101, 2025.
https://doi.org/10.1007/978-3-031-93564-0_6

across engineering, data science, human-computer interaction, and sustainability to address increasingly complex challenges [1, 2]. To keep pace with these technological developments, design education must continuously innovate and refine teaching strategies.

Design thinking, a widely adopted methodology in design education, consists of five stages: empathize, define, ideate, prototype, and test [3]. Among these, the empathize and define stages are particularly crucial, as they help students to develop a deep understanding of user needs and accurately frame design problems. Nevertheless, students often struggle with cognitive biases in these stages, leading to vague problem definitions and a lack of critical thinking and innovation [4].

Dual Process Theory (DPT) provides a theoretical framework for understanding students' cognitive processes during these stages, distinguishing between System 1 (intuitive, fast, experience-driven thinking) and System 2 (deliberate, analytical, and reflective thinking) [5]. In design education, students frequently rely on System 1 for quick decision-making, often neglecting the complexity of problems and the need for deeper analysis [6]. Conversely, when System 2 lacks experiential input from System 1, it struggles to generate meaningful insights into user needs, thereby compromising design feasibility. Therefore, effectively integrating both cognitive systems into design education remains a significant challenge.

As an embodied learning strategy, role-playing has the potential to bridge System 1 and System 2 by fostering emotional and physical engagement, allowing students to immerse themselves in user experiences during the empathize and define stages [7]. While theoretical research highlights the benefits of role-playing in cognitive integration, empirical studies on its application in design education remain limited.

On this basis, this study seeks to investigate how role-playing would affect students' ability to empathize and define design problems, and its influences on comprehension, memory retention, and knowledge transfer. There are two primary research questions: 1) How does role-playing influence the development of empathize and problem-definition skills in design education? 2) What are the key effects of role-playing on students' immediate comprehension, memory retention, and knowledge transfer?

To address these two questions, an experimental study was conducted with 90 undergraduate design students, who were randomly assigned to three groups: a high-embodiment role-playing group, a low-embodiment role-playing group, and a traditional lecture-based control group. Pre-tests, post-tests, and delayed tests were used to assess the influence of different embodiment levels on learning outcomes. The results provide empirical evidence for the effectiveness of role-playing in design education and offer insights into optimizing cognitive processes.

2 Literature Review

2.1 Design Thinking

Design thinking has evolved from a user-centered product development methodology into a systematic, interdisciplinary approach applied across business, education, and healthcare sectors [8]. It has transitioned from a linear problem-solving model to an iterative process that emphasizes feedback and optimization, thus enhancing organizational flexibility and adaptability [9]. The integration of emerging technologies such as AI, big data, and Virtual Reality (VR) has further expanded its applications, facilitating user research, rapid prototyping, and sustainability-driven design solutions [10].

In education, design thinking fosters innovation, problem-solving, and interdisciplinary collaboration, equipping students with the adaptability and self-directed learning skills needed in uncertain environments [11]. Furthermore, the shift towards problem-based learning (PBL) and experiential learning has reinforced the importance of practical skills and iterative design processes [10].

However, design thinking education still faces many challenges, including curriculum standardization, faculty expertise, and students' adaptation to exploratory learning [9]. Traditional assessment methods primarily focus on final outputs rather than evaluating students' iterative processes, limiting their ability to refine problem definitions and generate innovative ideas [10]. Additionally, the lack of access to digital tools and collaborative spaces remains a barrier to the effective implementation of design thinking in education [12].

Addressing these challenges requires curriculum refinement and the integration of experiential learning strategies, such as role-playing, to enhance cognitive engagement in design education.

2.2 Embodied Learning in Education

Previous studies have shown that embodied learning can enhance students' understanding of complex concepts through multimodal interaction, contextualized strategies, and gesture-based engagement. For instance, in physics education, the combination of haptic devices with visual simulations has been found to deepen students' comprehension of force dynamics [13]. Contextualized strategies, such as role-playing and storytelling, have proven effective in increasing students' motivation and attention [14]. Moreover, gesture-based interaction tools, such as Kinect, enable students to map their physical movements onto virtual environments, which further facilitate dynamic learning experiences [15]. Despite its effectiveness, embodied learning remains underexplored in design education, and its potential requires further investigation.

The wide adoption of embodied learning faces both technological and resource constraints, particularly due to the high cost of VR and haptic feedback devices, limiting accessibility in resource-constrained settings [16]. While it has proven effective in fostering creativity and problem-solving across disciplines, research in design education remains limited [17]. Hence, there is a need to focus on low-cost strategies, such as role-playing and contextual simulations, to enhance accessibility.

2.3 Dual-Process Theory

Since its introduction in the 1960s, DPT serves as a fundamental framework for understanding human cognition and decision-making. The theory distinguishes between System 1 (fast, intuitive thinking) and System 2 (slow, analytical thinking) [5, 18]. While initially viewed as opposing forces, later models, such as the Hypothetical Thinking Model [19] and the Tri-Process Model [20], emphasize their interaction in complex reasoning. DPT has been applied across various domains, including healthcare, economics, artificial intelligence, and education, demonstrating how cognitive biases affect decision-making and how balancing intuitive and analytical thinking are essential in improving learning outcomes [21].

In design education, DPT highlights several key learning challenges, primarily cognitive biases and perceptual gaps (see Fig. 1). Students often over-rely on intuitive thinking (System 1) during problem identification and decision-making, leading to rapid assumptions, superficial analysis, and incomplete user research, which compromises design feasibility. Additionally, many perceive design thinking as a fixed methodology rather than an adaptive process, limiting their ability to navigate complex and evolving challenges. Conversely, an excessive dependence on analytical reasoning (System 2) without experiential input results in weak knowledge transfer and difficulty applying prior insights to new design problems.

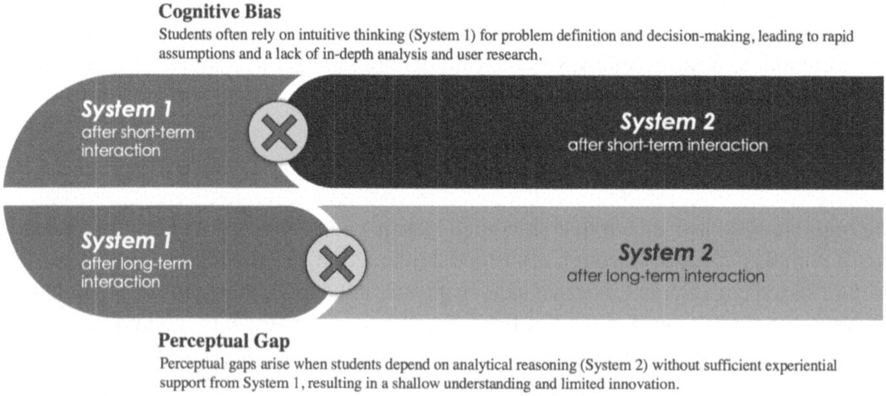

Fig. 1. Schematic diagram of the mechanisms of cognitive bias and perceptual discontinuity.

To overcome these challenges, it is essential to establish a balance between intuitive and analytical thinking in design education. Strengthening students' critical thinking and knowledge transfer abilities through the structured integration of System 1 and System 2 enables more flexible and effective responses to complex design challenges, ultimately enhancing their creativity and practical adaptability.

2.4 Core Elements in Embodied Learning

Embodied learning in non-technology-dependent settings is built on three core elements: sensori-motor engagement, congruency of bodily actions, and immersion/presence [22]. Originally applied in VR environments to enhance interactivity and knowledge acquisition [22], these principles have since been extended to traditional educational contexts, demonstrating significant learning benefits [23]. This study broadens the dimension of congruency of gestures to congruency of bodily actions, encompassing whole-body movements, postures, and physical states to better accommodate diverse learning settings.

Sensori-motor engagement emphasizes active participation, as research suggests that bodily involvement enhances multisensory cognition, attention, and memory retention. Engaging in physical actions rather than passive observation strengthens the connection between knowledge and experience.

Congruency of bodily actions extends beyond gestures to full-body movement, reinforcing spatial cognition and deepening understanding through intuitive representation of role behaviors. For example, in public speaking or drama courses, body language helps students grasp emotional and contextual nuances, while in science education, physical actions can simulate complex phenomena [24].

Immersion/presence enhances engagement by fostering a sense of "being present" in the learning environment through visual, auditory, and tactile stimuli [22]. In non-technology-dependent settings, role-playing, scenario-based learning, and problem-based approaches help recreate realistic experiences, making abstract concepts more tangible. Physical elements such as costumes, spatial arrangements, and interactive social roles further strengthen immersion, enabling learners to better understand user perspectives and engage deeply with the content [15].

Applying these principles in the empathize and define stages of design thinking is expected to enhance learners' ability to understand target roles and problem contexts, optimizing problem identification and definition. Through sensori-motor engagement, students actively perform role-related bodily actions, reinforcing physical and cognitive connections to user needs. The congruency of bodily actions ensures alignment between role behaviors and learning objectives, while immersion strengthens engagement by providing an authentic and emotionally resonant experience. Together, these elements create a holistic learning framework that fosters deeper understanding, critical thinking, and problem-solving adaptability in design education.

3 Methods

This study conducted an experimental investigation with 90 undergraduate design students, who were randomly assigned to three groups: a high-embodiment role-playing group, a low-embodiment role-playing group, and a traditional lecture-based control group. The study employed pre-tests, post-tests, and delayed tests to assess the impact of different embodiment levels on learning outcomes. The data analysis aims to provide empirical evidence for the application of role-playing in design education and offer insights for optimizing cognitive processes. The University Research Ethics Committee approved the study.

3.1 Participants

A total of 90 undergraduate design students (25 males, 65 females) participated in the study. Participants were recruited from a university and randomly assigned to one of three groups (i.e., high-embodiment, low-embodiment, and control), with 30 participants in each group ($n = 30$) to ensure balanced group sizes. Their ages ranged from 19 to 22 years ($M = 19.89$, $SD = 1.00$). Detailed demographic information is summarized in Table 1.

Table 1. Demographic information.

Variables		Group A	Group B	Group C
Gender	Male	9 (30.0%)	8 (26.7%)	8 (26.7%)
	Female	21 (70.0%)	22 (73.3%)	22 (73.3%)
Age	Mean	20.4	20.5	20.6
	Standard deviation	0.96	0.97	1.10

3.2 Apparatus

The teaching program, *Designing a Smart Mobility System for Older Adults*, was developed to replicate the physical, cognitive, and social challenges experienced by older adults. To create a fully immersive and experiential learning process, the program integrated sensori-motor engagement, bodily action congruency, and immersive presence, ensuring that participants could physically and cognitively engage with the challenges older adults confront (see Fig. 2).

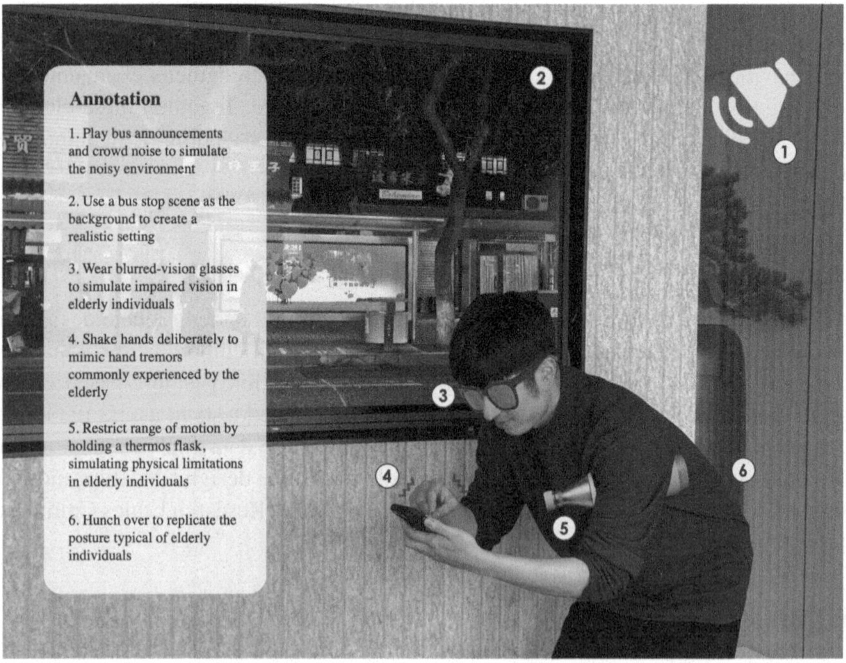

Fig. 2. Schematic diagram of high-embodiment role-playing in the project of designing a smart mobility system for older adults.

Sensori-motor engagement was achieved through the use of joint-restriction braces, blurred-vision glasses, and weighted gloves. These tools simulated restricted mobility, impaired vision, and hand tremors, enabling students to experience firsthand the physical limitations that older adults encounter. By navigating spaces, boarding buses, and performing everyday mobility tasks under these constraints, participants would be able to develop a more embodied understanding of mobility-related challenges.

Bodily action congruency was reinforced by requiring students to replicate the typical behaviors of older adults, such as walking slowly, cautiously gripping handrails, and adjusting their posture when checking their phones. These actions helped students understand movement limitations and behavioral adaptations necessary for mobility. A task accuracy test further evaluated their ability to maintain older adults' gait patterns, enhancing their awareness of physical constraints.

Immersive presence was established by incorporating multisensory stimuli and realistic settings. Environmental elements such as bus stop signage, seating arrangements, and directional signs created an authentic mobility context. To enhance realism, auditory and visual stimuli (e.g., bus announcements, crowd noise, and light reflections) were integrated. Moreover, the introduction of social roles such as passenger and driver enables students to engage in interpersonal interactions, allowing them to experience the psychological aspects of older adults when seeking assistance or navigating social situations.

By combining these three elements, the apparatus provided an immersive learning environment, fostering empathy and improving students' ability to identify and define design requirements for older adults effectively.

3.3 Procedures

A 3 × 3 factorial design was employed to evaluate the impact of role-playing strategies on comprehension, memory retention, and knowledge transfer. Participants were randomly assigned to one of three groups: 1) High-embodiment group. This group incorporated sensory-motor engagement, congruency of bodily actions, and immersion to simulate realistic scenarios; 2) Low-embodiment group. This group was limited to verbal interactions, where students performed oral rehearsals based on a script without engaging in physical actions or immersive contexts; 3) Control group. This group followed a traditional text-based instructional approach, where students completed tasks using reading materials without role-playing or interactive elements.

This study employed pre-tests, post-tests, and delayed tests to assess students' prior knowledge, immediate comprehension, memory retention, and knowledge transferability. The experiment followed a four-stage process: pre-test, intervention, post-test, and delayed test.

The pre-test (5 min) was conducted before the intervention to evaluate students' baseline understanding of the empathize and define stages in design thinking. Following the pre-test, the intervention phase (90 min) focused on *Designing a Smart Mobility System for Older Adults* and consisted of three parts: a 20-min lecture on design thinking concepts, a 25-min study of standardized materials on mobility challenges to ensure all participants had the same background knowledge, and a 45-min learning activity based on their assigned instructional approach. The high-embodiment group engaged in immersive role-playing, the low-embodiment group conducted verbal rehearsals, and the control group followed a traditional text-based learning approach.

The post-test (10 min) was administered immediately after the intervention to assess comprehension. It included six items: three repeated from the pre-test to measure theoretical understanding and three scenario-based questions evaluating students' ability to analyze user needs and apply their knowledge in practical contexts. The delayed test (10 min), conducted one week later, included four modified items from previous tests to minimize memory effects and three new items introducing a distinct design scenario, *Optimizing School Bus Experiences for Primary School Children*, to evaluate long-term memory retention and knowledge transfer.

4 Results

The effectiveness of embodied role-playing teaching methods on learning outcomes was evaluated through analyses of pre-test, post-test, and delayed test data. To ensure comparability across groups, a homogeneity of variance test was conducted on pre-test scores. Levene's test confirmed that the assumption of homogeneity of variance for ANOVA was satisfied ($F = 0.21$, $p = 0.81$). A subsequent one-way ANOVA showed no significant differences in prior knowledge levels among the groups ($F = 1.11$, $p = 0.33$) (see Table 2), indicating equivalent starting levels across the groups and providing a common basis for further comparisons.

Table 2. One-way ANOVA results of the pre-test data.

Variable	Groups	Numbers	Mean score	Standard deviation	F statistics
Pre-test	Exp. A	30	41.9	16.4	1.11
	Exp. B	30	48.0	18.9	
	Ctrl. C	30	47.8	18.7	

Note: Exp. = Experimental group, Ctrl. = Control group

The post-test data were analyzed to evaluate immediate learning outcomes. Levene's test confirmed the homogeneity of variance ($F = 0.46$, $p = 0.63$). ANOVA results revealed that teaching methods significantly influenced immediate understanding ($p < 0.05$). As given in Table 3, Tukey HSD post hoc tests indicated that both Experimental Group A and Group B achieved significantly higher scores than the Control Group C ($p < 0.05$), while no significant differences were observed between Group A and Group B.

The delayed test results were analyzed to evaluate memory retention and knowledge transfer. For the first four questions assessing memory retention, Levene's test confirmed homogeneity of variance ($F = 0.91$, $p = 0.41$). ANOVA results showed that teaching methods had a significant effect on memory retention ($p < 0.05$). Post hoc analyses revealed that Group A outperformed the Control Group C ($p < 0.01$), and Group B also outperformed Group C ($p < 0.05$), with no significant differences between Group A and Group B (see Table 4).

For the last three questions assessing knowledge transfer, Levene's test again confirmed homogeneity of variance ($F = 1.69$, $p = 0.19$). ANOVA results indicated a

Table 3. ANOVA results of the post-test data.

Variable	Groups	Numbers	Mean score	Standard deviation	F statistics	Partial Eta Squared	Post-hoc Test (Tukey HSD)
Post-test	Exp. A	30	67.2	12.5	3.92*	0.08	A > C*
	Exp. B	30	67.3	10.3			B > C*
	Ctrl. C	30	60.1	11.4			

Note: Exp. = Experimental group, Ctrl. = Control group, $^{*}p < 0.05$

Table 4. ANOVA results of the delayed test on memory retention.

Variable	Groups	Numbers	Mean score	Standard deviation	F statistics	Partial Eta Squared	Post-hoc Test (Tukey HSD)
Delayed test	Exp. A	30	76.2	16.3	6.18**	0.12	A > C**
	Exp. B	30	73.2	12.4			B > C*
	Ctrl. C	30	63.2	16.0			

Note: Exp. = Experimental group, Ctrl. = Control group, $^{*}p < 0.05$, $^{**}p < 0.01$

significant effect of teaching methods on knowledge transfer (p < 0.01). Tukey HSD post hoc tests indicated that Group A outperformed both Group B (p < 0.05) and the Control Group C (p < 0.01), and no significant differences were found between Group B and Group C (see Table 5).

Table 5. ANOVA results of the delayed test on knowledge transfer

Variable	Groups	Numbers	Mean score	Standard deviation	F statistics	Partial Eta Squared	Post-hoc Test (Tukey HSD)
Delayed test	Exp. A	30	70.2	17.3	7.37**	0.14	A > C**
	Exp. B	30	55.8	17.2			A > B*
	Ctrl. C	30	52.3	22.4			

Note: Exp. = Experimental group, Ctrl. = Control group, $^{*}p < 0.05$, $^{**}p < 0.01$

Furthermore, an analysis of average scores on comprehension, memory retention, and knowledge transfer confirmed that the results were not affected by floor or ceiling effects, ensuring the reliability of the findings. These results demonstrated the efficacy of embodied role-playing teaching methods in enhancing both immediate learning outcomes, as well as longer-term retention and transfer of knowledge.

5 Discussion

This study demonstrated the effectiveness of embodied role-playing in enhancing comprehension, memory retention, and knowledge transfer in the empathize and define stages of design thinking. Post-test results indicated that role-playing improves comprehension, as students actively engage with design concepts through physical and contextual experiences. This aligns with embodied cognition theory, which suggests that physical interaction and contextual experiences enhance the intuitive understanding of abstract concepts by grounding knowledge in real-world contexts.

Moreover, the delayed test results demonstrated that role-playing strengthens long-term memory retention, particularly in high-embodiment conditions. Compared to traditional lecture-based instruction, embodied strategies leverage multisensory stimuli (e.g., visual, auditory, and kinesthetic inputs) to facilitate multi-channel encoding, thus improving memory stability [26]. The emotional resonance also generated through role-playing strengthens memory traces, enhancing retention of the learning content.

The study also demonstrated that embodied learning promotes knowledge transfer, as the high-embodiment group showed the strongest ability to apply empathize and define frameworks to new design challenges. This supports prior research suggesting that experiential learning enhances flexible problem-solving by enabling learners to integrate abstract knowledge with real-world contexts [27].

From a cognitive perspective, the findings are consistent with DPT, which differentiates between System 1 and System 2 [4]. Role-playing facilitates the transition between these systems by reducing cognitive barriers, allowing students to engage intuitively during the empathize phase and analytically during the define phase. The results align with prior work suggesting that experiential learning enriches System 1's knowledge base, improving its ability to generate high-quality inputs for System 2, ultimately strengthening adaptability and critical thinking [28].

In this sense, these findings reinforced the effectiveness of embodied learning in strengthening comprehension, memory retention, and knowledge transferability, consistent with previous research in cognitive science and education. By bridging intuitive and analytical thought processes, embodied role-playing emerges as a valuable pedagogical strategy for enhancing cognitive flexibility in design education.

6 Conclusion

In conclusion, this study explored the use of embodied role-playing as a pedagogical strategy to address cognitive challenges in design education, particularly during the empathize and define stages of design thinking. By drawing on DPT, we demonstrated how the interplay between intuitive (System 1) and analytical (System 2) thinking affects students' ability to analyze user needs and define design problems. Role-playing was shown to enhance students' immediate comprehension, memory intention, and knowledge transfer while reducing cognitive biases, thereby improving the depth and accuracy of their design decisions. Despite its contributions, this study has several limitations to consider. First, individual differences (e.g., personality traits such as extraversion and openness) may have influenced the performance of students. For instance, extroverted students may engage more actively in role-playing, while introverted ones may benefit less due to reduced interaction. Future studies could integrate personality assessments to examine these effects in detail. Second, the simplified and controlled design scenarios used in this study may restrict the generalizability of results to more complex real-world design challenges. There is thus a need for future research to incorporate more diverse and multifaceted tasks to better reflect practical scenarios in real-world settings of design education.

Moreover, the findings of this study have notable implications for design education. First, embodied role-playing transforms traditional teaching models by shifting from passive knowledge transmission to experiential learning. By immersing students in real-world design scenarios, this approach enhances their ability to empathize with users and define design problems more effectively [29]. Integrating VR can further enhance authenticity and engagement, though challenges remain in ensuring its accessibility and scalability [11].

Second, this method strengthens practical skills by fostering teamwork, interdisciplinary collaboration, and adaptability to open-ended challenges. Future implementations could integrate role-playing into real design projects through academia-industry collaborations, reinforcing hands-on learning experiences [9]. However, aligning role-playing with existing curricula requires careful planning to balance theory and practice.

Lastly, technological integration can further optimize learning outcomes. AI and big data analytics can personalize learning paths and provide real-time feedback, helping students identify and overcome learning barriers [30, 31]. Additionally, metaverse-based role-playing could enable global, cross-disciplinary design collaboration, thereby broadening students' perspectives and skills [32].

While embodied role-playing offers significant benefits, further research is needed to refine its implementation, assess long-term impacts, and address challenges related to accessibility, scalability, and standardization.

References

1. Schwab, K.: The fourth industrial revolution. Crown Business, New York (2017)
2. Garca Ferrari, T.: Design and the fourth industrial revolution. dangers and opportunities for a mutating discipline. Des. J. S2625–S2633 (2017)
3. Liedtka, J.: Perspective: linking design thinking with innovation outcomes through cognitive bias reduction. J. Prod. Innov. Manag. **32**(6), 925–938 (2015)
4. Evans, J.S.B.: Dual-processing accounts of reasoning, judgment, and social cognition. Annu. Rev. Psychol. **59**(1), 255–278 (2008)
5. Milli, S., Lieder, F., Griffiths, T.L.: A rational reinterpretation of dual-process theories. Cognition **217**, 104881 (2021)

6. Moore, D., Sauder, J., Jin, Y.: A dual-process analysis of design idea generation. In: International Design Engineering Technical Conferences and Computers and Information in Engineering Conference, p. V007T07A017. American Society of Mechanical Engineers, New York (2014)
7. Kim, Y.S., Park, J.A.: Design thinking in the framework of visual thinking and characterization of service design ideation methods using visual reasoning model. Des. J. **24**(6), 931–953 (2021)
8. Lu, P., Li, Z., Li, J., Hsiao, S.W.: A consumer-oriented design thinking model for product design education. Interact. Learn. Environ. **31**(8), 4753–4771 (2023)
9. Pieroni, M.P., McAloone, T.C., Pigosso, D.C.: Business model innovation for circular economy and sustainability: a review of approaches. J. Clean. Prod. **215**, 198–216 (2019)
10. Lahiri, A., Cormican, K., Sampaio, S.: Design thinking: from products to projects. Procedia Comput. Sci. **181**, 141–148 (2021)
11. Wang, G.: Digital reframing: the design thinking of redesigning traditional products into innovative digital products. J. Prod. Innov. Manag. **39**(1), 95–118 (2022)
12. Magana, A.J., Balachandran, S.: Unpacking students' conceptualizations through haptic feedback. J. Comput. Assist. Learn. **33**(5), 513–531 (2017)
13. Hung, I.C., Hsu, H.H., Chen, N.S., Kinshuk.: Communicating through body: a situated embodiment-based strategy with flag semaphore for procedural knowledge construction. Educ. Technol. Res. Dev. **63**, 749–769 (2015)
14. Johnson-Glenberg, M.C., Megowan-Romanowicz, C., Birchfield, D.A., Savio-Ramos, C.: Effects of embodied learning and digital platform on the retention of physics content: centripetal force. Front. Psychol. **7**, 1819 (2016)
15. Dede, C.: Immersive interfaces for engagement and learning. Science **323**(5910), 66–69 (2009)
16. Castro-Alonso, J.C., Ayres, P., Paas, F.: Animations showing Lego manipulative tasks: three potential moderators of effectiveness. Comput. Educ. **85**, 1–13 (2015)
17. Tversky, A., Kahneman, D., Slovic, P.: Judgment under uncertainty: Heuristics and biases. Cambridge University Press, Cambridge (1982)
18. Evans, J.S.B.: Dual-process theories of reasoning: contemporary issues and developmental applications. Dev. Rev. **31**(2–3), 86–102 (2011)
19. Stanovich, K.E., West, R.F., Toplak, M.E.: The complexity of developmental predictions from dual process models. Dev. Rev. **31**(2–3), 103–118 (2011)
20. Reyna, V.F., Brainerd, C.J.: Dual processes in decision making and developmental neuroscience: a fuzzy-trace model. Dev. Rev. **31**(2–3), 180–206 (2011)
21. Ricco, R.B., Overton, W.F.: Dual systems competence-procedural processing: a relational developmental systems approach to reasoning. Dev. Rev. **31**(2–3), 119–150 (2011)
22. Johnson-Glenberg, M.C.: Immersive VR and education: embodied design principles that include gesture and hand controls. Front. Robot. AI **5**, 375272 (2018)
23. Kontra, C., Lyons, D.J., Fischer, S.M., Beilock, S.L.: Physical experience enhances science learning. Psychol. Sci. **26**(6), 737–749 (2015)
24. Johnson-Glenberg, M.C., Birchfield, D.A., Tolentino, L., Koziupa, T.: Collaborative embodied learning in mixed reality motion-capture environments: two science studies. J. Educ. Psychol. **106**(1), 86–99 (2014)
25. Slater, M., Wilbur, S.: A framework for immersive virtual environments (FIVE): speculations on the role of presence in virtual environments. Presence: Teleoperators Virtual Environ. **6**(6), 603–616 (1997)
26. Fischer, K.W., Immordino-Yang, M.H.: The fundamental importance of the brain and learning for education. Mind Brain Educ. **2**, 1–7 (2008)
27. Cross, N.: Designerly ways of knowing: Design discipline versus design science. Des. Issues **17**(3), 49–55 (2001)

28. Kahneman, D.: Thinking, fast and slow. Farrar, Straus and Giroux, New York (2011)
29. Kolb, D.A.: Experiential learning: Experience as the source of learning and development, 2nd edn. Pearson Education, New Jersey (2014)
30. Siemens, G.: Learning analytics: the emergence of a discipline. Am. Behav. Sci. **57**(10), 1380–1400 (2013)
31. Popenici, S.A., Kerr, S.: Exploring the impact of artificial intelligence on teaching and learning in higher education. Res. Pract. Technol. Enhanc. Learn. **12**(1), 22 (2017)
32. Mystakidis, S.: Metaverse. Encyclopedia **2**(1), 486–497 (2022)

Co-designing Lesson Plans for Supporting Human-Centred AI Literacy in K-12 Education

Linda Mannila[1], Susanne Hägglund[2](✉), and Mattias Wingren[2]

[1] University of Helsinki, Helsinki, Finland
linda.mannila@helsinki.fi
[2] Åbo Akademi University, Vasa, Finland
{susanne.hagglund,mattias.wingren}@abo.fi

Abstract. The fast AI development has resulted in governments as well as national and international organizations calling for "AI for all", highlighting the need for AI-related competences. At the same time human centered approaches to AI are underscored, in order to protect human rights, promote sustainable development, and equip individuals with the necessary values and skills for effective human machine collaboration in everyday life and work. Still, AI in education remains a nascent field, with no clear guidelines on what to teach or how to pedagogically leverage AI. Introducing AI competences, or AI literacy, in K-12 education poses additional challenges as the topic is unfamiliar to most teachers and seldom has a clear space in the curriculum. In this paper, we describe a human-centered process of co-designing AI lesson plans for grades 3–6 (students aged 9–13) together with students, teachers, IT educators, class teacher students, and teacher trainers. The paper presents the phases involved and lessons learned when creating educational experiences that 1) are suitable from both a teacher and student perspective, 2) can fit learning objectives in the current curriculum, and 3) prioritize the ethical, social, and human dimensions of AI.

Keywords: Co-design · Human-centred AI · AI literacy · K-12 education

1 Introduction

We are witnessing a transformation where artificial intelligence (AI) plays an increasing role in everyday life. AI has the potential to become a so-called general-purpose technology, much like electricity and the Internet, underpinning general and vital societal tasks [15,25]. The development extends beyond early adopters who actively seek out niche AI-supported solutions; it now affects everyone and permeates all aspects of society. Consequently, there has been a growing emphasis on human-centered AI (HCAI), aiming to design reliable, safe, and trustworthy systems that support human self-efficacy and sustainability and respect human rights, values and equality [37].

B. K. Smith and M. Borge (Eds.): HCII 2025, LNCS 15806, pp. 102–118, 2025.
https://doi.org/10.1007/978-3-031-93564-0_7

The importance of HCAI is underscored by UNESCO [43], highlighting the need to protect human rights, promote sustainable development, and equip individuals with values and skills for effective human-machine collaboration in daily life, education, and work. The UNESCO goal of "AI for all" aims to ensure that everyone can benefit from technological advancements, emphasizing the need for a broad understanding of AI's potential impact, capabilities, limitations and appropriate contexts of use [45]. This is also addressed in the EU framework DigComp 2.2, which outlines the competences all citizens need in an increasingly digital world [48].

Yang et al. [52] assert that "[t]he greater the impact that AI has on humans, the greater the need is for us to understand it". This naturally also extends to children and young people, as AI technology is embedded in services, tools, and devices they use [46]. The EU report "AI and the rights of the child" [5] presents 12 key recommendations to ensure that children can lead safe, secure, and active lives in an AI-dominated world. One of these recommendations emphasizes the critical role of schools in helping children develop adequate AI-related competences.

AI in education, however, remains a nascent field, with no clear guidelines on what to teach or how to pedagogically leverage AI [20]. While much of the current discourse on AI in education focuses on generative AI, it is crucial to adopt a broader perspective. This is highlighted by UNESCO [44] as the need to learn *about*, learn *with* and learn to *work and live with* AI, competences commonly framed as AI literacy [19,21,26,27].

Introducing AI literacy in K-12 education is challenging as it is unfamiliar to most teachers. A similar challenge was encountered when programming was introduced into K-12 curricula globally, as many teachers lacked experience in programming [22,36]. The surge in programming education led to an abundance of educational tools and material, making it difficult for teachers to discern which resources to use, while the absence of a specific computing subject in many countries posed further challenges in integrating new technology-related content into other subjects [22].

These challenges suggest that integrating AI in a human-centered manner into K-12 education requires collective design processes, or co-design [39], involving relevant stakeholders to develop approaches and resources that are practical and suitable for authentic classroom settings. Co-creating curricula and activities with the K-12 community has been proposed as a solution [18,40,51,53], although such initiatives have often involved only teachers, overlooking other important stakeholders. A more inclusive co-design approach, involving a range of stakeholders, could better ensure that the integration of AI literacy into K-12 education is suitable and reflective of real-world needs and contexts.

In this paper, we describe the human-centered process of co-designing AI lesson plans for K-12 education in Finland with students (n = 38), teachers (n = 3), teacher trainers (n = 4), class teacher students (n = 31), and an IT educator (n = 1). The aim was to create educational experiences that 1) are suitable from both a teacher and student perspective, 2) fit learning objectives in the current Finnish core curriculum, and 3) prioritize the ethical, social, and human dimensions of AI, preparing students to use AI technologies both responsibly and actively. The study is part of a close-to-practice research project, with the overarching goal of exploring and supporting the development of students' (aged 9–13) AI literacy.

The rationale behind human-centered design processes is often to produce new knowledge, design new services or products, or both [28]. We used co-design with educators and children to achieve two main goals: 1) generating new knowledge on children's AI literacy and 2) iteratively co-designing three lesson plans to bring light on AI from different perspectives adapted to grades 3–6. This paper focuses on the latter objective, addressing the following research questions:

- **RQ1:** How can AI literacy lesson plans be iteratively co-designed with students, teachers, and teacher trainers?
- **RQ2:** How can different stakeholders contribute to human-centered AI pedagogy and curriculum development?

To address these questions, we describe the co-design methods used and their practical application through various activities and degrees of stakeholder participation. Finally, we share initial reflections on benefits and challenges of using human-centered co-design processes when developing AI literacy curricula resources.

2 Background

2.1 AI Literacy in K-12 Education

AI literacy encompasses the knowledge, skills and attitudes necessary for individuals to navigate, make responsible decisions, and actively participate in a society increasingly shaped by AI technologies [19]. This literacy primarily pertains to the competencies of everyday users interacting with AI systems rather than AI professionals developing the technologies [17]. Determining what non-experts should know about AI is complex and varies depending on the educational context and level [10]. For students to use AI responsibly, ethically and actively, they need access to AI technologies, a basic understanding of how they work, and the ability to critically evaluate these systems [21].

Several studies have influenced the discourse on AI literacy in K-12 education. Although not specifically designed for the K-12 context, the framework by Long and Magerko [19] has been notably impactful. In addition to describing AI literacy as "a set of competencies that enables individuals to critically evaluate AI technologies; communicate and collaborate effectively with AI; and use AI as a tool online, at home, and in the workplace" (p. 2), they frame AI literacy around five questions: What is AI?; What can AI do?; How does AI work?; How should AI be used?; and How do people perceive AI?

Another well-cited contribution is the exploratory literature review by Ng et al. [26], which conceptualizes AI literacy based on four main components:

knowing and understanding, using, evaluating, and addressing ethical issues. More recently, Chiu et al. [7] developed an AI literacy framework in collaboration with experienced AI educators, highlighting five key elements: technology, impact, ethics, collaboration, and self-reflection.

Attempts have been made to define and operationalize AI literacy for K-12 contexts [45]. A large-scale initiative is AI for K-12 [41], which organizes AI competences around five big ideas: perception, representation and reasoning, learning, natural interaction and societal impact. Another categorization is provided by Kim et al. [13], who suggest framing AI education around three main competencies: fundamental ideas (AI Knowledge), programming and using AI tools (AI Skills), and aspects related to social impact and collaboration (AI Attitudes). Lin et al. [18] note that many AI curricula introduce the topic as an extension of computer science, making it challenging to integrate into other disciplines.

2.2 Co-design for HCAI

Co-design can be seen as an important part of a human-centered approach to AI in education. While HCAI still lacks a universal definition [35], it is suggested to differ from traditional AI by, for instance, integrating user experience design methods, such as user observation, stakeholder engagement, iterative design, and continuous evaluation in design processes.

Given that teachers have significant influence over the content and activities that reach students [16], it is crucial to involve them in the design of new materials and activities. This is especially important in countries where teachers have autonomy, as top-down reforms may not align with the local educational culture [14]. Viewing teachers merely as implementers of others' innovative ideas is problematic: when teachers are not sufficiently involved, there is a risk that reforms will be superficially adopted, leading to failed implementation and no real change in practice [8].

Involving students in the process is equally important [11]. Previous research suggests that children form their own perceptions of abstract digital technology and how it works (e.g., [3,24,30]). Therefore, when developing educational resources, it is important to consider children's prior knowledge and ideas to build on what they already know and address potential misconceptions. Moreover, the Finnish national curriculum [9] emphasizes that schoolwork should be based on student participation, ensuring that students' voices are heard (p. 36), for instance in planning activities.

In a multi-stakeholder study, Mannila et al. [21], present a co-created view on AI literacy, based on responses from a diverse and international expert panel. The authors found that the experts highlighted a wide range of knowledge, skills and attitudes regarding understanding and critically evaluating the role of AI, recognizing and using AI, and describing and developing AI solutions. The results underscore the need for including multiple perspectives when discussing and developing curricula for new areas, as no single expert group could have presented as broad a picture as the diverse panel as a whole.

3 Methodology

The process of co-designing teaching resources, activities and pedagogy for supporting AI literacy in grades 3–6 occurred over four phases during the 2023/2024 school year, involving 77 stakeholders (38 students, 31 class teacher students, three teachers, one IT educator, and four teacher trainers). The teachers were class teachers, meaning that they have the same student group in all subjects. The IT educator was responsible for the infrastructure and in-service teacher training in one of the schools, and the teacher trainers represented the teacher education programs at two universities.

The stakeholders participated in selected co-design activities online, during face-to-face workshops, or in classrooms in two geographically distant primary schools in Finland. As researchers we represent an interdisciplinary team spanning computer science, cognitive science, education and sociology.

Our methodological framework is design-based research, where participants (students, teachers, educators and researchers) are seen as design partners, following the principles of participatory design [4,38,42] and design research in education [1,23]. Additionally, we employed human-centered design (HCD) methods, often used when designing HCAI tools [37], to engage with and understand stakeholders' needs and values [35].

Our co-design approach also builds on the basics of self-determination theory (SDT), which assumes that individuals have three basic psychological needs that influence their motivation [34]: competence, autonomy, and relatedness. Competence refers to having the knowledge and skills necessary to successfully perform a task, autonomy to the feeling of control and freedom of choice, and relatedness to the sense of belonging to a community with a shared purpose. SDT has previously been used to understand how to prepare and motivate teachers to iteratively develop and implement new curricula [6,50].

A human-centered design process includes various degrees of stakeholder participation. Nyholm and colleagues [28] identify five levels of participation, inspired by typologies of children's participation: 1) information, where the (young) participants are listened to, 2) consultation, where the (young) participants are supported to express their opinions and viewpoints, which are treated seriously, 3) dialogue, where the (young) participants' opinions are considered, 4) influence, where (young) participants are involved in decision-making processes and lastly 5) shared decisions, where (young) participants fully share responsibility for decision-making.

In our study, stakeholder voices are included at levels 1–4. An initial literature review represents the lowest degree of stakeholder participation while the highest degree of decision-making, however without full control and responsibility for design choices, is manifested in co-designing content, form, and ambitions of lesson plan elements with teachers and educators.

Our study comprises four co-design stages: co-ideation, co-design, co-implementation and lastly co-evaluation (cf. [31]). Each phase has distinct goals and activities. The first two stages aim to design the right lesson plans by empathizing with stakeholders, ideating, and creating initial drafts of the plans.

These stages involved a scoping review, an informal focus group interview with teachers and educators, and a review discussion with teacher trainers. The interviews and discussions were recorded.

The last two stages focus on designing the lesson plans appropriately by testing them in classrooms with students, evaluating and re-designing them according to stakeholders' experiences and feedback. These stages involved classroom interventions (two for each lesson plan), where the lesson plans were evaluated, as well as recorded follow-up discussions with teachers, educators, class teacher students, and teacher trainers. All interventions were video recorded, resulting in 6×45 min of video material. The interviews and discussions were also recorded.

3.1 Ethical Considerations

Ethical research practices, as outlined in the guidelines on good scientific practices published by the Finnish National Board on Research Integrity, TENK [33], were applied in the research. Participation was voluntary, and consent was collected prior to the study from all participants and/or their caregivers. Data protection notices were similarly distributed and discussed before the study. All participants were informed of the possibility to withdraw from the study without providing any further explanation. According to TENK, this research design does not warrant an ethical review statement from a human sciences ethics committee [32].

4 Co-designing AI Literacy Resources

In this section, we present the four co-design stages in more detail based on the description and summary provided in Table 1.

4.1 Co-ideation

In the initial idea generation phase, we immersed ourselves in the concept of AI literacy and mapped the needs and wishes of class teachers and children in relation to AI literacy. An initial scoping review and a workshop with teachers provided a foundation for understanding stakeholders' needs and challenges.

The scoping review was based on literature published between years 2020–2023 in databases. We found that the concept of AI literacy varied from study to study [13]; that studies often based their learning goals on computer science concepts without necessarily considering which concepts are most suited to which age groups (e.g., [2,13]); that studies were sometimes conducted without a clear description of the material (e.g., [12,55]); and that teacher involvement in research was limited [29,54].

Next, building on the lessons learnt from the scoping review, we conducted a workshop with the teachers and the IT educator. The goal of this workshop was to explore experiences, needs, and wishes connected to teaching AI and strengthening children's AI literacy in the form of an informal focus group interview. The themes and questions guiding this discussion are presented in Table 2.

Table 1. Activities carried out in the four co-design stages: co-ideation, co-design, co-implementation and co-evaluation.

Process	Activities
Co-ideation: Engaging in open dialogue to find ideas for exploring and supporting K-12 students' AI literacy.	Reviewing existing literature, research and available teaching materials on AI for K-12 education. **Method:** Scoping review. **Degree of participation:** 2.
	Review of existing practices, teachers' needs for and preferences of AI teaching materials. Drafting of teaching material in a workshop with teachers and IT educator. Focus on learning together and co-ideating a valid path towards bolstering AI-literacy among children in grades 3–6. **Method:** Focus group interview. **Degree of participation:** 4.
Co-design: Describing and co-designing the teaching resources, activities and classroom implementation.	Review of the research team's drafts for teaching material in a workshop with teachers and IT educator. Focus on learning together and co-creating finalized lecture plans. **Method:** Focus group interview. **Degree of participation:** 4.
	Review and further co-design of the research team's lesson plan drafts in a workshop with teacher trainers. **Method:** Focus group interview. **Degree of participation:** 3.
Co-implementation: Implementing and observing lectures in authentic classroom settings.	School interventions. Three 45-min lessons taught in one 3rd grade classroom and one 6th grade classroom. **Method:** Video observation. **Degree of participation:** 4.
	Post-intervention interviews with teachers, three interviews per classroom. **Method:** Individual interview. **Degree of participation:** 4.
Co-evaluation: Summative co-interpretation of lectures, evaluating the feasibility in relation to the original aim.	Evaluation of the lesson plans and experiences from the classroom trials in a workshop with teachers and IT educator. Focus on designing together and co-creating finalized lectures to share with teachers nationally. **Method:** Focus group interview. **Degree of participation:** 4.
	Evaluation of the lesson plans and experiences from the classroom trials in a workshop with teacher trainers. **Method:** Focus group interview. **Degree of participation:** 3.
	Evaluation of the lesson plans in a workshop with class teacher students. **Method:** Focus group interview. **Degree of participation:** 1.

Table 2. Themes and questions covered during the first focus group interview.

General understanding	What do you think AI is? What do you think your colleagues know about AI?
Connections to broader educational goals	Do you see any connections between AI and the current goals in the curriculum with regard to digital competence, programming, or media literacy? Which ones? How could these be leveraged?
Current state of AI in the classroom	Do you talk about AI in your classes? If so, how and what terms are used? Do other teachers in your school talk about AI in their classes?
Need for AI literacy	Do you think children need to know about AI at this age? If so, what (knowledge, skills, attitudes)?
AI pedagogy	How could these topics be introduced to children in your classes? What kind of activities are suitable, how much variation is needed?
Integration	Could you integrate AI as content/subject matter into your teaching, and if so, how? How much time could you reasonably use?
Own questions	What questions do you have about AI? What questions do you think other teachers have?
Other people's questions	What questions or concerns, if any, do you hear about AI from a) children, b) other teachers, c) parents, d) social media?

Initial ideation of the lesson plans began during this workshop based on the teachers' comments and suggestions. To mitigate the risk of overwhelming teachers, we identified 1) the main aspects and content to be covered and 2) the resources required by teachers to do so. Based on the discussions we started planning three lessons, covering a minimum set of "must know" resources, accessible not only to the early adopters participating in our study but to a broader range of educators. These resources were later to be complemented with additional supplementary material.

4.2 Co-design

Building on the rough sketches and ideas for teaching AI co-designed in the first workshop, the research team drafted three lesson plans also taking into account previous work on AI literacy (e.g., [19]) and the three perspectives highlighted by UNESCO [44]: learning *with* AI, learning *about* AI and learning to *work and live with* AI. A summary of the three lesson plans is presented in Table 3.

Table 3. Rough draft of the three lesson plans.

Lesson 1: What is AI? Where can AI be found? What can AI do? How is AI perceived?	Exploring children's preconceptions and potential misunderstandings of AI. Discussing different types of AI technologies and where they can be found. Creative task of drawing an AI-enhanced everyday thing, followed up by generative AI doing the same.
Lesson 2: How does AI work?	Training a machine learning model based on own images. Discussions on data and bias.
Lesson 3: What should AI do?	Discussion heavy lesson exploring different ethical considerations based on, e.g., generative AI tools, deep fakes and challenges occurring when training the model in Lesson 2.

The first lesson plan introduces children to AI, covering questions such as "what is AI?", "where can AI be found", "what can AI do" and "how do you perceive AI"? The aim of this introductory lesson is twofold. First, we want to gain insight into students' previous conceptions and potential misconceptions of AI: what it is, where it can be found and what it can be used for. This is important as children's previous knowledge and skills in relation to AI may vary. This focus also gives us the possibility to build on children's examples and address potential misunderstandings. After initial discussions, we provide insights into what AI is by providing up-to-date and age-appropriate examples. The children are also asked to draw their own version of an AI-enhanced everyday thing (such as shoes or backpacks). Next the children's drawings are described in a prompt to an image generating AI solution, providing comparable AI versions for the children's ideas.

The second lesson covers *how AI works* and lets the children apply the knowledge from the first one in practice. We use the GDPR-compliant Teachable machine developed in the GenAI research project[1] in Finland, which makes it possible to train a machine learning model using own image data. The quality of the result depends on the amount and quality of the training data, opening up for discussions on for instance bias and prejudice in AI systems.

The third and concluding lesson builds on the previous ones, by focusing on ethics and risks with AI, that is what AI should – and should not – do. The discussions were planned around topics such as non-alignment with human values, bias and discrimination, also reflecting back to the activities in the first two lessons on generated images and the trained AI model. This lesson is mainly

[1] https://www.generation-ai-stn.fi.

discussion based, building on concrete examples such as deep fakes and other AI generated material.

The lesson drafts were collectively reviewed, evaluated, and redesigned in two workshops. The first one was arranged with the teachers and the IT educator. We provided suggestions and alternative examples for them to comment on, and their input was essential for selecting suitable examples and a realistic amount of material. The suggestions and ideas were noted and included in the material discussed during the second workshop, which took place with the teacher trainers. This workshop provided additional feedback on the suitability of the lesson plans, which was taken into account in the next phase.

4.3 Co-implementation

Co-implementation took place in two of the participating teachers' classrooms, as two research team members taught according to the co-designed lesson plans. All in all the researchers taught six 45-minute lessons, three per class. One class consisted of 22 third graders (aged 9–10), and the other one 16 sixth graders (aged 12–13). The teachers were passively present, yet offering support and participating in reflective discussions when needed. The aim was to test and evaluate the lesson plans, their structure and timing as well as the suitability of the activities with the children. The interventions were video recorded for qualitative analysis, but the recording data were not used for co-design purposes.

Design improvements were continuously made throughout this phase. For example, children in one class provided feedback on a drawing task, suggesting adding space on the design sheet for them to explain their idea and drawing in words. This child-led suggestion for improvement, along with the team's recognition of the need to discuss the idea behind the drawings, led to an instant redesign of the task, which was then tested with the second group. Similar improvements were made regarding the content of the lessons (e.g., the type of AI examples to include) and the software to use for in-class reflections on AI and the ways of accessing these tools (QR-codes instead of 8-digit codes).

At the end of each lesson, the researchers conducted brief individual interviews with the teachers to get just-in-time feedback on the lesson plans, the activities, student engagement and potential suggestions for improvement. When possible, the feedback was directly implemented in the lesson plans.

4.4 Co-evaluation

In this final stage, we summarized our subjective team reflections on how well the lesson plans succeeded in meeting our original aim, that is, to create educational experiences that are suitable from a teacher and student perspective, fit the current curriculum and focus on the ethical, social, and human dimensions of AI. The experiences were reviewed separately in a follow-up discussion with the teachers and the IT educator, as well as a similar discussion with the teacher trainers and class teacher students. While taking note of the positive feedback, we particularly focused on challenges and suggestions for improvements, such as ways for the lessons to be even more interactive and the most critical aspects to focus on given the limited amount of time and lessons available. We then re-designed and implemented these changes in the material before making them publicly available.

5 Discussion

When grounding research in a design-based methodology [1,4,23,38,42], stakeholders' collaboration is put in focus and gives them the opportunity to co-develop curricular content and methods with each other and us as researchers. A natural and concrete outcome of this design-based process was the iteratively refined and further developed curriculum and pedagogical approaches.

Human-centered design processes are associated with both benefits and drawbacks [47,49] for the research team and for the stakeholders devoting time and resources to participating in the process. While the level of participation for the different stakeholder groups varied throughout the process, it is clear that all groups were needed as they highlighted aspects and suggestions from their respective perspective. While previous co-design studies have focused mainly on teacher involvement [18,40,51,53], we found the collective experience and viewpoints of children, teachers and educators to be crucial; they hold valuable information defining and framing the teaching context that we as researchers and designers do not and cannot have knowledge of. They are the experts on teaching, on the needs of both teachers and children, on current curricula, procured technological solutions and personal data management policies of schools, affecting deployment of digital solutions in the lesson plans. It was evident in every co-design stage that for lesson plans on AI to be truly human-centered and aligned with the national core curriculum, it is imperative that at least these three stakeholder groups are engaged with various degrees of participation.

Leaving the desk and getting out in the field was a great opportunity for the researchers to learn about classroom environmental settings (infrastructure, routines, level of noise), children's immediate responses to and experiences of the educational content, and to stress test the lesson plans, for instance regarding time allocated to different activities. Many of the children's design suggestions were iteratively implemented. We find that the classroom interventions with young stakeholders, together with the co-design activities with teachers, IT educator and teacher trainers, enhance the human-centeredness of the lesson plans as the needs and experiences of the participants are reflected in the design. As such, we believe that the final versions of the lesson plans will serve as a basic material for introducing AI in a human-centered way for children in grades 3–6.

Another benefit of the HCD process was mutual learning. As an interdisciplinary team of researchers we learned throughout the process, in particular in the classrooms. The participating stakeholders reported the same. Apart from enhanced AI literacy, the children and teachers explored opportunities to learn collegially about a novel concept with and by each other, building on prior knowledge, experiences, and reflections that each child and teacher to various degrees have about AI. Thus, the process can be seen as adhering to SDT [34] in particular from a teacher perspective, as it built *competence*, gave teachers *autonomy* through continuous opportunities to affect the design and bring forward their own thoughts, and finally supported *relatedness* by bringing together teachers from different schools, and us researchers, sharing the same goal.

One identified drawback of co-design is the reality that every stakeholder is unique with individual resources, attitudes, and skill sets. Making a few teachers proxy voices for a whole group of professionals is inevitably not representative. This applies to the children in the classrooms as well, as only two student groups participated in the co-design process. Clearly, these classes do not represent all 3rd or 6th graders. Strengthening research reliability by engaging more participants in human-centered design processes would require more time and financial resources. It is also challenging for teachers and students to participate in longitudinal design processes as school days are full even without research projects.

Furthermore, our experience raised the question whether the teachers should have been trained to run the interventions in their classrooms, rather than having external researchers do the teaching. Students may perceive unfamiliar persons teaching a new subject as intimidating, perhaps hampering some activities such as joint discussions or think aloud-methods in class. However, the opposite is also likely, as the novel theme and break from the daily schedule might create added interest that is not entirely attributable to the AI lesson plans, resulting in validity challenges. On the other hand, the teachers could bypass many of the hurdles researchers new to the class must face, for example technical challenges and implicit knowledge regarding the children and class routines, prior skills of the children and their ability to access digital platforms. There may be disadvantages to this approach off-setting potential benefits, but it is still something worth considering in the future, as it could help scale the co-design process to include additional teachers, children and grade levels.

Lastly, observing children with video cameras present in the room may influence the co-designing process. Being observed, knowing that the data will be stored, analyzed, and potentially shared with others, can affect the children's experiences. Ethical research practices were, however, applied throughout the HCD process. Adults and caregivers provided written informed consent for participation, and the children were asked for their consent prior to each lesson. Thus, participation was voluntary, and all participants were informed of the possibility to withdraw from the study at any time, without the need for further explanation.

6 Conclusions and Future Work

We argue that AI literacy in K-12 education plays an antecedent role in meeting the goals of HCAI. Educating young people about AI helps them better understand, use, and critique AI systems, which in the long run can lead to more effective and responsible development and deployment of human-centered, ethical, and trustworthy AI solutions. Furthermore, AI-literate individuals are more likely to recognize ethical issues and biases in AI systems, aligning with the goals of HCAI and potentially leading to increased accountability and improved practices in AI development. Thus, AI literacy and HCAI are interrelated, with the former supporting the ambitions of the latter. The challenge lies in teaching these skills in an age-appropriate, motivating, and concrete way.

In this paper, we have illustrated a process of co-designing age-appropriate lesson plans for AI literacy in grades 3–6 with different stakeholder groups. Our experiences suggest that co-designing lesson plans from a human-centered design perspective, together with children, teachers, educators, and teacher trainers, is a successful approach, despite costs in terms of time, resources, and different starting points of participants. Stakeholder participation offers mutual learning opportunities and enhances human centeredness by acknowledging and addressing the diverse needs and values of different stakeholders in the design and deployment process. The HCD process and results highlighted are not relevant only in a Finnish context but also carry a wider international interest, as the results are language-agnostic. We expect that the co-designed lesson plans and suggestions for progression will be applicable in both Nordic and international contexts.

It is essential to involve those directly impacted by AI in the development process. We will continue to collaborate closely with practitioners, following a design-based research approach that emphasizes the co-creation of lesson plans for AI literacy, as outlined in this paper. In the coming years, we aim to deepen the understanding of and develop the conditions for implementing AI literacy in grades 3–9 from a student, teacher, teacher educator and curriculum perspective, while also involving additional schools and voices in the co-design process. By considering these four perspectives, we hope to contribute to an overall picture of how AI literacy can be integrated in grades 3–9 through co-design, thereby supporting the goals of HCAI to empower humans in a technologically advanced and ethically conscious society.

Acknowledgments. The study is part of the research project "AILIT - AI Literacy for K-12 education" funded by the Swedish Cultural Foundation in Finland. The authors thank all individuals, young and old, who contributed to our work.

References

1. den Akker, J.V., Gravemeijer, K., McKenney, S., Nieveen, N. (eds.): Educational Design Research. Routledge (2006). https://doi.org/10.4324/9780203088364
2. Akram, B., Yoder, S., Tatar, C., Boorugu, S., Aderemi, I., Jiang, S.: Towards an AI-infused interdisciplinary curriculum for middle-grade classrooms. In: Proceedings of the AAAI Conference on Artificial Intelligence 36(11), pp. 12681–12688 (2022). https://doi.org/10.1609/aaai.v36i11.21544
3. Brante, E.W., Walldén, R.: "internet? that's an app you can download": first-graders use linguistic resources to describe internet and digital information. Education Inquiry (2021). https://doi.org/10.1080/20004508.2021.1950273

4. Brown, N.: Scope and continuum of participatory research. Int. J. Res. Method Educ. **45**(2), 200–211 (2022). https://doi.org/10.1080/1743727X.2021.1902980
5. Charisi, V., et al.: Artificial Intelligence and the Rights of the Child: Towards an Integrated Agenda for Research and Policy. No. JRC127564 in EUR 31048 EN, Publications Office of the European Union, Luxembourg (2022). https://doi.org/10.2760/012329
6. Chiu, T., Chai, C.S.: Sustainable curriculum planning for artificial intelligence education: a self-determination theory perspective. Sustainability **12**(14), 5568 (2020). https://doi.org/10.3390/su12145568
7. Chiu, T.K., Ahmad, Z., Ismailov, M., Sanusi, I.T.: What are artificial intelligence literacy and competency? a comprehensive framework to support them. Comput. Educ. Open **6**, 100171 (2024). https://doi.org/10.1016/j.caeo.2024.100171, https://www.sciencedirect.com/science/article/pii/S2666557324000120
8. Couso, D.: Participatory approaches to curriculum design from a design research perspective. In: Psillos, D., Kariotoglou, P. (eds.) Iterative Design of Teaching-Learning Sequences. Springer, Dordrecht (2016). https://doi.org/10.1007/978-94-007-7808-5_4
9. FNAE: Grunderna för läroplanen för den grundläggande utbildningen. föreskrifter och anvisningar. Tech. Rep. 2014:96, Finnish National Agency for Education (2014). https://www.oph.fi/sites/default/files/documents/grunderna_for_laroplanen_for_den_grundlaggande_utbildningen_2014.pdf
10. Holmes, W., Porayska-Pomsta, K., Holstein, K., Sutherland, E., Baker, T., et al.: Ethics of AI in education: towards a community-wide framework. Int. J. Artif. Intell. Educ. **32**(3), 504–526 (2022). https://doi.org/10.1007/s40593-021-00239-1
11. Iversen, O.S., Smith, R.C., Dindler, C.: Child as protagonist: expanding the role of children in participatory design. In: Proceedings of the 2017 Conference on Interaction Design and Children (2017). https://dl.acm.org/citation.cfm?doid=3078072.3079725
12. Katuka, G.A., Auguste, Y., Song, Y., Tian, X., Kumar, A., Celepkolu, M., McKlin, T.: A summer camp experience to engage middle school learners in AI through conversational app development. In: Proceedings of the 54th ACM Technical Symposium on Computer Science Education V. 1, pp. 813–819, March 2023. https://doi.org/10.1145/3545945.3569864
13. Kim, S., Jang, Y., Kim, W., Choi, S., Jung, H., Kim, S., Kim, H.: Why and what to teach: Ai curriculum for elementary school. In: Proceedings of the AAAI Conference on Artificial Intelligence, vol. 35, pp. 15569–15576 (2021). https://doi.org/10.1609/aaai.v35i17.17833
14. Korhonen, T., J.L., Salo, L.: Towards an innovative school 2.0. In: Korhonen, T., K.K., Salo, L. (eds.) Invention Pedagogy: The Finnish Approach to Maker Education, pp. 219–235. Routledge Research in STEM Education, Routledge, London, 1st edn. (2022). https://doi.org/10.4324/9781003287360-19
15. Kukkonen, K.: Strategically Managing the Value Creation and Productivity Paradox of Artificial Intelligence: The General Purpose Technology View. Ph.D. thesis, University of Turku (2023). https://www.utupub.fi/handle/10024/175573
16. Larke, L.R.: Agentic neglect: Teachers as gatekeepers of england's national computing curriculum. Br. J. Edu. Technol. **50**(3), 1137–1150 (2019). https://doi.org/10.1111/bjet.12744
17. Laupichler, M., Aster, A., Schirch, J., Raupach, T.: Artificial intelligence literacy in higher and adult education: A scoping literature review. Computers & Education: AI 3 (2022). https://doi.org/10.1016/j.caeai.2022.100101

18. Lin, P., Van Brummelen, J.: Engaging teachers to co-design integrated AI curriculum for K-12 classrooms. In: Proceedings of the 2021 CHI Conference on Human Factors in Computing Systems. CHI '21. ACM, NY (2021). https://doi.org/10.1145/3411764.3445377, https://doi.org/10.1145/3411764.3445377
19. Long, D., Magerko, B.: What is AI literacy? competencies and design considerations. In: Proceedings of the 2020 CHI conference on human factors in computing systems. pp. 1–16 (2020)
20. Luckin, R., Cukurova, M., Kent, C., du Boulay, B.: Empowering educators to be AI-ready. Comput. Educ. Artif. Intell. **3**, 100076 (2022). https://doi.org/10.1016/j.caeai.2022.100076
21. Mannila, L., Hallström, J., et al.: Framing AI literacy for K-12 education: insights from multi-perspective and international stakeholder. In: Australasian Computing Education Conference (ACE 2025). ACM (2025)
22. Mannila, L., Heintz, F.: Introducing programming and computational thinking in grades 1–9: Sweden in an international context. In: Hallström, J., de Vries, M.J. (eds.) Programming and Computational Thinking in Technology Education: Swedish Perspectives. Brill (2023). https://doi.org/10.1163/9789004687912_004
23. McKenney, S., Reeves, T.C.: Conducting Educational Design Research. Routledge, 2nd edn. (2019)
24. Mertala, P., Fagerlund, J., Calderon, O.: Finnish 5th and 6th grade students' pre-instructional conceptions of artificial intelligence (ai) and their implications for ai literacy education. Comput. Educ. Artif. Intell. 3, Article 100095 (2022). https://doi.org/10.1016/j.caeai.2022.100095
25. Mollick, E.: Co-intelligence. Living and working with AI. Portfolio/Penguin, USA (2024)
26. Ng, D., Leung, J., Chu, S., Qiao, M.S.: Conceptualizing AI literacy: an exploratory review. Comput. Educ. Artif. Intell. **2**, 100041 (2021). https://doi.org/10.1016/j.caeai.2021.100041, https://www.sciencedirect.com/science/article/pii/S2666920X21000357
27. Ng, D, T.K., Lee, M., Tan, R, J.Y., et al.: A review of AI teaching and learning from 2000 to 2020. Educ. Inf. Technol. **28**, 8445–8501 (2023). https://doi.org/10.1007/s10639-022-11491-w, https://doi.org/10.1007/s10639-022-11491-w
28. Nyholm, L., et al.: Delaktighet genom samskapande metoder för utveckling av innovationer inom social- och hälsovård. Hoitotiede 34(4) (2022)
29. Ottenbreit-Leftwich, A., et al.: Lessons learned for AI education with elementary students and teachers. Int. J. of Artificial Intelligence in Education (2022). https://doi.org/10.1007/s40593-022-00304-3
30. Ottenbreit-Leftwich, A., et al.: How do elementary students conceptualize artificial intelligence? In: Proc. of the 52nd ACM Technical Symposium on CS Education, p. 1261 (2021). https://doi.org/10.1145/3408877.3439642
31. Pearce, T., Maple, M., Shakeshaft, A., Wayland, S., McKay, K.: What is the co-creation of new knowledge? a content analysis and proposed definition. Int. J. Environ. Res. Public Health **17**(7), 2229 (2020). https://doi.org/10.3390/ijerph17072229
32. Finnish National Board on Research Integrity (TENK), F.N.B.: The ethical principles of research with human participants and ethical review in the human sciences in Finland. finnish national board on research integrity tenk guidelines 2019. Tech. Rep. 2019:3, TENK (2019), https://tenk.fi/sites/default/files/2023-05/RI_Guidelines_2023.pdf

33. Finnish National Board on Research Integrity (TENK), F.N.B.: The finnish code of conduct for research integrity and procedures for handling alleged violations of research integrity in Finland. Tech. Rep. 2023:3, TENK (2023). https://tenk.fi/sites/default/files/2023-05/RI_Guidelines_2023.pdf
34. Ryan, R.M., Deci, E.L.: Intrinsic and extrinsic motivation from a self-determination theory perspective: Definitions, theory, practices, and future directions. Contemporary Educational Psychology 61, 101860 (2020). https://doi.org/10.1016/j.cedpsych.2020.101860
35. Schmager, S., Pappas, I., Vassilakopoulou, P.: Defining Human-Centered AI: A Comprehensive Review of HCAI Literature. In: Proc. of the 15th Mediterranean Conference on Information Systems and the 6th Middle East & North Africa Conf. on Digital Information Systems. Madrid, Spain (2023)
36. Sentance, S., Csizmadia, A.: Computing in the curriculum: Challenges and strategies from a teacher's perspective. Educ. Inf. Technol. **22**, 469–495 (2017). 10.1007/s10639-016-9482-0
37. Shneiderman, B.: Human-Centered AI. Oxford University Press, UK (2022)
38. Spinuzzi, C.: The methodology of participatory design. Tech. Commun. **52**(2), 163–174 (2005)
39. Steen, M.: Co-design as a process of joint inquiry and imagination. Des. Issues **29**(2), 16–28 (2013). https://doi.org/10.1162/DESI_a_002071306
40. Tedre, M., Kahila, J., Vartiainen, H.: Exploration on how co-designing with AI facilitates critical evaluation of ethics of AI in craft education. In: Langran, E., Christensen, P., Sanson, J. (eds.) Proc. of Society for Information Technology & Teacher Education International Conference, pp. 2289–2296. Association for the Advancement of Computing in Education (AACE), New Orleans, LA, United States (2023)
41. Touretzky, D., Gardner-McCune, C., Seehorn, D.: Machine learning and the five big ideas in AI. Int. J. Artif. Intell. Educ. **33**, 233–266 (2023). https://doi.org/10.1007/s40593-022-00314-1
42. Tuhkala, A.: Participatory Design: an Approach for Involving Teachers as Design Partners. Ph.D. thesis, JYU Dissertations (2019). http://urn.fi/URN:ISBN:978-951-39-7782-5
43. UNESCO: Beijing consensus on artificial intelligence and education. In: International Conference on Artificial Intelligence and Education, Planning Education in the AI Era: Lead the Leap. p. 70. Beijing (2019), https://unesdoc.unesco.org/ark:/48223/pf0000368303, also available. In: Português
44. UNESCO: AI and education: guidance for policy-makers. UNESCO (2021). https://unesdoc.unesco.org/ark:/48223/pf0000376709
45. UNESCO: K-12 AI curricula: a mapping of government-endorsed AI curricula. UNESCO (2022). https://unesdoc.unesco.org/ark:/48223/pf0000380602
46. UNICEF: Policy guidance on ai for children, November 2021. https://www.unicef.org/innocenti/media/1341/file/UNICEF-Global-Insight-policy-guidance-AI-children-2.0-2021.pdf. Accessed 08 July 2024
47. Viklund, E., Nilsson, I., Hägglund, S., Nyholm, L., Forsman, A.K.: The perks and struggles of participatory approaches: exploring older persons' experiences of participating in designing and developing an application. Gerontechnology **22**(1), 1–12 (2023). https://doi.org/10.4017/gt.2023.22.1.816.03
48. Vuorikari, R., Kluzer, S., Punie, Y.: DigComp 2.2: The Digital Competence Framework for Citizens - With new examples of knowledge, skills and attitudes. No. JRC128415 in EUR 31006 EN, Publications Office of the European Union, Luxembourg (2022). https://doi.org/10.2760/490274

49. Williams, O., Sarre, S., Papoulias, S.C., Knowles, S., Robert, G., Beresford, P., Rose, D., Carr, S., Kaur, M., Palmer, V.J.: Lost in the shadows: reflections on the dark side of co-production. Health Res. Policy Syst. **18**, 43 (2020). https://doi.org/10.1186/s12961-020-00558-0
50. Xia, Q., Chiu, T.K.F., Lee, M., Sanusi, I.T., Dai, Y., Chai, C.S.: A self-determination theory (sdt) design approach for inclusive and diverse artificial intelligence (ai) education. Comput. Educ. **189**, 104582 (2022). https://doi.org/10.1016/j.compedu.2022.104582
51. Xie, B., et al.: Co-designing AI education curriculum with cross-disciplinary high school teachers. In: Proceedings of the AAAI Conference on Artificial Intelligence, vol. 38, pp. 23146–23154 (2024). https://doi.org/10.1609/aaai.v38i21.30360
52. Yang, S.J., Ogata, H., Matsui, T., Chen, N.S.: Human-centered artificial intelligence in education: Seeing the invisible through the visible. Comput. Educ. AI **2**, 100008 (2021). https://doi.org/10.1016/j.caeai.2021.100008, https://www.sciencedirect.com/science/article/pii/S2666920X21000023
53. Yau, K.W., et al.: Co-designing artificial intelligence curriculum for secondary schools: A grounded theory of teachers' experience. In: Int. Symposium on Educational Technology (ISET), pp. 58–62 (2022). https://doi.org/10.1109/ISET55194.2022.00020
54. Yau, K.W., Chai, C.S., Chiu, T., Meng, H., King, I., Yam, Y.: A phenomenographic approach on teacher conceptions of teaching artificial intelligence (ai) in K-12 schools. Educ. Inf. Technol. **28**(1), 1041–1064 (2023). https://doi.org/10.1007/s10639-022-11019-6
55. Zammit, M., Voulgari, I., Liapis, A., Yannakakis, G.N.: Learn to machine learn via games in the classroom. Front. Educ. **7**, 913530 (2022). https://doi.org/10.3389/feduc.2022.913530

Taxonomies – Reuniting Art and Science via a Fascination with Nature

Emanuela Marchetti[1](✉), Andrea Valente[2], and Shanice Otersen[3]

[1] Department of Mathematics and Computer Science, University of Southern Denmark, Campusvej 55, 5230 Odense, Denmark
emanuela@imada.sdu.dk

[2] Department of Design, Media and Educational Sciences, University of Southern Denmark, Universitetsparken 1, 6000 Kolding, Denmark
aval@sdu.dk

[3] Department of Innovation and Entrepreneurship , BioTechLab Spinderihallerne, Spinderigade 11, 7100 Vejle Kommune, Denmark
SHMOT@vejle.dk

Abstract. This paper presents *Taxonomies*, a STEAM project placed on the intersection between art, science, and technology. In Taxonomies art is taking the lead role, providing a goal for action, while natural sciences and computation provide knowledge and means for artistic creation. The project is a collaboration between the University of Southern Denmark, the BiotechLab at Spinderihallerne and Rosborg Gymnasium, a Danish secondary school oriented towards the humanities. During the past year a series of 3 workshops was designed, implemented, and run at Rosborg, respectively focusing on: fabricating organic colors from plants, botanical painting with organic colors, and procedurally generating plant forms. Through our process, we found new insights on how to integrate art and science within STEAM, with art playing a sense-making role. Three forms of engagement were observed during the workshops: personal, sensorial, and exploratory. The students expressed appreciation of the theoretical modules at the beginning of the workshops, and voiced curiosity for more in-depth knowledge about natural inks. A new iteration of the workshops is being run at Rosborg with the involvement of sciences teachers, which will provide richer insights on the relations between the different disciplines and students' engagement.

Keywords: STEAM · Engagement · Botanical Art · Computational Thinking

1 Introduction

Art and science are currently regarded as separate subjects and consequently taught disconnected from each other. This was not always the standard practice: during the Renaissance and until the 19th and before the 20th century, art and science were regarded as two sides of the same coin, each discipline providing knowledge and skills to humans, who were seeking to understand the world around them, to the point that artistic and scientific achievements merged into one another.

B. K. Smith and M. Borge (Eds.): HCII 2025, LNCS 15806, pp. 119–138, 2025.
https://doi.org/10.1007/978-3-031-93564-0_8

To illustrate this, we can think about the achievements of da Vinci and Alberti, the former producing stunning drawings of human anatomy, the latter theorizing on how to draw perspective, during the Italian Renaissance. German poet Goethe wrote "Theory of Colors" in 1810, an analysis of the nature and perception of colors, providing precise insights on how our eyes respond to white light and complementarity in colors and light, these insights are still relevant today and discussed in textbooks on perception and graphic design [6, 14]. Furthermore, naturalist Ernst Haeckel and author Beatrix Potter produced stunning illustrations while conducting botanical studies.

Art and science were both driven by a fascination with the beauty of nature constantly informing each other, opening a space for exploration and innovation in art and science alike [1]. However, through history, art and science took separate ways, art shifted from being an integral part of the scientific investigation, to focusing on other subjects than realism. Hence scientific illustration is nowadays a niche practiced by a small minority of individuals, such as botanical and archaeological illustrators [1].

As we live in a time with many complex challenges and need for innovation, we see great potential in reviving the deep connections that art and science shared in the past, as resources for fostering learning and a passion in natural sciences, leading the way towards exploring out-of-the-box innovative solutions.

In this paper, we discuss findings from a 3-part workshop series named "Taxonomies", aimed at bridging art, science, and technology, to create an interdisciplinary learning experience driven by engagement with art and nature. The workshop series was conducted in collaboration with a high school art class in Vejle (Denmark) and is the outcome of a close collaboration between researchers from the University of Southern Denmark (SDU), the BioTechLab at Spinderihallerne, and Rosborg Gymnasium. Spinderihallerne is an innovation center, aiming at connecting art, design, science, and technology, offering open hands-on workshops to citizens of all ages. Our aim was to investigate the role of art in fostering learning from a STEAM perspective and how an interdisciplinary workshop series like Taxonomies, partly conducted in an alternative learning environment, could resonate with high school students. Each workshop aimed at developing different skills, such as experimentation with plants to make inks from nature, scientific note taking, observation and depiction of nature, and introduction to coding for aesthetic programming by using L-Systems [9, 22]. Our workshop series is grounded on the STEAM framework [2, 11]; however, the typical role of art in STEAM learning is being reconfigured, shifting from a motivational to a sense-making resource, where making becomes an epistemological act of inquiry and understanding.

Our data suggests that the students deeply engaged with the provided materials and activities. Overall, the workshop series resonated well with the high school students, they were open-minded, experimental and playful. They used the provided artefacts to enhance their learning, as well as to create their own artefacts, in the form of botanical illustrations and manipulated code from L-systems. The successful creation of their own artefacts can be seen as a physical manifestation of their combined learning experiences.

2 Theory – Reuniting Art and Science

The focus of this study lies at the intersection between arts, natural sciences and computational thinking (CT), intended as basic forms of algorithmic thinking and engagement with simple forms of coding. Our purpose is to rethink the relationship between art and science, to repair their connection as it was in the old days, back to the Middle Ages and the Renaissance until the modern time. Before audio-video technologies were invented, drawing was an integral part of the scientific methodological palette, as it was employed to gather and document visual data from scientific inquiries [1, 21]. In this sense, it is our aim to empirically investigate how art can be inspired and materially supported by science, building on fascination with the beauty of nature as a shared ground. Moreover, it is in the interest of the Taxonomies project to investigate the learning potential of integrating art making in scientific inquiry, in a way that could support knowledge and skill acquisition in both areas.

In this respect, botanical art emerged as an ideal discipline, as it was literally part of botanic inquiry [23]. Famous naturalists from the past, engaged in making compelling and aesthetically beautiful botanical illustrations as a form of data gathering, observational analysis and documentation. They were focusing on specific structural details and morphological development through the life of a plant specimen. According to Rakow [23] the interest for investigating plants can be traced back to the Antiquity, with civilizations like Egypt, Persia, Greece, and Rome, who built the first botanical gardens. The culture of botanical gardens developed further in Europe through the Middle Ages and the Renaissance [18, 23] with a main agenda of cultivating medicinal plants and investigating their therapeutic properties. Moreover, in the 16th and 17th centuries, botanical gardens were perceived as "teaching laboratories" for university students dedicated to disciplines equivalent to the fields of medicine, pharmacy, and botany [23]. At the time, naturalists were either hiring artists to support them in their data collection and to create illustrations for their publications, or they were making their own illustrations, in this way art and science were organically integrated with each other. Excellent examples of this practice are represented by Leonardo Da Vinci in the Renaissance, who can be seen as the first scientific illustrator, in him the scientist and the artist became "interdependent" [31], more recently by naturalist Ernst Haeckel [10] or Beatrix Potter, who was engaged in investigating the life of fungi before she became a famous author. Haeckel conveyed his aesthetic interest in nature through the title of his most famous work "Art Forms in Nature" in 1904 [10]. Moreover, in line with Anderson-Tempini [1], drawing is ultimately a method to "interrogate" forms and structures of natural organisms. Hence botanical drawing can be defined as a practice for botanical inquiry, in which naturalists closely observe the morphology of different types of plants, recording lines and shapes, communicating similarities and anomalies across multiple specimens, and documenting their growth across one or more species [1, 19].

Starting from similar premises, this study aims at leveraging botanical art as a platform for supporting empirical investigations of nature and CT, promoting knowledge and skills acquisition in science and art alike. Therefore, we build on STEAM, which is typically approached as an interdisciplinary pedagogical framework, promoting engagement and motivation in learning sciences with primary and secondary school pupils [2].

STEAM is a redefinition of STEM, which stands as an acronym for Sciences, Technology, Engineering and Mathematics, enriched with the "A" of art [2, 16]. STEAM has been mainly promoted to elicit interest for science and mathematics in young pupils, introducing creativity seen as one of the soft skills needed in our information-based society, which also belongs to the interdisciplinary concept of CT [6]. Moreover, it has been claimed that the A for art in STEAM would have empowered the all-interdisciplinary framework providing "possibility of longer-term socio-technical futures instead of short-term financial predictions that currently lead to uncontrolled economies" [2]. Hence the role of art in STEAM has been depicted mainly as a motivational one, supporting young pupils to develop an interest in science and mathematics through play, creativity and self-expression, hopefully leading to the desire to learn more on scientific subjects [17]. Boy [2] moves further in proposing arts as a way to define a new learning paradigm, in which "understanding" would have taken the lead on "knowing". Boy argues that knowing is useful only when providing support to solving problems in real world situations and not on a general level. Boy reconducts STEAM theoretical foundations to Vygotsky [30] and Piaget [20] and notions of situated learning, seen as a "designed multi-agent activity", in which pupils would engage in creative endeavor, aimed at enabling the pupils in building an understanding of science through use of technologies.

Regarding CT, our main aim was to expose humanities and art students to coding, framed as an aesthetic activity, and demystifying coding as a valid tool in an art drawing context, for art-skilled students. We adopted L-Systems, a grammar-like system to generate plants, that is very powerful if rather formal; we made L-Systems more accessible to the students, thanks to the *tangible computing* approach we developed for these workshops.

Mejias et al. [16] argues that the STEAM framework is being increasingly used, but that the role of art in science is ambiguous, therefore, the authors propose an analysis of STEAM in relation to the different relations that can coexist between art and science. The main dimensions proposed by Mejias et al. [16] are *pedagogical*, in relation to how the integration of art and science is aimed at supporting learning and *instrumentalism* in relation to how art and science are integrated with one another to address real world problems. Mejias et al. [16] propose a spectrum in which art and science are combined in different ways across two axes, the *pedagogical* and *non-pedagogical*, and the *One-Sides Instrumental* and the *Mutually instrumental.* The first integration of art and science is called "One-sided Instrumental and Non-pedagogical" in which the arts use STEM as a medium for artistic expression, for instance when practicing art making inspired by STEM knowledge, hence, botanical art can easily belong to this area. The second one is called "Mutually Instrumental & Non-pedagogical", in which arts and STEM embrace interconnections and defy disciplinary separation. The third form of integration is called "One-sided Instrumental & Pedagogical", in which art incorporates STEM "concepts, principles and practices" with the goal of supporting learning in the arts or in science. The fourth and last integration deals with a "Mutually Instrumental & Pedagogical", in which art and science are integrated organically to support learning in both areas "within and beyond boundaries".

Moreover, Mejias et al. argue [16] that many STEAM practices are not necessarily pedagogical, in this sense botanical art serving naturalistic inquiry, would be seen as a STEAM practice. However, these non-pedagogical practices can provide interesting perspectives on the pedagogical potential of STEAM practices.

In conclusion, we find that STEAM studies often approach artmaking as a recreational relief, enabling school pupils to enjoy their science lectures [17], not exploiting at full the learning potential of artmaking. Therefore, our study aims at proposing art not as a motivational resource, but rather as an epistemological resource, in which art making is materially supported and inspired by scientific knowledge, while fostering also learning about art, specifically about how to paint realistic and detailed plants. An ideal scenario for our inquiry, would be that art and science blend into one another, so that the artists/naturalists are driven to create art and science at the same time led by a fascination with the beauty of nature.

3 Method

Methodologically we adopted a research-through-design approach [32], in which our design process and the related outcome is aimed at gaining new knowledge with respect to rethinking the role of art in STEAM learning. Our data gathering was supported by focused ethnography [27, p. 3], which can be defined as an adaptation of traditional ethnography to address "more focused problems, for a more limited time, limited community or subpopulation, more applied results, and the inclusion of insider researchers". In the anthropological tradition, ethnography is expected to require long time commitment from the investigators, who should deeply immerse themselves in the culture they are investigating. In our studies, the population is represented by an art class of 17–19 years old gymnasium students, which emerged as being all female, and we involved them in 3 workshops, which run for circa one hour and a half each at a different day. Moreover, we have teamed up across institutions, where the art teacher from the gymnasium acted as an "insider researcher" [27], he prepared the students prior to the workshops and organized the activities in the school, acting as an intermediary among the BiotechLab, SDU, and his school.

During the workshops, observations were conducted as the main method for data gathering, as well as notetaking and sketches, experimental notes from students during workshop one and finally situated interviews after each workshop. The observations were captured in the form of photos, sketches and videos of how the students interacted with each other, in line with the methods of visual ethnography [Pink] supported by drawing [3, 15], which along with the artworks produced by the students, were subject to an interpretive analysis [7].

4 The Taxonomies Workshop Format

The taxonomies workshop series was formulated over a year of collaboration (Fig. 1), with the initial goal to arrange an art exhibition. Building around the making of natural materials and the notion of engaging the students in artmaking, botanical art emerged as an ideal core practice, already embodying scientific goals and meaning.

During this year, we experimented on how to make vibrant colors from plants that could allow for a broad range of nuances, how to adapt them to standard watercolor

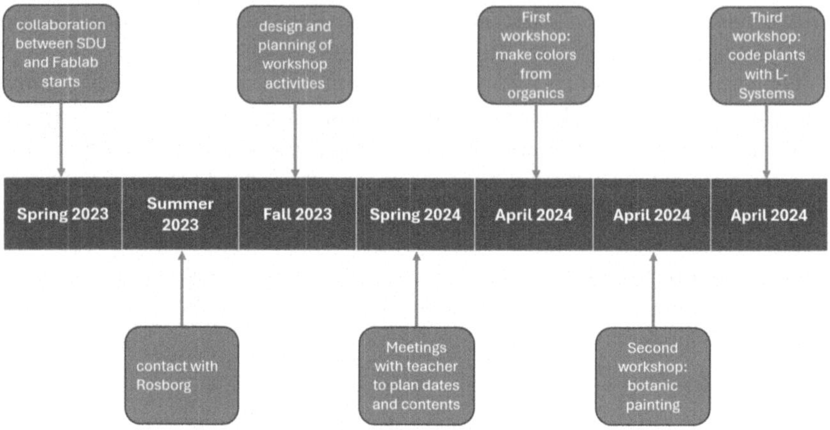

Fig. 1. Timeline of Taxonomies activities.

techniques applied to botanical art, which required fine details and precision. Finally we explored how to formulate a coding workshop for students with a solid art foundation, but no prior experience with coding. Hence, we produced a series of materials and exemplars to be used in the workshops such as:

- Colors - Different inks and recipes for preparation processes,
- Paintings - Exemplars of color mix and finished botanical paintings,
- Coding materials - Cards, drawing exercise, a digital simulator, and examples of procedurally generated plants.

The workshop series consisted of three parts (Fig. 1), which were designed to fit into an art module named "Humans in Nature", focused on the Anthropocene. It emerged as a collaborative project with the Danish high school Rosborg Gymnasium, the largest high school in Vejle. Each workshop set focus on different aspects of the overall series, collectively encouraging knowledge creation in art, science and technology alike. Acting as both the inspiration for and through which art was created, nature and natural elements embedded meaning into the creative process and provided a new basis to engage with botanical art.

As a final outcome, the students' artworks were exhibited publicly at Spinderihallerne Vejle, together with our exemplar materials, which emerged as a gratifying experience for the students, their teacher and their families. Moreover, the exhibition lasted for a month and showcased our initiative to a broad audience, as Spinderihallerne is open to the public and houses many different cultural events.

4.1 Workshop 1 – Natural Inks, Creating Colors from Plants and Foodwaste

As shown in Fig. 1, the first workshop was conducted at the "BioTechLab" in Spinderihallerne, while the consecutive workshops were taught in Rosborg's art classroom. The BioTechLab is an alternative learning space, where we initially aimed at conducting the whole workshop series, however, due to constraints on the teachers and students' side, we had to adapt our plan and hold the other workshops at the school.

The first workshop revolved around creating natural inks from plant matter and food waste (Fig. 2) and intended to bring students closer to the material (colors), they are working with in their regular art practice. Inspired by the notion of DIY-materials, a movement in which designers fabricate their own materials instead of industrially produced ones, [24], we challenged the students understanding of colors and how they can create with them. The DIY-approach encourages open experimentation and exploration, thereby promoting the creation of new aesthetic outputs.

Fig. 2. Students at the color making workshop.

At the beginning of the workshop, students received a brief introduction to the BioTechLab, exploring its possibilities and an overview of the entire workshop series. This was followed by a short lecture on creating plant-based colors. The lecture explained how different colors can be extracted from plant matter through various processes—some requiring heat, where ingredients are boiled for a specific time, while others needed cold extraction, by breaking down plant cells in a blender (Fig. 2). The lecture also highlighted the importance of pH-level in natural colors, explaining that adjusting them will change the color hue. Afterwards, the students were divided into groups of 3–4, with each group receiving a different manual for producing natural inks. Each manual contained two recipes: the first provided instructions to create the base color, while the second guided the students to use modifiers, such as baking soda and vinegar to produce various hues, by changing the colors pH-level. At this stage students were also encouraged to use plant matter they had brought in themselves, and to create and note down their own recipes. For this purpose, the groups were given a small research journal that also allowed them to document their observations, ingredient measurements, and reflections on the color-making process.

The manuals were laid out to ensure that the students would be provided with usable colors to paint with in the following workshop, while letting them engage freely with

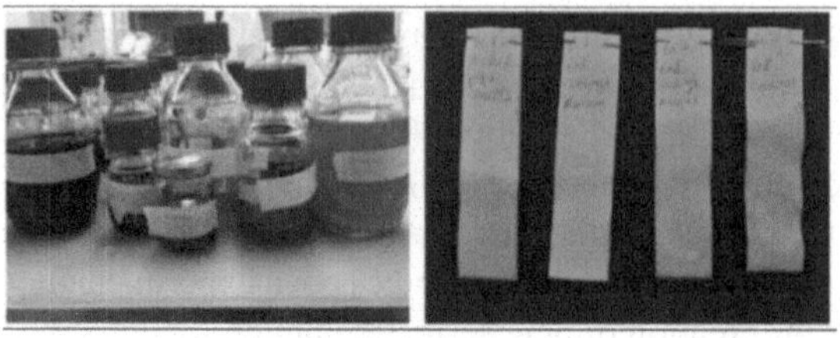

Fig. 3. Inks and strips of colors for Workshop 1.

trial-and-error processes. The base recipes were inspired by Logan [13] and included red cabbage, turmeric root, avocado stones and shells, grass, yellow onion peels, red onion peels, and rosehips. They were chosen according to two factors: seasonal availability and varied color output.

At the end of the workshop, students poured the inks they made into glass jars, which were labeled with their names and used recipes, linking each one to the groups research journal. Finally, the students dipped paper strips into their inks to create a shared color card for the next session. (Fig. 3) The color card would become an important tool for the students to plan their paintings in the consecutive workshop.

4.2 Workshop 2 – Botanical Art - How to Paint Plants with Plants

The second workshop focused on botanical illustration, as a scientific method for observation, analysis, and documentation of botanical research. In the start, the students were provided with an introduction on botanical illustration and its history. Instructions, on how to paint with plant-based colors, were provided through exemplars from images and small videos of the drawings made by the author acting as facilitator, shown at different stages (Fig. 4).

The students were instructed to adopt a wet-on-wet watercolor technique, in which a layer of water is applied to the paper with a wet, clean brush [19]. In this way, the water provides a substratum that can lead the color where desired and would prevent strong pigments, like the yellow gained from turmeric root, to stain the paper. In preparation, the students were asked to bring different plant species that they found inspiring and use them as subjects, observing them in depth, as according to Edwards' drawing method [8], and eventually dissect them to examine their inner structure; a common practice in botanical research and art [18, 19].

An important aspect to consider is that organic colors are less reliable than commercially available paints. For instance, these inks are more watering, which might result in excessive amounts of water, which would take long time to dray, ruining the paper and allowing for little nuance range.

A very fluid light ink cannot effectively be lightened with water, as it is done with regular watercolors. Moreover, in the drying process, these inks can shift their hues, so that more pre-knowledge on the specific ink and careful planning are required to gain the desired colors.

For instance, inks gained from red cabbage, blackberries, and blackcurrant appear purple when still wet, but shift towards slightly more blue-violet hues while drying, as

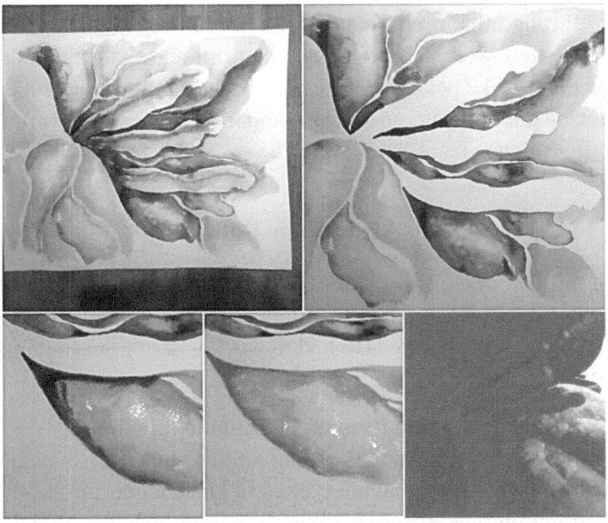

Fig. 4. Instructional example of a Bougainvillea painting, at different stages and reference image.

Fig. 5. Students at the workshop and workstation.

shown in Fig. 4 for red cabbage. This is probably caused by dehydration and oxidation of the pigment. Hence mixing these violet inks with a turmeric yellow, will give you a green hue instead of a warmer reddish one. Moreover, turmeric emerged as a difficult hue, despite giving a bright yellow, turmeric is not a good color to apply at first as it can leave greyish stains on the page, which cannot be removed. Therefore, the students were instructed in diluting the yellow ink with water, or to apply a more tamable ink like yellow peel onion, which gives a nice, non-staining peach hue and allows to alleviate the effect of the turmeric on the paper.

The students were challenged by these inks and were encouraged to experiment with different mixes on scrap of watercolor paper before painting. Unfortunately, they generally rushed through that preliminary phase, preferring to move to their botanicals (Fig. 5). In the end, they were able to create beautiful and delicate paintings, showing whole plants and details like petals or leaves. They also showed interest for the inks and their behavior during painting, an aspect we would like to investigate further in following iterations involving science teachers as well.

4.3 Use Code to Create Plants: Algorithmic Botany

The goals of the third workshop were: to expose humanities and art students to coding, framed as an aesthetic activity, and demystifying coding as a valid tool in an art drawing context, for art-skilled students. We also had to work within a set of constraints:

- The code should be very simple, we cannot adopt "no-code" solutions, since we want to introduce CT or at least some form of algorithmic thinking,
- The code should be easy to change for humanities students, to support a hands-on format and learning-by-doing that are typical in Danish education,
- Minimal programming language learning required, i.e. no complex syntax nor advanced data-structures,
- And the overall workshop should fit in a single slot of two times 45 min, a hard constrain from the school.

Given that the students and teachers in art classes tend to have no programming experience, they usually would not consider coding as a natural medium for botanical art. However, in our experience, digital art and game assets are created using algorithmic-based tools: in particular Lindenmayer Systems [22] are very common in 3D graphics software and generative art tools. Blender, Maya, 3ds Max and Houdini, all have variations of L-Systems for fractals, terrain or plants generation. Therefore, we decided to look closer at L-Systems and design our workshop around them. Introduced in 1968 by Aristid Lindenmayer (a botanist), they are string-rewriting systems, very similar to context-free grammars [4], and according to [22]:

> *"[...] were conceived as a mathematical theory of plant development. [...] The emphasis was on plant topology, that is, the neighborhood relations between cells or larger plant modules."*

L-Systems have become very famous in the 1990s and have been used to draw plants, algae and grass. Deterministic and probabilistic versions of L-Systems exist, but here we focus on the former for simplicity. A classic example of L-System is shown in Fig. 1: the symbols are F and X, the starting symbol.

These rewriting systems are very expressive, they can even generate iterated fractals (as in [25] chapter 8) and the resulting images are considered aesthetically pleasing. However, L-Systems do not satisfy all of our constraints: we found their formal nature problematic, since their syntax is based on context-free grammars, which belong to Computer Science, with formal methods and language theory. Moreover, the parallel rewriting process for L-Systems is a recursive algorithm, and both parallelism and recursion are advanced topics in programming. Two of the authors have been working with tangible models for computation [28, 29], so we decided to leverage on tangibles, and represented

Fig. 6. Derivation of a tree from L-Systems rules (on the right).

our L-Systems' elements (branches, leaves and possibly flowers) as cards: we call it *L-System concretization method*. Hence the rewriting and the rendering become simpler to explain and to simulate manually; the students only have to place cards on the table, match and change some of them, following the rules. We devised two versions of this method: in both we take the L-System and convert it into a deck of cards and a set of rules, but in the first version the rules are purely textual (see Fig. 7), while in the second version the rules are allowed to be more visual and based on placing and relative angles of the tangibles (as in Fig. 8). The advantage of the second version is that students can directly layout their plants, without reasoning in terms of LOGO commands, which are needed to draw plants with the first version.

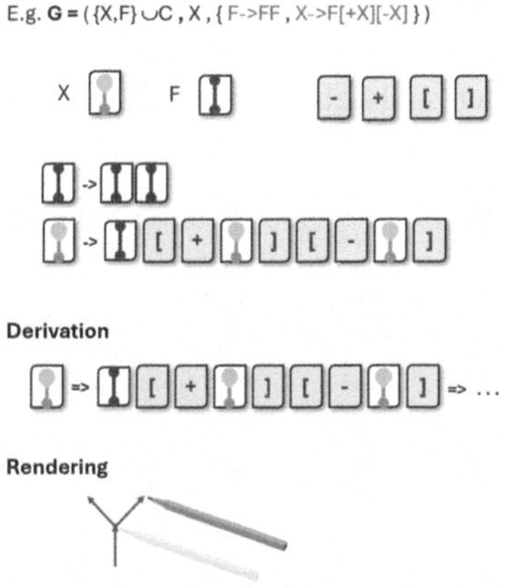

Fig. 7. Example of concretization, version one of our method.

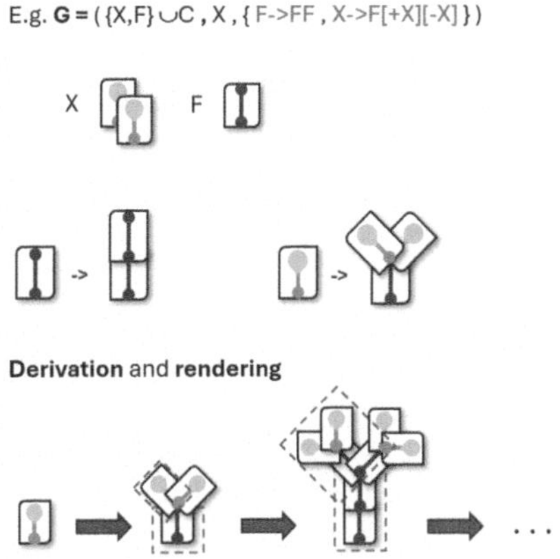

Fig. 8. Example of concretization, version one of our method.

We used both versions of the method for our workshop, starting from the second (see how the students use the visual rules in Fig. 9), and later the first, which required manual algorithm simulation (as visible in Fig. 10).

In addition, we implemented an L-System simulator in P5.js (freely available at https://editor.p5js.org/andrea270872/full/3Z0R3PxZW) and made it available to the students. In this software simulator a student can change the L-System parameters, but also write new sets of rules and see them in action. This is not coding, since it does not involve

Fig. 9. Students working with tangibles.

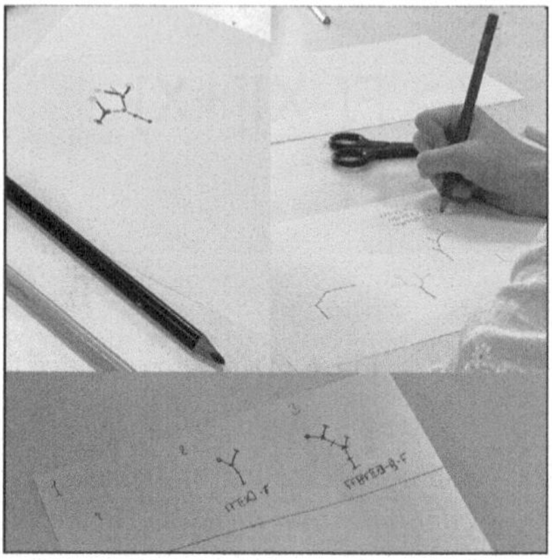

Fig. 10. Students drawing plants following LOGO commands.

understanding and using the actual syntax and semantics of a universal programming language, but still requires an understanding of a recursive rewriting algorithm and the implications of how changing rules reflects on the procedurally generate plants. A user-friendly interface is provided using a few HTML form elements, a usual praxis when coding with P5.js. The user of the simulator can write any L-System rules in a text area element, and adjust plant drawing parameters (Fig. 11). The user interface is highly responsive, so that each time any of the parameters or the rules change, the plant is redrawn, giving instant visual feedback to the user, and helping build an intuition of what the various controls actually mean for the plant begin generated.

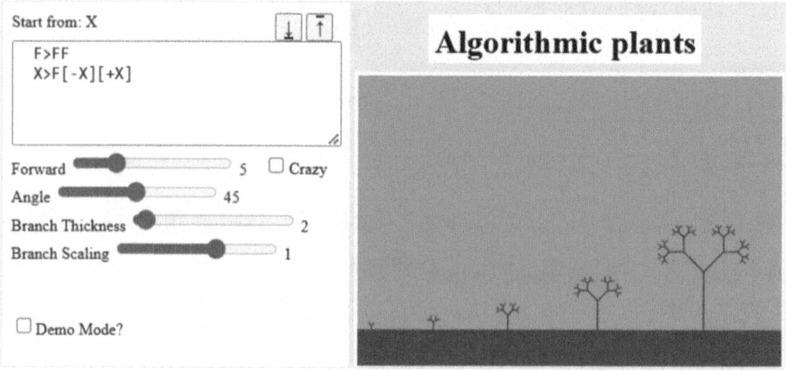

Fig. 11. Simplified view of the main elements of the L-System simulator's GUI.

During the first part of the workshop the students received a light lecture about L-Systems, supported by slides, showing examples of visual rules and derivation of plants. The students then were given a choice between using the prepared cards or drawing the plants with pencil and paper, using the LOGO-based algorithm; most students used the cards, but several also drew by hand. In the third part of workshop, the students got to play and explore the online simulator.

5 Analysis and Discussion

The workshops fostered engagement and interest in the students, they participated actively and were eager to experiment on their own beyond the provided instructions, which was our goal since the start. During the situated interviews conducted at the end of the third workshop, the students were asked about what they found interesting about the workshops, and they replied that they found the whole experience: "fun" and "interesting". Several students said that it was "funny" to create colors that they will use afterwards. One student remarked: "It is great to do the whole process, usually you just buy the colors, this process is more personal." Another student said that she found the colors that were produced from the natural ingredients to be "different from what she expected." Another outcome of the interviews was that the students would have all liked to be given more time for each workshop, especially the first one, as making the colors took time, and brewing the colors for a longer time would have given stronger inks. When asked if they would have liked to receive more theoretical input in the beginning of the workshop, most students said that they were interested in exploring further the chemistry of colors, as many of them also studied biology.

The art teacher and his students appreciated how the whole process communicated a deep interconnection between art and sciences. The teacher also asked us if we could run the whole module again and proposed to involve a biology and chemistry teacher, who has expressed interest to volunteer for the first workshop, as she herself is interested in art and in the chemistry of colors.

5.1 Engagement During the Workshops

During the workshops we observed three main types of engagements, which we call: personal, sensorial and exploratory.

During the first workshop, from a personal perspective the students enjoyed interacting within their own group. They were visibly excited by being in the lab and wearing lab coats, which provided a different environment than the classroom making them feel like scientists. Hence, they chatted and laughed, while they were boiling the plants and food waste in pots, joking on how "it feels like cooking soups!".

Sensorial and exploratory engagement emerged as interconnected. The students worked on the given recipes, but were keen on exploring further, adding their own plant materials, such as: pomegranate seeds and peel, tulip and rose petals, and leaves. In so doing they acted excited about the possible outcomes of their experiments. The students also engaged with color making through their senses, commenting on the smells of the ingredients, in positive and negative tones. A girl from a group, who was blending grass to obtain a green, said: "It really smells like summer!" The other group members leaned in to smell the grass and nodded in agreement. In another group, busy with gaining purple-pink from cabbage, a girl remarked making faces that it smelled really "unpleasant!".

The students did not always succeed in gaining the color they were hoping for, but they did not seem discouraged, instead they tried to adjust their recipes further or boil them down more, trying to gain their envisioned colors. They used paper strips to observe the intensity and hue of the colors they made. Overall, they seemed to value the making process over the final color outcomes, as reflected by the vast amount of natural inks the students created, despite the time limitations of the workshop.

The students took notes of their own recipes in their journals, but did not all engage in the same way. Therefore, the level of accuracy in their descriptions varied from group to group, as some groups recorded detailed observations, while others lacked them entirely. However, even the more scrupulous groups often did not record the exact amounts of the ingredients, which is essential information to replicate the recipes later. This shows that the students have not understood the importance of keeping an accurate lab journal, an essential task in natural inquiries.

During the second workshop, the students appeared equally engaged socially, they accommodated themselves at their tables chatting, laughing, and looking at each other's plants. Some brought flowers, others brought tree branches with or without leaves. The art teachers said that he encouraged them to find suitable plants in the green area around the school and this provided a new way to engage with the school environment, as a resource for naturalistic art inspiration.

The students engaged sensorially and exploratorily with the painting process. They were attentive enough to the introduction to botanical painting, especially on how to paint with the colors they made, which were available in glass jars on a cart. The students were well trained in watercolor basic technique, and this gave them an advantage, when diving into natural inks. However, this enabled them to feel confident so that they did not experiment color mixing enough before engaging with their botanicals, rushing to painting their botanical as soon as possible. As a result, the students were more challenged in mixing the colors than necessary. A main difficulty was found in managing the amount of water on the paper, some students laughed at each other while waiting for the paper to dry. Moreover, the fluidity of the inks made it difficult for the students to gain a good range of nuances, from dark to light; hence in their final works some compensated by adding layers of colored pencils in the darkest areas, rediscovering on their own the grisaille technique [19]. Watercolor painting also requires artists to simplify their subjects, especially when using watery inks, aiming at slightly more abstract forms, to keep a clear contrast between light and darker areas. This requires a little more planning and time to adapt to the new materials, which unfortunately was not available. In the end, they managed to create convincing botanical paintings, depicting plant from different angles and focusing on different details.

During the 3rd workshop, we noticed the same types of personal, sensorial and exploratory engagement. However, the students appeared a little nervous in the start, for the novelty of the experience and were not as chatty as in the other workshops. The paper-based activity, requiring them to cut our cards to assemble a plant form, acted as an icebreaker eliciting personal and exploratory engagement. The students laughed and chatted gaily while cutting out the cards, an activity that seems to evoke images of child play. They became more focused and quieter while in the process of understanding how to apply the instructions from the L-Systems grammars to correctly compose the plants. Interestingly they were dubious of their ability and were genuinely surprised when discovering that they did it right responding as: *"Really"* or *"I did it right? I did not think so!"* giggling. Sensorial engagement emerged while the students engaged with the cards, with drawing and with the digital simulator. Again, while busy with drawing and getting acquainted with the digital simulator the students were focused and quiet, limiting personal engagement. They observed closely the look of their plants, leaning towards their computer, but soon they started to freely explore different configurations and to target specific ones, altering the provided algorithms. The students often sat in pairs in front of their computer and laughed, while playfully generating unrealistic plants on the simulator. After each attempt, they turned the screens with their generated plants around to others to show off what they made.

Informal interviews were conducted asking the students about their experience, initiated with a simple question such as: "How was it for you to work with L-Systems?". In general, the students answered saying: "It was fun and really cool to see how it works, the outcome", "the program was fun", "it was very different than what we normally do" and "it was a more structured way of thinking and it was nice to put art and plants that are usually organic into a structure, we are not used to it in art class". A few comments pointed out the fact that in the 3rd workshop the images of the plants were created from a model, while in the previous workshops, art skills were applied to draw images from reality. In this sense, the outcome from the 2nd and 3rd workshops were found to be substantially different in terms of meaning making and visual quality of the represented plants. Historically, botanical art had a representational goal, visualizing features of real observed plants, on the other hand, L-Systems generate abstract archetype of a species, more than a specimen with its own characteristics.

Finally, the students suggested improvements to the L-System simulator, in particular they were interested in generating animations instead of static pictures of their plants, so that they could see how specific plants might grow and develop. In the end, a valuable outcome from the workshop, was that L-Systems provided the students with a basis to tinker and reason on plant forms through simple visual grammars, and gain some basic understanding of algorithmic thinking.

During our dialogue with the students, we asked if the students could see coherence among the three workshops of the Taxonomies project and all students nodded in agreement, a few pointed out that they could see that, although different, L-Systems could be another art material to represent plant forms, as the workshops were shifting from analogue, hand-crafted images, to digital, computer-generated ones.

The students were excited about having their works displayed in Spinderihallerne for a thematic exhibition (Fig. 12), together with the artefacts made by the authors, including: glass jars with inks, botanical paintings, and a video showing the development of plants from the L-Systems simulator. At the exhibition, the students' parents were proud of the students' work and satisfied with the workshops' outcome, so that they came to congratulate us for the module and the exhibition. A mother told us smiling that her daughter became fond of making her own ink: "…And now she keeps a shelf on the fridge for food waste to make her own inks!".

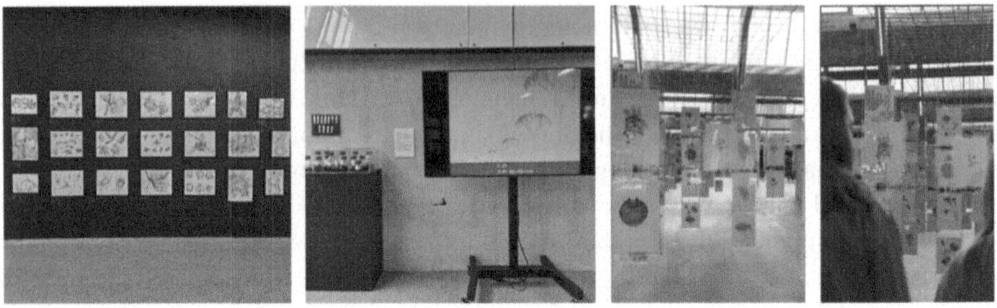

Fig.12. Taxonomies exhibition, from left: Exemplar paintings, colors and L-Systems videos, paintings made by the students.

5.2 What have We Learnt on Creating STEAM Learning Workshops

The Taxonomies workshops emerged as an inspiring experience for the students and their teacher, as well as for us, leading to new understanding of the role of art in STEAM and art-based learning activities.

Interdisciplinary entanglement driven by art making was the aspect that mainly led our creative process in combining our passions, in reconnecting botanical art to sciences, and to conceive the workshops format. Reflecting on current STEAM research [2, 17] we found that art was weakly added to activities with a scientific learning goal or for other purposes entirely. Art was generally seen as a recreational relieve and a motivational activity to foster interest for science, hence according to Mejias et al. [16] art is relegated to a secondary instrumental purpose. We identify a series of issues in this way of conceiving the role of art in STEAM activities, the first issue is that art is approached only as fun and games, hence the learners will not take it seriously in the sense that they will not fully engage with it or make something of value for themselves, devaluing art learning potential. Moreover, art is seen as a form of self-expression but deprived of technical skills, which are seen as too intimidating and not available to everybody. This can be seen as an instance of the conceptual trap [Edwards], according to which individuals intimidated by art practice find refuge in abstract or spontaneous unskilled art, which in the end does not provide intellectual engagement and might stop doing art all together. In this way, we find that art cannot do a significant difference in supporting learning of sciences [Boy, Mejia], apart from providing a pleasant break from learning.

Instead with our study, we place ourselves in Mejias' spectrum [16] where art and science are in a *mutually instrumental and pedagogical relation*, as we aimed at creating conditions in which art students, could learn about science making art and learn to make better art through science. Hence in our study:

- Botanical art serves an instrumental purpose for providing a purpose for engaging in scientific inquiry,
- The students are supposed to produce art inspired by science, as they are instructed to draw and paint plant forms,

- The students are supposed and instructed to make their own colors out of plants, extracting pigments and stabilizing colors with chemical mediums, hence gaining knowledge on organic pigments and their chemistry,
- Finally, in making botanical art through code, the students are encouraged to experiments and reflect on the mathematical proportions of plants, and how simple code can enable to create realistic plant forms.

Based on our experience, we advocate for a more organic integration of art and science, in which the students' art skills are challenged and fostered through instructions, as is their scientific knowledge. Both disciplines then should equally engage the learners on an intellectual level, as learning means and goals. This required us to provide technical and not only expressive instructions on how to make art, which can be mistakenly seen as a demotivating approach in STEAM, when art is employed mainly as motivational resource. This was positively commented by the art teacher, whose goal is to help his students improve in art making, technically and artistically.

An organic integration of art and science emerged by itself regarding the practice and learning of making colors. Colors and paints are themselves a product of scientific progress, they are gained through complex processes that evolved through time, to secure usable and durable colors. Colors are a product of chemistry, whose fabrication require chemical and biological knowledge in relation to treating natural (vegetal and animal) and mineral pigments, and which chemical medium to add to make the gained colors last for a long time. On the other hand, color essence is grounded in physics, as what the human eye consistently perceive as colors are different light wavelengths, which are reflected by the objects around us [5]. Moreover, the colors we perceive affect our nervous system in different ways and on this aspect are grounded the psychological, cultural, and expressive value of colors in art [Dabner, Edwards]. In a new iteration we plan to explore further the chemical and physical essence of colors and color perception, a central topic in both arts and sciences.

Taking art as the driving force of our work, led us to a new framing for coding, seen as algorithmic art material, transforming botanical art into a form of procedural digital art. This exploration led us to new understandings of coding and how coding could be framed as art material in STEAM. L-Systems provided an ideal resource, formulated explicitly with the purpose of replicating plant forms on a computer to conduct botanical investigations on the structures and proportions of plants through their development. Interestingly, the students noticed how coded plants were not specific specimens, they are not observed plants, which can show varying degrees of differences in proportions, forms, missing or defective parts. In this sense, we find that from a scientific perspective while engaging in botanical investigation, drawing can be seen as an inductive practice, as it allows us investigators to analyze and theorize about different species starting from individual plants, hence generalizing about one or more species from individually observed specimens. On the other hand, L-System are already theorized archetypes, algorithmic abstractions of different species, which can be used to generate individual plants of a specific species. In this sense, L-System embody a deductive approach to botany, as the authors [22] had to analyze in-depth different plants and weeds to formulate algorithms able to generate easily recognizable images of such plants; *stochastic L-Systems* can deal with this, but they are more complex to introduce and require discussions of probability.

A final aspect that emerged through our study is that a sensible integration between art and science, can lead learners to engage in trials and error processes, which in STEAM literature are seen as an integral part of the scientific process [2, 17]. However, these processes belong to arts and science alike, in the forms of lab repeated experiments and formative evaluations in design iterations, hence bridging lab and studio work, a perspective that could be further investigated from a mutually instrumental relationship among the different fields.

6 Conclusion

STEAM learning proposes a new approach to STEM, in which scientific disciplines are being complemented by art, as a motivational and enjoyable element. However, the results from our Taxonomies workshop series suggest that art could take a more significant role in fostering learning, bridging art and science making through naturalistic inspiration and representation, fabrication and use of organic color matters, reframing coding as material for botanical art. In this way, art has been approached as empirical mean for inquiry: to observe, analyze, and investigate nature forms.

The students participating to the workshops engaged with the proposed materials and activities on a personal, sensorial, and exploratory level, especially towards the practical parts of the workshops. The students appreciated the workshops as an integrated creative process, in which they made their art materials as well as their artwork. Moreover, during the 3rd workshop, the students' engagement grew from an initial intimidation, not being used to code, towards free play with the simulator and humor. We interpret their growing engagement, as a sign that our combination of tangibles and software contributed to a demystification of coding, and elicited aesthetic explorations of the potential of L-Systems as a valid tool in a botanical art drawing context.

Through the workshops, we leveraged a variety of materials: lab and kitchen equipment, plants and food waste, brushes and watercolor paper, computational tangibles, manual algorithm animation, and a light form of coding with our L-System simulator. Our workshop format, theme and simulators (paper and digital) emerged suitable for humanities students and to support open STEAM discussions with them.

New iterations of the workshop series are being conducted with Rosborg Gymnasium, involving science teachers, with the aim to strengthen scientific learning in relation to chemical alteration of organic colors and laboratory note-taking practices. Moreover, it is our goal to generalize our format into a *kit* that other high-schools teachers could use, to run similar workshops module by themselves. This kit should include: for the 1st workshop *recipes* and shopping lists to prepare colors with food and plants, for the 2nd resources on art and botanical painting tutorials as well as list of available material, and for the 3rd a teacher-level explanation of our L-System concretization method, templates for computational tangibles and instructions on how to use the simulator (already available online).

References

1. Anderson-Tempini, G. Drawing as a Way of Knowing in Art and Science. Intellect Books (2017)
2. Boy, G.A.: From STEM to STEAM: toward a human-centred education, creativity & learning thinking. In: Proceedings of the 31st European conference on cognitive ergonomics, pp. 1–7 (2013)
3. Causey, A.: Drawn to see: drawing as an ethnographic method. University of Toronto Press (2017)
4. Chomski, N.: On certain formal properties of grammars. Inf. Control. **2**(2), 137–167 (1959)
5. Dabner, D., Stewart, S., Vickress, A.: Graphic design school: the principles and practice of graphic design. John Wiley & Sons (2017)
6. Denning, P.J., Tedre, M.: Computational thinking. Mit Press (2019)
7. Dourish, P.: Reading and interpreting ethnography. In: Ways of Knowing in HCI, pp. 1–23. New York, NY: Springer New York (2014)
8. Edwards, B.: Drawing on the right side of the brain deluxe: the definitive. Penguin (2012)
9. Flake. G.W.: The computational beauty of nature: computer explorations of fractals, chaos, complex systems, and adaptation. MIT press (2000)
10. Haeckel, E.: Art forms in nature. Courier Corporation (2012)
11. Katanosaka, T., Khan, M.F.F., Sakamura, K.: A physics learning system using gamification for high-school students. In: 2023 11th International Conference on Information and Education Technology (ICIET), pp. 167–171. IEEE (2023)
12. Kharel, D.: Visual ethnography, thick description and cultural representation. Dhaulagiri J. Sociol. Anthropol. **9**, 147–160 (2015)
13. Logan, J.: Make Ink: A Forager′s Guide to Natural Inkmaking. Abrams (2018)
14. Lupton, E., Phillips, J.C.: Graphic design: the new basics (revised and expanded). Chronicle Books (2015)
15. Marchetti, E.: At observere gennem dine hænder: tegning som etnografisk praksis. In: Grønning, I A., Enemark Lundtofte, T., Kampmann Walther, B. (eds.) Medievidenskab Metoder og Teorier, pp. 83–97. Syddansk Universitetsforlag (2022)
16. Mejias, S., et al.: The trouble with STEAM and why we use it anyway. Sci. Educ. **105**(2), 209–231 (2021)
17. Namukasa, I.K., Hughes, J. Scucuglia, R.: STEAM and critical making in teacher education. In: Handbook of cognitive mathematics, pp. 939–970. Cham: Springer International Publishing (2022)
18. Neacşu, I.: On Contemporary Botanical Art. Bull. Transilvania Univ. Braşov Ser. IV: Philology Cult. Stud. **15**(Suppl), 25–34 (2023)
19. Oxley, V.: Botanical illustration. Crowood (2013)
20. Piaget, I.: Construction of reality in the child. Routledge & Kegan Paul, London (1957)
21. Pink, S., Sumartojo, S., Lupton, D., Heyes LaBond, C.: Empathetic technologies: digital materiality and video ethnography. Visual Stud. **32**(4), 371–381. (2017)
22. Prusinkiewicz, P., Lindenmayer, A. The algorithmic beauty of plants. Springer Science & Business Media (2012)
23. Rakow, D.A., Lee, S.A.: Western botanical gardens: history and evolution. Hortic. Rev. **43**, 269–310 (2015)
24. Rognoli, V., Bianchini, M., Maffei, S., Karana, E. DIY materials. Mater. Des. **86**, 692–702 (2015). https://doi.org/10.1016/j.matdes.2015.07.020
25. Shiffman, D.: The nature of code: simulating natural systems with javascript. No Starch Press (2024)

26. Solomon, C., et al.: History of logo. In: Proceedings of the ACM on Programming Languages 4 HOPL, pp. 1–66 (2020)
27. Trundle, C., Phillips, T.: Defining focused ethnography: disciplinary boundary-work and the imagined divisions between 'focused' and 'traditional' ethnography in health research–a critical review. Soc. Sci. Med. 116108 (2023)
28. Valente, A., Marchetti, E.: Programming turing machines as a game for technology sense-making. In: 2011 IEEE 11th International Conference on Advanced Learning Technologies, pp. 428–430. IEEE (2011)
29. Valente, A., Marchetti, E.: Playful learning and shared computational thinking: the PaCoMa case study. In: International Conference on Computers in Education ICCE 2020, vol. II, pp. 180–189. Asia-Pacific Society for Computers in Education (2020)
30. Vygotsky, L.S.: Mind in society: the development of higher psychological processes **86**. Harvard University Press (1978)
31. Wills, M.: Leonardo Da Vinci, Artist/Scientist. Leonardo was the first scientific illustrator. JSTOR (2016). https://daily.jstor.org/leonardo-da-vinci-artist-scientist/
32. Zimmerman, J., Forlizzi, J.: Research through design in HCI. In: Ways of Knowing in HCI, pp. 167–189. New York, NY: Springer New York (2014)

EcoPoetico: A Poetry Recommender System for Digital Literary Mediation

Daniel Mora Melanchthon[1(✉)] and Loreto Espallargas[2]

[1] Pontificia Universidad Católica de Valparaíso, Valparaíso, Chile
dimora@uc.cl

[2] Universitat Autònoma Barcelona, Barcelona, Spain
laespallargas@uc.cl

Abstract. This study presents EcoPoetico, a multimodal web app designed to enhance digital literary mediation by recommending poems based on semantic relatedness. The app addresses key challenges in digital reading platforms, such as the ambiguity of literary mediation in online contexts and the cognitive challenge of processing poetry, which is often problematic in curriculum design and not always favored by teachers. Using a corpus of ∼5,000 Spanish-language poems, EcoPoetico employs the BERT-based language model Beto and cosine similarity to offer personalized poetry suggestions. To evaluate its performance, the study conducted both usability and recommendation tests. The usability test showed that both students and teachers found EcoPoetico engaging and easy to use, with potential for teaching purposes. However, teachers emphasized the need for Explainable AI to enhance the platform's educational value by providing insights into how recommendations are generated. The recommendation test confirmed the system's effectiveness, as cosine similarity resulted in recommendations that aligned more closely with expert criteria for adequacy, significantly outperforming random suggestions. A cosine similarity analysis reveals that the similarity score is not the primary factor in determining the adequacy of a recommendation, but rather its variance among the recommended poems. Higher variance allows for better discrimination and leads to more effective recommendations. EcoPoetico's open-source code and modular architecture allow for easy adaptation to other languages or corpora.

Keywords: Digital literary mediation · Poetry recommendation system · Educational technology · Cosine similarity

1 Introduction

The shift towards digital reading and writing is clear with the growing use of digital platforms [31]. Access to digital texts depends not just on devices or facilities, but on the semiotic process that relates texts and their meanings [17]. Reading scaffolding, traditionally handled by educators and librarians, becomes

B. K. Smith and M. Borge (Eds.): HCII 2025, LNCS 15806, pp. 139–157, 2025.
https://doi.org/10.1007/978-3-031-93564-0_9

ambiguous in the digital realm, particularly with digital repositories [18]. This raises the key question: who mediates in a digital reading platform?

Poetry, as a cognitively demanding genre [6], presents an ideal case study for digital mediation. Its fragmented structure and dense language can make it challenging for readers and problematic for curriculum integration [3]. From a computational perspective, although advancements have been made in text-based recommender systems [15], automatic scansion [25], poetry generation as a writing aid [8], and fully autonomous poetry writing [2], progress in poetry recommendation systems remains limited.

To address this gap, this study presents and evaluates EcoPoetico, a multimodal web app designed to recommend poems based on semantic relatedness. The recommendation module leverages Beto [7], a LLM trained on Spanish for feature extraction, and the use of cosine similarity for ranking the most similar poems. The system uses a corpus of ~5,000 Spanish-language poems and offers an interactive, mosaic-style interface featuring horizontal scrolling and dynamic reading paths. Its open-source architecture makes it easily adaptable for other languages and corpora.

This study aimed to evaluate the usability and recommendation accuracy of EcoPoetico through qualitative and quantitative testing with adolescents and literary mediators. The usability test examined how participants navigated the platform and interpreted its features, while the recommendation test assessed the semantic relevance of suggested poems based on expert evaluations. By comparing the experiences of these two groups, we highlight the potential of digital platforms as mediators of literary exploration and propose improvements to enhance their educational value.

In what follows, Sect. 2 states the theoretical basis of digital literary mediation and related NLP work regarding poetry. Section 3 details the design and features of EcoPoetico, including its recommendation algorithm and user interface. Section 4 outlines the usability and recommendation test, followed by their results in Sect. 5. Finally, Sect. 6 discusses the implications of our study, and conclude with recommendations for future research in Sect. 7.

2 Theoretical Framework and Related Works

2.1 Literary Digital Mediation and Digital Libraries

The digital shift in reading and writing practices has transformed how readers interact with literary texts, as digital repositories and reading platforms become more prevalent [31]. However, many digital libraries and repositories still resemble traditional physical libraries, offering basic functions that rely on static metadata (e.g. author names, summaries, and book covers) rather than making use of the features inherent to the digital medium (e.g. personalized recommendations, interactive annotations, adaptive reading pathways). Evolving from analog reading to digital literacy represents not merely a change in reading devices but also a fundamental shift in literary engagement, comprehension, and meaning construction [5].

Despite the essentiality of the firsts steps on this matter (i.e. creating digital repositories, including multimodal loans as audiobooks), according to latest studies on Literature Didactics [26,27] the access to digital texts is not solely based on devices itself, but on the semiotic process that relates texts and its significance through meaning making [17]. Only literary mediation makes these learning possible [28]. Literary mediation, essential for facilitating this learning process, has traditionally been managed by experts such as teachers and librarians in physical contexts. However, its application and potential for improvement in the digital realm remain unclear due to the relative novelty of these platforms [18]. Addressing these uncertainties is crucial because, in the absence of adequate mediation in the digital reading era, the market effectively becomes the primary mediator [26]. Far from replacing analogue formats and physical libraries, we argue that new digital reading practices expand its reach and impact on new explorations in the reading field.

2.2 Related Poetic Applications

In the context of creative computing, digital humanities, and NLP tools tailored to the literary field, much of the efforts have gone towards poetry analysis and writing, and fewer efforts towards poetry recommendation. Regarding automatic scansion and poetic analysis, state-of-the-art results have been obtained using hybrid models that combine machine-learning techniques and models with knowledge-based rules designed by experts [19,25].

Regarding poetry writing, machine-learning models have been built for poetry generation, either as an assistance (machine-in-the-loop) which suggests while the human writer decides on how to continue the poem [8,9], or as an autonomous writer that generates a full poem starting from a proposed seed [2,12,29]. There are also free-to-use web applications (e.g. Verse by Verse[1] by Google AI or Co-PoeTryMe[2]) that help the author write poems based on initial cues or adopting different styles from well-known writers.

Books Recommender Systems, that directly relate to Literary Digital Mediation, have seen increasing attempts during the last years, specially on literary genres or closer tasks (e.g. Library Catalogue Management). For building Book Recommender Systems, common techniques used are Collaborative Filtering, Content-Based Filtering, K-Nearest Neighbour, Support Vector Machines, and Neural Networks [1,10,30,32]. During the last few years, both static and contextualized word embeddings have been widely adopted as features in various textual tasks, including building Book Recommender Systems with notable success [15], where cosine similarity has been used as the main metric [20].

One of the most used approaches for text-based recommendations is the use of cosine similarity as a metric of semantic relatedness between vectors [21]. The main intuition is to extract a vector representation of the text (e.g. document, book, poem) and compute the cosine of the angle between two vectors in a multidimensional space. Features used to obtain the vector vary and

[1] https://sites.research.google/versebyverse/.
[2] https://poetryme.dei.uc.pt/~copoetryme/.

depend mostly on the task at hand and available resources. It is common practice nowadays, due to their high performance on relevant text-based tasks that require syntactic-semantic knowledge, the use of Large Language Models as feature extractors [11,34].

3 EcoPoetico Web App

3.1 Overview

EcoPoetico[3] is an open-source[4] multimodal web application designed to mediate poetry by providing personalized recommendations based on the semantic content of poems. The platform was developed to address the challenges of digital literary mediation, offering an exploratory and engaging poetry reading experience. By encouraging non-linear navigation, the app transforms poetry discovery into a dynamic and personalized journey through interconnected texts.

The primary objective of EcoPoetico is to promote meaningful engagement with poetry by suggesting semantically related poems as users navigate the platform. The web app is designed for learners, educators, and poetry enthusiasts, offering an experimental reading environment that balances a user-friendly interface with an NLP-based recommendation system. The platform leverages a large corpus of ~5,000 publicly available Spanish-language poems and features a modular, open-source architecture, making it easily adaptable for other languages and corpora.

3.2 Recommendation System

The poetry recommendation system in EcoPoetico is designed to provide users with semantically related poems based on their selected readings. The system uses cosine similarity as a measure of semantic relatedness to generate personalized suggestions. In addition, TF-IDF (Term Frequency-Inverse Document Frequency) is used to extract relevant keywords from each poem.

Cosine Similarity for Semantic Recommendations. Cosine similarity is widely used in text-based recommendation systems due to its effectiveness in capturing semantic similarity between texts [21]. To represent the semantic meaning of poems, the system uses Beto [7], a BERT-based language model specifically trained on Spanish texts, for extracting features. The embedding corresponding to the [CLS] token from the last layer is extracted as a vector representation of the entire poem. This embedding condenses both syntactic and semantic information, making it suitable for this task that requires a high-level comprehension of each poem.

---

[3] https://www.ecopoetico.cl.

[4] https://github.com/melanchthon19/ecopoetico.

For each selected poem, the system computes a similarity matrix across the entire corpus by comparing their vector representations. Based on the cosine similarity scores, the system ranks the poems and presents the top 30 most semantically related poems. This approach ensures that users receive recommendations that are both thematically coherent and diverse, supporting a personalized and exploratory reading experience.

TF-IDF for Highlighting Relevant Keywords. To enhance interpretability, EcoPoetico uses Term Frequency-Inverse Document Frequency (TF-IDF) to highlight relevant keywords for each poem by computing their score within the author's body of work. Poems are grouped by author, and content words are extracted after preprocessing the poem. TF-IDF assigns higher scores to words that appear frequently in a poem but are less frequent across the author's other works. The number of selected keywords is proportional to the length of the poem, ensuring that longer texts provide more context-rich terms without overwhelming the reader. This approach highlights distinctive thematic and stylistic elements, supporting a deeper understanding of the semantic features that define each poem.

3.3 User Interaction

EcoPoetico guides users through an interactive reading experience that begins with an exploratory mosaic-style interface (Fig. 1a). The homepage displays excerpts of poems in a grid-like horizontal scroll view, inviting users to browse poetry fragments intuitively. This layout breaks from the conventional vertical reading flow, encouraging spontaneous discovery.

Upon selecting a fragment, a new window opens, showing the complete poem with key terms highlighted to guide the reader's attention. At this point, users can choose to either return to the initial mosaic-like view or *travel* further by receiving recommendations of semantically related poems. The *travel* button, inspired by the metaphor of a literary journey, records the selected poem as part of the user's reading path and presents a new mosaic-like view of the poems excerpts (Fig. 1b). This new layout displays only the recommended poems (i.e. the 30 most similar among the entire corpus), creating a cohesive exploration of interconnected texts.

At the top of the screen, a poetic route tracker visually maps the user's selections, allowing them to revisit previous poems and retrace their reading journey. Users can navigate back and forth along their path, repeating the process until they decide to download their completed poetic route, which contains all the poems they explored.

Multimodal Features. Following [13], the use of multimodal features can significantly enrich the mediation experience. Integrating these elements into the educational framework not only supports diverse learning preferences but also enhances engagement and comprehension. EcoPoetico integrates optional

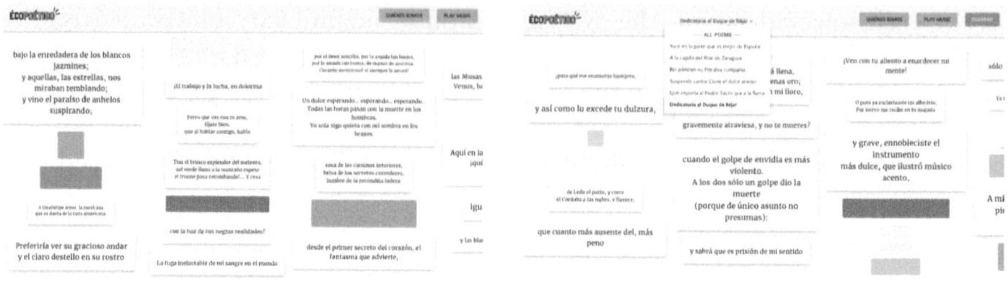

(a) Initial mosaic-like view showing excerpts (horizontal scroll).

(b) Suggestion view of the recommended poems. The traversed path is on top.

Fig. 1. Views of EcoPoetico's interface.

background music that users can enable or disable according to their preference. The minimalist synthesizer soundtrack was designed to enhance the reading flow. Future updates may introduce additional multimodal features, such as audio readings of poems, interactive annotations, and visual illustrations, further expanding the platform's immersive potential.

Poetic Corpus. The poems in EcoPoetico are drawn from a curated open-access corpus called Ciudad Seva[5]. Few filtering rules were applied to remove poems based on their length or to eliminate duplicates (i.e., the same poem with different titles). Out of the ~12,000 available poems, the resulting selection grouped approximately 5,000 poems. The collection predominantly features literary texts from Spanish-speaking authors, along with Spanish translations of internationally renowned poets. This digital library was automatically scraped, and the poems were stored in a suitable format for further processing.

Modular Architecture and System Pipeline. EcoPoetico was developed using open-source tools and libraries, with its code publicly available to encourage customization and collaboration. The recommendation system follows a modular architecture depicted in Fig. 2, where each component can be easily adjusted to support different languages, poetry collections, or similarity metric. This modularity allows the platform to adapt seamlessly to various contexts and use cases, such as thematic collections, literary festivals, or educational programs focused on poetry analysis.

The key parameters that must be defined include the corpus to be used, the feature extraction model, and the similarity metric. The corpus is preprocessed to clean the data and structure the poems for analysis. In the feature extraction step, any language model can be used to generate vector representations of each poem. These vectors are then compared using a similarity metric to build a

[5] https://ciudadseva.com/biblioteca/indice-autor-poemas/.

recommendation matrix, which is then accessed by the front-end interface to suggest semantically related poems to users.

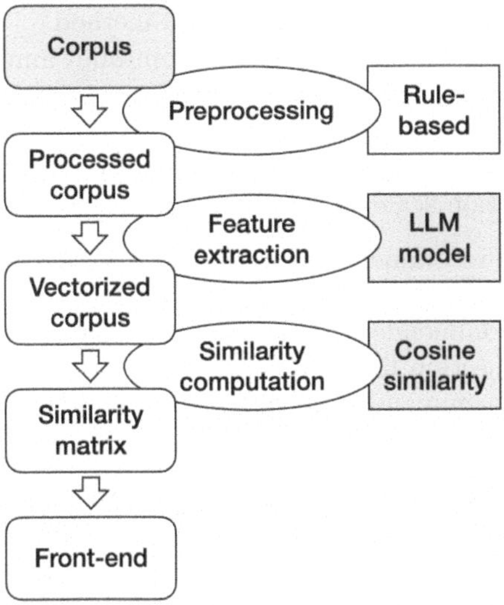

Fig. 2. Recomendation system's pipeline. Yellow blocks represent the main components that can be easily adapted for specific use cases: corpora in different languages or from particular literary streams, the LLM for feature extraction, and the similarity metric. (Color figure online)

4 Methodology

This study employed a qualitative approach to evaluate the usability and effectiveness of EcoPoetico as a tool for digital literary mediation. The methodology consisted of two key components: a recommendation test, conducted by literary experts, to evaluate the system's ability to provide semantically relevant poetry suggestions, and a usability test to assess user interaction, involving students and teachers.

4.1 Recommendation Test

The recommendation test aimed to provide a data-driven assessment of the system's ability to generate relevant and meaningful recommendations. Five expert literary mediators participated in the annotation task, each evaluating a set of 100 recommendations, resulting in a total of 500 annotations. The sample included 25 selected poems from the corpus, representing a diverse selection of authors, literary periods, and a wide range of topics and themes. Each poem was paired with 20 recommendations: 10 generated by the system based on cosine similarity ("true" recommendations) and 10 randomly selected ("random" recommendations) as a control group. This design enabled a comparison between system-generated and unrelated suggestions, providing valuable insights into the accuracy and relevance of the recommendation method.

To facilitate the annotation process, a custom-built annotation platform was developed specifically for this study. The platform provided an intuitive interface where annotators could view the base poem alongside its corresponding recommendations and assign ratings using a simple drop-down menu for the three-category evaluation scale:

- **Inadequate:** The recommended poem has little or no semantic relation to the original poem.
- **Neutral:** The recommended poem has some shared semantic features but lacks a strong connection to the base poem.
- **Adequate:** The recommended poem has a strong and clear semantic relation to the base poem.

Annotators were instructed to focus solely on the content derived from the poem itself, considering aspects such as themes, repetitions, literary devices, structure, style, motifs, and tone. They were explicitly asked to disregard external factors such as the poet's biography, historical context of production, nationality, or literary movement, as well as the characteristics of potential readers. This ensured that the evaluation was grounded in the syntactic-semantic qualities of the texts rather than prior knowledge of the authors or assumptions about what readers might typically enjoy, prefer, or find popular.

4.2 Usability Test

To explore the diverse ways students and mediators engaged with EcoPoetico, along with their opinions and interpretations, we adopted a qualitative approach for the usability test. The main workflow for all participants had three main stages. Firstly, a pre-experience questionnaire. Secondly, the experience using and testing the web application. Lastly, a post-experience interview. Drawing on [23], semi structured interviews were the main tool to gather perceptions from adolescents. Regarding mediators, we designed a focus group [24] to discuss their professional viewpoint of the web application.

Participants. Nine participants from various regions of Chile were recruited for the study through a convenience sample. Five key focus adolescents (three girls and two boys aged 16 to 18) took part in the study. Four teachers (three women and one non-binary person aged 30 to 37) participated in the focus group. Selection criteria included Chilean children between 15 and 18 who have not yet attended college and Chilean literary mediators of all ages who have professionally worked for more than 5 years. All participants are highly literate (on average, +100 books at home, +6 h of independent reading per week, easy access to digital literature, and a social environment with university degrees).

Procedure. First, adolescents, parents and mediators signed an informed consent that follows a rigorous ethical standard (see Ethics Statement). Once signed, all participants answered a pre-experience questionnaire that contained basic demographic information, technology uses, access to electronic devices, 10 Likert scale [14] questions about their feelings towards reading poetry and other literary genres, and two open-ended questions about their expectations of the web application and favourite ways of approaching/mediating poetry.

In the case of adolescents, a Zoom video call was conducted with each participant. Firstly, we presented ourselves and gave instructions on how to explore the webpage. The link was shared for the first time at this point of the interview. Adolescents used the platform at their will without any intervention, unless a direct question was asked, until they were ready to move on to the next stage. On average, students used the platform for around 30 min. We asked students to share their screen during the exploration to observe their movements through the platform. Finally, a semi structured interview post-experience was made to know their impressions about usability, design, content, reading experience and other holistic comments about the platform. The session with mediators followed the same structure but in a focus group modality.

Thematic Analysis of Interview Data. We used a thematic analysis to organise the answers given by the participants during the interviews [4]. After repeatedly reading data during a process of peer debriefing, we found patterns that were categorised under different themes, represented as a collection of quotes from the participants.

5 Results

5.1 Recommendation Test

The recommendation test revealed significant differences between the system-generated recommendations and the random control group ($\chi^2 = 91.36$, $p < 0.0001$), as Fig. 3 illustrates. The system's recommendations received "adequate" ratings significantly more often (143) compared to the random set (56) and produced far fewer "inadequate" ratings (35) compared to the random recommendations (128). These results suggest that the system better aligns with expert criteria when recommending poems based on semantic content compared to random suggestions, demonstrating the effective use of an LLM as a feature extractor and cosine similarity for grouping similar poems based on their textual content in the poetry genre.

To assess the alignment between the system-generated recommendations and expert annotations, an average recommendation score was calculated. This score was determined by assigning weights of 1, 2, and 3 to the annotation categories "inadequate", "neutral", and "adequate", respectively, and then dividing the weighted sum by the total number of annotations. The difference in average score between the system and random recommendations was computed for each

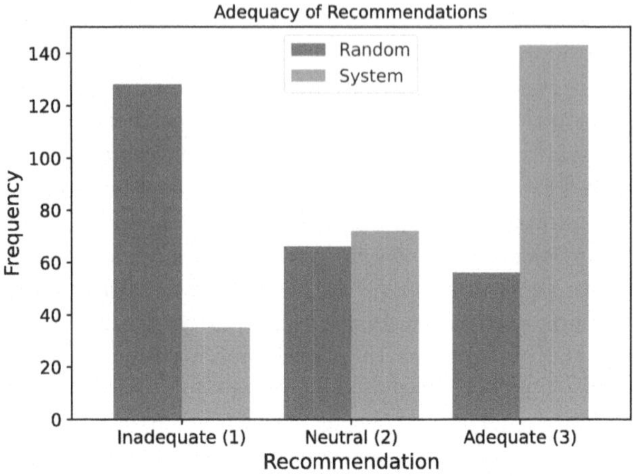

Fig. 3. Comparison of system and random recommendations.

poem, and a percentage improvement was calculated by normalizing the difference relative to the random average score. Figure 4 illustrates the 25 annotated poems ranked by their degree of improvement compared to the random baseline which illustrates the effectiveness of the system's recommendations for each specific poem.

To evaluate how cosine similarity influenced the system's performance, a further analysis was carried out considering three groups of poems: the top 3 (best alignment with expert criteria), the bottom 3 (worst alignment), and the middle 3. For each poem, the first 100 recommendations were analyzed to observe how similarity scores behaved. As shown in Fig. 5, cosine similarity values followed a similar pattern across all three groups. Interestingly, a high similarity score did not necessarily correlate with an adequate recommendation. For example, the worst group had a mean similarity score of 0.80, close to the best group's 0.83, while the middle group was significantly lower at 0.69.

A key distinction lies in the coefficient of variation (CV) of similarity scores within each group, as depicted in Fig. 6. The best and middle groups exhibited higher CVs (3.11% and 4.68%, respectively) compared to the worst group (1.65%). This low CV in the worst group indicates overly similar cosine similarity values, failing to adequately distinguish between poems and resulting in inadequate recommendations. Levene's test confirmed these differences were significant (Statistic = 87.6021, $p < 0.0001$). Thus, the absolute cosine value itself is not directly related to the adequacy of the recommendation, but rather its variance across the recommended poems.

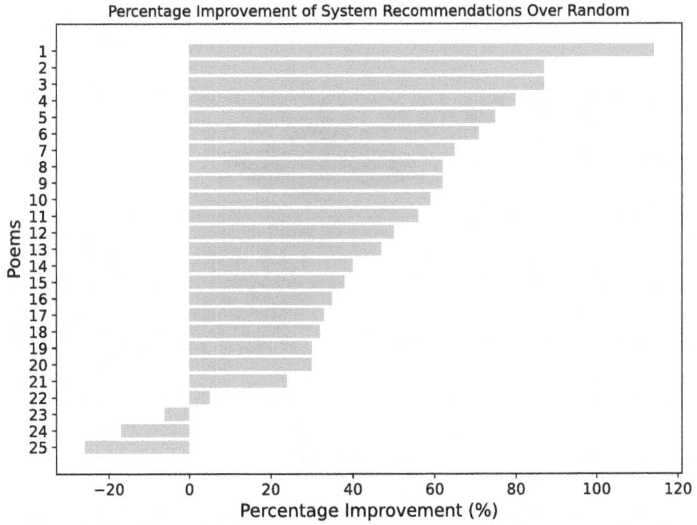

Fig. 4. Percentage improvement in recommendation adequacy for 25 annotated poems ranked by their improvement over the random baseline.

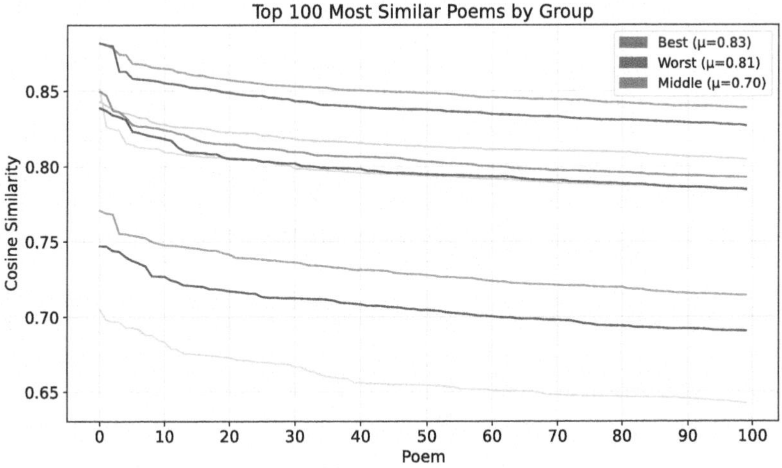

Fig. 5. Cosine similarity trends for the first 100 recommendations in the best, middle, and worst groups. Despite similar patterns across groups, high similarity scores did not consistently correlate with adequate recommendations.

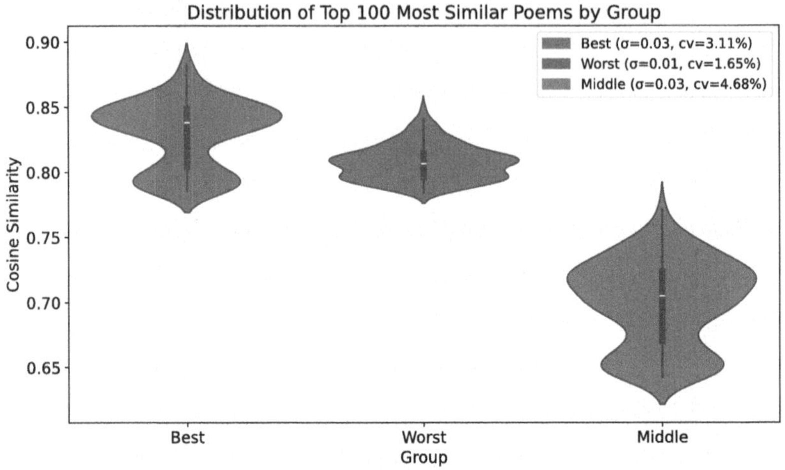

Fig. 6. Cosine similarity score distributions for the best, middle, and worst groups. Higher CV in the best and middle groups relates to better poem differentiation.

5.2 Usability Test

Peer debriefing revealed five key themes: valuable aspects, suggested features, literary mediation, multimodality, and usability. Table 1 highlights the most frequently mentioned themes by participants. As expected, the comparison between numbers reflects the diversion of interests and requirements of both groups.

Overall, both groups found the platform easy to use and motivating, with potential applications in school settings for teaching purposes. Students were generally more receptive to the recommendations, whereas teachers were more skeptical, expressing a desire for an explanation of how the system generated semantic recommendations. Interestingly, teachers were more drawn to a chaotic, exploratory experience, whereas some students preferred a more structured approach, favouring features like an index or search bar. However, the presentation of excerpts appealed to students, as they found it easier to engage with shorter poetry fragments.

Valuable Aspects. Both groups valued the ability to explore poetry through innovative features, but adolescents appreciated the option to download poems (6 mentions), as this allowed them to reflect offline and compare poems. Mediators did not reference this feature but appreciated the horizontal navigation (2 mentions for each group) and the excerpt-based presentation of poems (7 mentions total).

> AM: "It's great, I really like the fact that you can save the poem on your computer or mobile phone (...) (thinking of my friends who like to read) if they really like a poem, it would be very easy for them to download the poem and put it on their mobile phone, on their home screen".

Table 1. Most relevant themes and their topics mentioned by students (Stud) and teachers (Tchr) during the interviews and focus group.

Theme	Stud	Tchr	Total
Valuable Aspects			
Download poems	6	0	6
Horizontal navigation	2	2	4
Displaying of poems in excerpts	5	2	7
Saves time and effort	0	2	2
Saving the poetic route	0	2	2
Suggested Features			
Create a profile	3	1	4
Save favourite poems	4	0	4
Hyperlinks to authors	7	0	7
Literary Mediation			
The platform mediates your own poetic exploration	10	4	14
I need a technical explanation of how suggestions work	2	5	7
Suggested poems are similar in content and words	8	2	10
The platform invites them to keep reading	4	2	6
More information about the corpus selection	0	2	2
Multimodality			
Needs a different music genre	6	0	6
I would like illustrations related to the poem	4	0	4
Audio poems (reading aloud)	0	1	1
2D poetic platform game	0	2	2
Usability			
Intuitive (general use)	5	2	7
Confusing (specific aspects)	7	1	8
Needs human mediation for more effectiveness	2	3	5

Suggested Features. A commonly suggested feature was creating a profile to save poems (mentioned 4 times), share them with others, and add hyperlinks (mentioned 7 times, exclusively by students). For mediators, who typically have a broader knowledge of authors and literary movements, additional information about specific authors was not deemed necessary during navigation. In contrast, some students acknowledged having limited knowledge about poets' lives and their literary contexts. For these users, the ability to access information about the author or receive recommendations not only for related poems but also within the author's work could enhance and better organize their navigation experience.

RE: "I don't know many poets, that's why I think it would be the perfect application (if it included) like the author's stream, for example, show the kind of poems the author writes".
VG: "I would also like to have the option of a search bar with the authors (...) in my school if I have some homework to do regarding poetry, I would like to have all the options in one place, to be able to search like... all the works".

Literary Mediation. Both groups of participants understood the mediation offered by the webpage. There are 14 mentions in total that recognise the importance of the *poetic journey* as an exploration that guides the readers through new possibilities. Although adolescents and mediators understand these possibilities from different perspectives, both groups valued almost the same aspects.

NF: "perhaps you can discover a world you don't know through fragments (...) It reminds me of an echo, and the echo is heard repeatedly... so I suppose it repeats something that would be poetry and it expands, expands, expands".

Mediator E: "The platform also has this game where the child or the young person makes the journey, and you kind of take a back seat as a teacher (...) It seems to me that this is also very valuable, like giving the user, the young person, the chance to guide their own journey".

When it comes to interpreting the suggestions provided by the platform, the students were more receptive to the recommendations, whereas the mediators were insecure about the automatic selection and skeptical about how the mediation worked (7 mentions).

NF: "I could sort of connect them, like I could find something in one (poem) that reminded me of the other. I think the first two I chose were about the sea, so there was always something about the sea and then like a feeling about the sea, and then it continued in all the (poems) I chose".

Mediator V: "the truth is that I am very intrigued to see... why? Why did it suggest those poems? And I don't know... what I understood (...) was that it was either suggesting the same author or a group of authors or similar themes."

The mediation offered by the platform invited them to continue reading on similar topics, as they found it engaging, specially for students (6 mentions in total).

Multimodality. A relevant edge to test was the incorporation of multimodality. The exploration of this enhancement was made through a music button. Observing adolescent's navigation through the hotspots, it calls to our attention that the time they gave to the reproduction of music was very short. While mediators said that music was comfortable and appropriate for reading, children thought that music should be softer and more related to the poem.

> AM: "if in any poem they talk to you about a landscape (it could have) the sounds of that landscape".

In the same line of multimodality, there are many mentions asking for illustrations related to the poem as an aspect that might attract more readers. For example:

> NT: "(In a printed book) I can see images where I can infer the story. Here they explain it like in an excerpt of the poem... I think... so, that's the only thing, that doesn't really catch my attention visually. I would be interested in having a design or... I don't know... a design for each of the squares".

It seems that music and illustrations are not an issue for mediators, as they are already interested and attracted by the poems themselves. At the same time, they do not necessarily have constructed a relation between poetry and calmness, which makes strong music less impressive. But mediators agreed that there are other multimodal enhancements that could be more important. As seen in Table 1, they mentioned to include audio poems in the line of 'mashup poem creation' in which you can grab verses and mix them up or 2D-platform poetic games in which a character jumps from one poem-square to another.

Usability. Both groups considered that the platform is generally easy to use (7 mentions in total), but confusing on particular aspects, such as the initial tutorial or how the music changes according to the color of the background blocks. Additionally, the guidance of a human mediator while interacting with the platform might enhance its mediation effectiveness.

6 Discussion

6.1 Poety Recommendation System Applied to Educational Settings

One significant finding from the usability test is the necessity of Explainable AI (XAI) for educational purposes. Teachers, as key stakeholders in educational environments, are accountable for the tools and resources used in classrooms. It is crucial for educators to understand and interpret how EcoPoetico generates its recommendations. Providing explanations for why certain poems are suggested can increase teachers' trust in the system and enable them to justify its use to students and educational stakeholders. This aligns with the framework proposed by [16], which emphasizes the importance of transparency and trust in AI-supported educational tools. XAI not only fosters accountability but also ensures that educational AI tools meet specific pedagogical needs while avoiding potential pitfalls associated with black box models or opaque algorithms. Incorporating XAI features into EcoPoetico, such as visual explanations or textual summaries of the recommendation process, would significantly enhance its utility in classroom settings.

EcoPoetico directly addresses well-documented challenges in curriculum design related to the teaching of poetry. Poetry is often perceived as cognitively demanding due to its fragmented and dense language [3,6]. Teachers frequently face difficulties integrating poetry into their curricula, as many students find it inaccessible or unengaging. By providing semantically related poems, EcoPoetico helps educators present interconnected texts, making poetry more approachable and engaging for students. This functionality could be further enhanced by allowing teachers to monitor students' progress and engagement with the platform. Additionally, EcoPoetico can serve as a resource for finding similar poems to be used outside the platform, offering educators a broader selection of materials to integrate into their lesson plans.

6.2 Potential for Integration with Other Poetic Projects

EcoPoetico's modular architecture and open-source design make it a valuable tool for integration with other poetic projects. For example, it could complement existing initiatives like Poetree Treebanks [22], which provides an off the shelf API for downloading and using poetic corpora in 10 languages which account for more than 330,000 poems. Generating new recommendation matrices in different languages or corpora can be easily achieved by using suitable models from the Hugging Face platform [33]. This flexibility opens avenues for multilingual and cross-cultural exploration of poetry, expanding the platform's potential audience and educational impact.

6.3 Recommendation Algorithm and Cosine Similarity

EcoPoetico demonstrates the practical application of cosine similarity for literary recommendations, particularly in the underexplored genre of poetry. The study highlights an important insight: the effectiveness of cosine similarity is not solely determined by absolute similarity scores but also by the variance among recommended poems. A higher coefficient of variation in similarity scores within the group of recommended poems enables better discrimination, leading to more meaningful recommendations. This pattern suggests a way of interpreting cosine similarity values in the context of literary recommendation. Further exploration of this pattern could refine recommendation systems across different genres and enhance their interpretability.

While the current recommendation system effectively uses cosine similarity for semantic comparisons, it could be enhanced by incorporating handcrafted features specific to poetry. Features such as rhyme schemes, metaphor identification, or stanza structures could provide deeper insights into the poetic elements that influence recommendations. These features would not only enrich the recommendation algorithm but also offer users a more nuanced exploration of poetry.

7 Conclusion

This study addressed the challenge of literary mediation in online contexts, particularly in teaching poetry. We developed and evaluated EcoPoetico, a multimodal web application that uses a BERT-based model for feature extraction and cosine similarity for semantic recommendations. Its open-source design ensures adaptability and integration with other corpora.

EcoPoetico successfully generated meaningful recommendations, with usability tests highlighting its potential for teaching and exploration, and recommendation tests confirming cosine similarity's alignment with expert criteria. Greater variance in similarity scores proved critical for adequate recommendations.

Future work should focus on adding Explainable AI features to build trust among teachers and students in classroom settings, expanding the algorithm with handcrafted poetic features, and exploring multilingual and thematic corpora. Further studies on cosine similarity across specific genres could refine the system's interpretability and impact.

Acknowledgments. We would like to thank students, teachers/mediators and literary experts for their anonymous contribution to this research, as well as the anonymous reviewers for their valuable feedback.

Disclosure of Interests. The authors have no competing interests to declare that are relevant to the content of this article.

Ethics Statement. The research conducted adheres to international ethical standards concerning participant consent, confidentiality, and integrity of data. All participants provided informed consent, including their parents if under legal majority of age.

Limitations. The main limitation of this work is that the usability test is based on a small number of participants (9). Thus, main findings regarding usability are not generalizable to different contexts or populations beyond the study's scope. Additionally, the corpus used for testing the recommendation was Spanish only, and the behaviour, reading experience, and system's recommendations may lead to different conclusions if the language were different.

References

1. Anwar, K., Siddiqui, J., Saquib Sohail, S.: Machine learning techniques for book recommendation: an overview. SSRN Electron. J. (2019). https://doi.org/10.2139/ssrn.3356349

2. Badura, M., Lampert, M., Dreżewski, R.: System supporting poetry generation using text generation and style transfer methods. Procedia Comput. Sci. **207**, 3310–3319 (2022). https://doi.org/10.1016/j.procs.2022.09.389, knowledge-Based and Intelligent Information and Engineering Systems: Proceedings of the 26th International Conference KES2022
3. Blake, J., Snapper, G.: Poetry in education. Engl. Educ. **56**(1), 1–4 (2022). https://doi.org/10.1080/04250494.2022.2030974
4. Braun, V., Clarke, V.: One size fits all? What counts as quality practice in (reflexive) thematic analysis? Qual. Res. Psychol. **18**(3), 328–352 (2021). https://doi.org/10.1080/14780887.2020.1769238
5. Burnett, C., Merchant, G.: Stacking stories as method: research in early years settings. In: The Routledge International Handbook of Learning with Technology in Early Childhood, p. 12. Routledge (2019)
6. Castiglione, D.: Difficult poetry processing: reading times and the narrativity hypothesis. Lang. Lit. **26**(2), 99–121 (2017). https://doi.org/10.1177/0963947017704726
7. Cañete, J., Chaperon, G., Fuentes, R., Ho, J.H., Kang, H., Pérez, J.: Spanish pre-trained BERT model and evaluation data. In: PML4DC at ICLR 2020 (2020)
8. Chakrabarty, T., Padmakumar, V., He, H.: Help me write a poem: instruction tuning as a vehicle for collaborative poetry writing. In: Goldberg, Y., Kozareva, Z., Zhang, Y. (eds.) Proceedings of the 2022 Conference on Empirical Methods in Natural Language Processing, pp. 6848–6863. Association for Computational Linguistics, Abu Dhabi, United Arab Emirates (2022). https://doi.org/10.18653/v1/2022.emnlp-main.460
9. Clark, E., Ross, A.S., Tan, C., Ji, Y., Smith, N.A.: Creative writing with a machine in the loop: case studies on slogans and stories. In: IUI '18, Association for Computing Machinery, pp. 329–340. New York, NY, USA (2018). https://doi.org/10.1145/3172944.3172983
10. Das, R.K., Islam, M.S.U.: Application of artificial intelligence and machine learning in libraries: a systematic review (2021). https://doi.org/10.48550/arXiv.2112.04573
11. Gillioz, A., Casas, J., Mugellini, E., Khaled, O.A.: Overview of the transformer-based models for NLP tasks. In: 2020 15th Conference on Computer Science and Information Systems (FedCSIS), pp. 179–183 (2020). https://doi.org/10.15439/2020F20
12. Gonçalo Oliveira, H., Mendes, T., Boavida, A., Nakamura, A., Ackerman, M.: Co-PoeTryMe: interactive poetry generation. Cogn. Syst. Res. **54**, 199–216 (2019). https://doi.org/10.1016/j.cogsys.2018.11.012
13. Henkel, A.Q., Mygind, S., Svendsen, H.B.: Exploring reading experiences of three media versions: danish 8th grade students reading the story Nord. L1-Educ. Stud. Lang. Liter., 1–29 (2021). https://doi.org/10.17239/L1ESLL-2021.21.02.04
14. Hernández Sampieri, R., Fernández Collado, C., Baptista Lucio, P.: Metodología de la investigación. McGraw Hill España (2014). https://dialnet.unirioja.es/servlet/libro?codigo=775008
15. Kanwal, S., Nawaz, S., Malik, M.K., Nawaz, Z.: A review of text-based recommendation systems. IEEE Access **9**, 31638–31661 (2021). https://doi.org/10.1109/ACCESS.2021.3059312
16. Khosravi, H., et al.: Explainable artificial intelligence in education. Comput. Educ. Artif. Intell. **3**, 100074 (2022). https://doi.org/10.1016/j.caeai.2022.100074
17. Kress, G., Leeuwen, T.V.: Reading Images: The Grammar of Visual Design. Routledge (2020)

18. Kucirkova, N.: How and Why to Read and Create Children's Digital Books. UCL Press, London, UK (2018). https://doi.org/10.14324/111.9781787353473
19. Marco, G., De La Rosa, J., Gonzalo, J., Ros, S., González-Blanco, E.: Automated metric analysis of Spanish poetry: two complementary approaches. IEEE Access **9**, 51734–51746 (2021). https://doi.org/10.1109/ACCESS.2021.3069635
20. Nuipian, V., Chuaykhun, J.: Book recommendation system based on course descriptions using cosine similarity. In: Proceedings of the 2023 7th International Conference on Natural Language Processing and Information Retrieval, pp. 273–277. NLPIR '23, Association for Computing Machinery, New York, NY, USA (2024). https://doi.org/10.1145/3639233.3639335
21. Ostendorff, M.: Contextual document similarity for content-based literature recommender systems (2020). https://doi.org/10.48550/arXiv.2008.00202
22. Plecháč, P., et al.: PoeTree. Poetry Treebanks in Czech, English, French, German, Hungarian, Italian, Portuguese, Russian and Spanish (2023). https://doi.org/10.5281/zenodo.10008459
23. Powney, J., Watts, M.: Interviewing in Educational Research. Routledge, London (2018). https://doi.org/10.4324/9780429503740
24. Prieto Rodríguez, M.A., March Cerdà, J.C.: Paso a paso en el diseño de un estudio mediante grupos focales. Atención primaria: Publicación oficial de la Sociedad Española de Familia y Comunitaria **29**(6), 366–373 (2002). https://dialnet.unirioja.es/servlet/articulo?codigo=7441050, publisher: Doyma Section: Atención primaria: Publicación oficial de la Sociedad Española de Familia y Comunitaria
25. Pozo, P., de la Rosa, J., Ros, S., González-Blanco, E., Hernández, L., de Sisto, M.: A bridge too far for artificial intelligence?: Automatic classification of stanzas in Spanish poetry. J. Assoc. Inf. Sci. Technol. **73**(2), 258–267 (2022). https://doi.org/10.1002/asi.24532
26. Ramada Prieto, L.: Esto no va de libros. Literatura infantil y juvenil digital y educación literaria. Ph.D. Thesis, Universitat Autònoma de Barcelona (2017). https://www.tdx.cat/handle/10803/460770
27. Ramada Prieto, L.: Ficción digital en las bibliotecas. Xarxa de Bibliotecs Municipals (2021)
28. Ramírez, C.G.: Prácticas de mediación de lectura literaria en el contexto escolar chileno: el quehacer del profesor mediador. Revista Sophia Austral **28**, 13–13 (2022). https://doi.org/10.22352/SAUSTRAL20222813
29. Santillan, M.C., Azcarraga, A.P.: Poem generation using transformers and doc2vec embeddings. In: 2020 International Joint Conference on Neural Networks (IJCNN), pp. 1–7 (2020). https://doi.org/10.1109/IJCNN48605.2020.9207442
30. Sarma, D., Mittra, T., Hossain, M.S.: Personalized book recommendation system using machine learning algorithm. Int. J. Adv. Comput. Sci. Appl. (IJACSA) **12**(1) (2021). https://doi.org/10.14569/IJACSA.2021.0120126
31. Çeliktürk Sezgin, Z.: Systematic analysis of digital reading studies in the digital age. Participatory Educ. Res. **9**(1), 233–250 (2022). https://doi.org/10.17275/per.22.13.9.1
32. Wayesa, F., Leranso, M., Asefa, G., Kedir, A.: Pattern-based hybrid book recommendation system using semantic relationships. Sci. Rep. **13**(1), 3693 (2023). https://doi.org/10.1038/s41598-023-30987-0
33. Wolf, T., et al.: Huggingface's transformers: state-of-the-art natural language processing (2020). https://arxiv.org/abs/1910.03771
34. Zhang, E.Y., Cheok, A.D., Pan, Z., Cai, J., Yan, Y.: From turing to transformers: a comprehensive review and tutorial on the evolution and applications of generative transformer models. Science **5**(4), 46 (2023). https://doi.org/10.3390/sci5040046

Designing a 1-Bit Button-Based Back-Channel Tool to Facilitate Communication in Junior High School Lectures

Hiromasa Tanaka[1], Tatsuya Fukumoto[2], Kengo Yamamoto[3], Tomoaki Higashino[4], and Shogo Fukushima[1(✉)]

[1] Kyushu University, Fukuoka, Japan
shogo@ait.kyushu-u.ac.jp
[2] Izumi Municipal Gosho Junior High School, Osaka, Japan
[3] NTT Communications Corporation, Tokyo, Japan
[4] Think Future English Academy, Osaka, Japan

Abstract. Active participation is essential for enhancing learning outcomes in lecture-style classes. However, existing Personal Response System (PRS) software to promote active participation is implemented on PCs, requiring teachers to temporarily pause the instruction to operate the computer. Similarly, students are required to engage in actions beyond listening, such as operating computers. To address these issues, we designed a system with single-function button input that eliminates the need for device operation during the lecture and provides feedback perceivable through peripheral vision. We first implemented the buttons in a junior high school English class for over a month and observed behavior. Based on our observations, instructions were designed to reduce the shyness associated with pressing the buttons. Additionally, we developed a feedback mechanism that presented audio with sound effects while preserving the anonymity of students. To verify the effectiveness of this system, we conducted a control experiment in an English cram school with junior high school students. The results suggested that the button system changed the communication style and adjusted the speed of class progress. Moreover, voice feedback improved the evaluation of empathy and a sense of unity.

Keywords: Collaboration · User Experience Design · Schools/Educational Setting · Empirical study

1 Introduction

In lecture-style classes, active participation is essential, to engage voluntarily in higher-order thinking, such as analysis and interpretation rather than passively listening to the lecture [5,26–28]. Personal response systems (PRS) have been studied widely as a tool for promoting active participation in lecture-style

B. K. Smith and M. Borge (Eds.): HCII 2025, LNCS 15806, pp. 158–174, 2025.
https://doi.org/10.1007/978-3-031-93564-0_10

classes [6,7,11,15,19,21]. Recently, various learning systems, such as moodle [6], clicker [19], and Kahoot [11], have incorporated this PRS functionality. This integration motivates diligent preparation for quizzes as students are prompted to respond through a wireless keypad [7]. Results have indicated that such students have scored 25% higher on post-class exams than students that did not use PRS [15]. Murphy and Riddle (2003) and others have broadly reviewed these technologies [21]; however, many user interfaces are either hardware or software implementations of numerous buttons, such as a wireless keypad, and students vote or submit responses to questions or problems posed by the teacher. This demands attention and cognitive resources to focus on the device within their central vision and perform the necessary operations.

To develop an interface that mitigate cognitive resources to device operation, we drew inspiration from Ishii's ambientROOM [17]. Ishii et al. proposed the concept of cognitively-background interactions as distinct from cognitively-foreground interactions. Applying this concept to the design of a PRS system, we defined back-channel communication as "communication that minimizes cognitively foregrounded operations and cognitive resource demands". To realize PRS through this back-channel communication, we designed a single-function 1-bit input-button user interface and a simple feedback system for the teacher that used only sound effects and uniform blinking of the screen to confirm whether the student was nodding while explaining. Sound effects were employed as feedback for the teacher as the content design of the sound effects could return a positive emotional response to the explainer. Although not used within a lecture setting, it has been suggested that introducing a button with a positive sound effect during brainstorming sessions can result in a shift in the emotions of participants in group work. Leading to more positive outcomes and a greater number of generated ideas [29]. Thus we believe that this effect could be introduced in a lecture format class as well.

This study introduced a button system in a lecture-style English class at a junior high school and an English cram school. This decision was prompted by the reluctance of students to take risks, engage in verbal expression, or share their ideas during class, a common phenomenon observed particularly in Japanese junior high and high school English classes [16]. The button was implemented as a software application with the intention of being deployed on a large scale in various schools (Fig. 1). This application was a single large button on the screen that enabled push-only interactions. The UI was designed to eliminate all elements from the screen except for the button. This design choice aimed to prevent students from being distracted by irrelevant elements on the tablet device. Recognizing the social pressure associated with drawing attention to oneself in a classroom setting, no audible feedback was generated from the student's terminal when the button was pressed. Instead, when a student activated the button, the teacher's tablet device flashed green at the top, and positive sound effects were emitted by the teacher's device. This was intended to subtly disrupt the classroom atmosphere, while maintaining the anonymity of the student.

The main contributions of this study are as follows:

- We designed a mono-functional reaction button with only one bit of information for a lecture-style class, based on our observations in a junior high school class. Upon pressing the button, the teacher's tablet device glowed green and a positive voice was played.
- The button system and visual and sound feedback were tested, via an evaluation experiment with a small class of junior high school students. Despite the less number of participants owing to COVID-19, almost all the participating students expressed positivity toward the system and continued to use it until the end of the class.

Fig. 1. Proposed one-channel reaction button system at a cram school.

2 Related Work

One approach that encourages students to participate independently is active learning. In the Think-Pair-Share [18] method, students think individually about a problem given by a teacher, discuss it in pairs, and share each pair's opinions with the entire group. This encourages independence by sharing opinions in class. In peer instruction [9], all students answer questions from the teacher individually, discuss them in groups with other students, answer them again, and listen to the teacher's explanations. Students answer questions asked by the teacher by indicating the number of fingers on their hands or by sending them on a clicker. This method motivates the students to explore their answers. In these approaches, each student speaks and provides reaction feedback to the teacher without the use of tools.

One system that enables teachers to immediately understand their students' understanding is multimodal learning analysis (MMLA) [3,4,10,23,24], which uses sensors to collect and analyze physiological and behavioral data from students. Studies have focused on its application in game-based learning [13] and conceptual models used in its implementation [12]. Further, studies have focused on providing feedback to teachers during class based on the analysis results, thus helping to identify students requiring support and enabling teachers to provide appropriate instruction [2]. However, there are barriers to classroom use because of the high cost of installing data-collection devices and concerns about student privacy from constant data collection during class [10,23]. In contrast, PRS [6,7,11,15,19,21] can be implemented at minimal cost and sends each student's response to the teacher. The Response Analyzer System [22] uses students' mobile phones to select and send their learning statuses. Clicker [19], which is used in peer instruction [9], enables students to select the answer they believe is correct in response to a teacher's question. Further, using PRS devices facilitates the parallel reception of responses from many students and enables them to react anonymously.

When students use the PRS, they select and press a button from a list of multiple buttons to answer a question or quiz. Burnstein et al. [7] studied the input from a physical keypad with 12 buttons used to answer questions during a lecture-style class; the Kahoot input method in the study by Dellos et al. [11] involved utilizing buttons on a web browser or app to answer quizzes. Regardless of the hardware or software nature of the buttons used for input, in these systems, the student observed the device or screen at hand, selected the button they wanted to press, and pressed it as if voting. In contrast, certain systems use a single button for discussion, such as Conversation Votes [1] and the Naruhodo Button [29]. These button systems react to the speaker's statements during group work or brainstorming situations; their single function eliminates the need to check and select a button. In this system, we used single-function buttons as input interfaces to send nod-like responses without assigning cognitive resources to device operations (Table 1).

The data collected via a button system enables teachers to monitor the status of all students through educational support software such as Moodle [6]. Teachers can view graphs of voting data and effectively adjust the class progress and content. Furthermore, sharing student data with an entire class supports independent student participation [7]. Studies have used such methods to visualize student voting data; however, this study adopted a simple feedback method wherein the top of the teacher's tablet device lit green. This enabled the teacher to check the student's level of understanding while remaining aware of his/her surroundings such that he/she could concentrate on his/her instruction. Although not a button system, CommentScreen [8] facilitates communication among students by displaying comments and pictograms sent by students on a lecture material screen in real time. In addition, iPlayer, which specializes in remote classes, aims to improve the sense of community and togetherness by showing slides and videos to which other students are paying attention. Pallof and Pratt [25] noted the importance of fostering a sense of solidarity among students in distance classes; we believe that this is equally important in in-person classes. In addition, the Naruhodo button used in group work has been suggested to induce a shift toward positive emotions owing to positive voice sound effects when the button is pressed [29]. We believe that sharing positive emotions induced by positive voices within the class may facilitate a sense of togetherness. We considered a feedback system wherein positive voice sound effects were emitted by the teacher's device when a student presses a button (Table 1). We examined the potential of this feedback to provide students with a sense of togetherness and evoke positive emotions.

Table 1. Comparison of tools

Method	Parallelism	Anonymity	Input	Output
Think-Pair-Share [18]	No	No	-	Voice
Clicker [19]	Yes	Yes	Multi-bit	Sight
CommentScreen [8]	Yes	Yes	Keyboard	Sight
Proposed System	Yes	Yes	1 bit	Voice

3 Participant Observation in a Junior High School Class

To clarify the rationale for designing a button system usable in actual classes, we introduced a prototype of the button system in a middle school class and collected video data, data from participant observations, questionnaires, and log data of button presses. Participant observation is a qualitative research method, wherein a researcher joins a society or group to observe and collect data.

This observation had two purposes. First, to investigate whether students used buttons in class. Second, to determine the impact of using sound as feedback for pressing buttons.

The following two research questions were examined in middle school.

- RQ1: *Did the students use the button system?*
- RQ2: *Did the students prefer to have sound feedback?*

3.1 Prototype Introduced in Junior High Schools

A single-function button prototype was designed for use in middle school classrooms. Sound feedback is sometimes used to evoke positive emotions [14]; hence, we used sound effects to create an atmosphere wherein the students could react easily. The sound effects emitted from the buttons were the same nine positive sounds as those emmited by the Naruhodo Button [29]. This button is a software that can be switched with or without sound.

Because of a request from the Board of Education that the classes should not become too entertaining, no sound was emitted from the buttons at the time of introduction. We chose software buttons because they are easy for teachers to manage on a daily basis.

Each student and student used student and teacher devices, respectively. When a student tapped the button in the middle of the screen (Fig. 2(a)), information about the button press, including the student's account name, was sent to the server, and the number of presses displayed on top of the student's device increased. Pressing the RESET button at the bottom left of the screen reset the displayed count. The teacher device received press information from the server every second (Fig. 2(b)).

The upper part of the teacher's device screen displayed a graph showing the number of button presses for the entire class and time on the vertical and horizontal axis, respectively. The account name, number of button presses in the last three minutes, and total number of button presses were displayed at the bottom of the screen.

After certain observation time, the effects of device size and sound effects necessitated an analysis; therefore, we prepared three sizes of devices and used them in class with sound effects. Herein, the sound effects originated from the device of the button that was pressed.

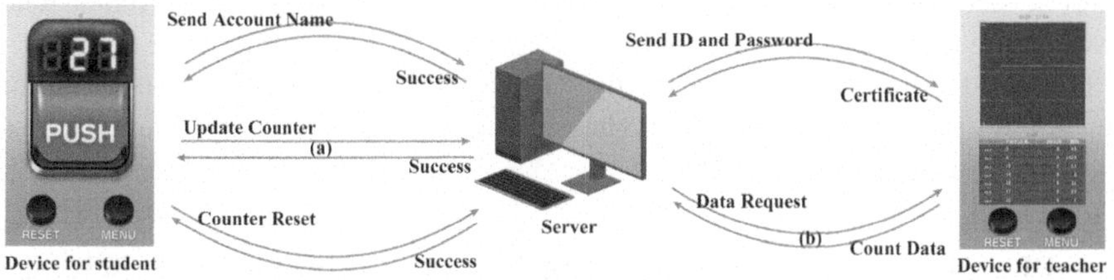

Fig. 2. Button System Configuration.

3.2 Methods

The prototype described in Sect. 3.1 was introduced for approximately one month starting from June 3, 2022, in the third-year second language (English) class at Gosho Junior High School in Izumi City.

Log data were collected using the button system from June 3rd to 16th to investigate its usage for participant observation. June 8th was excluded because log data could not be collected. During this period, the classes were divided into

Fig. 3. Desk Arrangement in the Classroom (Left) and Buttons (Top Right) and Classroom in Session (Bottom Right).

two groups according to proficiency level. Twenty students with an average score of 40 or higher for the previous year's test used the button system.

Participant observations were conducted on June 3rd, 6th, 7th, 16th, and July 4th. Consequently, the desk space was insufficient for placing buttons. To address this issue and for the investigation related to RQ2, on July 1st and July 4th, all classes with a total of 36 students participated; students used three different sizes of buttons (10.1, 6.53, and 2.5 in.) with sound as feedback when pressing the buttons.

For the timing of button pressing, the teacher informed the students that they should press the button when they thought "I see" as with the button used in group work [29].

3.3 Findings from the Implementation at the Junior High School

The data obtained from the observation, log data, questionnaire results, and the teacher's discussion regarding the button system after the class were transcribed and divided into three groups including those related to the button presses, sound from the buttons, and environment, using the online whiteboard application Miro [20].

Button Presses. An average of 93% students pressed the button at least once in each class. In a post-class questionnaire conducted on July 4th, when asked, "Did you hesitate to press the button at any point?" 80% responded with "No", with 20% responding "Yes". (Fig. 4). In the open-ended comments section of the questionnaire, one participant stated, "I do not know when I am convinced and

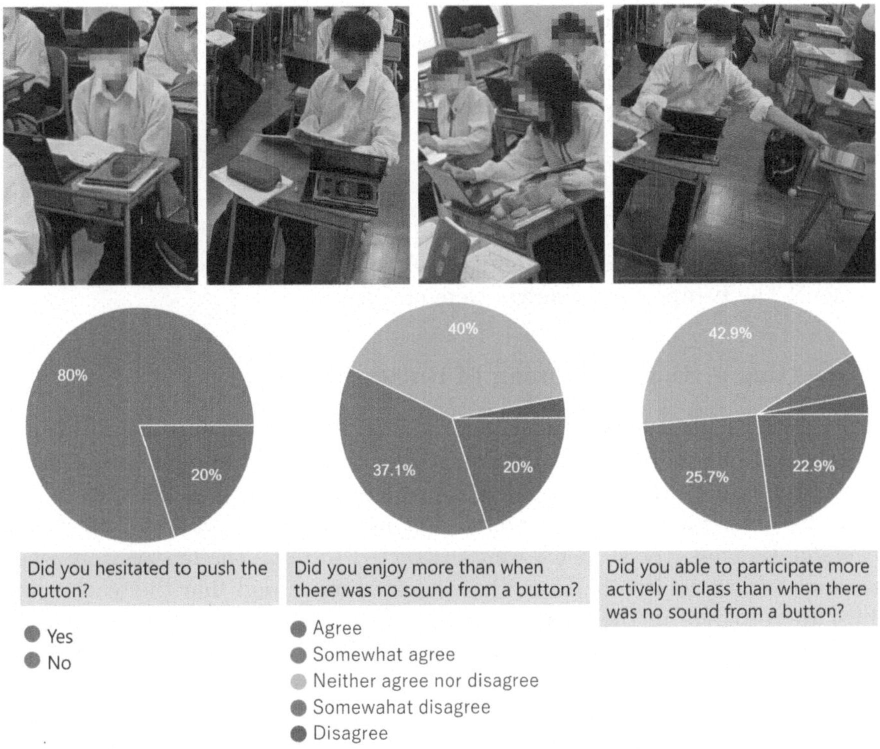

Fig. 4. Patterns of tablet placement. Desks in junior high schools are narrow, thus layouts need to be adjusted. (top). Questionnaire results. From left to right: hesitation to press, enjoyment when sound is present, and activeness when sound is present. (bottom).

when I should press the button", indicating that it can be challenging for certain students to determine the timing to press the button on their own.

Sound with Button. When the students were asked about their reaction to a voice from the button, they responded that they felt shame when the voice was played. During participant observation, there were instances when students turned off the volume on their devices and pressed the button.

Environment. As mentioned above, owing to limited desk space and the presence of other items, such as textbooks and notebooks, placing button devices on students' desks was challenging. During participant observation, the button device was often placed on an unused desk or hidden behind the devices used for class (Fig. 4).

Furthermore, when operating the button system, the student devices were charged for the total number of students. In this particular class, where the button system was introduced, each student already had one device. Thus, twice as many devices as the students required charging. When attempting to charge over 70 devices, some could not be charged owing to limitations in the school's charging environment.

4 Design

Based on our observations in middle school, we revised the button system used in school. The two primary changes were as follows:

4.1 Setting a Rule for Timing of Button Presses

In the junior high school, students were allowed to press buttons any time; however, certain students said that it was difficult to find the right time to press them. Therefore, in the experiment at the cram school, the teacher said, "*Press the button only when you understand. Not pressing it means that you do not understand*". Thus, the students were instructed to press the button only when they understood the lesson. Thus, the students understood that the teacher will adjust the progress of the class according to the students' button presses. We considered that as the progress of the class was adjusted by the students' pressing of the button, class ownership was with the students, thereby improving their understanding and satisfaction with the class.

4.2 Feedback Method Change

In the junior high school, students' button press information was sent to the teacher's tablet device; however, the tablet device was not shown to the students. Moreover, sounds were played by each student's device. Certain students expressed embarrassment when a sound was played when the button was pressed.

Hence, at the cram school, two tablets were placed front-to-back on the teacher's teaching table: one each for the teacher and student. In addition, the audio was played only from the teacher's tablet device and not from the student's device. We believed that this would enable us to provide feedback to students while maintaining their anonymity. This change allowed the students to receive button responses from students other than themselves. This could create a sense of empathy in situations such as "when I push the button with understanding, others push the button, too". We also believed that this would create a sense of community and unity among students in the same class.

5 System Evaluation in a Small Cram School Lesson

To verify the effectiveness of the improved button system described in Sect. 4, we conducted an experiment at to evaluate the system at THINK FUTURE English Academy, a junior high English cram school (Fig. 5). This experiment

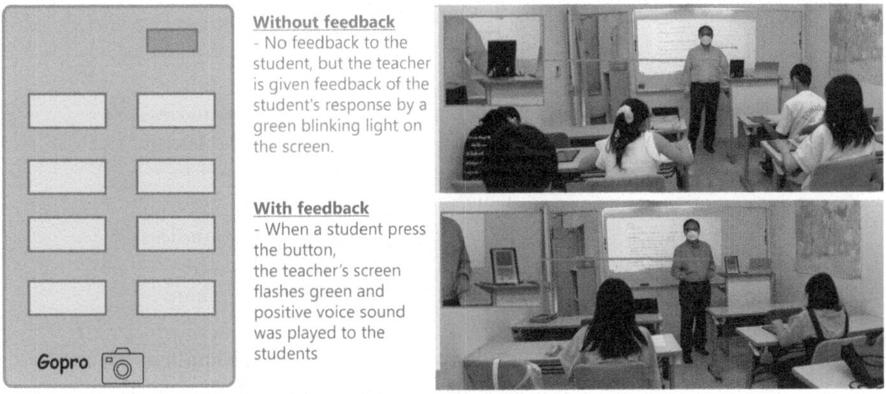

Fig. 5. Seating arrangement at the cram school and the feedback methods.

aimed to verify the effectiveness of a simple button system without audio or visual feedback (RQ1) and with audio and visual feedback (RQ2). Each research question was divided into three levels; this experiment determined the level that was reached.

- RQ1: Effectiveness of proposed button system
  - RQ1a (fluently press): *Did the button system encourage student responses?*
  - RQ1b (appropriate progression): *Did the feedback of the responses to the teacher facilitate appropriate adjustments in the speed of the class?*
  - RQ1c (understanding and satisfaction): *Did the system improve student understanding and satisfaction?*
- RQ2: Effectiveness of proposed visual and sound feedback to the students
  - RQ2a (awareness of the ambient feedback): *Did you become aware of other students' reactions?*
  - RQ2b (empathy): *Did the reactions of other students create a sense of empathy?*
  - RQ2c (a sense of unity): *Did the reactions of other students create a sense of community and unity among the students?*

All the lessons were in English, and the content of the lessons was equivalent to level 2 of "EIKEN", the English Proficiency test. All students were junior high school students, and the teacher had been teaching in the cram school for 37 years. The students were told before the lesson that the teacher's device confirmed that they had pressed the button, that they had to press the button in response to the teacher's confirmation of their level of understanding, such as "Press the button when you understand", and that the teacher would adjust the lesson progress according to the button presses. Lessons using the button system without feedback, using the button system with feedback, and without using the button system were held on September 3, 17, and 24, respectively. The

Table 2. Questionnaire 1

Evaluation	Question
Appropriate Progression	When you were using the soundless button, was the speed of the lesson appropriate for you compared to usual?
Understanding	When you were using the soundless button, did you understand the content of the lesson better than usual?
Satisfaction	When you were using the soundless button, were you more satisfied with the lesson than usual?

Table 3. Questionnaire 2

Evaluation	Question
Awareness of the ambient feedback	Did you know if others were pressing the button?
Empathy	Did you feel empathy for others pushing the button?
A sense of unity	Did you feel a sense of unity in the entire classroom?

total number of participants in the two groups was seven without feedback, four with feedback, and four without the button system.

Two questionnaires were administered for each research question. One was to be completed after all lessons (Questionnaire 1). The other questionnaire was answered after the students used the button with feedback during the lesson (Questionnaire 2). Questionnaire 1 was to be answered after both the with- and without-feedback conditions were experienced; therefore, it was asked after the completion of all the lessons. The questionnaire was rated on a 7-point Likert scale (7: strongly agree, 6: agree, 5: somewhat agree, 4: neither agree nor disagree, 3: somewhat disagree, 2: disagree, 1: strongly disagree).

6 Results and Discussion

Table 4 presents the visualized responses to the questionnaire on RQ1. Table 2 The responses to questions Q1, Q2, and Q3 on a 7-point Likert scale corresponded to appropriate progression, understanding, and satisfaction in the table. Red and blue cells indicate scores above and below 4, respectively. Table 4 shows that seven participants provided positive answers to all three questions, one participant provided neutral answers to Q1 and Q2, one participant provided

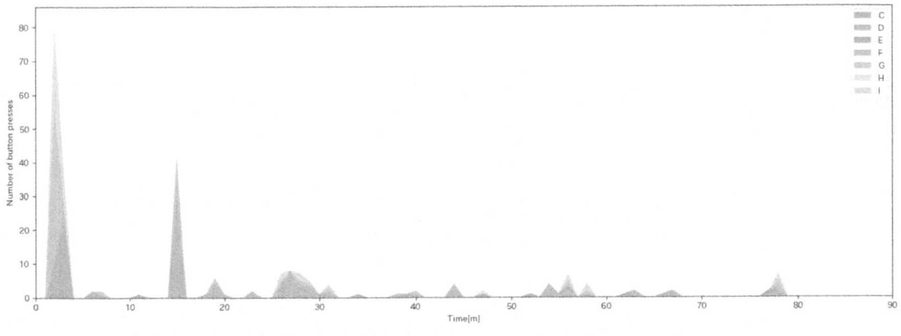

Fig. 6. Log data for seven students for the September 3 lesson.

positive answers to Q3 and the remaining two provided neutral answers. More than half of the experimental participants responded positively to all questions and no experimental participant responded negatively to any of the three questions; hence, the three-step goal of RQ1 was achieved.

Table 5 presents a visualization of the questionnaire for RQ2, similar to that in Table 4. The responses to questions Q4, Q5, and Q6 in Table 6 on a 7-point Likert scale correspond to visible, empathy, and a sense of unity, respectively, in Table 3. Red and blue cells indicate scores above and below 4, respectively. Participants C, D, and E responded positively to all questions, indicating that they achieved the three-step goal of RQ2. Participant H provided positive answers to Q4 and Q5, and neutral answers to Q6. This may indicate that RQ2-1 (visibility) and RQ2-2 (empathy) were achieved, but RQ2-3 (sense of unity) was not. Experimental participant K responded negatively to Q4 and Q5 and positively to Q6. We speculate that this was because Q4 and Q5 were questions about others pressing the button, whereas Q6 was a question about the sense of unity in the entire classroom created by pressing the button. Although Participant K did not directly empathize with others pressing the button, he/she may have felt a sense of unity when it was done many times during the lesson.

Table 4. Visualization of Questionnaire Results Regarding RQ1. Red and blue cells indicate scores above and below 4, respectively.

Participants	Presses	Progression	Understand	Satisfaction
A	9	6	6	6
B	10.5	6	6	6
C	10	6	6	5
D	56	6	6	5

6.1 RQ1a: Did the Button System Encourage Student Responses?

Figure 6 shows a stacked line graph of the log data from the lesson on September 3; each color corresponds to a different student. As the button was pressed from the beginning to the end of the class, it successfully prompted a response from the students. The timing of the button presses was the same among the students; thus, the buttons were pressed as per the teacher's confirmation of the students' understanding. Except at the beginning of the lesson, when the teacher instructed the students to press the button extensively to get accustomed to it, there were no extreme number of button presses. Thus, the buttons were not being used for purposes unrelated to the class; rather, they were used for the teacher's intended purpose.

During the lesson, there were changes in the teachers' remarks to the students to confirm their understanding. At the beginning of the lesson, the teacher asked, "Did you understand? Press it if you understand". However, in the middle of the same lesson, when the teacher said, "Do you understand?" Students pressed the buttons. The students started to press the button when the teacher said, "Do you understand?" Thus, rules for using the button system were established between the teacher and students during the lesson and these rules became familiar to the teacher and students. Thus, reactions to buttons influenced verbal communication.

6.2 RQ1b: Did the Feedback of the Responses to the Teacher Facilitate Appropriate Adjustments in the Speed of the Class?

The appropriate progress column in Table 4 presents the students' responses to the question, "When using the soundless button, did you understand the content of the lesson better than usual?"

The speed at which a class progresses is subjective and does not necessarily mean that the student will score high on a test, even if it is considered appropriate. Even if the actual progress is not appropriate for the student, the student can feel that he or she is influencing the progress of the class by regularly telling the teacher whether he or she has understood the lesson.

Table 5. Visualization of Questionnaire Results Regarding RQ2. Red and blue cells indicate scores above and below 4, respectively.

Participants	Visible	Empathy	A sense of unity
A	6	7	6
B	6	6	6
C	5	6	6
E	1	1	6

6.3 RQ1c: Did the System Improve Student Understanding and Satisfaction?

The understanding and satisfaction column in Table 4 presents the students' responses to the question, "When using the soundless button, did you understand the content of the lesson better than usual?" and "When using the soundless button, were you more satisfied with the lesson than usual?".

Comprehension was evaluated subjectively by the students, and it is unclear whether they understood the lesson content more deeply.

6.4 RQ2a: Did You Become Aware of Other Students' Reactions?

The awareness of the ambient feedback column in Table 5 presents the answers of the students to the question, "Did you know if others were pressing the button?".

The student-chosen "Uh-huh" was initially used as the feedback voice; however, this was changed to "I see" by the teacher in the middle of the lesson. In the lesson using the button system with feedback, students were observed pressing the button after checking that another student had pressed it, as if they were following others.

Table 5 shows that all but one student indicated that they knew whether another student was pressing a button in class with feedback.

6.5 RQ2b: Did the Reactions of Other Students Create a Sense of Empathy?

Table 3 shows the students' responses to the question, "Did you feel empathy for others pressing the button?" The reason for Participant E's reluctant response to the question about whether he empathized was most likely owing to a discrepancy in his response to the other students. In a class with buttons with feedback, there were times when other students were pressing the buttons; however, this student was not pressing the buttons; we speculate that when he did not understand the lesson content, the other students did, and he did not empathize.

6.6 RQ2c: Did the Reactions of Other Students Create a Sense of Community and Unity Among the Students?

Table 5 shows the students' responses to the question, "Did you feel a sense of unity in the whole classroom?".

In Q2 (Table 5), when asked, "When did you feel a sense of unity?" students responded "when other students pushed their buttons simultaneously". It is highly likely that other students' reactions led to a sense of unity.

7 Conclusion and Future Work

Students learn more by actively participating in class. Thus, in recent years, various active-learning methods have been developed. Many of these can switch to multiple UIs and modes depending on the class type, and input interfaces range from keyboards to mice. In contrast, we implemented a monofunctional reaction button with only one bit of information that could only be pressed as a single button in a lecture-style class. The button was implemented as a software application. This application was simply a large button on the screen, which could only be interacted with by pressing. The UI was designed to eliminate all elements from the screen except for the button; thus, the students were not distracted by the tablet device, which was not relevant to the class. To mitigate the social pressure associated with drawing attention to oneself in a classroom setting, no sound was played from the student's terminal when the button was pressed; however, a positive sound effect was played from the teacher's terminal, thereby enhancing empathy and a sense of unity in the classroom.

We conducted an evaluation experiment with a small class of junior high school students to test the effectiveness of this button system and the visual and sound feedback. Despite the less number of participants owing to COVID-19, almost all participating students were positive about the system and continued to use it until the end of the class.

However, many issues remain to be addressed, particularly because the small number of student participants in the cram school experiment did not facilitate statistical processing; future experiments will be conducted with a larger sample size. One interesting aspect of this button system is that the way in which the rules for using the buttons are determined can significantly change student behavior. In the junior high school experiment, the students were allowed to press the buttons freely without setting any specific rules; however, certain students were confused by unfamiliar devices; for example, because they did not know when to press the buttons. In contrast, in the cram school experiment, when the students were allowed a thorough practice of the rules on how to press the buttons before the experiment, they did not appear puzzled by the press. It is expected that the effectiveness of such a button system will vary significantly depending on the method of introduction by the teacher.

Acknowledgments. This work is supported by JST-Mirai Program Grant Number JPMJMI21D3, Japan.

References

1. Bergstrom, T., Karahalios, K.: Vote and be heard: adding back-channel signals to social mirrors. In: Gross, T., et al. (eds.) INTERACT 2009. LNCS, vol. 5726, pp. 546–559. Springer, Heidelberg (2009). https://doi.org/10.1007/978-3-642-03655-2_61
2. Bhattacharya, S., Shah, V.B., Kumar, K., Biswas, U.: A real-time interactive visualizer for large classroom. ACM Trans. Interact. Intell. Syst. **11**(1) (2021). https://doi.org/10.1145/3418529
3. Blikstein, P.: Multimodal learning analytics. In: Proceedings of the Third International Conference on Learning Analytics and Knowledge, pp. 102–106 (2013)

4. Blikstein, P., Worsley, M.: Multimodal learning analytics and education data mining: using computational technologies to measure complex learning tasks. J. Learn. Anal. **3**(2), 220–238 (2016)
5. Bonwell, C.C., Eison, J.A.: Active learning: creating excitement in the classroom. 1991 ASHE-ERIC higher education reports. ERIC (1991)
6. Brandl, K.: Review of are you ready to Moodle? Language Learning & Technology (2005)
7. Burnstein, R.A., Lederman, L.M.: Using wireless keypads in lecture classes. Phys. Teach. **39**(1), 8–13 (2001)
8. CommentScreen: Commentscreen (2022). https://www.commentscreen.com
9. Crouch, C.H., Mazur, E.: Peer instruction: ten years of experience and results. Am. J. Phys. **69**(9), 970–977 (2001). https://doi.org/10.1016/j.inffus.2009.01.002
10. Cukurova, M., Giannakos, M., Martinez-Maldonado, R.: The promise and challenges of multimodal learning analytics. Br. J. Edu. Technol. **51**(5), 1441–1449 (2020)
11. Dellos, R.: Kahoot! A digital game resource for learning. Int. J. Instruct. Technol. Distance Learn. **12**(4), 49–52 (2015)
12. Di Mitri, D., Schneider, J., Specht, M., Drachsler, H.: From signals to knowledge: a conceptual model for multimodal learning analytics. J. Comput. Assist. Learn. **34**(4), 338–349 (2018)
13. Emerson, A., Cloude, E.B., Azevedo, R., Lester, J.: Multimodal learning analytics for game-based learning. Br. J. Edu. Technol. **51**(5), 1505–1526 (2020)
14. Fukushima, S., Hashimoto, Y., Nozawa, T., Kajimoto, H.: Laugh enhancer using laugh track synchronized with the user's laugh motion. In: CHI'10 Extended Abstracts on Human Factors in Computing Systems, pp. 3613–3618. Association for Computing Machinery (2010)
15. Hake, R.R.: Interactive-engagement versus traditional methods: a six-thousand-student survey of mechanics test data for introductory physics courses. Am. J. Phys. **66**(1), 64–74 (1998)
16. Hammond, C.D.: Culturally responsive teaching in the Japanese classroom: a comparative analysis of cultural teaching and learning styles in japan and the united states. Kyoto Gakuen Univ. J. Econ. **17**(1), 41–50 (2007)
17. Ishii, H.: Tangible bits: towards seamless interfaces between people, bits and atoms. In: Conference on Human Factors in Computing Systems CHI/ACM Press (1997)
18. Lyman, F.: Think-pair-share: an expanding teaching technique. Maa-Cie Cooperative News **1**(1), 1–2 (1987)
19. Martyn, M.: Clickers in the classroom: an active learning approach. Educ. Q. **30**(2), 71 (2007)
20. Miro.com: Miro (2019). https://miro.com/
21. Murphy, P., Riddle, R.: Interactive Learning Tools and Techniques: Personal Response Systems, [resource guide]. Duke University Center for Instructional Technology (2003)
22. Nagaoka, K.: A response analyzer system utilizing mobile phones. In: Proceedings of the 4th IASTED International Conference on Web-Based Education (WBE'05), pp. 579–584 (2005)
23. Ngoon, T.J., et al.: An Instructor is [already] able to keep track of 30 students: Students' perceptions of smart classrooms for improving teaching & their emergent understandings of teaching and learning. In: DIS '23: Proceedings of the 2023 ACM Designing Interactive Systems Conference, pp. 1277—1292 (2023)
24. Olive Co., L.: La cause (2020). https://www.01ive.co.jp/

25. Palloff, R.M., Pratt, K.: Building learning communities in cyberspace: effective strategies for the online classroom. Jossey-Bass Higher and Adult Education Series, ERIC (1999)
26. Prince, M.: Does active learning work? A review of the research. J. Eng. Educ. **93**(3), 223–231 (2004)
27. Taba, H.: The dynamics of education. Harcourt, Brace (1932)
28. Weaver, R.R., Qi, J.: Classroom organization and participation: college students' perceptions. J. Higher Educ. **76**(5), 570–601 (2005)
29. Yoshida, N., Fukushima, S., Aida, D., Naemura, T.: Practical study of positive-feedback button for brainstorming with interjection sound effects. In: Proceedings of the 2016 CHI Conference Extended Abstracts on Human Factors in Computing Systems, pp. 1322–1328 (2016)

User-Centered Design for Career and Academic Motivation in Student-Athletes

Sanethia V. Thomas(✉), Jasmine McKenzie, Alaina Smith, and Juan E. Gilbert

University of Florida, Gainesville, FL 32607, USA
sanethiat@ufl.edu

Abstract. Student-athletes, especially football players, face unique challenges in balancing academics and athletics, often viewing sports as their only path to success despite less than 2% advancing to professional levels. To address this gap, "I AM PRO" was created as a career exploration tool to help these young athletes broaden their aspirations and academic focus, featuring a culturally relevant Embodied Conversational Agent (ECA) integrating advanced technology with career counseling strategies. Developed with principles from Human-Centered and Culturally Relevant Computing, the ECA reflects the characteristics and experiences of African American football players through tailored interactions, serving as a virtual mentor that guides personalized career exploration aligned with the National Career Clusters Framework and offering Individual Development Plans (IDPs) for various career paths. A mixed-methods approach evaluated the app's effectiveness, involving quantitative surveys and qualitative interviews with 79 participants from the Texas Youth Football Association, focusing on changes in athletic identity and career motivation. Participants reported a shift from an intense athletic identity toward increased academic motivation and awareness of diverse career options, with usability testing confirming that the app exceeded standards. This research highlights the need for culturally relevant career counseling technologies, demonstrating how tools like "I AM PRO" can empower under-served populations by promoting holistic development and advocating for integrating early career exploration in educational settings.

Keywords: User-Centered Design · Human Computer Interaction · Relevant · Natural Language Processing · Embodied Conversational Agent · Career Development · Athlete Development

1 Introduction

The lifestyle of a professional athlete is lavish and glamorized by news and media. Media has portrayed images that infuse catchphrases such as 'Be Like

B. K. Smith and M. Borge (Eds.): HCII 2025, LNCS 15806, pp. 175–194, 2025.
https://doi.org/10.1007/978-3-031-93564-0_11

Mike,' 'Bo Knows,' or 'Hoop Dreams,' to subconsciously instill hope in aspiring young athletes of "making it" to the professional level. Due to the overwhelming influence of media and imaging, aspiring athletes are swayed to concentrate more on athletic training and success [13]. Athletes who are trained for elite sports maintain a strong sense of self-efficacy in making it to the professional level. Within the African-American community, 70% of males believe with a high degree of certainty that they will have a career in sports, particularly in football and basketball [7]. Yet only 1.7% of college football players and 0.08% of high school players play in the NFL [5]. Lapchick stated, "the overemphasis on sports among Blacks and the obstacles for social mobility leads many young Black men on a 'treadmill to oblivion' which offers faint hopes of high-paying professional jobs for a select few [32]." According to the 2010 census, there are 30,000 Black physicians and only 3,500 Black professional athletes [8]. This concludes that Black males are more likely to become medical doctors than professional athletes. Yet, in some instances, sport is more glorified and time consuming than education.

Incorporating a preventative program with early adolescent student-athletes will provide many benefits. In the early adolescent years, students develop advanced reasoning skills and transition to high school, where they can begin to shape their career interests and their athletic abilities are trained for elite sports [3]. However, the cur-rent preventative programming resources for athlete development and sports retirement are targeted at college and professional athletes. Additionally, interventions are ad-ministered through in-person dialogue or paper-based, and if technology is used, the tools tend to be antiquated and/or challenging to implement [16]. Therefore, there is an opportunity to employ sophisticated technologies to develop a more robust preventative program to assist athletes with athlete development at the start of their athletic career.

Human-like conversational agents have been used to enhance educational, personal, and career development [1,14,23,30]. Conversational agents have expanded their roles to include motivators, mentors, learning companions, change agents, and life-long learning partners [15,47]. Recent advancements have shown that these agents can be powerful technological mediators that impact motivational outcomes such as self-efficacy and attitude change [6,10]. Additionally, research has shown that adolescent learners benefit from interacting with conversational agents more than adult learners [25]. Therefore, this research explores the concept of using conversational agents to motivate early adolescent football student-athletes, focusing on African American students, to prepare for life after sports retirement.

Most technology for athletes focuses on performance rather than career development, and traditional career counseling methods often fail to capture athletes' true aspirations [39,41]. This research aims to design, develop, and evaluate an innovative preventative program using an intelligent embodied conversational agent to help early adolescent African American football players explore career paths beyond sports. By incorporating culturally relevant design and leveraging the National Career Clusters Framework, the technology will create Individual

Development Plans with suggested courses and majors. The goal is to serve as an early intervention, guiding student-athletes in building a career identity and academic plan for their future. The research addresses the following four questions:

RQ1: Is I AM PRO a usable and engaging tool for early adolescent African American football players?
RQ2: Does I AM PRO help reduce over-reliance on athletic identity?
RQ3: Does I AM PRO increase academic motivation?
RQ4: Does I AM PRO improve career awareness and motivation?

2 Lit Review/Related Works

All athletes must transition out of sports, which can result in significant personal, social, and psychological challenges. Normative transitions are predictable events, such as progressing from junior to senior levels or retiring after achieving career milestones, while non-normative transitions are unpredictable and involuntary, often caused by injuries or unexpected termination from the sport. Regardless of the type, athletes who are unprepared for life after sports may experience depression, anxiety, and a loss of identity due to their reliance on the athletic role [11,21,33,42].

Athletic identity is described as the degree to which an individual identifies with the athletic role and looks to others for acknowledgment of that role [12]. Athletes with a strong athletic identity are considered individuals with identity achievement. These athletes are also influenced by their surroundings and thus settle in identity foreclosure without considering alternatives. Concurrently, early adolescent athletes are at a growth stage experiencing an identity moratorium.

Athletes who fail to explore their identity beyond sports often struggle during retirement [37]. They may face cognitive, emotional, and behavioral challenges, including adjustment difficulties, financial instability, and social or psychological issues, sometimes leading to depression or substance abuse [11,24,37]. Identity foreclosure, when athletes have a hard time identifying with anything outside of sports, further complicates this transition, as they define their self-worth solely through their athletic achievements [20]. This tunnel vision leaves little time to develop alternative skills, making career transitions difficult regardless of whether they are anticipated or sudden [46].

Historically, African-American athletes disproportionally face identity foreclosure due to societal and cultural pressures, such as the glamorization of sports as a path out of poverty. However, even though 70% African American male athletes believe that they will have a professional sports career, only 1.7% of college football players make it to the NFL. Therefore, preparing students with other options before this is important in helping them form other identities and career options outside of sports.

2.1 The Role of Technology in Career Development

Technology has become a unique and powerful influence on adolescent development. Using technology to develop career development resources can provide innovative, creative, and exciting tools that can be more engaging and impressionable for early adolescent athletes. Technology has contributed to an increase in brain placidity in terms of becoming more adaptable in response to the demands of the environment [18]. Adolescent learning has expanded as they have immediate access to content and information about any topic imaginable. Technology has allowed adolescents to effectively and critically evaluate data, synthesize content, and apply it to real-world problem-solving. Additionally, technology-enhanced learning can be more effective and efficient by incorporating a culturally relevant pedagogy, especially through interventions like Embodied Conversational Agents (ECA) than traditional methods that fail to engage students effectively [19].

ECAs are virtual agents that simulate human interaction through speech, gestures, and visual cues. They can increase engagement and motivation by mimicking human-like mentorship and create a trustworthy environment through relatable cultural and social characteristics. Incorporating cultural relevance in ECAs can align the technology with the user's cultural identity to improve relatability and perceived authenticity. For example, an African American student-athlete interacting with an ECA modeled after a professional athlete from their cultural background may feel more connected than one that does not reflect their background.

Some technological approaches have focused on sports career transitioning, including ReadyAthlete and GamePlan. ReadyAthlete is a mobile application designed to support the identity development of student-athletes. The application allowed student-athletes to receive messages on a variety of topics related to healthy identity development and measured changes in identity development. In the pilot study, 27 student-athletes received three texts weekly for 5 weeks. ReadyAthlete was beneficial for student-athletes because it allowed them to access information and guidance on their own time. It challenged them to think critically about their future selves, provided helpful action steps to implement in increasing identity, and reinforced positive steps [24].

GamePlan is a commercial software application. It is a platform designed for athletic departments to build athlete development within their program and develop relationships with potential employers for their student-athletes. Athletic directors can track engagement and performance through data analytics and an intuitive dashboard. There has not been formal peer-reviewed research on GamePlan, but their website has reported that over 40 colleges and universities use their system within their athletic department [34].

Although these applications have had some success, they only target college or professional athletes, excluding early adolescents. Additionally, within each, there is a lack of cultural specificity.

2.2 Culturally Relevant Computing

Culturally relevant cues (CRCs) in technology use a student's cultural background to enhance engagement and learning outcomes [6,19]. Ladson-Billings argued the academic success of African-American students has not been well nurtured due to a lack of cultural relevance [31]. Research suggests that culturally relevant teaching leads to higher motivation and academic success, particularly for African American students who often lack culturally inclusive curricula [12,31]. CRCs ensure that educational content is socially meaningful and tailored to the experiences of specific groups, making them valuable for African American student-athletes, who navigate both racial and athletic identities [13,16].

The life of a student-athlete is vastly different from the life of a non-student athlete [13,16]. Athletes have different demands, languages, practices, and traditions; generally, they have different cultures. African American athletes face unique challenges, including negative stereotypes that portray them as athletically gifted but academically inferior [17,26,28,29]. Educational institutions must combat these biases by integrating culturally responsive support systems [10,12,26,31]. Leadership programs have been developed to help Black athletes challenge stereotypes and embrace their identities, while initiatives like the National Urban Alliance provide customized training to enhance student-athlete well-being [2,38].

Embodied Conversational Agents (ECAs) have successfully incorporated CRCs to improve student engagement. Studies show that same-race ECAs foster stronger connections with Black students, as demonstrated in Project Mango, which used hip-hop and sports themes to teach mathematics, increasing student interest by 63% [22]. Similarly, programs like My Sports Pulse and virtual career fairs have leveraged sport-themed narratives to promote STEM education, with 75% of participants reporting satisfaction [35]. While ECAs have proven effective in education and career counseling, their application in athlete development remains under-explored. Future research should refine ECA design by considering appearance, personality, and motivational messaging to better support student-athletes' broader career aspirations beyond sports.

2.3 Early Adolescent Athletes

Most athletic development resources focus on college or professional athletes, but introducing career transition preparation in early adolescence (ages 11–14) may be more effective [43,45]. At this stage, students undergo significant cognitive and athletic development, shaping their academic and career trajectories as they transition into high school [40,43]. More specifically, early adolescent male athletes often engage in early specialization, an intense focus on one sport to maximize elite potential [12,27].

Neurological research shows that early adolescence is a critical period for cognitive growth, including advanced reasoning, abstract thinking, and 21st-century skill development such as critical thinking, problem-solving, communication, and adaptability [43,45]. Academic choices made during this period strongly influence long-term career paths, highlighting the need for career planning systems in middle schools to help students make intentional academic and career decisions [4,44]. Career exploration at this stage maximizes impact, fostering both athletic and academic development [16].

3 Design and Features of "I AM PRO"

This research utilized a user-centered approach to design and develop I AM PRO. I AM PRO is an intelligent intervention tool for career exploration targeted to African-American adolescent football athletes, whom, for this paper, will be referred to as "students." I AM PRO design includes culturally relevant cues related to football and the African-American football athlete. The system features an Embodied Conversational Agent (ECA), referred to as an "avatar," designed to represent a National Football League (NFL) player who transitioned from playing professional football to being a computer engineer. The ECA engages the student-athlete in a conversation about football and their career goals. Student-athletes can explore careers from the sixteen career clusters set forth by the National Careers Cluster Framework [13]. Students can also view former NFL players who have developed a career in each career cluster. Once students choose a career, an Individual Development Plan (IDP) of recommended courses in secondary school provides post-secondary education to the student-athlete. I AM PRO uses principles from Human-Centered Computing, Natural Language Interfaces, and Culturally Relevant Computing. The system incorporates cultural cues based on Impression Management and Social Cognitive Theory.

3.1 Key Features

At the start of the system, students are introduced to Coach Mike. Coach Mike is an avatar that is characterized as a football coach. He sets the tone for the session and explains the purpose of the study. Coach Mike serves as a guide and instructs the students on how to navigate the system. Anthony is the main avatar that interacts with the students. Anthony is characterized as an older peer who experienced playing in the NFL and is now a computer engineer. Anthony is programmed to control the conversation and has the ability to talk about football and careers. He is designed to be relatable and motivating. Anthony establishes the rules of interaction before the student engages in the conversation. Anthony starts the conversation by asking the student about their football experience as a way to establish rapport. He then encourages the students to view the career clusters and player profiles. Anthony concludes the conversation when the student has picked a career of interest.

After the students pick a career, they are given an Individual Development Plan (IDP). The IDP includes suggestive high school courses and college majors according to the career cluster. Coach Mike ends the session by thanking the student for their participation and encouraging them to do well in both school and football. At the end of the study, the student has an option to give verbal feedback through an in-person interview.

The design of I AM PRO incorporates several key elements to enhance engagement and effectiveness for African-American adolescent football players exploring career options. The system considers early adolescence, a critical developmental stage (ages 10–14), when students experience cognitive growth, define their athletic identity, and begin shaping their academic trajectories. Given that African-Americans comprise 68% of football players and 70% believe they will play professionally-though only 1.2% make it to the NFL—the intervention emphasizes cultural impact and shared experiences. Football's demanding schedule often limits career exploration, contributing to lower academic performance and graduation rates among African-American players.

To foster engagement, I AM PRO features "Coach Mike", an authoritative figure who provides credibility and guidance, and "Anthony", a peer mentor who represents a successful transition from the NFL to a career in software engineering. Their roles align with impression management, social cognitive theory, and mentorship principles. The system also implements structured interaction rules to minimize distractions and ensure meaningful dialogue. Rapport-building strategies, such as football-related discussions, help establish trust and maintain engagement, while situated dialogue ensures focused, goal-oriented conversations.

Career exploration is supported through the inclusion of 16 career clusters, based on industry standards from Advance CTE, and player profiles featuring former NFL athletes to reinforce career diversity. Additionally, a Career Cluster Plan of Study offers students a tailored roadmap for relevant high school coursework. The system concludes with a closing message that acknowledges students' participation and encourages future career planning, reinforcing key principles from social cognitive theory. Through these integrated elements, I AM PRO aligns with research-based strategies to enhance career identity, academic motivation, and self-efficacy among student-athletes.

Content and Design Decisions. I AM PRO is comprised of four content areas. The first and second content areas are the conversation elements of the avatars. The third content area is the National Career Clusters, and the fourth content area is the NFL player profiles.

Coach Mike represents the authority figure of one similar to a football coach. Coach Mike explains the purpose of the study, guides them through the system, and introduces Anthony. Coach Mike's voice is deep, and he has a no-nonsense yet welcoming personality. Coach Mike's script affirms and motivates the students.

Anthony represents an older peer or mentor who has played in the NFL and has a successful career. Anthony's voice is mid-tone, and he uses colloquialisms and football terminology to connect with the students. Anthony uses a guided conversation method to control the conversation.

Advance Career Technical Education (CTE) created the National Career Clusters. Advance CTE comprises state directors and state leaders responsible for secondary education across the United States [13]. There are sixteen career clusters. Each cluster contains an overall career description, sample occupations, pathways, and career-ready practices. According to the career cluster, the Individual Development Plan includes suggestive courses they can take yearly in high school and college majors.

The player profiles contain informational content of former football players who have pursued a career within a career cluster. The profile includes the player's name, a picture from playing in the NFL, a picture of his career, his college, the NFL team he played for, his position, NFL career highlights, and his current job title.

3.2 Design Iteration

I AM PRO was designed using the Interaction Design (ID) methodology framework, which emphasizes early-stage design to ensure user needs are met. The development process included personas, storyboards, wireframing, and a heuristic evaluation conducted by trained university students. The persona featured Michael, a 6th-grade African-American football player who believed football was his only path to success. The storyboard expanded on this, depicting how Michael discovered computer science through I AM PRO and gained confidence in planning his academic future. The heuristic evaluation assessed usability based on Nielsen's principles, leading to design refinements that improved system intuitiveness and user experience.

The interface design evolved through multiple iterations. The initial version allowed students to create an avatar and included motivational content but was not approved due to usability concerns. The second iteration introduced a peer-mentor avatar but was deemed unrelatable. The final iteration featured an avatar resembling a football-playing peer mentor, integrating National Career Clusters icons and a football arena background with a chalkboard overlay to balance sports and academics. This design, which aligned with usability standards and the target audience's expectations, was ultimately approved. Figure 1 is the final design.

I AM PRO Navigation. The researcher created three additional scenes to add to the experience of I AM PRO. Coach Mike dressed in a suit to reflect his professionalism. A backdrop of six football silhouettes with different team jerseys is a cultural cue of football. The picture of the football silhouettes came from Google stock photos. As the students navigate through the system, Coach Mike has different outfits to appeal to them in a more welcoming and relaxed way.

The I AM PRO navigation follows a structured sequence guided by Coach Mike. The first scene introduces Coach Mike, who welcomes students and explains the program. After clicking "Begin Now", students complete part one

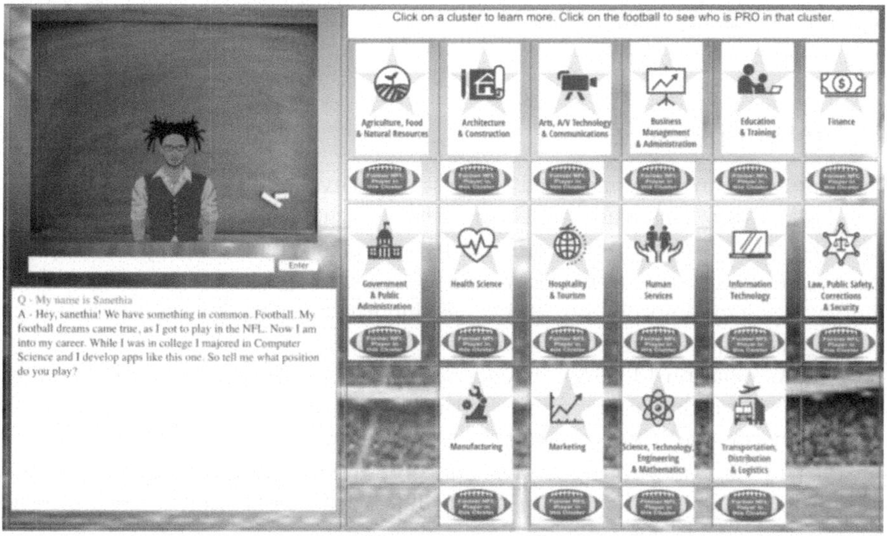

Fig. 1. Final Design of I AM PRO

of the pre-survey. The main navigation screen assigns students a random color, determining whether they take the AIMS or SAMSAQ survey first. After completing their respective survey, they return to the main screen and proceed to Step 2, where they interact with Anthony. Anthony then directs them to their assigned post-survey via a color-coded button. Upon completion, students return to the main screen, where Coach Mike guides them to Step 3 End, leading to the evaluation page. The session concludes with the System Usability Scale (SUS) survey and a thank-you message.

Software Design. I AM PRO is a web-based system built using Oddcast Media Technologies and Artificial Intelligence Markup Language (AIML), accessible through any internet browser. Developed with Flash-based ASP, JavaScript, HTML, and CSS, it features an interactive graphical interface supporting keyboard, mouse, and touchscreen inputs. The system leverages Oddcast's VHost Sitepal to create fully animated 2D avatars with real-time text-to-speech capabilities, enabling natural language interactions. AIML, developed by Richard Wallace, powers the conversational AI, using predefined and standard AIML files to generate user responses. The system architecture integrates the VHost SitePal interface, AIML Converter, Natural Language Speech Engine, and National Career Cluster database to deliver dynamic career exploration experiences. Unlike existing programs such as GamePlan and ReadyAthlete, which focus on college athletes, I AM PRO uniquely targets adolescent African-American football players, offering culturally relevant, interactive career guidance. It empowers students to explore careers, align high school courses with future aspirations, and engage in decision-making at a formative stage, setting it apart from other athlete development platforms.

4 Methodology

Purpose. Researchers conducted a user study to evaluate the impact and usability of I AM PRO. This study aimed to gather insights from students of the target population on the effectiveness of I AM PRO. The study aimed to provide quantitative and qualitative feedback from users to show positive effects on athletic identity, academic motivation, and career identity.

The researchers conducted the study in Austin, Texas, with the Texas Youth Football Association (TYFA). Texas was the desired location because it ranks the highest in producing top football athletes [36]. After receiving positive feedback in Austin, the Vice President of TYFA invited the researcher to replicate the study in San Antonio, Texas. The zip codes in San Antonio indicated a population from a higher socioeconomic status [9]. A total of 85 students volunteered to evaluate I AM PRO.

Participants. The study recruited students from TYFA during football team registration, with 56.6% African American (the target group), 28.9% Caucasian, 10.5% Hispanic, and the rest identifying as Hawaiian, Indian, or mixed. San Antonio had greater diversity, while both locations had a similar number of African American students. Due to technical issues, data from nine participants were excluded, leaving 76 evaluations (31 from Austin, 45 from San Antonio).

Most participants were early adolescents (11–12 years old), aligning with the Identity vs. Role Confusion stage of development. The majority (67.1%) were in 6th grade, followed by 26.3% in 7th and 6.6 in 8th. Since Texas schools use letter grades rather than GPA, students self-reported: 6.6% had straight As, 72.4% had A's and B's, 19.7% had B's and C's, and 1.3% had C's and D's. Three Austin participants reported they could not read, reflecting district data showing nearly half of African American students read below grade level by second grade.

Regarding football experience, 43.5% had played all their lives, 46% for a few years, and 10.5% were in their first year. Participants used touchscreen Lenovo Yoga laptops with headphones and accessed I AM PRO via Mozilla Firefox. The study included four online surveys (demographics, AIMS, SAMSAQ, SUS) and one in-person interview, administered through Qualtrics.

Instruments. Students completed four online surveys via Qualtrics and one in-person interview. The surveys included a demographics survey, the Athlete Identity Measurement Survey (AIMS), the Student-Athletes Motivation Towards Sports and Academics Questionnaire (SAMSAQ), and the System Usability Scale (SUS).

The demographics survey, designed by the researcher, included seven multiple-choice questions on race, grade, school performance, football experience, and career aspirations. It provided descriptive statistics and confirmed the study's target population. The AIMS survey, a 10-item, seven-point Likert scale with a Cronbach's alpha of .93, measured athletic identity and its variance based on race, football experience, and career aspirations. The SAMSAQ, modified for the target audience, assessed academic and career motivation using an 11-item, seven-point Likert scale (Cronbach's alpha = .82). The SUS, a widely used usability assessment tool (Cronbach's alpha = .92), measured the ease of use of I AM PRO on a 100-point scale, with scores above 68 indicating above-average usability. These surveys provided key quantitative insights into research questions on athletic identity, motivation, and system usability.

Procedure. The study was held at two Texas Youth Football Association (TYFA) registration sites. At each site, TYFA provided two tables, two tablecloths, ten chairs, and one support staff member for assistance. The researcher set up five laptop stations with headphones, as shown in the figure. There was a poster-sized flyer for the study on display at each site.

There were 34 teams at the first site and 90 teams at the second site. The support staff talked with the coaches about the opportunity for their players to use I AM PRO. The coaches communicated the message to the players and their parents. The researcher explained the study to those interested in participating, asked them if they had any questions, and instructed them to complete a consent form. Once the parent and the student completed the consent form, the student was assigned a color and escorted to a laptop station. The researcher started I AM PRO and instructed them to wear headphones. The students interacted with I AM PRO. Once the students were done using the system, the researcher asked if they would participate in an interview about the system. If the student agreed, the researcher conducted the interview. The session with I AM PRO was audio, video, and screen recording using Camtasia. The researcher recorded the in-person interviews using a Google Pixel. After the students completed the session, the researcher handed them a twenty-five dollar Amazon gift card for participating in the study.

Statistical Treatment. The power analysis revealed a sample size estimation of thirty-four to affect the statistical analysis. Each student had forty-five data points. The independent variables were location, race, grade, and academic performance. A p-value of ff 0.05 was used for all inferential statistical analyses. Error bars in all figures show 95% confidence intervals. Results may be imprecise because students expressed challenges in comprehending the survey questions, and some students pacified the questions. Additionally, researchers observed that some students haphazardly answered the survey questions by creating patterns with the dots.

The researcher used Qualtrics, Google Analytics, and IBM SPSS Statistics to analyze the quantitative data. The initial results on the SUS showed a bimodal distribution. Therefore, the data was transformed to a normal distribution using percentile ranking. The inverse distribution function was used to compute normality. A 95% Confidence Interval was constructed to determine the SUS's statistical significance. An independent t-test was performed to determine the statistical significance of the AIMS and SAMSAQ. To analyze the qualitative data, the researcher transcribed the audio files and conducted a content analysis. The content was coded and categorized, and assertions were derived from the students' responses [4].

5 Results and Discussion

The experimental design used a mixed-methods approach. The analysis consisted of data from the SUS, AIMS, SAMSAQ, and SUS surveys and the in-person interview. Two graduate students in the Computer and Information Science and Engineering Department at the University of Florida crossed-referenced the results.

5.1 Quantitative Analysis

System Usability Scale. Seventy students completed the SUS with an average score of 69.8 (SD = 12.6, min = 42.5, max = 95), above the average score of 68. The score indicates that I AM PRO is a usable tool. The most frequent SUS scores were 62.5 and 80.0, given by nine students for each score. A Shapiro-Wilks test ($p < .05$) and a visual inspection of the bimodal histogram in the figure confirmed that the SUS scores were not normally distributed. The critical t-value of 1.9955 at 0.05 yielded a margin of error 3.03. Therefore, the 95% CI is (66.77, 72.83). Since the national average SUS score of 68 falls within this CI, the mean SUS score of 69.8 for I AM PRO is not statistically different from the national average.

Athletic Identity. Athletic Identity refers to the degree of strength and exclusivity a person identifies with the athlete role. Athletic Identity can also be defined as giving special attention to sports relative to other activities. The athletic identity score provides insight into reasons for the lack of participation in different activities, such as education and social interactions [17]. Students with a low athletic identity score identify themselves in other roles outside of an athlete. This study produced a Cronbach's Alpha score of .805. Seventy is the highest score one can achieve on the AIMS. The population's mean score for football athletes is 52. The mean total score for this study was (M = 46.00, SD = 10.8). =The mean total score is six points below the population average, resulting in a low athletic identity.

An independent sample t-test was conducted to determine whether students who used I AM PRO (M = 49.51 SD = 9.93) had a lower athletic identity than students who did not use I AM PRO (M = 41.91, SD 11.16). The groups did not differ significantly $t(25) = .781$, $p = .442$. The mean for students who used I AM PRO was not statistically significantly lower than students who did not use I AM PRO.

Academic Motivation. Academic motivation refers to how students are motivated toward academic-related tasks. Academic motivation is a significant factor in predicting grade point averages. SAMSAQ was used to understand students' academic motivation better. The highest score for SAMSAQAM is 42. This study produced a Cronbach's Alpha of .544. The mean total score for this study was ($M = 35.71$, $SD = 4.62$).

An independent sample t-test was conducted to determine whether students who used I AM PRO ($M = 36.80$ $SD = 4.97$) had higher academic motivation than students who did not use I AM PRO ($M = 34.80$, $SD = 4.39$). The groups did not differ significantly $t(54) = -1.129$, $p = .264$. Although the score was a bit higher, the mean for students who used I AM PRO was not statistically significantly higher than for students who did not use I AM PRO.

Career Motivation. Career Motivation refers to how motivated participants were to obtain a sports career. The questions measure how motivated participants were in obtaining a career outside of sport. The highest score for career motivation is 35. To better understand student-athletes' career motivation, they were evaluated using the SAMSAQCM survey. The Cronbach's Alpha score was .099. The mean total score for this study was ($M = 30.85$, $SD = 8.35$).

An independent sample t-test was conducted to determine whether students who used I AM PRO ($M = 31.29$ $SD = 11.78$) had higher career motivation than students who did not use I AM PRO (M 30.46, SD 2.90). The groups did not differ significantly $t(64) = .385$, $p = .702$. Although the score was a bit higher, the mean for students who used I AM PRO was not statistically significantly higher than for students who did not use I AM PRO.

5.2 Qualitative Analysis

System Usability Scale. The in-person interview was conducted after the session with I AM PRO. The researcher asked three reflective questions about their experience and whether they would recommend I AM PRO to their friends. The goal of the interview was to gain verbal feedback on the students' perception of I AM PRO, measure students' increase of awareness of the careers, and gather suggested improvements for I AM PRO. The interview was voluntary. Twenty-two students agreed to participate in the interview. Students who did not volunteer for the interview were camera shy, rushed by their parents, or eagerly wanted the $25.00 gift card.

The first question in the interview, "What did you think about the system?" revealed that I AM PRO helped students think about their future and increased their career motivation. Responses were categorized into three main codes: Thought-Provoking, Educational, and Helpful. Many students found the system thought-provoking, encouraging them to consider careers beyond professional football, with comments like, "It made you think about football and school" and "Think about the future." Students also reported learning valuable information about their educational and career options, such as, "I learned a lot that I didn't know" and "I learned about what I can do after my football career." The system was viewed as helpful in guiding students toward future goals, with responses like, "It helped me want to know what I want to do when I get older so I won't struggle." In summary, I AM PRO was effective in broadening students' career awareness and motivating them to think beyond athletics.

The second question was: Did you learn about something you did not know before?" The two principal codes were Careers and Possibility. In terms of careers, students responded with the names of the career clusters they learned about. Regarding the possibility, some students did not know they could be professional football players and have another career. One student said, "I didn't know a football player could be an engineer." Another student said, "I did not know football players could be astronauts." The key assertion derived from these responses is: "I AM PRO taught students about careers and enlightened them that they could have a professional sports career and another career. Students became aware that they could do both. Therefore, the dream of becoming a professional football player is not crushed, and they are more prone to develop another career path. This attributes to a decrease in athletic identity.

The third question was: "How would you improve the system?" The three codes were No Improvements, Careers, and Features. The majority of the students said the system did not need any improvements. One student said, "I think it's perfect." Another student said, "There's nothing to improve." A couple of the students said the system needed more information about the careers and more career options. One student indicated the system needed better graphics. The key assertion derived from these responses is: "Students liked I AM PRO. The system can be improved by offering more careers and enhancing the graphics."

Question Added to SUS. An open-ended question was added to the end of the System Usability Scale (SUS) to help interpret the SUS scores and provide additional insights. This question asked students for their overall thoughts on I AM PRO. The key assertion derived from their responses was that students liked I AM PRO, found it easy to use, and believed it was helpful for learning about careers. Many students used positive language to describe the system, with responses categorized into three main codes: Like, Helpful, and Easy. In terms of Like, students used phrases like, "It is a cool way to help what you want to be in the future" and "It's pretty LIT," indicating they had a positive impression of the system. Regarding Helpful, students shared that I AM PRO aided in career planning and academic achievement, with comments such as, "It helped me think about some options if I don't go pro" and "I think I AM PRO would help kids get their career choices accomplished." Lastly, for Easy, students found the system user-friendly, with remarks like, "It is easy and fun to use" and "I thought it was very easy to use." In summary, students viewed I AM PRO as a useful, easy-to-navigate tool for career exploration and academic support.

6 Discussion

This work evaluated the effect of I AM PRO on usability and academic and career motivation in early adolescent African-American student-athletes. This work aimed to develop an intelligent career exploration tool for student-athlete football players. Specifically, this work focuses on designing, implementing, and evaluating I AM PRO, which allows student-athlete football players to identify a career path for life after sport. The system design was inspired using three constructs. First, the researcher used a Human-Centered Computing approach and interface design principles and tools to develop the system; second, the system leveraged design principles for developing Embodied Conversational Agents; third, the system encapsulated culturally relevant pedagogy.

I AM PRO is easily accessible through a web browser, and the interface is multi-modal to support text and audio interactions. The system architecture included licensing software, SitePal, to develop the avatar. The researcher used the Artificial Intelligent Markup Language (AIML) to program the avatar. The National Career Clusters informed the content of this work. The evaluation consisted of capturing qualitative and quantitative results through pre and post-online surveys and an in-person interview.

Early adolescent African-American football players consider I AM PRO a usable tool based on the SUS score and the qualitative analysis. The SUS score revealed the student-rated usability was above average. Many students verbalized that I AM PRO helped them learn about careers and think about their future. Most of them said they liked the system and would recommend it to their friends. Students expressed in the survey and the interview that I AM PRO effectively identified a career outside of sport. One student stated that I AM PRO helped him realize that he must be good in school and sports.

The student's qualitative responses were positive regarding career motivation for I AM PRO. A couple of students were shocked to know that an athlete could be a football player, astronaut, or engineer. Students reported that I AM PRO introduced careers to them that they did not know previously, and there were instances where students switched careers once they explored other career clusters. Students who initially wanted to pursue a career solely in professional sports were encouraged to explore alternate careers.

6.1 Implications

This work contributes to three areas: Human-Computer Interaction, Athlete Development, and Education.

Human-Computer Interaction Findings inform the design recommendations for specialized groups such as adolescent student-athletes. Aligned with previous research, we recommend that the Embodied Conversational Agent represent the same race as the user or the predominant race in that sport, paying particular attention to hair, facial features, and clothing. Additionally, we recommend that the ECA be credible and authentic. Within I AM PRO, the ECA shared his biography of playing professional sports and emphasized the importance of an alternate career. We also recommend using culturally relevant cues with the same interest as the user. For instance, in I AM PRO, we used the football theme for the background, icons, and football vernacular for communication flow. Strategically, we incorporated a chalkboard in the background to give a sense of the seriousness of education and work, and his character reflected an everyday look within the NFL. Regarding pedagogy, we recommend the ECA initially develop rapport on a shared interest with the user. This allows the user to open and share things that are important to them. Developing a common ground provides a smooth transition, increased engagement, and promising results. Our final design recommendation is to incorporate known role models poised as the ECA or featured in another part of the system. I AM PRO uses professional football player profiles within each career cluster to motivate and encourage student-athletes to a promising life after they retire from the sport.

Athlete Development This research presents an option for having innovative tools for academic and career development customized by sport. Through the research methodology, we offer insights and recommend academic and career interventions for athletes starting in their early adolescent years when they begin forming their identities. Incorporating a value system by emphasizing the importance of career exploration using a culturally relevant pedagogy provides an engaging way to motivate athletes.

Education There is a significant concern about African-American athletes' academic performance and graduation rates. I AM PRO is a model system that demonstrates an effective strategy for preventative programming. This research has shown effectiveness with students with low comprehension and academic achievement. Students were engaged and expressed an increase in academic motivation. I AM PRO is a multi-modal intervention tool that can reach students who may have challenges when it comes to academics.

6.2 Future Work

First, this research could progress into a longitudinal study by incorporating career development activities and monitoring students' progress each year until graduation. The results will aim to impact grade point averages and graduation rates. Second, additional system developments can be made to feature more information on each career: salary, functions, career path, colleges, and companies. Third, since most students report that parents help them choose career goals, developments can be made to incorporate a parental component into the system. Fourth, design, develop, and evaluate tools on a lower-grade reading level to accommodate all students. Finally, I AM PRO can be designed to target other sports student-athletes and even expand to non-sport students.

6.3 Limitations

This study faced several limitations that may have impacted the results. A last-minute change in the experiment design reduced student interaction with I AM

PRO from two sessions to one, limiting exposure and potential effects on athletic identity, academic motivation, and career exploration. Additionally, some students struggled with reading comprehension, affecting survey accuracy, while others rushed through the session due to time constraints or parental pressure. Technical and internet issues resulted in data loss, and the National Career Clusters content proved overwhelming for students to process on a single page. Some desired careers were not represented in the system—one student, for instance, wanted to be a cowboy—while career cluster selection was sometimes influenced by icons rather than genuine interest, with many students choosing Finance simply because of the dollar bill symbol.

7 Conclusion

Findings inform design recommendations for adolescent student-athletes. Consistent with previous research, we recommend that the Embodied Conversational Agent (ECA) match the user's race or the predominant race in that sport, with attention to hair, facial features, and clothing for authenticity. The ECA should be credible, as demonstrated in I AM PRO, where it shared its professional sports background while emphasizing the importance of alternate careers.

Culturally relevant cues should align with the user's interests; I AM PRO incorporated a football-themed background, icons, and vernacular to enhance engagement. A chalkboard was added to reinforce the importance of education. Additionally, ECAs should build rapport by establishing shared interests, fostering trust and engagement. Finally, incorporating known role models as ECAs or elsewhere in the system—such as I AM PRO's inclusion of professional football player profiles—can further motivate student-athletes toward post-sports careers.

This research also presents an option to have innovative tools for academic and career development customized by sport. Through the research methodology, we offer insights and recommend academic and career interventions for athletes starting in their early adolescent years when they begin forming their identity. Incorporating a value system by emphasizing the importance of career exploration using a culturally relevant pedagogy provides an engaging way to motivate athletes.

Finally, there is a major concern within the education of academic performance and graduation rates of African-American athletes. I AM PRO is a model system that demonstrates an effective strategy for preventative programming. This research has shown effectiveness with students with low comprehension and academic achievement. Students were engaged and expressed an increase in academic motivation. I AM PRO is a multi-modal intervention tool that can reach students who may have challenges when it comes to academics.

Acknowledgments. Financial support for this study was provided by the National Science Foundation Graduate Research Fellowship Program (NSF GRFP). The authors wish to thank Dr. Juan E. Gilbert for his support and guidance, the Texas Youth

Football Association for allowing us to conduct the study, and the Human Experience Lab for help with research and analysis.

References

1. Abdullah, A., et al.: Pedagogical agents to support embodied, discovery-based learning. In: Beskow, J., Peters, C., Castellano, G., O'Sullivan, C., Leite, I., Kopp, S. (eds.) Intelligent Virtual Agents: 17th International Conference, IVA 2017, Stockholm, Sweden, August 27-30, 2017, Proceedings, pp. 1–14. Springer International Publishing, Cham (2017). https://doi.org/10.1007/978-3-319-67401-8_1
2. National Urban Alliance. 2014. Ncaa/aasp/nua scholar athlete transformation initiative. (2014). https://www.nuatc.org/our-work/nua-higher-educationstudent-athletes/
3. Ashby Plant, E., Baylor, A.L., Doerr, C.E., Rosenberg-Kima, R.B.: Changing middle-school students' attitudes and performance regarding engineering with computer-based social models. Comput. Educ. **53**(2), 209–215 (2009). https://doi.org/10.1016/j.compedu.2009.01.013
4. Bangor, A., Kortum, P., Miller, J.: Determining what individual sus scores mean: adding an adjective rating scale. J. Usability Stud. **4**, 114–123 (2009). http://uxpajournal.org/wp-content/uploads/sites/8/pdf/JUS_Bangor_May2009.pdf
5. Barber, R.: NCAA student-athlete commercial (2011). https://www.youtube.com/watch?v=9UzO4DJBoWw
6. Baylor, A.: Beyond butlers: intelligent agents as mentors. J. Educ. Comput. Res. **22**(4), 373–382 (2000). https://doi.org/10.2190/1EBD-G126-TFCY-A3K6
7. Beamon, K.K.: Are sports overemphasized in the socialization process of African American males? A qualitative analysis of former collegiate athletes' perception of sport socialization. J. Black Stud. **41**(2), 281–300 (2010). https://doi.org/10.1177/0021934709340873
8. Beamon, K., Bell, P.A.: Academics versus athletics: an examination of the effects of background and socialization on African American male student athletes (2025). https://psycnet.apa.org/record/2006-09170-003
9. BestPlaces: comparison: san antonio, Texas - Austin, Texas (2015). https://www.bestplaces.net/compare-cities/san_antonio_tx/austin_tx/economy
10. Bickmore, T., Cassell, J.: Relational agents. In: Proceedings of the SIGCHI Conference on Human Factors in Computing Systems (2001). https://doi.org/10.1145/365024.365304
11. Brandt, T., Harmsen, N., Walsh, A., Bonura, K., Galli, N.: Career transitions in sport athletic identity and transitions. Soc. Sport, Exercise Perf. Psychol. **4**, 1 (2016)
12. Brewer, B., Van Raalte, J., Linder, D.: Athletic identity: Hercules' muscles or Achilles heel? Int. J. Sport Psychol. **24**(2), 237–254 (1993)
13. Tim Carmody. Athletes are different from you and me (2010). https://kottke.org/10/08/athletes-are-different-from-you-and-me
14. Cassell, J., Bickmore, T., Campbell, L., Vilhjálmsson, H., Yan, H.: Human conversation as a system framework: designing embodied conversational agents. The MIT Press eBooks, pp. 29–63 (2000). https://doi.org/10.7551/mitpress/2697.003.0004
15. Clore, G.L., Ortony, A.: Psychological construction in the OCC model of emotion. Emot. Rev. **5**(4), 335–343 (2013). https://doi.org/10.1177/1754073913489751

16. Advance CTE. Career exploration in middle school: setting students on the path to success. Assoc. Career Tech. Educ. (ACTE) (2017). https://careertech.org/resource/career-exploration-in-middle-school-setting-students-on-the-path-to-success/
17. Akilah R Francique. Black female collegiate athlete experiences in a culturally relevant leadership program. Black College Athlete and Culturally Relevant Program **7**(2), 87–106 (2013). https://www.researchgate.net/publication/267026428_Black_female_collegiate_athlete_experiences_in_a_culturally_relevant_leadership_program
18. Giedd, J.N.: The digital revolution and adolescent brain evolution. J. Adolesc. Health **51**(2), 101–105 (2012). https://doi.org/10.1016/j.jadohealth.2012.06.002
19. Gilbert, J.E., Arbuthnot, K., Hood, S., Grant, M.M., Eugene,W.: Teaching algebra using culturally relevant virtual instructors. Int. J. Virtual Reality **7**, 21–30 (2008). https://www.researchgate.net/publication/220222148_Teaching_Algebra_Using_Culturally_Relevant_Virtual_Instructors
20. Gordon, S., Lavallee, D.: Career Transitions. The New Sport and Exercise Psychology Companion, pp. 567–582 (2012)
21. Gordon, S., Lavallee, D.: Career transitions. Abertay University, pp. 567–582 (2011). https://rke.abertay.ac.uk/en/publications/career-transitions
22. Gosha, K.: Supplemental instruction animations to teach introductory college mathematics for student-athletes. Int. J. Adv. Res. Comput. Commun. Eng. ISO Certified **3297**, 6 (2017). https://doi.org/10.17148/IJARCCE.2017.6601
23. Gosha, K.: The application of embodied conversational agents for mentoring african american stem doctoral students (2025). https://open.clemson.edu/all_dissertations/1099/
24. Harris, P.C., Pusser, B., Kelly, D., Hull, M., Desmond, R.: Identity promoting identity development in student athletes: there's an app for that. **2**(2), 34–55 (2018). https://www.researchgate.net/publication/328858037_Identity_Promoting_Identity_Development_in_Student_Athletes_There
25. McGraw Hill. Avatars and instruction: how pedagogical agents can improve digital learning (2017). https://medium.com/inspired-ideas-prek-12/avatars-and-instruction-how-pedagogical-agents-can-improve-digital-learning-e7930f3b1e01
26. Hodge, S., Burden, J., Robinson, L., Bennett, R.: Theorizing on the stereotyping of black male student-athletes: issues and implications. J. Study Sports Athletes Educ. **2**(2), 203–226 (2008). https://doi.org/10.1179/ssa.2008.2.2.203
27. Jayanthi, N., Pinkham, C., Dugas, L., Patrick, B., LaBella, C.: Sports specialization in young athletes. Sports Health Multidisc. Approach **5**(3), 251–257 (2013). https://doi.org/10.1177/1941738112464626
28. Jones, B.W.: Success is required: the experiences of high-achieving black male football players at predominantly white division 1 institutions in the south (2015). https://mavmatrix.uta.edu/edleadershippolicy_dissertations/122/
29. Keith, H.C., Lawrence, S.M.: Female and male student athletes' perceptions of career transition in sport and higher education: a visual elicitation and qualitative assessment. J. Vocat. Educ. Training **56**(4), 485–506 (2025). https://eric.ed.gov/?id=EJ753705
30. Kerry, A., Ellis, R., Bull, S.: Conversational agents in e-learning. In: Allen, T., Ellis, R., Petridis, M. (eds.) Applications and Innovations in Intelligent Systems XVI, pp. 169–182. Springer, London (2009). https://doi.org/10.1007/978-1-84882-215-3_13
31. Ladson-Billings, G.: Toward a theory of culturally relevant pedagogy. Am. Educ. Res. J. **32**(3), 465–491 (1995). https://doi.org/10.3102/00028312032003465

32. Lapchick, R.E.: Fractured Focus. Free Press (1986)
33. Lavallee, D.: Theoretical perspectives on career transitions in sport. In: Lavallee, D., Wylleman, P. (Eds.) Morgantown, WV (2000). https://rke.abertay.ac.uk/en/publications/theoretical-perspectives-on-career-transitions-in-sport
34. McCaffrey, V.: Game plan (2017). https://www.wearegameplan.com/
35. Metcalf, D., Milrad, M., Cheek, D., Raasch, S., Hamilton, A.: My Sports Pulse: increasing student interest in STEM disciplines through sports themes, games and mobile technologies. In: Proceedings - 5th IEEE International Conference on Wireless, Mobile, and Ubiquitous Technologies in Education, WMUTE 2008, pp. 23–30 (2008). ISBN: 0769531083. https://doi.org/10.1109/WMUTE.2008.38
36. New, J.: Racial Gaps in the Power 5 (2016). https://www.insidehighered.com
37. Evelyn Monteal Oregon. An examination of athletic identity and identity foreclosure among male collegiate student-athletes (2010). https://cdr.lib.unc.edu/concern/dissertations/qf85nc52f
38. DISC Profile. What is disc (2021). https://www.discprofile.com/what-is-disc
39. Samuel, R.D., Tenenbaum, G., Mangel, E., Virshuvski, R., Chen, T., Badir, A.: Athletes' experiences of severe injuries as a career change event. J. Sport Psychol. Action **6**(2), 99–120 (2015). https://doi.org/10.1080/21520704.2015.1012249
40. Sanders, R.A.: Adolescent psychosocial, social, and cognitive development. Pediatrics Rev. **34**(8), 354–359 (2013). https://doi.org/10.1542/pir.34-8-354
41. Stambulova, N.: To Plan or Not to Plan: The Five-Step Career Planning Strategy. Halmsted University, Sweden, Tech. rep (2014)
42. Taylor, J., Ogilvie, B.C.: A conceptual model of adaptation to retirement among athletes. J. Appl. Sport Psychol. **6**(1), 1–20 (1994). https://doi.org/10.1080/10413209408406462
43. Thornburg, H.D.: Is early adolescence really a stage of development? (1983). https://doi.org/10.2307/1477147
44. Trusty, J., Niles, S., Carney, J.: Education-career planning and middle school counselors. Prof. Sch. Couns. **9**(2), 136–143 (2005)
45. Unicef: Early and Late Adolescence (2011). https://www.unicef.org
46. Vickers, E.: Life after sport: depression in the retired athlete (2013). https://members.believeperform.com/life-after-sport-depression-in-retired-athletes/
47. Wiggins, J., Mott, B., Pezzullo, L., Wiebe, E., Boyer, K., Lester, J.: Conversational UX design for kids: toward learning companions (2017). https://www.semanticscholar.org/paper/Conversational-UX-Design-for-Kids-%3AToward-Learning/dd3644c001f95fb4c8272400ee0699ce9eb02514

Technological Innovation in Education

Knowledge Sharing in the Context of E-Learning: A Bibliometric Analysis

Jorge Cruz-Cárdenas[1,2(✉)], Carlos Ramos-Galarza[3], Andrés Palacio-Fierro[4], and Jorge Guadalupe-Lanas[5]

[1] Facultad de Administración y Negocios, Universidad Indoamérica, Quito, Ecuador
jorgecruz@uti.edu.ec

[2] Research Center in Business, Society, and Technology, ESTec, Universidad Indoamérica, Quito, Ecuador

[3] Facultad de Psicología, Centro de Investigación en Mecatrónica y Sistemas Interactivos - MIST, Universidad Indoamérica, Quito, Ecuador
carlosramos@uti.edu.ec

[4] Universidad Internacional del Ecuador – UIDE, Quito, Ecuador
andrespalacio@uide.edu.ec

[5] Instituto de Altos Estudios Nacionales – IAEN, Quito, Ecuador
jorge.guadalupe@iaen.edu.ec

Abstract. Distance education mediated by technologies, also called e-learning or online learning, has experienced tremendous growth. This growth has been supported by the advancement of disruptive technologies and the rapid expansion of the Covid-19 pandemic. Among the various benefits that this type of education offers is the possibility of knowledge sharing (KS) between individuals in a fast, fluid, and storable way. The present study, using bibliometric techniques, seeks to contribute to the academic and professional world of KS in technology-mediated learning environments. We identified 1,167 relevant documents (articles, conference papers, book chapters, and books) in the Scopus database on which the different analyses were carried out. It was established that KS publication in technology-mediated learning environments is experiencing rapid expansion, that this is a multidisciplinary field of study, and that it is carried out by institutions associated with developed and emerging countries. The science mapping analysis allowed us to identify three relevant research areas: 1) KS in the context of organizational education or employee training using e-learning; 2) psychological and social aspects in the adoption and practices of KS; and 3) KS in the context of e-learning in higher education institutions or universities. An analysis called the overlay visualization of terms allows us to identify a change in emphasis from the techniques and technologies behind KS to the people and communities that are protagonists of KS. This article concludes by discussing these results and their implications for research and professional practice.

Keywords: Knowledge Sharing · E-Learning · Online Learning

B. K. Smith and M. Borge (Eds.): HCII 2025, LNCS 15806, pp. 197–205, 2025.
https://doi.org/10.1007/978-3-031-93564-0_12

1 Introduction

The rapid advance of disruptive technologies, such as artificial intelligence, cloud computing, augmented reality, and blockchains, and their confluence, are generating great changes in education. These changes are reflected in the rapid expansion of e-learning, which is distance education in a digital format and uses the Internet as a means of dissemination. E-learning can be a complete education method in itself or combined with face-to-face education in models called blended learning [1], where there is flexibility to incorporate different percentages of each type of education.

Due to the type of recipients, e-learning can be oriented toward university education or professional training and coaching. E-learning generates advantages such as convenience and flexibility for students. Another advantage is the possibility of knowledge sharing (KS), which can be defined as the process of sharing knowledge resources with other people [2]. These other people may be fellow students, co-workers, or members of an online community.

KS brings many benefits to e-learning. When e-learning includes KS, students value e-learning better and have a greater intention to use this type of education [2]. Additionally, KS increases student engagement and improves learning outcomes [3]. In the organizational field, that is, in the education and training of employees, KS as a component of e-learning is a source of competitive advantage because it leads to organizational learning and innovation [4].

The impact of KS on e-learning has attracted great interest from academics and professionals; this interest is reflected in the growing number of publications [5]. In scenarios of this type, studies that tend to describe and organize the literature that is generated become necessary [1]. This is the objective of the present study. Literature organization and systematization efforts can be approached from bibliometric perspectives if there is a large number of relevant documents, or from literature reviews if the relevant documents are few [6]. Considering the large number of studies on KS and e-learning, the present study adopts a bibliometric approach, and its objective is formulated as follows:

- To establish performance measures and mapping of science in knowledge sharing in the e-learning framework from a bibliometric perspective.

To the best of our knowledge, this specialized objective is a distinctive characteristic of this article, since the closest previous studies focused on a much broader scope, such as addressing the entirety of e-learning.

This article is organized into four sections. The first section already presented is the Introduction. Next, the Methods section describes the steps taken to deploy the bibliometric tools. In the third section, Analysis of Results, two types of bibliometric tools were deployed: those aimed at measuring performance and those focused on the mapping of science [7]. Finally, the last section, the Discussion, Conclusions, and Implications, details the theoretical and practical implications of the results.

2 Methods

The present bibliometric study followed a series of steps recommended for this type of research [6], namely: 1) formulating the research objectives, 2) designing the methodology and research tools, and 3) conducting the analyses of the selected body of documents and discussing the results. The objectives are stated in the Introduction.

A first decision of the present study was to choose Scopus as the database. This decision was made based on the balance that this database has between quality and content coverage [8]. The next step was to define the search string by seeking two types of terms that were present: a term related to the type of education and "e-learning" was used as the starting term and another term had to be related to the practice of interest, with "knowledge sharing" being the starting term. Next, a search was carried out for the most frequent alternative terms to the starting terms using the Scopus database. After this exploration, the final search string was defined as follows: ("e-learning" OR "online learning" OR "online teaching" OR "virtual learning" OR "online education") AND ("knowledge sharing" OR "knowledge-sharing" OR "share knowledge" OR "sharing knowledge" OR "knowledge creation" OR "knowledge exchange."

With the established search chain, the search for documents in the Scopus database was carried out in August 2024. Two delimitations were applied to the search. The first was to select only articles, conference papers, book chapters, and books—that is, documents that have undergone editorial and peer review. The second delimitation was to include only documents in English to carry out science mapping analyses. By applying these two filters, 1,167 documents were obtained, which were the basis for the analyses developed in the following section.

3 Analysis of Results

To achieve the objectives of the present study, two groups of very common analyses in bibliometric studies were carried out: performance analysis and science mapping [7]. In the performance analysis, we sought to describe the historical evolution of production and the role of different actors, such as institutions and countries. In science mapping, we aimed to establish the characteristics of the field under study based on the relationships in the documents.

A first approach in the performance analysis was to establish the annual evolution of the number of documents published on KS in the e-learning framework. Figure 1 presents this evolution until 2023, the last full year included. As can be seen in the aforementioned figure, the academic field of KS in e-learning starts approximately at the beginning of the 21st century. Until 2004, the growth rate was quite modest. Subsequently, since 2005, growth has accelerated, which is reflected in a steeper curved line. That is to say, this academic field is in the process of rapid growth.

A second approach to performance was to find the most active academic areas in KS research in the context of e-learning. As can be seen in Table 1, this field of study is a multidisciplinary field that is nourished by contributions, especially from two areas, computer science and social sciences. In both cases, more than 40% of the documents were associated with one of these areas. This multidisciplinary character has also been

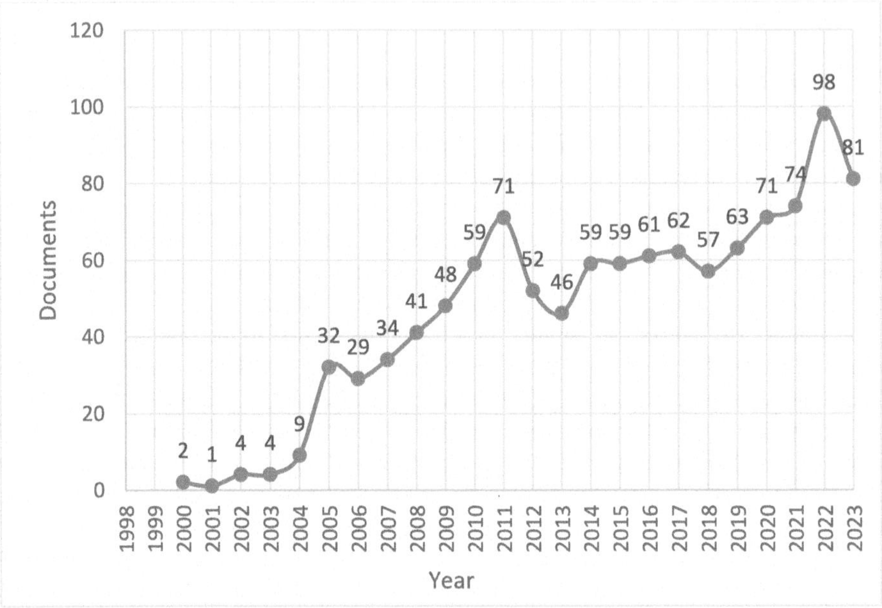

Fig. 1. Historical evolution of the annual publication of documents (source: Scopus).

found in other studies on education and technology topics [e.g., 1, 9]. It is necessary to indicate that the same document can be associated with more than one area, which is why the percentages in Table 1 add up to more than 100%.

Table 1. Main disciplines' contributions.

Subject area	Documents	%
Computer science	751	64.4%
Social sciences	536	45.9%
Engineering	265	22.7%
Mathematics	131	11.2%
Decision sciences	110	9.4%
Business, management, and accounting	102	8.7%

Regarding the most frequent type of documents, two types stood out: Conference papers (627 documents or 53.7%) and articles (472 documents or 40.4%). This result is logical, as conference papers are a common way of disseminating studies in computer science. Three publication vehicles or means stood out with more than 20 published documents. The first was "Lecture Notes in Computer Science" (50 documents), followed by the "ACM International Conference Proceeding Series" (29 documents) and "Communications in Compute and Information Science" (28 documents). These results are consistent with the results previously found, referring to the contribution of the computer science discipline and the popularity of conference papers.

Finally, Table 2 presents the most prominent institutions or universities and the countries in which these institutions are located. As a cut-off point, only institutions with 10 or more associated documents were included. As can be seen in Table 2, no institution clearly stood out. Additionally, it can be observed that the most prominent institutions are associated with developed and emerging countries, with a great lack of institutions from developing countries. This trend has also been observed in other studies on education and technology [e.g., 1, 9].

Table 2. Most notable institutions in research.

University/Institution	Country	Associated documents
Helsingin Yliopisto	Finland	14
Universiti Teknologi Malaysia	Malaysia	14
The University of Hong Kong	China	12
Central China Normal University	China	12
Norges T-N Universitet	Norway	10
University of Technology Sydney	Australia	10
Bina Nusantara University	Indonesia	10
Ahlia University	Bahrain	10

A second group of analysis was oriented toward science mapping. Of the various types of possible analysis, the analysis of the co-occurrence of words or terms and the analysis of the overlay visualization of terms were selected. These two tools were chosen for their capacity to structure a field of science and allow visualization of its historical evolution [10, 11].

Thus, using VosViewer Software 1.6.20 [11], a co-occurrence analysis of keywords was carried out based on the contents of titles and abstracts. This analysis is a good approach to the areas or lines of research on the topic being analyzed [12]. In total, 22,189 terms were identified. Using a minimum frequency of 20 occurrences, the most relevant terms were 193. Additionally, cleaning was done by eliminating terms that had more to do with the characteristics of the documents and their methodologies. Thus, terms such as "chapter," "design methodology approach," "future research," "literature review," and "practical implication" were eliminated. Finally, 177 terms and keywords were obtained.

Figure 2 presents the results of the co-occurrence analysis of the terms; each thematic cluster is represented by a different color. Additionally, each term is represented by a node whose size reflects the importance or frequency of the appearance of said term in the titles and abstracts of the documents.

As can be seen in Fig. 2, Cluster 1 (red color, 81 items) had "e-learning" as its central node. Other relevant nodes or terms were "knowledge management," "training,"

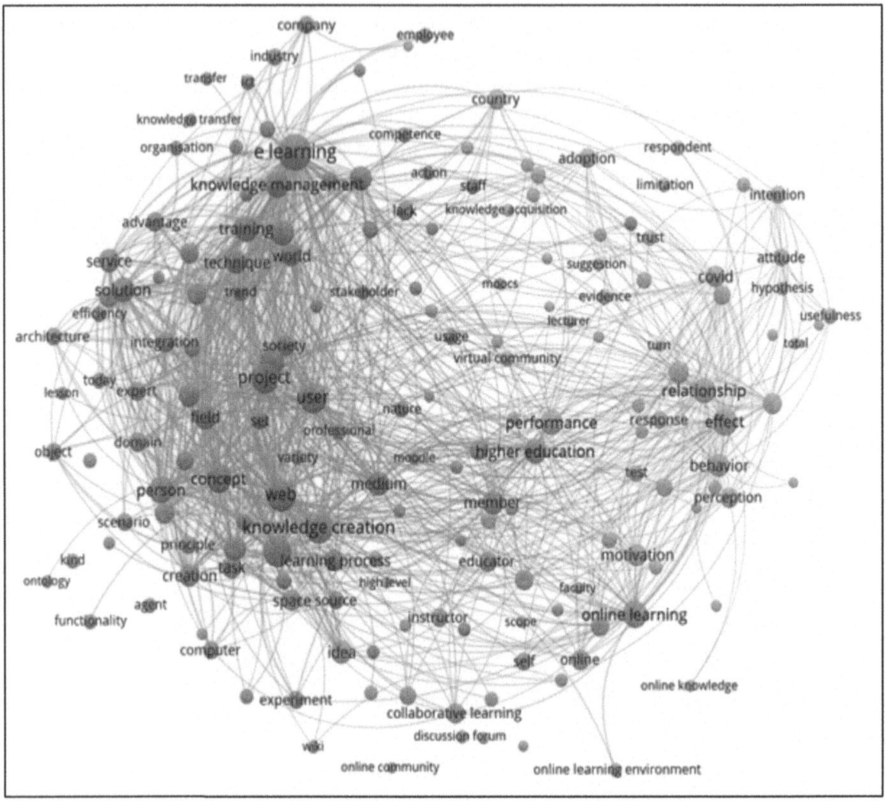

Fig. 2. Co-occurrence analysis of terms.

"solution," "service," "company," "organization," "industry," and "employee." Based on these relevant terms, it is possible to conclude that this cluster is associated with KS in the context of training and enabling employees of organizations within the framework of e-learning.

Cluster 2 (green color, 57 items) had as its central nodes "relationship," "performance," "effect," "covid," and "behavior." Among other nodes also present were "perception," "motivation," "intention," "adoption," and "virtual community." Based on these terms, it was possible to associate this cluster with psychological and social aspects that influence the adoption and practice of KS in e-learning environments.

Finally, Cluster 3 (blue color, 39 items) had "online learning," "knowledge creation," and "higher education" as central nodes. Other relevant terms were "educator," "instructor," "student," "forum," "discussion," and "collaborative learning," among others. Based on these terms, it was concluded that this cluster was associated with KS in the context of higher or university education based on e-learning.

An additional analysis within the science mapping approach was that of the overlay visualization of terms. This type of analysis allows us to see the historical evolution of interest in research based on the popularity (frequency) of the terms used in the documents and their ages [11]. This analysis was also based on the contents of the titles and abstracts. The results of this analysis are presented in Fig. 3.

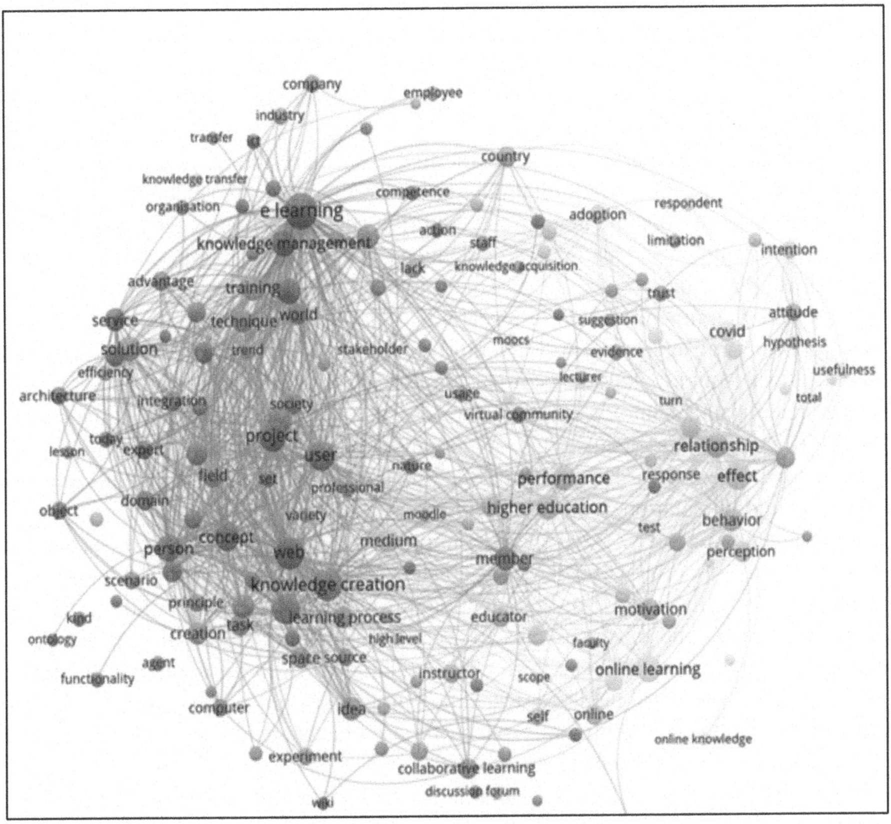

Fig. 3. Overlay visualization of terms.

In Fig. 3, the topicality of the terms is represented in different colors. Thus, terms that were popular further back in time are represented in purple. The most current terms are represented in green and yellow. Additionally, and similar to the analysis of the co-occurrence of terms, the size of the nodes is proportional to the importance (frequency) of a certain term or word.

As can be seen in Fig. 3, some terms, such as "e-learning," "project," "knowledge creation," "architecture," "web," "domain," and "ict," were popular years ago. Currently, the most popular terms are "online learning," "covid," "usefulness," "motivation," "performance," "behavior," and "relationship," among others. In short, the emphasis has moved from more technical aspects related to the enabling technologies of KS to aspects more related to the protagonists of KS, which are people and their interrelationships. Evidently, Covid 19 has also attracted great attention, which has also been identified in other studies on technology-mediated education [e.g., 1].

4 Discussion, Conclusions, and Implications

The rapid advances of digital and information and communication technologies and their confluence are completely reconfiguring the way in which people receive training and education and the way in which KS occurs among people. For these reasons, KS in the context of e-learning is attracting great attention from academics and practitioners [5]. Therefore, the present study seeks to contribute by generating a bibliometric approach to KS in the context of e-learning.

Using the Scopus database, applying the search string resulting from an exploratory study, and imposing certain delimitations, 1,167 documents were selected. The performance analysis of this documentary group confirmed the growing interest in KS in digital education environments. This interest is deduced from a steep growth curve in annual publications, particularly since 2005. Therefore, KS in e-learning environments is an attractive and recommended field of research.

KS in e-learning environments is a multidisciplinary field, with strong prominence in computer science and social sciences. This multidisciplinarity is a characteristic of studies on education and technology [1, 9]. Therefore, this study recommends the integration of multidisciplinary work teams. This recommendation is valid for researchers interested in conducting research on KS topics in e-learning environments and for professionals seeking its implementation.

Science mapping analyses have led to important conclusions regarding areas or lines of research and work [10]. Three thematic clusters emerged very clearly. The first cluster is related to KS in the context of organizational training and capacity building through e-learning. The second cluster relates to the psychological and social aspects of the adoption and practice of KS. The third cluster relates to KS in the context of higher or university education distributed by e-learning. Future research could position their work based on these clusters. Additionally, each of these clusters can be the objects of more focused studies using bibliometric techniques.

Regarding professional practice, although KS practices in digital education in the organizational world and in higher education look like two separate worlds (clusters), the experiences obtained in each of these worlds can enrich the other. That is, there can be a mutually beneficial transfer of experiences between the worlds of organizations and companies and of higher education. Finally, it is necessary not to lose sight of the fact that KS generation does not occur only in e-learning contexts. Thanks to digital and communication technologies, KS goes beyond the world of companies and universities. In this sense, people in their roles as citizens and consumers are very active in the generation of digital KS [13, 14].

Within the same science mapping analyses, another interesting result was obtained with the application of the overlay visualization of the terms tool. It can be seen how the emphasis of studies on KS in the context of e-learning has changed from an emphasis on the techniques and technologies to generate KS to greater attention to the people and communities that are the protagonists of KS. This phenomenon has also been observed in other studies focusing on education and technologies [e.g., 1, 9]. Additionally, another current topic revealed in the analysis of the overlay visualization of terms is the influence of the Covid-19 pandemic. This pandemic had its greatest effect between 2020 and 2023. Covid-19 forced a large number of countries to adopt quarantine and social isolation measures, which, in turn, led to the rapid adoption of technologies so that the world could continue to function [5, 12].

References

1. Cruz-Cárdenas, J., Parra-Domínguez, J., Zabelina, E., Deyneka, O., Ramos-Galarza, C.: Blended learning and higher education: a bibliometric analysis. In: Zaphiris, P., Ioannou, A. (eds.) Learning and Collaboration Technologies. HCII 2023. Lecture Notes in Computer Science, vol. 14041. Springer, Cham (2023). https://doi.org/10.1007/978-3-031-34550-0_33
2. Al-Emran, M., Teo, T.: Do knowledge acquisition and knowledge sharing really affect e-learning adoption? Empirical Study. Educ. Inf. Technol. **25**, 1983–1998 (2020)
3. Huan, X., Li, H., Huang, L., Jiang, T.: Research on the development and innovation of online education based on digital knowledge sharing community. BMC Psychol. **11**, 295 (2023)
4. Matzler, K., Muller, J.: Antecedents of knowledge sharing examining the influence of learning and performance orientation. J. Econ. Psychol. **32**(3), 317–329 (2011)
5. Yilmaz, F.G.K., Yilmaz, R.: Examining the factors influencing students' knowledge-sharing behavior in the social media-based learning community. Psychol. Sch. **60**(11), 4637–4652 (2023)
6. Donthu, N., Kumar, S., Mukherjee, D., Pandey, N., Lim, W.M.: How to conduct a bibliometric analysis: an overview and guidelines. J. Bus. Res. **133**, 285–296 (2021)
7. Guleria, D., Kaur, G.: Bibliometric analysis of ecopreneurship using VOSviewer and RStudio bibliometrix, 1989–2019. Libr. Hi. Tech. **39**(4), 1001–1024 (2021)
8. Pranckuté, R.: Web of Science (WoS) and Scopus: the titans of bibliographic information in today's academic world. Publications. **9**(1), 12 (2021)
9. Cruz-Cárdenas, J., Zabelina, E., Deyneka, O., Palacio-Fierro, A., Guadalupe-Lanas, J., Ramos-Galarza, C.: Smartphones and higher education: mapping the field. In: Salvendy, G., Wei, J. (eds.) Design, Operation and Evaluation of Mobile Communications. HCII 2023. Lecture Notes in Computer Science, vol. 14052. Springer, Cham (2023). https://doi.org/10.1007/978-3-031-35921-7_17
10. Van Eck, N.J., Waltman, L.: Software survey: VOSviewer, a computer program for bibliometric mapping. Scientometrics **84**(2), 523–538 (2010)
11. Van Eck, N.J., Waltman, L.: Manual for Vosviewer version 1.6.20 (2023). https://www.vosviewer.com/documentation/Manual_VOSviewer_1.6.15.pdf
12. Cruz-Cárdenas, J., Zabelina, E., Guadalupe-Lanas, J., Palacio-Fierro, A., Ramos-Galarza, C.: Covid-19, consumer behavior, technology, and society: a literature review and bibliometric analysis. Technol. Forecast. Soc. Change. **173**, 121179 (2021)
13. Bigne, E., Ruiz, C., Curras-Perez, R.: How consumers process online review types in familiar versus unfamiliar destinations. a self-reported and neuroscientific study. Technol. Forecast. Soc. Change **199**, 123067 (2024)
14. Boyd, E.D., Clarke, B.T., Spekman, E.R.: The emergence and impact of consumer brand empowerment in online social networks. J. Brand Manag. **21**, 516–531 (2014)

'You Told the Students?': Experts' Views on Design and Measurement of Active Learning in Higher Education

Pedro Isaias[1,2(✉)], Paula Miranda[3], and Sara Pifano[4]

[1] University of New South Wales (UNSW – Sydney), Sydney, Australia
pedro.isaias@unsw.edu.au
[2] Universidade Aberta–Portuguese Open University, Lisbon, Portugal
[3] Setubal School of Technology, Polytechnic Institute of Setubal, Setúbal, Portugal
[4] ISRLab – Information Society Research Laboratory, Lisbon, Portugal

Abstract. The higher education sector is constantly pivoting towards innovation and adopting new strategies to improve education delivery. Active learning is at the centre of various teaching approaches that focus on the increasing participation of the students in their own learning process. While it is becoming a widespread strategy in higher education, its adoption remains limited and it continues to be surrounded by some uncertainty, in particular at the level of its design and effectiveness. This paper aims to examine the viewpoints of university lecturers with concern to active learning′s design and instructional impact measurement, which were collected in a two-phase research strategy combining an online questionnaire and semi-structured interviews. The findings portray active learning as a valuable teaching strategy and enable the proposition of an assortment of design guidelines, as well as recommendations for measuring the instructional impact of active learning initiatives that can contribute to a more fruitful implementation.

Keywords: Active Learning · Higher Education · Instructional Design · Instructional Impact Measurement · Mixed Method Research

1 Introduction

There are several studies arguing active learning′s capacity to promote learning more effectively in comparison with traditional methods, based solely on transmission of content [1, 2]. In addition, educators and researchers are increasingly sharing their experience with different applications of active learning strategies and supporting technologies, adding to a considerable body of research on the subject [3–6]. Despite the extensive inventory of benefits provided by the literature, some teachers still question its effectiveness, they fear the preparation time involved and the students' resistance to this method. Moreover, they have some reservations regarding their capacity to cover the entirety of the syllabus [7].

Despite the popularity of active learning and the abundance of research focusing on it, there seems to be a lack of specific studies that address its design and the measurement of its impact. Although some studies do approach these questions, in terms

B. K. Smith and M. Borge (Eds.): HCII 2025, LNCS 15806, pp. 206–224, 2025.
https://doi.org/10.1007/978-3-031-93564-0_13

of design they concern specific subjects [8, 9] or individual activities [10, 11], and in terms of measurement they focus solely on one or two methods [12]. Furthermore, active learning's benefits call for its implementation, but instruction seems to remain mostly focused on teacher-centred practices [13]. This paper examines design guidelines, which can be used transversally in any subject, and a variety of measurement instruments, with the potential to provide a more comprehensive depiction of the impact of active learning. Thus, it intends to answer two main research questions: a) what design strategies can be used to develop active learning in higher education, in order to maximise its effectiveness; b) what measurement instruments can be used to assess active learning's instructional impact.

The paper begins with a brief overview of active learning's design guidelines and measurement instruments to assess its instructional effectiveness. The methods section ensues describing the data collection instruments and prefaces the results section. The paper concludes with a discussion of the most significant results.

2 Designing and Measuring Active Learning in Higher Education

Higher education is concerned with providing students with the competences that they require to address real-world problems and to become skilled professionals and lifelong learners. Active learning emerges in a context of growing student empowerment, of promoting student engagement with their own learning and fomenting student proactivity [14]. Active learning is connected with social-constructivist paradigms and promotes the delivery of content in inquiry-based practices [15].

2.1 Design Recommendations

The literature is abundant with recommendations when it comes to active learning design. The studies that were reviewed for this paper seem to focus especially on recommendations that underline the importance of explaining the context, starting early and in a simple manner, planning the learning activities carefully, fostering student participation and measuring the outcomes of active learning.

Given that active learning demands students to be more responsible for the learning process and it represents a significant change in relation to transmission-based instruction, it is important to clarify the context. Explaining the rationale behind the implementation of active learning, identifying and elucidating the structure of the course and the purpose of the learning activities can reduce the students' resistance [7]. When lecturers explain the value of active learning and its requirements, early in the semester, students can more swiftly adhere to it [16]. Lecturers can resort to interactive digital maps and visualization tools, such as online infographics to illustrate the advantages and expectations of active learning as a teaching strategy, helping students to become more informed and less reticent.

In addition, to ease the transition into active learning it is important to start the implementation early in the course and with simple activities that represent lower risk to the teachers and the learners. This type of activities (for example pause procedure and minute papers) enables the teachers to make only a few changes and gives the students the opportunity to adapt. The activities and the rationale behind them should be clearly explained to students [1]. Using interactive tutorials and simulations can represent an appealing start for the students and using microlearning platforms and assist them to acquire knowledge in a more progressive and manageable manner.

With regards to planning the activities, students welcome active learning activities that have meaning, represent an appropriate challenge [1] and that are unambiguously connected to the learning objectives and assessment, as it is defended by constructive alignment [17]. In order to foster student participation, some best practices include navigating the room and engaging directly with the students, inviting students to ask questions, approaching students who seem disengaged and trying to include them in the activity, and grading the students' participation as a manner to elicit their contribution [7]. Learning Management Systems can be valuable allies in this phase, as they can be used by lecturers to store the classes' planification. In addition, polling and survey tools can be integrated in the class to offer real-time feedback from the students.

Some studies also mention the importance of student reflection, using an adequate space and obtaining feedback. Students' reflection has a fundamental role in the promotion of lifelong learning, and it plays a central part in supporting decision-making [18]. Active learning is improved with reflection [19]. Concerning feedback, teachers can begin by consulting and asking for feedback from colleagues, which can be a useful strategy when designing active learning courses [1]. Feedback can come equally from students, by asking them to provide feedback about how the course is going and addressing their concerns [16]. The physical space is an important aspect of designing active learning courses [20]. There are several examples in the literature that report the conversion of traditional rooms into rooms suitable for active and collaborative learning with the support of technology [21]. Interactive whiteboards and annotation tools can support active learning inside the classroom and to foment reflection, students can be asked to compile e-portfolios with activities featuring relevant content covered in the lectures.

2.2 Methods for Evaluating Active Learning's Effectiveness

Concerns about active learning's effectiveness [7], place an emphasis on the importance of evaluating its impact. Self-reporting instruments are useful to obtain information on the views of different stakeholders, but they are limited in scope, and they can only assess a restricted number of factors. Additionally, observation-based instruments are valuable [22], but they can sometimes miss important cues.

In the literature, comparative studies assess the effectiveness of active learning in comparison with the conventional lecture format, in some cases using student performance [23]. Some authors report having used a combination of methods, such as surveys and students' final grades, paired with demographics [24].

There are also other tools such as the Active Learning scale in the Australasian Survey of Student Engagement (AUSSE) with 11 items to measure active learning [12] and observational tools such as the Active-Learning Inventory Tool [22]. When active learning is supported by technology there is equally the possibility of using the technology itself to obtain data on student's engagement and other metrics. Clickstream data, for example, can provide insight into students' use of resources, but the information it provides is limited [25]. Given the advantages and disadvantages of each method portrayed in the literature, this paper posits that each method on its own is insufficient to provide the width of data to comprehensively understand if an active learning initiative has been effective and argues that it is important to resort to more than one method to assess how the students perceived the experience, and what impact it had on the concrete learning performance and attainment of learning objectives. With this respect, technology can play an important role in gathering insight, learning analytics platforms can be used, as well as online survey services and digital peer and self-assessment tools.

3 Materials and Methods

This paper is based on a mixed method research approach [26] using an online questionnaire [27] and semi-structured interviews [28] to address its two main research questions: a) what design strategies can be used to develop active learning in higher education, in order to maximise its effectiveness; b) what measurement instruments can be used to assess active learning's instructional impact. Research Ethics Committee approval was sought for this research.

3.1 Data Collection Instruments

The questionnaire had three main parts: a) demographic questions about the respondents; b) questions concerning the definition, learning activities, design and measurement of active learning; and c) Likert scale questions regarding design guidelines, including measurement. There was a question at the end asking the respondents if they would be interested in participating in a subsequent interview. After the pilot and the necessary adjustments deriving from it, the final version of the questionnaire was distributed via email invitation, on the SurveyMonkey platform. The semi-structured interviews' script was designed following a preliminary analysis of the results of the questionnaire and it was directed at exploring its key conclusions. The script was divided into two sections: a) questions pertaining to definition, learning activities, design and measurement; and b) questions concerning some of the answers that the respondents had provided in the questionnaire. Depending on the availability of the interviewees, the interviews were conducted via Skype and email.

3.2 Sample and Subsample

The questionnaire's sample of respondents was the result of convenience and purposive sampling [29], in the sense that they were selected due to their expertise and their accessibility to the researchers. They were selected from a population of university lecturers, from several subjects and various countries. The interviews were conducted with a subsample of the questionnaire's respondents, who at the end of the questionnaire volunteered their contact information to be part of a subsequent interview. From this population of volunteers, a sample was selected via theoretical sampling [30], based on their answers in the Likert scale questions. This sampling technique was used to select respondents who had, in the questionnaire, used either a neutral score (neither agree nor disagree), a disagreement score (totally disagree or disagree), or a "I don't know" reply. Since the items in the Likert scale questions were supported by previous literature as per Sect. 2, it was more valuable to examine this type of responses, for the insight it could provide.

3.3 Data Analysis

The data deriving from the questionnaire was analysed in SPSS 21, where a preliminary analysis based on descriptive statistics was conducted. Following this analysis, the Likert scale questions were further examined by resorting to a factor analysis also in SPSS 21. The results of the questionnaire were then used as the basis for the analysis of the data provided by the interviews. The scripts and transcripts of the interviews were introduced in Aplasia 9 where they were coded using the main subjects that emerged in the questionnaire and explored for any additional themes.

4 Results

Due to the volume and coverage of the data collected in the online questionnaire and the semi-structured interviews, this paper will focus, as per its research questions, solely on the data concerning design and measurement. Focusing only on these sections of both data collection instruments, will enable a more in-depth and reflective analysis of the results. Hence, although the questionnaire and interviews are part of a larger study, for the purpose of this paper, this section will present the data pertaining exclusively to design and measurement. The online questionnaire received 338 valid responses, and 12 semi-structured interviews were conducted.

4.1 Participants

The majority of the participants, 71%, was between the age of 41 to 60 years old. Only 1% was under 30 years old, 19% was between 30 and 40 and a small percentage (9%) was over 60. Circa 61% were female participants and 39% were male. The questionnaire was completed by respondents from 62 countries, such as Spain, Portugal, Turkey, Romania, United States and Russia. Most participants were professors (31%) or associate professors (32%), while lecturers and senior lecturers were accounted by 14% each. Other positions included tutors and assistant and adjunct professors. When directly citing their contribution, to safeguard their anonymity, codes will be used (R#1-R#338). With regards to the interviews, in total, 105 respondents volunteered in the questionnaire, but due to a limitation of resources relating mainly to time, 64 were contacted to participate in the interviews. From the 22 respondents who responded affirmatively, 12 completed the interview. For the purpose of maintaining their anonymity they are referred in the paper as I#11-I#22.

Table 1. Design strategies.

Design strategies	Percentage
Ask for feedback from students	80%
Carefully plan the activities that will be used	62%
Promote student reflection	60%
Foster student participation	60%
Start the implementation of active learning at the beginning of the course	55%
Engage the students through explaining why active learning will be used in the classroom	53%
Measure the outcomes of your active learning experience	43%
Start with simple activities	41%
Ensure the space facilitates active learning	30%
Ask for feedback from colleagues	19%
Other	2%

4.2 Active Learning Design Roadmap for Maximising Effectiveness

In the questionnaire, the respondents were asked to select the strategies that they have used to ensure an effective design (Table 1).

Asking students for feedback was the most valued design strategy. The participants were asked in an optional open question to identify what other design best practices they would recommend. A total of 123 responses were given, which can be divided into three clusters:

- Activities and tools –games, interactive pools, modelling technologies, argumentation, video discussions, mind mapping, log book entries, text analysis, quizzes, jigsaw reading;
- Best practices –addressing the students' interests, using authentic case studies and evaluation, co-teaching, creating a community of learning, and the adaptation of methods to the course, topic and students' readiness;
- Teaching methodologies –flipped classroom, project-based learning, inquiry-based learning, problem-based learning and cooperative learning.

With respect to the interviews, the participants were asked to compile five main design principles (Fig. 1).

There is a predominance of sub-codes concerning the design of the learning activities, which the interviewees placed at the centre of their design efforts. According to them, learning activities, in the context of active learning design need to be: purposeful in the sense that they are directed at a specific problem; personalised to suit student's individually; supported by technology deployment; compatible with the learning objectives that were set in the course; designed creatively; inclusive of complex problems to challenge the students; and subject to a wrap-up upon completion. With reference to content, it is required to use real life projects and cases and it needs to be based on subjects

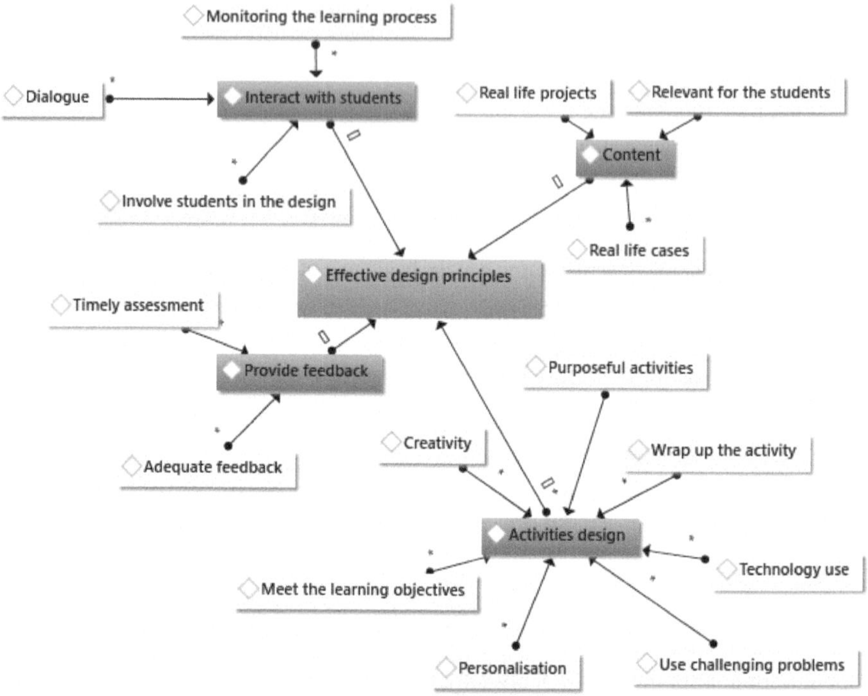

Fig. 1. Network map for the code effective design principles, in the interviews (generated in Aplasia 9).

that are relevant for the students. Interacting with the students include the promotion of dialogue, increasing communication; the monitoring of the learning process while it is happening in the classroom; and the improvement of the students' involvement. Involving the students in the process seems to be key to a successful implementation, as I#19 describes "a lot of my colleagues arrive to me and say 'I tried to do active learning or flip the class activity, and it fail.' And the first thing I ask them, 'you told the students that they had to work a little bit more, or in a different way?' –'Yes, more or less', but at the end of the day, the answer is no". Finally, concerning the provision of feedback the participants determined that it should be appropriate to the activity and offered in a timely manner.

The questionnaire explored effective design further through a set of Likert scale questions where the respondents were asked to manifest their agreement or disagreement level toward statements pertaining to several guidelines for active learning effective design and where they could add any comment. The first group of guidelines is explaining the context (Fig. 2).

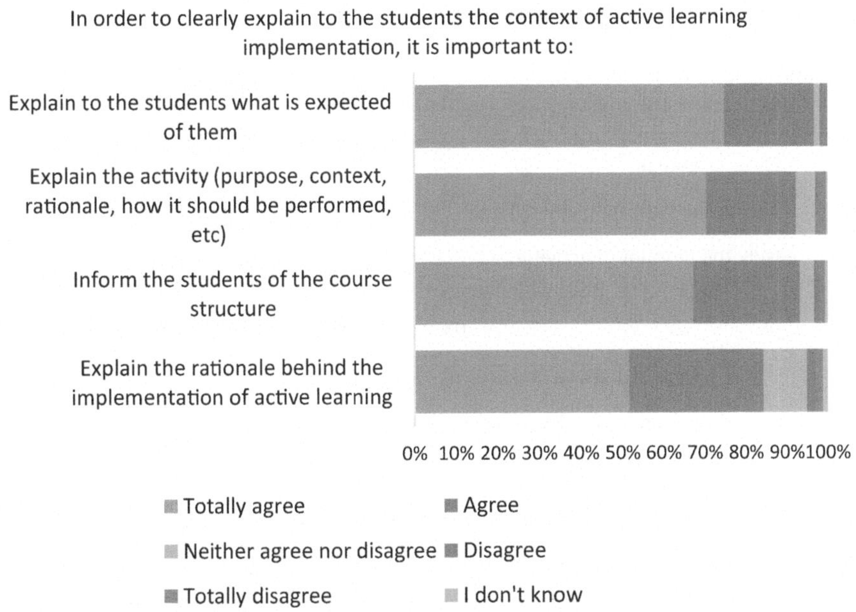

Fig. 2. Statements pertaining to the explanation of context

The respondents' total agreement levels (totally agree and agree scores) were above 80% for the items related to the need to explain the context, with the first item receiving 96% of total agreement. Comments left by the respondents highlighted the importance of informing the students of what is expected of them and of the benefits of active learning, as one respondent added "If students are not informed of what they have to do and why, they are naturally reluctant" (R#46).

In the interviews, explaining her response of "neither agree nor disagree" in the item "explaining the rationale behind the implementation of active learning", I#16 said that her students already know that "doing" is required in statistics, so there is no need to explain the pedagogical choice. Also, one interviewee, who had selected the option "neither agree nor disagree" in the item "explain the activity", justified it by arguing that if the students "are actively engaged in the development of the learning programme, explaining the details mentioned above is irrelevant. Moreover, going over such details BEFORE the activity might "spoil" the "surprise" aspect of the lesson (which can be a motivational element)" (I#20).

The second set of design guidelines, posits that it is important to start early and simple (Fig. 3).

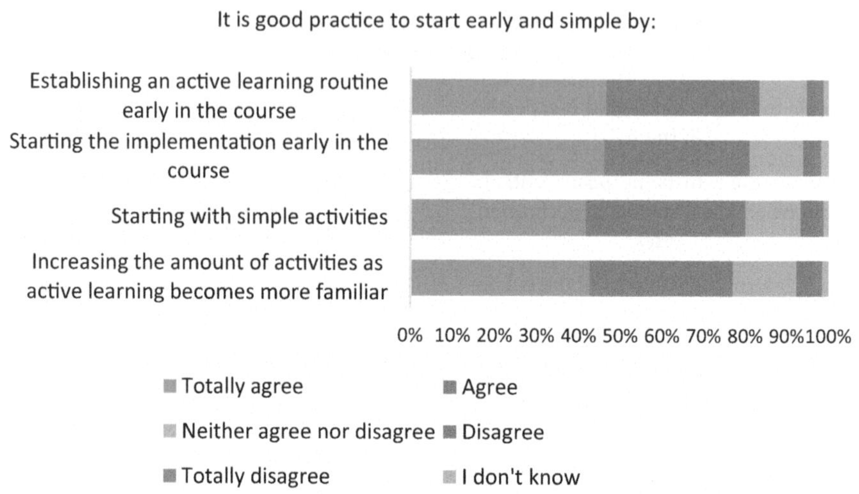

Fig. 3. Statements concerning an early and simple start

The total agreement percentage concerning an early and simple start were higher than 80%, with the difference that they gathered more neutral and disagreement ratings. The comments added by the participants clarified that it depends mainly on the learning goals. In addition, the interviews provided some insight into these results (Table 2).

Table 2. Explanation of responses to starting early and simple items.

Item	Response	Reasons for response
Starting with simple activities	Neutral (I#11)	Depends on the level of the students. With master students or more experienced students, for example, it is possible to start with complex activities
	Disagreement (I#16)	Starting early is important, but it doesn't necessarily mean that the activities need to be simple. They need to be challenging and relevant
Increase of the amount of activities as active learning becomes more familiar	Neutral (I#19)	It depends on the situation, but there can be an increase in intensity rather than in number
	Disagreement (I#16)	"Starting activities should be the same as the activities that are going to be used throughout the entirety of the course, to ensure a similar structure between the weeks" (I#16)

The third group of guidelines, regarding the need to carefully plan the activities, gathered similar agreement in the questionnaire (Fig. 4).

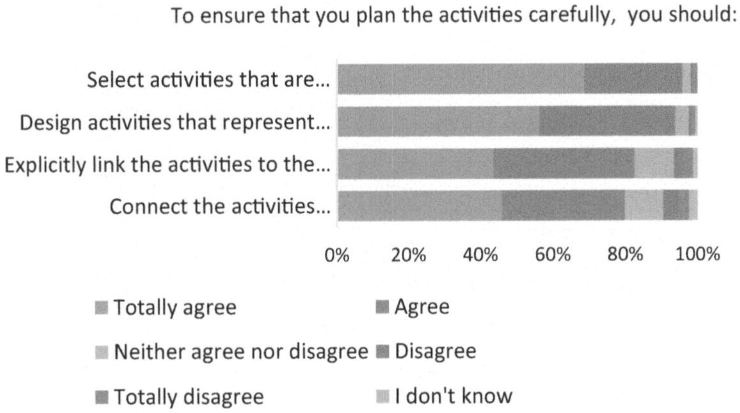

Fig. 4. Items related to carefully planning the activities.

All statements had a high level of total agreement with 80% or over. The selection of activities that are meaningful to the learning context even reached 96% of total agreement scores. In the comments, one respondent added a different perspective, contrary to connecting the activities to assessment, "this frees me up as a teacher to focus on the students' learning, not their grades. Likewise, by being separated from assessment, students are given the opportunity to experiment and try new things. When tied to assessment, students understandably become more narrowly focused and risk averse." (R#108). In the interviews, I#18 argued that he had selected the option "neither agree nor disagree" in the item "explicitly link the activities to the learning assessment" because "there are certain learning outcomes that cannot really (and effectively) be measured. That is why I would go (mainly) for learner feedback as it provides indications of the achievement of these "invisible" outcomes. "(I#18).

The set of guidelines that follows concerns the promotion of student participation (Fig. 5).

The items associated with this guideline had different levels of total agreement. The first two items had 86% and over of total agreement. Grading the students' participation had the agreement of 70% of the sample, but 18% of neutral scores, while navigating the room had 65% of total agreement and 21% of neutral scores. The comment section was used mainly to suggest other forms of engaging the students, namely activity design, getting to know them and their interests better, defining their role and encouraging them to share their ideas. Table 3 shows some of the reasons behind the respondents' answers, which became evident during the interviews.

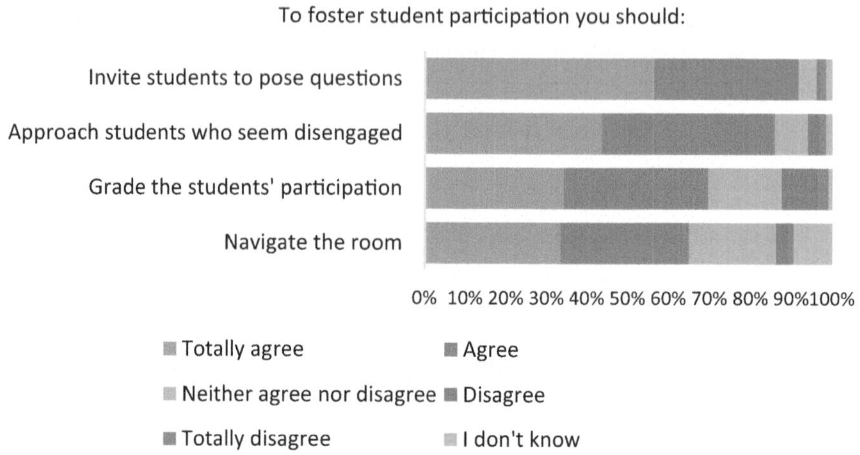

Fig. 5. Student participation items.

Table 3. Items pertaining to student participation discussed in the interviews

Item	Response	Reasons for response
Navigate the room	Neutral (I#14)	It will not in itself engage students, but it is good to maintain them alert
Approach students who seem disengaged	Neutral (I#20)	It is unrealistic to approach large numbers of students
Grade the students' participation	Neutral (I#19)	Grading participation isn't always the solution. It depends on the context and on the content
	Disagree (I#18, I#20)	"I strive for the opposite: peer learning and healthy collaboration" I#20
		It can "force participation just to get a good grade, not because learners are truly participating." (I#18)

Design guidelines pertaining to measurement will be analysed in the next sub-Sect. (4.3). The last question combined several recommendations. The six items connect essentially to student reflection, learning space and feedback (Fig. 6).

Consulting with colleagues and using active learning rooms gathered only 66% and 59% of agreement respectively. In the comments, one participant said that although the space does facilitate active learning, the absence of it should not be an impediment. Another respondent highlighted the value of studying the literature, similar implementation cases and the experiences of others. The interviews provided data on all items pertaining to this question (Table 4).

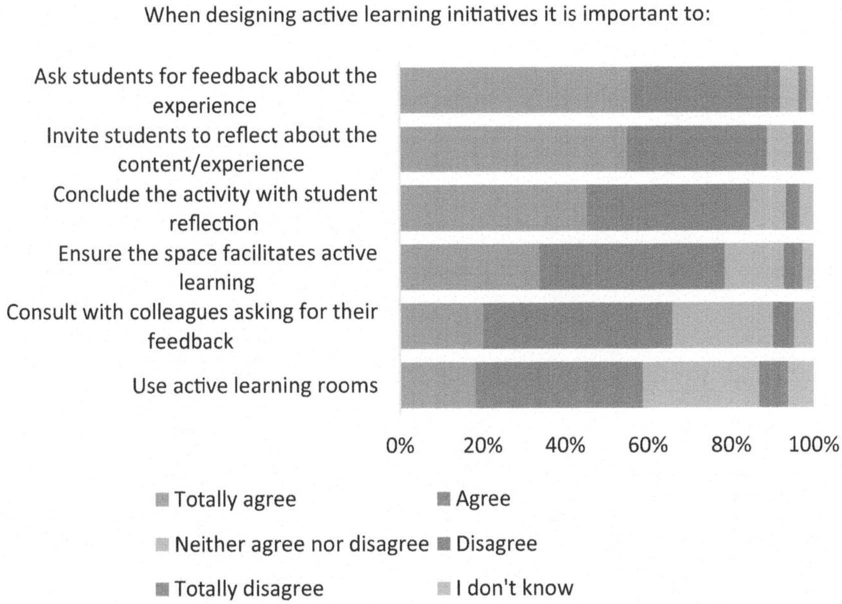

Fig. 6. Other guidelines for active learning design.

Table 4. Interviewees' responses to various design guidelines.

Item	Response	Reasons for response
Consult with colleagues asking for their feedback	Neutral (I#11, I#20)	Some teachers do not have the time to spare, and academic competition can hinder its usefulness
		It is dependent on experience, but it is not crucial
	Disagreement (I#12)	Some teachers aren't interested in new ideas
Ask students for feedback about the experience"	Neutral (I#12, I#14)	Despite the neutral rating, student feedback would be welcomed
		Can be used only if there is any free time
Use active learning rooms	Neutral (I#18, I#19, I#20)	With massification it is important to be creative and use the resources that are available

(*continued*)

Table 4. (*continued*)

Item	Response	Reasons for response
		It can have an important role in planning, but there is no need to create special rooms
		Although it can be a problem, it is more often "an excuse not to do active learning (…) Spaces, if you are creative, are not a problem. That is not the key point" (I#19)
	Disagreement (I#14)	Active learning does not require a specific facility
Ensure the space facilitates active learning	Neutral (I#19, I#20)	Massification requires teachers to use what they have
		The room is not essential
	Disagreement (I#14)	Active learning needs to be "more mental than manual/physical."(I#14)
Invite students to reflect about the content/experience	Neutral (I#12, I#16)	Would rather invite students to reflect
		It can sometimes be useful, but it is not always required
Conclude the activity with student reflection	Disagreement (I#16)	It is important to have some type of "wrap-up (whether it be reflection or a discussion), (…) reflection felt too narrow of a term to use." (I#16)

4.3 Measurement Instruments to Assess Active Learning's Instructional Impact

In the interviews, the university lecturers were asked about the benefits of evaluating the effectiveness of active learning. They were unanimous in defending the importance of measuring their experiences, mainly because the data that they collect assists them to determine if their work is being successful, it offers feedback about the students' views, and it can be used to further perfect the design of prospective active learning initiatives. According to the interviewees, evaluation methods can, similarly, be used to evaluate the performance of both students and teachers; to determine if the learning strategy is meeting the learning objectives, both in general to the course and in particular to the activity; and to determine the aspects that are working and those that are just inefficient and result in superficial learning, In addition it serves as a motivation, as stated by I#18 "seeing that these methods are effective, motivates teachers/lecturers to invest more in developing such learning programmes".

In the questionnaire, the participants were asked to list the methods that they have used (Table 5).

Table 5. Evaluation methods to assess active learning's effectiveness

Evaluation methods	Percentage
Learning outcomes measurements (i.e. grades of exams, tests or assignments)	77%
Observation	59%
Student surveys	56%
Number of assignments/activities completed	40%
Student interviews	34%
Student focus groups	24%
Data analytics from technology deployment	21%
Other	6%
I do not assess the effectiveness of my active learning initiatives	2%

The majority of the participants reported using students' learning outcomes, such as their grades in exams and assignments, relying on observation and using students' surveys. Only an exceedingly small percentage of respondents (2%) claimed not to assess the effectiveness of the active learning initiatives. Some participants added other methods to the list in the questionnaire, including analysis of the quality of interventions, attendance and dropout rates, open feedback sessions, and teacher reflections. A frequency and mean analysis of the number of options selected by the respondents showed that on average each respondent selected 3 evaluation instruments (mean = 3.21) and that only 9% of the respondents selected just one method.

The interviews also included a question to list specific instruments, which half of the participants responded by identifying only one method. Similarly, to the results in the questionnaire, 7 interviewees identified some type of learning outcomes measurement, such as formative and/or summative tests and assessment obtained from projects, portfolios or essays. In addition, observations and students' surveys were mentioned by 4 interviewees each. One of the university lecturers reported using all three methods combined. I#14, who mentioned only learning outcomes, argued: "I don't use any specific instrument for active learning effectiveness measurement as I can't spend teaching hours for it". Observation, in its turn, was described as being more sensitive by I#15, and student surveys were defended by I#18 as "a true reflection of what the learners "get" from the learning experience".

In the questionnaire, measurement of active learning' outcomes were equally included as a design guideline in the Likert scale questions (Fig. 7).

Most measurement instruments had total agreement levels of 79% or higher, with the exception of data analytics, which reached just 57% of total agreement rates. This item also had 29% of neutral responses, which is substantially high. The comments offered by the respondents pertained to data analytics from technology, with one respondent stating

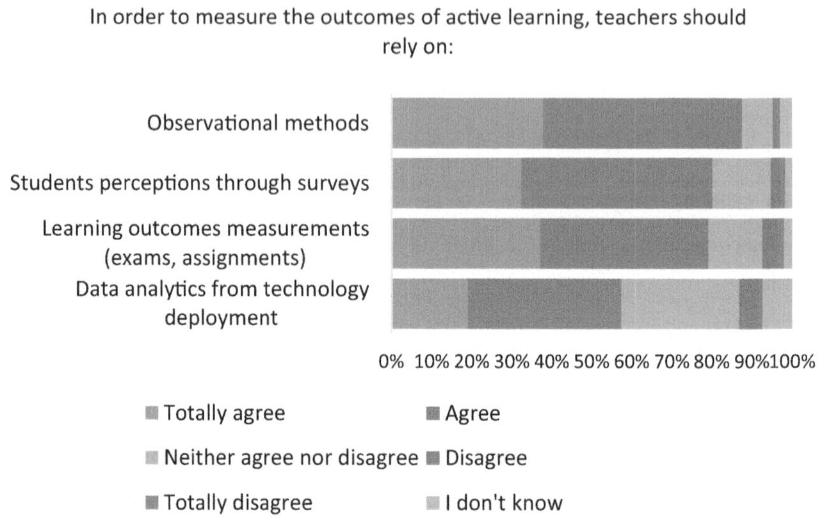

Fig. 7. Items for measuring the outcomes of active learning.

that it is "questionable whether the right data could be collected, analysed and interpreted correctly" (R#57). With concern to student surveys one participant argued that he has "observed oftentimes that students' perceptions through survey are not honestly evaluated by students" (R#205). Also, exam results, one respondent argued, provide incomplete data, being necessary to observe the behaviour of the students. Table 6 illustrates some of the arguments behind the selection of neutral scores to the measurement items.

Table 6. Examination of responses to measurement items in the interviews

Item	Response	Reasons for response
Data analytics from technology deployment	Neutral (I#11, I#14, I#18, I#20)	Prefer formative learning
		Prefer student feedback questionnaires/interviews, as they provide insight into what the students obtained
		No experience with data analytics
		Teachers can extract the data themselves and analyse it
	I don't know (I#16)	Didn't understand what it meant
Students' perceptions through surveys	Neutral (I#14)	They only provide an estimation and do not have a direct link to actual knowledge

Finally, the interviewees were asked to identify the challenges associated with measuring active learning and they all voiced different concerns. According to the respondents the challenges pertaining to measurement concern the need for platform readiness, difficulty in preserving student representativeness, student excessively positive feedback, survey design bias, evaluation bias in observational methods, subjectiveness of evaluation, lack of time to develop adequate instruments and complexity of qualitative data analysis.

4.4 Factor Analysis of Design Guidelines

The Likert scale questions were further analysed through a factor analysis. To determine the factorability of the items, The Kaiser-Meyer-Olkin test resulted in 0.908, above the recommended 0.5 value [31]. In addition, the Bartlett's test of sphericity had a 0.00 value signifying that the data is not normally distributed, it is skew and since it is lower than 0.05 [31] it is significant. Both tests confirmed the appropriateness of conducting a factor analysis. This adequacy was further confirmed by the communalities table, which displayed values above 0.3, attesting the items common variance. Factor analysis was selected due to its ability to provide a summary of the data in a manner that simplifies the interpretation and understanding of relationships and patterns. It can reorganise variables, narrowing them into clusters established on their common variance [32]. Factor analysis was performed using principal axis factoring extraction technique, since it is the best option for data which is not normally distributed [33] and direct noblemen rotation, due to an assumed correlation between the items [33]. Based on the items' eigenvalues (>1) and on a visual examination of the scree plot, five components were extracted. In examining the pattern mix and the items factor loadings, it was possible to detect the items that were associated with each factor, enabling their characterisation. The items associated with factor 1 pertained mostly to learning activities, factor 2 to reflection and feedback, factor 3 to measurement, factor 4 to space and factor 1 to early implementation. These five components do summarise the overall findings in the sense that both respondents and interviewees emphasised the centrality of learning activities in terms of their design and of informing the students about their context and rationale; argued the significance of student reflection and feedback as an approach to improve design; and defended the deployment of several measurement instruments as an important design strategy. In addition, they were supportive of the idea of using active learning rooms, but characterised the guidelines pertaining to it as dispensable, and promoted the idea of a timely implementation, rooted early in the routine of the course.

5 Discussion

This paper intended to contribute to active learning research by focusing on design and measurement guidelines, to assist the development of more effective learning experiences in higher education. The results offered a panoply of guidelines and recommendations in term of design and measurement that can provide teachers, across multiple subjects, with a structure to enhance their courses whether they are just starting to implement active learning or are more experienced.

Responding to the first research question, on a preliminary approach to design guidelines, in the questionnaires, the overall results underlined the importance of obtaining feedback from the students, carefully planning the learning activities, student reflection, starting early and explaining the rationale behind active learning's use. The interviews echoed the centrality of the learning activities and of the students' role. A preliminary analysis of the Likert scale items frequencies confirmed the central design themes that emerged from previous research. Explaining the context as argued by Tharayil, Borrego [7] received a sound support by the respondents, with high agreement levels and with comments and interviewees reiterating the importance of keeping the students informed. Starting early and in a simple manner defended by previous research [1, 16], received a high percentage of agreement, which was more pronounced in terms of starting early rather than in a simple manner. Planning the learning activities judiciously as theorised in the literature [1, 17], gathered the agreement of an expressive majority of the respondents, while fostering student participation, as advocated by Tharayil, Borrego [7] was defended by the participants, but with more restraint in terms of navigating the room and grading participation.

As per the literature [18, 19], overall the respondents underlined the importance of student reflection and, in line, with previous studies [16], an overwhelming majority of the participants were in agreement with asking students for feedback, but contrary to what [1] defended they were much less inclined to do so in relation to colleagues. Finally, the items pertaining to space registered a lower level of agreement. Although the literature argues for the value of rooms designed to facilitate active learning [20, 21] and the majority of the respondents also agrees, it was deemed as nonessential by some respondents and interviewees. In response to the second research question, the instruments for measuring the outcomes of active learning inventoried in previous studies [12] had the support of the majority of the respondents in the Likert scale questions, but with varying degrees. The instrument that gathered less agreement was data analytics, while observational methods, student surveys and exams and assignments were more popular. It equally became evident that the best approach to a more comprehensive measurement is the use of several methods, each providing data about an aspect of the experience. A further examination of the Likert scale items, using factor analysis enabled the reduction of these items down to five components, which were defined as learning activities, reflection and feedback, measurement, active learning spaces and early implementation.

6 Conclusion

As it is true for any teaching approach, active learning's pedagogical value is greatly dependent on the outcomes that stem from its adoption. This becomes even more relevant for strategies that require considerable effort and time. Although this research set out to provide a comprehensive and general set of guidelines for design and measurement, it became evident that even the most straightforward practices were not a one-size-fits-all solution. The findings show that some of the best practices that teachers can use to guide the implementation of active learning depend on a variety of factors to be successful. Nonetheless, and recognising that these guidelines cannot be universalised, they do seem to constitute the pillar, as per the respondents and interviewees, of a more effective implementation and measurement.

The main limitations of this study pertain to the samples, both in the questionnaire due to the lack of probability sampling and in the interviews due to a low number of interviewees. The fact that the interviewees were volunteers can also introduce some bias, as it speaks to a specific type of respondent. Since not all the items of the guidelines were covered by the interviews, limited insight was obtained about the reasons behind the agreement and disagreement with certain items. Further research can focus on case studies of active learning implementation to examine the strategies that are used in its design and to assess its instructional impact. Moreover, given that there is still some teacher resistance to active learning, it would be important to its advancement, to examine the reasons behind this opposition. It is fundamental to examine the viewpoints of university lecturers and to study their experiences. The more active learning pioneers and adopters share their experience, more knowledge will be accessible to teachers to judge if this teaching approach is suitable for their courses and more data will be available to guide a more successful implementation.

References

1. Brame, C.: Active Learning. Vanderbilt University Center for Teaching (2016)
2. Kozanitis, A., Nenciovici, L.: Effect of active learning versus traditional lecturing on the learning achievement of college students in humanities and social sciences: a meta-analysis. High. Educ. **86**(6), 1377–1394 (2023)
3. Isaias, P.: Flipping Your Classroom: A Methodology for Successful Flipped Classrooms. In: Demetrios, G., Sampson, D.I., P. I. (ed) IADIS International Conference Cognition and Exploratory Learning in Digital, International Association for Development of the Information Society., Budapest, Hungary (2018)
4. Isaias, P., McKimmie, B., Bakharia, A., Zornig J.: Flipping the classroom effectively: evaluation results from a course at the university of Queensland. In: EdMedia+ Innovate Learning, pp. 1864–1873. Association for the Advancement of Computing in Education (AACE) (2018)
5. Nordmann, E., et al.: Lights, camera, active! appreciation of active learning predicts positive attitudes towards lecture capture. High. Educ. (2021)
6. Velde, R.V.D., et al.: The idea is nice... but not for me: first-year students' readiness for large-scale 'flipped lectures'—what (de)motivates them?. High. Educ. (2020)
7. Tharayil, S., et al.: Strategies to mitigate student resistance to active learning. Int J STEM Educ **5**(1), 7 (2018)
8. Sandrone, S., et al.: Active learning in psychiatry education: current practices and future perspectives. Front. Psychiatry **11** (2020)
9. Borda, E., et al.: Initial implementation of active learning strategies in large, lecture STEM courses: lessons learned from a multi-institutional, interdisciplinary STEM faculty development program. Int. J. STEM Educ. **7**(1), 4 (2020)
10. Campbell, L.O., Heller, S., Pulse, L.: Student-created video: an active learning approach in online environments. Interact. Learn. Environ. 1–10 (2020)
11. Kannan, V., et al.: Flip & Pair – a strategy to augment a blended course with active-learning components: effects on engagement and learning. Smart Learn. Environ. **7**(1), 34 (2020)
12. Carr, R., Palmer, S., Hagel, P.: Active learning: the importance of developing a comprehensive measure. Act. Learn. High. Educ. **16**(3), 173–186 (2015)

13. Børte, K., Nesje, K., Lillejord, S.: Barriers to student active learning in higher education. Teach. High. Educ. **28**(3), 597–615 (2023)
14. Faustino, P., Simões, D.: The contribution of the technology acceptance model for an active teaching and learning process in higher education: a bibliometric analysis. In: Handbook of Research on Digital Learning, pp. 242–261. IGI Global (2020)
15. Reilly, C., Reeves, T.C.: Refining active learning design principles through design-based research. Act. Learn. High. Educ. **25**(1), 81–100 (2024)
16. Deslauriers, L., et al.: Measuring actual learning versus feeling of learning in response to being actively engaged in the classroom. Proc. Natl. Acad. Sci. **116**(39), 19251–19257 (2019)
17. Hailikari, T., et al.: Student perspectives on how different elements of constructive alignment support active learning. Active Learn. High. Educ. **23**(3) (2021)
18. López-Cuello, J., Uitdewilligen, S., Sambeth, A.: Triggers and conducive factors for reflection in university students: a focus group study. Reflective Pract. 1–15 (2024)
19. Van den Beemt, A., et al.: Remote labs in higher engineering education: engaging students with active learning pedagogy. J. Comput. High. Educ. **35**(2), 320–340 (2023)
20. Park, E.L., Choi, B.K.: Transformation of classroom spaces: traditional versus active learning classroom in colleges. High. Educ. **68**(5), 749–771 (2014)
21. Rands, M.L., Gansemer-Topf, A.M.: The room itself is active: how classroom design impacts student engagement. J. Learn. Spaces **6**(1), 26 (2017)
22. Van Amburgh, J.A., et al.: A tool for measuring active learning in the classroom. Am. J. Pharm. Educ. **71**(5), 85 (2007)
23. Freeman, S., et al.: Active learning increases student performance in science, engineering, and mathematics. Proc. Natl. Acad. Sci. **111**(23), 8410–8415 (2014)
24. Duran, P.A., et al.: Student attitudes and achievement in active learning calculus. Int. J. Math. Educ. Sci. Technol. **55**(3), 759–780 (2024)
25. Seo, K., et al.: Active learning with online video: the impact of learning context on engagement. Comput. Educ. **165**, 104132 (2021)
26. Creswell, J.W., Creswell, J.D.: Research design: Qualitative, quantitative, and mixed methods approaches, 5th ed. Sage, Los Angeles (2018)
27. Wright, K.B.: Researching Internet-based populations: advantages and disadvantages of online survey research, online questionnaire authoring software packages, and web survey services. J. Comput. Mediated Commun. **10**(3), JCMC1034 (2005)
28. Dicicco-Bloom, B., Crabtree, B.F.: The qualitative research interview. Med. Educ. **40**(4), 314–321 (2006)
29. Lavrakas, P.J.: Encyclopedia of survey research methods. Sage Publications: Thousand Oaks, California (2008)
30. Robinson, O.C.: Sampling in interview-based qualitative research: a theoretical and practical guide. Qual. Res. Psychol. **11**(1), 25–41 (2014)
31. Field, A.: Discovering statistics using IBM SPSS statistics. 4th ed.: Sage (2013)
32. Yong, A.G., Pearce, S.: A beginner's guide to factor analysis: focusing on exploratory factor analysis. Tutorials Quant. Methods Psychol. **9**(2), 79–94 (2013)
33. Costello, A.B., Osborne, J.: Best practices in exploratory factor analysis: four recommendations for getting the most from your analysis. Pract. Assess. Res. Eval. **10**(1), 7 (2005)

Evaluating the Transformative Digital Pedagogies for Higher Education Training Programme: Insights into Participants' Perceptions

Elis Kakoulli Constantinou[1](✉), María Victoria Soulé[2], Stavroulla Hadjiconstantinou[1], and Nicoletta Pantela[1]

[1] Cyprus University of Technology, Limassol, Cyprus
elis.constantinou@cut.ac.cy
[2] University of Cyprus, Nicosia, Cyprus

Abstract. The adaptation of education and training systems to the digital age is one of the priorities of the European Commission. Aiming at promoting high-quality, inclusive education, Higher Education (HE) institutions are working towards digital and pedagogical transformation; however, lack of both pedagogical skills for using digital technologies and digital skills for implementing innovative teaching practices make this a challenging task. The Erasmus+ funded Transformative Digital Pedagogies for Higher Education (TDP4HE) project addresses this challenge by developing a training programme for HE staff designed to enhance academic staff's pedagogical and digital competencies, enabling them to effectively transition to digital education. This paper examines the first implementation and evaluation of this online training programme, delivered to EUt + university staff in May-June 2024. The results show participants' positive perceptions about the training programme's innovative approach to transformative digital pedagogies. They also identify certain challenges encountered and reveal ways in which the training programme could be improved to better meet educators' needs.

Keywords: Digital Pedagogies · Online Training Programme · Digital Competence · Higher Education · Programme Evaluation

1 Introduction

Among the most important initiatives of the European Commission is the support of the adaptation of the education and training systems of Member States to the digital age creating opportunities for high-quality, inclusive education for all [1]. For many years now, the development of digital competences of citizens in general and educators in particular has been a priority of the European Commission [2]. This focus stems from the realisation that digital literacy is crucial for navigating the increasingly digital world and participating fully in society. EU's emphasis on digital transformation is manifested in a) the Digital Competence Framework for Citizens (DigComp) [3], which provides a

B. K. Smith and M. Borge (Eds.): HCII 2025, LNCS 15806, pp. 225–244, 2025.
https://doi.org/10.1007/978-3-031-93564-0_14

common understanding of digital competence, b) the Digital Competence Framework for Educators (DigCompEdu) [2], which focuses on the specific digital competencies that educators need in order to effectively integrate technology into their teaching practices, and c) funding programmes such as Erasmus+ and Horizon 2020 to support initiatives that promote digital skills development among citizens and educators. Furthermore, according to the International Association of Universities [4], digital transformation is among the strategic priorities of Higher Education (HE) institutions accelerated during COVID-19 pandemic.

Nevertheless, there are several challenges to be considered, such as the digital divide that may exist between countries and educational institutions, which prevents equitable access to technology and digital resources. Another challenge is the fact that technology is advancing rapidly, which requires continuous learning and adaptation for both citizens and educators. Last but not least, one of the greatest challenges is the provision of adequate training and professional development opportunities for educators to effectively use digital tools in their teaching. On the one hand, the lack of pedagogical competences linked to the use of digital technologies, and on the other hand, the lack of digital competences linked to the implementation of innovative and transformative teaching practices, make this effort more complicated.

Inspired by these facts, the Transformative Digital Pedagogies for Higher Education (TDP4HE) project, an ERASMUS+ project submitted under the action KA220-HED - Cooperation partnerships in Higher Education [5], proposes a transformative pedagogical model for the development of pedagogical competences of academic staff. One of the major activities of the project is the design and implementation of an online training programme aiming at developing the transformative digital pedagogies of academic teaching staff. The TDP4HE training programme aims to empower academic teaching staff with both pedagogical and digital competences and to increase their capacity and readiness to manage a real shift towards digital education with their teaching practices. This paper focuses on the implementation and evaluation of the training programme, which was offered online to members of the academic teaching staff of the Universities of the European University of Technology alliance (EUt+) between May – June 2024.

2 Literature Review

2.1 Digital Transformation in HE

According to Mahlow and Hediger [6], digital transformation refers to the transformation of organizational processes and building of new competencies and models through digital technologies in a profound and strategic way. In other words, it does not only concern the use of digital technologies, but it also involves a change of culture, and the acquisition of new skills to facilitate the effective utilisation of technology in order to achieve better outcomes. Bygstad et al. [7], use different terms to define digital transformation in HE. First, they refer to "dual digitalisation" which involves a combination of digital tools, such as Learning Management Systems (LMS), MOOCs, course websites, etc., and digital subjects developed by academics. Then they add that, currently, this "dual digitalisation" has been viewed in a more holistic and comprehensive way, leading to a reconsideration of the learning process; the authors refer to the term "digital learning space", which involves a combination of the technical, pedagogical and organisational perspective.

During the last decades, emphasis has been placed on digital transformation in HE due to various reasons. First of all, the needs and the expectations of digital native students are changing, and employability skills seem to hold a prominent position in academic curricula, equipping students to meet today's challenges in the modern workplace [8]. Moreover, emerging technologies offer new possibilities for teaching, learning and research, making education more accessible and inclusive [9]. Additionally, HE institutions face increasing competition, both domestically and internationally, and digital transformation can help them stand out and excel both in the achievement of better learning outcomes and in research. The need for digital transformation was intensified with the abrupt shift to remote learning during the COVID-19 pandemic, which forced HE institutions to quickly adapt and offer flexible learning options. This primarily involved leveraging digital platforms, adopting innovative teaching methods, and creating new digital learning materials [10].

In the 2030 Agenda for Sustainable Development, adopted by all United Nations Member States in 2015, quality education is one of the fundamental human rights and a cornerstone of the 17 Sustainable Development Goals [11]. Digital transformation is fundamental in the improvement of HE. It must be carefully guided to enhance quality education, while proactively mitigating potential risks and negative impacts [4].

2.2 Transforming Pedagogy in Higher Education

The Digital Education Action Plan (2021–2027) is a renewed EU policy initiative that sets out a common vision of high-quality, inclusive and accessible digital education in Europe; it promotes the development of a high-performing digital education ecosystem and enhances digital skills and competences for digital transformation [1]. Teachers' lack of digital competence and pedagogical knowledge in HE is one of the major barriers to the realisation of this vision. Members of academic staff need to undergo training that will equip them with the digital skills and pedagogical knowledge to effectively integrate technology into their teaching [12]. They also need to be provided with the appropriate support in adapting to this evolving digital landscape.

Over the last couple of decades there has been an increase in literature pertaining to the professional development of lecturers; however, literature that combines professional development of academics and educational innovation with the use of new technologies in the context of HE is scarce [13]. According to Ter Beek et al. [13], educating lecturers to apply and integrate innovative technology in their curricula is essential for the future of education, and it is up to HE institutions to facilitate effective forms of lecturer professional development to scale up the pace of change. A study by Bitar and Davidovich [14] provides an exploration of lecturers' experiences in terms of the Digital Learning initiative implemented by the Council for Higher Education (CHE) and the Planning and Budgeting Committee (PBC) in Israel. The results of the study reveal four key domains that shape lecturers' experiences with Digital Learning: educational, personal, cultural and social, and institutional. These domains interact in complex ways, influencing the adoption and effectiveness of Digital Learning strategies. The study also shows that effective Digital Learning implementation, apart from the integration of technological, pedagogical, and content knowledge, requires an understanding of the cultural and institutional landscape.

The efforts to digitalise and transform pedagogy in HE takes place along with a shift to more learner-centred and active learning approaches to education [12]. Such approaches place emphasis on student engagement in real-life problems and challenges through activities like group work, discussions, problem-solving, and hands-on projects. According to Santoveña-Casal and López [15], in general, an analysis of the topics and research in the last years reflects the COVID-19 pandemic's impact on HE as well as the need of HE institutions to significantly expand the use of digital pedagogy by adapting their teaching methodologies. This demands a significant increase in research conducted in this area of knowledge. Even though the shift to digital technologies was massive during the pandemic, many academics did not embrace student-centered teaching approaches, and the need for education and support on the pedagogical use of new technologies was strengthened [16].

The TDP4HE project proposes a transformative pedagogical model for the development of pedagogical competences of academic staff, that makes integral use of digital technologies [5]. Research conducted in the project is based on the view that the digitalisation of teaching and learning processes is not simply the application of digital technologies to enhance traditional teaching methods. Digitalisation in classrooms is revolutionary in that it makes it easier to adopt radically different and innovative student-centred approaches. By adopting transformative pedagogical approaches, this project aims to develop a model that links transformative pedagogies (learner-centred, opposed to transmissive, teacher-centred, approaches) to the use of digital technologies and to develop a transdisciplinary training programme to foster innovative ways of teaching and learning for academic teaching staff from different disciplines.

3 The TDP4HE Training Programme

The Training Programme on Transformative Digital Pedagogies for academic teaching staff aims not only at improving teachers' technological competency but also their understanding of how to integrate content, pedagogy and technology together in an innovative and transformative way. More specifically, the programme aims to contribute to the general objectives of the project by training academic teaching staff to understand and apply effective teaching methodologies in HE, recognise technology's role in modern pedagogy, design courses, implement diverse teaching methods, integrate new technologies, employ varied assessment techniques, use digital resources effectively, and adapt pedagogical strategies to evolving educational environment.

Grounded in the literature described in the previous section, the programme was designed based on the results obtained from needs analysis on the pedagogical practices implemented in the eight universities that form the European University of Technology (EUt+). Among the results of the needs analysis was the need to focus on transformative approaches (learner-centred) as opposed to transmissive (teacher-centred) approaches. Furthermore, the main topics foregrounded by needs analysis were summarised: learner-centred approaches, inquiry-based approaches, problem-based learning and problem-solution skills, project-based learning, case-based learning, critical thinking, social-collaborative learning, inter and transdisciplinary thinking skills, and lifelong learning.

The designed online course training programme on transformative digital pedagogies for academic teaching staff includes five different modules, which were incorporated into the project's learning management system (LMS: Moodle). Delivered fully online, the programme features synchronous webinars with pre-tasks, sessions, and assessments. Teaching methods include lectures, demonstrations, small group collaboration, discussions, and assigned readings. The five modules cover teaching in the digital era, using emerging technologies, study process principles, psychology, inclusive education, and academic staff development. Participants are expected to actively engage in theoretical discussions and hands-on activities, integrating theory with practice through evaluated tasks. The first, pilot phase of the implementation of the training programme took place online in Fall 2024 with academics from the European University of Technology (EUt+); the participants included teaching staff from different departments of the project partner universities and associate partners.

A trainer's guide is also planned as a deliverable from the Training Programme on Transformative Digital Pedagogies. This will focus on the content and methodology of the training programme for academic teaching staff and will be available in the project's Open Community of Practice and the project website.

Continuous evaluation of training programs like the TDP4HE is essential to ensure they remain effective, relevant, and aligned with the evolving needs of educators and learners. By systematically assessing the programme's design, delivery, and outcomes, stakeholders can identify areas for improvement and ensure that the training equips educators with the necessary skills to adapt to technological advancements and pedagogical shifts [17]. Continuous evaluation was a key component in the design of the TDP4HE programme as a way of fostering a culture of accountability and reflective practice, enabling participants and shareholders to provide feedback and share insights that can refine the programme's content and methodologies. Moreover, as digital tools and teaching strategies evolve rapidly, continuous assessment helps maintain the program's relevance, ensuring that it consistently supports educators in fostering engaging and transformative learning experiences in higher education [18].

Incorporating principles of design-based research (DBR) into the evaluation process allows for iterative testing and refinement of the program in real-world contexts, ensuring that it responds dynamically to practical challenges and evolving educational environments [19].

4 Methodology

This study is based on the principles of Design-based research (DBR), an interventionist research method [20]. DBR is a methodology designed by and for educators that seeks to increase the impact, transfer and translation of education research into improved practice [21]. In addition, it stresses the need for theory building and the development of design principles that guide, inform and improve both practice and research in educational contexts [22]. As already mentioned, the design of the training programme described in this paper reflected the outcome of the needs analysis and is in the process of being refined through two cycles of implementation, data collection, analysis and revision. DBR follows iterative cycles of (1) problem identification and definition, (2) context analysis, (3) design and development, (4) implementation, (5) evaluation, (6) reflection and redesign, and (7) communication and dissemination. Phases (1) to (4) of this study were reported in Soule and Kakoulli Constantinou's [23] paper. The present paper focuses on phases (5) to (7), aiming at presenting the way the TDP4HE training programme was evaluated by the participants, discussing their reflections and suggestions for the redesign of the programme and last but not least, communicating the results to different experts and stakeholders interested in transformative digital pedagogy in the HE context.

4.1 Research Questions

The research questions underpinning the study were the following:

1. What are participants' perceptions about the TDP4HE training programme?
2. What are the challenges that participants faced during the implementation of the programme?
3. What are participants' suggestions concerning improvements that need to be made?

4.2 Research Tools

Both qualitative and quantitative data were collected to evaluate the TDP4HE training programme and explore participants' perceptions. The data were collected through a focus group discussion and an online questionnaire which were used to highlight strengths and identify improvement areas. The focus group session lasted 45 min and was video-recorded and transcribed for analysis. The focus group included 10 questions designed to gather detailed participant feedback. The questions were:

1. What are your initial thoughts about the overall experience of this training programme?
2. How do you feel the training programme has impacted your knowledge/understanding of teaching methodologies?
3. Has this programme helped you understand how important technology is in contemporary pedagogy in HE?
4. How confident are you in your ability to formulate learning objectives, design course content, and establish learning outcomes after attending the training programme?
5. Do you feel the programme objectives align with your personal and professional development goals?
6. How much do you think that this programme has helped you become familiar with some learner-centred approaches and teaching methodologies like project-based learning, social collaborative learning, etc.?
7. How much do you think the programme has helped you with integrating emerging technologies into your teaching practices?
8. How do you expect this programme to impact your teaching practices in the short term and long term?

9. How do you feel about the structure and content of the TDP4HE training programme? Do you have any suggestions for improving the programme to better meet your needs?
10. Any final comments/ thoughts?

The data from the focus group were analysed using thematic analysis, which involved manually identifying and categorising key themes and patterns within the responses. This process entailed a careful review of the focus group transcripts, allowing for an in-depth understanding of recurring ideas and insights. By organising the data into distinct themes, we were able to draw meaningful conclusions and gain a comprehensive view of the participants' feedback.

The online questionnaire included 12 questions designed to gather detailed feedback from the participants. In particular, questions 1, 2 and 12 were open-ended and aimed at prompting participants to elaborate on their experience (e.g. what they liked the most/least and suggestions for improvements. Questions 3 to 11 were five-point Likert statements measuring participants' agreement (Strongly Disagree-Strongly agree). All questions are listed below:

1. What was the one aspect you found most interesting or useful in the TDP4HE Training programme?
2. What was the one thing you liked the least, or which you would change about in the TDP4HE Training programme?
3. The TDP4HE Training programme contents met my expectations.
4. The content has been clear and understandable.
5. The LMS/ Moodle platform worked well.
6. The synchronous sessions were organised to allow all participants to fully participate.
7. The pre- and post-activities were useful.
8. The asynchronous materials were useful.
9. The TDP4HE modules were useful, so that I am more confident about its topic now.
10. I think this training programme is useful for my professional/academic training.
11. I would recommend this training programme to other colleagues.
12. Please provide any other comment, suggestion or feedback about the training programme that was not covered in the questions above.

The data from the online questionnaire were analysed manually using participants' written responses to the open-ended questions, and the graphs were generated automatically using Google Forms. Both research tools allowed gaining a comprehensive understanding of their feedback.

4.3 Participants

A total of 106 members of the academic staff of all nine Universities of the EUt + alliance registered in the course. Participants represented Riga Technical University, University of Technology of Troyes, Cyprus University of Technology, Technical University of Cartagena, Technological University Dublin, Technical University of Sofia, Technical University of Cluj-Napoca, Darmstadt University of Applied Sciences, and The University of Cassino and Southern Lazio. Almost half of the 106 academics participated actively in the synchronous sessions. Twenty-four academics across the EUt+

Alliance completed the online questionnaire. In addition, four academic staff members from the EUt + Alliance who attended the TDP4HE Training Programme sessions participated in the focus group conducted by two interviewers from the Cyprus University of Technology.

5 Results

The findings of the focus group discussions and online questionnaire provide insights into participants' perceptions of the TDP4HE training programme highlighting its strengths, challenges, and areas for improvement.

The findings section presents eight key thematic areas, each illustrated with relevant excerpts from focus group discussions and visual representations from the online questionnaire, such as graphs, to enhance clarity and depth of analysis. By integrating qualitative and quantitative data, this section provides a holistic understanding of the programme's impact and effectiveness.

5.1 Interesting/Useful Aspects of the Programme

In the focus group discussion, participants expressed initial curiosity and motivation to improve their teaching methods and stay updated with the latest advancements in the field. This was driven by a desire to find their place within a larger network of professionals and specialists.

The following extracts illustrate this theme:

So I have to, I must admit that my initial thoughts were most of curiosity and how to find my own connection, to find my own spot into this large network of professionals, of specialists in the field. (Participant 1)

So, once again, I, you gave me the confidence and you're-motivated me that I am on the right track, according to the methodologies I use with my students. (Participant 1)

So it made us, made me at least, consider differently how to use technology in the classroom and how the lesson can be more interactive and that students could gain more motivation when using these technologies in classroom. (Participant 3)

Also, the question, "*What was the one aspect you found most interesting or useful in the TDP4HE Training programme?*", shows as the most interesting or useful the diverse trainers' backgrounds, the selected topics and materials presented utilising theoretical and practical means at a great level, the communication between them and exchange of ideas. Participants' responses are also shown in Table 1 below:

Furthermore, participants found the asynchronous materials useful, as 91.6% strongly agreed or agreed with the statement, while a few remained neutral or disagreed (Fig. 1).

Participants also think that the training programme is useful for their professional/academic training, as 91.7% of them strongly agreed or agreed with the statement, while a few remained neutral (Fig. 2).

Table 1. Interesting and useful aspects of the training programme

• The internationalisation aspect of the team of trainers from different universities/countries in EUT+.
• The diversity of the selected topics, the up-to-date references, materials and cases presented.
• The communication between the participants and the opportunity to share experiences.
• The group discussions and interactions they had in the break-out rooms.
• The multifaceted approach to the problem was a skillful combination of theoretical background and interactive, hands-on activities and practical tools.
• The innovative teaching and learning techniques/ teaching through new/ emerging technologies.
• The modules' content particularly Module 2, "Didactic Foundation of Learning/Teaching through the use of new/ emerging technologies".

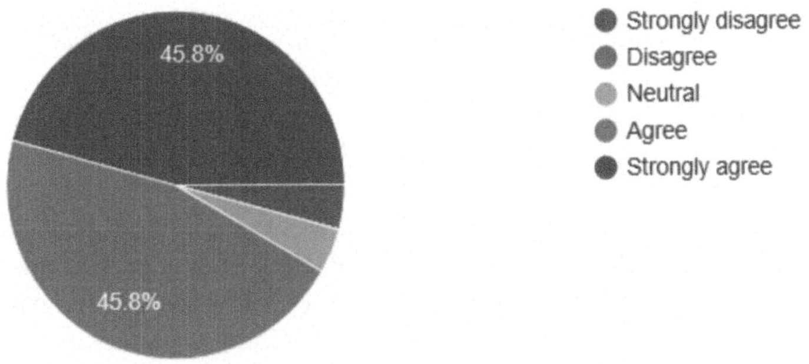

Fig. 1. The asynchronous materials were useful

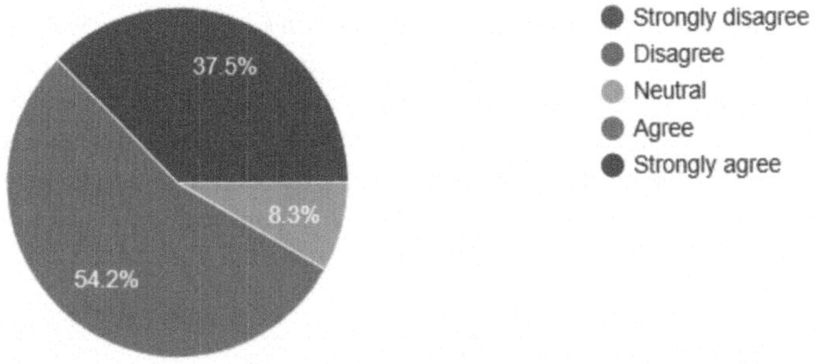

Fig. 2. This training programme is useful for my professional/academic training

5.2 Things that Participants Liked/Didn't Like

Participants liked the fact that the programme reassured them about the validity of their existing teaching methodologies, such as project-based learning and student-centred approaches. They appreciated knowing that their methods aligned with contemporary practices.

The excerpts below showcase this theme:

I came across your course and I am thankful to that it's actually that you highlighted the fact that I knew it was the right way to do it. It is the right way to do it. So, project-based learning, student-centered approach, and technologies to be used in the delivery, in the teaching and the learning and the assessment part of our students should be incorporated and not neglected. (Participant 1)

Yeah..It's actually, it was very reassuring and very comfortable, you know, to know that what you do, you do it in the right way. Because there are episodes, moments in our careers when we question our approach, our teaching methodologies as a result of the experience, since we have got or with the discussions. (Participant 1)

Another aspect that participants highly valued was the programme's structure, which involved collaboration with trainers from different universities. Participants appreciated the opportunity to interact with colleagues from various disciplines and share diverse perspectives:

So it was convenient for us. And I also really liked that we had the chance, it was interactive, we had the chance to speak about our minds, we had the breakout rooms, so we were meeting with the other colleagues and we had to discuss about certain things. So it was overall a very fruitful and thoughtful experience full of new knowledge. (Participant 3)

On the other hand, the question "What was the one thing you liked the least, or which you would change about in the TDP4HE Training programme?" revealed the least favourite parts of the training programme and/or suggestions mainly focused on the overall organisation, training content and teaching approach. A few of them stated that nothing should be changed (Table 2).

Participants also considered the time allocated for each breakout room insufficient. They suggested extending these sessions to allow for more thorough discussions and exchange of ideas.

Talking about the length of the breakout rooms, you know, because you try to keep the balance between the theory and the presentations and then the interaction in the breakout rooms. And it worked as it worked, but we felt like, and I'm sure you heard the complaint, it was too little time. We needed more time to, you know, maybe to expand a little bit the timing for how the breakout rooms work next time you organize a new program, right, to provide each and every speaker who is willing to share their experiences the amount of time they need to do that. (Participant 1)

5.3 Meeting Participants' Expectations

Regarding whether the TDP4HE Training programme contents met their expectations, as Fig. 3 illustrates, 75% of participants strongly agreed or agreed with the statement, while a few remained neutrals, disagreed or strongly disagreed.

Table 2. The least favourite parts of the training programme

Category	Specific points that could change
Overall organisation	• Follow-up emails from different persons made it difficult to retrieve the information sent • In some cases, long synchronous sessions coincided with personal/family time; they could be kept only for questions • A workshop could be organised in person to complete the programme
Training content	• Presentations could be less theoretical and more interactive, with more practical aspects, guidelines, examples, and best practices guidelines for teaching and implementing relevant pedagogical theories • Some sessions were at a basic level • Some of the information is redundant across the modules • The last two modules aimed to cover too many topics • More training on digital transformation tools for teaching • Methods to improve pedagogical resources for too many students in a classroom • Focusing on fields other than language teaching, such as mechanical engineering and robotics, would be beneficial
Teaching approach	• The collaborative tasks with other colleagues were challenging due to the lack of time to meet with them • More time to be dedicated to practical activities such as group discussions/activities

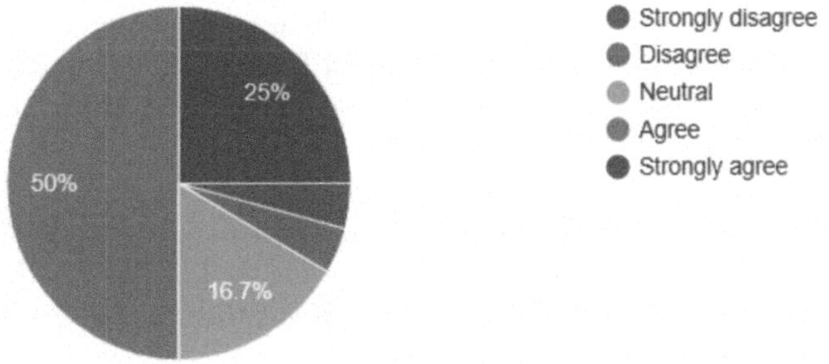

Fig. 3. The TDP4HE Training programme content met my expectations.

Also, regarding whether the synchronous sessions were organised to allow all participants to participate fully, 83.4% strongly agreed or agreed with the statement, while a few remained neutral or strongly disagreed (Fig. 4).

5.4 Content/Materials/Tools/Moodle Platform

Concerning the content and whether it was clear and understandable, 95.9% of participants strongly agreed or agreed with the statement, while one remained neutral (Fig. 5).

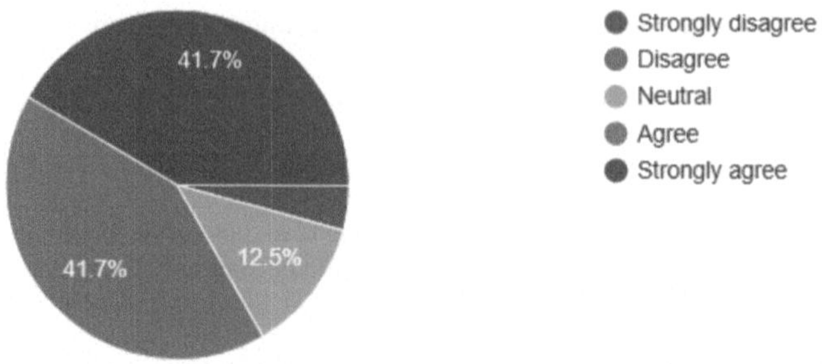

Fig. 4. The synchronous sessions were organised to allow all participants to fully participate.

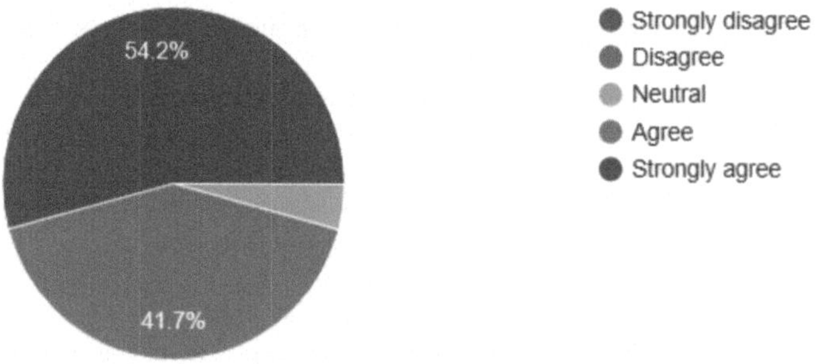

Fig. 5. The content has been clear and understandable.

Also, the organisation of content, along with the use of the Moodle platform, were appreciated. Participants valued the availability of further readings, presentations, and video recordings, which allowed them to revisit and deepen their understanding of the material.

The following excerpts highlight this theme:

I want to underline the fact that I really enjoyed the way you organised your content and how you used the Moodle platform with underline the fact that I really enjoyed the way you organised your content and how you used the Moodle platform with all those topics connected and the details (Participant 1).

So I don't know if you have the tracks on how many times people check your platform, but I have to say that I was interested in here and there to go back to one topic or to try to find out more about something else (Participant 1).

Results from the questionnaire report that the LMS/ Moodle platform worked well (Fig. 6), 83.4% of participants strongly agreed or agreed with the statement, while a few remained neutral or strongly disagreed.

The focus group discussion also highlighted the value of the online format and the use of interactive tools like breakout rooms. Participants found the programme's flexibility and the ability to engage in meaningful discussions with peers beneficial.

The excerpts below showcase this theme:

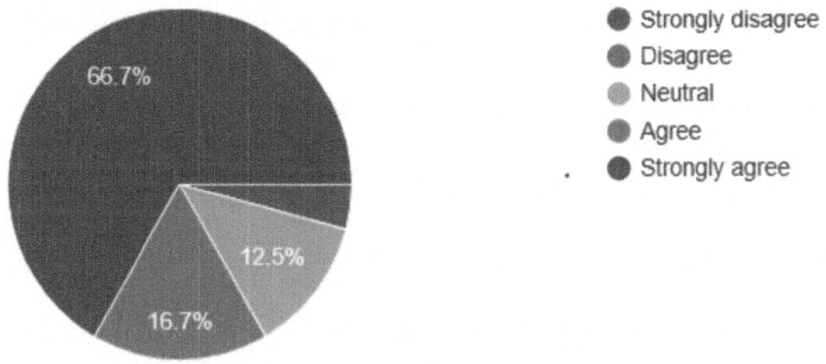

Fig. 6. The LMS/ Moodle platform worked well.

In this way, it's very useful to break the groups into different groups, smaller groups. I think that this has been a very good idea from Patrick, and I think that we can do it more frequently (Participant 4).

I think it was really nice to keep this combination of the plenaries, the sessions, the online sessions, and the interaction in the breakout rooms (Participant 1).

Regarding whether the pre- and post-activities were useful, 79.2% of participants strongly agreed or agreed with the statement, while a few remained neutral or strongly disagreed (Fig. 7).

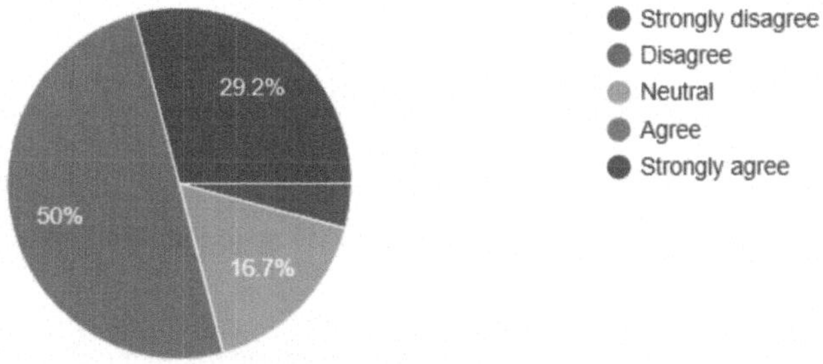

Fig. 7. The pre- and post-activities were useful

The integration of technology was another aspect of the content highlighted in the programme. Participants recognised the need to move beyond basic digital tools to more advanced technologies like virtual reality to enhance student engagement and motivation.

The excerpts below illustrate this theme:

I would say that nowadays in the 21st century we can't speak about technology only using, for example, a presentation or a video in our classroom, just to use technology for the sake of technology. So it was very insightful that we had also a module concerning the virtual reality and all of its aspects (Participant 3).

So you can see different ideas how you could improve yourself and your approaches, which was very useful from my personal perspective. And of course, the digital, the use of digital tools is very important, just because the students, they live in this kind of environment, so we have to try to be closer to them, to try to, I know, a part of their lives, so the education won't be just something they have to pass to get the degree or something like that, to involve them really in as many activities as possible. So technology is different tools, it provides these possibilities. (Participant 2).

I want to underline the fact that I really enjoyed the way you organized your content and how you used the Moodle platform with underline the fact that I really enjoyed the way you organized your content and how you used the Moodle platform with all those topics connected and the details the details about the further readings and the PowerPoint presentations and the video recording of your presentation (Participant 1)

5.5 Modules

Regarding the question of whether the training programme modules were helpful so that they are more confident about its topic now, most participants strongly agreed or agreed with the statement for all modules (Fig. 8). Participants tend to strongly agree or agree about being more confident for Modules 2 and 5. On the other hand, Modules 1 and 4 concentrated some neutral responses. Only one participant strongly disagreed with the statement on all occasions.

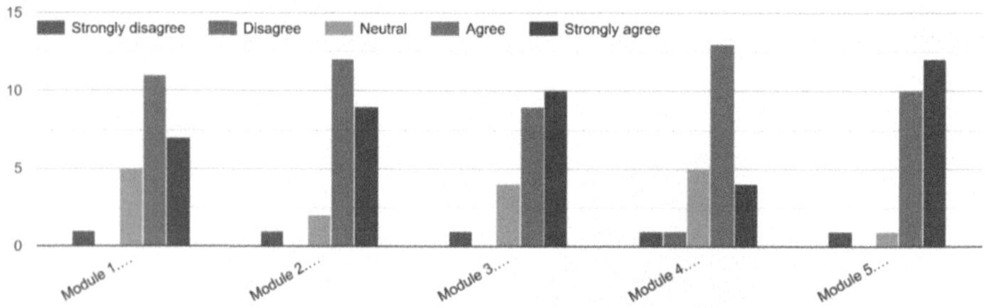

Fig. 8. The TDP4HE modules were useful, so that I am more confident about its topic now.

They would also recommend this training programme to other colleagues, as 75% of them strongly agreed or agreed with the statement, while a few remained neutral (Fig. 9).

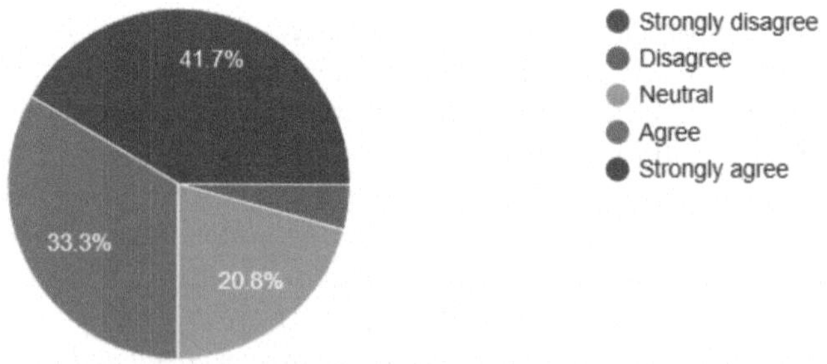

Fig. 9. I would recommend this training programme to other colleagues.

5.6 Challenges Faced

Despite acknowledging the importance of technology, participants pointed out significant challenges, including financial constraints and the complexity of integrating advanced technologies into their teaching practices:

Of course, we talked about any challenges that we may have about the equipment and that it costs a lot of money. However, it is very important to face these challenges and integrate technology in our classroom and not just a presentation or a video (Participant 3). [...] *Yeah, I totally agree with you, [the participant calls the name of another participant here]* [...] *And again, right, I agree with this aspect about the, I mean, with the financial aspect that it might be challenging in all institutions too.* (Participant 1).

5.7 Suggestions for Changes/Improvements

Participants suggested several improvements, including more active engagement with the underutilised community of practice to enhance course development and discussions despite time constraints. Future changes could involve reorganising the programme with additional or different partners and incorporating workshops or small conferences to enrich face-to-face interactions. Additionally, there is a need for more relevant examples and modules focused on designing virtual or augmented reality tools tailored to various specializations and scenarios, as current examples may not suit all teaching contexts.

The excerpts below showcase this theme:

I think that the community of practice is a tool that we have to use and we are not using it. Because many of the ideas, many of the things, many of the thoughts that we have covered in the course can be developed and discussed in the community of practice. We have to feed the community of practice. I think that it's not easy because we have a lack of time for doing so many things, but I think that we have to encourage ourselves and encourage our colleagues to use the community of practice. I think that it's just to ignite it. So, we start interchanging ideas in the community of practice. This is one of the things that I think could improve a lot the courses and our regular teaching because it is with the interaction, it is with the change of ideas, how this thing can flourish (Participant 4).

My first suggestion is to do it again next year maybe to involve more partners or to separate different activities to different partners so everyone will be involved in these activities that's just suggestion of course and the second thing I think it will be very useful if we have a workshop or a small conference or something like that and we can meet in person. I mean divided in different groups of different tasks. I think that the work face to face could never be the same. I mean, it's much more useful and enrich all the people participating in it (Participant 2).

I really enjoyed the one with Dali that you had as an example included in your course, but I'm not sure of how relevant that is in my teaching context. So maybe one extra module that you could include or at least one session would be to create those groups groups in which we might design one particular virtual reality tool or augmented reality tool that could work or not, I'm not sure. But I felt at that stage of the module that further into specific scenarios, cases for different specializations (Participant 1).

But in the two sessions I attended, what I miss what's more focus in specific problems. Let's say, to use technology is very far from easy. When you want to integrate, for example, virtual reality in your class is not something that you can do easily. You need, I think, I think my experience, at least in the things that I am teaching, for me is not easy. And there is another thing that I miss is how to provide interaction with technology. (Participant 4)

5.8 Recommendations

Based on the results of the focus group and the evaluation questionnaire, several recommendations can be proposed.

Firstly, it would be beneficial to engage participants before the programme begins to maintain and boost initial curiosity and motivation.

In terms of pedagogical validation and reassurance, the programme could incorporate case studies or testimonials from educators who have successfully implemented similar methodologies. This not only provides practical validation but also inspires participants by showcasing real-world applications. Furthermore, hosting interactive Q&A sessions where participants can discuss their existing methods with experts and receive constructive feedback can be highly beneficial. This approach reinforces the validity of their practices while offering opportunities for improvement.

Participants would also be interested in more practical approaches, particularly in handling large class sizes, which would improve the relevance of university teaching contexts.

To address the theme of integrating technology, the programme should include hands-on workshops that focus on using advanced technologies like virtual reality, augmented reality, and AI tools in teaching. These workshops can provide practical experience and confidence in using new tools. Additionally, providing comprehensive guides and tutorials tailored to various teaching contexts can support participants in effectively integrating these technologies into their classrooms.

Recognising the challenges in implementing technology, it is crucial to discuss strategies for resource allocation, such as acquiring funding or grants to overcome financial constraints. Simplifying the integration process by offering step-by-step guides can also help participants incorporate technology with minimal complexity and resources. This dual approach addresses both financial and practical barriers.

The programme's collaborative learning and networking aspect can be enhanced by organising participants into smaller, themed groups based on their disciplines or interests. This facilitates more relevant and in-depth discussions. Additionally, planning periodic online meetups can help maintain and strengthen professional connections, fostering a robust network of educators. The TDP4HE Community of Practice can assist in this effort.

Enhancing the interactive and flexible learning environment is another key area for improvement. Providing flexible scheduling options can also accommodate participants' diverse needs and time zones, ensuring everyone can participate fully.

Regarding suggestions for improvement, it is advised to make greater use of the underutilised TDP4HE Community of Practice, which can significantly enhance discussions despite time constraints. Furthermore, there is a need to integrate more relevant examples and modules that focus on designing virtual or augmented reality tools specific to various specialisations and scenarios, as the current examples may not apply to all teaching contexts.

To address the need for longer interaction periods, extending the time allocated for breakout room interactions can allow for more thorough discussions and exchanging ideas.

In general, the results indicate that participants appreciated the training programme's innovative approach to transformative digital pedagogies. These insights have supported refining the training strategy and addressing the identified issues to better meet educators' needs and enhance overall satisfaction with the programme.

6 Discussion

Digital transformation and the acquisition of pedagogical competence is vital, and for this reason it has been listed among the strategic priorities of the European Commission [1]. By embracing technological change and equipping faculty with the necessary skills, HE institutions can better serve their students and contribute to a more digitally literate and globally competitive workforce. Digital transformation is not just about using technology for technology's sake. It rather concerns the thoughtful and strategic integration of technology to enhance teaching and learning, prepare students for the future, and drive innovation in HE. This task requires a significant investment in faculty development to ensure that academics have the support they need in order to develop the pedagogical competence to effectively utilise technology in their teaching practices. The purpose of the study was the evaluation of the pilot version of the TDP4HE training programme offered online to members of the academic teaching staff of the Universities of the European University of Technology alliance (EUt+) in Spring 2024. Through the administration of an online questionnaire and the organisation of semi-structured focus groups, useful results were obtained in relation to participants' perceptions about the programme, challenges faced during its implementation and suggestions and recommendations for future improvements.

First and foremost, the study revealed a common characteristic in all the participants; this was the fact that they all recognised how important it was to develop their pedagogical competences in combination with the integral use of digital technologies dur-ing the teaching and learning process. This is found in literature in many different contexts [16, 24]. According to Bitar and Davidovich [14], educators are prompted to rethink their instructional roles and enhance their teaching strategies, placing emphasis on continuous professional growth.

In relation to participants' perceptions about the training programme, this was positively perceived by the participants, who characterised it as useful for their profes-sional training. In general, participants spoke highly of the training programme, stat-ing that it met their expectations, and that they were satisfied with the platform use, the organisation, the material as well as the content. In addition, participants appreciated the fact that the trainers had diverse backgrounds, since this enriched their learning experience. Moreover, the selected topics and the fact that theory was combined with practice and that there were opportunities for communication and exchange of ideas were viewed positively by the participants. Bragg et al. [25] support that online professional development for teachers is more productive than traditional face-to-face professional development when it is relevant to teachers' professional learning needs promotes social aspects of learning includes content that is readily transferred to classroom environments, and when it encourages self-reflection. Participants' positive comments in the present study pertaining to the content of the training programme show that they valued the aspects of transformative digital pedagogies covered in the training, and that the fact that the programme was well-structured and well-organised on the Moodle platform facilitated this process.

As far as challenges encountered are concerned, participants reported financial constraints and the complexity of integrating advanced technologies into their teaching practices. These kinds of constraints and lack of appropriate equipment is a challenge faced in HE in many parts of the globe, as illustrated in the systematic literature review by Forde and O'Brien [26].

Furthermore, the study also yielded insightful results with regards to improvements that need to be made in the second cycle of the TDP4HE training programme implementation. These suggestions mainly related to the inclusion of more interactive and practise-based activities during the training, which is in line with ElSayary's [27] view that it is essential to provide teachers with realistic experiences for integrating digital technologies into the teaching and learning process. According to ElSayary [27], training should focus on collaborative work to reduce anxiety and create opportunities for exchange of good practices, and this is in fact what the TDP4HE training programme aimed to offer. Nevertheless, participants stated that despite the opportunities for interaction and discussion and collaboration in breakout rooms during the synchronous webinars, they still needed less theoretical presentations and more time for interaction and practice during the training.

The evaluation of the TDP4HE training programme yielded important insights for the improvement of the programme and its re-implementation with a wider audience, outside the bounds of EUt+. The study also carried important implications for HE institutions, teacher educators, academics and researchers in the field of digital trans-formation and education in general. The iterative process of DBR, on which this study is based, is hoped to deliver richer results that could further facilitate the extraction of more solid conclusions and could inspire further research on the topic.

7 Conclusion

In conclusion, the evaluation of the Transformative Digital Pedagogies for Higher Education (TDP4HE) training programme has provided valuable insights into participants' perceptions, highlighting both its strengths and areas for improvement. The programme represents a significant step towards advancing digital pedagogies in higher education by equipping academic staff with the necessary skills to effectively integrate technology into their teaching practices. The findings from this study underscore the importance of aligning professional development initiatives with the real-world challenges and expectations of educators. By addressing participant feedback, future iterations of the programme can enhance its impact by incorporating more hands-on activities, fostering greater interaction among participants, and expanding the range of technological tools covered. Furthermore, the recommendations put forth highlight the need for sustainable support structures, including access to funding opportunities, dedicated mentorship, and continuous engagement through professional networks like the TDP4HE Community of Practice. Implementing these improvements will ensure that the programme not only remains relevant but also becomes a model for digital transformation in higher education. Ultimately, by fostering a culture of innovation and collaboration, the programme has the potential to empower educators, enhance student learning experiences, and contribute to a more digitally literate and globally competitive academic landscape. The next implementation of the programme is expected to build upon these insights by offering an even more refined and interactive learning experience, reaching a wider audience beyond the EUt+ alliance and further solidifying its role as a key driver of digital pedagogical transformation. As research suggests, professional development programmes that effectively integrate digital pedagogies, provide hands-on experiences, and encourage collaboration are essential for fostering meaningful educational innovation [25].

Acknowledgments. The work presented in this publication has been partially funded by the European Union's Erasmus Plus programme, grant agreement 2022-1-LV01-KA220-HED-000085277. This publication reflects the views only of the authors, and the European Commission cannot be held responsible for any use which may be made of the information contained therein.

Disclosure of Interests. The authors have no competing interests to declare that are relevant to the content of this article.

References

1. European Commission. Digital education action plan (2021–2027): resetting education and training for the digital age (2021). https://ec.europa.eu/education/education-in-the-eu/digital-education-action-plan_en. Accessed 31 Jan 2025
2. Redecker, C., European framework for the digital competence of educators. In: Punie, Y. (ed.) DigCompEdu, Publications Office of the European Union, Luxembourg (2017)
3. Vuorikari, R., Kluzer, S. and Punie, Y.: DigComp 2.2: The digital competence framework for citizens with new examples of knowledge, skills and attitudes, EUR 31006 EN, Publications Office of the European Union, Luxembourg, 2022, ISBN 978–92–76–48883–5, https://doi.org/10.2760/490274, JRC128415 (2022)
4. International Association of Universities. Transforming higher education in a digital world for the global common good: policy statement of the International Association of Universities (IAU) (2022). www.iau-aiu.net. Accessed 31 Jan 2025
5. Transformative digital pedagogies for higher education (2025). https://transformative-pedagogies.univ-tech.eu/goals. Accessed 31 Jan 2025
6. Mahlow, C., Hediger, A.: Digital transformation in higher education—buzzword or opportunity?. eLearn **5**(13) (2019)
7. Bygstad, B., Øvrelid, E., Ludvigsen, S., Dæhlen, M.: From dual digitalization to digital learning space: exploring the digital transformation of higher education. Comput. Educ. **182** (2022). https://doi.org/10.1016/j.compedu.2022.104463
8. Tushar, H., Sooraksa, N.: Global employability skills in the 21st century workplace: a semi-systematic literature review. Heliyon **9**(11) (2023)

9. Haleem, A., Javaid, M., Qadri, M.A., Suman, R.: Understanding the role of digital technologies in education: a review. Sustain. Oper. Comput. **3**, 275–285 (2022)
10. Tuffnell, C.: Digital transformation of post-pandemic learning and teaching: utilising TPACK to support educator development in a flipped learning pilot. Stud. Technol. Enhanced Learn. **3**(2) (2023)
11. United Nations: transforming our world: the 2030 agenda for sustainable development (2015). https://sdgs.un.org/publications/transforming-our-world-2030-agenda-sustainable-development-17981. Accessed 31 Jan 2025
12. Røe, Y., Wojniusz, S., Bjerke, A.H.: The digital transformation of higher education teaching: four pedagogical prescriptions to move active learning pedagogy forward. Front. Educ. **6** (2022)
13. Ter Beek, M., Wopereis, I., Schildkamp, K.: Don't wait, innovate! preparing students and lecturers in higher education for the future labor market. Educ. Sci. **12**(9) (2022)
14. Bitar, N., Davidovich, N.: Transforming pedagogy: the digital revolution in higher education. Educ. Sci. **14**(8) (2024)
15. Santoveña-Casal, S., López, S.R.: Mapping of digital pedagogies in higher education. Educ. Inf. Technol. **29**(2), 2437–2458 (2024)
16. Kakoulli Constantinou, E., Verchier, Y., Flynn, P.: Defining the teaching profiles of academic staff across a European universities alliance: Lessons learned after the pandemic and the way into the future. Int. J. Innovative Res. Sci. Stud. **8**(1), 369–379 (2025)
17. Kirkpatrick, J.D., Kirkpatrick, W.K.: Kirkpatrick's Four Levels of Training Evaluation. ATD Press, Alexandria, VA (2016)
18. Darling-Hammond, L.: Accountability in teacher education. Action Teacher Educ. **42**(1), 60–71 (2020)
19. Anderson, T., Shattuck, J.: Design-based research: a decade of progress in education research? Educ. Res. **41**(1), 16–25 (2012)
20. Hoadley, C., Campos, F.C.: Design-based research: what it is and why it matters to studying online learning. Educ. Psychol. **57**(3), 207–220 (2022)
21. Barab, S., Squire, K.: Design-based research: putting a stake in the ground. In: Barab, S., Squire, K. (eds.) Design-based Research, pp. 1–14. Psychology Press (2016)
22. Collective, T.D.B.R.: Design-based research: an emerging paradigm for educational inquiry. Educ. Res. **32**(1), 5–8 (2003)
23. Soule, M.V., Kakoulli Constantinou, E.: Digital pedagogies for higher education: the design of an online training programme for academic staff. In: Zaphiris, P., Ioannou, A. (eds.) Learning and Collaboration Technologies 11th International Conference, LCT 2024 Held as Part of the 26th HCI International Conference, HCII 2024, LNCS 14722, pp. 91–102 (2024)
24. Almazova, N., Krylova, E., Rubtsova, A., Odinokaya, M.: Challenges and opportunities for Russian higher education amid covid-19: teachers' perspective. Educ. Sci. **10**(12), 1–11 (2020)
25. Bragg, L.A., Walsh, C., Heyeres, M.: Successful design and delivery of online professional development for teachers: a systematic review of the literature. Comput. Educ. **166** (2021)
26. Forde, C., O'Brien, A.: A literature review of barriers and opportunities presented by digitally enhanced practical skill teaching and learning in health science education. Med. Educ. Online **27**(1) (2022)
27. ElSayary, A.: The impact of a professional upskilling training programme on developing teachers' digital competence. J. Comput. Assist. Learn. **39**(4), 1154–1166 (2023)

Experiences with Collaborative Online International Learning (COIL) in STEM Projects: A Report on Work-in-Progress

Ute Klotz and Luca Mazzola(✉)

HSLU - Lucerne University of Applied Sciences and Arts, School of Computer Science and Information Technology, Campus Zug-Rotkreuz, Suurstoffi 1, 6343 Rotkreuz, Switzerland
{ute.klotz,luca.mazzola}@hslu.ch

Abstract. Graduates of bachelor's and master's degree programs at universities of applied sciences are expected to possess not only cutting edge specialist knowledge, but also language skills, a cosmopolitanian perspective and intercultural competences. To address these demands, an experimental approach was undertaken within the English-language bachelor's program in International IT Management and the German-language bachelor's program in Business Information Technology to deepen working in virtual, multinational teams and to raise cultural awareness. This was done with the help integration of Collaborative Online International Learning (COIL) projects. Over the course of this experiment six different COIL projects were conceptualised, four realised, across different semesters within the same module. The primary objective was to provide students with practical experience in multinational collaboration. The results stem from module evaluations and personal experiences as lecturers. Student feedback on the COIL projects varied significantly, influenced by their individual learning experiences, language proficiency, and personal time availability. COIL projects are a valuable tool to complement the internationalisation of universities, raise awareness of intercultural issues and equip students for multinational collaboration and project teams. This paper offers a detailed account of the experiences of both students and lecturers engaged in these COIL projects and suggests possibilities for improvement.

Keywords: Collaborative Online International Learning · COIL · Cultural Awareness · Business Information Technology · IT Management · Digital Skills · Employability · Multinational Teams

1 Introduction

Swissuniversities, the umbrella organisation of Swiss universities, regularly supports relevant topics based on cooperation projects. This includes the P8 project "Strengthening Digital Skills in Teaching", which was carried out from 2019-2024

B. K. Smith and M. Borge (Eds.): HCII 2025, LNCS 15806, pp. 245–260, 2025.
https://doi.org/10.1007/978-3-031-93564-0_15

and was made possible with financial contributions from the Swiss Confederation. The objective of the P8 project is to strengthen the digital skills of three stakeholder groups: students, teachers, and the university as an institution [20]. At the Lucerne University of Applied Sciences and Arts (HSLU), the P8 project was expanded in terms of its scope, meaning the aspects of interculturality and internationalisation were included, and, was conducted together with the three schools - Business, Computer Science and Information Technology and Social Work - as well as the Lucerne University of Teacher Education. The P8 project was carried out under the title "Digital Skills Intercultural (DSI): Internationalisation and Multi-perspectivity through Digital Cooperation". The self-imposed, overarching project goals relate, among other things, to the development and implementation of educational content at university level that enables international experiences, provides initial answers regarding forming international relationships and gives first-hand experience in how different levels of knowledge and areas of expertise must be handled. Finally, the findings from the various school-specific projects should be collected, analysed and used for further process optimisation and knowledge transfer [12]. In addition, these objectives are particularly important, because the School of Computer Science and Information Technology is in the Canton of Zug, in the city of Rotkreuz, where various multinational companies and corporate headquarters, keen to employ graduates with international experience. The Canton of Zug has been offering English-language apprenticeships at international companies for many years (bildxzug, n.d.), which can then be followed by a bachelor's degree at the university. The Lucerne School of Computer Science and Information Technology has decided to implement the P8-project with various partner universities across different bachelors' degree programmes and modules. This initiative involves collaboration with different lecturers as part of Collaborative Online International Learning (COIL) projects in the years 2021 - 2024. This publication refers to three specific COIL Projects foreseen in the Intercultural Project module of the English language bachelor's degree programme in International IT Management and three successive editions of the Data Engineering module foreseen in the German language bachelor's degree programme in Business Information Technology.

2 Theoretical Background

According to Durand and Balhasan [8] and Zaby [25], today's workforce is expected to have the ability to work in interdisciplinary and multinational teams, be innovative and contribute to the competitiveness of international companies with foreign language skills and a cosmopolitanian mindset. This includes developing an understanding of the practical challenges involved, such as organising meetings that need to be scheduled in different time zones, project management that considers different country-specific regulations, finding solutions to technical problems when face-to-face meetings are not possible, and facilitating online discussions between various experts.

The internationalisation of higher education, now widely acknowledged in society, contributes to this. Additionally, despite the large numbers of international degrees and international mobility programs, internationalisation also includes ≪Internationalisation at home≫ [21,23]. This approach encompasses the internationalisation of teaching material or degree programmes, the enhancement of language skills, and the development of internationalisation initiatives at a strategic level [3]. In 2020, the mobility rate at Swiss universities was 15.7% [5]. This highlichts that not all student can afford international mobility costs [1] or compensate for the absence from an existing part-time job and the potential loss of employment. ≪Internationalisation at home≫ offers a viable possibility here, although Alvarez and Steiner [1] caution against viewing it as a second-best solution. Nevertheless, as Veugelers [21], suggests this approach still holds considerable potential for further development.

One way of promoting internationalisation at home is through International Collaborative International Online Projects (COIL), which are integrated into existing modules. It is an approach that brings students and professors together across cultures to learn, discuss and collaborate as part of their class. The professors work together to design the intercultural experience, and the students work together to realise the planned activities. *"COIL becomes part of the class, enabling all students to have a significant intercultural experience within their course of study."* [19] According to [1], a COIL project is not a simple solution that can be integrated into every university as standard but must be thought through in relation to each specific university. Rather, COIL can be seen as a method of virtually linking two universities and providing students with intercultural experiences [4].

There are universities that have already conducted COIL projects in the STEM field, which are briefly summarised in the following paragraphs.

Zolbanin and Gosalia [26] conducted a COIL project with a university from the USA and one from the Middle East. In this four-week group project, students had to design a database using the entity-relationship model, justify and document the design and document their cultural experiences on PowerPoint slides. The students of each university were prepared for the COIL project separately, but there seems to be no theme-specific input. Unfortunately, no further information regarding the assessment scheme or assessment process is available. The students were asked about the effectiveness of the COIL project, among other things, as part of an online survey. Based on the experience of more than 20 COIL projects, the authors made 17 recommendations relating to both the planning and implementation phases of a COIL project. The aim of these recommendations is to increase the benefits for students and minimise the risks. One aspect that the authors believe needs more research is gender-related aspects, which should be considered in future research projects.

Durand and Balhasan [26] describe the structure and experiences of a COIL project between one university from the USA and one from the United Arab Emirates, each representing different engineering disciplines. In this project, students were tasked with conducting a cost analysis and an economic evaluation of a technical case study, which they then presented to their peers from the other engineering discipline. The receiving students were responsible for understanding and critiquing the economic evaluation. Together, the students then discussed, proposed, and ultimately documented potential process improvements based on the case study. Additionally, each student was required to submit an individual reflection, critically assessing their learning experiences and identifying ways to improve their future engagement These reflections revealed that students valued the more relaxed discussions with their fellow students, which meant that the lecturers did not have to be present. The students said that this encouraged them to think less about right and wrong and instead focus more on creative exchange. However, the students in each discipline expressed a desire for more knowledge about the other students' discipline in advance.

Gutiérrez-González et al. [10] describe another COIL project, where bachelor's students from Peru collaborated with master's students from Spain over six weeks. According to the authors, the age difference and the varying levels of expertise posed significant challenges. The master's students in Spain were tasked with evaluating the energy efficiency of selected buildings, while the bachelor's students in Peru were tasked to apply their theoretical knowledge to these given and selected buildings and analyse the findings in terms of similarities or differences. The results were then reported through oral presentations. Following the project, an online survey revealed that students had a strong interest in future intercultural training opportunities because of this COIL project, believing it provides them with a competitive advantage over other students. However, the students also highlighted several challenges. Interpersonal difficulties arose, which often required the lecturer to intervene as a mediator. Additionally, the time difference between the two groups made synchronous collaboration difficult.

Munoz-Escalona et al. [16] describe a COIL project involving 82 students across three universities from two different academic years. In this project, students were tasked with analysing photos of micro components from various cars and discussing them regarding specified aspects as part of a reverse engineering process. Their findings were then summarised and presented in the form of a poster. Once again, students were asked about their experiences using an online survey. Most students responded positively, reporting increased self-confidence and, as in Gutiérrez-González et al. [10], a competitive advantage over other students. However, students also noted several challenges, including lack of commitment from some students, technical problems and the timing of the COIL project within the academic semester.

Based on the literature and the project objectives of the project "Digital Skills Intercultural (DSI): Internationalisation and Multiperspectivity through Digital Cooperation", the following central questions are to be answered:

- What are the experiences of students and lecturers from the STEM field with COIL projects and what improvements could be made in the upcoming COIL projects?
- What improvements can be made to enhance the effectiveness of COIL projects in the future?

Table 1. Overview of literature on exemplar COIL projects, in computer science-related and technical degree programmes (in descending chronological order).

Overview COIL Projects	
Authors, Publication year	Zolbanin & Gosalia, 2024 [26]
Semester	Fall 2023
Countries Partner Universities	USA — Middle East
Number of students per university	27/15
Educational content/Scientific methods	Database Design & Entity-Relationship (ER) Model
Length of COIL Project	4 weeks
Information and Communication Tools	E-Mail, Forum per Learning Platform
Authors, Publication year	Duran & Balhasan, 2023 [8]
Semester	Fall 2021
Countries Partner Universities	USA — VAE
Number of students per university	23-30/6
Educational content/Scientific methods	Cost analysis/Economic assessment of a technical scenario
Length of COIL Project	Nearly the whole semester
Information and Communication Tools	MS Teams, Zoom
Authors, Publication year	Gutiérrez-González et al., 2023 [10]
Semester	Spring 2021
Countries Partner Universities	Peru — Spain
Number of students per university	40/3
Educational content/Scientific methods	Analysing and discussing energy efficiency in buildings
Length of COIL Project	6 weeks
Information and Communication Tools	Miro, Moodle, Zoom
Authors, Publication year	Munoz-Escalona et al., 2022 [16]
Semester	*not specified*
Countries Partner Universities	Scotland — Spain — Venezuela
Number of students per university	46/11 /25
Educational content/Scientific methods	Analysing a car and its components in terms of functionality, material, manufacturing process, etc.
Length of COIL Project	3 weeks
Information and Communication Tools	Moodle, WhatsApp, Wiki

To this end, a set of four modules was adapted for a COIL collaboration, one of which was run over multiple semesters. Table 2 presents a synoptic view.

3 Data Collection

As part of the "Digital Skills Intercultural (DSI): Internationalisation and Multi-perspectivity through Digital Cooperation" project, four out of six COIL projects were completed in different semesters within two bachelor study programs. Table 2 provides an overview of the COIL projects realised between 2021 and 2024. Two of the COIL projects originally planned could not or only partially be

Table 2. COIL Projects in the bachelor degree programmes in International IT-Management and Business Information Technology (adapted and expanded from [11]

Description of COIL projects @ HSLU	
Number of COIL-Project	1/failed
Semester	Fall 2021
Country Partner University	Ireland
Number of students per university	10/no details
Educational content/Scientific methods	Photo competition (focus on the respective university)
Length of COIL Project	5 weeks
Information and Communication Tools	E-Mail, Learning Platform
Number of COIL-Project	2
Semester	Fall 2022
Country Partner University	Canada
Number of students per university	34/31
Educational content/Scientific methods	Mutual individual student interview, focused on an intercultural topic
Length of COIL Project	4 weeks
Information and Communication Tools	Zoom, MS Teams, Email, Learning platform
Number of COIL-Project	3
Semester	Fall 2022
Country Partner University	Ukraine
Number of students per university	25/15
Educational content/Scientific methods	Group discussion on Big Tech & Diversity based on given research articles, individual preparation per university
Length of COIL Project	4 weeks
Information and Communication Tools	E-Mail, Learning platform
Number of COIL-Project	4a
Semester	Spring 2023
Country Partner University	South Africa
Number of students per university	25 (4)/31 (5)
Educational content/Scientific methods	Group projects, individual tutoring
Length of COIL Project	6 weeks
Information and Communication Tools	E-Mail, Zoom, Videos
Number of COIL-Project	4b
Semester	Fall 2023
Country Partner University	South Africa
Number of students per university	30 (12)/19 (9)
Educational content/Scientific methods	Group projects, individual tutoring
Length of COIL Project	5 weeks
Information and Communication Tools	E-Mail, Zoom, Videos
Number of COIL-Project	4c/failed
Semester	Spring 2024
Country Partner University	USA
Number of students per university	31 (0)/28
Educational content/Scientific methods	Asynchronous, pre-registered videos, group works, individual tutoring
Length of COIL Project	8 weeks
Information and Communication Tools	E-Mail, Zoom, IM Chats

realised for various reasons. The findings from the COIL projects obtained are based on methods in which quantitative and qualitative data are collected and analysed separately. The data collections approaches are detailed in Tables 3 and

Table 3. Overview Quantitative Data Collection and Data Analysis

Semester	Method Data Collection	Method Data Analysis
Spring 2023, Fall 2024, Spring 2024	Online Anonymous Surveys 5 questions on a 5-likert scale [13] (Dommeyer et alii, 2004 [7])	Simple data aggregation [2], after elimination of empty values (Nardi, 2018 [17])

4 with the second column outlining the quantitative and qualitative approaches, respectively.

For the quantitative data collection, an anonymous survey [7] was conducted using a 5-point Likert-scale [13] and a minimal number of questions (5) aimed at capturing students' self-reported perceptions. This approach is also helpful as it facilitates a clear and transparent comparisons of multiple editions of the same module [15], and can be effectively integrated with qualitative approaches [18].

For the qualitative data collection, a department-wide, standardised, anonymous module evaluation was carried out for each of the two modules, whereby the optional text relating to the COIL project was evaluated [24]. Additionally, the individual student feedback, questions or comments submitted via email were included, based on a feedback request for the COIL project.

Participation in the quantitative and qualitative data collection was voluntary and anonymous. There were no consequences for the participants and no further obligations.

4 Data Analysis

The approaches for data analysis are reported in Tables 3 and 4 in the third column, for the quantitative and qualitative approaches, respectively.

In the quantitative analysis, the small number of students participating in the voluntary, anonymous online survey limited the scope to simple statistical methods [6]. After eliminating the values for questions skipped by individual respondents [17], the data aggregated [2], using a straightforward approach of calculating the mean value for every question.

In the qualitative analysis, the data were analysed according to Gioia [9,14] using first-order codes, second-order themes and aggregate dimensions. The data were analysed separately by two researchers, then discussed and the corresponding codes were assigned based on the discussion. The results were summarised

Table 4. Overview Qualitative Data Collection and Data Analysis

Semester	Method Data Collection	Method Data Analysis
Fall 2022	Online Module Evaluation	Gioia-Methodology (Gioia, Corley and Hamilton, 2016 [9]; Miles and Huberman, 2020 [14])
Fall 2023	Individual feedback based on emails	

Table 5. Survey results COIL Project No. 4a in Spring 2023 (HSLU side only).

COIL Project No. 4a	Spring 2023			
	COIL	no COIL	Delta	Delta %
No. of students	4	21		
Responses	4	9		
Effort	5.23	5.12	0.11	0.02
Satisfaction	5.11	4.97	0.14	0.03
Innovativeness	5.29	4.55	0.74	0.16
Motivation	5.87	4.79	1.08	0.23
Self-Evaluation	5.02	5.13	−0.11	−0.02
Knowledge Acquisition	5.45	5.04	0.41	0.08
GAIN: Reality vs. Perception	−0.43	0.09		

based on the aggregate dimensions. As with the quantitative data, the qualitative data are limited due to voluntary participation.

5 Results

There are two perspectives on the COIL projects realised. One is the students' perspective, and the other is the lecturers' perspective. The data collection and data analysis in Tables 3 and 4 relate to the student perspective, while the lecturers' impressions are presented in Table 8.

Table 6. Survey results COIL Project No. 4b in Fall 2023 (HSLU side only).

COIL Project No. 4b	Fall 2023			
	COIL	no COIL	Delta	Delta %
No. of students	12	18		
Responses	11	11		
Effort	5.19	5.15	0.04	0.01
Satisfaction	4.99	4.79	0.20	0.04
Innovativeness	5.54	4.51	1.03	0.23
Motivation	5.53	4.39	1.14	0.26
Self-Evaluation	5.21	5.35	−0.14	−0.03
Knowledge Acquisition	5.23	4.78	0.45	0.09
GAIN: Reality vs. Perception	−0.02	0.57		

The results from the quantitative data analysis are presented in Tables 5, 6, and 7 which display the numerical results of the survey conducted in this module (students perspective), in the context of the bachelor's program Business Information Technology. The module is offered as an elective and is particularly recommended to students aiming for a major in Data Engineering. As a note, participation in the COIL component of the module was voluntary and based on the interest of the individual student groups. Consequently, the number of students who actively participated in the COIL differs from the total number of students enrolled in the class, with the actual number of participants indicated in brackets in Table 2.

Table 7. Survey results COIL Project No. 4c in Spring 2024 (failed, no participation on HSLU side).

COIL Project No. 4c	Spring 2024		
	COIL	no COIL	Delta
No. of students	0	23	
Responses	–	6	
Effort	–	5.12	N.A.
Satisfaction	–	4.81	N.A.
Innovativeness	–	4.45	N.A.
Motivation	–	4.34	N.A.
Self-Evaluation	–	5.25	N.A.
Knowledge Acquisition	–	4.98	N.A.

The survey measured five specific dimensions each corresponding to direct questions posed to the students:

1. The ***effort*** required by the module is for student completion,
2. The level of ***satisfaction*** concerning the content, modality and perceived knowledge acquisition,
3. The ***innovativeness*** of the format and the experience it provided,
4. The ***motivation*** this modality instilled in the students,
5. The ***self-evaluation*** of the mastered knowledge (in terms of expected grades),

Additionally, the final grade received in the module was used retrospectively as a proxy, for:

6. The ***knowledge acquisition*** measurement.

An initial observation from the data for [COIL Project No. 4c] [see Table 2] is that none of the students opted to participate in the COIL experience, resulting in the absence of any measurement. At HSLU, grades are assigned on a scale from 1 (minimum, equivalent to an F) to 6 (maximum, best performance, equivalent to A+). The same scale was used for the students' surveys, but was rescaled to a 10 point system for consistency in the figures. The radar graphs in Figs. 1, 2, and 3 represent these results for an easier comparison. Although the small sample size limits the possibility of drawing broad generalisations, the radar graphs enable

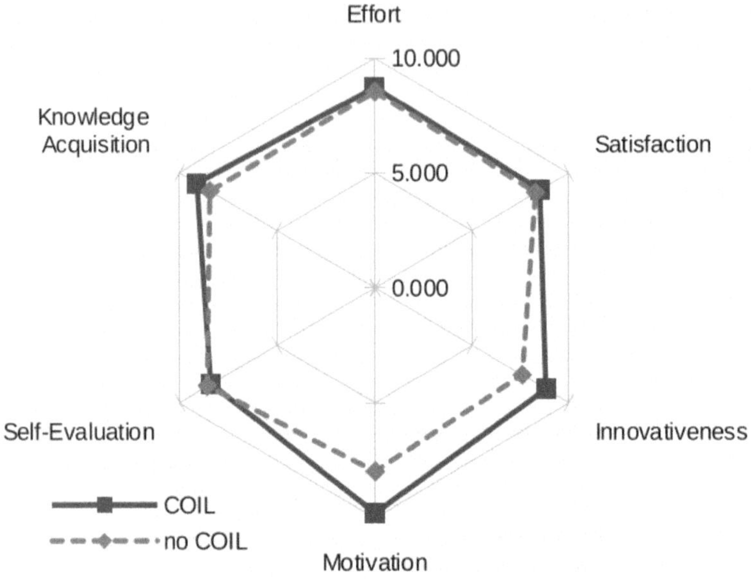

Fig. 1. Survey results - COIL Project 4a [Table 5] - Spring 23

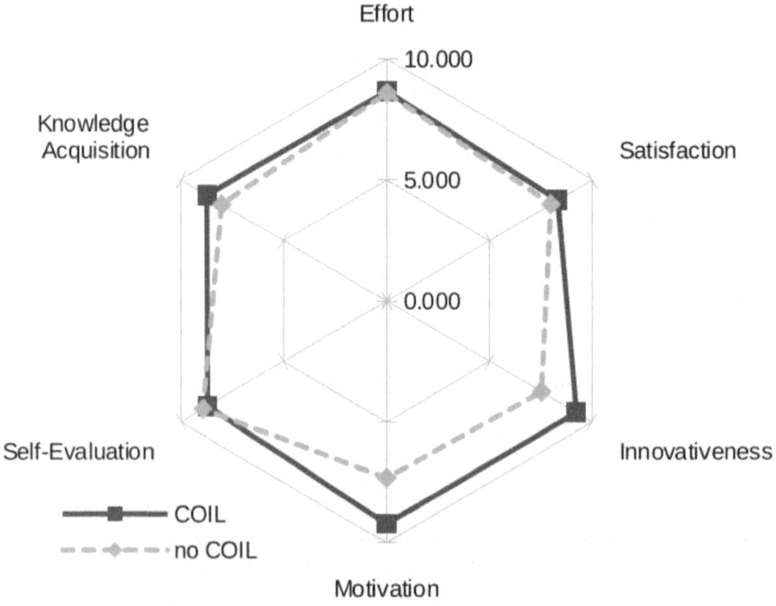

Fig. 2. Survey results - COIL Project 4b [Table 6] - Fall 23

a comparison between the "COIL" and the "no-COIL" versions of the module in each semester. This allows for (isolating any changes unrelated to the COIL, such as variations in schedule, content, etc.) supporting a preliminary evaluation of the COIL project's effects on the students' experiences and performances.

The results from the qualitative data are summarised as follows: Overall, the students' feedback was contradictory. On the one hand, students appreciated the experience of the COIL project, despite all the challenges. On the other hand, students criticised mandatory participation. Age differences between the students, the lower level of professional experience and gaps in specialist knowledge, and failure to adhere to commonly accepted norms such as punctuality led to significant frustration among some students within the COIL project. However, theses issues were reported by individual students, as other participants reported more positive experiences in the opposite direction. Students reported that misunderstandings during the COIL project led to hostility and aggression, making a peaceful and constructive discussion difficult. The students expressed a desire for more active involvement and a more intensive presence from the lecturers in the next COIL project so that misunderstandings can be addressed immediately. Furthermore, they suggested the project be scheduled at the start of the semester, as when motivation potentially leading to greater engagement and participation.

From the lecturers' perspective, Table 8 presents the experiences with the four COIL projects realised based on the selected best practices (Columns 1 and

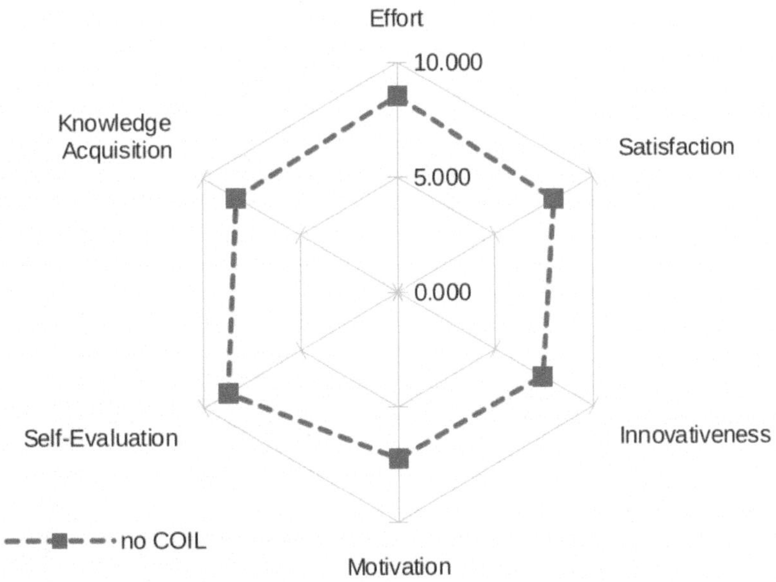

Fig. 3. Survey results - COIL Project 4c [Table 7]- Spring 24

Table 8. Lecturers' experiences regarding COIL-Projects realised at HSLU and categorised based on the best practices according to [26]

≪ *BestPractice* ≫	Description	Lecturers' experiences regarding COIL-Projects realised at HSLU
Agreement on the project details	Creating a common understanding of the project goals, tasks and results	An agreement on key aspects of the project is needed, including its duration, the tasks of the lecturers and students, the content (topic, scientific methods), the teaching materials, the format of instructions in terms of synchronous/asynchronous teaching units, assessment scheme and group division. This should be discussed in an initial, informal online meeting. A first impression that can help determine whether a collaboration between the two lecturers is feasible on a personal and professional level.
Creating learning experiences for all	Difficulty creating a good, positive learning experience for all students, despite different prerequisites	Significant differences between students from various universities which may not be immediately apparent, can emerge during collaborative projects. These differences may include not only age, subject knowledge and language skills, but also interculturality, and travelling experience. Often these differences are often only noticed during or after the project. In such case, the lecturers must take a more active role, acting as mediators. The project workload and tasks must be manageable for students from both universities, ensuring they are overwhelmed by the content or the time the project requires.
Different time zones	Online meetings despite different time zones to enable/enhance the learning experience	Significant time differences (eight hours and more) can make a collaboration difficult. And the larger the group of students working together, the more challenging it is to coordinate individual schedules. To make scheduling simpler, appointments between students and between lecturers should always be held on the same day and at the same time each week.
Developing a group contract	Discuss expectations of the group members and define the tasks and their scope	Most students expect effective collaboration and a fair distribution of tasks. However, students may be are difficult to reach, arrive late or fail to turn up for the scheduled online meetings. In such cases, students should promptly inform their lecturers timely as the project duration is limited. Students must carefully consider whether they are willing and able to support students, that may need extra assistance, especially in terms of the time commitment this may require.
Equal weighting of the project in the evaluation	Equal weighting of the project in the evaluation	Ideally, both the assessment scheme and the weighting of this assessment/grade should be consistent for both universities. However, the assessment can no longer be changed if the semester has already started.
Feedback/evaluation of the project between the lecturers	Evaluation of the project after completion	In general, lecturers are interested in long-term collaboration and are willing to facilitate this to keep the workload of such a project manageable. It is thus crucial to establish a personal, uncomplicated connection between the lecturers involved, and to organise and allocate the work fairly.

2) from Zolbanin and Gosalia [30]. Column 3 describes the experiences that have been made and shows the possibilities for improvement.

6 Discussion

This study analysed the experiences of STEM students and lecturers with COIL projects [see Table 2] and used the data collected to identify improvement opportunities. While previous quantitative studies have primarily focused on student satisfaction within the COIL projects, the dimensions measured in this study extend the previous results of [8,10,16,26]. Notably, students who participated in a COIL project rated their efforts for the module higher across all four dimensions Effort, Satisfaction, Innovativeness, and Motivation than students who did. However, the only dimension measured where COIL project participants rated themselves lower is Self Evaluation in terms of the expected module grade. However, this Self-assessment was too low when compared to their actual grades, as reflected in the Knowledge Acquisition dimension. In contrast, non-COIL students overestimated their expected grades relative to their actual performance. These results represent new findings compared to the existing literature, but they also present a limitation as they cannot be easily explained. One possible interpretation of the data suggests that the students who took part in the COIL project had a more heightened awareness of the topic's complexity. This may be partly due to the interaction with other students which may have enabled them to recognise aspects that would have otherwise been overlooked without interaction. This perceived complexity of the subject may lead them to believe that they need to invest more time in exam preparation and, if they are unable to do so, they may interpret it as poorer exam preparation. The Knowledge Acquisition dimension, however, may warrant further discussion, as this was not directly measured, but inferred from the module grade received. Additional research is needed to interpret and discuss the data.

A critical aspect of the qualitative student feedback concerns the voluntary nature of participation. Dissatisfaction with the COIL project gave subsequently rise to this question in the qualitative feedback, particularly in contrast to COIL project 4c, where the option for voluntary participation taking part. Here, too, further research is needed to better understand students' reasons for or against participation and its consequences.

This study also reflects on and expands upon based the lecturers' experience based on the best practices of [25]. However, since only four COIL projects were carried out as part of this study, it is more accurate to describe the findings as extended observations and suggestions for improvements. Six key best practices were selected and discussed. However, also best practices that are related more to the administrative processes could be explained in more detail, such as selecting a partner. For example, creating and sending of a collaboration request form with relevant information could support the partner search. It is also essential to clarify whether authorisation processes are necessary within a university and in what time frame these can be processed. This requires time to be scheduled.

For three editions of an English-language module in a German-language bachelor's degree programme, the official module description and the enrolment procedure indicate that English language proficiency (minimum at level B2, but preferably C1 or C2 of the European CEFR levels [13] are required for participation in this COIL project. This ensures that students possess the English language skills necessary for a meaningful, synchronised, in-depth exchange with their fellow students at the partner university [22].

An additional aspect not explicitly mentioned in [26] is the teaming up of students from two universities which presents a delicate challenge. While students can choose peers from their own university, but students cannot choose students from the partner university they cannot select students from their partner university as they have yet to meet each other, and the time available is limited. As a result, students are often allocated to groups randomly by the respective lecturers. However, where possible, meaningful allocation criteria should be considered. The success of the collaboration between the students of both universities, their motivation and the work results, depend heavily on the group's structure. Though there is no definitive list of causal relationships that can be run through, a few criteria that could be considered. Further research is needed to identify and define decision making criteria that can improve group formation and thus the project results.

An important consideration from the students' perspective is having formal proof of their participation in a COIL project. A certificate of participation could be issued based on a reciprocal arrangement, ensuring their involvement.

7 Conclusion

In this study, four out of six planned COIL projects were carried out in both a German-language and an English-language STEM bachelor's degree programme. Both quantitative and qualitative data were used to analyse the experiences of students and lecturers, with the aim of proposing possible improvements for future COIL projects. The quantitative data revealed that, among other things, students who participated in the COIL project perceived the complexity of the subject matter more deeply through the aspects of self-evaluation and knowledge acquisition.

However, this interpretation should be approached with caution, as the Knowledge Acquisition dimension was inferred from the module grade. Further research is necessary in this regard. The quantity and quality of the qualitative data could be enhanced to obtain more reliable and perhaps also more nuanced statements and insights on learning experiences and cultural awareness. Ultimately, the aim of these COIL projects was to practice collaboration in virtual, multinational teams. While significant progress has been made toward this objective, it is evident that students' individual learning experiences vary widely, and the effort required from lecturers and instructors to design and deliver COIL-enabled modules is considerable.

References

1. Alvarez, L., Steiner, M.: Collaborative online international learning. ASEM Educ. Digit. World Bridging Continents-connecting People 18–29 (2019)
2. Batterton, K.A., Hale, K.N.: The likert scale what it is and how to use it. Phalanx **50**(2), 32–39 (2017)
3. Burren, S., Le Breton, M., Porta, C., Böhnel, M.: Zur Reproduktion von Differenz im Kontext von Internationalisierungsprozessen an Fachhochschulen. Schweizerische Zeitschrift für Soziale Arbeit/Revue suisse de travail social **27**, 73–90 (2020). https://doi.org/10.33058/szsa.2020.0195
4. Ceo-DiFrancesco, D., Bender-Slack, D.: Collaborative online international learning: students and professors making global connections. In: Kramer Moeller, A. (ed.) Fostering Connections, Empowering Communities, Celebrating the World, pp. 147–173. 2016 Report of the Central States Conference on the Teaching of Foreign Languages, Terry, Robert M. (2016)
5. Crameri, A.: Mobilitätsquoten und Internationalisierungsindex der Schweizer Hochschulen: executive Summary. Movetia. Austausch und Mobilität. (2023), https://www.movetia.ch/fileadmin/user_upload/Dokumente/Bereich_4/Medienmitteiliungen/230119_Mobilit%C3%A4tsindex/230119_Medienmitteilung_Movetia_Index.pdf, Mobility rates and internationalization index of Swiss universities: Executive Summary. Movetia. Exchange and mobility
6. Cress, U., Hesse, F.W.: Quantitative methods for studying small groups. In: The International Handbook of Collaborative Learning, pp. 93–111. Routledge (2013)
7. Dommeyer, C.J., Baum, P., Hanna, R.W., Chapman, K.S.: Gathering faculty teaching evaluations by in-class and online surveys: their effects on response rates and evaluations. Assess. Eval. High. Educ. **29**(5), 611–623 (2004)
8. Durand, H., Balhasan, S.: An example of using collaborative online international learning for petroleum and chemical engineering undergraduate courses. Int. Rev. Res. Open Distrib. Learn. **24**(3), 225–233 (2023). https://doi.org/10.19173/irrodl.v24i3.7227
9. Gioia, D.A., Corley, K.G., Hamilton, A.L.: Seeking qualitative rigor in inductive research: notes on the gioia methodology. Organ. Res. Methods **16**(1), 15–31 (2013). https://doi.org/10.1177/1094428112452151
10. Gutiérrez-González, S., Coello-Torres, C.E., Cuenca-Romero, L.A., Carpintero, V.C., Bravo, A.R.: Incorporating collaborative online international learning (COIL) into common practices for architects and building engineers. Int. J. Learn. Teach. Educ. Res. **22**(2), 20–36 (2023). https://doi.org/10.26803/ijlter.22.2.2
11. Klotz, U.: Projekt P8 / Swissuniversities / <<Digitale Lehre - Digitale Präsenz - Digitales Studium>> Digital Skills Interkulturell (DSI): Internationalisierung und Multiperspektivität durch digitale Kooperation (2024), Unveröffentlichter Abschlussbericht
12. Kürsteiner, B., Kessler, O.: Digital Skills Interkulturell (DSI): Internationalisierung und Multiperspektivität durch digitale Kooperation: Kickoff: Projekt P8 / Swissuniversities <<Digitale Lehre - Digitale Präsenz - Digitales Studium>>. (2021), Unveröffentlichte Präsentation
13. Louangrath, P.: Reliability and validity of survey scales. Int. J. Res. Methodol. Soc. Sci. **4**(1), 50–62 (2018). https://doi.org/10.5281/zenodo.2545038
14. Miles, M.B., Huberman, A.M., Saldaña, J.: Qualitative Data Analysis: A Methods Sourcebook (Fourth). SAGE (2020)

15. Mohler, P.P., Johnson, T.P.: Equivalence, comparability, and methodological progress. In: Harkness, J.A., et al. (eds.) Survey Methods in Multicultural, Multinational, and Multiregional Contexts, pp. 17–29. Wiley Series in Survey Methodology, John Wiley & Sons Inc., Hoboken (2010). https://doi.org/10.1002/9780470609927.ch2
16. Munoz-Escalona, P., de Crespo, Z.C., Marin, M.O., Dunn, M.: Collaborative online international learning: a way to develop students' engineering capabilities and awareness to become global citizens. Int. J. Mech. Eng. Educ. **50**(1), 89–104 (2022). https://doi.org/10.1177/0306419020934100
17. Nardi, P.M.: Doing Survey Research: A Guide to Quantitative Methods. Routledge (2018)
18. Singh, R.K., Neuert, C.E., Raykov, T.: Assessing conceptual comparability of single-item survey instruments with a mixed-methods approach. Qual. Quant. 1–27 (2023). https://doi.org/10.1007/s11135-023-01801-w
19. State University of New York (Ed.): Suny COIL. collaborative online international learning: connect. Engage. Collaborate [Welcome] (2023). https://coil.suny.edu/. Accessed12 June 2024
20. Swissuniversities (Ed.): P-8 Staerkung von Digital Skills in der Lehre. (2024). https://www.swissuniversities.ch/themen/digitalisierung/digital-skills, Unveröffentlichte Präsentation
21. Veugelers, R.: Internationalisierung der Hochschulbildung und Auswirkungen auf die Wirtschaft (EENEE - Policy Brief No.4) (2020). http://www.education-economics.org/de/dms/EENEE/Policy_Briefs/German/DE_PolicyBrief4_2020.pdf. Accessed 02 May 2024
22. Villar-Onrubia, D., Rajpal, B.: Online international learning: internationalising the curriculum through virtual mobility at coventry university. Perspect. Policy Pract. High. Educ. **20**(2-3), 75–82 (2016). https://doi.org/10.1080/13603108.2015.1067652
23. Watkins, H., Smith, R.: Thinking globally, working locally: employability and internationalization at home. J. Stud. Int. Educ. **22**(3), 210–224 (2018). https://doi.org/10.1177/1028315317751686
24. Williams, R., Brennan, J.: Collecting and using student feedback date: a guide to good practice. https://oro.open.ac.uk/11875/
25. Zaby, A.: Internationalisierung der HAW–Perspektiven der Auslandsmobilität. In: 50 Jahre hlb. pp. 235–244. Nomos Verlagsgesellschaft mbH & Co. KG (2022). https://doi.org/10.5771/9783748935193-235
26. Zolbanin, H.M., Gosalia, S.S.: Collaborative online international learning (COIL) for information systems education: best practices and implementation strategies. Commun. Assoc. Inf. Syst. **54**(1), 773-791 (2024). https://doi.org/10.17705/1CAIS.05428

From Chance to Systematization: Shedding Light on the Formation Phase of University-SME Cooperation

Paul Kruse(✉), Sebastian Reiners, Janis Joshua Elmer, and Jörg Becker

University of Muenster, Schlossplatz 2, 48149 Münster, Germany
{kruse,reiners,elmer,becker}@ercis.de

Abstract. The adoption of digital technologies is far from trivial. Especially for Small and Medium-sized Enterprise with their limitations in resources. To overcome these limitations, cooperation with academia has proven to be useful. However, these cooperation are heavily dependent on personal connections. Despite research regarding the formation process, the initial step, identifying a contact person, remains ambiguous. By conducting 15 interviews with academia and practitioners who successfully establish such cooperation, we provide insights for forming cooperation between academia and Small and Medium-sized Enterprise. The interviews were analyzed using an inductive approach. This resulted in 381 codes, 13 2nd-order themes, and four dimensions. Ultimately, four exemplary strategies for how to leverage the framework are demonstrated. These strategies provide actionable pathways for both Small and Medium-sized Enterprise and academia to initiate and maintain successful cooperation and illustrate how the developed framework can be used by Small and Medium-sized Enterprise and universities to identify suitable strategies for improving their ability to establish contact with potential partners.

Keywords: University-SME Cooperation · University-Business Cooperation · UBC · Formation

1 Introduction

Digital technologies have played a pivotal role over the past few decades, driving waves of digitalization across businesses and societies [17]. Research shows broad agreement that adopting digital technologies can benefit organizations [25]. However, the adoption and deployment of digital technologies are far from trivial. Compounding this issue, many Small and Medium-sized Enterprises (SMEs) lack the appropriated resources, have knowledge gaps, or missing capabilities-factors that hinder these digital endeavors [7,9]. At the same time, in the DACH region (Germany, Austria, and Switzerland), the performance of SMEs critically shapes the economic success of their countries [26]. Hence, their challenges must

B. K. Smith and M. Borge (Eds.): HCII 2025, LNCS 15806, pp. 261–280, 2025.
https://doi.org/10.1007/978-3-031-93564-0_16

be addressed due to their sheer number of employees, their share in exports, and their portion of the economy [9,21].

A specific group of organizations (i.e., German Mittelstand) within the DACH region showed remarkable resilience to keep up with the ever-changing environment and technological development [9]. Those organizations partnering with the local ecosystem overcome limitations through innovation enabled by external networks [3,27]. A vital connection within external networks is the partnership with local research centers and universities [3,27]. Many cooperations between organizations and universities rely heavily on personal connections [24]. Without these personal ties, organizations often find it challenging to identify the appropriate contact within a university to initiate a partnership. In this sense, Schaeffer et al. [24, p. 189] mentioned a "need for a more automatic process to connect local demands with academic expertise."

While there is some research conceptualizing the University-Business Cooperation (UBC) formation process [1], the initial step, the identification of a contact person, remains ambiguous [21,22]. The guidelines from business associations, governments, and universities, more often than not, simplify the identification process with "find a partner" [16, p. 6]. There is a gap in current research describing the "how". More precisely, understanding "how [...] businesses identify suitable researchers, teams, and universities" [21, p. 76].

This research endeavor aims to systematize the process of forming UBC. We accomplish this by developing a comprehensive framework that delineates the steps and strategies concepts for initiating UBC, explicitly focusing on the needs of SMEs. By integrating existing research on the UBC formation process with insights from interviews with both practitioners and academics, we provide a robust foundation for this framework. Our contribution to the field includes an exemplary demonstration of the framework for UBC that transcends personal connections by offering detailed insights and strategies. We enhance the understanding of establishing cooperation by introducing a systematic instrument that clarifies the "how" of identifying and engaging in UBC.

2 Theoretical Background

2.1 University-Business Cooperation

The topic of cooperation between universities and companies is not new, and its relevance is undisputed [12]. This type of cooperation can take various forms and benefit all stakeholders (e.g., universities and businesses). The cooperation with businesses, for example, enables universities to integrate real-world scenarios into their teaching [24] or can be seen as another source of income to finance research activities or research groups [24]. From a business perspective, the "race for innovation and growth" [21, p. 67] is a constantly rising challenge. To face this challenge, businesses need to integrate and exploit new digital technologies, which is "one of the biggest challenges that companies currently face" [15, p. 1]. The integration and exploration of new digital technologies is not an easy endeavor. Support from external units is essential as they can equip the business with the necessary digital skills to transform it in step with its fast-paced environment [4,13]. These skills are typically possessed by young professionals who are technically proficient and aligned with the latest developments [13]. People like this are usually found at universities, so universities can be seen as a link between well-educated students and the business world [10]. Hence, universities provide the (human) foundation for future innovation [24]. Businesses expect "students - as digital natives - and researchers to provide an outside-in view into digital opportunities in their industries and to help them to innovate and develop digital business models, products and services" [17, p. 302].

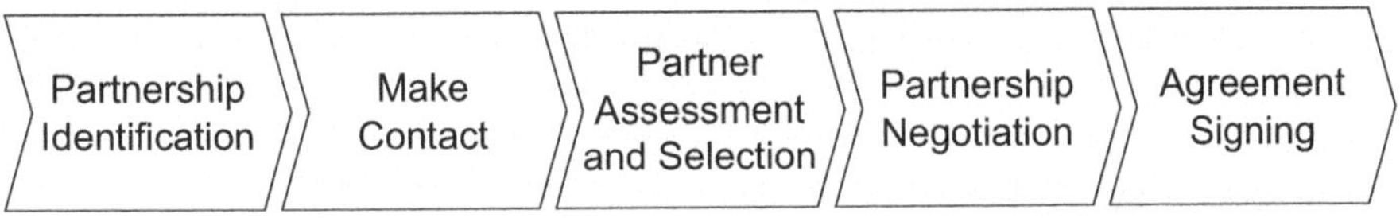

Fig. 1. UBC formation process adopted from [1]

The formation process of UBC has been investigated and structured in research. On the foundation of literature research, Ankrah and AL-Tabbaa [1] proposed five stages (see Fig. 1) describing the process: (1) Partnership identification: The purpose and goals are established, and the capabilities of potential partners are assessed, possibly leveraging existing relationships. (2) Make contact: Identify prospective partners who align with the desired objectives. (3) Partner assessment and selection: This involves evaluating strategic interests and actual capabilities and ensuring the right cooperation mix. (4) Partnership negotiation: Detailed negotiations define the partnership's mission, goals, structure, and management responsibilities, including establishing clear plans, milestones, and success indicators. (5) Agreement signing: Preparing and signing cooperation and intellectual property agreements legally cements the partnership and delineates the terms of engagement. These stages collectively provide a systematic framework for developing and implementing practical and mutually beneficial UBC.

2.2 University-SME Cooperation

The cooperation formation process is tedious when considering SMEs compared to larger enterprises. SMEs struggle from resource limitations or missing contacts with universities, in contrast to large enterprises [9,13,21–23]. To actively participate in such cooperation, relational capabilities are necessary [20]. However, SMEs struggle with these capabilities as they have problems building up and managing the necessary relationships with specialists for digital technologies or the respective service providers [18]. Transforming a business by integrating innovation is difficult as it compromises more than just developing new products and processes [20]. As new knowledge often lies outside the known [13], such a transformation can be better handled in cooperations [27].

The academic literature focuses on barriers to University-SME cooperation instead of delivering results from successful cooperation to inspire other SMEs to cooperate [22]. A common approach to initiate contact between universities and other organizations, such as SMEs, is the Technology Transfer Center. However, Technology Transfer Centers are more likely to be contacted for legal advice on intellectual property issues due to additional bureaucracy [24]. In this regard, informal relationships are considered much more efficient [22, 24]. Informal relationships mean direct or indirect (you know someone who knows someone) personnel contact between a business and a university. Without this informal relationship, it is difficult to identify the right contact person to initiate cooperation [24].

2.3 Success Factors

Research exists on barriers, facilitators, and success factors for UBC. However, research indicates that dismantling barriers is not necessarily supporting UBC [12]. Instead, the focus should be more on the facilitators and success factors. Rybnicek and Königsgruber [23] derive a conceptual model focussing on these success factors. Their model consists of institutional, relationship, output, and framework factors, each with management recommendations (e.g., flexibility, honesty, clarity, and awareness) [23]. In addition, four potential moderators (scale, level, phase, and discipline) complement their conceptual model. Before a sophisticated identification process can be conducted, one's requirements have to be known (**institutional factors**) [23]. There is only a chance for successful cooperation when the roles and responsibilities are clarified from the beginning and a willingness for change (*flexibility*) is present. Both parties must listen and understand their cooperation partner (**relationship factors**). The basis for this is a good personal relationship and a "reciprocal communication" (*honesty*) [23, p. 231]. Besides, previous experience with joint projects is beneficial, as a basis of trust already exists [22]. If it is the start of a new partnership without personal contacts, smaller projects are seen as a good starting point to facilitate trust [5]. Especially the cooperation objectives received a lot of attention (**output factors**). Due to the different foci, understanding each other's objectives is highly relevant. Besides, a proper partner selection and evaluation is necessary [23]. To have these points clear (*clarity*) is highly important to the overall cooperation. Lastly, the environment (**framework factors**) is highly important for building cooperation. Establishing cooperation often depends on governmental support [23]. Next, factors such as intellectual property, contracts, and geographical distance are essential in cooperation and should not be ignored (*awareness*).

3 Method

The status quo needs to be identified to derive a framework for strategies to initiate contact between universities and SMEs. Therefore, a semi-structured interview study is prepared to aim at interviewing "knowledgeable agents" [14, p. 17] for the formation of UBC. In our case, a knowledgeable agent works for an SME or university and cooperates with the other party. These people are considered knowledgeable, as they are working in such cooperation and can explain their "thoughts, intentions, and actions" [14, p. 17]. We prepared two guidelines for each group (university and SME), which follow the same structure but differ in the design of the questions. In our interview sample, different criteria need to be fulfilled. First, the interviewee should have experiences with cooperation in the context of universities or SMEs and vice versa. Second, the university or the respective SME must be in the DACH region. Third, the SMEs needs to fulfill the criteria of the European definition for SMEs[1].

We published two LinkedIn posts and shared them through the university account for each group to identify possible interview partners. Next, another post was published in a dedicated SMEs LinkedIn group. Last, a list of 150 SMEs was derived from *Verband Innovativer Unternehmen e. V.* and *Berufsstart*. These 150 SMEs were then cold-called by mail regarding university cooperation and their willingness to share their thoughts and experiences. For the academic interviewees, the researchers' network from previous projects, conferences, and former coworkers was addressed with the request to forward the inquiry to a respective person. The final sample for the conducted interviews is listed in Table 1 and contains SMEs and researchers from Germany and Austria.

Table 1. Interview Sample

ID	Organization (#Employees)	Role	Years of Experience	Interview Time
I01	SME (10)	Consultant	5 years	37 min
I02	SME (25)	Engineer	1.5 years	19 min
I03	SME (30)	CEO	15 years	25 min
I04	SME (220)	Division Manager	16 years	37 min
I05	SME (25)	CEO	6 years	40 min
I06	SME (20)	Team leader	8 years	48 min
I07	SME (2)	Team leader	3 years	52 min
I08	SME (9)	Project Manager	4 years	30 min
I09	Technical University	Research Assistant	4 years	26 min
I10	Research Institut	Post Doc	4 years	26 min
I11	University	Junior Professor	3.5 years	35 min
I12	University	Professor	6 years	28 min
I13	University	Managing Director	11 years	52 min
I14	University	Post Doc	8.5 years	30 min
I15	University	Professor	2 years	20 min

The conducted interviews were then transcribed with the tool *aTrain* of the University of Graz[2] and the following settings: *model = Medium (accurate), lan-*

[1] SMEs are defined by the EU as enterprises that "*employ fewer than 250 persons and which have an annual turnover not exceeding EUR 50 million, and/or an annual balance sheet total not exceeding EUR 43 million.*" [8].

[2] https://business-analytics.uni-graz.at/de/forschung/atrain/.

guage = German, Multispeaker = yes, Number of speaker = two. We checked the final transcripts for correct transcription and imported them to *MaxQDA*. The applied coding approach is inductive, where just the relevant and demarcable sentences (i.e., topics, challenges, opportunities, and stories) are highlighted (1st-order Concepts) [14]. The 1st-order concepts represent the language of the domain experts and are just translated from German to English with DeepL. The translation is then checked to ensure that the meaning is accurate. The coding was conducted by three researchers and resulted in 381 codes. Next, we further discussed 1st-order concepts and clustered them into 13 2nd-order themes. Subsequently, the 13 2nd-order themes were further aggregated into four dimensions. In the final step, the aggregated dimensions with their respective 2nd-order themes were integrated into the existing process model by Ankrah and AL-Tabbaa [1] (Fig. 2).

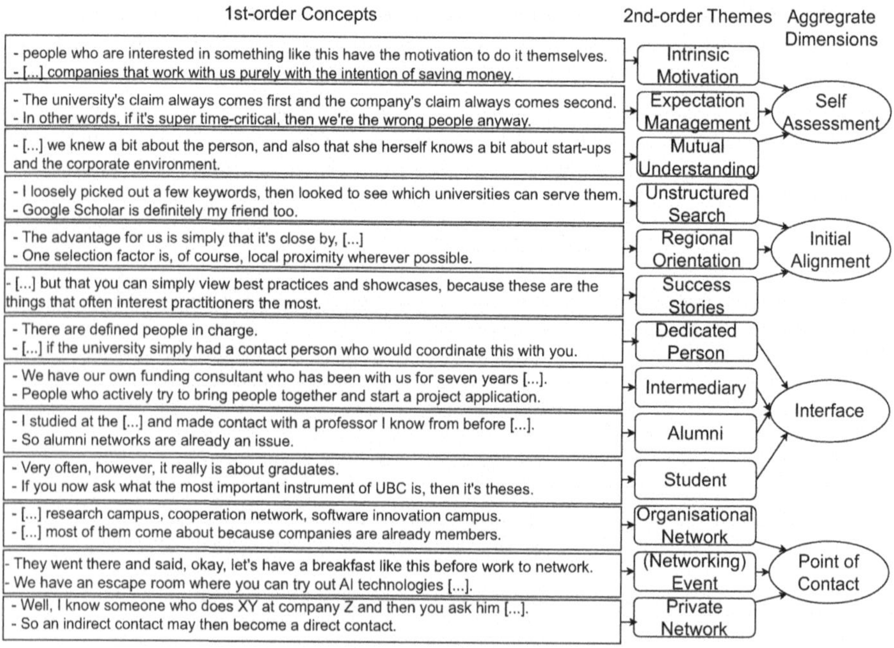

Fig. 2. Data structure based on [14]

4 Findings

This chapter presents a process framework illustrating the UBC process derived from combining our interview study with academic literature. The framework is based on the conceptual process framework for university-industry collaboration by Ankrah and AL-Tabbaa [1]. In our framework (see Fig. 3), we alter the "partnership identification" and "make contact" stages of the Ankrah and AL-Tabbaa [1] framework. The latter three stages of the original framework [1] are not changed within the scope of this work. In the following, we describe the newly proposed stages **Self Assessment** and **Establish Contact**.

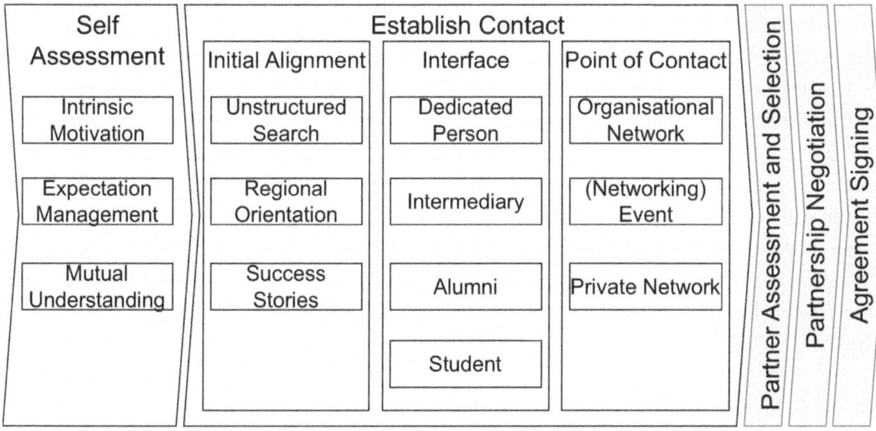

Fig. 3. Updated UBC-process adopted from [1]

4.1 Self Assessment

Intrinsic Motivation: In the context of the UBC formation process, intrinsic motivation is crucial during the self-assessment stage. For many SMEs, this motivation naturally arises, as those interested in cooperation often "*[...] have a kind of self-motivation*" (I14). This involves recognizing and understanding the benefits of such partnerships and being driven by more than just cost-saving measures. Cooperation motivated purely by financial savings, such as those where companies try to engage students merely to cut costs, are "*[...] not a fruitful cooperation*" (I11). In contrast, it is observed, "*the companies that are really interested, there is actually nothing negative*" (I11), underscoring the positive outcomes from intrinsically motivated partnerships. Proactively, they look for "*suitable universities for the topics*" (I06) they are interested in, valuing the strategic expansion that academic partnerships can offer. This forward-thinking approach often results in a "*long list of ideas*" (I04) that are concrete enough to be turned into opportunities. These statements highlight the importance of approaching the other party with concrete ideas or problems that are also relevant to them.

Expectation Management: Effective expectation management is crucial in the self-assessment stage of UBC formation. It begins with clearly communicating the cooperation's phases, roles, and outputs to all involved parties. That means one should prepare a "*little outreach slide deck*" (I10) where the respective roles and outcomes are connected to the phase of the cooperation. The cooperation partner can use the slide deck to understand the expected investment, costs, and outcomes and consider their commitment. A clear expectation management is essential to avoid situations with frustrated cooperation partners. Managing expectations around time sensitivity is also essential, as academia may not meet "*super time-critical*" (I12) demands. To further manage expectations, partnerships often need to navigate the complexities of public sector requirements, such as "*the structures, the requirements [...] in terms of tenders, purchasing processes, etc.*" (I07). This means, especially for academic institutions, to think about "*[...] assistance [and] how far this can go [...]*" (I07). In projects involving students, one needs to know that this is always a "*surprise package*" (I13). That means SMEs should not expect to "*have hired McKinsey for half the price or a third of the price*" (I11). Ensuring that "*the university's requirements always come first*" (I08) in project scopes prevents unrealistic demands on student contributors.

Mutual Understanding: Fostering mutual understanding ensures smooth interaction and cooperation between academic institutions and SMEs. This requires the business and academic spheres to bridge the language and culture gap. That means one should "*adapt linguistically*" (I09) to the respective target group. For example, SMEs do not appreciate consulting language (e.g., "*[...] it's not about a CRM strategy, [...], but about a customer loyalty solution.*" (I09)). I09 formulates this aspect in one sentence: "*Simply so that those who want to take advantage of these offers are also accepted as they are, picked up at the level of knowledge where they are.*" (I09). Another approach is to use moderators (i.e., people who understand the academic and practitioner language), as they can help translate. The moderator can help to identify a possible solution as "*[e]verything sounds good at first. It's a bit like all the trees in the forest. You just can't see the wood for the trees*" (I09). In other words, the moderator can provide guidance on the available solutions. Additionally, mutual understanding is enhanced when partners bring multifaceted experiences. For instance, cooperation with individuals who are familiar with both start-ups and the corporate environment means "*we don't have to explain much*" (I07), as these individuals already possess a valuable perspective that does not solely rest within a university context.

4.2 Establish Contact

Initial Alignment: The process phase *Establish Contact* consists of three different dimensions. The first dimension, i.e., Initial Alignment, covers the starting opportunities for academia and SMEs to establish contact with the other part. Based on the conducted interviews, three 2nd-order themes (e.g., unstructured search, regional orientation, and success stories) were allocated within this dimension.

Unstructured Search: Most universities publicly display information regarding their interest. Searching for this information may be time-consuming, but it can provide a first impression of the players available. A straightforward way to gain an initial understanding of the various opportunities is to perform a Google search. Hence, one approach can be a search by "*loosely [pick] out a few keywords, then [look] to see which universities can serve them*" (I06). Another valuable approach for researching universities is to utilize databases like Scopus or Google Scholar. These platforms provide access to a vast collection of publications from various sources and allow users to perform keyword searches to identify relevant research and publications. Especially SMEs can leverage platforms like Google Scholar to identify researchers specializing in specific topics. Persons in academia usually display their publications, indicating their research focus. I06 mentioned that "*Google Scholar is definitely my friend too*" when searching for Universities. I04 "*[looks] at people's publication lists to assess whether [they] are on the same page and whether a conversation is worthwhile.*"

Regional Orientation: From the interviews, it became evident that regional cooperations have a better chance of success than large-distance cooperations. Regionality is critical for academia and SMEs. For academia, it is evident that most SMEs prioritize their local region, making them primarily interested in cooperating with nearby academic institutions. Interviewee I11 addresses this particular point in the interview by stating, "*many SMEs, even if they have international customers, are keen to somehow have a value chain in their town to somehow strengthen their location, to somehow leave money there*" (I11). The Interviewees strengthen this view from the SMEs. "*The advantage for us is simply that it's close by, we don't have to travel across Germany for it, we can learn a bit about how it works without having to go to a huge expense*" (I01). This statement is supported by I06 ("*one selection factor is, of course, local proximity wherever possible*") and I04 ("*We simply wouldn't address a university in Berlin across the board because we have a regional focus.*").

Success Stories: Academia could provide their previous experiences with SMEs by presenting best practices and success stories. This information is suitable for practitioners and may lead to further cooperation. The last 2nd-order theme for initial alignment addresses, in particular, academia. For SMEs, it is often hard to identify a matching scientific counterpart. As one interviewee notes, "*it's incredibly complicated to even get in touch with people, to find the right contact person somehow*" (I03). Academia could simplify the search for SMEs by providing success stories or examples from previous cases. For SME, these previous cases may function as an exemplary guideline or motivational input to engage with similar problems. Consequently, these cases may motivate SMEs to also participate in UBC. I09 has experiences with SMEs cooperation and proposes to "*[create a kind of empowerment for SMEs]*". Thereby, this empowerment needs to be "*as long-lasting as possible, as sustainable as possible, preferably in such a way that they are not associated with high hurdles*" (I09). With that statement, I09 means to provide examples such as use cases and best practices without an over-engineered bureaucratic registration procedure. Instead, grab their attention and trigger an outreach by using best practices and success stories as "*these are the things practitioners often care about most*" (I09).

Interface. In this context, "interface" refers to bridging the gap between academia and SMEs. This dimension encompasses four distinct 2nd-order themes: dedicated personnel, intermediaries, alumni, and students.

Dedicated Person: Dedicated persons are beneficial for the coordination of UBC. Hence, both organizations should clearly define responsible employees. It could also be helpful for academia to have a dedicated, responsible person per chair. To manage cooperation with academia, I04 created the role of university cooperation manager, ideally a younger employee of the organization. Initially, the organization supported four students but has grown to accommodate up to 50 students. I04 highlights that they wanted to be "*well prepared so that the expectations are clear.*" I04 mentioned that "*there are defined people in charge. I no longer have this role of university cooperation manager because I think that the students might need younger identification figures than me*". Similarly, I03 calls for a dedicated contact person in charge of the coordination. "*Well, it would be cool if the university simply had a contact person who would coordinate this with you.*"

Intermediary: Someone must take the initiative and proactively engage with potential partners. Whether this person is an external funding consultant or a motivated individual from the organization is less important than ensuring the effort is made. Such intermediaries include funding consultants, transfer centers, press offices, or initiatives led by a network member who leads the connection. I05 had good experiences with funding consultants, while I01 appreciated the clear communication with a press office.

> "*We have our own funding consultant who has been with us for seven years and who submits the grants to us.*" (I05)
> "*So there are people you can talk to, for example, [Name of a University of Applied Sciences], where there is a very clear press office, and then you have a very clear group of people to talk to.*" (I01)

Alternatively, the intermediary can be a SME or someone from academia who takes over the project manager role and brings people together. I12 had this experience and stated:

> "*People who actively try to bring people together and start a project application. We once had that in a network, which was super good. He basically got to know everyone and said, there's a call here, you're working on this and that, would that be something? Why don't we get together? So very active, personal, direct. It worked very well in that sense [...].*" (I12)

Alumni: Alumni are well-connected in academia. This potential should be leveraged, especially by SMEs. However, academia should also keep track of their former students by establishing and maintaining alumni networks. Both sides benefit considerably from the alumni and should actively leverage this asset. "*One point, for example, is that there are now graduates here in [Location] who have founded companies or are working. So alumni networks are already an issue*" (I12). An example in this direction is provided by I01, who used his connections to the former university. "*I studied at the University of Applied Sciences in [location] and made contact with a professor I know from before, and they also have a project module in their course, and I got involved, or we as a company got involved and offered a project module for the students.*" (I01). A more systematic and long-lasting approach is the one by I04. They "*[...] hired people who were active here at the universities relatively early on, and they brought the relationships with them.*" (I04). In addition, I04's company hires graduates and focuses on doctoral candidates who are experienced in supervising theses.

> "*There are also a relatively large number of people with doctorates who are not just graduates, but who have also had contact with several universities, several professors, who know how research methodology works, who can also supervise a thesis well because they know what the requirements are.*" (I04)

Student: Students provide a good entry point in UBC. However, students should not be viewed as a cheap workforce to be exploited. If a business hires students and establishes a connection with the university through them, the terms of cooperation should be clearly defined. When this is done, it can pave the way for multiple future connections. Students act as essential interfaces for academia and SMEs. Academia can offer practical cases for students while SMEs gain access to well-trained individuals: "*If you now ask what the most important instrument of university cooperation is, then it's theses*" (I04). I12 mentioned something similar, noting that their most common form of cooperation is also based on graduates: "*Very often, however, it really is about graduates. Master's theses, then people working in SMEs and also saying there that we would like to write the Master's thesis in cooperation would also be a point*" (I12). One SME addresses this topic in a very systematic way. I04 comments, "*[we] started with four at the time*" and "*should have around 50 students under contract, working students, final theses, internships, all types of contracts*" (I04). At first glance, this seems to be the most straightforward way to establish cooperation. However, a genuine interest is essential. If, mainly, the SMEs are merely interested in implementing standard software and need someone (a student) to execute it, then it "*is clearly a knockout*" (I12). I11 supports the statement by claiming that "*companies that work with us purely with the intention of saving money[, are] generally not the most fruitful cooperation*" (I11). One needs to understand the purpose of the thesis, which is to get an academic degree. I08 found a way to accomplish this by accepting that "*[t]he university claim always comes first, and the company claim always comes second*" (I08). I04 applies a similar approach, clearly defining contracts with the students to provide a safe space in a stressful situation. They made contracts "*that state that this is a contract for the joint preparation of a Master's thesis with the following content*" (I04). This should assure the student that the organization is not using them for a spontaneous need.

Point of Contact: The point of contact is not with the person directly but with the environment in which the person is active. The dimension consists of three 2nd-order themes: Organizational Network, (Networking) Event, and Private Network.

Organisational Network: Networks, in general, are a key element in getting in contact with the other party. Networks may vary in form and offerings, but most universities provide networks where businesses can join. "*We have an An-Institute*[3] *at the University of Applied Sciences [...]. And through this An-Institute, we have created a sort of satellite, which then ensures networking [for] SMEs*" (I09). At the University of I14, different institutions such as "*[...] research campus, cooperation network, software innovation campus*" are available. Besides, different international, national, or regional research networks, start-up centers, and university associations are available. Also, government-sponsored programs are available, too (e.g., "*Mittelstand-Digital*" (I03, I09)). These institutions and networks are especially valuable for setting up cooperation between SMEs and academia as "*[...] most of [the Cooperation] come about because companies are already members [of a network]*" (I14). Hence, joining such networks or institutions close to universities offers an excellent starting point for establishing cooperation with academia.

(Networking) Event: Attending (networking) events is time-consuming. However, getting out of the daily routines provides space for getting in touch. Talking at these events creates space for new ideas and innovation. Events are often related, but not necessarily limited, to organizational networks. The impact of such events should not be underestimated by academics and SMEs. Particularly for SMEs, participating in events can be a transformative experience. "*[SMEs] are often so busy with the operational tasks that they don't often take the time to think outside the box.*" (I12). That is why, as an example, I12 organized and had good experiences with an economic or business breakfast. The idea of the breakfast is "*to tear them away from their operational activities*" (I12) due to a location change, which is not happening during the day but before the actual work starts. "*They went there and said, okay, let's have a breakfast like this before work to network*" (I12). Besides, "*there are also regular networking and workshop events where you can at least talk about certain topics [...]*" (I14). A more hands-on experience is provided by I09 as "*[they] have an escape room where you can try out AI technologies and then have to break out of this escape*

[3] An-Institute is a term for "legally independent institutions at [German] universities that are interlinked with them in terms of organization, personnel, and space but do not form an integral part of the respective university" [11, p.31].

room with AI, allowing you to get to grips with such technologies in a playful way" (I09). Typically, a sort of reception after the event is organized where you can "*[...] talk to each other [...] and that's how contact is established*" (I11). I12 also supports that talking after networking events is a classic case of getting in contact.

Private Network: Previous research has shown that private networks are valuable for establishing UBC [24]. The key is to talk to each other and participate in previously mentioned events to build up (in)direct contacts. As previously discussed, networks are vital for establishing successful cooperation. Nonetheless, being part of a formal, organized network is not always a prerequisite for effective cooperation. Instead, one's network can prove to be exceptionally valuable. Almost everyone has connections to individuals in various roles and positions, and strategically leveraging these relationships can foster new opportunities for cooperation. It is beneficial to distinguish these personal connections into direct contacts—those with whom one has a personal relationship—and indirect contacts, who can be reached through mutual acquaintances. Cultivating and utilizing both types of connections can significantly enhance one's ability to initiate and sustain productive partnerships.

For academia, it seems to be easier as "*[the direct contacts] are often people who have studied with you, so personal network, three Fs, family, fools and friends*" (I10). I14 had similar experiences as "*you know people who are somehow employed in these companies and have somehow established contact on a kind of personal level.*" For the organization of I10, the personal connections from the CEO were important. "*[Our] managing director was also relatively influential in the beginning because he naturally has a lot of contacts*" (I08). The interview coding indicated that these personal connections are essential for establishing cooperation. I01's statement is in the same direction: "*If I hadn't had the contact, it wouldn't have happened.*"

Even when direct personal contact is unavailable, indirect personal contact certainly exists. "*If there is already a contact, does not mean that there has to be a direct contact, but there is an indirect contact*" (I11). I14 and I13 mentioned something similar by stating that:

> "*Well, I know someone who does XY at company Z, and then you ask him, we have this and that in mind. [...] Who would be the right contact person for you internally and so on? Then you feel your way around.*" (I14)
> "*The preferred way is to know someone who knows the company.*" (I13)

I13 also supports the fact that indirect personal contacts are important. They were searching for a business partner from a certain sector where they had no previous experience. Through a network, they got in contact with a "*[Smart City Alliance], and suddenly there were three super companies, [local companies], who were also on fire [passionate about the issue]*" (I13). The importance of such connections is summarized by I11 as follows:

> "*There is only contact where there is already contact. So an indirect contact may then become a direct contact.*" (I11)

To break up this chicken-egg problem, one can, for example, start with the own employees. "*In other words, you ask your employees where they studied, or you know where they studied and take the route*" (I01)

4.3 Exemplary Demonstration of Framework

The developed framework can help decision-makers at both universities and SMEs to pursue UBC by highlighting key topics in the process of the successful formation of contacts between SMEs and universities. Not every topic in the framework will be relevant for all organizations or institutions. For example, companies already part of a networking organization will likely not need to rethink their current point of contact significantly. Nevertheless, there might still be room for improvement, for example, if they have not yet set up a dedicated person to handle incoming requests from universities. Thus, using the framework, decision-makers can better understand what is part of the process for establishing contacts and relations between universities and SMEs. Through this understanding, they can formulate strategies along the proposed themes and process steps that improve their organization's capabilities to identify and utilize contact persons for UBC. In the following, some example strategies will be given for SMEs and universities to illustrate how the framework can be applied.

For instance, the expectations towards UBC, especially from SMEs, are often not well aligned with what universities are capable and willing to provide, particularly in the early stages of cooperation projects. As found through the interviews, a significant problem arises if the SME views the universities as simple service providers who can deliver solutions to the SMEs problems and ideas. For example, I14 showed concern when they noted, "*I often have the feeling that we are perceived as a service provider [...] who will come [into the company] and improve everything [...] when in reality we can only provide some support*". This leads to situations where the output of early UBC falls far beneath SME's expectations. At the same time, the findings have shown that students as intermediaries provide a great entry point for long-lasting relations between SMEs and universities and are a significant factor in pursuing more extensive projects. As I08 put it: "*[...] if someone comes for a thesis and does a very good job on the project, there is always the opportunity to continue it with us [...]*". Considering these two themes, a worthwhile strategy for SMEs to pursue if they have no strong relationships with universities yet is to **start small**. SMEs should, in the beginning, align their expectation towards UBC with smaller-scale projects that universities must pursue in the hope of building long-lasting relationships that allow the future partners to engage in larger projects down the road with a more tangible payoff for the SME. For example, SMEs might start building relationships with universities through tendering exploratory student theses and creating more personal contacts with university employees, which can create leverage to suggest and outline more significant project ideas.

Similarly, it is often difficult to perceive the value of organizational networks. I07, for example, about a national network aiming to connect SMEs to research projects, reported that "*[...] it has to be worth it, but it has never been worth it [...]*". Yet, our findings suggest that most cooperation projects come about through contacts within such networks. However, I07 has shown that it can be challenging to find the right contact person, even if the SME is part of a network, "*[...] because the difficulty is simply there, who to speak to [...]*". This visibility problem can be overcome through **active engagement within organizational networks** by regularly attending or hosting events and seeking out discussions with other network attendees, including university contacts. In addition, these events offer lower barriers to starting conversations with universities and exploring complex topics together. These "*initial interviews*" (I06) foster a mutual understanding, which is integral to a successful UBC.

Because networking events remain a lower barrier to entry for SMEs, universities should consider increasing their commitment to **hosting open and accessible network events**. Not only can these events be used to discuss the ideas and topics of SMEs, but universities can also present their research projects, success stories, ideas, and artifacts. As such, these events allow companies to break from their rigid organizational reality as universities can offer an "*unbiased approach, with knowledgeable individuals, who can approach the problems without prior knowledge*" (I03) and who can provide "*novel perspectives on the daily doings*" (I02) of companies. Universities should consider networking events at times that do not conflict with SMEs' organizational responsibilities to increase their appeal. For example, I12 reported much success with "*Business-breakfasts*": *"In the end, it was relatively good because they went there and said, okay, I'll have a breakfast like this before work to network and see others. And I can get out of this world of thought for a bit. And I think you have to create this situation so that they're ready.*" (I12).

Another strategy universities could use to improve their situation regarding establishing cooperation with SMEs is to give specific employees the explicit responsibility for interfacing with businesses and inquiring about ideas for cooperation projects. The proposed framework indicates that active expectation management and the establishment of a mutual understanding are essential components of a successful UBC, which can be effectively achieved through a direct channel of communication between SMEs and employees at the university who are close to the subject matter. Yet, SMEs often struggle to find the correct person to contact. For example, it was noted that "*it's incredibly complicated to even get in touch with people and find the right contact person somehow. You have some secretaries on the line who then don't know. Then they call the department. You don't have a concentrated point where this matchmaking takes place [...]*" (I03). **Dedicated contact persons** on the university's side, preferably closely related to its various departments, can make the phase in which contact is established much more efficient by eliminating much of the overhead from searching for the right person to contact. Simultaneously, a dedicated person close to the issues benefits the establishment of a mutual understanding and the active alignment of expectations, as they allow for early and direct discussions about ideas, potential projects, and research. While nominating a dedicated contact person can arguably constitute a significant improvement for

UBC, universities must simultaneously ensure they are easily identifiable. As the framework suggests, *unstructured search* for potential cooperation partners is a frequently used method for SMEs to identify university partners. Yet, during the interviews, it was frequently suggested that it was challenging to find the necessary information. When asked how they identified their contact person (I07) answered: "*Well, I think it starts with the fact that is simply no information you can find on the websites.*" Hence, it is critical to the strategy of nominating a dedicated person for coordinating UBC that this person is also prominently advertised on the university website.

5 Discussion

Our derived process model aids SMEs and academia to address the previously mentioned success factors by Rybnicek and Königsgruber [23]. For the **institutional factors**, understanding one's own needs and requirements, clearly defining roles and responsibilities, and maintaining a willingness to adapt is essential. Through our process step *Self Assessment* with its 2nd-order themes *Expectation Management* and *Instrinsic Motivation*, two critical aspects of this step are addressed. Additionally, the theme *Dedicated Person*, found in the *Interface* dimension, contributes significantly to meeting these institutional factors. The **Relationship factors** contains aspects such as listening, understanding, personal relations, reciprocal communication, and smaller projects. We address these topics through our 2nd-order themes *Mutual Understanding*, *Expectation Management*, *Dedicated Person*, and through the suggested strategies like *starting small*, and *active engagement within organizational networks*. The **Output factors** cover understanding and objectives and partner selection and evaluation. This section is partly covered through our extension. The criteria for the selection and evaluation steps were not part of the research presented in this work. However, these steps are addressed in the framework by Ankrah and AL-Tabbaa [1]. Lastly, the **Framework factors** with outside support and geographical distance are addressed. The aggregated dimension *Point of Contact* addresses the outside support, while the geographical distance is covered by our 2nd-order theme *Regional Orientation*.

By combining selected themes of the developed framework with additional, reported experiences from the interview participants, we illustrated how universities and SMEs might use our framework to formulate grounded strategies for establishing contact with potential partners for UBC. Research on establishing contact between universities and SMEs is currently limited [21,22]. At the same time, academic literature has primarily focused on barriers to university-SME cooperation [22]. Thus, our proposed, exemplary strategies provide one of the first attempts to come up with actionable pathways specifically for both SMEs and universities to initiate and maintain successful cooperation. Earlier literature, such as Bjerregaard [6] or Awasthy et al. [2], addresses contact-making strategies to some extent. However, they are focused on larger-scale industry-university collaboration [2] or remain un-prescriptive, merely reporting on the effectiveness of existing personal contacts [6]. Instead, the developed framework and, by extension, the developed strategies are directly grounded in the experiences of universities and SMEs. They are enriched with insights from cooperation projects and directly extend previous attempts at providing strategies for establishing contact in UBC through more actionable pathways.

5.1 Limitations

We acknowledge that our research may have two limitations. The first concerns the number of interviewees. In particular, interviewing participants from the SME sector proved challenging. We specifically sought SMEs that have engaged or are currently engaged in some form of cooperation with academia. These criteria, combined with our focus on the DACH region, resulted in a limited number of SMEs responding to our invitation and participating in the study. Nevertheless, the insights gained from these interviews were valuable and offered essential perspectives on establishing contact with academia. The second limitation relates to the research focus of our academic interviewees. All the participants from academia have backgrounds in IT and business economics. While this focus may limit the range of possible insights, it also aligns with the critical role of digitalization, which is considered one of the significant challenges of our time [15]. Furthermore, Information Systems research is inherently connected to real-world applications. In summary, although we acknowledge these limitations, we believe the setup is appropriate for the study.

5.2 Further Research

The limitations of this study lend themselves to potential avenues for future research. By addressing these areas, future research can build on our findings and provide a more comprehensive understanding of how academia and industry can effectively cooperate, ultimately enhancing the value and impact of these cooperations. First, future research expands beyond the DACH region to include SMEs from diverse geographic locations. This broader scope would help capture various experiences and insights regarding cooperation with academia. Additionally, efforts to engage a more significant number of SMEs could provide a more comprehensive understanding of the challenges and successes in this area. Future studies could also include participants from a broader range of academic disciplines. By incorporating perspectives from fields outside of IT and business economics, researchers could gain a richer and more varied understanding of how different disciplines engage with industry partners, potentially uncovering unique cooperation models and strategies.

As per the conducted study, we promote the idea of conducting longitudinal research to track the evolution of SME and academic cooperation over time, similar to the study by Müller et al. [19]. This approach would provide insights into how initial contacts develop into long-term partnerships and the factors influencing their success or failure. Lastly, alternative models of UBC that are not centered around traditional roles and responsibilities should be investigated. This could include exploring co-creation models, innovation labs, and open innovation ecosystems where roles might be more fluid and collaborative.

6 Contribution

The first and initial step of UBC has not yet been specified in research [16]. That is why our research sheds light on the formation of UBC by conducting interviews with practitioners and researchers. The derived insights extended the framework from Ankrah and AL-Tabbaa [1] through the introduction of new stages—**Self Assessment** and **Establish Contact** (see Fig. 3). These additions provide a more comprehensive understanding of the initial phases of UBC, offering a refined model that addresses specific challenges faced by academic and business partners. This research contributes to the literature by highlighting critical themes such as intrinsic motivation, expectation management, and mutual understanding. It emphasizes the importance of these factors in forming and sustaining effective cooperation. These insights offer a basis for further empirical studies exploring the dynamics of UBC. The proposed process model is a tool for practitioners and researchers, facilitating the strategic selection and integration of relevant elements within UBC. We illustrate this by outlining practical strategies, including growing partnerships through smaller starting projects, active engagement with networking events, hosting accessible events, and employing dedicated intermediaries. These strategies provide actionable pathways to establish cooperation for SMEs and academia. In this sense, our framework enhances the theoretical and practical understanding of effectively establishing UBC.

Disclosure of Interests. The authors have no competing interests to declare that are relevant to the content of this article.

References

1. Ankrah, S., AL-Tabbaa, O.: Universities-industry collaboration: a systematic review. Scand. J. Manage. **31**(3), 387–408 (2015)
2. Awasthy, R., Flint, S., Sankarnarayana, R., Jones, R.L.: A framework to improve university-industry collaboration. J. Ind. Univ. Collab. **2**(1), 49–62 (2020)
3. Baker, W.E., Grinstein, A., Harmancioglu, N.: Whose innovation performance benefits more from external networks: entrepreneurial or conservative firms? J. Prod. Innov. Manag. **33**(1), 104–120 (2016)
4. Banerjee, P.K., Ma, L.C.: Routinisation of B2B e-commerce by small firms: a process perspective. Inf. Syst. Front. **14**, 1033–1046 (2012)
5. Barnes, T., Pashby, I., Gibbons, A.: Effective university - industry interaction: a multi-case evaluation of collaborative R&D projects. Eur. Manag. J. **20**(3), 272–285 (2002)
6. Bjerregaard, T.: Universities-industry collaboration strategies: a micro-level perspective. Eur. J. Innov. Manag. **12**(2), 161–176 (2009)
7. Brunswicker, S., Ehrenmann, F.: Managing open innovation in SMEs: a good practice example of a German software firm. Int. J. Ind. Eng. Manage. **4**(1), 33–41 (2013)

8. Commission of the European Communities: Commission recommendation concerning the definition of micro, small and medium-sized enterprises (2003)
9. De Massis, A., Audretsch, D., Uhlaner, L., Kammerlander, N.: Innovation with limited resources: management lessons from the German Mittelstand. J. Prod. Innov. Manag. **35**(1), 125–146 (2018)
10. D'Este, P., Perkmann, M.: Why do academics engage with industry? the entrepreneurial university and individual motivations. J. Technol. Transf. **36**(3), 316–339 (2011)
11. Federal Ministry of Education and Research: Bundesbericht Forschung 2004. Forschungsbericht, Federal Ministry of Education and Research, Berlin, Germany (2004)
12. Galán-Muros, V., Plewa, C.: What drives and inhibits university-business cooperation in Europe? A comprehensive assessement. R&D Manage. **46**(2), 369–382 (2016)
13. Gerling, C., Bickel, F., Haskamp, T., Uebernickel, F.: Collaborate to innovate: utilizing design patterns cards for accelerating the digital transformation of small and medium-sized enterprises. In: Proceedings of the 55th Hawaii International Conference on System Sciences, pp. 5335–5344. Virtual (2022)
14. Gioia, D.A., Corley, K.G., Hamilton, A.L.: Seeking qualitative rigor in inductive research: notes on the Gioia methodology. Organ. Res. Methods **16**(1), 15–31 (2012)
15. Hess, T., Benlian, A., Matt, C., Wiesböck, F.: Options for formulating a digital transformation strategy. MIS Q. Exec. **15**(2), 123–139 (2016)
16. Kruse, P.: A design-driven approach to facilitate university-SME cooperation. In: Thrity-Second European Conference on Information Systems (ECIS2024). Paphos, Cyprus (2024)
17. Legner, C., et al.: Digitalization: opportunity and challenge for the business and information systems engineering community. Bus. Inf. Syst. Eng. **59**(4), 301–308 (2017). https://doi.org/10.1007/s12599-017-0484-2
18. Levy, M., Loebbecke, C., Powell, P.: SMEs, co-opetition and knowledge sharing: the role of information systems. Eur. J. Inf. Syst. **12**, 3–17 (2003)
19. Müller, L.S., Nohe, C., Reiners, S., Becker, J., Hertel, G.: Adopting information systems at work: a longitudinal examination of trust dynamics, antecedents, and outcomes. Behav. Inf. Technol. **43**(6), 1096–1128 (2024)
20. Ngugi, I.K., Johnsen, R.E., Erdélyi, P.: Relational capabilities for value co-creation and innovation in SMEs. J. Small Bus. Enterp. Dev. **17**(2), 260–278 (2010)
21. Orazbayeva, B., Plewa, C., Davey, T., Muros, V.G.: The future of university-business cooperation: research and practice priorities. J. Eng. Tech. Manage. **54**, 67–80 (2019)
22. Pereira, R., Franco, M.: Cooperation between universities and SMEs: a systematic literature review. Ind. High. Educ. **36**(1), 37–50 (2022)
23. Rybnicek, R., Königsgruber, R.: What makes industry-university collaboration succeed? a systematic review of the literature. J. Bus. Econ. **89**(2), 221–250 (2019)
24. Schaeffer, P.R., Guerrero, M., Fischer, B.B.: Mutualism in ecosystems of innovation and entrepreneurship: a bidirectional perspective on universities's linkages. J. Bus. Res. **134**, 184–197 (2021)
25. Soluk, J., Kammerlander, N.: Digital transformation in family-owned mittelstand firms: a dynamic capabilities perspective. Eur. J. Inf. Syst. **30**(6), 676–711 (2021)

26. Thrassou, A., Uzunboylu, N., Vrontis, D., Christofi, M.: Digitalization of SMEs: a review of opportunities and challenges. In: Thrassou, A., Vrontis, D., Weber, Y., Shams, S., Tsoukatos, E. (eds.) The Changing Role of SMEs in Global Business. PSCBRIAEAB, pp. 179–200. Springer, Cham (2020). https://doi.org/10.1007/978-3-030-45835-5_9
27. Uhlaner, L.M., van Stel, A., Duplat, V., Zhou, H.: Disentangling the effects of organizational capabilities, innovation and firm size on SME sales growth. Small Bus. Econ. **41**, 581–607 (2013)

The Effects of Integrating Information Technology into Inquiry-Based Instruction on Students' Learning in Taiwan a Meta-analysis

Win Chieh Lo[1](✉) and Meng Ping Tsuei[2]

[1] Department of Science, National Taipei University of Education, Taipei, Republic of China
lwj4334@ms14.hinet.net

[2] Graduate School of Curriculum and Instructional Communications Technology, National Taipei University of Education, Taipei, Republic of China
mptsuei@mail.ntue.edu.tw

Abstract. This study aims to conduct a meta-analysis of research on inquiry-based instruction facilitated by information technology (IT) integration in Taiwan from 2000 to 2024. We searched by using keywords "information technology integration", and "inquiry teaching". The results gathered 63 studies (with 5,928 participants). The moderator variables in the study were categorized including three dimensions: (1) IT Integration Dimension: Assistive learning IT, IT integration methods, and timing of IT use. (2) Inquiry Teaching Dimension: inquiry levels, inquiry models, guidance methods, group settings for inquiry, timing of inquiry activities, and types of textbooks used. (3) Instruction Information: Subjects and participant age. The results of this study were as follows: The weighted average effect size ($g = 0.611$, $p < .01$) indicates that there was a significant effect of integrating information technology into inquiry-based instruction on students' learning. The crucial parameters for optimizing the effectiveness of integrating information technology into inquiry-based instruction on students' learning are identified as follows: (1) Used in elementary schools; (2) Applying in the science subject; (3) Use structed inquiry; (4) Achieve the inquiry level of "drawing conclusions and verifying;" (5) Apply interaction and communication to integrate IT into inquiry teaching; (6) The IT integration study devices were provided through classroom information equipment. The meta-analysis of moderator variables in this study can be applied to similar research, providing a comprehensive overview of IT integrated inquiry learning in Taiwan.

Keywords: Meta-Analysis · Information Technology Integration · Information Technology · Inquiry Teaching · Inquiry Learning

1 Introduction

1.1 Reviewing the Effectiveness of IT Integration Through Inquiry Teaching and Learning Standards

The benefits of technological advancement for education are evident, and its integration into education significantly influences the future development of information technology (IT). In digital learning (E-Learning), the "E" is not only defined as "Electronic", but

B. K. Smith and M. Borge (Eds.): HCII 2025, LNCS 15806, pp. 281–299, 2025.
https://doi.org/10.1007/978-3-031-93564-0_17

also carries meanings such as Exploration, Experience, Excitement, Extend, Expand, Easy, and Effective (Kao, 2006). This characteristic has driven the rapid growth of platforms that integrate IT into education, and these platforms have become a common trend in modern education, influencing various subjects. Research in meta-analysis of the effectiveness of IT integration in teaching shows its impact on student performance. Looking back at relevant studies in meta-analysis of IT integration, it is found that subject's achievement or attitudes related to learning are commonly used as indicators of the effectiveness of IT integration in teaching. For example, the impact of virtual reality teaching on students' attitudes and skills (Liao, 2023), a comprehensive review of 30 years of research on the impact of technology integration in primary and secondary school mathematics education (Liao, & Chen, 2021), and the impact of mobile learning on academic achievement among Taiwanese students (Liao, Chen, & Yang, 2020). Moreover, Yen, & Huang, (2019) conducted a meta-analysis from the cognitive and affective perspectives to explore the impact of flipped classrooms on middle and primary school students' learning outcomes, identifying factors such as subject area, digital learning platform, self-study materials, self-assessment mechanisms, student-centered activities, and instructional time as having a positive impact. Hsiao (2019) also found through meta-analysis that integrating creativity into the curriculum can enhance students' creativity, with publication type, research design, subject area, research tools, and educational level being important factors influencing the effectiveness of creativity-based teaching.

However, from the findings of the above studies, it remains difficult to see the transformational relationship between teachers and students in the process of teaching and learning in IT integrated education. That is, "purposeful teaching by teachers does not necessarily translate into meaningful learning for students". However, research on inquiry-based teaching, which emphasizes students as the center of learning, and the development of various concrete teaching and learning models, can be applied in various subjects and remains a widely applicable teaching method. This could serve as one of the effectiveness indicators in meta-analysis of IT integration in education. Although the concept of inquiry originated early and was formally defined by John Dewey in the early 20th century, it has since undergone various developments, such as Problem-based Learning (PBL) and Experiential Learning, which emphasize the student-centered role in learning. Moreover, in recent years, the 5E teaching model, which includes five learning phases: Engagement, Exploration, Explanation, Elaboration, and Evaluation, has specifically outlined the context of inquiry-based learning. This approach is also consistent with Herron, (1971) proposal of four progressively deeper levels of inquiry in curriculum design: Structured Inquiry, Controlled Inquiry, Guided Inquiry, and Open Inquiry. These levels must align with a gradual, step-by-step process. The tiered learning stages unique to inquiry-based teaching can guide teachers in integrating different modes of "inquiry-based teaching" into their curriculum design. These stages can also be used to evaluate students' abilities at different levels during the inquiry learning process, thus serving as an effectiveness indicator for the integration of IT into teaching. Furthermore, inquiry-based teaching is not limited to natural or mathematical sciences. A review of the implementation of inquiry-based teaching in Taiwan over the past 20 years shows that many subjects have already incorporated inquiry-based teaching, such as music (HRao, 2001; Zeng, 2003), Chemistry (Wang, 2002), Earth Science (Cai, 2003; Li,

2005; Zhou, 2006; Lin, 2009; Chen, 2010), Mandarin (Zhao, 2004; Qiu, 2012), Visual Arts (Zhang, 2005), English (Lin, 2007; Ma, 2010; Su, 2012; Wu, 2019), Social Studies (Zheng, 2010), and Computer Science (Wu, 2010; Wu, 2011) all show that inquiry-based teaching can be applied to most subjects today and even helps college students enhance problem-solving and self-directed learning abilities (Li, 2012).

Therefore, if we can review the integration of IT into teaching from the perspective of inquiry-based teaching and learning, we will be able to identify, from another angle, the effectiveness of technology integration and the interconnection between teachers and students in the teaching and learning process.

1.2 Research Purpose and Questions

This study conducted a comprehensive meta-analysis of the use and distribution of IT integration in teaching, as well as the types and levels of teacher-student interaction during integration. The purpose of this study is to perform a meta-analysis to examine the overall effectiveness of IT integration into teaching in Taiwan. The research selected studies related to IT and inquiry-based teaching in Taiwan from 2000 to 2024. The study first analyzed the moderating effects of IT integration on the effectiveness of inquiry-based learning. Secondly, it aimed to identify the mutual influences among moderating variables during the process of IT integration into inquiry-based teaching. The research questions were as follows:

Research Question 1 (RQ1): What are the frequency and overall distribution of IT integration in inquiry-based teaching? Which moderating variables influence the overall frequency and distribution?

Research Question 2 (RQ2): During IT integration in inquiry-based teaching, how do the teacher-planned inquiry teaching models differ from students' self-directed inquiry learning levels? Which moderating variables influence the correlation between the two?

Research Question 3 (RQ3): Based on the comparative effects of moderating variables, what combinations are effective when integrating IT into teaching?

2 Literature

2.1 Inquiry-Based Learning

Inquiry-based teaching was introduced by John Dewey in the early 20th century. Dewey's experiential learning approach emphasized guiding students to develop reflective thinking through hands-on experiences, enabling them to transform acquired knowledge into deeper understanding. He argued that learning is not solely about acquiring knowledge but also about exploring the processes and methods behind it (Dewey, 1935). Similarly, Bruner, (1960) advocated for fostering intuitive and analytical skills through scientific inquiry activities, a perspective that influenced the developmental framework of the National Science Education Standards (NSES) in the United States. Lederman, and Lederman, (2005) elaborated on the importance of teaching students the methods of scientific inquiry within the context of the nature and history of science. This includes formulating questions, developing hypotheses, designing research procedures, interpreting evidence and data, critically evaluating findings, and analyzing the role of scientific evidence and information. Through this process, inquiry-based learning transforms students into active learners. Today, this approach remains highly relevant and integrates seamlessly into various emerging curriculum models. A key characteristic of inquiry-based teaching is its hierarchical learning structure. Trevor MacKenzie (2016) emphasized that curriculum design often includes four levels: structured inquiry, controlled inquiry, guided inquiry, and open inquiry, likening the progression to learning to swim. Other researchers have proposed similar hierarchical frameworks, such as guided, structured, and recipe-based inquiry (Bainchini, & Colburn, 2000). Herron (1971) categorized inquiry into four levels based on the extent of teacher involvement in questions, procedures, and solutions: (1) Confirmation/Verification Inquiry: Teachers provide the questions, procedures, and expected results. Students follow the steps to verify known outcomes. (2) Structured Inquiry: Teachers provide the questions and procedures. Students follow the steps to derive results. (3) Guided Inquiry: Teachers pose the questions, but students design their own procedures and methods to solve the problems. (4) Open Inquiry: Students independently propose questions related to the topic and design their own inquiry procedures. These inquiry models have become mainstream in inquiry-based teaching and are linked to the depth of student learning across 13 science process skills: observing, measuring, using space-time relationships, communicating, classifying, predicting, using numbers, inferring, controlling variables, defining operationally, interpreting data, formulating hypotheses, and experimenting.

The Predict-Observe-Explain (POE) teaching method (White & Gunstone, 1992), later modified to include "Comparison" (POEC) by Chiu et al. (2005), organizes these skills into a sequential process: prediction, observation, explanation, and comparison. This structured framework simplifies the integration of the 13 science process skills, offering teachers a streamlined approach to inquiry-based teaching and providing students with a progressive learning strategy. Moreover, inquiry-based learning extends beyond science education and finds applications in STEM fields (science, technology, engineering, and mathematics) through Process-Oriented Guided Inquiry Learning (POGIL). It is also adaptable to other subjects, such as history, where it encourages critical analysis and evidence-based reasoning (Monte-Sano, Bordonaro, & Aumen, 2020).

2.2 Information Technology

Information technology (IT) serves as a vital tool for integrating education and technology. With rapid advancements, IT has revolutionized traditional teaching methods, fostered the modernization and accessibility of global education while reducing disparities in resource allocation. IT enhances learning efficiency and student engagement, refines teaching methods, and supports personalized and differentiated learning, contributing to the universalization of educational resources. In Taiwan, the Ministry of Education introduced its Comprehensive Blueprint for Information Education in Elementary and Secondary Schools in 2001, aiming for IT integration to account for 20% of total teaching hours (Shen, 2004). Today, IT's role in education has become indispensable, profoundly influencing both how students learn and how teachers teach. The "E" in e-learning is widely interpreted to encompass aspects such as Electronic, Exploration, Experience, Excitement, Extend, Expend, Easy, and Effective (Kao, 2006).

The synergy between IT and e-learning has broadened the educational landscape, with notable applications including: (1) Personalized Learning and AI Technology: Pane, Steiner, Baird, and Hamilton, (2015) demonstrated that AI-based personalized learning systems significantly improve student performance. (2) Distance and Blended Learning: Means, Toyama, Murphy, Bakia, and Jones, (2009) found that blended learning is more effective than traditional face-to-face teaching. (3) Collaboration and Interaction: Johnson, Johnson, and Holubec, (1998) highlighted IT's ability to enhance collaborative learning and teamwork among students. (4) Virtual and Augmented Reality: Merchant, Goetz, Cifuentes, Keeney-Kennicutt, and Davis, (2014) confirmed that virtual reality technology significantly improves learning outcomes, particularly in STEM education. (5) Bridging Educational Resource Gaps: UNESCO's 2012 Open Educational Resources (OER) initiative addressed inequalities in digital learning and resource allocation, promoting educational equity. (6) Improving Teacher Efficiency: Koehler, and Mishra, (2009) emphasized the importance of digital literacy for teachers and the effectiveness of integrating technology into teaching practices.

Research demonstrates that these emerging technologies empower learners by enabling access to knowledge anytime and anywhere, tailoring learning experiences to individual needs, and supporting educators in various ways. IT facilitates the analysis of student performance, the creation of engaging multimedia learning environments, and enhanced teacher-student interaction through collaborative platforms. As IT continues to evolve, its integration into education will remain a cornerstone of modern pedagogical strategies.

3 Method

3.1 Literature Search

First, keywords including 'IT integration', 'information technology', 'inquiry teaching', and 'inquiry learning' were used to conduct a bibliographic search in the Airity Library and the National Master and Doctoral Thesis System databases Taiwan. The articles selected were published from 2000 to 2024. There were 451 articles selected consisting of 329 papers, 114 journal articles, and 8 conference papers. Subsequently, the abstracts were reviewed for preliminary screening, and articles not related to online learning or lacking full-text downloads were excluded. Then, 87 articles were selected for in-depth review, with 63 of them focusing on online learning and containing information on experimental groups, control groups, sample numbers, means, standard deviations, and F-values or t-values.

3.2 Coding Framework

Meta-analysis of the study was conducted. The moderator variables of this study included the: Learning stage (elementary school, junior high school, high school and university), Domain subjects (Chinese, English, mathematics, natural science, social science and art), Inquiry model (structured inquiry, guided inquiry, open inquiry), Inquiry levels (analyze the problem, make plans and verification conclusion), Guidance methods (teacher-led, student-led and teacher & student-led), Grouping methods (whole class, group, personal, mix), Teaching material (self-made media, ready-made video, written information, other), IT device (Paper, teaching aids, fixed information equipment, notebook/mobile device, traditional learning machine, intelligent learning machine, tool learning machine, mix, unspecified), IT integration methods (interaction and communication, WebQuest, game, mobile learning, flipped classroom), Intervention duration (1–4 weeks, 5–8 weeks, 9–12 weeks, 13 weeks above).

Researchers and co-researchers separately registered the 63 papers and journals, and discrepancies in registrations were resolved through discussion to reach a consensus. The registration content of Table 1 underwent a consistency test, achieving an observer reliability of more than 78.6% through Cohen's Kappa calculation.

Table 1. The distribution of codes in studies.

no	Author	A	B	C	D	E	F
1	Chen, Yu-Lung (2000)	2	n	2	4	4	w
2	Huang, Fu-Nuan (2001)	3	a	1	2	3	w
3	JAO, Kueih-Siang (2001)	2	a	1	2	4	w
4	Wang, Chien-Chin (2003)	3	n	2	3	4	w
5	Zeng, Pei-Yi (2004)	2	a	1	2	3	w
6	Tsai, Peng-Hen (2003)	1	m	1	3	3	w
7	Chang, Yi-Yu (2005)	2	a	1	2	4	w
8	Li, Hsin-Yi (2005)	3	n	3	4	4	w
9	Yang, Kai-Ti (2007)	1	n	1	3	4	w
10	Lin, Chiou-Tsen (2007)	1	e	1	2	3	i
11	Tsai, Chung-Chieh (2007)	1	n	1	4	4	i
12	Chou, Shih-Yao (2008)	3	s	3	3	3	i
13	Lin, Tai-An (2008)	2	n	3	4	3	i
14	Chen, Ming-Hui (2009)	2	n	2	4	3	w
15	Chen, Chien-Hua (2009)	1	n	2	4	1	i
16	Chen, Mei-hua (2009)	2	m	2	4	1	i
17	Liao, Wen-Shioung (2009)	1	c	1	3	6	m
18	Tsai, Peng-Hen (2010)	1	m	1	3	3	g
19	Wu, Fang-Tsai (2010)	4	n	3	3	4	i
20	Chern, Mei-Shian (2010)	1	n	2	3	4	w
21	Weng, Hsiao-Lan (2010)	2	n	2	2	3	w

(*continued*)

Table 1. (*continued*)

no	Author	A	B	C	D	E	F
22	Ma, Ming-Xiao (2010)	2	e	1	2	3	w
23	Hou, Ming-Xian (2010)	1	s	2	3	4	w
24	Liao, Chia-Min (2010)	1	n	1	4	3	i
25	Chen, Xuan-Der (2011)	1	c	1	3	4	i
26	Wu, Jen-Chung (2011)	4	n	1	4	7	i
27	Wang, Chung-Ming (2011)	1	c	1	3	3	i
28	Wang, Mei-Yun (2012)	1	n	3	4	u	i
29	Li, Chi-Chia (2012)	4	s	3	4	1	i
30	Lin, Shu-Wen (2012)	1	n	1	3	2	i
31	Chang (2012a)	4	s	3	4	3	w
32	Chang (2012b)	1	n	3	4	2	i
33	Chang and Chiueh (2012)	1	s	2	3	2	g
34	Chen, Yi-Hsing (2012)	1	s	1	2	3	i
35	Yen, Bai-Hung (2012)	1	c	1	3	4	g
36	Wang, Tzu-Ching (2013)	1	n	1	3	2	i
37	Lee, Sheng-Lung (2013)	1	s	1	3	2	i
38	Sun, Yu-Wen (2013)	2	n	1	3	8	w
39	Peng, Yih-Jen (2013)	2	m	2	3	3	i
40	Huang, Tsui-Wen (2013)	2	s	2	4	4	w
41	Liao, Chia-Yu (2013)	1	n	2	3	4	g
42	Tsai, Shu-Hui (2013)	2	a	1	2	7	g
43	Chung, Chang-Hung (2014)	2	n	2	4	3	i
44	Lien, Hsin-Hsin (2014)	1	c	1	2	4	m
45	Chen,Ching-Chi (2015)	1	s	1	2	3	i
46	Yang, Su-Wan (2015)	3	n	1	4	3	i
47	Hsieh, Ming-Feng (2015)	2	m	1	3	5	i
48	Kao, Juo-Hsin (2016)	3	n	1	3	2	i
49	Chuang, Her-Wen (2016)	1	n	2	2	4	w
50	Wen, Mei-Yun (2016)	2	n	1	2	5	g
51	Chang, Wan-Jen (2017)	4	n	2	4	6	i
52	Tu, Yi-Lien (2018)	2	n	1	2	6	m
53	Wu, Tzu-Ying (2019)	3	e	1	3	4	i

(*continued*)

Table 1. (*continued*)

no	Author	A	B	C	D	E	F
54	Wu, Yun-Yan (2019)	1	e	1	2	3	g
55	Huang, Siu-Shiang (2019)	3	c	3	4	8	i
56	Lu, Chiu-Hui (2020)	3	o	1	3	4	m
57	Lin, Chih-Lung (2020)	2	n	1	2	4	m
58	Peng, Chia-hui (2020)	2	c	1	3	1	i
59	Hsu, Kuan-Pu (2021)	2	n	1	2	4	i
60	Huang, Tzu-Yang (2022)	2	n	1	4	7	i
61	Wang, Wan-Ting (2023)	1	n	2	4	7	m
62	Liou, Yu-Ching (2023)	1	s	1	2	3	g
63	Chen, Huei-Hsiung (2024)	3	n	2	4	3	i

Note:
A (Learning stage): 1. Elementary school, 2. Junior high school, 3. High School, 4. University, o.other
B (Domain subjects): a. art, c. Chinese, e. English, m. mathematics, n. natural, s. society
C (Inquiry model): 1. Structured inquiry, 2. Guided inquiry, 3. Open inquiry
D (Inquiry levels): 1. Found the problem, 2. Analyze the problem, 3. Make plans, 4. Verification conclusion
E (IT device): 1. Paper, 2. Teaching aids, 3. Fixed information equipment, 4. Notebook/mobile device, 5. Traditional learning machine, 6. Intelligent learning machine, 7. Tool learning machine, 8. Mix, u. unspecified
F (IT integration methods): i. interaction and communication, w. WebQuest, g. game, m. mobile learning, f. flipped classroom

The effect size of this study is determined using the g value (formula 1), as calculated by Yen, and Huang, (2019), employing Hedges and Olkin's (1985) method. The effect size is then categorized according to Cohen's (1988) guidelines: $|g| < 0.2$ indicates no effect size; $0.2 < |g| < 0.5$ suggests a low effect size; $0.5 < |g| < 0.8$ implies a medium effect size; and $|g| > 0.8$ indicates a high effect size.

$$g = \frac{x_1 + x_2}{s} \quad s = \sqrt{\frac{(n_1 - 1)s_1^2 + (n_2 - 1)s_2^2}{n_1 + n_2 - 2}} \tag{1}$$

After registering the coding content from the 63 papers and journals into an Excel spreadsheet, Comprehensive Meta-Analysis V3 software was utilized to conduct meta-analysis.

4 Results

4.1 Effect Sizes of Studies on IT Integration in Inquiry-Based Learning

This section explains the results of meta-analysis. In this context, it discusses the calculation of effect sizes and the variations found within the subcategories. Among the 63 research papers on IT integration in inquiry-based learning, there were 3031 participants in the experimental group and 2897 participants in the control group, totaling 5928 individuals.

Study name	Hedges's g	Standard error	Variance	Lower limit	Upper limit	Z-Value	p-Value
	Statistics for each study						
Chen, Ming-Hui (2009)	0.337	0.171	0.029	0.003	0.671	1.975	0.048
Hou, Ming-Xian (2010)	0.558	0.250	0.062	0.068	1.048	2.233	0.026
Chen, Xuan-Der (2011)	1.528	0.268	0.072	1.003	2.052	5.710	0.000
Wu, Jen-Chung (2011)	0.142	0.340	0.116	-0.525	0.809	0.417	0.677
Chung, Chang-Hung (2014)	5.021	0.310	0.096	4.412	5.629	16.171	0.000
Chen, Huei-Hsiung (2024)	-1.371	0.282	0.079	-1.923	-0.819	-4.869	0.000
Chen, Yu-Lung (2000)	0.493	0.265	0.070	-0.027	1.014	1.860	0.063
Huang, Fu-Nuan (2001)	1.255	0.229	0.052	0.806	1.704	5.481	0.000
JAO, Kueih-Siang (2001)	0.441	0.125	0.016	0.195	0.686	3.521	0.000
Wang, Chien-Chin (2003)	0.553	0.233	0.054	0.096	1.010	2.371	0.018
Zeng, Pei-Yi (2004)	0.929	0.122	0.015	0.689	1.169	7.583	0.000
Tsai, Peng-Hen (2003)	0.228	0.239	0.057	-0.240	0.696	0.955	0.339
Chang, Yi-Yu (2005)	0.115	0.178	0.032	-0.234	0.465	0.646	0.518
Li, Hsin-Yi (2005)	0.072	0.204	0.041	-0.328	0.471	0.352	0.725
Yang, Kai-Ti (2007)	22.268	1.042	1.086	20.226	24.310	21.370	0.000
Lin, Chiou-Tsen (2007)	0.233	0.203	0.041	-0.165	0.630	1.145	0.252
Tsai, Chung-Chieh (2008)	0.585	0.161	0.026	0.269	0.901	3.629	0.000
Chou, Shih-Yao (2008)	0.591	0.213	0.046	0.173	1.009	2.770	0.006
Lin, Tai-An (2008)	1.334	0.262	0.069	0.820	1.847	5.091	0.000
Chen, Chien-Hua (2009)	0.971	0.184	0.034	0.610	1.333	5.264	0.000
Chen, Mei-hua (2009)	0.498	0.201	0.040	0.105	0.891	2.481	0.013
Liao, Wen-Shioung (2009)	1.425	0.229	0.052	0.976	1.874	6.219	0.000
Tsai, Peng-Hen (2010)	0.387	0.172	0.030	0.049	0.725	2.247	0.025
Wu, Fang-Tsai (2010)	0.384	0.153	0.023	0.084	0.685	2.508	0.012
Chem, Mei-Shian (2010)	0.325	0.180	0.033	-0.028	0.679	1.803	0.071
Weng, Hsiao-Lan (2010)	0.068	0.169	0.029	-0.264	0.400	0.403	0.687
Ma, Ming-Xiao (2010)	0.338	0.257	0.066	-0.165	0.841	1.316	0.188
Liao, Chia-Min (2010)	0.230	0.250	0.062	-0.260	0.719	0.920	0.357
Wang, Chung-Ming (2011)	1.659	0.296	0.088	1.078	2.240	5.596	0.000
Wang, Mei-Yun (2012)	0.735	0.201	0.040	0.342	1.128	3.668	0.000
Li, Chi-Chia (2012)	0.428	0.248	0.062	-0.058	0.914	1.726	0.084
Lin, Shu-Wen (2012)	0.181	0.318	0.101	-0.443	0.805	0.570	0.569
Chang, Hsu-Wei (2012)	0.363	0.281	0.079	-0.188	0.913	1.292	0.196
Chang, Su-Fen (2012)	0.175	0.251	0.063	-0.318	0.667	0.695	0.487
Chang, Yung-Chin (2012)	1.774	0.163	0.026	1.455	2.092	10.916	0.000
Chen, Yi-Hsing (2012)	0.162	0.300	0.090	-0.426	0.750	0.541	0.589
Yen, Bai-Hung (2012)	0.302	0.225	0.051	-0.138	0.743	1.345	0.178
Wang, Tzu-Ching (2013)	0.022	0.188	0.035	-0.346	0.390	0.119	0.905
Lee, Sheng-Lung (2013)	0.220	0.264	0.070	-0.298	0.738	0.834	0.405
Sun, Yu-Wen (2013)	0.930	0.264	0.070	0.412	1.448	3.517	0.000
Peng, Yih-Jen (2013)	0.131	0.195	0.038	-0.251	0.513	0.673	0.501
Huang, Tsui-Wen (2013)	0.515	0.247	0.061	0.030	1.000	2.081	0.037
Liao, Chia-Yu (2013)	1.096	0.274	0.075	0.560	1.633	4.004	0.000
Tsai, Shu-Hui (2013)	0.794	0.228	0.052	0.347	1.241	3.481	0.001
Lien, Hsin-Hsin (2015)	0.090	0.212	0.045	-0.325	0.505	0.424	0.671
Chen,Ching-Chi (2015)	2.239	0.249	0.062	1.751	2.727	8.991	0.000
Yang, Su-Wan (2015)	0.561	0.181	0.033	0.207	0.915	3.106	0.002
Hsieh, Ming-Feng (2015)	0.727	0.268	0.072	0.202	1.252	2.716	0.007
Kao, Juo-Hsin (2016)	0.010	0.204	0.041	-0.389	0.409	0.049	0.961
Chuang, Her-Wen (2016)	0.469	0.232	0.054	0.015	0.923	2.025	0.043
Wen, Mei-Yun (2016)	0.520	0.257	0.066	0.016	1.024	2.021	0.043
Chang, Wan-Jen (2017)	0.695	0.187	0.035	0.329	1.061	3.718	0.000
Tu, Yi-Lien (2018)	0.463	0.340	0.115	-0.203	1.128	1.363	0.173
Wu, Tzu-Ying (2019)	1.984	0.292	0.085	1.412	2.556	6.797	0.000
Wu, Yun-Yan (2019)	0.855	0.281	0.079	0.305	1.405	3.047	0.002
Huang, Siu-Shiang (2019)	0.811	0.241	0.058	0.338	1.284	3.363	0.001
Lu, Chiu-Hui (2020)	0.928	0.272	0.074	0.395	1.460	3.415	0.001
Lin, Chih-Lung (2020)	0.266	0.285	0.081	-0.294	0.825	0.931	0.352
Peng, Chia-hui (2020)	0.170	0.332	0.110	-0.481	0.821	0.512	0.609
Hsu, Kuan-Pu (2021)	0.378	0.259	0.067	-0.130	0.887	1.459	0.145
Huang, Tzu-Yang (2022)	0.457	0.196	0.039	0.072	0.842	2.326	0.020
Wang, Wan-Ting (2023)	0.422	0.293	0.086	-0.152	0.997	1.440	0.150
Liou, Yu-Ching (2023)	0.041	0.287	0.082	-0.521	0.603	0.143	0.886
	0.611	0.028	0.001	0.557	0.665	22.105	0.000

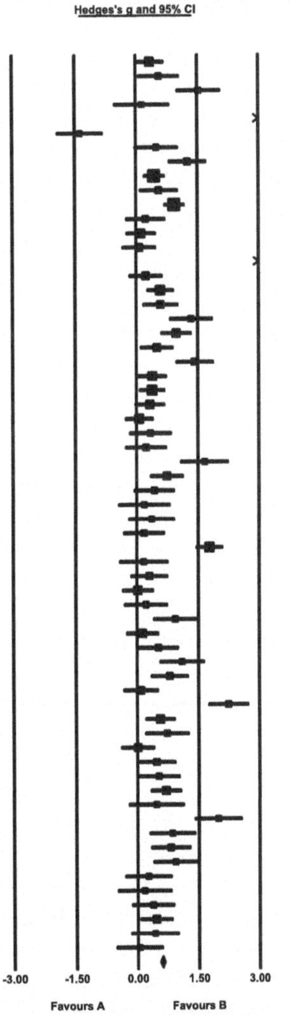

Fig. 1. Forest plot.

The meta-analysis results, as presented in Table 2 with the g value and forest plot, indicated that the effect size of 50 research papers reached a significant level ($|g| > 0.2$), while the effect size of 13 research papers did not reach a significant level ($|g| < 0.2$). The overall effect size after weighting was calculated to be 0.611 ($p < .01$), demonstrating the existence of an experimental effect in online inquiry learning. Subsequently, the g value, standard error, and standard deviation in the forest plot were reviewed, and samples with significant numerical differences were removed. This resulted in 55 papers being retained for meta-analysis, as illustrated in Fig. 1. The forest plot displaying the distribution of Hedges' g effect sizes of the studies included in the research is presented.

4.2 Publication Bias

To prevent extreme values of effect size (g) and standard error from biasing the interpretation, 8 research papers were excluded. The funnel plot shown in Fig. 2 showed that the symmetry line of the 55 research papers was at 0.47. Notably, the distribution of the 25 research papers on the right side of the symmetry line appeared to be more dispersed compared to the 30 research papers on the left side of the symmetry line.

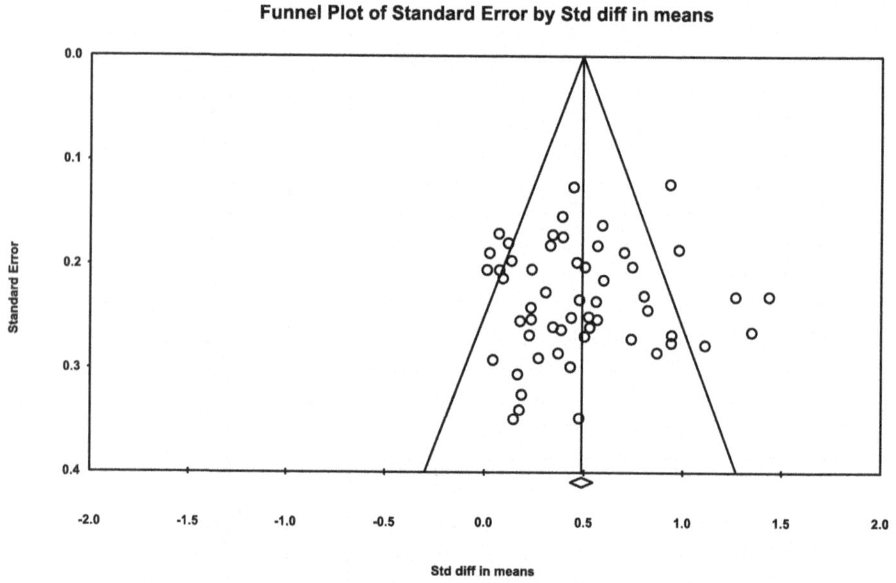

Fig. 2. Funnel plot

In this meta-analysis, publication bias was assessed using a Funnel plot, Classic fail-safe N. The Funnel plot revealed a symmetrical distribution of studies. Classic fail-safe N values were 5,250 exceeding the critical threshold of 5K + 10. These results indicated there were no publication bias existed in the study.

Using the rank correlation test proposed by Begg and Mazumdar (1994), The Tau value obtained from Kendall's tau with continuity correction was 0.02963, with z-value for tau of 0.31942 and p-values for tau of 0.74941 (2-tailed).

Using Egger's regression intercept test, the results of standard error was 0.86853 and t-value was 0.19495. The corresponding p-values was 0.84618 (2-tailed).

4.3 Moderator Analyses

From the distribution of research papers in each category (moderator variable) as shown in Table 2, which outlines the number of studies cited for each category of moderating variables, we can observe the level of attention given to various topics related to integrating information technology (IT) into inquiry-based teaching in Taiwan. The effect size (g-value) further substantiates the quality and credibility of research in each category. By referencing these two metrics, we can provide an overview of how IT has been integrated into inquiry-based teaching in Taiwan.

The primary focus of integrating IT into inquiry-based teaching has been on elementary and junior high school students (76.4%), with fewer studies conducted at the high school and university levels. However, studies at the high school level reported a higher effect size ($g = 0.549$). Regarding subject areas, natural sciences were the most commonly studied (28 studies), while the arts demonstrated the highest effect size ($g = 0.664$), indicating the potential for diverse applications and better outcomes in these subjects. Subjects such as Chinese, English, mathematics, and social sciences also showed varying degrees of implementation and effect sizes, suggesting that IT integration is well-represented across disciplines.

In terms of inquiry teaching models and levels of student learning, structured inquiry was the most commonly used approach (32 studies), followed by guided inquiry (14 studies), and open inquiry (9 studies). Despite this, student learning outcomes reached higher levels of inquiry, with all studies achieving at least the problem-analysis stage (second level), and 19 studies advancing to the stage of drawing conclusions and verification, accompanied by a strong effect size ($g = 0.536$). This indicates that through the indicators of inquiry teaching and learning, the effectiveness of integrating information technology into teaching can be observed, as well as the extent to which teachers' instruction is effectively transformed into students' autonomous learning. Another key indicator of the effectiveness of IT integration is the technologies used and strategies. Since IT is widely accessible in Taiwan's classrooms, common tools such as computers, projectors, and laptops were utilized in most studies (34 studies). Emerging technologies, while less frequently used (3 studies), showed significant potential with a high effect size ($g = 0.906$), demonstrating their effectiveness in teaching. In terms of strategies for integrating teaching, the primary approach involves interaction between humans and machines or interpersonal communication methods, as evidenced by 25 studies, followed by theme-based learning using WebQuests (17 studies). Although game-based learning (7 studies, $g = 0.541$) and mobile learning (6 studies, $g = 0.616$) were less common, they exhibited strong effect sizes, showcasing the diverse possibilities for IT integration.

Table 2. The overall effect sizes of the studies according to moderator analyses.

	Effect size and 95% confidence interval							Heterogeneity			Comparison between groups
	K	*g*	*SE*	low limit	up limit	*Z*	*p*	*Q*	*df*	*p*	
Over all	-	.48	.03	.43	.54	16.72	.00***				
Category											
Learning stage / Homogeneity test								1.31	3	.73	
g1	22	.45	.05	.36	.55	9.51	.00***				
g2	20	.50	.05	.41	.59	1.83	.00***				
g3	8	.55	.08	.40	.70	7.13	.00***				
g4	5	.45	.10	.26	.64	4.70	.00***				
Domain subjects / Homogeneity test								13.54	6	.04*	
aa	5	.66	.07	.53	.80	9.39	.00***				
ac	5	.58	.11	.37	.79	5.41	.00***				
ae	3	.41	.14	.14	.69	3.00	.00***				
am	5	.37	.09	.19	.55	3.99	.00***				
an	28	.45	.04	.37	.53	1.98	.00***				
as	8	.39	.09	.21	.57	4.31	.00***				
ao	1	.93	.27	.40	1.46	3.41	.00***				
Inquiry model / Homogeneity test								.17	2	.92	
im1	32	.48	.04	.41	.56	12.58	.00***				
im2	14	.48	.06	.37	.59	8.47	.00***				
im3	9	.51	.07	.37	.65	7.04	.00***				
Inquiry levels / Homogeneity test								1.90	2	.39	
il2	17	.47	.05	.38	.57	9.51	.00***				
il3	19	.44	.05	.34	.54	8.65	.00***				
il4	19	.54	.05	.44	.63	1.78	.00***				

(continued)

Table 2. (*continued*)

	Effect size and 95% confidence interval							Heterogeneity			Comparison between groups
	K	*g*	*SE*	low limit	up limit	*Z*	*p*	*Q*	*df*	*p*	
IT device / Homogeneity test								34.59	8	.00***	
td1	4	.62	.11	.40	.84	5.54	.00***				td2 > td6*** td2 > td1,td3, td8** td4 > td6** td2 > td4,tdu* td6 > td3*
td2	5	.09	.10	-.11	.30	.89	.37				
td3	17	.50	.05	.40	.60	1.06	.00***				
td4	17	.41	.05	.32	.51	8.37	.00***				
td5	2	.62	.19	.26	.98	3.34	.00***				
td6	3	.91	.13	.64	1.17	6.80	.00***				
td7	4	.51	.12	.27	.75	4.11	.00***				
td8	2	.87	.18	.52	1.21	4.86	.00***				
tdu	1	.74	.20	.34	1.13	3.67	.00***				
IT integration methods / Homogeneity test								2.41	3	.49	
tii	25	.45	.04	.37	.54	1.49	.00***				
tiw	17	.48	.05	.38	.57	1.09	.00***				
tig	7	.54	.09	.37	.72	6.07	.00***				
tim	6	.62	.11	.41	.83	5.76	.00***				

Note:
Learning stage: g1(elementary school), g2(junior high school), g3(high school), g4(university)
Domain subjects: aa(art), ac(chinese), ae(English), am(mathematics), an(natural science), as(social science), ao(other)
Inquiry model: im1(structured inquiry), im2(guided inquiry), im3(open inquiry)
Inquiry levels: il2(analyze the problem), il3(make plans), il4(verification conclusion)
IT device: td1(paper), td2(teaching aids), td3(fixed information equipment), td4(notebook/mobile device), td5(traditional learning machine), td6(intelligent learning machine), td7(tool learning machine), td8(mix), tdu(unspecified)
IT integration methods: tii(interaction and communication), tiw(WebQuest), tig(game), tim(mobile learning)

5 Conclusions

To explore the current status of Information Technology into Inquiry-based Instruction on Students' Learning in Taiwan, a meta-analysis was conducted on 8 journals and 63 papers. The weighted average effect size was calculated to be 0.611, indicating the validity of the experimental group, control group numbers, means, standard deviations, and other values in the experimental studies.

Through the collection of moderator variables including Publication types, Learning stage, Domain subjects, Inquiry models, Inquiry levels, Guidance methods, Grouping methods, Inquiry timing, Teaching material, IT device, IT integration methods, IT integration timing, Intervention duration, significant consistency was achieved using Heterogeneity test. This indicates that the contents of the moderator variables are consistent, and findings and explanations are available for reference.

The crucial parameters for optimizing the effectiveness of integrating information technology into inquiry-based instruction on students' learning are identified as follows: (1) Used in elementary schools; (2) Applying in the science subject; (3) Use structed inquiry; (4) Achieve the inquiry level of "drawing conclusions and verifying;" (5) Apply interaction and communication to integrate IT into inquiry teaching; (6) The IT integration study devices were provided through classroom information equipment.

This study examines the guidance and learning of online inquiry in Taiwan from 2000 to 2024, describing it in terms of breadth and depth. It provides a reference for subsequent discussions on the overall trend in this area.

References

Bruner, J.S.: *The process of education.* Cambridge. Harvard University Press, MA (1960)

Cai, S.H.: The impact of online earth science online teaching courses on student learning [Unpublished master's thesis]. National Taiwan Normal University (2003). https://www.airitilibrary.com/Article/Detail/U0021-2603200719133351

*Chang, W.J.: A Design of Augmented Reality Learning Sysyem to Support College Students' Rural Experiential Learning. J. Liberal Arts and Soc. Sci. **13**(1), 29–64. (2017). https://www.airitilibrary.com/Article/Detail/18197205-201703-201704100021-201704100021-29-64

Bainchini, J.A., Colburn, A.: Teaching the Nature of Science through Inquiry to Prospective Elementary Teachers: A Tale of two Researchers. J. Res. Sci. Teach. **37**, 177–209 (2000)

Begg, C.B., Mazumdar, M.: Operating Characteristics of a Rank Correlation Test for Publication Bias. Biomet. **50**(4), 1088–1101 (1994)

*Chang, H.W.: A Study of the Impact on Metacognition by Integrating WebQuest with Concept Mapping Strategies [Unpublished master's thesis]. Tamkang University. (2012a). https://doi-org.metalib.lib.ntue.edu.tw/10.6846/TKU.2012.01276

*Chang, S.F.: The Impact of Problem-Based Learning Activities on Fourth graders' Views of the Nature of Sicence [Unpublished master's thesis]. Chung Yuan Christian University. (2012b). https://doi.org/10.6840/cycu201200426

Chang, Y.C., Chiueh, Y.W.: A Study on Teaching Basic Economic Concepts in the Social Studies Curriculum of Fourth Grade School Students. J. Univ. Taipei. Educ. **43**(2), 87–129 (2012). https://doi.org/10.6336/JUTe/2012.43(2)4

*Chang, Y.Y.: A Experimental Study on the Learning Effect of Integrated Information Technology into Visual Arts Appreciation Instruction [Unpublished master's thesis]. National Taiwan Normal University. (2005). https://www.airitilibrary.com/Article/Detail/U0021-2004200715270297

*Chen, C.C.: Investigation on Learning Effects of Summary-Strategies Integrated into the Social Studies for the Elementary Students [Unpublished master's thesis]. Tamkang University (2015). https://doi.org/10.6846/TKU.2015.00471

*Chen, C.H.: The Effectiveness of Problem-Based Learning on Problem Solving, Critical Thinking and Conceptual Change of Fourth-Grade students [Unpublished master's thesis]. Chung Yuan Christian University. (2009). https://doi.org/10.6840/cycu200900737

*Chen, H.H.: PhET Interactive Virtual Experiments Incorporate Guided Inquiry Teaching to Promote Physics Learning Effectiveness for High School Students [Unpublished master's thesis]. National Kaohsiung Normal University (2024)

*Chen, M.H.: The Impact of Problem-Based Learning on the Mathematics Learning Attitudes and Mathematics Learning Strategies of Eighth Graders [Unpublished master's thesis]. Chung Yuan Christian University. (2009). https://doi.org/10.6840/cycu200900733

Chen, M.H., Yang, T.Y., Lin, K.Y., Wang, K.H.: Effects of Using the WebQuest Instructional Model on Students' Science Learning with Different Learning Styles. J. Nat. Pingtung Univ. Educ. **32**, 393–424 (2009)

*Chen, Y.H.: The Effects of Applying Elaboration Theory of Instruction with Prezi Presentation Software in Social Studies on Elementary Students' Learning Motivations and Learning Outcomes [Unpublished master's thesis]. National Taipei University of Technology. (2012). https://doi.org/10.6841/NTUT.2012.00173

*Chen, Y.L.: Using Conceptual Guidance Mechanism to Support Web-Based Authentic Inquiry Learning Environment [Unpublished master's thesis]. National Taiwan Normal University. (2000). https://www.airitilibrary.com/Article/Detail/U0021-2603200719110466

*Chen, X.D.: The effects of Web 2.0 Cooperative Learning on Sixth Graders [Unpublished master's thesis]. National Taiwan Normal University. (2011). https://www.airitilibrary.com/Article/Detail/U0021-1610201315223440

*Chern, M.S.: Explore the impact of scaffolding on web-based identifying scientific issue learning content on 6th grade students' abilities of identifying scientific issue and inquiry [Unpublished master's thesis]. National Chiao Tung University. (2010). https://doi.org/10.6842/NCTU.2010.00665

Chiu, M.H., Lin, S.C., Tang, W.J., Chou, J.C., Chang, R.Y., Wang, J.H.: Scientific creative experiment book. Hungyeh Publishing, Taipei (2005)

Chou, S.Y., Chen, C.M.: Fulfilling Global Education in High School Geography Curriculum: The Teaching Design Case of Internet Cooperative Learning for Students on Both Sides of Taiwan Strait. J. Geograph. Res. **48**, 63–84 (2008). https://doi.org/10.6234/JGR.2008.48.04

*Chuang, H.W.: The Research of System Design and User Satisfaction of the Panorama Environmental Education System - A Case Study of Barclay Memorial Park [Unpublished master's thesis]. Chang Jung Christian University (2016)

Chung, C.H., Wang, K.H.: The Effect of Different Models of Integrating Computer Simulation in Argument-based Inquiry on Student Science Learning-Learning Genetics as an Example. Int. J. Dig. Learn. Technol. **6**(3), 19–40 (2014)

Dewey, J.: Liberalism and Social Action. G. P. Putnam's Sons, New York (1935)

Herron, M.: The nature of scientific enquiry. School Rev. **79**, 171–212 (1971)

*Hou, M.X.: The Effects of Task Scaffolding Strategy on WebQuest Learning [Unpublished master's thesis]. National Taiwan Normal University. (2010). https://www.airitilibrary.com/Article/Detail?DocID=U0021-1610201315203027

Hsiao, C.C.: Meta-Analysis of The Effect of Creativity Teaching Model on Domestic Students' Creativity. Bull. Spec. Educ. **44**(3), 93–120 (2019). https://doi.org/10.6172/BSE.201911_44(3).0004

*Hsieh, M.F.: The effect of integrating electronic textbook with cooperative learning on math learning motivation and achievement for ninth graders [Unpublished master's thesis]. Tamkang University. (2015). https://doi.org/10.6846/TKU.2015.00232

*Hsu, K.P.: Research on the Influence of Virtual Reality on the Physiological Learning Achievement in Junior High Schools Take the "Lens Imaging" Course as an Example [Unpublished master's thesis]. Tamkang University. (2021). https://doi.org/10.6846/TKU.2021.00015

*Huang, F.N.: An Experimental Study of Applying Network Resources Learning in Senior High School Music Appreciation Curriculum [Unpublished master's thesis]. National Taiwan Normal University. (2001). https://www.airitilibrary.com/Article/Detail/U0021-2603200719114482

*Huang, S.S.: A Study on the Influence of Literacy-Oriented Teaching on Students' Creativity and Learning Effectiveness: Take Language Field of Technical High School as an Example [Unpublished master's thesis]. Chang Jung Christian University. (2019). https://doi.org/10.6840/cycu201900179

*Huang, T.W.: A Study to Promote Problem-Solving Ability for Junior High School Students through Incorporating WebQuest into Geographical Thematic Integrated Curriculum [Unpublished master's thesis]. Tamkang University. (2013). https://doi.org/10.6846/TKU.2013.00501

*Huang, T.Y.: Research on the Computational Thinking Learning Effect of the Micro: bit of Eighth-grade students in the Information Technology Curriculum [Unpublished master's thesis]. Tamkang University. (2022). https://doi.org/10.6846/TKU.2022.00208

*Jao, K.H.: The Experimental Study of Application of Web-Based Learning Community [Unpublished master's thesis]. National Taiwan Normal University. (2001). https://www.airitilibrary.com/Article/Detail/U0021-2603200719114481

Johnson, D.W., Johnson, R.T., Holubec, E.J.: Cooperation in the Classroom. Association for Supervision and Curriculum Development (1998)

*Kao, J.H.: The effect of applying astrology software Stellarium on high school students' learning of "Diurnal motion" [Unpublished master's thesis]. Chung Yuan Christian University. (2016). https://doi.org/10.6840/cycu201600271

Kao, Y.J.: Digital Learning: New Trends in Learning. J. Internet Soc. Commun. **57**(22). (2006). https://student.hlc.edu.tw/action/file/64/20211007165637724.pdf

Koehler, M., Mishra, P.: What is technological pedagogical content knowledge (TPACK)? Contemp. Issues Technol. Teacher Educ. **9**(1), 60–70 (2009)

Lederman, J.S., Lederman, N.G.: Developing and Assessing Elementary Teachers' and Students' Understandings of Nature of Science and Scientific Inquiry. [Conference presentation] April, 2005 Annual Meeting of the National Association for Research in Science Teaching, Dallas, Texas. (2005). https://www.researchgate.net/publication/228891001_Developing_and_assessing_elementary_teachers'_and_students'_understandings_of_nature_of_science_and_scientific_inquiry

*Lee, S.L.: The Application of the Inquiry Teaching Method in the Smart Classroom - Taking the Social Area as the Example [Unpublished master's thesis]. Tamkang University. (2013). https://doi.org/10.6846/TKU.2013.00068

*Li, C.C.: The Effects of Integrating ADDIE Model into Project-Based Learning on Problem Solving Ability and Self-Directed Learning Readiness of Undergraduates [Unpublished master's thesis]. National Taipei University of Technology. (2012). https://doi.org/10.6841/NTUT.2012.00178

*Li, H.Y.: The Application of the Problem-Based Learning Strategy for Teaching Coastal Problems in Senior High School Geography [Unpublished master's thesis]. National Taiwan Normal University (2005). https://hdl.handle.net/11296/xhmca7

*Liao, C.M.: A Study of Learning Attitudes and Achievement Comparison between Web-based, Project-based Learning and Traditional Learning in an Elementary Level Life and Environment Course [Unpublished master's thesis]. Tamkang University (2010). https://doi.org/10.6846/TKU.2010.00331

Liao, C.Y., Lien, C.J., Lu, Y.L.: A Study of Developing a Computer Educational Game for Elementary Science Teaching on Moon and the Effectiveness. Contemp. J. Sci. Educ. **21**(3), 317–344 (2013). https://doi.org/10.6173/CJSE.2013.2103.04

*Liao, W.S.: Research on Integrating Podcast into idiom teaching for 6th graders [Unpublished master's thesis]. Tamkang University. (2009). https://doi.org/10.6846/TKU.2009.00020

Liao, Y.K.: A Meta-Analysis of Applying Virtual Reality in Teaching on Taiwan Students' Affective and Skill Outcomes. Res. Educ. Commun. Technol. **131**, 33–62 (2023). https://doi.org/10.6137/RECT.202304_(131).0004

Liao, Y.K., Chen, Y.H.: Integrating Technology in Mathematics Instruction on Grade School Academic Achievement in Taiwan: A Meta-Analysis. Bull. Educ. Psychol. **52**(4), 781–806 (2021). https://doi.org/10.6251/BEP.202106_52(4).0003

Liao, Y.K., Chen, C.H., Yang, Y.C.: A Meta-Analysis of the Effects of Mobile Learning on Students' Academic Achievement in TAIWAN. Contemp. Educ. Res. Q. **28**(3), 67–102 (2020). https://doi.org/10.6151/CERQ.202009_28(3).0003

*Lien, H.H.: The Effectiveness of Integrating E-Storybook with Shared-Book Reading and Inferential Comprehension Instruction on Elementary Students'Reading Comprehension [Unpublished master's thesis]. Tamkang University. (2014). https://doi.org/10.6846/TKU.2014.00582

Lin, C.L., Lin, F.J.: The Effect of Using Augmented Reality on Students' Learning Motivation and Academic Achievement in Science Instruction - A Case Study of a Minth Grade Lesson in Electromagnetism. J. Liberal Arts and Soc. Sci. **16**(4), 345–367 (2020)

*Lin, C.T.: The Effectiveness of Web-based Lessons on English Classes: A Case Study—The Multi-Language Learning Website by Tamkang University [Unpublished master's thesis]. Tamkang University. (2007). https://doi.org/10.6846/TKU.2007.00220

*Lin, S.W.: The Study of Influence on Learning Motivation and Science Learning Effect Applying Interactive Whiteboard in Elementary Science Curriculum [Unpublished master's thesis]. Chung Yuan Christian University. (2012). https://doi.org/10.6840/cycu201200478

*Lin, T.A.: The study on the impact of problem-based learning by integrating web-based cooperative learning in Shihmen Reservoir Watershed geography environmental education [Unpublished master's thesis]. National Taiwan Normal University (2009). https://etds.lib.ntnu.edu.tw/thesis/detail/bc5d6949108ba7358a4f2a147d94e4f2/

*Liou, Y.C.: Investigating Game-based Learning Performance and Motivation on Fifth Graders - Unit in Japanese Occupation Period in Taiwan [Unpublished master's thesis]. Chang Jung Christian University. (2023). https://doi.org/10.6840/cycu202301283

*Lu, C.H.: A study of the effect of integrating ARCS with APPs on learning motivation and achievement in accounting instructions [Unpublished master's thesis]. Tamkang University. (2020). https://doi.org/10.6846/TKU.2020.00267

*Ma, M.X.: The Effects of the Use of WebQuest on Taiwanese Middle School Students' English Motivation and Learning Outcomes [Unpublished master's thesis]. Chung Yuan Christian University. (2010). https://doi.org/10.6840/cycu201000864

MacKenzie, T.: Dive Into Inquiry: Amplify Learning and Empower Student Voice. EdTechTeam Press (2016)

Means, B., Toyama, Y., Murphy, R., Bakia, M., Jones, K.: Evaluation of Evidence-Based Practices in Online Learning: A Meta-Analysis and Review of Online Learning Studies. U.S. Department of Education (2009)

Merchant, Z., Goetz, E.T., Cifuentes, L., Keeney-Kennicutt, W., Davis, T.J.: Effectiveness of virtual reality-based instruction on students' learning outcomes in K-12 and higher education: A meta-analysis. Comput. Educ. **70**, 29–40 (2014)

Monte-Sano, C., Bordonaro, A., Aumen, J.: Successes and Challenges in Learning to Teach History as Inquiry. Hist. Teach. **53**(4), 675–706 (2020)

Pane, J.F., Steiner, E.D., Baird, M.D., Hamilton, L.S.: Continued Progress: Promising Evidence on Personalized Learning. RAND Corporation (2015)

*Peng, C.H.: Impacts of Computational Thinking Integrating into Teaching on Chinese Language Course for Junior High School Students' Learning Motivation and Achievement in Remote Areas [Unpublished master's thesis]. Tamkang University. (2020). https://doi.org/10.6846/TKU.2020.00339

*Peng, Y.J.: A Study of using Improved Polya's approach to learn Mathematics on Setting Equations in the one-Variable-First for Junior High School Students [Unpublished master's thesis]. Tamkang University. (2013). https://doi.org/10.6846/TKU.2013.00799

Qiu, C.Y.: An Action Research of Applying Inquiry-based Teaching in Elementary School Newspaper Education [Unpublished master's thesis]. Tamkang University (2012). https://doi.org/10.6846/TKU.2012.00190

Rao, K.H.: The Experimental Study of Application of Web-Based Learning Community [Unpublished master's thesis]. National Taiwan Normal University (2001). https://www.airitilibrary.com/Article/Detail/U0021-2603200719114481

Shen, C.H.: Integrating Information Technology into Instruction: Concept, Application and Activity Planning. J. Educ. Media & Library Sci. **42**(1), 139–155 (2004)

*Sun, Y.W.: A Study on Future Classroom: Applying Innovative Green Cloud-based Education Software Services System to Natural Science in Junior High School [Unpublished master's thesis]. National Taipei University of Technology. (2013). https://doi.org/10.6841/NTUT.2013.00020

*Tsai, C.C.: The Study of Self-regulation Learning strategy for WebQuest Learning System [Unpublished master's thesis]. National Taiwan Normal University. (2007). https://www.airitilibrary.com/Article/Detail/U0021-2910200810560396

*Tsai, P.H., Huang, T.Y.: The Study of Cognitive Learning Style and Locus of Control Affecting the Internet Multimedia Learning. J. Xingguo **11**, 71–85 (2010). https://doi.org/10.29950/JHKUM.201001.0005

Tsai, P.H., Chan, H.G., Huang, T.Y.: A study of Elementary Third Grade Students Learning Solid Grape with Network Digital School. J. Internet Technol. **4**(2), 79–84 (2003). https://doi.org/10.6138/JIT.2003.4.2.04

*Tsai, S.H.: The Effect of Integrating the Digital Simulation Game into Cooperative Learning on Achievement and Motivation of Junior High School Students' Rhythm Learning [Unpublished master's thesis]. Tamkang University. (2013). https://doi.org/10.6846/TKU.2013.00082

*Tu, Y.L.: The Effects of interactive eBook with Question Prompts on Reading Comprehension of Junior High School Students [Unpublished master's thesis]. Tamkang University. (2018). https://doi.org/10.6846/TKU.2018.00787

UNESCO: Open educational resources (OER): Opportunities and challenges (2012)

*Wang, C.C.: Research on the effectiveness of integrating molecular model simulation website into high school chemistry teaching [Unpublished master's thesis]. National Taiwan Normal University. (2002). https://www.airitilibrary.com/Article/Detail/U0021-2603200719122616

*Wang, C.M.: Improving Fifth-graders' Writing Attitude and Performance by Limited Writing Instruction with Interactive Whiteboard [Unpublished master's thesis]. Chung Yuan Christian University. (2011). https://doi.org/10.6840/CYCU.2011.00245

*Wang, M.Y.: The Influence of the STS Instructional Model Integrated into the Second-grade Living Class on Students' Academic Achievement [Unpublished master's thesis]. Ling Tung University. (2012). https://doi.org/10.6823/LTU.2012.00033

*Wang, T.C.: Elementary Natural Science Learning Through Digital Storytelling in Cooperative Learning Groups [Unpublished master's thesis]. National Taipei University of Technology. (2013). https://doi.org/10.6841/NTUT.2013.00046

*Wang, W.T.: A Study on Effectiveness of Head-mounted VR with 5E Inquiry Model in Astronomy Knowledge and Stargazing Skills for Elementary School Students [Unpublished master's thesis]. Tamkang University. (2023). https://doi.org/10.6846/tku202300237

*Wen, M.Y.: A Study of the Effect on Teaching Physics And Chemistry with Song to Students with Different Learning Styles – the Case of Junior High School Students in Taoyuan [Unpublished master's thesis]. Chien Hsin University of Science and Technology (2016)

*Weng, H.L.: Research on different levels of scaffolding web-based identifying scientific issues learning on junior high students' identifying scientific issues ability [Unpublished master's thesis]. National Chiao Tung University. (2010). https://doi.org/10.6842/NCTU.2010.00709

White, R., Gunstone, R.F.: Prediction-observation-explanation : Probing Understanding. The Falmer Press, London (1992)

*Wu, F.T.: A Study of Learning Performance of Collaborative Learning on the Programming Language [Unpublished master's thesis]. Tamkang University. (2010). https://doi.org/10.6846/TKU.2010.01089

Wu, J.C.: An Effectiveness of E-learning Services Designed for 3D Computer Aided Design Software Learning. Elementary Educ. **51**(5), 50–60 (2011). https://doi.org/10.6476/JNE.201106.0050

*Wu, T.Y.: Action Study on Integrating Inquiry Learning into High School English Writing and Student's Writing Ability Improvement [Unpublished master's thesis]. National Chengchi University (2019a). https://hdl.handle.net/11296/c465jw

*Wu, Y.Y.: A research on Integrating English Musical Film into Team Games Tournament for Promoting English Listening Ability [Unpublished master's thesis]. Tamkang University. (2019b). https://doi.org/10.6846/TKU.2019.00606

*Yang, K.T.: Investigating the Effectiveness of Different e-Learning Material Development Model in Improving Sixth Grade Students' Photosynthesis Conceptions [Unpublished master's thesis]. National Taiwan Normal University. (2007). https://www.airitilibrary.com/Article/Detail/U0021-2910200810532226

*Yang, S.W.: A Study of the Effects of Using Online Learning Platform with Cooperative Learning Strategy on Computer Programming Language Learning for Offshore Island Senior High School Students [Unpublished master's thesis]. Tamkang University. (2015). https://doi.org/10.6846/TKU.2015.00189

*Yen, B.H., Ou Tang, Y.: The Effects of Using Different Incentive Mechanisms on Sixth Graders' Internet Learning Activities. Journal of Education, 27, 221–262. (2012). https://doi.org/10.6479/JE.201206.0221

Yen, M.C., Huang, B.Y.: A Meta-Analysis of the Learning Effects of Flipped Classroom on Elementary School and Junior High School Students. Bull. Educ. Psychol. **51**(1), 23–50 (2019). https://doi.org/10.6251/BEP.201909_51(1).0002

*Zeng, P.Y.: The Experimental Study of Integrating Information Technology on Music Instruction [Unpublished master's thesis]. National Taiwan Normal University. (2004). https://www.airitilibrary.com/Article/Detail/U0021-2603200719114481

Zhao, T.C.: The Effects of Web-based Peer Assessment on Lowering Senior High Students' Writing Apprehension [Unpublished master's thesis]. National Taiwan Normal (2004). https://www.airitilibrary.com/Article/Detail/U0021-2004200709292004

Zhang, Y.Y.: A Experimental Study on the Learning Effect of Integrated Information Technology into Visual Arts Appreciation Instruction [Unpublished master's thesis]. National Taiwan Normal University. (2005). https://www.airitilibrary.com/Article/Detail/U0021-2004200715270297

Zheng, C.H.: The Use of Moodle Learning Platform to Integrate into Teaching on the Impact of Learning Outcomes and Attitudes—To an Elementary School in Taichung County as an Example of Teaching the Social Course. [Unpublished master's thesis]. Chaoyang University of Technology (2010). https://hdl.handle.net/11296/jc87gf

Zhou, Y.P.: Explore the impact of applying different "teaching methods" to WISE courses on earth science learning for junior high school students [Unpublished master's thesis]. National Taiwan Normal University (2006). https://hdl.handle.net/11296/3f33j2

Zeng, P.Y.: The Experimental Study of Application of Web-Based Learning Community [Unpublished master's thesis]. National Taiwan Normal University. (2001). https://www.airitilibrary.com/Article/Detail/U0021-2603200719114481

Enhancing IT Education Through Tailored Course Selection: A Case Study from Estonian General Education School

Birgy Lorenz[1](✉), Diana Poudel[2], and Ago Luberg[1]

[1] Tallinn University of Technology, Tallinn, Estonia
{birgy.lorenz,ago.luberg}@taltech.ee
[2] University of Tartu, Tartu, Estonia
diana.poudel@ut.ee

Abstract. The study explores enhancing elective course selection in Information Technology (IT) education within Estonian general schools by developing a pre-selection assessment tool. Aimed at aligning student interests and competencies with course offerings, the tool evaluates academic skills, prior exposure to IT, and personal preferences. Results from surveys conducted among high school and university students reveal significant disparities in preparedness and engagement levels, emphasizing the importance of early exposure to IT-related activities. Key findings include the strong influence of mathematics and digital safety skills on ICT interest, the value of hands-on learning approaches, and persistent gender disparities. The study highlights the potential of structured pre-selection processes to improve academic outcomes, reduce dropout rates, and address gender imbalances. However, challenges such as superficial evaluations and evolving student interests underscore the need for iterative tool refinement. Future directions include integrating AI-driven, adaptive assessments to provide personalized guidance, ultimately fostering equitable and inclusive pathways to ICT education and careers.

Keywords: IT Education Elective Courses · Student Pre-Selection · Skills Assessment of Programming and Mathematics · Student Interests · Adaptive Learning · Gender Challenges in STEM

1 Introduction

To find your path is a matter of success in life. To test out different possibilities as well. On the one hand, it gives ideas for choosing a future career; on the other hand, it gives everyone a fair chance to be active in shaping it. Choosing optional courses and modules in Estonian general education institutions offers teachers and students unique opportunities and challenges. With so many different course options available, from programming and robotics to IT and robotics, cyber security, technology fundamentals, information society, innovation, and community, there has never been a more important need for an efficient way to match students with courses that suit their interests and skill levels.

B. K. Smith and M. Borge (Eds.): HCII 2025, LNCS 15806, pp. 300–314, 2025.
https://doi.org/10.1007/978-3-031-93564-0_18

By using a pre-selection test to evaluate students' experiences and competencies across a range of subjects and interests, including math, physics, social studies, handicrafts, informatics, volunteer work, teaching others, comprehending devices, logical problem-solving, building, involvement in robotics clubs, programming experiences, teamwork, and participation, this study seeks to close the gap between course offerings and student capabilities.

This study is motivated by observing a gap between the elective courses offered in IT and related fields in Estonian general education schools and the students' ability to choose upper-level BA and MA study paths that best suit their interests and capabilities. It has been noted that this discrepancy may deter students, especially those who lack basic knowledge or comprehension of the requirements of each course, which could result in lower success rates and even a complete disinterest in IT disciplines. Given the growing significance of IT skills in the contemporary economy and the gender differences in IT-related educational pathways and professions, this worry is more pressing.

Our primary research question is whether a structured pre-selection test can effectively direct students toward elective courses that match their current skills and interests and promote sustained engagement and success in IT education. The test is intended to evaluate students' interests and capabilities across relevant subjects and skills.

This study is based on the hypothesis that we can improve educational outcomes, deepen students' interest in IT fields, and possibly close the gender gap in IT-related subjects if we give students a better understanding of their abilities and interests concerning the course content and direct their elective choices accordingly.

2 Background

Choosing a career path can feel like navigating a maze, especially in STEM. However, how do young students decide if STEM is their calling?

Positive experiences in foundational subjects such as mathematics, science, and coding are critical for sparking interest in STEM (Science, Technology, Engineering, and Mathematics) careers. Research highlights that enjoyment and confidence in these areas play a pivotal role, with strong mathematics skills and exposure to computational thinking serving as essential foundations for STEM success. Students who enjoy coding are more likely to pursue STEM fields [18]. So, positive attitudes towards coding are vital in inspiring students' interest in STEM careers. A robust link exists between STEM learning attitudes and computational thinking skills among primary school students [23]. By highlighting this relationship, there is room to test educational interventions focusing on cognitive development and cultivating positive attitudes towards STEM subjects to foster better outcomes in computational thinking capabilities. Schools can better prepare students for success in various academic domains by emphasizing critical thinking development within educational frameworks. Students with these skills were likely to excel in mathematics and science [4].

Recognizing and integrating students' hobbies into educational practices is important to enhance motivation and engagement in learning. By designing interest-driven learning environments, educators can better support student success and foster a lifelong love of learning for everyone [2]. Pre-college engineering courses significantly increase students' likelihood of pursuing STEM majors. Completing these courses, especially with math and science classes, boosts readiness and interest in STEM, highlighting the need for more engineering-focused curricula in high schools [19]. Positive experiences in these areas shape students' confidence and ignite aspirations for future STEM pursuits.

Additionally, integrating computer science into mathematics education fosters engagement and broadens participation in STEM disciplines. Therefore, to cultivate even better results, strong mathematics skills are essential for STEM success, so there is a need to improve high school math education. For example, many students lack the advanced math background, such as calculus, needed for STEM fields, which impacts course selection and career readiness [7]. The crucial role of mathematics and science self-efficacy in shaping students' interests and aspirations toward STEM careers is also pointed out in another study by Kwon [15]. By focusing on building self-confidence through targeted educational strategies, educators can significantly influence students' pathways into STEM fields, ultimately contributing to a more diverse and capable workforce. Integrating computer science into mathematics education can effectively engage students and enhance their quantitative reasoning skills. By framing mathematical concepts within creative contexts like art, courses can enrich students' learning experiences and align with contemporary educational goals to broaden participation in STEM disciplines [9].

2.1 Diversify IT!

Gender disparities in STEM remain a pressing issue. Card and Payne [6] found that high school course selection impacts gender disparities in STEM enrollment. While females match males in STEM readiness overall, fewer take advanced courses like physics and calculus, which are key for STEM success. Targeted strategies are needed to boost female participation. STEM-related high school education heavily influences also higher education choices. Gender disparities persist, with males favouring engineering and females leaning towards life sciences. There is a need for early STEM engagement, effective counselling, and targeted policies to enhance participation and equity [10]. Also, Kordaki and Berdousis[14] found significant gender differences in computer science course selection, with males favouring technical courses and females leaning towards social or theoretical topics. They highlight societal stereotypes and male-dominated environments as barriers for females, advocating inclusive strategies and diverse course offerings to promote gender equity in computer science education.

Some studies have revealed that women face significant internal barriers, including self-doubt and a lack of confidence, alongside external obstacles such as a chilly or hostile classroom environment and an excessively demanding curriculum. These factors collectively undermine women's persistence in engineering programs. Designing targeted interventions to improve retention rates among female students is important to improve possibilities for everyone – both men and women [11]. Challenges that women face are not different from those faced by people when they do not have previous competencies and experiences and are rushed into proposing at the highest level (for example, higher-level programming exercises).

Canaan and Mouganie's [5] research highlights the significant role that female academic advisors can play in encouraging female students to pursue and persist in STEM majors. Their findings provide actionable evidence for educational institutions and policymakers aiming to reduce the gender gap in STEM fields by promoting mentorship opportunities that connect female students with female role models in science.

Despite lower completion rates, selective STEM programs provide significant economic benefits for less-prepared students. Earnings gains of 30–40% highlight the value of encouraging these students to enroll, addressing STEM workforce shortages and improving economic outcomes [17].

Early STEM engagement and effective counselling are key to enhancing gender equity in higher education and career pathways. At the same time, STEM stereotypes harm students' confidence and career expectations, reducing interest in STEM careers. Improving self-efficacy and outcome expectations can mitigate these effects and boost engagement in STEM fields [16].

2.2 How to Tweak the Future?

Looking to the future, developing valid assessment tools can help gauge and enhance student interest in computationally intensive careers. Addressing stereotypes and fostering inclusive educational strategies are key to broadening participation in STEM and building a capable workforce. By leveraging these insights, educators and policymakers can design targeted interventions and curricula to inspire diverse student populations to pursue and succeed in STEM careers.

Some solutions to be considered:

- If universities offered online courses to high schools, For example, 20 years ago, Shay and Rees [22] concluded that understanding the motivations behind students' selections of online courses is vital for educational institutions aiming to improve their online offerings. By addressing factors such as flexibility, resource access, perceived quality, social interaction, and student characteristics, institutions can better cater to the needs of prospective online learners and enhance their educational experiences.
- 2024 Sevrin [21] also concludes that by focusing on relevant curricula, innovative pedagogical strategies, inclusivity, transfer pathways, and industry partnerships, we can effectively contribute to meeting the growing demands of the technology sector over the next decade.
- The positive impact of project-based learning can affect middle school students' interest, knowledge, and career aspirations in artificial intelligence [1]. Educators can enhance student motivation by fostering an engaging learning environment that emphasizes practical application and prepares them for careers in rapidly evolving fields like AI. Integrating project-based learning with informal educational experiences can significantly enhance students' interest in STEM majors and careers [3]. By fostering an engaging and practical learning environment, educators can better prepare students for future opportunities in these critical fields, ultimately contributing to a more skilled workforce in science and technology.
- It might be an option to develop valid assessment tools to gauge student interest in computationally intensive science careers [20]. Using a validated instrument and exploring related interventions, one gets insights into enhancing STEM education and encouraging young students to pursue careers integrating computational thinking and scientific inquiry.

- When it comes to the university level, the stress is also up with students there. Depending on how the university deals with students' anxieties varies the results and success of the student as well. For example, if instructors knowingly mitigate student stress and anxiety, it will positively affect students' academic performance [12].
- Some universities have started developing forecasting models to determine who is more likely to drop out. Even with a limited dataset, machine learning techniques can yield accurate predictions. So, one way to go in the future is to integrate predictive modelling into institutional strategies to enhance student retention and optimize resource allocation. This might also mean that students get different suggestions from the analytical tools or tools of AI that can act as a personalized tutor solution [13].

So, our solution proposes developing a pre-assessment tool that considers students' interest in math and STEM lessons, experiences and competencies in participating in competitions, university and industry programs, project-based learning and others. The tool considers the possibilities available for both general education and vocational schools and recommends near-development zones, as effective teaching involves identifying each student's zone [24] and tailoring instruction to meet those needs [8]. However, we also will investigate students coping mechanisms and fears at the university level and solutions to ease it.

3 Methods

Our methodology involved creating and administering a thorough test and analyzing its effects on student engagement, course selection, and success rates to determine how well a pre-selection test could improve elective course selection in IT and related fields. The pre-selection exam was created to cover various topics and abilities related to the offered elective courses. These topics and abilities included qualitative and quantitative elements, such as teamwork and interest in volunteer work, as well as quantitative subjects like physics and mathematics. We included questions on prior robotics, programming, and technology competition participation to comprehensively understand each student's interests and talents. We also discussed the issue with university students, adding discussions around fear and anxiety.

The process comprised three steps:

1. The pre-selection test was created with educators and subject matter experts. It consisted of academic and interest-based questions to determine students' preparedness for and interest in particular IT-related elective courses.
2. Students took the test at the start of the school year before choosing their elective courses. To enable a thorough analysis, we gathered information on students' responses.
3. We discussed the results and challenges of studying IT with university students to understand their perceptions and fears when they had previous IT skills and when they did not. We also could compare the 2024-year results to the 2019 year results of some topics as we had some data on previous experiences and backgrounds of students studying informatics in the same program. We also included remarks from program managers to understand how they dealt with the challenges of people dropping out too early due to gaps in skills or lack thereof.

The developed tool (survey) aims to gather data for designing a test better to understand students' choices of ICT elective modules. This information will help evaluate preferences, motivations, and prior exposure to technology education, thereby supporting curriculum development and improving the alignment of course offerings with student needs.

Target groups were a. General students in secondary schools and higher education institutions who study programming (A). b. Specific subgroup: one of the Estonian high schools that provides several ICT modules and courses linked to university B (before course enrollment, everyone who studies in that school) and C (when enrolled in ICT elective module programming or cyber security), focusing on their decision-making process. C. Students at Tallinn University of Technology who were already studying at informatics course (D). The survey is biased toward male participants in 75% of the answers.

Survey structure was o ask about demographics, educational background, influence factors, self-assessment statements, skill self-evaluation, and participation in competitions of other ICT programs in Estonia. The expected outcome of what we were looking for gives us an overview of insights into factors influencing ICT elective choices, how prior exposure to STEM education and competitions correlates with module preferences, interest and skill levels across different groups and its comparisons.

The limitation of the study is that the test addresses various abilities and interests, from robotics and programming to mathematics and volunteer work. While comprehensive, this broad scope may lead to superficial evaluations in some areas, potentially reducing the test's precision in matching students to specific courses. Also, students' interests and competencies might evolve, and the test timing may not fully capture their long-term preferences or potential. The tool's effectiveness relies on focus group discussions with students and teachers to evaluate feedback on course choices and test scores.

The study is specific to Estonian general education schools, and its findings and tools may not be directly applicable to other educational contexts with differing curricula, resources, or cultural attitudes towards IT and STEM.

4 Results

4.1 Results from the Questioner

The comparison between high school students (Groups B and C) and IT university students (Group D) reveals intriguing insights into their preferences and skills (see Table 1). Across all groups, there is a strong interest in understanding how devices work, with university students scoring the highest. This highlights the alignment between their academic pursuits and natural curiosity about technology. Highschool students, while also interested in this area, appear to have a more general focus, which could benefit from targeted exposure to technology-related subjects.

University students demonstrate slightly higher averages in logic-based activities such as solving puzzles and playing chess or sudoku, suggesting that logical reasoning skills become more refined or appreciated as they progress into IT studies. Group D also shows a greater preference for teamwork, reflecting the collaborative nature of

IT projects in higher education. In contrast, high school students display a more balanced approach between teamwork and working independently, likely influenced by their diverse learning environments.

Overall, the results indicate that students pursuing IT studies exhibit stronger preferences for activities that align with the demands of their field, such as logical thinking, teamwork, and creativity. For high school students, fostering these skills and interests through project-based learning or extracurricular opportunities could better prepare them for higher education and careers in technology.

Table 1. Comparison of Statements by Group BCD.

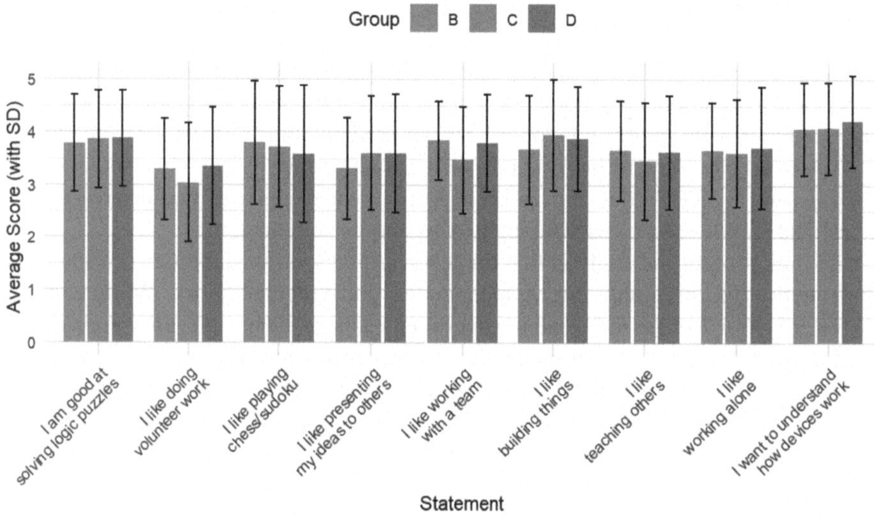

The comparison between Group A, which consists of students from a science-focused school, and Groups BCD, representing those more involved in IT-related activities, reveals notable differences in preferences (see Table 2). Group A students, while inclined towards logic and problem-solving due to their educational background, display comparatively less enthusiasm for IT-specific skills like understanding how devices work or engaging in team-oriented activities, such as collaborative building or presenting ideas. This suggests that Group A's interest in technology might stem more from general problem-solving than direct exposure to IT practices.

However, it is important to note that these data are not directly comparable, as Group A responded to a binary choice (selecting statements that apply to them), whereas Group BCD assessed the same statements on a 5-point Likert scale. While this difference in response method may influence the results, the trends still highlight how early exposure to IT-related activities could foster stronger engagement and interest in technology fields. Additionally, Group A's focus on science suggests that the general high school population may exhibit even more significant differences when compared to IT-focused students.

Table 2. Comparison of Preferences Between Group A and BCD.

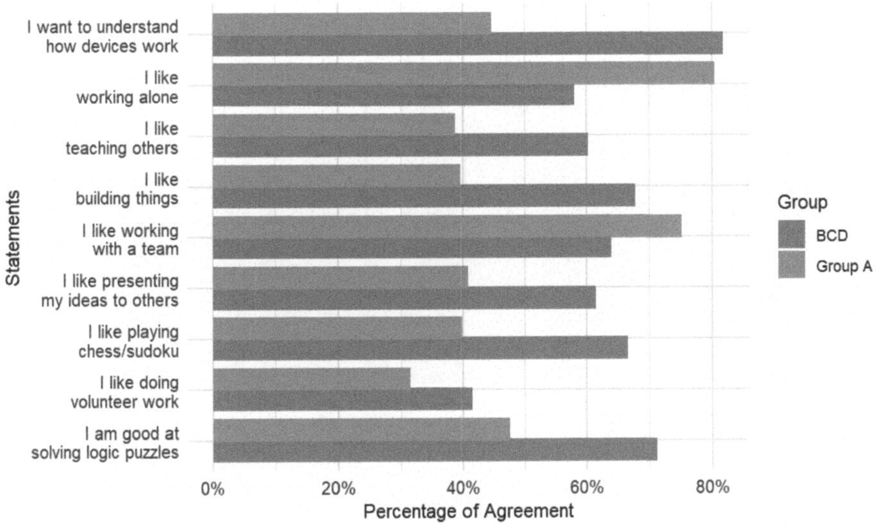

The analysis of subject preferences across the three groups (B, C, and D) reveals interesting patterns (see Table 3). Group D students who have pursued IT studies generally express stronger preferences for Informatics compared to Groups B and C. Their educational focus likely influences this and the fact that in many Estonian schools, the first exposure to Informatics often happens only at the gymnasium level. Therefore, it is logical that university students in ICT-related fields would be more interested in this subject. Meanwhile, Physics receives slightly lower scores, which is expected given that students with a stronger passion for Physics often pursue related fields such as engineering or pure sciences rather than ICT.

Of particular concern is the relatively low interest in Social Studies, which is consistent across all groups. As ICT becomes increasingly intertwined with major societal processes, current ICT students and STEM-oriented youth must better understand how their work impacts broader social and economic systems. This highlights the importance of integrating interdisciplinary perspectives into ICT education to ensure that students are equipped to address the societal implications of their work.

The graph reveals a notable trend: ICT-oriented students (Group BCD) show a significantly higher interest in all subjects than the general pool (Group A) (see Table 4).

This increased interest spans traditionally technical subjects such as Math, Physics, Informatics, and Social Studies. Interestingly, even in Social Studies, where one might expect a lower engagement from ICT-focused individuals, Group BCD demonstrates a considerably higher preference than Group A. This highlights a broader intellectual curiosity among ICT-inclined students, which may reflect their interdisciplinary thinking.

Another noteworthy difference lies in the preference for Manual Work. Group BCD shows a significantly higher percentage of interest in this subject than Group A. This

Table 3. Comparison of Subject Preferences by Group BCD.

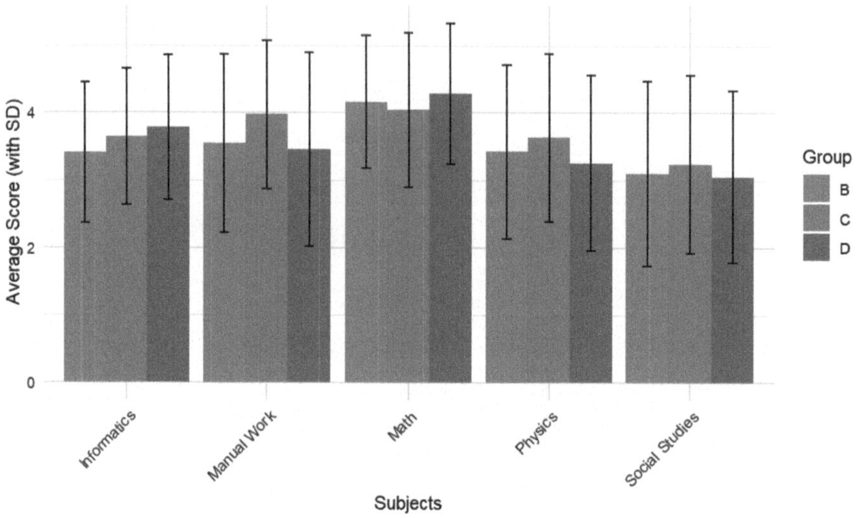

Table 4. Comparison of Subject Preferences by Group A and BCD.

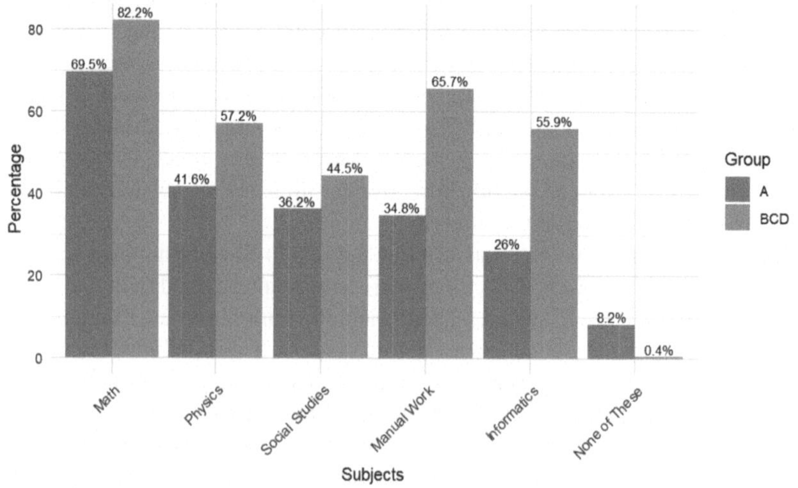

is intriguing, as manual skills often complement technical expertise, particularly in engineering or robotics.

An interesting point for further exploration is the difference in interest in Manual Work based on gender. Understanding whether gender shapes this preference within the ICT-oriented group could provide deeper insights into how traditional subject stereotypes align with modern educational pathways.

We now have a precise gender distribution within groups B, C, and D, allowing us to analyze subject preferences based on gender (see Table 5). It is important to note that this analysis will exclude group A, as gender information is unavailable.

The distribution shows that 63.56% of participants identify as male, 33.90% as female, and 2.54% preferred not to disclose their gender. This provides a solid foundation to examine how subject interests, such as manual work or informatics, differ between male and female participants in the given groups.

Table 5. Affordable small PC hardware systems (generated by authors).

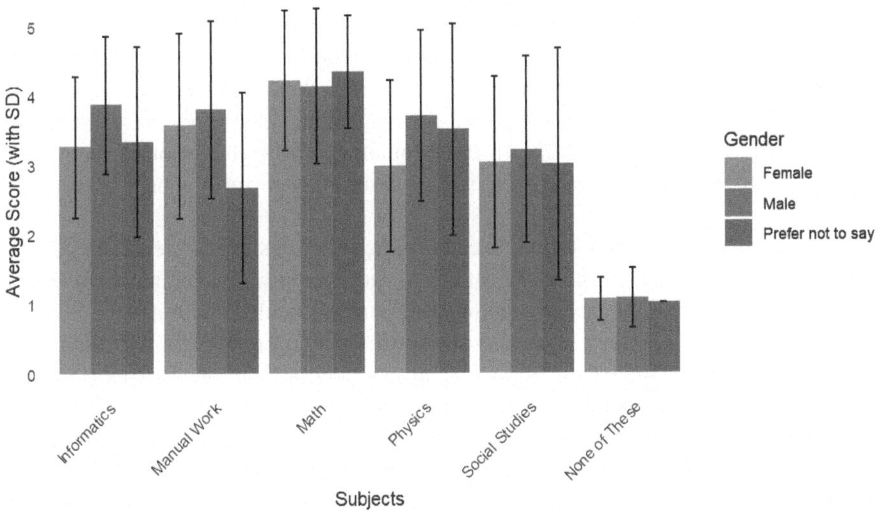

The analysis of subject preferences by gender reveals some interesting patterns. While there are no substantial differences between male and female respondents in their preference for manual work, it is notable that manual work consistently scores highly among those interested in ICT. This finding warrants further exploration because manual work is traditionally associated with hands-on, tangible activities rather than abstract or linguistic problem-solving, often linked to software development. This raises an intriguing question: why does manual work resonate more strongly with ICT-oriented individuals than mathematics, typically perceived as a foundational discipline for technology and programming? Understanding this dynamic could show how diverse interests and competencies contribute to developing ICT skills and career pathways.

4.2 Results from the Discussion with the University Students and Managers

Results from university students show that they come to university with very different backgrounds. Every year, more people have had some IT or programming experience in their high school years, as teaching STEM and programming at the high school level is becoming popular in Estonia. When we asked about their experience, about 15% said they had no computer experience. About 5 years ago, the result was around 25–30%. About 33% said they have some experience but not related to programming. About 40% have had experience with programming or are already working somewhere related to IT. About 5 years ago, only around 25% said they had experience with programming.

We also asked about their fears and what problems they possibly see coming up during the studies. There are some fears related to working alongside the school and finding enough time for studies. However, about 25% of the students said they fear their lack of programming experience can cause problems. Although they might have some experience with computers in general, they have not done any programming. Most of the IT study programs in universities start with extensive programming courses.

Students also shared that universities nowadays set up our courses so that people with no programming experience could pass those courses and get enough practical experience. Those with fewer skills must work harder than others with previous backgrounds, decreasing motivation. They feel that others are better than them and that they do not belong there. There are good examples where a total beginner achieves an excellent level of knowledge, but this takes much effort, and many students cannot bring themselves up to withstand this pressure. However, in most cases, they perform poorly or even drop out.

Solutions to ease the dropout rate, the course has been designed by educational psychologists, who advised boosting the students' motivation and teaching them overall learning skills like studying better and dealing with difficult situations (like exams). During the course, students evaluate their motivation and try to explain why their motivation is dropping (or increasing). Students are already helping themselves cope with problems by reflecting on their emotions and progress in their studies. The program manager organizes a discussion session with education psychologists where students can openly discuss their problems. Those sessions are always very popular; even older students from higher-level courses come to discuss their issues and solutions to cope with the stress. The university also organizes a lot of teamwork projects and events. This has increased their motivation and lowered the dropout rate even more. Working in a team allows the student to be socially active and get accurate help from their peers, and other students also tend to motivate each other to continue with the project or their studies. The "No one is left behind" solution works well in IT when you have fewer skills.

Managers also pointed out that one of the main problems with students who start their studies at university is the considerable difference in how they are organized compared to their previous studies. University students often have more freedom to choose their courses, whether to attend lectures etc. However, for the most, it makes them anxious about whether there is much freedom. They might feel that they have made wrong choices, affecting their future. It is recommended that students be provided with a fixed schedule or course plan at the beginning of their studies, but they should be open to providing a personal learning path to those who already have the appropriate skills to deal with the flexibility. This means we need tools or ways to detect who is more ready than others. For now, the tool is being tested or discussed in lectures. As AI is widely used in homework or help from peers, where there is no supervision and lectures are not mandatory, it is hard for the university to divide the students accurately and provide help when the student is not asking for it. So, it all depends on the students' choices, and if some have higher esteem, they tend to make poor choices that they can't handle later. Alternatively, if they stay silent (are afraid of other issues, like want to solve the challenge themselves) when they don't have the needed skills, all might end up with the same result – dropout.

Due to the COVID-19 lockdown, the university has switched to offering introductory programming courses online. This is suitable for students who live far away or have an otherwise strict schedule, for example, due to already working. Offering online courses has resulted in even fewer classroom students, which also provides less feedback for the lecturer on how the students are performing. This has spiked discussions among educators about returning students to real classrooms, especially those starting their studies. This allows the university to provide tutoring and consultations from the learning assistants we have hired. It has given good results but requires many assistants and might not be feasible for each course. Another possibility is to let the students discuss different topics in the classroom and guide them through the material, but this means they need to study the materials first at home, as reading the material together in the classroom to have a discussion seems to be a waste of time. Also, there is a discussion about whether these lessons should be mandatory, as some need it and some do not. Understanding who needs help and who does not and how to provide appropriate support is vital to helping students learn.

5 Discussion

The findings of this study suggest that it is possible to profile students with a higher potential for success in ICT fields, but the differences between groups are not significant enough to justify steering students away based on pre-selection results. This underscores the need for an inclusive approach, ensuring that all students have access to opportunities in ICT education, regardless of their initial level of interest or competency. Such inclusivity is essential to maintain equity in education and prevent unintentional exclusion.

One of the main challenges in developing the pre-selection test for the high school was determining the appropriate level of flexibility in the criteria for course recommendations. For example, ICT modules aligned closely with students' existing skill levels required less flexibility in recommendations, while modules like cybersecurity, which provided broader foundational knowledge, could be offered to a wider range of students. Despite these efforts, the registration data revealed higher interest in the ICT module (62 students) than the cybersecurity module (28 students), suggesting that students may gravitate toward courses that align with their interests rather than foundational knowledge.

Students with no prior ICT experience were less motivated to enrol in high school ICT courses, highlighting the importance of building a strong ICT foundation at the primary school level. Early exposure to ICT concepts and activities can significantly lower barriers to entry, boost confidence, and generate sustained interest in the field. Without such groundwork, fostering enthusiasm and engagement among students who have not encountered ICT-related topics before high school is difficult.

The anonymity of the pre-selection tool eliminated potential ethical concerns about pressuring students into ICT pathways. However, this anonymity also limited the ability to analyze the tool's detailed impact and gather feedback from educators. While the generic nature of the tool allowed for broad application, it hindered the capacity to establish transparent cause-and-effect relationships between the recommendations and student outcomes. A non-anonymous implementation could provide richer insights but must be carefully managed to avoid creating undue pressure on students.

When it comes to university students, this kind of tool gives them information on how much help they need. At the same time, there needs to be solutions that are met with the results – for example, if you have good learning skills and high motivation, you need less practice and go through the exercises more quickly than those who have less time due to working, older computer, noisy environment, not that good learning skills and motivation and poos ICT related overall skillset. University can give support via materials, tutoring and discussions, but it needs to fit the learner as well, and only the learner knows what he or she needs. However, as the learner does not know, no one knows how to help.

Therefore, given the rapid advancements in artificial intelligence, future iterations of the tool could benefit from integrating discussion-based assessments powered by large language models (LLMs). Such models could interact with students to understand their interests and ambitions more deeply, providing highly personalized recommendations. This approach could offer a more dynamic and engaging experience while generating valuable data for refining the AI's ability to guide students effectively.

Ultimately, this study emphasizes that introducing ICT education at the high school level is insufficient to create widespread interest in the field. A comprehensive ICT curriculum starting from primary school is essential to ensure that students understand the diverse ICT opportunities. Until such curricula can be implemented, the responsibility falls on parents, as data indicate that engagement in robotics and similar hobbies during primary school is associated with higher interest in ICT during high school and, presumably, at the university level. If students are equipped with this knowledge early on, they may not require external tools to guide their course selection, as they will already have the confidence and awareness needed to make informed decisions about their ICT education and career pathways.

6 Conclusion

This study focused on the importance of tailored approaches in IT education to address gaps in preparedness, engagement, and inclusion at both the secondary and university levels. By employing a pre-selection assessment tool, schools and universities can better align course offerings with students' interests and competencies, ensuring a more personalized and supportive educational journey.

Key findings highlight that early exposure to IT-related activities, strong foundational skills in mathematics, and opportunities for hands-on learning are pivotal for fostering interest and success in IT fields. Gender disparities remain a challenge, requiring targeted interventions to encourage equitable participation. Moreover, university students face unique issues, such as a lack of prior programming experience, fears of falling behind, and the overwhelming freedom of course selection, which can lead to anxiety and dropout. Structured support mechanisms have effectively mitigated these challenges, including introductory courses, peer mentoring, and practical learning opportunities.

The study also emphasizes the evolving nature of student interests and skills, suggesting the need for iterative refinement of assessment tools. Future iterations should incorporate dynamic, AI-driven assessments to provide deeper insights and personalized student recommendations. Additionally, integrating interdisciplinary perspectives into IT education—such as the societal impacts of technology—can prepare students for the broader challenges of the digital era.

Ultimately, enhancing IT education through adaptive, inclusive strategies improves academic outcomes and cultivates a diverse, capable workforce to meet the demands of the rapidly evolving technology sector. Collaboration between educators, policymakers, and industry stakeholders will be critical in realizing this vision, ensuring that students of all backgrounds are equipped to thrive in IT and related fields.

References

1. Aliabadi, R.: The Impact of an Artificial Intelligence (AI) Project-Based Learning (PBL) Course on Middle-School Students' Interest, Knowledge, and Career Aspiration in the AI Field. Robert Morris Univ. (2023)
2. Azevedo, F.S.: The tailored practice of hobbies and its implication for the design of interest-driven learning environments. J. Learn. Sci. **22**(3), 462–510 (2013)
3. Bicer, A., Lee, Y.: Effect of STEM PBL embedded informal learning on student interest in STEM majors and careers. J. Math. Educ. **12**(1), 57–73 (2023)
4. Bounou, A., Lavidas, K., Komis, V., Papadakis, S., Manoli, P.: Correlation between high school students' computational thinking and their performance in STEM and language courses. Educ. Sci. **13**(11), 1101 (2023)
5. Canaan, S., Mouganie, P.: The impact of advisor gender on female students' STEM enrollment and persistence. J. Hum. Resour. **58**(2), 593–632 (2023)
6. Card, D., Payne, A.A.: High school choices and the gender gap in STEM. Econ. Inq. **59**(1), 9–28 (2021)
7. Enderson, M.C., Ritz, J.: STEM in general education: Does mathematics competence influence course selection. J. Technol. Stud. **42**(1), 30–41 (2016)
8. Felder, R.M., Brent, R.: Teaching and learning STEM: A practical guide. John Wiley & Sons, US (2024)
9. Friend, M., Swift, A. W., Love, B., Winter, V.: A Wolf in Lamb's Clothing: Computer Science in a Mathematics Course. In: Proceedings of the 54th ACM Technical Symposium on Computer Science Education Vol. 1, pp. 256–262. (2023)
10. Gill, T., Vidal Rodeiro, C., Zanini, N.: Higher education choices of secondary school graduates with a Science, Technology, Engineering or Mathematics (STEM) background. J. Furth. High. Educ. **42**(7), 998–1014 (2018)
11. González-Pérez, S., Martínez-Martínez, M., Rey-Paredes, V., Cifre, E.: I am done with this! Women dropping out of engineering majors. Front. Psychol. **13**, 918439 (2022)
12. Hsu, J. L., Goldsmith, G. R.: Instructor strategies to alleviate stress and anxiety among college and university STEM students. CBE—Life Sci. Educ. **20**(1), es1 (2021)
13. Kabathova, J., Drlik, M.: Towards predicting student's dropout in university courses using different machine learning techniques. Appl. Sci. **11**(7), 3130 (2021)

14. Kordaki, M., Berdousis, I.: Course selection in computer science: Gender differences. Procedia Soc. Behav. Sci. **116**, 4770–4774 (2014)
15. Kwon, H., Vela, K., Williams, A.M., Barroso, L.R.: Mathematics and science self-efficacy and STEM careers: A path analysis. J. Math. Educ. **12**(1), 74–89 (2023)
16. Luo, T., So, W.W.M., Wan, Z.H., Li, W.C.: STEM stereotypes predict students' STEM career interest via self-efficacy and outcome expectations. Int. J. STEM Educ. **8**, 1–13 (2021)
17. Ng, K., Riehl, E.: The returns to STEM programs for less-prepared students. Am. Econ. J. Econ. Pol. **16**(2), 37–77 (2024)
18. Ogegbo, A.A., Aina, A.Y.: Exploring young students' attitude towards coding and its relationship with STEM career interest. Educ. Inf. Technol. **29**(8), 9041–9059 (2024)
19. Phelps, L.A., Camburn, E.M., Min, S.: Choosing STEM college majors: Exploring the role of pre-college engineering courses. J. Pre-Coll. Eng. Educ. Res. (J-PEER), **8**(1), 1 (2018)
20. Rachmatullah, A., Wiebe, E.N.: Exploring middle school students' interests in computationally intensive science careers: The CISCI instrument validation and intervention. Sci. Educ. **107**(2), 333–367 (2023)
21. Servin, C., Hawthorne, E.K., Postner, L., Tang, C., Tucker, C.S.: Curricular and Pedagogical Considerations in Computer Science Education: The Role of Community Colleges for the Next Decade. In: Proceedings of the 55th ACM Technical Symposium on Computer Science Education Vol. 1, pp. 1196–1201. (2024)
22. Shay, M., Rees, J.: Understanding why students select online courses and criteria they use in making that selection. Int. J. Instruct. Technol. Distance Learn. **1**(5), 23–30 (2004)
23. Sun, L., Hu, L., Yang, W., Zhou, D., Wang, X.: STEM learning attitude predicts computational thinking skills among primary school students. J. Comput. Assist. Learn. **37**(2), 346–358 (2021)
24. Wass, R., Golding, C.: Sharpening a tool for teaching: the zone of proximal development. Teach. High. Educ. **19**(6), 671–684 (2014)

Improving Cybersecurity Education in Schools: An Assessment of the "Digitally Safer School" Proposal

Birgy Lorenz(✉)

Tallinn University of Technology, Tallinn, Estonia
birgy.lorenz@taltech.ee

Abstract. As technology becomes increasingly integrated into education, ensuring robust cybersecurity practices in schools is essential. This paper examines the "Digitally Safer School" initiative in Estonia, which aims to enhance cybersecurity awareness and practices among students, teachers, and the broader school community. Using a mixed-methods approach, the study evaluates the current state of cybersecurity in schools, identifying strengths, weaknesses, and opportunities for improvement. Key findings highlight gaps in documentation, staff training, and the integration of cybersecurity into curricula, alongside strengths in technology accessibility and IT support. The study introduces a maturity model and self-assessment tool that schools can use to measure and enhance their cybersecurity readiness. Schools are encouraged to foster a culture of digital safety through staff training, student engagement, and community involvement, supported by secure IT infrastructure and effective incident management protocols. The findings demonstrate that significant challenges remain while schools have progressed in some areas. The "Digitally Safer School" initiative offers a scalable framework for improving cybersecurity education and practices, serving as a model for global adoption in educational settings. This paper's results support the claim that we still need to push for collaboration between policymakers, educators, and communities to create resilient, digitally secure learning environments.

Keywords: Cybersecurity Awareness · Educational Sector · Digitally Safer School · Digital Security Practices · Cybersecurity Maturity Tool Development for Schools

1 Background

The rapid advancement of technology, COVID-19, in the Estonian case and the global situation, has fundamentally transformed our environment, making cybersecurity as essential as following traffic rules or using smoke detectors. Changing people's habits requires more than just occasional training or campaigns; it necessitates the creation of a supportive environment and backing a broad supportive network. Schools can serve as community hubs, connecting various generations and groups, and thus play a crucial role in influencing students and their families in cybersecurity practices.

In this paper, I will examine schools' challenges regarding cyber security policy, uses of safer technology, and awareness-related human resources possibilities in Estonia.

B. K. Smith and M. Borge (Eds.): HCII 2025, LNCS 15806, pp. 315–327, 2025.
https://doi.org/10.1007/978-3-031-93564-0_19

1.1 Policy

National cybersecurity strategies are pivotal in shaping and improving cybersecurity education by providing necessary frameworks, fostering partnerships, ensuring resource allocation, and promoting international collaboration. These elements are essential for building a resilient cybersecurity workforce that addresses contemporary digital threats [3]. It is important to develop structured e-safety initiatives, like the example available for Zimbabwean secondary schools, to mitigate the risks associated with ICT usage and promote a culture of digital safety among students[24]. It is also important to emphasize collaboration among educators, parents, and policymakers, which is lacking in most countries in providing a safe digital environment for students.

Not every school knows their cybersecurity awareness situation, and the gaps are becoming more visible when they start to evaluate themselves. So, to start, one needs to find these "low hanging fruits" to tackle. Usually, schools lack comprehensive training for staff and students, undermining their potential effectiveness [33]. Some findings show that not only the staff is the issue, but a more integrated approach that prioritizes awareness and proactive measures to enhance student safety in digital environments would benefit everyone.

While governments, like Estonia, force governmental institutions, including local authorities and schools, to implement technical standards, schools focus on student behaviour online [11]. Legislators tend to talk pass schools, and therefore push schools to deal with security role identification, threat assessments, IT management, incident response, remote work, and a small part of employee training, when they are not ready to do it. At the same time, what is important to teachers and parents, is not regulated anywhere. Schools, if the policy does not tackle students' and parents' fundamental challenges, curriculum, and extracurricular work, face implementation challenges as technical security is not the school's primary responsibility and goal. Schools sometimes see themselves as in the "safe bubble" where no hacker would attack them as in the real world.

Therefore, frameworks for schools should serve as a vital resource for educators aiming to create safe digital learning environments while fostering essential skills in students to navigate the complexities of the online world. Schools can relate, when asked, to better students' rights and responsibilities, resilience and risk, and practical whole-school approaches that are integrated and specific to the curriculum. Educators understand better if the risks are explained and associated with online learning environments or student behaviour online [36].

Addressing other existing challenges and fostering collaboration among stakeholders also have significant potential to enhance overall cybersecurity awareness and preparedness despite the challenges. These challenges usually include a lack of resources, insufficient training for educators and schools IT-supporting personnel, varying levels of student engagement, and the need for continuous updates to curricula to keep pace with evolving cyber threats [32].

1.2 Content and Students

At the same time, even cybersecurity education faces challenges. For now, it is usually developed as a standalone, but it should be integrated into the broader educational process. For example, it is useless if informatics teachers follow the GDPR rules, if no one else at the school, does not. A systemic approach where everyone is involved in providing a safer environment and binding the rules is essential to foster lasting changes in children's online behaviour and awareness [26]. A structured and integrated approach to evaluating and improving cybersecurity education can effectively enhance students' understanding and behaviours related to online safety [6]. This also means that sometimes there is a need to start with a lower level, like discussing how multimedia tools are used in real life and then connecting with cybersecurity education while fostering awareness among non-expert end-users [38].

Developing practical assessment tools and emphasizing educational strategies can also contribute to better cybersecurity practices among learners. It is eminent that formal education plays a significant role in shaping students' cybersecurity behaviours, and it cannot be left to be the responsibility of parents or society, that sometimes can happen. Those schools that already incorporate comprehensive cybersecurity education into their curricula tend to provide students with higher levels of cyber awareness, which becomes helpful in personal and work life, not just school life [37]. It would not be possible if schools focused only on providing a safe environment.

1.3 Teachers

There is also a need to improve digital safety education within teacher training programs, curricula, and practical experiences to boost pre-service teachers' confidence and competence in this essential area [35]. Many teachers feel unprepared due to insufficient training and resources, which affects their ability to deliver comprehensive cybersecurity education or even give low-level support to the students [9]. Teachers also need educational institutions to develop clear policies regarding digital technologies, ensuring all stakeholders understand their roles and responsibilities in digital learning. All is not lost as in the EU. Some examples include cybersecurity evaluations of the teacher's digital competence. One example is the SELFIE tool, which allows institutions to evaluate their use of digital technologies and identify areas for improvement. These self-assessments are crucial for fostering a continuous enhancement culture in digital education and improving digital citizenship among students and teachers [23].

Schools and teachers also need to understand that cybersecurity always brings new challenges, such as rising data usage and creation among young people. This pushes privacy concerns, data ownership, and the impact of algorithms on daily life to be the topics that schools need to tackle and explain. As issues with AI emerge, new challenges are faced daily. Some research findings suggest that educators should incorporate critical data education into existing curricula rather than treating it as an isolated subject or only being responsible for informatics teachers. This integration can help foster a culture of critical engagement with data among students and teachers as a community [27].

The schoolteachers and staff should also improve their practices as they are seen as role models. Schools need to implement security as part of the culture, not something that needs to be tackled separately. By adopting effective training strategies and fostering a culture of security, organizations can significantly reduce their vulnerability to cyber threats [19].

1.4 Assessment

Institutions need to conduct self-assessments to determine their current cybersecurity maturity level. It helps identify weaknesses and outlines necessary mitigation strategies, fostering an environment of proactive security management [4].

Schools that effectively integrate digital innovations tend to see also improvements in educational outcomes, including enhanced student motivation and better academic performance. Successful implementation requires a clear vision, ongoing support, and adaptability to changing circumstances [28].

Schools need a straightforward solution that provides a structured framework to easily follow to assess their cyber-safety practices, identify gaps, and implement necessary changes. The framework must also push schools for collaboration among various stakeholders, including educators, parents, and local authorities, to ensure a holistic approach to cyber safety education and improvement of the situation in the school (environment, policies, etc.). This collaborative effort is crucial for creating a supportive student environment [20].

Any framework or tool built needs to connect to the real world as one needs to apply these methods in real-world scenarios to test their usability. The effectiveness of an assessment method can be enhanced when it is well-documented, easy to learn, supported by tools, and previously applied in similar contexts [22].

The issue for schools is that existing cybersecurity frameworks can be complex and poorly suited for the education sector. One issue is that the solution must consider that the staff lacks extensive cybersecurity expertise, but another is that the school is in some sense in the "bubble" where you can "play real life". For example, if a cyber security incident emerges with students or teachers, the schools, instead of giving it to the police, discuss it with parties and push them to reconcile. However, in real-world cyber security, schools are like whatever a company needs to protect its assets [34].

Some models are available for schools, but for example, even inside the education sector, adopting ideas from school to school can be challenging. For instance, what higher education is using, is not always reasonable for basic and secondary or vocational schools. Example higher education incorporates better industry feedback, practical training, and ongoing assessment to prepare students for careers in cybersecurity effectively, therefore universities also perform better as an organization, when it comes to cyber security performance. That is not expected from basic education, even when they sometimes provide cybersecurity special education [15]. However, what is common to most schools is to use rubrics solutions where they can identify strengths and weaknesses in their digital integration efforts, and it also guides what to do next if that challenge or area is on the priority list to be improved [8].

So, in the end, there is a need for assessment tools that allow schools to measure their current level of digital maturity systematically according to the real world and for educational challenges they especially face and what allows them to integrate digital technologies into school teaching, learning, and real-world organizational practices. Schools must also have access to benchmark their digital maturity against others, track progress over time, and develop strategic plans to enhance their digital capabilities.

1.5 Situation and Needs Analysis in Estonia

As mentioned in the Sect. 1.1. Estonia pushes schools to implement the Estonian Cyber Security Standard, which is rather technical. For schools there are several other laws the schools must also comply with: Basic and Upper Secondary School Act [7], General Data Protection Regulation [14], Personal Data Protection Act [30], Cybersecurity Act [10] and NIS 2 Directive [25], Public Information Act [31]. All of these must be understood to assess schools' maturity level in cybersecurity. Implementing the E-ITS (Cybersecurity Information Technology Standard) in 2024 and starting to implement non-mandatory computer science curricula in 2023 [12, 13] has significantly impacted schools. The availability of educational materials and various support programs also plays a crucial role. Significant impact has been observed from the Harno (formerly HITSA, Tiger Leap) initiative [18] and the "Smartly on the Internet" activities [2], which focus on training teachers and conducting activities for youth. For instance, both programs have implemented updates in computer science education (curriculum and material development), as mentioned above. Other influential factors include competitions series, like the Cyber Olympiad program [1] initiated by Estonian Ministry of Defense and carried out by Tallinn University of Technology.

Also, it seems that Estonia, dealing with overall technical readiness to challenges and optional support for students, is in a good position in the world. On the other hand, good initiatives do not always align, and not all schools are on board, even in Estonia. Challenges within schools include:

- Lack of accountable and knowledgeable staff. There is low awareness of information security, insufficient or inadequate training, lack of centralized community support, and a lack of fundamental knowledge about cybersecurity;
- There is no clear understanding of how technical park security is organized, which in reality can be random or unmanaged;
- Activities with the school community (students, teachers, staff, parents) are occasional and project-based, without agreed-upon actions, measurements, or funding;
- There is no systematic monitoring, resulting in a lack of understanding of the current situation and future development needs;
- There are issues with reaching the target group with mass-level educational opportunities, a lack of differentiation, and management activities related to talents that make it inaccessible to everyone.

Given the significant demands on schools, any cybersecurity program implemented must efficiently use existing resources. Achieving the desired impact requires unified goals and the application of shared principles and measures. The "Digitally Safer School" proposal outlines various activity areas and measures to enhance the cybersecurity awareness of students, teachers, and the broader community. Cybersecurity, in the context of this paper, encompasses both digital competence and cyber hygiene. The proposal provides a solution for different levels that help schools organize their cybersecurity activities more effectively and measure outcomes in their situation. These areas include enhancing students' and teachers' awareness of cybersecurity, involving students in creating a secure school environment, engaging students in cybersecurity competitions, and contributing to community-wide cybersecurity awareness that is already available but not used by every school.

2 Methods

This study utilized a mixed-methods approach to assess the impact of the "Digitally Safer School" proposal in Estonia, focusing on enhancing cybersecurity practices and awareness within educational settings.

The creation of the "Digitally Safer School" self-assessment tool was inspired by several models and tools, including the digital maturity assessment tool from Digipeegel(Digital Mirror)[21], the Capability Maturity Model (CMM) [29], the Concerns-Based Adoption Model (CBAM) [5, 16], and the Estonian Information Security standard measurement tool developed by Information System Authority. Measurable domains, questions, and levels were developed in collaboration with schools and involved experts. Components for the assessment tool were designed to address various aspects of a school's environment, education processes, and people, ensuring a comprehensive evaluation framework that supports schools in effectively enhancing their cybersecurity situation.

For collecting the data, interviews and focus groups with key stakeholders (administrators, teachers, and IT staff) from schools participating in the proposal development initiative provided depth and context to the data, exploring subjective experiences and the perceived effectiveness of the program. This was carried out in 2021 and 2024 to see what has changed. Eighteen experts participated in the progress 2021, and 8 evaluated the changes 2024.

A specific evaluation tool was developed to measure schools' cybersecurity readiness across multiple dimensions. Seventy-five schools participated in the testing in 2021 and 25 in 2024. Schools were selected based on various criteria to ensure a representative mix across different geographical locations and resource levels, providing a generalizable data set. This tool facilitated a structured and standardized assessment of schools' cybersecurity capabilities and needs. Surveys were administered to a broader audience within the schools, including staff and students, before and after the tool's implementation. These surveys quantitatively assessed changes in cybersecurity awareness and practices. At the evaluation of the categories, questions were asked to be filled in privately, including those of the board, teachers, IT personnel, parents, and students' representatives. After that, a focus group discussion followed, usually about why this information is unavailable to every group in the school and how the school can gather additional proof. The third layer meeting evaluated the results and decided which areas the school will focus on in the next two years to improve.

Analysis of the results: I examined the program implementation process, participants' engagement levels, and challenges. By comparing pre- and post-implementation data, the tool usually improved cybersecurity measures and awareness, as all the schools in 2021 chose 1–5 areas to improve. While developing the tool, cybersecurity and educational experts contributed to developing the proposal and analyzing the collected data, ensuring the reliability and validity of the results. Quantitative data from the surveys were analyzed using statistical methods to identify significant changes and trends in cybersecurity awareness and practices, providing empirical evidence of the program's impact. Continuous feedback mechanisms were integrated throughout the program, allowing for real-time adjustments and improvements based on interim findings. In 2024, the tool was improved by adding more valuable questions to analyses specific evidence like availability of GDPR regulations, how well schools had already stated implementing E-ITS, or how they were coming with emerging AI use and its privacy concerns.

This comprehensive approach enabled systematically evaluating the impact of the "Digitally Safer School" proposal and identifying key factors contributing to its success or challenges. The findings from this study are expected to contribute to the broader knowledge base of effective cybersecurity practices in educational settings and guide future program development and implementation.

3 Results and Discussion

The proposal "Digitally Safer School" emphasizes the role of schools as pivotal community hubs, influencing not only students but also parents, creating a ripple effect of awareness and behavioural change. It introduces a multi-level maturity model inspired by international frameworks, assessing schools across documentation, infrastructure, education, and stakeholder engagement. The model includes a scale* from 0 (no action) to 5 (innovative redevelopment), allowing schools to measure their progress systematically. Other stages in which schools can position themselves are orientation (1), preparing (2), mechanical use (3), routines, and systematic usage (4).

The school level is evaluated in four sub-categories; every category has 5–8 sub-areas in which schools must provide proof of their actual situation. Category A is **Documentation** – schools need to explain and showcase how well E-ITS, GDPR and other legal responsibilities have been implemented at the school. Everyone working and studying in the school must be on the same page. For example, are rules for learning and teaching visibly written down, and are there guidelines on properly using technologies? If not, the level cannot be high. Category B – **The Environment** - are other rules and legislation results about educating students visible on the strategies and real environment? What level of accessibility is there to technologies, and is there a policy for cybersecurity and incident management agreements? In this section, schools need to provide proof of real life, like pictures, information on the website or other information. Category C - **Education** – This category focuses on what is on the curriculum and how students benefit from awareness or talent programs. Does the school even do digital safety awareness provide extracurricular or curricular training for students around cyber security? Do the students and teachers participate in the competitions or other initiatives? Does the school cooperate with different organizations and industries to improve education? Category D - **Competences of adults that work with students** – this area focuses on the digital safety of users and adults' awareness. For example, is there someone responsible for cyber security at the school? What is the teacher's maturity level in cyber hygiene? Are educational technologists, IT-help, or Informatic teachers available? Are they up to their tasks? Does the school provide training to the parents (that is not mandatory, but would help the overall situation)?

The evaluation process for creating the solution involved developing a tool for self-assessment that was piloted in 75 schools, revealing gaps in every area, especially in cybersecurity documentation, staff training, and student involvement in digital safety (see Table 1. Analysis Results of the Schools Testing 2021).

Table 1. Analysis Results of the Schools Testing 2021.

Area	School Documentation and Compliance	School Environment	Education and Talent Development	Adult Competencies
Average result out of 0–4* - how well the schools are performing	2,5*	2,61*	1,68*	1,58*
Description	Schools demonstrate moderate performance in maintaining organizational documentation and legal compliance	Schools generally provide reasonable access to technology (3.5*) and maintain updated ICT tools (3.0*)	Students' education situation at the school	People who work with students, at what level are their competencies?
Strengths	Compliance with general regulations (2.8*) and establishing educational agreements and strategies (2.7*)	IT/HT support availability (3.4*) inside the school is average	Some schools sometimes focus on the topics systematically	Some improvement is seen in IT support staff competencies (2.3*) and informatics teachers' cybersecurity knowledge (1.8*)
Weaknesses	Implementing the Estonian Information Security Standard (E-ITS) scored very low (0.9*), indicating limited adoption	IT strategy and cybersecurity integration into school development plans (1.7*) and incident management (1.7*)	Extracurricular activities such as clubs (1.1*), self-assessment tests for students (1.3*), and cybersecurity education integration (1.7*). Collaboration with businesses (1.8*) and opportunities for advanced IT education, including cybersecurity (1.6*)	Teachers' basic digital hygiene skills (1.2*), leadership in digital safety within schools (1.5*), and parent engagement (1.1*)

This analysis underscores the critical need for schools to adopt a systematic approach to digital safety by focusing on infrastructure, education, and stakeholder engagement. While foundational elements like technology availability and general compliance are present, the lack of targeted initiatives in cybersecurity presents a significant barrier to creating a digitally safer school environment. Addressing these gaps requires collaborative efforts among schools, governments, and businesses, with a strong emphasis on capacity building and innovation in both student and adult education.

The second assessment in 2024 showed that schools that had started E-ITS implementation were improving significantly in the documentation category and somewhat in the Competencies of adults who work with students. Areas like Environment and Curriculum were not so much affected as the effort went on to make "the papers" friendly. Main issues arose in 2021 that got some ease, like low integration of cybersecurity standards. However, technology and IT support availability have remained the same due to insufficient teacher and parent engagement and limited student extracurricular opportunities.

Schools should also prioritize staff training, integrate cybersecurity strategies into development plans, and enhance student engagement through clubs, competitions, and targeted education programs. Recommendations from the proposals focus on fostering collaboration between schools, local governments, and national bodies and promoting teacher training, student activities, and public awareness. This is vital for various reasons, such as the emerging use of AI and the fact that we have seen information war attacks on schools [17].

3.1 Discussion and Suggestions on What Schools Should Learn from the Results?

Schools can evaluate their security practices by examining several critical areas to ensure a safe and secure digital environment for students, staff, and the community. A comprehensive approach begins with establishing robust privacy and digital safety policies. These include creating a clear and accessible privacy notice, maintaining a data processing register, and implementing guidelines to handle digital safety issues for students, parents, and staff. Codifying these practices into the school's official regulations or code of conduct ensures consistency and accountability.

IT systems form the backbone of digital safety, and their security is crucial. Schools should ensure that staff and students log into devices with unique accounts while guests and shared devices operate under restricted permissions. Network security is enhanced by password-protected WiFi segmented into secure sub-networks. All devices must be equipped with antivirus software, regularly updated, and monitored for potential threats. Schools can also implement secure printing systems and firewalls to protect internet usage. Proper policies regarding using and scanning external devices like USB drives reinforce safety.

Cloud services and email systems also play a significant role. Schools often utilize centralized cloud platforms for learning, ensuring data is stored securely. Email protocols should enforce multifactor authentication, particularly for remote access, and prevent spoofing to protect against phishing and other cyber threats. Clear guidelines help staff understand the appropriate use of school email for personal or professional purposes.

Internal practices around data protection are equally important. Schools need transparent processes for obtaining consent for data use and ensuring staff know the boundaries of data disclosure. Conducting audits on data protection compliance and using AI-related tools helps identify improvement areas that can be addressed promptly. Digital safety incidents should be logged, analyzed, and used as learning opportunities to update policies and guidelines. Trained personnel capable of reporting breaches and managing cybersecurity incidents are essential for maintaining a proactive stance on safety.

Public-facing initiatives like publishing the informatics curriculum and sharing digital safety plans help build transparency and trust. However, one should be aware not to disclose anything too deep (as exact guidelines or other), as this is the possible guidebook for the attacker. At the same time, parents, teachers, and students should know how to behave when different situations arise. Schools should also actively engage with their community by organizing workshops and awareness events that enhance the digital safety knowledge of parents and local stakeholders.

Training and education are pivotal for fostering a culture of safety. Teachers benefit from regular cybersecurity and AI-related training, ensuring they stay current with best practices. Students gain valuable knowledge through workshops on digital safety, personal data protection, and the ethical use of AI. Parents, too, are included in this educational effort, receiving guidance on maintaining digital safety at home.

Participation in national and international initiatives strengthens the school's commitment to cybersecurity. Schools raise awareness and inspire students to explore careers in this critical field by celebrating events like Safer Internet Day and competing in cybersecurity challenges. Advanced programs and competitions help identify and nurture talent, creating global opportunities for students to excel.

Finally, schools can contribute to the broader educational community by sharing their best practices in digital safety. Collaborative efforts to enhance training, refine strategies, and adopt innovative solutions ensure that schools remain at the forefront of fostering a secure and inclusive learning environment.

The proposal also introduces a certification system for recognizing schools' achievements in cybersecurity, with tiers like Bronze, Silver, Gold, and Diamond, based on their progress. Schools are encouraged to document and share best practices to create a supportive network for continuous improvement. Overall, the "Digitally Safer School" proposal seeks to institutionalize cybersecurity practices, ensuring sustainable and scalable solutions to prepare schools for the digital era while fostering a safety culture and awareness in educational communities.

4 Conclusion

Policymakers and schools play a crucial role in strengthening cybersecurity in educational institutions. To achieve this, policymakers should develop a unified national strategy that provides clear cybersecurity guidelines tailored specifically for schools. This strategy should emphasize integrating cybersecurity into curricula, providing consistent staff training, and enhancing student awareness. Additionally, dedicated funding must be allocated to ensure schools have access to modern cybersecurity technologies, support systems, and educational materials. Standardized cybersecurity education frameworks should be created to ensure regular training for teachers, staff, and students while promoting best practices for digital hygiene and online safety.

Policymakers can further support schools by fostering research and collaboration between educational institutions, universities, and industry experts. This will help develop innovative tools and share knowledge effectively. National-level evaluations should be implemented to measure progress, with incentives for schools that excel in cybersecurity preparedness. In Estonia, the Estonian Information Security Standard is the most influential regulation for schools. Investment in secure IT infrastructure is critical. Schools must ensure that all systems, including WiFi, devices, and software, are secure, up-to-date, and protected by antivirus software, firewalls, and secure login protocols. Incident preparedness should also be a priority, with clear protocols for managing and logging cybersecurity incidents to ensure quick and effective responses.

Schools, on their part, have also started to integrate cybersecurity into their institutional policies. These policies cover areas such as privacy, data protection, incident response, and cybersecurity measures, and they should be regularly updated to align with national standards. Regular training for teachers and administrative staff is essential to improve their digital hygiene and cybersecurity awareness.

Schools should also incorporate cybersecurity topics into the curriculum to engage students and organize extracurricular activities like clubs and competitions to nurture interest and talent. Community engagement is equally important; schools should involve parents and local stakeholders through workshops and awareness programs to build a collective commitment to digital safety.

Finally, schools should foster a culture of continuous improvement by regularly assessing and adapting their cybersecurity practices to meet evolving threats. Self-assessment frameworks and external audits can help identify areas for improvement and ensure ongoing progress.

By implementing these measures, policymakers and schools can work together to create safer digital environments, equipping educational institutions to meet the digital era's challenges effectively.

Acknowledgements. Digitally Safer School proposal origin report was ordered and funded by the Ministry of Economic Affairs and Communications 2021.

References

1. About the project. CyberOlympics competitions in Estonia. https://sites.google.com/view/kyberolympia/eng/about-the-project, last accessed 2025/01/14
2. About the project. Safer Internet Centre in Estonia homepage, https://www.targaltinternetis.ee/en/about-the-project/, last accessed 2025/01/14
3. AlDaajeh, S., Saleous, H., Alrabaee, S., Barka, E., Breitinger, F., Choo, K.K.R.: The role of national cybersecurity strategies on the improvement of cybersecurity education. Comput. Secur. **119**, 102754 (2022)
4. Almomani, I., Ahmed, M., Maglaras, L.: Cybersecurity maturity assessment framework for higher education institutions in Saudi Arabia. PeerJ Comput. Sci. **7**, e703 (2021)
5. Anderson, S.E.: Understanding teacher change: Revisiting the concerns-based adoption model. Curric. Inq. **27**(3), 331–367 (1997)
6. Antunes, M., Silva, C., Marques, F.: An integrated cybernetic awareness strategy to assess cybersecurity attitudes and behaviours in school context. Appl. Sci. **11**(23), 11269 (2021)
7. Basic and Upper Secondary School Act, https://www.riigiteataja.ee/akt/126042024012?leiaKehtiv, last accessed 2025/01/14

8. Begicevic Redjep, N., Balaban, I., Zugec, B.: Assessing digital maturity of schools: framework and instrument. Technol. Pedagog. Educ. **30**(5), 643–658 (2021)
9. Childers, G., Linsky, C.L., Payne, B., Byers, J., Baker, D.: K-12 educators' self-confidence in designing and implementing cybersecurity lessons. Comput. Educ. Open **4**, 100119 (2023)
10. Cybersecurity Act, https://www.riigiteataja.ee/akt/121062024015?leiaKehtiv, last accessed 2025/01/14
11. E-ITS Profile for Educational Institution homepage, https://eits.ria.ee/api/2/main_menu/asset/Haridusasutuste_profiil_v2023.pdf, last accessed 2025/01/14
12. Elective subject "Informatics" for Basic School, https://www.riigiteataja.ee/aktilisa/1080/3202/3005/18m_pohi_lisa10.pdf, last accessed 2025/01/14
13. Elective subject "Informatics" for Highschool, https://www.riigiteataja.ee/aktilisa/1080/3202/3001/18m_gym_lisa9.pdf, last accessed 2025/01/14
14. General Data Protection Regulation, https://eur-lex.europa.eu/legal-content/ET/TXT/PDF/?uri=CELEX:32016R0679, last accessed 2025/01/14
15. Hajny, J., Ricci, S., Piesarskas, E., Levillain, O., Galletta, L., De Nicola, R.: Framework, tools and good practices for cybersecurity curricula. IEEE Access **9**, 94723–94747 (2021)
16. Hall, G.E.: The Concerns-Based Adoption Model: A Developmental Conceptualization of the Adoption Process Within Educational Institutions (1974)
17. Harper, D.: Lithuanian schools receive hundreds of bomb threats for third consecutive month. Euronews (2023). https://www.euronews.com/2023/12/06/lithuanian-schools-receive-hundreds-of-bomb-threats-for-third-consecutive-month, last accessed 2025/01/14
18. How it all began? From Tiger Leap to digital society. Education Estonia homepage, https://www.educationestonia.org/tiger-leap/, last accessed 2025/01/14
19. Khando, K., Gao, S., Islam, S.M., Salman, A.: Enhancing employees information security awareness in private and public organizations: A systematic literature review. Comput. Secur. **106**, 102267 (2021)
20. Kritzinger, E., Lautenbach, G.: Cyber-Safety Awareness: Assisting Schools in Implementation Guidelines. In Science and Information Conference, pp. 617–629. Cham, Springer International Publishing (2022)
21. Laanpere, M., Sillat, L.H., Luik, P., Lehiste., P., Pozhogina, K.: National Policies and Services for Digital Competence Advancement in Estonia. In: IFIP World Conference on Computers in Education, pp. 675–686. Cham: Springer Nature Switzerland (2022)
22. Leszczyna, R.: Review of cybersecurity assessment methods: Applicability perspective. Comput. Secur. **108**, 102376 (2021)
23. Morze, N.V., Kucherovska, V O.: Ways to design a digital educational environment for K-12 education. In: CTE Workshop Proceedings, Vol. 8, pp. 200–211. (2021)
24. Moyo, A., Tsokota, T., Ruvinga, C., Chipfumbu Kangara, C.T.: An e-safety framework for secondary schools in Zimbabwe. Technol. Knowl. Learn. **27**(4), 1133–1153 (2022)
25. NIS 2 Directive, https://eur-lex.europa.eu/legal-content/ET/TXT/PDF/?uri=CELEX:32022L2555, last accessed 2025/01/14
26. Ondrušková, D., Pospíšil, R.: The good practices for implementation of cyber security education for school children. Contemp. Educ. Technol. **15**(3), ep435 (2023)
27. Pangrazio, L., Selwyn, N.: Towards a school-based 'critical data education.' Pedagog. Cult. Soc. **29**(3), 431–448 (2021)
28. Pata, K., Tammets, K., Väljataga, T., Kori, K., Laanpere, M., Rõbtsenkov, R.: The patterns of school improvement in digitally innovative schools. Technol. Knowl. Learn. **27**(3), 823–841 (2022)
29. Paulk, M.C., Curtis, B., Chrissis, M.B., Weber, V.V.: Capability maturity model, version 1.1." IEEE software **10**(4), 18–27 (1993)
30. Personal Data Protection Act, https://www.riigiteataja.ee/akt/104012019011?leiaKehtiv, last accessed 2025/01/14

31. Public Information Act, https://www.riigiteataja.ee/akt/122032011010?leiaKehtiv, last accessed 2025/01/14
32. Shillair, R., Esteve-González, P., Dutton, W.H., Creese, S., Nagyfejeo, E., von Solms, B.: Cybersecurity education, awareness raising, and training initiatives: National level evidence-based results, challenges, and promise. Comput. Secur. **119**, 102756 (2022)
33. Siyam, N., Hussain, M.: Cyber-safety policy elements in the era of online learning: a content analysis of policies in the UAE. TechTrends **65**(4), 535–547 (2021)
34. Torres, M., Mullins, A., Thompson, N.: Education Cybersecurity Assessment Tool: A cybersecurity self-assessment tool for the Australian K-12 sector (2022)
35. Torres-Hernández, N., Gallego-Arrufat, M.J.: Toward an Education for Digital Safety Based on the Self-Perceived Competences of Pre-service Teachers. Comput. Sch. **41**(3), 307–327 (2024)
36. Walsh, K., et al.: Best practice framework for online safety education: Results from a rapid review of the international literature, expert review, and stakeholder consultation. Int. J. Child-Comput. Interact. **33**, 100474 (2022)
37. Witsenboer, J.W.A., Sijtsma, K., Scheele, F.: Measuring cyber secure behavior of elementary and high school students in the Netherlands. Comput. Educ. **186**, 104536 (2022)
38. Zhang-Kennedy, L., Chiasson, S.: A systematic review of multimedia tools for cybersecurity awareness and education. ACM Comput. Surv. (CSUR) **54**(1), 1–39 (2021)

Innovating IT Ethics Education: The Role of AI in Course Development

Birgy Lorenz(✉) and Kaido Kikkas

Tallinn University of Technology, Tallinn, Estonia
{birgy.lorenz,kaido.kikkas}@taltech.ee

Abstract. This article outlines the evolution of the course "Social, Professional and Ethical Aspects of IT" at Tallinn University of Technology. Before 2022, the course relied on lectures, papers, and seminar presentations, culminating in an oral or essay exam. However, in 2023, the Estonian-language version of the course (the English-language version was essentially unchanged) introduced problem-solving challenges and small group projects while maintaining lectures. By 2024, the course structure had become modular, with IT history, professional ethics, intellectual property, human-computer interaction, and sustainability offered as e-learning modules. Large language models, particularly ChatGPT, played a pivotal role in developing course materials, problem scenarios, and test questions later refined and evaluated by instructors. Participation in e-learning modules with practice session attendance increased from 68% in 2023 to 95% in 2024. The average course result rose from 70% to 85%, and ethical issues related to LLM use were partially resolved. Student feedback highlighted the value of AI in fostering critical thinking, collaborative learning, and real-world problem-solving. However, the study also identified gaps in AI integration for creative tasks and lingering concerns about LLMs' reliability and ethical implications. Faculty adoption of AI tools such as LLMs remains limited, underscoring the need for institutional support, more precise guidelines, and training (including risk awareness). This paper explores the transformative potential of LLMs in education, emphasizing bridging the gap between academic objectives and industry-relevant skills while addressing challenges to ensure ethical and effective implementation.

Keywords: Artificial Intelligence in Education · Large Language Models · Challenge-Based Learning (CBL) · ChatGPT in Course Design · Critical Thinking in IT · Ethical AI Use in Education

1 Introduction

Integrating artificial intelligence (AI), specifically Large Language Models (LLMs), into higher education has sparked a dynamic conversation about its potential to transform teaching and learning. Some researchers have explored the opportunities and challenges posed by tools like ChatGPT in academic settings. Their findings underscore the dual nature of AI's impact: while these technologies can enhance student engagement, motivation, and personalized learning, they raise pressing ethical and practical concerns.

B. K. Smith and M. Borge (Eds.): HCII 2025, LNCS 15806, pp. 328–338, 2025.
https://doi.org/10.1007/978-3-031-93564-0_20

Issues such as academic integrity, reliability of AI outputs, and the risk of over-reliance on technology have prompted calls for a balanced approach to AI adoption. To leverage AI's benefits while addressing its limitations, we must highlight the need for thoughtful integration of AI technologies, supported by innovative teaching strategies and ethical frameworks, to reshape education in meaningful and sustainable ways.

2 Background

Below, we will look at some recent studies concerning the use of AI in higher education, mainly focusing on adoption and restrictions. Rasul [7] highlights both the transformative potential and the significant challenges of integrating ChatGPT into higher education. While recognizing its ability to enhance learning experiences, the authors caution against uncritical adoption without addressing ethical concerns and reliability issues. The study advocates for a balanced approach that maximizes benefits while mitigating risks.

Several authors have discussed integrating AI technologies in creating and enhancing educational resources [10]. These tools streamline the process of creating content, allowing teachers to focus on pedagogical strategies rather than administrative tasks and offer more engaging and interactive learning experiences.

Some results [2] also indicate a significant positive relationship between using AI educational tools and student engagement. Students reported increased motivation and participation when using AI-driven platforms. Students who frequently utilized AI tools demonstrated improved academic performance, as evidenced by higher grades and enhanced critical thinking skills. Specific AI tools, such as adaptive learning platforms and intelligent tutoring systems, were identified as particularly effective in supporting personalized learning experiences. As a cautionary note on academic integrity, we see that this could also work both ways - while the importance of critical thinking in battling academic dishonesty has been covered for decades [8], utilizing critical thinking on 'the dark side' is also possible (for instance, to hide one's tracks, or find weak spots in procedures - the latter is a definite risk in the broader adoption of AI tools in education, and can also be a factor in the formal improvement, e.g. better grades).

Some results [4] also indicated that students who received AI-driven personalized recommendations exhibited significantly higher levels of learning engagement than those who did not. Participants who utilized AI-enabled recommendations demonstrated better academic performance, including higher grades and improved comprehension of course content. The findings support the flipped classroom model as a practical pedagogical approach, particularly when enhanced by AI technologies. However, there are cautionary notes, as LLMs are still prone to hallucinations [5], and unthinkingly following AI recommendations may lead students to trouble. Here again, the possible key for the solution is to cultivate critical thinking coupled with personal responsibility ("my errors are my own").

Ibrahim [6] studied the capabilities of ChatGPT and found its performance comparable or superior to that of students in nine out of the 32 courses assessed. The LLM particularly excelled in factual knowledge-based questions. This also raises concerns about academic integrity and plagiarism detection as most current detection algorithms struggle to accurately identify AI-generated responses, often misclassifying human responses as AI-generated and vice versa. There is a notable divide between students' willingness to use AI tools for educational assistance and educators' concerns about potential plagiarism.

Also, in some studies [9], students reported moderate comfort with AI educational applications. However, this comfort did not translate into increased course satisfaction when these technologies were hypothetically adopted. The study found that projected course satisfaction dropped in response to the proposed adoption of AI tools. This decline was particularly notable for applications that assigned summative grades or provided course support, eliciting higher student discomfort. Students expressed greater comfort with AI tools that offered career support, formative feedback, and administrative assistance than those involved in grading or well-being management. The findings suggest that while AI tools can potentially enhance educational experiences, their implementation must be approached cautiously. Institutions should consider student perceptions and discomfort levels when integrating these technologies.

According to Tayan [11], there is a need to assess how ChatGPT and similar tools affect teaching methodologies and learning outcomes in higher education technology courses. The integration of ChatGPT can facilitate enhanced learning experiences through personalized feedback, instant access to information, and support for diverse learning styles. However, there are concerns regarding over-reliance on AI tools, which may hinder critical thinking skills and reduce face-to-face interactions between students and educators.

First [3] suggests that many students recognized the potential of ChatGPT to enhance learning experiences by providing instant access to information, aiding in research, and facilitating personalized learning. Teachers noted that AI tools could assist in automating administrative tasks, allowing educators to focus more on teaching and student engagement. Some educators expressed apprehension about the potential for AI tools to replace traditional teaching methods, leading to a loss of interpersonal interactions between students and faculty.

To summarise, institutions must prioritize curriculum redesigns incorporating AI literacy and ethical considerations. By fostering an environment that balances technological advancements with traditional educational values, higher education can harness AI's potential to create a more engaging, efficient, and inclusive learning experience.

3 Methods

In this article, we look at the Bachelor course "Social, Professional and Ethical Aspects of IT" (Estonian-language version) and its transition from a traditional lecture-based format to a more interactive, problem-based and challenge-based learning approach in response to the COVID-19 pandemic 2023 and the rise of artificial intelligence (AI) tools 2024. The key questions that we want to address are:

- Does the AI-developed and assisted e-learning combined with a challenge-based approach increase student participation compared to the lecture-based model?
- How do students perceive using AI tools in their learning process, and which ethical considerations arise?

The course participants were undergraduate IT students enrolled across two academic years. The sample consisted of approximately 120 students per year. Year 1 (2023) used a partially integrated AI-assisted approach with problem-solving challenges, while Year 2 (2024) utilized a fully integrated e-learning and AI-assisted approach.

The study will employ a mixed-method approach, combining quantitative (scores, participation rates, etc.) and qualitative data (student feedback, instructor observations, peer reviews). The collected data reflects knowledge and skill acquisition before and after the course, including Moodle logins, forum participation and task completion rates, mid-course reflections and end-of-course surveys, and focus group discussions. We have also collected instructor observations like notes on student participation, teamwork dynamics, and problem-solving approaches to achieve extra insights into group collaboration and critical analysis.

The ethical considerations included anonymity and confidentiality for the students (in all the surveys and logs analyzed). Students were aware of the role of AI tools in generating course content and the research process. All materials were inspected by external reviewers (to detect AI hallucinations and text changes and to verify facts). Some limitations result from the variations in instructor delivery styles and student familiarity with AI tools (affecting engagement and outcomes).

4 Course Methodology

The course redesign methodology was grounded in a structured approach that combined problem-based learning (PBL), challenge-based learning (CBL), and AI-assisted content generation (see Fig. 1). This approach aimed to address both the pedagogical challenges imposed by the COVID-19 pandemic and the evolving landscape of IT education, which increasingly integrates artificial intelligence and digital learning tools.

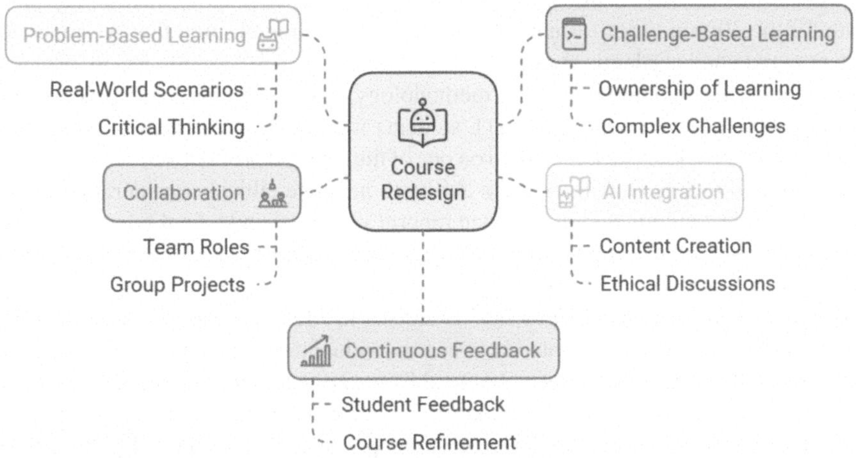

Fig. 1. Overview of CBL, PBL, and AI Impact on the Course Redesign

The first step in the course redesign was to introduce PBL to engage students in real-world scenarios, encouraging them to explore IT's social, ethical, and professional dimensions by tackling relevant challenges. CBL complemented this by posing more complex, open-ended challenges where students had to identify solutions and take ownership of the various aspects of the learning process. These methods involved creating 60 problem scenarios aligned with the core themes of the course: IT history, intellectual property, data protection, risk management, human-computer interaction, and ethics. The scenarios were developed using ChatGPT, where the entire course material (600 pages) was fed into the AI tool to generate potential problem statements. Out of the 100 LLM-generated problems, 60 were selected by instructors based on their relevance, complexity, and suitability for group work. These problems were further tested during the 2024 course to ensure they aligned with learning outcomes and provided appropriate challenges for students.

By 2024, the course structure had shifted towards e-learning modules that replaced traditional lectures. Six core topics were identified: IT history and media development, IT law and intellectual property, Professional IT frameworks, Online communication and data protection, Human-computer interaction, IT ethics, and sustainability. These modules were developed using existing lecture materials from 2022 and 2023, enhanced with AI-driven explanations and conceptual clarifications. ChatGPT generated additional explanatory texts to support student learning, particularly complex concepts. The modules were designed for asynchronous learning on Moodle, allowing students to engage with content at their own pace while ensuring it was interactive and aligned with the course's objectives.

The LLM played a central role in content creation and assessment design. In addition to generating problem-based learning scenarios, ChatGPT was utilized to develop multiple-choice questions and problem-solving test cases for the final e-test by generating a pool of test questions based on course materials. The instructors critically evaluated these to ensure they were challenging yet fair, aligned with course objectives, and appropriate for the 30-min exam format. This iterative evaluation ensured that AI-generated content maintained academic rigour.

Another critical component of the methodology was the emphasis on collaboration. Based on Belbin's team role model [1], students were assigned to diverse teams with balanced strengths. Each group worked on one of the selected problems over two months, which required technical skills and the ability to navigate ethical considerations in IT. The group project culminated in a written report (30 points) and a final presentation (15 points), with peer review (up to 10 points) fostering additional engagement and critical analysis of fellow students' work.

Students were assigned 12 practical exercises in Moodle forums besides the core modules. These exercises alternated between individual tasks and pair work, where students applied theoretical concepts to practical IT scenarios, reinforcing their understanding through discussion and collaboration. These exercises were evaluated on a pass/fail basis, and AI tools were permitted as a resource, provided that students did not directly copy their assignments from AI outputs. Students were encouraged to use AI to inspire and critically assess the information provided.

To ensure the ethical use of AI in the course, students were required to develop ethical guidelines for AI usage. This involved group discussions on the acceptable use of AI tools in their projects, fostering an understanding of AI's limitations and promoting critical thinking. The course aimed to instil a sense of responsibility in students, making them aware of the potential risks of over-reliance on AI and encouraging them to evaluate AI-generated information critically.

The course design incorporated continuous feedback loops. Throughout the course, students provided feedback on the effectiveness of the AI-generated content and the overall learning experience. This feedback was instrumental in refining the course structure for future iterations, particularly in ensuring the balance between AI-driven learning support and student-driven critical thinking.

The course transitioned into a dynamic, flexible learning environment by combining traditional pedagogical methods with AI-enhanced learning. Using PBL and CBL, complemented by AI tools, has enhanced student engagement, encouraged active learning, and bridged the gap between academic knowledge and practical application in the IT field.

5 Results and Discussion

The comparison between the 2023 and 2024 runs shows significant improvements in student engagement, participation, and performance, with notable contributions from integrating AI technologies in 2024. Due to changes to the course deadlines and active involvement, the results have improved (see Table 1).

Table 1. Comparison of the Annual Results of the Courses.

Year	2023	2024	Comments
Participation (e-learning)	Video session participation ranged from 80% for the first to 10% for the last session. Visits to the course wiki increased as the exam date was approaching	Moodle e-learning modules showed a participation rate of 100%, and Moodle exercises (12) were 98%. Constant use throughout the course due to many deadlines set all over the course	2024 related to AI usage
Presence in practice sessions	68%	95%	Presence and absence of students
Hackathon participants	Three groups	Seven groups	A hackathon was offered as an alternative to participating in some practice lessons

(*continued*)

Table 1. (*continued*)

Year	2023	2024	Comments
Smooth group work process (no disruption)	77%	98%	2024 related to AI usage (LLM as a tutor)
Provided feedback to other groups	64%	77%	Feedback was given 2 times in a course time and was not mandatory
Took the exam	64%	77%	The exam was not mandatory
Average result of the exam	63%	72%	In 2023, all materials (both online and offline) were allowed except AI, while in 2024, only printed-out extra materials were permitted
Average result of the course	70%	85%	Example, grade 5 (91% and more) to grade 1 (at least 51%)
Failures	9	3	Participants of the course
Ethical issues with the use of AI or other aspects in academic work identified	2	0	Related to AI over usage or plagiarism

The two runs of the course provided us with the following notions. In 2023, the data highlights that while students actively engage with core, assessment-driven content, optional and supportive resources are underutilized. The low participation in collaborative and forum activities indicates a need to redesign or incentivize these aspects to foster a more interactive learning environment. Strategies to address these challenges included:

- Integrate forum discussions into graded assignments or provide real-time virtual collaboration sessions.
- Make slides and videos directly relevant to assessments by embedding them into problem-solving tasks and adding comments to e-learning materials.
- Group-based gamification techniques or rewards boost team activity and peer feedback engagement.
- Utilize reminders and progress tracking to prompt students to explore non-assessment-based resources.

Furthermore, in 2024 the changes demonstrate effective engagement in assessment-focused and module-based e-learning activities, indicating that structured, outcome-driven tasks are the primary motivators for students. Examples of thought exercises and paired tasks show substantial interaction: Module 1 Thinking Exercise: 1217 views by 130 users; Module 2 License Task: 868 views by 124 users; Module 6 Ethics Exercise: 869 views by 122 users and Practical The slides (923 views by 126 users) indicate consistent engagement, likely tied to their relevance to hands-on work. At the same time, spikes in activity correlate with major deadlines and exams. Engagement tends to drop for non-assessment-related activities, such as optional forums or complementary reading.

5.1 Attitudes Towards AI at the Course

ChatGPT was used to co-develop the course modules, exercises, challenges, and exam tests, and students were also allowed to use the LLM as a tutor, place to improve text and ideas, and even co-create the solution or business value proposition or personas. Now, let us look at the results of AI use in the course compared to those of other courses. What would happen when students are permitted to use AI for coursework? Will the students take advantage of it or find an academic balance - where it should be used or not? Were the exercises AI-resistant, meaning they needed more human-related skills than AI skills? (See Table 2).

Integrating AI tools into the course appears to have positively influenced students' engagement, participation, and academic performance. Several key attitudes and trends emerge based on the data:

- Students demonstrated greater willingness to engage with course activities in 2024, as seen in higher attendance rates for practice sessions and improved participation in group work and feedback activities. AI tools likely made tasks more accessible and manageable, encouraging consistent interaction with course materials and activities.
- The increase in average scores from 70% to 85% suggests that students viewed AI as a valuable resource for learning. Adaptive learning tools, personalized feedback, and other AI-driven support mechanisms may have enhanced their understanding and exam preparation. The reduced number of students failing the course highlights that AI tools helped bridge learning gaps for students who might have struggled previously.
- The absence of ethics-related problems in 2024 indicates that students were comfortable and accountable for using AI tools. This reflects growing trust in AI as a legitimate aid rather than a shortcut or unethical resource.
- The growth in group work participation and feedback activities suggests that AI tools facilitated collaboration and communication, making these processes more engaging and less burdensome for students. The rise in hackathon participation (from 3 to 7 groups) shows that students were motivated to apply their knowledge creatively.
- While students embraced AI for learning support, collaboration, and personalized feedback, there is still hesitation towards AI-driven assessments or grading (as reflected in other courses). Ensuring transparency in AI applications could address any lingering discomfort.

Table 2. AI Usage Comments and Survey Results from Students Year 2024.

Usage in the 2024 course	Usage in other courses
Tasks with the highest usage of AI: • Completing module tasks: 59% found AI helpful • Refining ideas or clarifying focus questions: 51% • Acting as a tutor for new topics: 45% • Tasks with Moderate AI Use • Writing personas: 34% • Text enhancement in reports: 33% • Developing the core solution: 31% • Generating ideas for report sources: 30% • Answering module tests: 29% • Tasks with Low AI Utility • Feedback writing for ideas: 14% • Solving internal team issues: 18% • Writing emails: 19% • Presentation preparation: 19% • General AI Adoption • Many students did not use AI for various tasks: the usage percentages were especially low at interviews, presentations, and feedback generation (less than 30%)	98% of students use generative AI daily in their studies, reflecting high adoption and reliance on these tools for academic work 91% have found effective ways to use AI to support their learning, demonstrating that students are resourceful in leveraging these technologies 55% trust AI in academic tasks, while the rest express reservations, primarily due to: The need for verification: "Cannot trust 1:1 but good for ideas and starting points." Typical AI Applications by Students Highly Used: • 79% for programming tasks • 86% for idea generation or refinement • 76% for completing various homework tasks Moderately Used: • 58% for language improvements • 59% as an analysis tool • 35% for report writing

5.2 AI Use in Teaching and University Regulations

Compared to student use, only 56% of faculty use generative AI in teaching. Of those who do, 52% explain how AI can support learning, 27% introduce suitable AI applications, and 55% explain academic integrity rules regarding AI. Clear university rules for AI usage are reported by 86% of respondents, indicating institutional clarity but limited faculty-driven implementation.

Concerning the future of AI tools, 96% of students find AI suitable for developing interactive learning materials (e.g., simulations) and 95% as a personal learning assistant. Students (64%) also agree with using AI for automated grading of homework and reports. At the same time, students would welcome additional guidance in using AI: 94% would like to learn more about proper AI use in education, 92% want a recommended list of AI tools, 90% would like to receive examples and best practices, and 76% are interested in AI training workshops.

Ultimately, students are exploring AI tools independently due to the limited institutional or faculty-led guidance. This disparity highlights a gap between the institutional availability of tools and the integration of these tools into teaching methods. There are still concerns about AI accuracy and ethical implications that contribute to only moderate trust levels. Students use AI as a starting point, but if they rely only on their judgment for validation, especially in critical or high-stakes tasks, it is not the goal of academia. At the same time, there is hesitancy in integrating AI due to concerns about academic integrity or perceived risks. While the university provides rules for AI use, students and faculty desire more specific, actionable recommendations and real-world examples. Students use AI mainly for ideation, programming, and analysis, reflecting AI's strengths in providing rapid suggestions and technical support. Lower use in creative or collaborative tasks (e.g., presentations, media creation) indicates a gap in understanding how AI can support these areas.

Students are leading the way in adopting AI tools, particularly for ideation and technical tasks, but they need more apparent institutional support to maximize their potential. Faculty engagement and trust-building are key areas for development. By aligning institutional resources with practical training, universities can bridge the gap between innovation and practical implementation, fostering a more cohesive and efficient learning environment.

6 Conclusion

Integrating AI technologies, such as ChatGPT, into the "Social, Professional, and Ethical Aspects of IT" course demonstrates the transformative potential of AI in higher education. The course's evolution from a traditional lecture-based format to an AI-enhanced, challenge-based learning model significantly improved student engagement, participation, and academic performance. Key successes include increased e-learning participation (100%), higher practice session attendance (95% in 2024), and improved average course outcomes (rising from 70% to 85%). Moreover, ethical concerns about AI usage were largely alleviated, suggesting a practical implementation of clear guidelines and responsible use practices.

The study highlights the ability of AI to support personalized learning, foster critical thinking, and enhance collaboration through tailored feedback and problem-solving activities. Students demonstrated high adoption and trust in AI for academic tasks, particularly in ideation, programming, and analysis. However, gaps remain in integrating AI for creative tasks, such as presentations and team conflict resolution, and faculty engagement with AI tools was notably limited.

To fully harness AI's potential in education, institutions must bridge the gap between student-led adoption and faculty-driven implementation. This requires comprehensive guidelines for ethical AI use, targeted faculty training, and the development of innovative, interactive AI-driven learning materials. By aligning these efforts, higher education can create a cohesive, future-ready learning environment that balances technological advancements with academic integrity and human-centred teaching practices.

References

1. Aritzeta, A., Swailes, S., Senior, B.: Belbin's team role model: Development, validity and applications for team building. J. Manage. Stud. **44**(1), 96–118 (2007)
2. Boubker, O.: From chatting to self-educating: Can AI tools boost student learning outcomes? Expert Syst. Appl. **238**, 121820 (2024)
3. Firat, M.: What ChatGPT means for universities: Perceptions of scholars and students. J. Appl. Learn. Teach. **6**(1), 57–63 (2023)

4. Huang, A.Y., Lu, O.H., Yang, S.J.: Effects of artificial Intelligence-Enabled personalized recommendations on learners' learning engagement, motivation, and outcomes in a flipped classroom. Comput. Educ. **194**, 104684 (2023)
5. Huang, L., Yu, W., Ma, W., Zhong, W., Feng, Z., Wang, H., Chen, Q., Peng, W., Feng, X., Qin, B., Liu, T. A: Survey on Hallucination in Large Language Models: Principles, Taxonomy, Challenges, and Open Questions. ACM Trans. Inform. Syst. https://doi.org/10.1145/3703155 (2024)
6. Ibrahim, H., et al.: Perception, performance, and detectability of conversational artificial intelligence across 32 university courses. Sci. Rep. **13**(1), 12187 (2023)
7. Rasul, T., et al.: The role of ChatGPT in higher education: Benefits, challenges, and future research directions. J. Appl. Learn. Teach. **6**(1), 41–56 (2023)
8. Roberts-Cady, S.: The role of critical thinking in academic dishonesty policies. International Journal for Educational Integrity Vol. 4 No. 2 December 2008 pp. 60–66 ISSN 1833–2595. (2008)
9. Rodway, P., Schepman, A.: The impact of adopting AI educational technologies on projected course satisfaction in university students. Comput. Educ.: Artif. Intell. **5**, 100150 (2023)
10. Rudik, I. V., Onyshchuk, I. Y.: Artificial inteligence tools for developing educational resources: enhancing digital learning experience for teachers and learners. (2024)
11. Tayan, O., Hassan, A., Khankan, K., Askool, S.: Considerations for adapting higher education technology courses for AI large language models: A critical review of the impact of ChatGPT. Mach. Learn. Appl. **15**, 100513 (2024)

Integrating GDPR in the School Through Digital Tools – The Teacher as a Mediator

Emanuela Marchetti[1(✉)], Andrea Valente[1], Claus Witfelt[2], Daniel Amo-Filva[3], Alicia Garcia-Holgado[4], Lucia Garcia-Holgado[4], Elisabetta Vidotto[5], Francisco Jose Garcia-Penalvo[4], David Fonseca[3], Tihomir Orehovacki[6], Maria Elena Garzotto[7], Marjan Krasna[8], Igor Pesek[8], and Ivan Ruzic[9]

[1] University of Southern Denmark, Odense, Denmark
emanuela@imada.sdu.dk, aval@sdu.dk
[2] Oerestad Gymnasium, Copenhagen, Denmark
[3] La Salle, Ramon Llull University, Barcelona, Spain
{daniel.amo,fonsi}@salle.url.edu
[4] University of Salamanca, Salamanca, Spain
{aliciagh,luciagh,fgarcia}@usal.es
[5] Arborio Comprehensive School, Arborio, Italy
elisabetta.vidotto.d@icarborio.edu.it
[6] Juraj Dobrila University of Pula, Pula, Croatia
tihomir.orehovacki@unipu.hr
[7] I.I.S. Bona, Biella, Italy
mariaelena.71@iisbona.edu.it
[8] University of Maribor, Maribor, Slovenia
{marjan.krasna,igor.pesek}@um.si
[9] Primary School Čakovec, Čakovec, Croatia

Abstract. This paper reports on the Erasmus+ Spadatas project, focused on supporting schools in their integration of European GDPR data protection in their practices. We see schools as ecologies, characterized by groups of actors interacting within a locality, defined by physical spaces, shared culture and tools. Teachers emerged as the main actors, experiencing the problems created by the digitization of the school, such as the way that digital platforms and social media were compromising the privacy and safety of the school ecology. Building on these insights, we have reconfigured our original aim, conducting a participatory, citizen science inquiry with teachers as central actors, and their students, mediating across other actors and ecologies beyond their immediate sphere of influence. It was decided to provide a *digital suite* composed of two tools: the first tool is a series of self-evaluation questionnaires, enabling teachers and colleagues to be aware of their level of proficiency in adopting competences, practices, and tools to effectively protect the pupils from data breaches. The second tool is a digital game-simulation, called *Viral Sphere*, addressing teachers' and their students' desires for resources to foster a dialogue on GDPR. This paper presents insights from summative evaluations of the *Spadatas* digital suite with partners and schools in Denmark and Italy, focusing on three emerging, intersecting dimensions: *ecological boundaries*, *technology and practice*, and *dialogue and identity*.

B. K. Smith and M. Borge (Eds.): HCII 2025, LNCS 15806, pp. 339–357, 2025.
https://doi.org/10.1007/978-3-031-93564-0_21

Keywords: School Digitization · GDPR · Citizen Science

1 Introduction

The aim of the Erasmus+ project *Spadatas* is to investigate how to support schools in integrating European GDPR (General Data Protection Regulation) [38] norms in their practices, via a research-through-design inquiry. Through our studies, an ecological [20], multiplanes [26, 27] perspective emerged, centered on the teacher as a main actor, whose professional role affects their own and their students' personal, interpersonal, and community planes of participation, in the innovation of the school practice. This became evident in the case of the implementation of GDPR norms. Schools can be seen as ecologies, characterized by groups of actors (like teachers and students) interacting within a specific "locality", defined by physical spaces, shared culture and tools. Through the digitization of the school, the teachers were the first to experience how digital platforms and social media were compromising the privacy and safety of the school ecology, blending personal and professional ecologies of both teachers and students. This situation was caused by the digitization of the school, which was accelerated by the Covid-19 pandemic [1, 2, 17, 18] imposing a strict regime of distant learning [10]. Moreover, additional challenges were introduced by the increasing use of social media by primary and secondary school students, constantly posting content related to their daily activities. Hence, teachers have seen their sphere of responsibility expanding beyond the walls of their schools, experiencing the need to educate themselves on the correct application of GDPR and at the same time to educate their students in the same subject.

Building on these insights, the aim of the project shifted towards the teacher as a main actor, mediating across other actors and ecologies beyond their immediate sphere of influence. Therefore, the design process focused on providing two main digital tools, which could address the institutional challenges of securing staff awareness and correct application of GDPR in the schools (community planes), and the teachers' challenges in educating themselves on GDPR, while educating their students on the same subject at the same time (personal/interpersonal planes) [18, 26, 27].

The first tool is represented by a series of self-evaluation questionnaires, enabling teachers, and their colleagues (principals and data protection officers, and IT administrators) to gain an awareness about their readiness to secure a correct implementation of GDPR in their schools. Other central stakeholders of this tool are school principals, who will have an overview of the data, to support monitoring and decision-making about existing and new staff, acquiring new updated tools or initiatives for training and information, also targeting families.

The second tool is a digital game-simulation, named *Viral Sphere* [6], which was developed together with a group of engineering students from the University of Southern Denmark, and students from Oerestad technical Gymnasium (in Copenhagen). Viral Sphere was developed to address teachers' and their students' desires for resources to foster a dialogue on GDPR. The game leverages network theory [32], to simulate social exchanges on a typical social media network and illustrate the potential harm of content sharing. Methodologically, the study builds on participatory design supported by co-design and focused ethnography [3, 29, 32], situated and online. Teachers and students were design partners in the project and contributed to the iterative development and evaluations of the questionnaires and of the Viral Sphere game.

This paper discusses insights gathered during a series of summative evaluations of our two tools, considered together as a *digital suite*. These evaluations, conducted in collaboration with the project partners and schools in Denmark and Italy, focus on the perspective of students and teachers on the integration of GDPR and how our digital suite is enabling them to educate themselves and engaging in a dialogue with each other.

2 The Digitization of the School – An Ecological Multiplane Perspective

Schools can be analyzed as complex ecologies, as according to [20, 24], schools are incorporating an intertwining of skilled practices, performed by competent actors, facilitated by material artefacts, also including digital technologies. In our studies, concerning the digitization of schools and the related task of incorporating GDPR norms in the school, main actors like teachers, school principals, janitors, IT support practitioners, and of course students [18]. Ecologies are biological metaphors [20, 24] to support the construction of analytical perspectives on human context of practice, highlighting their uniqueness, unity and at the same time their complexity, as their unity emerges from the interaction among different actors, their specific goals, and their mutual intertwining as they play their role within their shared ecology. In this sense, Nardi and O'Day [20] argue that contexts of practice can be compared to a natural niche, hosting different species (the actors), more or less directly interacting and affecting each other, while pursuing their goals, interacting with different resources and tools [18]. The individual actors are then observed in relation to their interconnections with tools, also seen as actors, practices, and other human actors within their ecological network.

Important aspects of ecologies that have deep implications for our studies, are locality and interconnectedness [20]. Locality deals with how ecologies are linked to a specific geographical and material placement (e.g. country and building), which can affect how different species interact with each other through materiality of buildings, environmental factors, and sociocultural and political dimensions. When looking at the digitization of the school, locality is related for instance to which actors have the responsibility of defining policies for innovation and acquisition of new technologies, related steps and information flows, organizational configurations for participation of different actors.

In this respect, we refer to Rogoff [27] and her notion of the three planes of analysis for sociocultural practice: personal, interpersonal and community. According to Rogoff [26, 27], individuals learn by participating in shared sociocultural activities, which could be running in schools or within other communities; in this respect she has investigated children learning how to cook together with their parents and scout girls learning to bake cookies for sales [26–28]. In such communities, learners are facilitated by adults, who have the responsibility of framing and segmenting the ongoing activities into smaller goal-oriented activities, and by more experienced peers. Participation learning practice can be analyzed with respect to how the individual acts and gains new knowledge in the process, how small groups participate in learning activities playing their respective role with each other, for instance as facilitators or learners, and how specific learning activities fit with community-related values, in the way the activities are being performed and in their learning outcomes.

Linking Rogoff's perspectives with an ecological perspective on practice, can allow us to better understand the individual role of different actors within the school ecology and their mutual intertwining, with regards to digitization and integration of GDPR in teaching and learning practice.

2.1 The Digitization of the School, Orchestration and Data Fragility

The digitization of schools has emerged as a massive innovation trend in schools, as part of a general trend in the digitization of public institutions, affecting the public administration, and cultural institutions like museum or nature centers increasingly adopting digital communication and learning practices [5, 37]. Moreover, through the pandemic schools were affected by an increasing pressure to adopt digital platforms that could effectively support distant teaching and learning practices, such as: lecturing, managing assignments and assessment for students, and sharing insights among teachers, as everybody was virtually participating in the school from their home [10]. The shift from the analog to the digital school was also pushed by emerging trends in research and IT industry, proposing future scenarios of personalization of learning, effectivity, self-assessment and motivation, facilitated by tools incorporating Artificial Intelligence, Machine Learning, and Learning Analytics [1, 2, 33]. More recently the emergence of generative AI has added pressure towards the adoption of AI-based tools in education, building on a strong premise that there is a need for "fundamental changes in our approaches to education and learning" [25] and these changes can be better pursued through the further integration of digital tools and practices. The proposed innovative scenarios of the digital school emphasize how digital technologies will facilitate personalized forms of learning through forms of self-assessment, facilitated by Self-assessment features, Analytics and AI, to the point of arguing that automatic measurements of performance can secure unbiased formative evaluation and measurable forms of assessment, and, therefore, a higher quality to the learners in keeping track of their performance than in traditional test-based evaluation performed by teachers [5, 14].

Interestingly, despite claims that the digitization of school has grown rapidly [23], different European countries experienced the digitization of the school at a different rate and with specific challenges. For instance, in Denmark the school have gradually started to move towards a digital school model before the pandemic. On the other hand, in Italy the digitization of the school took place mainly during the pandemic, which caused additional pressures and uncertainties for schools and families, while adapting to exclusive distant teaching and learning practices [10, 17].

However, the digitization of schools has already affected the school in significant ways, bringing different advantages and disadvantages. During this project, handling of academic data [1, 17] has emerged as a practice embodying increasing flexibility in data sharing and storing, while at the same time compromising the security of data through technical malfunctions, leading to leaks or data loss, and intentional or non-intentional misuse of data from human actors [16]. Moreover, educational challenges and a feeling of invasion of the school within family ecologies were also identified [8, 9]. General Data Protection Regulation (GDPR) consists of a series or norms on data security and protection to be implemented by public and private organizations as well as private individuals. GDPR was published on May 2018 by the EU as the "toughest" corpus of rules in data protection [38]. Individuals and organizations are receivers of the norms, so that they are compelled to follow the rules in respect of others, while at the same time they are supposed to feel safer when purchasing services or products, engaging in bureaucratic or simple social practices on the Internet.

Deep changes have already happened as the introduction of digital platforms in the school has acted as a transformative force, affecting multiple organizational levels [1, 17], forcing new pedagogical and organizational practices, and challenging existing roles and relations among different school practitioners, students, and their families. However, there is still a need for in depth, multilevel organizational analytical studies on the digitization of schools [23], hence, digitization scenarios often address poorly the role of the teachers [5, 14], focusing on the dialogue emerging between learners and technologies. However, the teacher stands out as a central figure in the school, to whom students, their families and the school administration refer to as the education practitioners [10]. Teachers play the main role in education, they are responsible to educate students in first place, setting the framework for their students to achieve learning goals, applying educational principles to specific activities to be run in the classroom [31]. Teacher are the practitioners who should secure that students reach their learning goals with regard to curricular knowledge and soft skills such as collaboration, creativity and digital literacy [21, 22], the latter embodying also notions of GDPR and data fragility. The notion of orchestration is proposed [12, 35] as a key concept to describe the role of the teachers in supporting students' learning in the classroom, including lecturing and providing independent tasks. Through the process of digitization of the classroom, the teachers were challenged in their orchestration practice, as they were required to quickly learn to master new digital platforms well enough to use them in class and to instruct their students. Among the teachers' tasks, there was also a need to educate themselves with respect to GDPR and the handling academic data in the new platforms, and responsibilities in relation to students' improper use of the platforms [9, 10, 17].

3 Methodology – Participatory Design and Citizen Science

It is a main goal of the Spadatas project to develop a digital tool that could provide support to schools in raising awareness on GDPR competences among their staff. Therefore, a *participatory design* process was initiated, in combination with a *citizen science* perspective, so that data gathering on the impact of GDPR and the development of the tool could be based on a dialogic data gathering strategy, in collaboration with our user base.

The two approaches can easily be combined [7, 30] as they both aim at facilitating an active involvement of citizens, seen as potential user of a solution to be developed, with an agenda of democratizing data gathering practices and the development of new solutions [3, 29]. Therefore, in our study the teachers and students involved played the role of co-investigators, as they played an active role in gathering data from other teachers and students, in designing and evaluating the solutions, through an iterative, open-ended and incremental approach.

According to the methodology of research through design [36], the design process conducted in this project has a double role of developing a usable tool while at the same time gaining an understanding of the integration of GDPR within schools. Moreover, participatory design methodology, with its dialogic and iterative workflow provided a solid grounding for formative testing for the tool under development, which in turn provided opportunities to prove or disprove our understanding of the experiences of GDPR of school staff and in particular teachers and students.

Similarly to participatory design, the citizen science approach aims at involving citizens as co-investigators in scientific inquiries of different kinds [7, 30]. The notion of citizen science emerged in the 90's as a growing interdisciplinary research field, with the aim of affecting policy making and education [7]. Similarly to participatory design, there have been multiple interpretations on the requirements for conducting citizen science inquiries [34]. However, a series of 10 principles have been proposed by the European Citizen Science Association, which can be summarized as: a requirement for open-ended research inquiries, to which individual citizens or communities can contribute from their perspective, and a focus on real-world problems, such as ecological issues, urban planning, social sciences and technology development, this last overlapping with the participatory design methodology [11, 30]. Moreover, citizens volunteering as co-investigators should have access to practices related to data collection and analysis related to the specific disciplines. Co-creation practices provide a natural connection between citizen science and participatory design approaches, and are being increasingly adopted to secure adequate degrees of citizen's participation [30].

In this study, higher education teachers and students are involved as co-researchers, in data collection, co-design, and evaluation through a series of iterations across European borders. Several iterations were previously conducted [17, 18] so this paper discusses findings from the 4th design-testing iteration (Table 1).

Table 1. Design Iterations.

Iterations	Schools Involved	Outcome
Field Study	Syddansk University Students (DK) from engineering and design, Oerestad Gymnasium, Copenhagen (DK), Arborio School (IT), I.I.S. Bona, Biella (IT)	Interviews and observations regarding experiences with GDPR in the school
1st Iteration-Spring 2023	Oerestad Gymnasium, Copenhagen (DK) Syddansk University Students (DK)	Preliminary data: 7 initial sketchy prototypes and data from local schools point

(*continued*)

Table 1. (*continued*)

Iterations	Schools Involved	Outcome
2nd Iteration – Winter 2023	Oerestad Gymnasium Copenhagen (DK) Arborio School (It) – 3 classes and 10 teachers I.I.S. Bona, Biella (It) – 2 classes and 6 teachers	Second turn of data collection: 5 prototypes from Oerestad gymnasium, tested with teachers and students at the two Italian school
3rd Iteration – Spring 2024	Syddansk University Students (DK) from engineering and design, Oerestad Gymnasium, Copenhagen (DK)	Development of self-evaluation questionnaire based on previous data SDU students have developed a simulation, based on the data from the previous iterations and testing with Oerestad Gymnasium
4th Iteration – Fall 2024-Spring 2025	Syddansk University Students (DK) from engineering and design, Oerestad Gymnasium, Copenhagen (DK), I.I.S. Bona, Biella (IT)	Development and testing of the digital suite (questionnaires and game), new testing round with Oerestad Gymnasium and the Italian Schools
5th Iteration – Spring 2025 (planning)	Arborio School	Additional data on the use of the suite, fix final bugs

Our design process started with involving students from Oerestad Gymnasium in conducting data gathering, together with the research team, interviewing other students and their teachers, including members of the research team, we refer to this stage as "Field Study" (Table 1). Based on these initial data, the students were supposed to create a series of apps-games aimed at supporting learning on GDPR eliciting a playful dialogue between teachers and students. Data from the sessions were collected through ethnographic observations in situ and online [32], supporting by notetaking and ethnographic sketching [4, 19], so to capture essential aspects of ongoing verbal and non-verbal interactions among teachers and students.

4 The Spadatas Digital Suite

The design outcome of our project is the Spadatas digital suite, which includes two tools: a series of self-evaluation questionnaires addressed to school staff, and a game-simulation targeted at teachers and students. In our study, the teachers emerged as core actors in the school ecology, as they were expected to educate themselves and their students in digital literacy educating them in acquiring a responsible online conduct, in the moment they were posting images and videos regarding their classmates. This has caused a sort of "cascading effect" as through the teachers were held increasingly accountable for students' online misconduct, which was affecting the classroom and school, their private circle of friends and even their families in unpredictable ways as we have investigated in previous studies [1, 17, 18].

4.1 The Self-evaluation Tool

A main goal of the project was to develop a tool for self-assessment composed of a series of questionnaires addressing school professionals. The questionnaires were developed by the team composed of researchers and teachers, who contributed to the formulation of the questions, to create questionnaires that would be sharp, meaningful and short, not to be perceived by the school staff as an additional bureaucratic task; the team also provided translations of the questionnaires into multiple languages. The data gathered through the questionnaires should be publicly accessible in anonymized and aggregated form, moreover, school principals should be able to access the anonymized data specific to their own school. In this way, the self-assessment tool is conceptualized to provide a *digital observatory* of how school staff perceive their own competencies in applying GDPR to their respective practice, aggregate per schools across EU. This in turn is supposed to provide first-hand information to the principals about the areas of GDPR knowledge and practices in which school employees might need further investments with regards to professional development, purchase of technical equipment, adjustment of school workflow so to provide better mutual support.

In the analysis phase of the tool's development, we identified 4 categories of users: principals, teachers, IT administrators and Data Protection Offices. The website was implemented as a way for school principals and administrators to be able to create an institution page, and from this page send links for surveys to each of the 4 categories of users. The central user stories/requirements were:

- The principal to be able to create a new institution, and save a link to that institution's page in the tool; using that link, open the dashboard page for an institution, and look at the statistics on the surveys submitted by all 4 categories of uses; finally, the principal can send an invitation-link to surveys for all 4 user-types
- A teacher (IT administrator, DP manager, or principal) receives a link to a survey page, is able to fill the form and submit; the data is stored by the backend in a database table specific to the user-type, indexed by institution and with an automatic timestamp
- All user-types can see an "observatory dashboard", that shows anonymized, aggregated statistics and diagrams calculated on all surveys data (i.e. not grouped by institution)

The system is built around a classic three-tiers architecture. Given that the entire system was to be hosted on SDU servers, we were subject to strict limitations, for example the backend had to be implemented in PHP, and the Database had to be SQL-based. Responsive Web Design (RWD) is achieved by using the bootstrap 5 framework, and it allows users to fully operate the website from mobile devices.

Figure 1 shows the overall organization of the *Spadatas* tool website: the main page (on top) gives access to the "new survey space" page (bottom left in the figure) where the user can create a new institution, the "find institution" which allows the user to get access to an institution, provided the right encrypted key is known, and two dashboard pages (bottom center and bottom right respectively, in Fig. 1). The first called "Auto

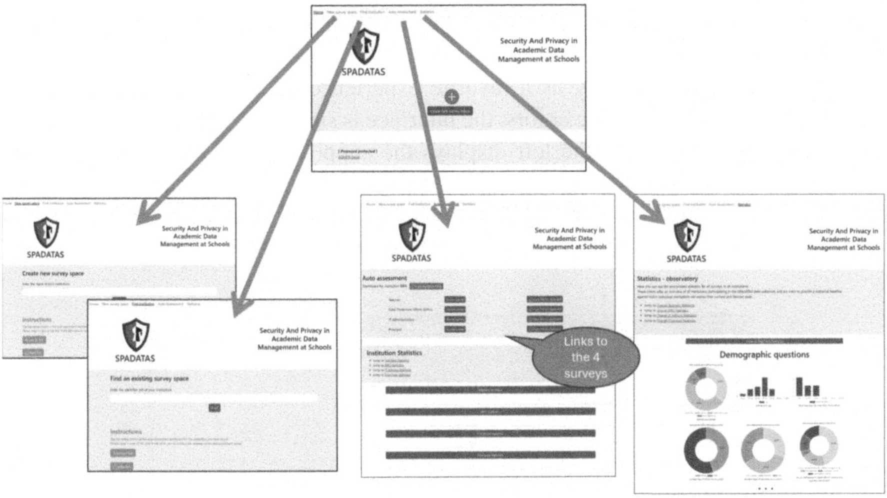

Fig. 1. Spadatas tool website.

assessment" can only be accesses by users that know the encrypted key for a specific institution, while the "Statistics" page shows global statistics and diagrams, and it is publicly accessible. The site also provides an "about" menu. From the "Auto Assessment" page the users can share links to the four kinds of surveys, also running within the tool; each survey has versions in English, Italian, Portugues, Serbian and Croatian, and they all submit data to the same databased, hosted at SDU.

In the data layer, a database was created to accommodate questionnaire answers for all four categories of users; a principal table stores data about the institutions created in the system, and four tables store surveys answers. Each of these tables refers back to the institutions in the principal table (via foreign keys), and to comply with GDPR and SDU regulations, no email nor personal information are kept in any of the tables.

4.2 The Viral Sphere Game

Since our data from field study suggested that teachers felt particularly vulnerable to the impact of the integration of GDPR in the school, we thought of addressing their needs with the design of a simple game-simulation to be used in the classroom to facilitate an open and constructive dialogue on GDPR with their students.

The simulation is called *Viral Sphere* and it was developed by a group of master students from the engineering program at SDU [6]. The game is implemented in Unity and can run on many platforms, in browsers and on mobile devices. The design of the simulation is based on data and stories collected through the previous stages of the project (as in Table 1). The game aimed at providing support to discuss typical ambiguous situations related to posting apparently innocent content on social media and without a malicious agenda, and about how the same content taken out of context might be misinterpreted as ill-meant, attract undesired attention to those represented in the content.

The interface of the game is inspired by suggestions from Italian students about reproducing the experience of sharing Instagram stories, which was indicated by most students in Denmark and Italy as a favorite experience on social media. Hence, the students chose a pinkish-purple colors, the interface is structured according to a palette-canvas structure: a panel on the left displays the supposed posts shared by the main user, a hypothetical Danish girl named Sam Nielsen, on the right a pink-purple canvas visualizes Sam's social network and how new posts shared by Sam can reach unknown people causing her social network to constantly grow (Fig. 2).

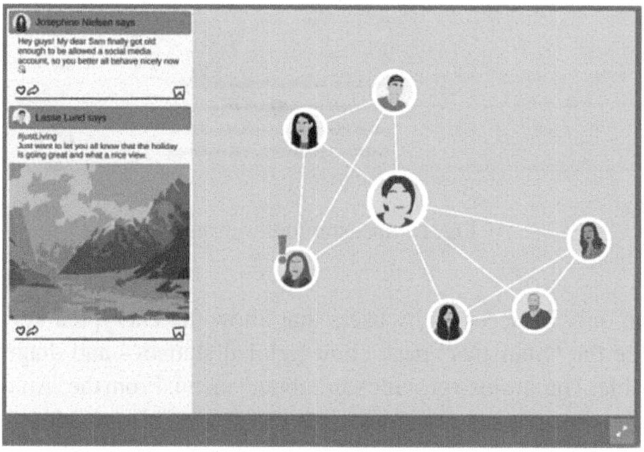

Fig. 2. Viral *Sphere simulation interface.*

The visualization of the social network is based on social network theory [6, 12], where actors are represented as nodes and their exchanges as arcs, to help students playing the game in understanding what a social network is and how complicated it can easily become. To play the game, the students should click on the appearing interjection symbols, signifying that one actor in the social network has something to say and has shared a post.

Playing the simulation takes a short time, circa 10 min, so to be easily included within classroom activities without monopolizing the lecture. In this way, Viral Sphere play sessions can easily be combined with other materials, open discussions, and exercises that the teachers find relevant. Moreover, Viral Sphere was supposed to be simple and straightforward also for non-gamers, not requiring specific training to be able to play it, allowing the students to play almost instantly. In this sense Viral Sphere was conceived as a *casual game* [15], as it does not require high profile gaming skills, it builds on a simple narrative, it can be played in a short time and on mobile devices.

The game aims at representing ambiguous sharing scenarios, in which apparently innocent posts about experiences with friends and classmates, can lead to unexpected conflicts, like showing a classmate mopping the floor, a post showing two friends dancing together or crossing a Pride parade. In the game these posts are shared to engage with friends commenting on own experiences, but as showed by our previous data this could lead to misunderstandings in the real world, conflicts and even disciplinary consequences.

The game has been through a double series of tests, first with Oerestad Gymnasium, where the design iterations started with the involvement of the students, and then with the Italian schools (Table 1); results from testing are discussed in the final section of this paper.

5 Testing Across Denmark and Italy – Analysis and Discussion

A series of formative evaluations complemented by co-design tasks, have been performed through the project, which has now reached the stage of summative evaluations on high-fidelity digital prototypes. The evaluations were run at Oerestad Gymnasium (Denmark) and at IIS Bona (Italy), new sessions are being planned also with the Arborio school (Italy). The goal of this final evaluations are to gather data to fine tune our digital suite from secondary schools located in Denmark and Italy, to better understand how teachers and students are experiencing the integration of GDPR in their schools and their lives, and their needs for support. The gathered data from these tests are analyzed from the perspective of Rogoff's three planes of participation (personal, interpersonal, and community) [27] and three intersecting dimensions such as: *Ecological boundaries, Technology and practice, Dialogue and identity*. The ecological dimension emerged as relevant since the first stages of our design process [17, 18], in relation to how use of social media platforms tends to blur the boundaries between personal and professional/school ecologies, causing unintended and unforeseen consequences. More specifically the *Ecological boundaries* dimension deals with the perceived dissolvement of the locality of the school ecology, as defined in [20, 24], affecting the sphere of responsibilities of the actors and consequences for their actions. In turn responsibilities and actions of the actors are affected by the *Technology and practice* dimension, which deals with how school digital platforms and students' parallel use of social media are reconfiguring the practice and social roles of the actors (mainly teachers and students) in the school. Finally, the *Dialogue and identity* dimension deals with how teachers and students see themselves as being affected by their use of digital platforms in general, and by their involvement in the project. In the following sections, it is discussed how teachers and students responded to our prototypes and how the developed digital suite aims at connecting these dimensions together, supporting institutional and actors' awareness in negotiating meaning on the application of GDPR in the school, from their own perspective.

5.1 Teachers' Training Tool

The first tool of the digital suite developed for the Spadatas project, includes a series of questionnaires for self-evaluation addressed at teachers, principals, IT administrators and data protection officers; this paper will focus on the teachers' self-evaluation, which included 12 teachers from Oerestad and 4 teachers from Bona. These questionnaires have the goal to raise awareness on how the teachers perceive their own knowledge of GDPR as well as their engagement with the topic. The questionnaires should also make it possible for the teachers to communicate areas of competencies and of uncertainties, requiring additional training or readjustment in the school workflow.

Regarding the dimension *Ecological boundaries*, the teachers appear as the actors most affected by the digitization of the school and the consequent integration of GDPR.

As according to Rogoff [27], the planes of analysis are intertwined with each other, so that it is not easy to distinguish which aspects of human experience belong to which plane, similarly in our study we noticed how the digitization of the school was initiated from a community/institutional plane and acquired a *circular* dynamic, as from the institution it was addressed to the teachers, in turn affecting their individual relationship with their work and development of new skills, and then affecting the students with consequences with respect to the relationship between families and the school. This complex dynamic seems to reinforce the notion of the role of the teachers as mediators between the school and the families ecologies, from an interpersonal and community planes [22, 31].

Our data suggest that the teachers experience the digitization of the school as forced onto them, as they were required to adopt digital platforms to record data on the students, such as presence, evaluations, and grades, and to communicate with families. The increasing use of social media by the students emerges from our data as the main source of issues and unpredictability in both countries, requiring teachers to educate the students in their data sharing practice, while educating themselves at the same time, an issue we started discussing in [17]. One of the teachers from Bona said during our interview: "They told us that we should have been of support to the parents of the youngest kids, but were not able even to be of support for ourselves!".

New insights emerged in relation to the need for good training for teachers and school staff. In Denmark one of the teachers said: "We all received a course from a company, but it was not relevant for schools and after a few months most colleagues have forgotten about it." Therefore, our collaborator from Oerestad has created an online course to share with his colleagues, that was commented as "useful", "clear" and most times "relevant". On the other hand, our collaborator from the Bona Institute said: "I had a course on a mobile platform, I took it on my phone on the train or while ironing, but it was not so useful!" Another teacher from Bona said that: "At school we are left to chance, we are faced with the need of erasing data – and added giggling –like: this message will self-destruct in…" From this perspective, the self-evaluation tool was found useful as a way for the school administration, in particular the principal, to keep updated on the areas in which school staff might need additional training. One of our interviewees said that she "wished" that there could be more communication and mutual support with the principals. Thus, teachers have started to organize themselves generating a series of good practices, which have been collected into a handbook available online (as part of the Spadatas project's output), creating shared, meaningful policies. In a way teachers took over and applied orchestration strategies [13, 35] to their own learning process, including peer support, regular meetings and sharing of resources. Hence, new forms of peer learning have emerged among the teachers, in which teachers who feel more competent in IT or who had taken courses in GDPR act as tutors for their colleagues, generating small communities of peer support, similarly to group work in schools [26, 28]. Our two collaborators from the institutions have taken initiative in covering that role, initiating a dialogue on the issue and in facilitating our tests. Moreover, the use of regular social media platforms has been increasingly limited through time, so that currently in both countries these open platforms are used only to send warnings about a new message being shared on the institutional email or school platform.

A dimension of *Technology and practice* emerged from our data, in relation to the teachers' perception of the use of different platforms in the school use and implication for teaching and learning practices. In ecologies technologies are seen as vital actors in their own right [20, 24], mediating meaning as well as procedures for meaning making and exchange. Schools are adopting different platforms, some connected to major IT companies, like Microsoft and Google. Some teachers have highlighted how their experiences with social media platforms have made them skeptical also of the platforms authorized by the schools, when linked to major IT companies. In Denmark we found a moderate skepticism, but a critique on the usability of the systems selected by the schools, which might "not work as well" as desired, or the file systems were found "unclear" compared to the platforms used privately despite regular improvements. The Italian teachers have argued that they do not feel safe as "We receive personalized advertisement, as they know everything we buy or just search (on the web)". Another teacher said that she is not sure about how data is protected if all the schools use Google platforms. A question that emerged during our interviews was "What happens to all the data stored in the school platforms?!" indicating doubts about how trustworthy the official platforms are.

For the final dimension, *Dialogue and identity*, it emerged how the digitization of the school in parallel to teachers' and students' presence on social media, are challenging the dialogue between teachers and students, and their families, and their respective identities. First, social media has pushed the dialogue between teachers and students beyond the boundaries of the school ecology, as teachers and students ended up seeing each other's personal content on social media can find themselves more or less willingly to interact with their students online. This dialogue can be taken in unexpected and sometimes sinister directions from what is experienced in the classroom, for instance in the ambiguous cases that were represented in the game Viral Sphere, but also students criticizing teachers or the school on their social media "walls". At the same time, teachers might be posting news about themselves and their family lives, unexpectedly revealing their personal life to their students and families more than desired. A difference was detected in the communication flow between high schools and family in Denmark and Italy. In Italy parents are involved in the school life of their kids until the final year, with regular communication and dates for parents-teachers meetings. Instead in Denmark students are seen as young adults, so teachers communicate to families only during the first year, but by the second-year teachers only address their students, apart from serious accidents requiring disciplinary intervention. Hence, our data shows that in Denmark teachers feel less pressure from families than in Italy, and Danish teachers did not mention any specific issues with respect to how their personal sharing can affect their professional lives in relation to their students. Instead, Italian teachers have said that they feel "exposed" to critics, from families or colleagues, while sharing or even just liking posts related to news and politics, so they have stopped giving likes to such posts. A teacher elaborated by saying that she felt that they cannot afford any freedom of thought online and the privacy might be "just a word in the dictionary", as any online action could lead them into conflict. In this respect, it emerged from our study, that the involvement of families in the students' school life, and the more contact among teachers and families, can lead to increasing pressure on the teachers and their online presence.

Moreover, it has also emerged how teachers have little trust in available training resources and activities. Hence, a limitation of our approach can be found in the fact that even if schools will be made aware of the teachers' needs, it is not guaranteed that the principals will be able to find satisfactory solutions, as one of the Italian teachers pointed out: "Some projects proposed are of little use to us!" The teachers from both schools stated that they learned more during our tests than through specific learning activities and suggested that they would have liked to take courses or topic-specific seminars at universities as training activities.

In this sense, the Spadatas suite seems to fill a hole with respect to enabling school staff in gaining an overview on the perception of the staff's competencies and which competencies are available in the schools, explicitly enabling to initiate peer-tutoring as well as external tutoring practices.

5.2 Viral Sphere

The evaluation of the Viral Sphere was a little more complex than the one run for the self-evaluation tool, as it required active involvement of students and teachers at the same time. The game was tested with two classes of 15 to 20 students at Oerestad and at Bona, so a total of 72 students in four classes. The tests involved our collaborator from Oerestad, who teaches "informatics", and two teachers from Bona during their classes in "citizenship" and "English". The test included: an introduction to GDPR, to the game, a gaming session of circa 15 min, a short online questionnaire on how the students perceive their knowledge of GDPR and the game, closing. The questionnaire included 13 questions, half of the questions were multiple choice, each of them completed by a follow up open question, where students could share some personal experience. The first 7 were about their knowledge of GDPR and experience with social media, the remaining 6 were about their evaluation of the game.

The interaction dynamics during the tests was similar in both schools, the students were initially noisy but became increasingly engaged with the introduction of the teachers on GDPR and were concentrated while playing the game. The evaluation at Oerestad took place in November-December 2024 and provided a reference to fine tune the test with Bona, which took place in January 2025 (Fig. 3).

Regarding the dimension *Ecological Boundaries,* the game appeared as a valuable resource in representing how quickly a social network can expand. The teacher at Oerestad took initiative in using the game to prompt questions for the students on what they learned on GDPR. For instance, while going through the scenarios illustrated in the game, the teacher would ask: "Are these personal or sensitive data?" and then "Do you remember the difference?", or "How do you expect that those who see the post would respond?" Or "Could you recall a post after it has been shared?" These questions acted as framing for the students to approach the game and provided inspiration for the creation of a guide for teachers about how to use the game in teaching, which has been published together with game, hence the game was used as orchestrating resource to build a dialogue on GDPR and what the students have learned about it. During the test at Bona, the researchers helped the teachers in reproducing the same kind of orchestration, prompting the students with retrieving notions on GDPR that were shared by the teachers. On a personal plane perspective, one of the teachers pointed out that "We are all on

Fig. 3. Left: *Students from Oerestad during test. Right: Students from Bona.*

social media, but nobody has a clear idea about how easy it is for people to judge based on an image, without really looking into the intention behind it." From the questionnaires, we gained data mainly on the personal perspective of the students' experience, especially on their knowledge of GDPR and experience of social media. The students honestly evaluated their knowledge "A little good" (Fig. 4), so average, providing in the follow up questions correct definitions of GDPR, while others simply wrote that they did not know much. From the perspective of the planes of sociocultural activities, sharing content online starts as an individual activity with implications on the interpersonal and community planes, as it is aimed at interacting with friends. Data from the questionnaire shows that students from Denmark and Italy use the same platforms, mainly TikTok, Instagram, and Snapchat. They also share the same type of content: videos or selfies of themselves and their friends engaged in various activities, this action expanding from a personal to a community plane.

Fig. 4. Diagrams *from the game test with Danish and Italian students.*

From the dimension *Technology and practice,* we tried to gather data on how the game could positively affect learning or reflections on the application of GDPR to online activities. Most students evaluated the game as fun, interesting, while a few settled with "decent" (Fig. 4). In the follow up questions, most students gave positive comments, such as that it was a “good game” or “useful, in whosing how data on social media get spread”. A few students added that it was a little “boring” or “too easy”, and that it could have been more “entertaining”, eventually playing in first person; this aspect could be further investigated, even if the short play time can provide limitations. Some students even stated that the game made them more “conscious” of their online activity and “the consequences” of their actions, which was the goal of our design process. The teachers acknowledged the game as a good resource to use in class and foster a dialogue with the students. One of the Italian teachers said that: “We are all on social media, but nobody has ever seen how you have drawn the network structure… it is taken for granted” and that “we have had the police to come and explain how posts spread across the web,” but that without a visualization the discussion on social media remains abstract. This is an interesting comment, suggesting that visualizing technical knowledge on social network could help concretizing the discussion on GDPR, hence suggesting an educational value for theoretical technical knowledge. Interestingly, being the game in English, the second test with the Italian school was conducted during an English lecture, where the teacher encouraged the students to translate the situations shown in the game, recognizing interdisciplinary potential in the game.

With respect to the dimension *Dialogue and identity,* circa 53% of the students experienced occurrences similar to the stories illustrated in the game (Fig. 4). In the follow up question they wrote that they experienced or heard of acquaintances who posted images picturing someone else, sometimes not fully dressed, and these pictures were reshared to others without any consent, affecting the “victims” as well as their family and friends, from personal to community planes [27]. A few students wrote that they, or their friends, regretted later having shared a specific picture, another reported of several friends having experienced the same. Moreover, the students proposed solutions to make the game more relatable such as: allowing students to play in first person, adding new personal and romantic stories, for instance showing young people kissing or nudes. We do not find the latter particularly appropriate and we consider a success that the students were thinking spontaneously of such occurrences. More interestingly some students suggested to add specific stories about school and classmates. On the other hand, other students replied that they could not think of improvements as the game as good as it could be. The teachers from both countries, found relevant that the game showed how individuals could be “blamed” or “criticized” without having any intention of causing harm to others, as “it is easy to simply judge or misunderstand people based on an image, without knowing the context!” This can be seen as directly connected to the loss of locality and blurring of boundaries in the school and family ecologies [20]. It seemed like these teachers were referring both to themselves and their students, to whom they feel responsible. Moreover, an interesting aspect that emerged in both schools is how the teachers sympathized with their students, acknowledging that they are all facing the same challenges when acting online, an awareness that led teachers, especially from Italy, to drastically self-limit their online activities. In conclusion, in both schools it was appreciated that we addressed the teachers’ need for pedagogical materials, providing a concrete visual representing of posting online and related consequences.

6 Conclusion

In this paper we report on the findings of the Erasmus+ Spadatas project. The main goal of the project is to supporting schools in their integration of European data protection regulations. We designed and provided a *digital tool suite* composed of two digital tools, addressing both the institutional challenges of securing staff awareness and correct application of GDPR in schools, and the teachers' challenges in educating themselves on GDPR, while educating their pupils on the same subject.

Results from different schools in Denmark and Italy show that the two suite tools work well individually, allowing to collect and visualize self-assessment data from teachers and other school practitioners, about their awareness of data privacy matters in their contexts (thanks to the self-evaluation questionnaires), and to foster awareness and discussion in the classroom, and across teachers and students (via the Viral Sphere game-simulation).

The two tools in the suite also showed to work well together, as they complement each other, and offer multiple affordances for teachers, as we observed how the tools can be seamlessly adopted in the classroom, across various subjects.

We are currently planning a final set of tests with the Arborio school (Italy). Finally, the digital suite is currently deployed via the Spadatas' website, and can be freely accessed by schools.

References

1. Amo-Filva, D., et al.: Assessing and promoting data fragility in schools: open questionnaires for auto-evaluation in educational roles. In: Gonçalves, J.A.D.C., Lima, J.L.S.D.M., Coelho, J.P., García-Peñalvo, F.J., García-Holgado, A. (eds.) Proceedings of TEEM 2023: The Eleventh International Conference on Technological Ecosystems for Enhancing Multiculturality, 1st edn., pp. 1285–1292 (2024)
2. Amo-Filva, D., et al.: Open educational resources to enhance students' data protection in schools (2022)
3. Björgvinsson, E., Ehn, P., Hillgren, P.A.: Participatory design and democratizing innovation. In: Proceedings of the 11th Biennial Participatory Design Conference, pp. 41–50 (2010)
4. Causey, A.: Drawn to See: Drawing as an Ethnographic Method. University of Toronto Press (2017)
5. Cope, B., Kalantzis, M., Searsmith, D.: Artificial intelligence for education: knowledge and its assessment in AI-enabled learning ecologies. Educ. Philos. Theory **53**(12), 1229–1245 (2021)
6. Davis, J.F., Gaudesen, H.G., Genster, N., Rasmussen, S.L., Sørensen, J.K., Marchetti, E.: Viral sphere: fostering healthy social media practice through playful simulation. In: Proceedings of the 18th European Conference on Games Based Learning, 1st edn., vol. 18, pp. 1025–1029. Academic Conferences and Publishing International (2024)
7. Dickinson, J.L., Zuckerberg, B., Bonter, D.N.: Citizen science as an ecological research tool: challenges and benefits. Annu. Rev. Ecol. Evol. Syst. **41**(1), 149–172 (2010)
8. Foster, C.A.: Your home, the new classroom: how public-school zoom use encroaches into family privacy. J. High Tech Law **22**(131), 131–175 (2021)
9. Garcia-Morales, V., Garrido-Moreno, A., Martin-Rojas, R.: The transformation of higher education after the COVID disruption: emerging challenges in an online learning scenario. Front. Psychol. **12**, 616059 (2021)

10. Garzotto, M.E., Marchetti, E.: Distant yet personal: equality in distant education during Covid-19 lockdown in Italy. Aktualitet **15**(3), 40–51 (2021)
11. Haklay, M., et al.: What is citizen science? The challenges of definition. Sci. Citizen Sci. **13** (2021)
12. Hogan, B.: Online social networks: concepts for data collection and analysis. In: The SAGE Handbook of Online Research Methods, pp. 241–258 (2017)
13. Hordvik, M., Fletcher, T., Haugen, A.L., Engebretsen, B., Møller, L.: Using the metaphor of orchestration to make sense of facilitating teacher educator professional development. Eur. J. Teach. Educ. **46**(3), 417–434 (2023)
14. Jensen, E.L., Archer, L., Ali, S.: Addressing social inequalities using AI, big data, and machine learning. J. Nonprofit Innov. **4**(2), 2 (2024)
15. Kultima, A.; Casual game design values. In: Proceedings of the 13th International MindTrek Conference: Everyday Life in the Ubiquitous Era, pp. 58–65 (2009)
16. Lakkaraju, H., Bastani, O.: How do I fool you?: Manipulating user trust via misleading black box explanations. In: AIES 2020, New York, NY, USA, pp. 79–85 (2020)
17. Marchetti, E., et al.: Teachers' perspective on the implementation of GDPR in schools – a design-oriented case study. In: Zaphiris, P., Ioannou, A. (eds.) Learning and Collaboration Technologies. HCII 2024. Lecture Notes in Computer Science, vol. 14723, pp. 182–199. Springer, Cham (2024). https://doi.org/10.1007/978-3-031-61685-3_14
18. Marchetti, E., et al.: Designing games for GDPR: negotiating understandings of GDPR in EU schools. In: Proceedings of the 18th European Conference on Games Based Learning: ECGBL 2024, pp. 863–871 (2024)
19. Marchetti, E.: At observere gennem dine hænder: tegning som etnografisk praksis. In: Grønning, A., Enemark Lundtofte, T., Kampmann Walther, B. (eds.) Medievidenskab - Metoder og Teorier. Syddansk Universitetsforlag, Odense, pp. 83–97 (2022)
20. Nardi, B.A., O'Day, V.: Information Ecologies: Using Technology with Heart. MIT Press (2000)
21. O'Halloran, E.: Exploring the influence of boundary objects on the relationships between elementary preservice teachers and cooperating teachers (2024)
22. Perignat, E., Katz-Buonincontro, J.: STEAM in practice and research: an integrative literature review. Thinking Skills Creativity **31**, 31–43 (2019)
23. Pettersson, F.: Understanding digitalization and educational change in school by means of activity theory and the levels of learning concept. Educ. Inf. Technol. **26**(1), 187–204 (2021)
24. Raptis, D., Kjeldskov, J., Skov, M.B., Paay, J.: What is a digital ecology? Theoretical foundations and a unified definition. Aust. J. Intell. Inf. Process. Syst. **13**(4), 5 (2014)
25. Resnick, M.: Generative AI and creative learning: concerns, opportunities, and choices. Medium (2023). https://mres.medium.com/ai-and-creative-learning-concerns-opportunities-and-choices-63b27f16d4d0. Accessed 14 Feb 2025
26. Rogoff, B.: Conceiving the relationship of the social world and the individual. In: Science Education: Major Themes in Education, pp. 38–60 (2006)
27. Rogoff, B.: Observing sociocultural activity on three planes: participatory appropriation, guided participation, and apprenticeship. In: Pedagogy and Practice: Culture and Identities, pp. 58–74 (2008)
28. Rogoff, B.: Mutually constituting, fractal: individual and cultural aspects of holistic process. Rev. Res. Educ. **47**(1), 60–83 (2023)
29. Sanders, E.B.N.: From user-centered to participatory design approaches. In: Frascara, J. (ed.) Design and the Social Sciences. Taylor & Francis Books Limited (2002)
30. Senabre Hidalgo, E., Perelló, J., Becker, F., Bonhoure, I., Legris, M., Cigarini, A.: Participation and co-creation in citizen science. In: Vohland, K., et al. The Science of Citizen Science, pp. 199–218. Springer, Cham (2021). https://doi.org/10.1007/978-3-030-58278-4_11

31. Siljebo, J.: Digitalization and digital transformation in schools: a challenge to educational theory? Education in the North (2020)
32. Trundle, C., Phillips, T.: Defining focused ethnography: disciplinary boundary-work and the imagined divisions between 'focused' and 'traditional' ethnography in health research–a critical review. Soc. Sci. Med., 116108 (2023)
33. Van Dijck, J., Poell, T.: Social media platforms and education. In: The SAGE Handbook of Social Media, pp. 579–591 (2018)
34. Vohland, K. et al.: Editorial: the science of citizen science evolves. In: Vohland, K., et al. The Science of Citizen Science, pp. 1–12. Springer, Cham (2021). https://doi.org/10.1007/978-3-030-58278-4_1
35. Xu, L., Mesiti, C.: Teacher orchestration of student responses to rich mathematics tasks in the US and Japanese classrooms. ZDM–Math. Educ. **54**(2), 273–286 (2022)
36. Zimmerman, J., Forlizzi, J.: Research through design in HCI. In: Olson, J., Kellogg, W. (eds.) Ways of Knowing in HCI, pp. 167–189. Springer, New York (2014). https://doi.org/10.1007/978-1-4939-0378-8_8
37. https://www.ft.dk/samling/20101/almdel/udu/bilag/334/1026036/index.htm. Accessed 14 Feb 2025
38. https://gdpr.eu/what-is-gdpr/?cn-reloaded=1. Accessed 14 Feb 2025

Adaptive Learning Platforms and Their Influence on Higher Education: A Scoping Review

Corina Núñez-Hernández[1], Fátima Avilés-Castillo[2], and Jorge Buele[3](✉)

[1] Carrera de Educación Básica, Facultad de Ciencias de la Educación, Universidad Tecnológica Indoamérica, Ambato 180103, Ecuador
[2] Facultad de Ingenierías, Universidad Tecnológica Indoamérica, Ambato 180103, Ecuador
[3] Centro de Investigación en Mecatrónica y Sistemas Interactivos (MIST), Carrera de Ingeniería Industrial, Universidad Tecnológica Indoamérica, Ambato 180103, Ecuador
jorgebuele@uti.edu.ec

Abstract. Over the past decade, adaptive learning platforms have transformed higher education by adjusting content and activities based on students' abilities and progress. This approach personalizes learning and optimizes academic performance, particularly in complex disciplines such as engineering and science. However, challenges remain related to their technological implementation and acceptance by both students and educators. This scoping review analyzes the impact of adaptive learning platforms in higher education, focusing on their influence on academic performance, student motivation, practical implementation challenges, and future implications for research. An exploratory literature review was conducted using the PRISMA-ScR method, identifying recent studies published between 2019 and 2024 in databases such as ERIC, Scopus, IEEE Xplore, Web of Science, and APA PsycNet. Quantitative and qualitative research studies were selected, evaluating the impact of these platforms in university settings and the outcomes they produce. The results indicate that adaptive learning platforms significantly enhance academic performance by providing personalized experiences and immediate feedback. They also increase student motivation and engagement, particularly in online learning environments. However, challenges were identified, including the need for adequate technological infrastructure and specialized training for educators. Adaptive learning platforms hold transformative potential in higher education but require overcoming technological and pedagogical barriers. Further qualitative research is recommended to better understand user experiences and maximize their effectiveness across diverse educational contexts.

Keywords: Adaptive Learning · Educational Platforms · Personalized Learning · Higher Education · Educational Technologies

1 Introduction

Throughout history, education has facilitated the development of societies by continuously adapting to social, economic, and cultural changes [1]. From the earliest universities to modern institutions, pedagogical approaches have evolved to meet the needs of a

B. K. Smith and M. Borge (Eds.): HCII 2025, LNCS 15806, pp. 358–370, 2025.
https://doi.org/10.1007/978-3-031-93564-0_22

constantly changing world [2]. In this regard, the Industrial Revolution introduced more structured and standardized teaching methods designed to train competent professionals [3]. However, these methods, which emphasized memorization and repetition, left little room for personalized learning [4].

In the 21st century, the exponential advancement of technology has challenged these traditional paradigms. The emergence of digital tools and online platforms has democratized access to information and diversified teaching methods [5]. En particular, el concepto de aprendizaje a lo largo de la vida ganó relevancia, reconociendo que el conocimiento ya no se adquiere exclusivamente en las aulas, sino que se construye de forma continua en entornos cada vez más dinámicos y flexibles. Este In particular, the concept of lifelong learning has gained prominence, recognizing that knowledge is no longer acquired exclusively within the classroom but is continuously constructed in increasingly dynamic and flexible environments. This shift has laid the foundation for the adoption of more innovative approaches that place students at the center of the educational process.

In this context, technologies such as robotics, artificial intelligence, big data, and machine learning have begun to revolutionize educational environments [6]. These tools enable the analysis of large volumes of data related to student performance and learning needs, facilitating the implementation of personalized pedagogical strategies. This approach contrasts with the traditional model, which relies on a standardized curriculum that does not always accommodate the unique characteristics of each student.

The concept of personalization in education has gained traction over the past decade, emphasizing the need to adapt teaching content and methodologies to students' individual characteristics [7, 8]. These include cognitive abilities, learning styles, progress rates, and specific areas of interest. This trend has been driven by the growing diversity within classrooms, where students with different cultural, linguistic, and academic backgrounds converge [9].

Within this framework, adaptive learning platforms have emerged as one of the most promising innovations in educational technology [10]. These platforms utilize algorithms that analyze student behavior and performance in real-time, automatically adjusting content and activities to optimize learning outcomes [11]. Unlike other digital approaches, adaptive learning provides personalized access to educational resources.

The integration of these platforms into education could be particularly relevant in addressing challenges such as student attrition, lack of engagement, and academic performance gaps [12]. Compared to traditional methods, adaptive platforms may offer greater flexibility, allowing students to progress at their own pace while receiving immediate feedback. Moreover, these technologies are particularly valuable in disciplines where concepts are complex and require deep comprehension, such as science, engineering, and medicine.

This article aims to conduct an exploratory review of the impact of adaptive learning platforms in higher education. Their contributions to academic performance, learning personalization, and student motivation will be analyzed, along with the practical implications and challenges associated with their implementation. Through this review, the objective is to provide a comprehensive perspective that may guide future research and practices regarding the use of adaptive technologies in educational contexts.

2 Methodology

2.1 Search Strategy

The review was conducted following the PRISMA-ScR guidelines. A systematic search was performed in academic databases such as ERIC, Scopus, IEEE Xplore, Web of Science, and APA PsycNet to identify relevant studies published from the inception of the databases up to 2024. Keywords such as "adaptive platforms," "higher education," "academic performance," and "learning personalization" were used, combined with Boolean operators to optimize search results. Additionally, advanced filters were applied to include only peer-reviewed articles published in academic journals.

2.2 Inclusion Criteria

Inclusion criteria were established to ensure the relevance and quality of the selected studies. The studies included were those that: (i) were published in English; (ii) were conducted in higher education contexts; (iii) provided empirical data evaluating the effectiveness of adaptive platforms; and (iv) employed robust methods for the implementation and evaluation of these platforms.

2.3 Exclusion Criteria

Studies were excluded if they: (i) focused solely on primary or secondary education contexts; (ii) lacked empirical data and were limited to theoretical reviews or conceptual essays; (iii) presented preliminary results without statistical validation; or (iv) consisted of conference abstracts or articles without full-text availability.

2.4 Data Extraction

Data extraction was carried out using a structured spreadsheet to systematize the information from each study, including the author(s) and year of publication, study objective, educational context and discipline, methodological design, number of participants, evaluated variables, main findings, conclusions, and reported limitations. This strategy ensured a rigorous organization and analysis of the collected data, maintaining a transparent and systematic approach throughout the review process.

3 Results

3.1 Data Synthesis

The initial search yielded a total of 1,748 articles retrieved from five databases. After removing 512 duplicates, 1,236 abstracts were screened, of which 1,072 were excluded for not meeting the inclusion criteria. Subsequently, 164 articles were selected for full-text review, and 22 articles were included in the final analysis. The study selection process followed the PRISMA-ScR guidelines and is summarized in Fig. 1.

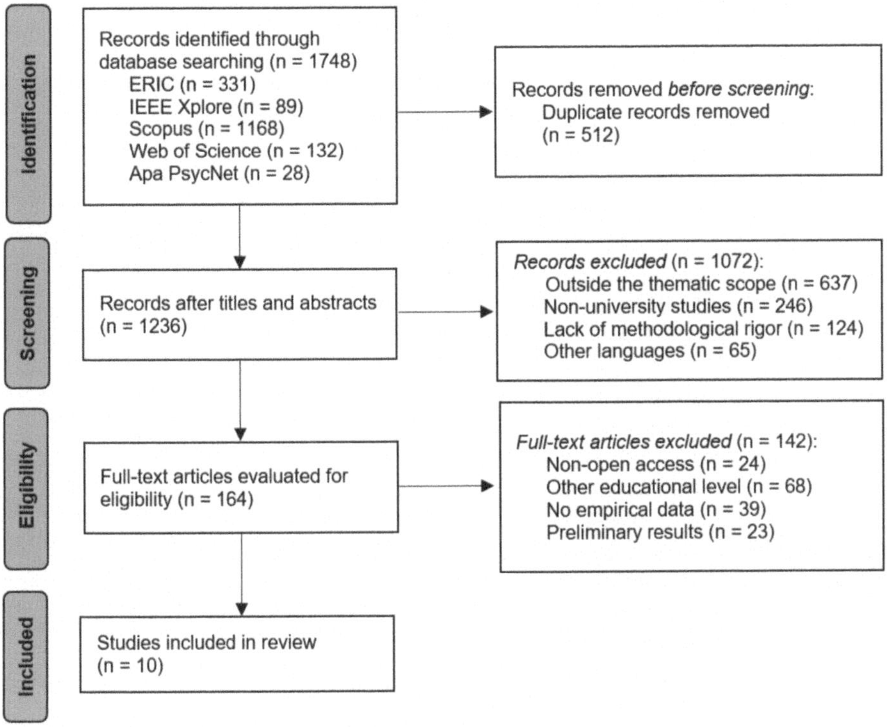

Fig. 1. Study selection diagram.

3.2 Study Characteristics

In the review of 10 studies on adaptive platforms in higher education, four case studies, three longitudinal studies, and three pretest-posttest studies were identified (see Table 1). The case studies provided a detailed analysis of specific contexts [13, 14], while the longitudinal studies examined the impact of the platforms over extended periods [15, 16]. On the other hand, the pretest-posttest studies allowed for the measurement of the immediate impact of the platforms on academic performance [17–19].

Most studies were conducted in higher education settings in the fields of science, engineering, and economics. For instance, Alwadei et al. [17] evaluated the impact in dentistry, while Naseer et al. [23] focused on general sciences. Meanwhile, Boehm et al. [18] explored applications in biomedical systems, and Eau et al. [21] investigated macroeconomics courses. Longer interventions, such as that of Sari et al. [16], demonstrated sustained effects over time, whereas shorter interventions, such as that of Xiao et al. [19], focused on specific tasks with immediate outcomes.

3.3 Analyzed Variables and Results

The most analyzed variables included academic performance (n = 10), student satisfaction (n = 5), and motivation (n = 3) (see Table 2). Four studies specifically assessed

Table 1. General studies information.

Reference	Study objective	Educational context	Number of participants	Methodology
Alwadei et al., 2023 [17]	To evaluate adaptive platforms in dental students	Higher education in dentistry	50	Pretest and posttest
Naseer et al., 2024 [20]	To measure the impact of AI on academic performance and motivation	Higher education in sciences	342	Correlational analysis
Sari et al., 2024 [16]	To assess the effectiveness of adaptive systems on student performance	Various educational settings	120	Pretest and posttest
Das y Malaviya, 2024 [13]	To explore the adoption of adaptive platforms in India	Universities in India	210	Surveys and quantitative analysis
Oroke et al., 2023 [15]	To analyze educational resilience through adaptive platforms	Computer science education	98	Longitudinal study
Xiao et al., 2024 [19]	To optimize adaptive learning pathways in advanced English	Advanced English in higher education	40	Genetic algorithm and cluster analysis
Boehm et al., 2024 [18]	Comparing adaptive platforms with traditional methods	Biomedical systems course	80	Retrospective study
Eau et al., 2019 [21]	To evaluate adaptive platforms in macroeconomics and metacognition	Macroeconomics course	992	Metacognition analysis

(*continued*)

Table 1. (*continued*)

Reference	Study objective	Educational context	Number of participants	Methodology
Demartini et al., 2024 [14]	To analyze the impact of AI on personalized learning	Polytechnic of Turin and schools	Not specified	Qualitative and quantitative analysis
Ayob et al., 2024 [22]	To compare educational methods before, during, and after COVID-19	Mathematics in EFL in the United Arab Emirates	300	Method comparison using ANOVA

improvements in metacognition [19, 21], while others focused on student engagement [13, 16].

Table 2. Findings of the included studies.

Reference	Evaluated variables	Main findings	Conclusions	Limitations
Alwadei et al., 2023 [17]	Academic performance	A 15% increase in academic performance; students showed improvement in understanding key concepts and solving clinical problems	Useful for personalized learning	Small sample size, limited to dentistry

(*continued*)

Regarding impact, nine studies reported significant improvements in academic performance, with average increases ranging from 15% to 25%. For example, Alwadei et al. [17] reported a 15% improvement in dentistry, while Naseer et al. [23] reported a 25% improvement in general sciences. Increases in student satisfaction and motivation were also observed, particularly in environments with immediate feedback and personalized learning experiences, as highlighted in the studies by Das and Malaviya [13] and Demartini et al. [14].

Interventions based on personalized learning pathways also showed positive outcomes. Xiao et al. [19] reported a 15% reduction in learning time, while Demartini et al. [14] highlighted improvements in time management due to content personalization. Additionally, Oroke et al. [15] emphasized academic resilience as an added benefit in situations of global disruptions.

Table 2. (*continued*)

Reference	Evaluated variables	Main findings	Conclusions	Limitations
Naseer et al., 2024 [20]	Academic performance, motivation	A 25% increase in academic performance and motivation; improvements observed among students with positive attitudes toward technology	AI enhances learning and motivation	Lack of qualitative analysis
Sari et al., 2024 [16]	Academic performance, satisfaction	Final grades increased by up to 20%; students reported higher satisfaction with adaptive learning compared to traditional methods	Effective in improving learning outcomes	Lack of longitudinal follow-up
Das y Malaviya, 2024 [13]	Satisfaction, engagement	A 30% increase in student satisfaction; higher participation and engagement in online sessions	Greater student engagement and satisfaction	Limited to the Indian context
Oroke et al., 2023 [15]	Resilience, performance	An 18% increase in academic resilience; students maintained stable performance during disruptions caused by the pandemic	Resilience in response to global disruptions	Small and specific sample

(*continued*)

Table 2. (*continued*)

Reference	Evaluated variables	Main findings	Conclusions	Limitations
Xiao et al., 2024 [19]	Effectiveness of learning pathways	Significant improvement in post-test performance, particularly in grammar and advanced vocabulary; learning time reduced by 15%	Recommended for advanced English learning	Applicable only to advanced English
Boehm et al., 2024 [18]	Academic performance, feedback	Similar results in academic performance; immediate feedback helped improve practical skills and self-assessment	Feedback is important for learning	Specific sample, limited generalizability
Eau et al., 2019 [21]	Metacognition, outcomes	Improvement in self-assessment and learning planning abilities; no significant changes in academic performance	Metacognition is key to improving learning	Lack of control in experimental design
Demartini et al., 2024 [14]	Personalization, academic outcomes	Personalization reduced task completion time by 10%; educators highlighted improved time management among students	AI enables educational personalization	Preliminary results
Ayob et al., 2024 [22]	Academic performance in different modalities	Blended learning was the most effective, with a 12% increase in average performance compared to face-to-face and online learning	Hybrid methods improve mathematics outcomes	Limited to mathematics and a specific local context

4 Discussion

4.1 Impact on Academic Performance and Personalized Learning

The reviewed studies indicate that adaptive learning platforms significantly enhance academic performance by adjusting content and activities based on individual student progress and capabilities. This personalization allows students to advance at their own pace, optimizing content comprehension and retention, particularly in complex disciplines such as science and engineering. Additionally, the ability to provide immediate feedback contributes to improved mastery of key skills [11]. These platforms have been particularly effective in assisting students with low mathematical proficiency in overcoming challenges in foundational courses, ultimately improving their success rates [24]. Similarly, the ALiS project demonstrated performance improvements in statistics by integrating adaptive platforms into a flipped classroom model [25, 26].

4.2 Student Motivation and Engagement

Adaptive learning platforms have also proven effective in increasing student motivation and engagement. By offering learning experiences that align more closely with students' needs and preferences, these platforms foster greater involvement and motivation to continue learning. This is especially beneficial in online learning environments, where the lack of physical interaction can reduce motivation. Studies suggest that personalized content promotes greater active participation, leading to improved learning outcomes [27]. A notable example is the use of Area9 Rhapsode™ in nursing programs, which significantly enhanced study habits and class preparation, resulting in increased active student engagement [28].

4.3 Practical Implications

For adaptive learning platforms to be effectively implemented in higher education, certain practical challenges must be addressed [29]. One of the main obstacles is the technological infrastructure, which must be robust enough to support the continuous use of advanced platforms that require intensive data handling. Additionally, instructors require specialized training to maximize the potential of these tools and use them effectively in their classrooms. Educational institutions should invest in staff training and infrastructure upgrades to ensure successful implementation [30]. This aligns with the emphasis on the need for clear adoption and implementation strategies in the Middle East and North Africa (MENA) region [31]. Furthermore, the role of generative artificial intelligence in shaping post-pandemic educational ecosystems is highlighted [32, 33].

4.4 Research Implications

Despite advancements in the adoption of adaptive learning platforms, research still presents gaps. Most of the reviewed studies rely on quantitative methodologies, such as surveys and standardized test analyses, which limit the understanding of the mechanisms underlying the success of these platforms. Future research should explore qualitative approaches that provide deeper insights into user experiences and the cognitive and emotional impact of adaptive platforms on learning. The evaluation of AI as an educational tool and the design of virtual classrooms are examples of how technology can address these gaps and maximize learning personalization [34–36].

5 Conclusion

Adaptive learning platforms have become effective tools for optimizing higher education, as personalization enhances student motivation and, consequently, academic performance. The ability of these platforms to adjust content and activities based on each student's progress and needs facilitates the comprehension and retention of concepts, particularly in highly complex fields such as science and engineering. Additionally, by promoting learning experiences aligned with students' interests and learning styles, these platforms foster greater active participation and engagement in the educational process.

However, the implementation of adaptive learning platforms presents significant challenges due to the need for robust technological infrastructures and specialized teacher training. These are critical aspects that must be addressed to maximize the potential of these tools. Furthermore, student perceptions of this type of learning remain an area of interest, as some users may prefer traditional methods.

Despite advancements, current research presents methodological limitations. It is essential to explore qualitative approaches that provide a deeper understanding of how these platforms impact cognitive and emotional learning processes. This would enable the development of more comprehensive strategies that not only improve educational outcomes but also enhance the overall learning experience in diverse and globalized contexts.

Acknowledgments. A special thanks to Universidad Tecnológica Indoamérica for its support through project IIDI-022-25 titled "Innovación en la Educación Superior a través de las Tecnologías Emergentes" and to the EDUTEM research network for assisting in the dissemination of results.

References

1. Heng, K., Sol, K.: Online learning during COVID-19: Key challenges and suggestions to enhance effectiveness. Cambodian J. Educ. Res. **1**, 3–16 (2021)
2. Singh, J., Steele, K., Singh, L.: Combining the best of online and face-to-face learning: hybrid and blended learning approach for COVID-19, post vaccine, & post-pandemic world. J. Educ. Technol. Syst. **50**, 140–171 (2021). https://doi.org/10.1177/00472395211047865
3. Spöttl, G., Windelband, L.: The 4th industrial revolution – its impact on vocational skills. J. Educ. Work (2021)
4. Halkiopoulos, C., Gkintoni, E.: Leveraging AI in E-learning: personalized learning and adaptive assessment through cognitive neuropsychology—a systematic analysis. Electronics **13**, 3762 (2024). https://doi.org/10.3390/electronics13183762

5. Campaña-Cordova, M., Castillo-Ledesma, F., Oleas-Orozco, J., Moncayo, H., Avilés-Castillo, F.: Enhancing the teaching of natural sciences in rural environments through educational videos. In: Proceedings of the 2023 IEEE Seventh Ecuador Technical Chapters Meeting (ECTM), pp. 1–5 (2023). https://doi.org/10.1109/ETCM58927.2023.10309022
6. Varela-Aldás, J., Buele, J., Jadan-Guerrero, J., Andaluz, V.H.: Teaching STEM competencies through an educational mobile robot. In: Zaphiris, P., Ioannou, A. (eds) Learning and Collaboration Technologies. Human and Technology Ecosystems. HCII 2020. Lecture Notes in Computer Science, vol. 12206, pp. 560–573. Springer, Cham (2020). https://doi.org/10.1007/978-3-030-50506-6_38
7. Jadán-Guerrero, J., Avilés-Castillo, F., Buele, J., Palacios-Navarro, G.: Gamification in inclusive education for children with disabilities: global trends and approaches - a bibliometric review. In: Gervasi, O., et al. Computational Science and Its Applications – ICCSA 2023 Workshops. ICCSA 2023. Lecture Notes in Computer Science, vol. 14104, pp. 461–477. Springer, Cham (2023). https://doi.org/10.1007/978-3-031-37105-9_31
8. López, V.M.: Realidad Virtual y Aumentada en la Educación Contemporánea. Soc. Educ. Lens. **1** (2024). https://doi.org/10.56931/sel.2024.e5
9. Lwande, C., Muchemi, L., Oboko, R.: Identifying learning styles and cognitive traits in a learning management system. Heliyon **7** (2021). https://doi.org/10.1016/j.heliyon.2021.e07701
10. Alamri, H.A., Watson, S., Watson, W.: Learning technology models that support personalization within blended learning environments in higher education. TechTrends **65**, 62–78 (2021). https://doi.org/10.1007/s11528-020-00530-3
11. Sajja, R., Sermet, Y., Cikmaz, M., Cwiertny, D., Demir, I.: Artificial intelligence-enabled intelligent assistant for personalized and adaptive learning in higher education. Information **15**, 596 (2024). https://doi.org/10.3390/info15100596
12. Núñez-Hernández, C., Buele, J.: Factors influencing university dropout in distance learning: a case study. J. High. Educ. Theory Pract. **23**, 29–38 (2023). https://doi.org/10.33423/jhetp.v23i14.6379
13. Das, A., Malaviya, S.: Adoption of adaptive learning-based E-learning platforms among university students in Uttarakhand, India: a study. J. Inform. Educ. Res. **4** (2024)
14. Demartini, C.G., Sciascia, L., Bosso, A., Manuri, F.: Artificial intelligence bringing improvements to adaptive learning in education: a case study. Sustainability. **16**, 1347 (2024). https://doi.org/10.3390/su16031347
15. Oroke, A.: Adaptive learning resilience: evaluating the transformative impact of adaptive learning platforms on computer education amid global disruptions. In: Proceedings of the fifteenth ICT for Africa Conference, Yaounde, Cameroon (2024)
16. Sari, H.E., Tumanggor, B., Efron, D.: Improving educational outcomes through adaptive learning systems using AI. Int. Trans. Artif. Intell. **3**, 21–31 (2024). https://doi.org/10.33050/italic.v3i1.647
17. Alwadei, A.H., et al.: Effectiveness of an adaptive eLearning intervention on dental students' learning in comparison to traditional instruction. J. Dent. Educ. **84**, 1294–1302 (2020). https://doi.org/10.1002/jdd.12312
18. Boehm, T.K.: better recall, but worse course evaluations – switching from lectures to adaptive learning. J. Educ. Online. **19** (2022). https://doi.org/10.9743/JEO.2022.19.1.12
19. Xiao, H.: An adaptive learning path optimization model for advanced English learners. Appl. Math. Nonlinear Sci. **9** (2024). https://doi.org/10.2478/amns-2024-2666

20. Naseer, F., Khan, M.N., Tahir, M., Addas, A., Aejaz, S.M.H.: Integrating deep learning techniques for personalized learning pathways in higher education. Heliyon **10** (2024). https://doi.org/10.1016/j.heliyon.2024.e32628
21. Eau, G., Judah, K., Shahid, H.: How can adaptive platforms improve student learning outcomes? A case study of open educational resources and adaptive learning platforms (2019). https://papers.ssrn.com/abstract=3478134. https://doi.org/10.2139/ssrn.3478134
22. Ayob, H.H., Hamada, T.I.: Teaching mathematics in an EFL context at higher education; before, during and after the COVID-19 pandemic: a comparative study. J. Appl. Res. High. Educ. **16**, 2262–2272 (2024). https://doi.org/10.1108/JARHE-05-2023-0186
23. Nasser, B.S.A., Abu-Naser, S.S.: Artificial intelligence in digital media: opportunities, challenges, and future directions. Int. J. Acad. Appl. Res. IJAAR **8**, 1–10 (2024)
24. Wang, P.: Using an adaptive learning platform to promote underprepared students' success in corequisite mathematics courses: a logistic regression analysis (2024)
25. Briggs, A., Anderson, T., Gebrekristos, S., Simon, A., Mei, A.: Evaluation of Adaptive Learning in Statistics (ALiS): Testing an Online Adaptive Learning Platform at Nine Postsecondary Institutions in Maryland (2019)
26. Camino-Morejón, V.M.: Plataformas de gamificación educativa para la enseñanza de segundas y terceras lenguas. Soc. Educ. Lens. **1** (2024). https://doi.org/10.56931/sel.2024.e7
27. Mirata, V., Hirt, F., Bergamin, P., van der Westhuizen, C.: Challenges and contexts in establishing adaptive learning in higher education: findings from a Delphi study. Int. J. Educ. Technol. High. Educ. **17**, 32 (2020). https://doi.org/10.1186/s41239-020-00209-y
28. Tretow-Fish, T.A.B., Andersen, B.L., Møller, T.E., Nortvig, A.-M.: what does it mean to prepare for class? A case study on students' study habits in a nursing educational programme. J. Learn. Dev. High. Educ. (2024)
29. Hassan, M.A., Habiba, U., Majeed, F., Shoaib, M.: Adaptive gamification in e-learning based on students' learning styles. Interact. Learn. Environ. **29**, 545–565 (2021). https://doi.org/10.1080/10494820.2019.1588745
30. Alam, A.: Cloud-based E-learning: scaffolding the environment for adaptive E-learning ecosystem based on cloud computing infrastructure. In: Satapathy, S.C., Lin, J.CW., Wee, L.K., Bhateja, V., Rajesh, T.M. (eds) Computer Communication, Networking and IoT. Lecture Notes in Networks and Systems, vol. 459, pp. 1–9. Springer, Singapore (2023). https://doi.org/10.1007/978-981-19-1976-3_1
31. Al-Zahrani, A.M., Alasmari, T.M.: A comprehensive analysis of AI adoption, implementation strategies, and challenges in higher education across the Middle East and North Africa (MENA) region. Educ. Inf. Technol. (2025). https://doi.org/10.1007/s10639-024-13300-y
32. Gupta, S., Dharamshi, R.R., Kakde, V.: An impactful and revolutionized educational ecosystem using generative AI to assist and assess the teaching and learning benefits, fostering the post-pandemic requirements. In: Proceedings of the 2024 Second International Conference on Emerging Trends in Information Technology and Engineering (ICETITE), pp. 1–4 (2024). https://doi.org/10.1109/ic-ETITE58242.2024.10493370
33. Sabando-García, Á.R., Moreira-Choez, J.S., Bazurto-Loor, A.A., Bravo-Madrid, A.B.: Alfabetización en inteligencia artificial en modalidades de estudio presencial y virtual entre estudiantes universitarios. Soc. Educ. Lens. **1** (2024). https://doi.org/10.56931/sel.2024.e4
34. Funda, V., Mbangeleli, N.B.A.: Artificial intelligence (AI) as a tool to address academic challenges in South African higher education. Int. J. Learn. Teach. Educ. Res. **23**, 520–537 (2024)

35. Nurhasanah, F., Nugraheni, A.S.C., Kusharjanta, B., Ardiansyah, R., Widono, S., Saddhono, K.: A design of virtual classrooms through AI, ML and DL to improve the level of learning. In: Proceedings of the 2024 4th International Conference on Advance Computing and Innovative Technologies in Engineering (ICACITE), pp. 940–945 (2024). https://doi.org/10.1109/ICACITE60783.2024.10616641
36. Chuquitarco-Aguayo, A.: Entornos inmersivos y rehabilitación motriz: Un enfoque con realidad virtual y gamificación. Soc. Educ. Lens. **1** (2024). https://doi.org/10.56931/sel.2024.e3

Development of a Platform for Nonformal Education Services: A Case Study in the Field of STEM in Estonia

Kristel Rillo(✉) and Birgy Lorenz

Tallinn University of Technology, Tallinn, Estonia
kristel.rillo@gmail.com, birgy.lorenz@taltech.ee

Abstract. The objective of this paper was to suggest a design for a platform solution that consolidates the delivery, funding and use of nonformal educational services and products. The contribution of STEM nonformal education to shaping the future of the field is significant, providing practical learning opportunities that help young people develop an early interest in science and technology career opportunities. For this, the authors mapped the current state of the sector in Estonia, including relevant regulations and frameworks, identified evolving needs in the demand and supply of STEM (Science, Technology, Engineering and Math) and ICT nonformal education (hereinafter referred as STEM nonformal education), specified business and user requirements and proposed a potential architecture and design for the platform solution. The study included sector mapping and needs analysis, focusing on designing a business platform by conducting a SWOT analysis, applying the Lean Canvas approach, creating business architecture and processes, developing user personas and journey maps, and prioritizing functional and non-functional requirements. Potential biases were addressed through stakeholder engagement and thorough risk assessment. When developed accordingly, the platform will benefit all parties—funders, learners, parents, and service providers—by ensuring transparency in funding and increasing the accessibility to activities for learners. The proposed solution may also be expandable to other activity domains, as well as related services and funding areas like educational software and student competitions, bringing together user-centric analytics based on the interests and needs of end-users. This paper is based on a master's thesis at Tallinn University of Technology.

Keywords: Educational Services · System Architecture · User Interface and Experience Design · STEAM · Nonformal Education

1 Background

Several significant global trends influence education funding and the nature of services, including the design of learner-centred and personalized educational services and technological advancements. The OECD report [17] highlights a growth in community-based and private education initiatives, where parental involvement and flexible learning options are becoming increasingly important. It is also predicted that traditional

B. K. Smith and M. Borge (Eds.): HCII 2025, LNCS 15806, pp. 371–383, 2025.
https://doi.org/10.1007/978-3-031-93564-0_23

bureaucratic management models and accountability at the system level will diminish as digital learning platforms and decentralized learning networks introduce new methods and forms of learning.

One important academic contribution to comprehending the dynamics of education governance in the context of globalization is Public-Private Partnerships (PPP) in Education. It highlights the necessity of carefully evaluating how PPPs are created and carried out to genuinely improve educational outcomes globally, offering insightful information to educators and policymakers interested in the nexus of public policy and education reform [25]. For example, Bray's research [3] highlights how community financing and decentralization can improve educational access and quality. Nevertheless, to optimize these advantages and tackle the inherent difficulties of this strategy, meticulous planning, capacity building, and fair resource distribution are also necessary. To ensure the private sector's contributions align with more general educational objectives and ethical norms, thorough evaluation and alignment of regulatory frameworks and cooperative models is required, even though these can improve access and introduce novel methods to educational content and delivery [11]. Well-established platforms built on blockchain technology can facilitate the decentralization and administration of educational data, enabling organizations to expedite certification and record-keeping procedures. This change also lessens the administrative strain on relevant stakeholders while increasing efficiency [1]. Also, some studies confirm that STEM nonformal education significantly contributes to developing skills among girls and boosting their self-esteem, interest, and participation in STEM activities. This is a crucial intervention for breaking stereotypes and promoting equality [27].

1.1 Situation in Estonia

The structure of the Estonian economy is significantly influenced by the technology sector, mainly information and communication technology (ICT). Top ICT and engineering specialists, as well as technicians and mid-level specialists, are expected to see the most significant job growth, according to OSKA's forecast [26].

An analysis of admissions data from higher education institutions over the past decade reveals that the decline in the number of entrants to STEM fields has slowed over the last five years. However, the proportion of graduates in this sector stood at 26.5% in 2023, falling short of the target of 30% and representing a 2.4 percentage point decline compared to 2021 (1.6%) [12], demonstrating the mismatch between the supply of qualified professionals and the demands of the labour market. According to an analysis by the Estonian Association of Engineers, nearly 70% of the required engineers will be lacking in the coming years, significantly hindering companies' capacity to produce and export high-tech products[8].

The selection of STEM-related specializations among graduates of general education schools (introductory or upper secondary school) is heavily impacted by prior exposure to the field, including in school or through nonformal activities [20] and according to the study conducted by the Estonian Association of Science Education, nonformal education providers noted that the field is underfunded [32]. The stakeholders of the nonformal education sector have indicated that decreasing financing of the sector could result in inconsistent service quality and restricted accessibility for students, in addition to the shortage of qualified tutors to conduct quality teaching [5]. The study [32] mentioned above supports the same: only 54% of STEM-related organizations receive full funding from the local government, 10% receive partial funding, and the remaining portion is paid for by parents (the local government's support also includes state budget support). While project grants account for 11% of funding sources, parents fund 17% of nonformal education groups. There is also an increased emphasis on social justice, as the growing number and share of private, fee-based initiatives in nonformal education highlight the need to address social inequality [2]. Ensuring equitable access to STEM opportunities is crucial to reaching children from less advantaged families.

In Estonia, learner participation in STEM nonformal education is significantly lower than in other fields. According to the Education Registry EHIS data for 2023/2024 academic year, the share of learners in the STEM and ICT fields was only 9% of the total learners participating in nonformal education services provided by the hobby schools [16]. To increase the number of admissions to the STEM and ICT curricula, the Ministry of Education and Research, The Estonian ICT Association and The Estonian Association of Engineers have initiated a programme, "Academy of Engineers". In addition to the other measures foreseen within the initiative, one main activity stream is introducing the field within the formal, informal, and nonformal learning settings [14]. The goal of encouraging interest in STEM fields is to raise young people's awareness of engineering and its career opportunities [9].

Next to the registered hobby schools, the diversity of the service providers in the STEM nonformal education sector is increasing, including schools, museums, libraries, non-profit organizations, and the private sector. For instance, the Estonian Museum of Natural History provides a range of educational initiatives to encourage natural education. Throughout Estonia, the company Mercury provides mobile STEM workshops and interest groups. Other forms, like the competition, formats Robotex and First Lego League or different learning camps, have also surfaced to popularize the field and guide learning. The field's supply has changed, and maintaining service quality is becoming more crucial, as is the financing model.

1.2 Regulatory Landscape for Developing the Platform

For the study, two core domains were essential to analyze: the regulatory environment applicable to nonformal education and possible restrictions on developing digital service in the education sector.

The legal framework of nonformal education in Estonia is defined by the Education Act [33], Youth Work Act [23], and Hobby Schools Act [22], which provides general standards for nonformal education but lacks specific quality criteria for the services. In Estonia, public digital services are regulated by the Ministry of Justice and Digital Affairs, while nonformal education falls under the jurisdiction of the Ministry of Education and Research. However, no specific national regulations govern e-services or educational services provided by the private sector.

International organizations recommend guiding standards for educational e-services. The "SEAL" quality label, which is specific to the service type (e.g., assessment tools, curriculum, platforms, professional development), is provided by the International Society for Technology in Education (ISTE). ISTE assesses, assigns labels, and publishes reports to improve platform reputations. The criteria for a platform include user interface and agency, learning design, digital pedagogy, inclusivity and assessment and data [29]. The "EdTech for Good" framework, developed by UNICEF's Global Centre for Learning Innovations, provides a tool for evaluating educational technology solutions, focusing on their quality and impact in improving children's learning experiences. The framework emphasizes safety and responsible data management, ensuring the privacy and security of children. Additionally, it values the effectiveness of solutions in enhancing learning outcomes and highlights the importance of learner-centred design tailored to children's cognitive and developmental needs. The framework also underscores the significance of cost-effectiveness, adaptability, and scalability [34].

Processing personal data, which is governed by the Estonian Personal Data Protection Act (IKS) and Regulation (EU) 2016/679 of the European Parliament and the Council (GDPR), is the most significant aspect of the platform's development. Any information that makes it possible to identify a natural person is considered personal data under the GDPR [10]. These include the learner's name, IP address, contact information, and personal identification code, as seen from the platform's perspective. Processing such data must adhere to purpose-based processing and minimization principles while being legal, equitable, and transparent. According to Sect. 8(2) of the Estonian Personal Data Protection Act (IKS) Riigikogu, the processing of children's data is subject to additional requirements to protect their rights and interests [24] and Article 6(1)(a) of the General Data Protection Regulation (GDPR), obtaining consent from a legal representative is mandatory for processing the personal data of children under the age of 13.

Furthermore, the purposes and scope of data processing must be communicated clearly and comprehensibly to the child or their legal representative. For information systems handling children's data, it is critical to ensure that the system can readily verify their age. Currently, the Population Register and the Estonian Education Information System (EHIS) are not integrated with the consent service [21].

In conclusion, platform dependability is mainly dependent on data security and protection. International standards and public digital service guidelines can guide the development of educational technology, even if Estonia does not have rules for private educational e-services. Monitoring relevant national databases for consent service use and nonformal education quality requirements is also relevant.

2 Methods

A multi-phase approach was implemented: a. Analysis of the current challenges faced by STEM nonformal education in Estonia; b. Examine existing stakeholders, including potential portal solution providers and developers, to evaluate their strengths and weaknesses in delivering the proposed service; c. Development of the portal design based on personas, their user journeys, and the payment system; d. Validation of the proposed solution through consultations with target group representatives.

The primary target group to investigate is nonformal education funders, including ministries, local governments, the private sector, philanthropists and donors. The second target group is education service providers, i.e., the STEM nonformal education sector, including hobby schools, general education schools, vocational schools, universities, companies, and non-profit organizations. In technology and nature, 26 hobby schools are registered with EHIS [15]; in addition to this, as mentioned above, organizations other than registered as nonformal schools also provide services in the field. The third target group is young people. In Estonia, the target group of youth services, which also includes informal education, is young people aged 7–26. In 2024, there were 288,117 young people in this age group [6].

The author conducted a survey to understand the attitudes, concerns and expectations of the target groups. The survey mapped the opinions and views of funders, service providers, and learners of STEM nonformal education. The questionnaire also focused on collecting attitudes and opinions on the proposed platform. The survey was conducted between 6 and 18 November 2024 and was shared in Facebook-related groups and the author's timeline. In addition, the link to the survey was forwarded to the mailing list of the principles of hobby schools in Tallinn. Respondents were asked to answer nine questions. Thirty-five people replied to the questionnaire.

The Lean Canvas model was utilized to structure the strategy by focusing on critical components such as customer problems, value propositions, competitive advantages, and revenue streams. A SWOT analysis complemented this by evaluating organizational strengths, weaknesses, opportunities, and threats, supporting strategic decision-making and resource prioritization when the platform was developed based on the designed solution. The methodology incorporated personas and customer journey maps (CJMs) to gain insights into user needs and interaction points with the solution. These tools identified key touchpoints and obstacles in the customer experience.

With the structure of a motivation model, the author identified and visualized the drivers, associated challenges, goals, and requirements per stakeholder group [30]. The mapping of the value streams identified the activities and capabilities necessary to support the development of the proposed platform service and ensure its alignment with the needs of stakeholders [31]. The author developed the business processes and sub-processes using BPMN (Business Process Model and Notation) [18].

The functional user requirements in this study were presented as epics and user stories, a common approach in agile software development for defining requirements. The user stories captured the target groups' needs, expectations, and desired values, making them easy to prioritize and suitable for estimating development efforts. The MoSCoW method was employed to prioritize requirements, categorizing system functionalities by their importance [19]. Non-functional requirements were classified using the FURPS + framework for software requirements classification [35].

The authors analyzed system architecture frameworks and selected a microservices architecture, considering the trends and potential changes in the field. High-fidelity prototypes were designed to visualize the potential layouts of the platform. To validate the design, semi-structured interviews were conducted with one financier, two service providers, and three learners, focusing on user stories and the initial prototype design. Feedback from these interviews was used to refine the requirements and user stories, ensuring the solution was better aligned with the target audience's needs.

Methodological limitations, such as potential biases in research methods and the author's subjective perspective, were mitigated through a SWOT analysis to identify organizational risks and involve stakeholders via questionnaires and interviews to validate and enhance the proposed solution. The Lean Canvas further contextualized the challenges and opportunities associated with the platform.

3 Results and Discussion

3.1 Analyzing the Current Challenges of STEM Nonformal Education in Estonia

Users' situation on this matter was gathered through the survey. According to the survey participants, the three most important problems are in the context of STEM nonformal education:

- limited financial support (61%);
- substantive quality of learning (56%);
- professionalism of the tutor or teacher (44%).

The support and funding of the local government (69%) was assessed as the most important factor in the availability of STEM nonformal education to learners (69%), followed by the answer option "possibility of another source of funding" (37%). Equally important (37%) were considered the capacity of nonformal schools and only then the strategic directions of the MoES (34%). It is important to specify that the support allocated by the MoES is also given to the local government, which then uses it accordingly.

The survey respondents highlighted several additional challenges in the field of nonformal education: young people have a lack of time, which makes it challenging to participate in STEM informal education; opportunities are limited at the local level; the difference between the skill levels and individual needs of young people, which places heightened demands on teaching and adaptation of activities; Children with special educational needs often have limited access to suitable nonformal activities.

According to the respondents, interest in STEM nonformal education often exceeds the offer, so young people often do not get into circles of interest. It also found that teachers lack sufficient practical skills and that the organization of studies is often one-sided, which does not motivate young people sufficiently. The availability of information was also assessed as a problem – young people and their families do not have a clear overview of what nonformal activities and development opportunities are available to them, and there is already an overabundance of information channels (different channels at national, local level, service providers, funders). The responses to the survey show that, above all, they know how to see and want to see a solution for the quality and availability of services in a potential service platform.

3.2 Analyzing the Current Actors to Provide the Portal Solution

The authors compared information systems that offer solutions for gathering and organizing information about nonformal education and nonformal activities to assess their suitability for achieving the same goals. The purpose of the comparison was to understand the strengths and shortcomings of the existing systems and their compliance with the requirements described in the project. The selection was based on including different types of owner portals (public (Infohunt) [13], local government (Tallinn) [28], umbrella organization (huviring.ee) [7], private sector (Edumus) [4]). A comparison of solutions is presented in Table 1.

Table 1. Comparison of alternative solutions.

Criterion	Infohunt	Tallinn nonformal platform	Huviring.ee	Edumus
Brief description of the system	Brings together activities and events for young people in their home region	Gather information on nonformal education in Tallinn. Registration for the service is not facilitated in the system but is directed to the specific service provider	Consolidates the offer on nonformal education services and events in STEM and ICT. Registration for the service is not facilitated in the system but is directed to the service provider	An online course platform for adults and students Registration for the service takes place on the platform
Funding the use of services for learners	Funding is not facilitated in the system	Funding is not facilitated in the system	Funding is not facilitated in the system	Funding is provided through the platform. The student or other paying body (school) pays an individual service or fixed fee to the platform operator, and the platform operator pays to the service provider

(*continued*)

Table 1. (*continued*)

Criterion	Infohunt	Tallinn nonformal platform	Huviring.ee	Edumus
Quality control of services	The specialist responsible for youth information in the region sets up the user account of a rural municipality or city. This person will then create user accounts for service providers in their area to enter information*. There is no additional service-based quality control embedded in the platform	There is no quality assurance built/foreseen in the system. Information with the request to add the service offered on the platform must be sent to a specific e-mail address	A registered user adds the service. Quality assurance of service offers is not foreseen within the platform	Edumus supports the service provider (teacher) in different ways for quality assurance, such as course templates, training, etc
Personalized service for learners	Recommendations to the learners are given based on the keywords marked by the learner	No	No	None – packages are designed according to the order of the funder (e.g. school)
Scalability	Regional use	Regional use	Initially, STEM focus, now scaling up to other fields	Ability to scale across disciplines
Platform development and management	State budget	Local government budget	ETHL budget	Edumus business model

* A statewide institution, representative or umbrella organization can add information about nationwide opportunities.

Infohunt.ee stands out from other alternatives by providing local governments and service providers with statistics on the opportunities for youth work, informal education and nonformal activities in the region. It includes the number of activities, statistics on participants (if registration takes place through the portal) and an overview of the areas and distribution of activity types. In addition, the portal motivates young people through a bonus system, where points can be accumulated for participation and redeemed in exchange for prizes.

The described platforms provide an important reference base but do not fully cover the functionalities and objectives of the platform proposed in the master's thesis. They also lack a comprehensive user-centric funding management mechanism that connects the learner, the service provider, and the funder. In addition, these systems' quality control and impact assessment tools are insufficient to provide stakeholders with a transparent overview of the effectiveness of services. The platform solution should seek to fill these gaps by offering a more comprehensive and adaptable solution to support STEM nonformal education.

3.3 Design Solution Base Through Personas and Customer Journey Maps

In order to get to know the parties involved in the service for whom to design the platform, the author compiled three personas: the learner, the service provider and the funder, according to the analysis of documents in the field and the results of the survey: a. the funder, Mari Kask, a 45-year-old local government specialist, seeks to improve the availability and quality of STEM nonformal education through simplified administration and data-driven decision-making; b.the service provider, Andres Mets, a 38-year-old robotics school leader, faces challenges like tutor shortages, unstable funding, and high administrative burdens, aiming to expand offerings and ensure sustainability; c. the learner, Laura Tamm, a 14-year-old student, struggles with fragmented information and limited opportunities, seeking engaging and practical learning experiences to develop her IT skills, influenced by family, peers, and accessibility. These personas highlight diverse needs and challenges, driving the platform's user-centred design.

On customer journey maps, the author described the user journey of the platform as steps from the emergence of the need and contact with the platform to the achievement of the goal. The purpose of user journey cards is to understand better the customer's needs and the processes used to address them. The platform's design accommodates the distinct journeys of its three key stakeholder groups, highlighting its potential to drive engagement and efficiency. For learners, the journey begins with raising awareness, exploring the platform, mapping personal interests, and selecting activities, followed by skill development during participation. Feedback mechanisms and personalized recommendations ensure ongoing engagement and long-term development. Service providers embark on their journey by familiarising themselves with the platform, adding activities, creating tailored offers, managing participants and resources, and collecting feedback to enhance service quality. They conclude with data-driven analysis to refine their offerings.

On the other hand, funders map sectoral needs, explore platform functionalities, and make informed funding decisions. Their journey continues with monitoring and reporting on funding impacts, culminating in performance assessments and updated strategies. These diverse, interconnected journeys demonstrate the platform's capacity to foster collaboration, improve user experiences, and deliver measurable outcomes.

3.4 Business Architecture and System Analysis

With the structure of the motivation model, the key drivers, such as economic sustainability and access to quality services, along with associated challenges, including insufficient funding and a shortage of teachers and mentors, were visualized and identified. Such structured visualization and alignment were carried out per each stakeholder group. The model also outlined goals relevant to the stakeholders, such as offering diverse services and updating funding models and requirements, including data-driven quality assurance mechanisms and a consolidated overview of learning opportunities.

Based on the business and target group analysis, functional requirements included features such as personalized learner recommendations based on interests and skills, payment systems fit to ensure transparency and administrative tools for service providers to enhance usability. The identified non-functional requirements, classified using the FURPS +framework, highlighted critical considerations such as system scalability to accommodate growing user demand, data security measures compliant with GDPR, and high availability to ensure uninterrupted service delivery.

For the architectural design of the proposed platform, the component diagram outlined its core modules and interactions. Key components foreseen include the user management module for administrating learner, service provider, and funder roles and accounts, the payment system for managing transactions, and the analytics module for generating data-driven insights to improve service quality and decision-making. The diagram also highlights integration capabilities with external systems, such as national education databases, ensuring interoperability and data exchange. Such architectural design is planned to ensure scalability, modularity, and adaptability to meet the evolving needs of stakeholders and the platform's strategic objectives.

3.5 Results Validation

To validate and refine the functional requirements of the proposed design, semi-structured interviews were conducted with one funder, two service providers and three learners. The interviews aimed to obtain feedback on the user stories and the initial prototype design.

- According to the funder's representative, the user stories were understandable and met their expectations for the planned platform. The service provider's representative assessed that adding services to the platform was straightforward and justified. It is recommended that a guiding visual workflow or checklist be included to identify ambiguities in entering services and meeting the planned quality criteria.
- Service providers emphasized the importance of transparency in how money is distributed.
- For learners, the users, their priorities, and the proposed designs were appropriate and understandable. Young people wanted the opportunity to share their activities and achievements with friends. Also highlighted was the need to add more visuals to the design in the case of authentication HarID or e-government authentication solution (13- and 14-year-old girl) and the complexity of the design to present their progress on the platform. A 17-year-old young man considered it very important that the platform offer him automatic and personalized recommendations, as he may not

always know the right keywords or be able to identify the offer of his interests. He also suggested adding e-sports activities and competitions to the platform, which he believes would increase interest and participation opportunities among young people.

Based on the results of the interviews, requirements and user stories were adjusted to better meet the target group's needs.

4 Conclusion

The design developed for developing a platform for nonformal education services in Estonia addresses critical challenges in STEM education, including limited financial support, inconsistent service quality, and a shortage of qualified tutors. By consolidating funding, service delivery, and user engagement into a user-centric digital platform, the project seeks to enhance accessibility, ensure transparency, and elevate the quality of STEM nonformal education.

The platform's proposed features include an innovative payment system, advanced data analytics for personalized recommendations, and quality assurance mechanisms to improve user experience. Validation through surveys and interviews with funders, service providers, and learners affirmed the platform's relevance and usability.

Key strengths of the platform include its adaptability, data-driven decision-making capabilities regarding financing and service delivery, and potential scalability across other educational and funding domains. Nonetheless, challenges remain, including securing sustainable funding, navigating resistance to change in the education sector, and adhering to data protection regulations. Successful implementation will require collaboration with stakeholders, innovative funding strategies, and a strong technical infrastructure.

The proposed solution aims to bridge the gap between demand and supply in STEM nonformal education, fostering inclusivity and equipping youth with the skills needed for a technology-driven future. Its scalability and focus on innovation position the platform as a model for similar initiatives in other domains.

References

1. Alam, A.: Platform utilising blockchain technology for elearning and online education for open sharing of academic proficiency and progress records. In: Asokan, R., Ruiz, D.P., Baig, Z.A., Piramuthu, S. (eds) Smart Data Intelligence. Algorithms for Intelligent Systems. Springer, Singapore (2022). https://doi.org/10.1007/978-981-19-3311-0_26
2. Keskus, A.: Huvihariduse kättesaadavus Eestis (2025)
3. Bray, M.: Decentralization of Education: Community Financing, vol. 36. World Bank Publications (1996)
4. Ruiz-Bartolomé, E., Greca, I.M.: Extracurricular program for girls to improve competencies and self-concept in science and technology. Educ. Sci. **13**(1), 70 (2023)
5. E-Education. Edumus. https://school.edumus.ee/. Accessed 25 Jan 2025
6. Eesti Huvihariduse Liit. Avalik pöördumine haridus-ja teadusministrile (2024)
7. Eesti Statistikaamet. Eesti Statistika: Noored (2024). https://www.stat.ee/et/avasta-statistikat/valdkonnad/heaolu/noored

8. Eesti Teadushuvihariduse Liit. Huviringid. https://www.huviring.ee/. Accessed 25 Jan 2025
9. Estonian Association of Engineers. Analüüs: Eestil puudub süsteemne plaan inseneride põua lahendamiseks. Postimees (2023)
10. Estonian Association of Engineers. Eesti Inseneride Liit: Tehnoloogiahüpe (2023)
11. European Parliament, European Council. Regulation (EU) 2016/679 of the European Parliament and of the Council. Official Journal of the European Union (2016). L_2016119EN.01000101.xml
12. Hanemann, U.: Non-state actors in non-formal youth and adult education, 109–110. UNESCO (2021)
13. Haridus - ja Teadusministeerium. Tark ja tegus rahvas" 2023. aasta tulemusaruanne (2024)
14. Haridus-ja Noorteamet. Infohunt. https://infohunt.ee/. Accessed 25 Jan 2025
15. Haridus-ja Teadusministeerium. Huviharidusstandard. Riigi Teataja (2007). https://www.riigiteataja.ee/akt/12809661
16. Haridus-ja Teadusministeerium. Huvikoolid. Haridussilm (2024). https://haridussilm.ee/ee/huviharidus/huviharidus/huvikoolid
17. Haridussilm. Haridussilm: Huvikoolis õppijad. Ministry of Education and Research (2025)
18. OECD. Trends Shaping Education 2022, 28–29 (2022)
19. Object Management Group. Business Process Model and Notation (2013). https://www.omg.org/spec/BPMN/2.0.2/PDF
20. Paradigm, V.: Prioritizing Requirements with MoSCoW Method: A Guide for Agile Projects. https://guides.visual-paradigm.com/prioritizing-requirements-with-moscow-method-a-guide-for-agile-projects. Accessed 25 Jan 2025
21. Pedaste, M., Külli, K., Tõnisson, E., Palts, T., Altin, H., Rantsus, R.: What happens to it education? the case in estonia with some recommendations for international discussion. Int. J. Inform. Educ. Technol. **7**(3), 204–211 (2016)
22. Riigi Infosüsteemide Amet. Nõusolekuteenus (2025). https://www.ria.ee/riigi-infosusteem/inimkeskne-andmehaldus/nousolekuteenus
23. Riigikogu. Huvikooli seadus. Riigi Teataja (2017). https://www.riigiteataja.ee/akt/13339594?leiaKehtiv
24. Riigikogu. Noorsootöö seadus. Riigi Teataja (2020). https://www.riigiteataja.ee/akt/116062020010?leiaKehtiv
25. Riigikogu. Personal Data Protection Act. Riigi Teataja (2025). https://www.riigiteataja.ee/akt/131122024044
26. Robertson, S., Mundy, K., Verger, A. (Eds.): Public Private Partnerships in Education: New Actors and Modes of Governance in a Globalizing World. Edward Elgar Publishing (2012)
27. Rosenblad, Y., Leoma, R., Krusell, S.: OSKA üldprognoos 2022–2031: Ülevaade Eesti tööturu olukorrast, tööjõuvajadusest ning sellest tulenevast koolitusvajadusest. Kutsekoda (2023)
28. Tallinn, Huvitegevus noortele. Tallinn. https://www.tallinn.ee/et/huvitegevus-noortele/huvikoolid. Accessed 25 Jan 2025
29. The International Society for Technology in Education. ISTE Seal Standard –Canva Finding Report (2024). https://cms-live-media.iste.org/iste-seal/reports/Canvas_Findings_Report_May_2024.pdf?_ga=2.215398992.677092759.1736244770-372082815.1728312315
30. The Open Group, "ArchiMate® 3.2 Specification: Motivation elements"(2009). https://pubs.opengroup.org/architecture/archimate32-doc/ch-Motivation-Elements.html
31. The Open Group, "TOGAF® Series Guide: Value Streams."(2022). https://pubs.opengroup.org/togaf-standard/business-architecture/value-streams.html
32. Tohver, E.: Loodus - ja täppisteaduste ning tehnoloogia (LTT) valdkonna huvitegevus ja -haridus Eesti üldharidus - ja huvikoolides (p. 36). Eesti Teadushuvihariduse Liit (2023)
33. Ülemnõukogu. Eesti Vabariigi haridusseadus. Riigi Teataja (2022). https://www.riigiteataja.ee/akt/115032022004

34. UNICEF. EdTech for Good. A Global Framework for Safe, Inclusive and Impactful EdTech. Unicef Learning Innovation Hub. https://www.unicef.org/digitaleducation/edtech-for-good. Accessed 25 Jan 2025
35. Ziemek, M.: Documenting non-functional requirements using FURPS+ (2022). https://marcinziemek.com/blog/content/articles/8/article_en.html

Bridging the Gap: The Role of Effective Communication Strategies in Fostering a Supportive Academic Environment for Students

Renee Swaby-Frazer[1(✉)] and Glenda Gay[2]

[1] The University of the West Indies, Global Campus, Kingston, Jamaica
renee.swaby-frazer@uwi.edu

[2] The University of the West Indies, Global Campus, Saint Michael, Barbados

Abstract. This study examines the challenges students face in higher education institutions, specifically the disconnect between centralized support systems and individualized student needs. This paper explores the delays experienced by graduate students at the online campus of a higher education institution in the Caribbean when contacting their administrators or faculty. Data were collected from 87 graduate students through a comprehensive survey measuring demographic information, communication experiences, needs, expectations, and preferences. Analysis revealed that students predominantly utilized email communication with facilitators and direct contact with academic advisors. Primary challenges identified include delayed response times, difficulty identifying appropriate institutional contacts, and inconsistent information dissemination. The findings suggest that clear communication protocols may reduce the overwhelming number of emails. Students preferred a dedicated team over automated systems or FAQs. Future research could involve focus groups to explore the role of human interaction.

Keywords: Higher Education · Communication · Frequently Asked Questions

1 Introduction

Effective communication between higher education institutions and their students is essential to promote a supportive academic environment. As universities strive to provide students with the necessary tools and resources, the ability to exchange information efficiently and accurately becomes increasingly important [1]. The level of responsiveness expected is not merely about information dissemination; it is a collaborative process that involves understanding students' needs, responding to their inquiries, anticipating potential challenges, promoting a sense of belonging and participation [2]. However, many graduate students report challenges in their interactions with faculty and administrative staff, revealing a gap between institutional intentions and students' experiences [3]. In measuring the ability to transmit information accurately and in a timely manner, communication strategies must not only be timely but also resonate with the values and

B. K. Smith and M. Borge (Eds.): HCII 2025, LNCS 15806, pp. 384–395, 2025.
https://doi.org/10.1007/978-3-031-93564-0_24

identities of its students [4]. The navigation of the complex layers of support services therefore requires a clear understanding of the available resources, which can still be undermined by poor communication practices [5].

The challenges faced by students in higher education institutions often originate from a disconnect between the centralized support systems and students' individual needs. For example, digital transformation in higher education has not always led to better communication; instead, it has occasionally exacerbated the existing barriers [6]. This perspective is shared by [7], who reported that communication strategies must evolve to face the main challenges of accessibility and inclusion. The impression that these deficiencies can significantly affect the commitment of students, and their general academic experience cannot be underscored.

In the exploration of the perceptions of graduate students, there is a growing demand for customized communications tailored to the unique circumstances of the students [8]. This requires a deviation from unique communication models, pushing higher education institutions to develop more nuanced strategies. The implementation of intelligent assistants could serve as a means of improving the effectiveness of communication in higher education to provide students with custom-made information in formats that are more useful, potentially filling the gaps in communication [9]. Alternatively, centralized support systems serve as precious resources for graduate students, their effectiveness depends largely on the underlying communication strategies employed by the institutions [10]. Recognizing the complex interaction of these factors is essential to promote an engaging and support learning environment. Therefore, continuous evaluation and the improvement of communication strategies will be fundamental to overcoming existing challenges and improving the experiences of graduate students in higher education institutions [11, 12]. It is therefore important to understand the effectiveness and timeliness of various methods of communication when students make requests for information or support. This includes their use of electronic mail, calls to faculty or administrators, as well as in-person visits. This study examined their perceptions regarding which communication channels provided quicker or more satisfactory responses to their inquiries. This paper therefore sought the opinions of graduate students registered at the online campus of a higher education institution in the Caribbean to address the following questions:

1. What challenges do graduate students encounter when attempting to seek academic or administrative support?
2. How do graduate students evaluate the effectiveness of different communication channels for their requests?

2 Literature Review

The paper seeks to determine the best practices that could reduce the unique challenges faced by graduate students who require speedy responses in order to make decisions as they progress in their academic journey. It also evaluated their perceptions of three methods of communication chosen in an attempt to reduce the frequency of delays in response to their queries.

Email Communication. Electronic mail (email) is a typical form of communication in personal, professional and educational settings, by providing a method of electronically exchanging information [13]. However, this method is known to have delays based on the asynchronous nature of this type of communication, resulting in difficulty in determining the urgency or importance of an email [14]. This delay in responding to an email message can lead to frustration, especially when its contents are time sensitive. In an education setting, students often email faculty and administrators with urgent queries such as those relating to course registration and fee payments. However, responding to numerous emails usually takes some time to provide information which results in delays. More so, some email messages are overlooked at peak times during the semester when the high volume of email messages received by faculty and administrators could become overwhelming, resulting in delays to student queries [15].

Frequently Asked Questions (FAQs). FAQs are usually placed on the campus' website as a self-service option to lessen the burden of administrative personnel by proactively addressing common queries. FAQs are particularly beneficial in providing easily accessible and detailed information to help students quickly find answers to their questions without the need to await a faculty or staff response [16]. However, while it may address common queries, FAQs may not address every specific or nuanced query, which leads to situations in which students do not find the answers they need. In addition, the static nature of FAQs could become outdated if they are not reviewed regularly, and students could become discouraged if they perceive that these questions lack depth or specificity [17].

Dedicated Communication Teams. The presence of a team of dedicated staff could play a key role in filling the gap between students and administrative services. These teams aim to manage various requests on campus websites – by responding to communications across multiple platforms, including email, helpdesk channels, and FAQs. [18]. These teams cater to the needs of students in order to improve responsiveness and satisfaction in communication. Additionally, these teams can proactively address common issues concerning students, thus improving their overall experience [19]. However, it is essential that these teams maintain visibility and accessibility since the lack of proactive communication may cause students to feel isolated or not supported [20].

Challenges Faced by Graduate Students. Despite the advantages of each communication method, they have unique challenges that depend mainly on the nature of the inquiry. For example, although email allows for detailed information and sharing of documents, there are inherent delays in responses, significantly impacting urgent issues, registration deadlines and financial requirements [14]. On the contrary, FAQs can effectively provide immediate access to commonly sought information but may fall short of addressing specific or unforeseen student inquiries [16]. Additionally, dedicated communication channels such as AI chatbots can offer quick responses but lack the ability to understand the complexities of specific student queries [15]. Other challenges are noted below.

Overload of Information. This is a widespread problem that complicates the process of providing appropriate academic support. The overwhelming volume of information available on institutional websites and communication platforms could lead to significant confusion among students. With several sources of information available, students find it difficult to discern relevant and precise content linked to their requests [21]. This deluge of information contributes not only to anxiety but can also lead to unanswered critical questions, ultimately stifling academic progress and satisfaction.

Insufficient Support Resources. Another critical aspect is insufficient support resources available for graduate students. The importance of accessible, timely, and sufficient academic support services is linked to student satisfaction; however, many institutions struggle to meet the demand of these queries [22]. Graduate students frequently point out that the response times of support staff can be excessively long, leaving them to browse for solutions without the necessary guidance. This exacerbates students' feelings of uncertainty and anxiety especially as they make research-related decisions [23]. Faced with such inadequate resources, students frequently express feelings of helplessness and distress, which can again lead to their disengagement from their studies.

Response Times and Academic Success. The complexity of students' research process requires rapid and precise feedback to allow effective decision-making during their academic journey. The effectiveness of response times as they seek academic support has important implications for their academic experiences. Therefore, the speed of responses by faculty and administrative staff is an essential factor that impacts their academic success [24]. The response time of academic support systems also significantly influences student satisfaction. Faster answers to inquiries not only improve the perception of support services but are also key in reducing students' levels of frustration.

When students receive timely responses, they are more likely to feel appreciated and satisfied, which positively affects their academic activities [24]. Conversely, delays in responses can exacerbate feelings of frustration and disengagement, leading to negative perceptions and delays in their educational journey [25]. Response delays can increase students' stress levels which can negatively affect their academic results. The delay in receiving essential information, such as clarifications on course fees or deadlines for assignments, often aggravates the situation and can lead students to feel disconnected from faculty and a loss of interest in their studies. The purpose of this study, therefore, was to evaluate the responses of students in graduate programmes regarding their reported communication experiences, needs and expectations, and preference for a method of communicating with faculty and administrators for academic support.

3 Research Methodology

This study was conducted at an online campus of a regional university comprising about 250 graduate students enrolled in either master's or doctoral programmes.

Survey Instrument. An online survey instrument comprised four sections including the capture of demographic data such as gender, age range, year of study and graduate programme. The other three sections focused on students' communication experiences, needs and expectations, and preference for a method of communication. Since most of the responses focused on key areas, the data was easier to summarise for analysis.

Communication Experiences. This section comprised three open-ended items that asked students, "How do you currently seek support for administrative or academic inquiries", "How often do you experience delays in getting responses to your queries?"

and "What are the most common challenges you face when seeking administrative or academic support?".

Needs and Expectations. This section also comprised two open-ended items, namely, "Which type of information or support do you seek most frequently?" and "How important is it for you to have a centralized communication channel for all your queries?".

Feedback and Suggestions. This section also comprised three closed-ended items, namely, "Would you find a centralized Frequently Asked Question (FAQ) document useful for common queries?", "Do you think having a dedicated team to respond to queries will improve your academic experience?" and "Do you believe this centralized communication plan will address your current challenges effectively?" The options provided for each question were Yes, No, or Not Sure.

Analysis. The items were reviewed by a group of research supervisors for relevance to this cohort, and possible re-wording of any items for clarity and conciseness. The instrument was revised based on their recommendations and then created using Google Forms. The instrument was pre-tested before posting in the general forum of the graduate courses at mid-semester. To ensure data integrity, the survey instrument was set to allow only one submission from the students. Responses were downloaded and imported into Microsoft Excel for coding and data analysis. Incomplete responses or responses that appeared to be outliers were removed, and the final data set was subsequently organized into themes based on the sections of the instrument. The data was then analyzed using frequencies, percentages and descriptive statistics to provide answers to the research questions.

Ethical Considerations. The graduate students were informed in the description of the survey instrument about the purpose of the study and how the results would be summarized. Since the survey was anonymous, there were no personal identifiers attached to the responses that were captured in the online form. Completion of the survey served as their consent to collect their data. Only summaries of the data provided were reported in this study.

4 Results

The survey captured 87 responses, representing 34.8% of the 250 graduate students served by the campus. The demographic details are summarized in Table 1, reflecting the gender, age range, and years of study. The table shows that most graduate students were female, with most students in the 36 to 45 age range. They were registered for three or more years with slightly more students registered for the master's programme than the professional doctorate programme.

- **Communication Experiences. Research Question 1:** What challenges do graduate students encounter when attempting to seek administrative and academic support?

The first research question explored graduate students' experiences when communicating with their facilitators, advisors, and other offices of student services. Respondents

Table 1. Sample Demographics (N = 87).

Demographic Variable	Doctoral		Masters		Total	
	#	%	#	%	#	(%)
	38	43.7	49	56.3	87	100
Gender						
Male	6	15.8	9	18.4	15	17.2
Female	32	84.2	40	81.6	72	82.8
Age Range						
18–25 years	0	-	2	4.1	2	2.3
26–35 years	0	-	13	26.5	13	14.9
36–45 years	18	47.4	22	44.9	40	46.0
46–55 years	16	42.1	11	22.4	27	31.0
56–65 years	4	10.5	1	2.0	5	5.8
Year of enrollment						
One or two	-	-	14	28.6	14	16.1
Three or more	38	100.0	35	71.4	35	83.9

were asked about methods that they used to seek support for both administrative and academic inquiries. The survey items corresponding to this research question focused on the methods used and challenges experienced in directing their queries, as well as the length of time in receiving responses to their queries.

Table 2 shows the results to survey item, "*How do you currently seek support for administrative or academic inquiries*?" Students selected multiple methods used to contact faculty or administrators for support. An average of 82% across both cohorts reported emailing their facilitators as a priority. This was followed by 58.6% of both cohorts who reported that they contacted their advisor. Specifically, 81.6% of the doctoral students (31 of 38) chose to contact their advisor as a second option, compared to 40.8% of the master's students (20 of 49). The methods of communication also show the order of contact by the students which includes contacting academic support to contacting the department for assistance.

The item, "*How often do you experience delays in getting responses to your queries?*" aimed at reviewing the standard of responding to students' queries within 48 working hours. About half of the students across the cohorts indicated that they sometimes experienced delays. Although 35.6% of the students reported frequent delays, notably, 44.8% of the doctoral students experienced frequent delays compared to 28.5% of the masters students. (See Table 3). In response to the item, "*What are the most common challenges you face when seeking support*?", half of the students again reported lack of a timely response to queries, 30.1% experienced difficulty in identifying the support personnel for their query, and 20.3% received inconsistent information (See Table 4).

Table 2. Methods used by graduate students for administrative or academic inquiries.

Methods of communication	Doctoral		Masters		TOTAL	
	# 38	% 43.7	# 49	% 56.3	Total 87	% 100
Emailing Facilitators	30	78.9	41	83.7	71	81.6
Contacting Advisor	31	81.6	20	40.8	51	58.6
Academic support	20	52.6	16	32.7	36	41.4
Helpdesk	13	34.2	16	32.7	29	33.3
The UWI website	7	18.4	12	24.5	19	21.8
The Department	1	2.6	2	4.1	3	3.4

Table 3. Frequency of delays experienced in receiving responses to queries.

Delay experienced	Doctoral		Masters		TOTAL	
	# 38	% 43.7	# 49	% 56.3	Total 87	% 100
Sometimes	18	47.4	26	53.1	44	50.6
Frequently	17	44.8	14	28.5	31	35.6
Rarely	3	7.9	9	18.4	12	13.8

Table 4. Most common challenges when seeking support.

Challenge	Doctoral		Masters		TOTAL	
	# 54	% 43.9	# 69	% 56.1	Total 123	% 100
Lack of timely responses	28	32.2	33	47.8	61	49.6
Finding the right contact	15	17.2	22	31.9	37	30.1
Inconsistent information	11	12.6	14	20.3	25	20.3

- **Needs and Expectations. Research Question 2**: How do graduate students evaluate the effectiveness of different communication channels for their requests?

This question addressed whether the types of information or support that graduate students seek align with the implementation of a centralized communication system for their queries. To answer this question, the type of information sought was first analysed along with the level of importance that the students attributed to the information. Table 5 shows that almost 90% of the students in both cohorts reported that the type of information they require was extremely or very important, with 55.2% of them noting that administrative processes such as registration or payment of fees was a top priority followed by research related guidance. Interestingly, 60.5% of the doctoral students paid more importance to administrative processes, while 34.7% of the masters students placed their focus on research-related guidance. Nine (10.3%) respondents rated administrative processes and research-related guidance as moderately important. Similar outcomes were noted for gender and age range across the two cohorts.

Table 5. Factors influencing the level of importance regarding students' queries.

Level of importance	Doctoral		Masters		TOTAL	
	# 38	% 43.6	# 49	% 44.4	Total 87	% 100
Extremely/Very Important	**34**	**89.5**	**44**	**89.8**	**78**	**89.7**
- Access to resources (Library, journals, software, etc.)	1	2.6	2	4.1	61	3.4
- Administrative processes (Registration, fees, etc.)	23	60.5	25	51.0	37	55.2
- Research-related guidance	10	26.3	17	34.7	25	31.0
Moderately/Not Important	**4**	**10.5**	**5**	**10.2**	**9**	**10.3**
- Administrative processes (registration, fees, etc.)	3	7.9	3	6.1	6	6.9
- Research-related guidance	1	2.6	2	4.1	3	3.4

The students were then asked about the level of importance they would place if they had access to a centralized communication channel for responses to these queries. Almost 90% of the students agreed that a centralized communication channel would benefit them compared to 10% who attributed minimal importance to this method of communication (Table 6).

Table 6. Level of importance of a centralized communication system for student queries.

Level of importance of a centralized communication system	Doctoral		Masters		TOTAL	
	# 38	% 43.6	# 49	% 44.4	Total 87	% 100
Extremely/Very Important	34	89.5	44	89.8	78	89.7
Moderately/Not Important	4	10.5	5	10.2	9	10.3

Feedback and Suggestions. While 90% of the students initially indicated that a communication channel would be very important to them. Table 7 shows that this percentage dropped to 72.4%. Students were also asked about their interest regarding a dedicated team to respond to their queries or a list of Frequently Asked Questions (FAQ) on the campus website. While all three options were well received by the students, 93.1% of the respondents chose a dedicated team as their best choice for responding to their queries. There was still some uncertainty among the students as 25.3% of them not sure about the level of importance of the communication system, while 19.5% were also unsure about the FAQs on the website. These results were similar across both cohorts of students.

Table 7. Responses to options of a central communication versus a FAQ document, or dedicated team.

Response	Centralized communication		Dedicated team to respond to queries		Frequently Asked Questions (FAQ)	
	# 87	% 100	# 87	% 100	# 87	% 100
Yes	63	72.4	81	93.1	63	72.4
Not sure	22	25.3	5	5.7	17	19.5
No	2	2.3	1	1.1	7	8.0

5 Discussion and Recommendations

The two cohorts of graduate students reported that they prioritized emailing their facilitators, followed by contacting their advisors for their queries. This is expected, since facilitators should be able to respond to questions concerning students' course information. The top three common challenges that students experienced were a lack of timely responses, difficulty finding the right contact, and receiving inconsistent information. About half of the students noted that these challenges were experienced sometimes, with 36% indicating that they were a frequent occurrence. This was compounded by an inability to identify appropriate support personnel for matters such as fee payments or specific registration concerns. In cases of non-academic queries, facilitators or advisors may not know specific details to assist their students. Clear communication could therefore help to avoid the overwhelming number of emails sent by students to various staff to receive timely, appropriate responses to their queries.

The results also indicated that students choose all three options, namely, an FAQ document, a dedicated team, and central communication system, since multiple access points could serve to have their queries quickly answered. However, as their first choice, students preferred a dedicated team to respond to their queries. Perhaps the implication of an automated centralized communication system or the static list of Frequently Asked Questions could have been perceived as impersonal. Future focus groups could ascertain whether this choice depends on the human interaction associated with a team dedicated to responding to their queries. Based on these findings, the following recommendations are proposed:

Implement a Dedicated Team. With 93.9% of respondents expressing support for a dedicated team to respond to their queries, establishing a team to handle various student queries should be implemented. Team members must be knowledgeable to quickly respond to queries related to registration, payment of fees and research-based guidance. This should be scheduled especially during the peaks times of the semester to reduce delays. Continuous training must be scheduled to ensure that advisors and other staff remain equipped to efficiently respond to both routine and complex queries.

Maintain a Comprehensive FAQ Document. Given that 72.4% of participants favor the use of an FAQ document, efforts should focus on creating a thorough and easily accessible FAQ resource. This document should be continuously updated based on common student inquiries and feedback, providing a first point of reference for students. It would also potentially reduce the volume of queries directed towards the various support teams.

Strengthen Centralized Communication Systems. Since 73.5% of the students supported this option, ensuring that all communication, such as emails and notices, is funneled through a single, cohesive channel not only simplifies the process for students but also streamlines monitoring trends and the type of queries to proactively address them.

Interrogate "Not Sure" Responses. Approximately 25% of the students in this study were not quite sure about the effectiveness of the three options available. As more students become involved in the process through feedback or focus groups, it may be possible to identify other options or potential improvements when designing the solutions that they require.

Integrate Automated Communication Tools. Considering various chatbots, a support tool for both academic and administrative functions should be explored to minimize delays, in addressing queries efficiently in real time scenarios.

This research highlights the importance of effective communication strategies in supporting graduate students throughout their academic careers. Student satisfaction could be improved by providing multiple efficient communication practices, reducing delays, and ensuring accurate information when responding to student queries. More so, exploring additional technological advancements, such as integrating AI-driven support tools alongside human resources, could further optimize communication and resource accessibility for students. Future research should focus on evaluating the impact of these initiatives with different groups of students at various levels over time, demographic factors, such as part- or full-time student status, or the preferred methods of communication among undergraduate students.

Disclosure of Interests. The authors have no competing interests to declare that are relevant to the content of this article.

References

1. Heffernan, T., Wilkins, S., Butt, M.M.: Transnational higher education: the importance of institutional reputation, trust and student-university identification in international partnerships. Int. J. Educ. Manag. **32**(2), 227–240 (2018)
2. Naheen, F., Elsharnouby, T.H.: You are what you communicate: on the relationships among university brand personality, identification, student participation, and citizenship behaviour. J. Mark. High. Educ. **34**(1), 368–389 (2024)
3. Scott, S., Aquino, K.: COVID-19 transitions: higher education professionals' perspectives on access barriers, services, and solutions for students with disabilities (2020)
4. Pringle, J., Fritz, S.: The university brand and social media: using data analytics to assess brand authenticity. J. Mark. High. Educ. **19**(1), 19–44 (2019)
5. Oleksiyenko, A., et al.: Global crisis management and higher education: agency and coupling in the context of wicked COVID-19 problems. High. Educ. Q. (2023)
6. Akour, M., Alenezi, M.: Higher education future in the era of digital transformation. Educ. Sci. **12**(1), 784 (2022)
7. Khahro, S.H., Javed, Y.: Key challenges in 21st century learning: a way forward towards sustainable higher educational institutions. Sustainability **14**(23) (2022)
8. Ramísio, P.J., Pinto, L.M.C., Costa, H., Arezes, D.: Sustainability strategy in higher education institutions: Lessons learned from a nine-year case study. J. Clean. Prod. **222**, 300–309 (2019)
9. Sajja, R., Sermet, Y., Cwiertny, D., Demir, I.: Platform-independent and curriculum-oriented intelligent assistant for higher education. Int. J. Educ. Technol. High. Educ. **20**(1), 42 (2023)
10. Rayburn, S.W., Anderson, S., Sierra, J.J.: Future thinking continuity of learning in marketing: a student perspective on crisis management in higher education. Mark. Educ. Rev. **31**(3), 241–255 (2021)
11. Michael, J.J., Elser, N.: Personal waste management in higher education: a case study illustrating the importance of a fourth bottom line. Int. J. Sustain. High. Educ. **20**(2), 341–359 (2019)
12. Belanger, B., Steele, A., Philhower, K.: Tailoring higher education options for smaller institutions to meet veterans' needs: enhancing inclusion in higher education: practical solutions by veterans for veterans. J. Veterans Stud. **7**(1) (2021)
13. Stoyanova, M., Nikoloudakis, Y., Panagiotakis, S., Pallis, E., Markakis, E.K.: A survey on the Internet of Things (IoT) forensics: challenges, approaches, and open issues. IEEE Commun. Surv. Tutorials **22**(2), 1191–1221 (2020)
14. Bailey, D.R., Lee, A.R.: Learning from experience in the midst of COVID-19: benefits, challenges, and strategies in online teaching. Comput. Assist. Lang. Learn. Electron. J. **21**(2), 178–198 (2020)
15. Sandu, N., Gide, E.: Adoption of AI-Chatbots to enhance student learning experience in higher education in India. In: Proceedings of the 18th International Conference on Information Technology Based Higher Education and Training (ITHET) (2019)
16. Zarandi, N., Soares, A., Alves, H.: Strategies, benefits and barriers–a systematic literature review of student co-creation in higher education. J. Mark. High. Educ. **34**(2), 895–919 (2024)
17. Arasaratnam-Smith, L.A., Northcote, M.T.: Community in online higher education: challenges and opportunities. Electron. J. E-Learn. **15**(2), 188–198 (2017)
18. Schwartz, S.E., et al.: I'm having a little struggle with this, can you help me out?": Examining impacts and processes of a social capital intervention for first-generation college students. Am. J. Community Psychol. **61**(1–2), 166–178 (2018)
19. Alruwais, N., Wills, G., Wald, M.: Advantages and challenges of using e-assessment. Int. J. Inf. Educ. Technol. **8**(1), 34–37 (2018)

20. Al-Nofaie, H.: Saudi University Students' perceptions towards virtual education during Covid-19 pandemic: a case study of language learning via blackboard. **11** (2020)
21. Ferri, F., Grifoni, P., Guzzo, T.: Online learning and emergency remote teaching: opportunities and challenges in emergency situations. Societies **10**
22. Alam, A.: Cloud-based e-learning: scaffolding the environment for adaptive e-learning ecosystem based on cloud computing infrastructure. In: Computer Communication, Networking and IoT: Proceedings of 5th ICICC 2021, Singapore (2022)
23. Zhang, W., Bray, M.: Comparative research on shadow education: achievements, challenges, and the agenda ahead. Eur. J. Educ. **55**(3), 322–341 (2020)
24. Baik, C., Larcombe, W., Brooker, A.: How universities can enhance student mental wellbeing: the student perspective. High. Educ. Res. Dev. **38**(4), 674–687 (2019)
25. McCallen, L.S., Johnson, H.L.: The role of institutional agents in promoting higher education success among first-generation college students at a public urban university. J. Divers. High. Educ. **13**(4), 320

Author Index

B. K. Smith and M. Borge (Eds.): HCII 2025, LNCS 15806, pp. 397–400, 2025.
https://doi.org/10.1007/978-3-031-93564-0